A TEXT BOOK OF

INFRASTRUCTURAL ENGINEERING II

SEMESTER – VI

THIRD YEAR (T. E.) DEGREE COURSE IN CIVIL ENGINEERING

As Per New Revised Syllabus of
North Maharashtra University, Jalgaon.
(Pattern 2012)

D. R. PATHAK
Formerly Professor in Civil Engg. Deptt.,
Government College of Engineering,
PUNE

H. K. GITE
Assistant Engineer Grade – 1
Water Resource Department, Govt. of Maharashtra
Formerly Assistant Professor Civil Engg. Deptt.
JSPM's Rajarshi Shahu College of Engiering
Tathwade, PUNE

VAISHALI T. THAKARE
Assistant Engineer Grade I
Central Design Organization,
Nashik

N 3345

Infrastructural Engineering II (TE CIVIL SEM. VI – NMU) ISBN 978-93-5164-398-2
First Edition : January 2015
© : Authors

The text of this publication, or any part thereof, should not be reproduced or transmitted in any form or stored in any computer storage system or device for distribution including photocopy, recording, taping or information retrieval system or reproduced on any disc, tape, perforated media or other information storage device etc., without the written permission of Authors with whom the rights are reserved. Breach of this condition is liable for legal action.

Every effort has been made to avoid errors or omissions in this publication. In spite of this, errors may have crept in. Any mistake, error or discrepancy so noted and shall be brought to our notice shall be taken care of in the next edition. It is notified that neither the publisher nor the authors or seller shall be responsible for any damage or loss of action to any one, of any kind, in any manner, therefrom.

Published By :
NIRALI PRAKASHAN
Abhyudaya Pragati, 1312, Shivaji Nagar,
Off J.M. Road, PUNE – 411005
Tel - (020) 25512336/37/39, Fax - (020) 25511379
Email : niralipune@pragationline.com

Printed By :
REPRO INDIA LTD
Mumbai.

DISTRIBUTION CENTRES
PUNE

Nirali Prakashan
119, Budhwar Peth, Jogeshwari Mandir Lane
Pune 411002, Maharashtra
Tel : (020) 2445 2044, 66022708, Fax : (020) 2445 1538
Email : bookorder@pragationline.com

Nirali Prakashan
S. No. 28/25, Dhyari,
Near Pari Company, Pune 411041
Tel : (020) 24690204 Fax : (020) 24690316
Email : dhyari@pragationline.com
              bookorder@pragationline.com

MUMBAI
Nirali Prakashan
385, S.V.P. Road, Rasdhara Co-op. Hsg. Society Ltd.,
Girgaum, Mumbai 400004, Maharashtra
Tel : (022) 2385 6339 / 2386 9976, Fax : (022) 2386 9976
Email : niralimumbai@pragationline.com

DISTRIBUTION BRANCHES

NAGPUR
Pratibha Book Distributors
Above Maratha Mandir, Shop No. 3, First Floor,
Rani Jhanshi Square, Sitabuldi, Nagpur 440012,
Maharashtra, Tel : (0712) 254 7129

BENGALURU
Pragati Book House
House No. 1, Sanjeevappa Lane, Avenue Road Cross,
Opp. Rice Church, Bengaluru – 560002.
Tel : (080) 64513344, 64513355,
Mob : 9880582331, 9845021552
Email:bharatsavla@yahoo.com

JALGAON
Nirali Prakashan
34, V. V. Golani Market, Navi Peth, Jalgaon 425001,
Maharashtra, Tel : (0257) 222 0395
Mob : 94234 91860

KOLHAPUR
Nirali Prakashan
New Mahadvar Road,
Kedar Plaza, 1st Floor Opp. IDBI Bank
Kolhapur 416 012, Maharashtra. Mob : 9855046155

CHENNAI
Pragati Books
9/1, Montieth Road, Behind Taas Mahal, Egmore,
Chennai 600008 Tamil Nadu, Tel : (044) 6518 3535,
Mob : 94440 01782 / 98450 21552 / 98805 82331, Email : bharatsavla@yahoo.com

---

RETAIL OUTLETS
PUNE

Pragati Book Centre
157, Budhwar Peth, Opp. Ratan Talkies,
Pune 411002, Maharashtra
Tel : (020) 2445 8887 / 6602 2707, Fax : (020) 2445 8887

Pragati Book Centre
Amber Chamber, 28/A, Budhwar Peth,
Appa Balwant Chowk, Pune : 411002, Maharashtra,
Tel : (020) 20240335 / 66281669
Email : pbcpune@pragationline.com

Pragati Book Centre
676/B, Budhwar Peth, Opp. Jogeshwari Mandir,
Pune 411002, Maharashtra
Tel : (020) 6601 7784 / 6602 0855

PBC Book Sellers and Stationers
152, Budhwar Peth, Pune 411002, Maharashtra
Tel : (020) 2445 2254 / 6609 2463

MUMBAI
Pragati Book Corner
Indira Niwas, 111 - A, Bhavani Shankar Road, Dadar (W), Mumbai 400028, Maharashtra
Tel : (022) 2422 3526 / 6662 5254, Email : pbcmumbai@pragationline.com

---

www.pragationline.com   info@pragationline.com

PREFACE

We take an opportunity to present this book entitled **'Infrastructural Engineering - II'** to the students of Third Year Civil Degree Engineering. The book is strictly written according to the New Revised Syllabus prepared by North Maharashtra University, Jalgaon (2012 Pattern).

The book will also be very useful for the students preparing for Engineering Service Examination and AMIE Examination.

The subject mater is presented in simple and easy form so as to enable the students to understand the subject easily. Sufficient care is taken to present the subject matter in the point wise form in most of the chapters.

Also, it is important to mention invaluable moral support of our beloved family members, who consistently encouraged us for better work.

We are thankful to the Publisher Shri. Dineshbhai Furia, Shri. Jignesh Furia and Shri M.P. Munde and staff of Nirali Prakashan namely Mrs Deepali Lachake (Co-ordinator), Mrs. Roshan Khan, Mrs. Shilpa Kale, Mrs. Ulka Chavan, Miss Kalyani Rathod, Miss Megha Khedkar who really have taken keen interest and untiring efforts in publishing this text. We express our deep sense of gratitude towards all the dear friends and students for their direct or indirect help in making this venture a success.

We are also thankful to **Mr. Pruthviraj M. More**, Branch Manager, Jalgaon office for his valuable help and efforts for promotion of our book.

Inspite of having taken all the precautions, it is possible that some errors may have escaped our attention. The readers are kindly requested to bring to my notice such corrections for being rectified in the next edition.

January 2015   **Authors**

SYLLABUS

Unit 1 (8 hours, 16 marks)

(a) Highway Planning and Development: Highway planning in India, development, rural and urban roads, road, departments in India, road classification, road authorities i.e. IRC, CRRI, NHAI, etc., Financing of road projects, road safety audit.

(b) Field Surveys: Reconnaissance, aerial surveys, location surveys, location of bridges.

Highway alignment: Basic requirements of an ideal alignment and factors controlling it, special requirements for hill roads.

(c) Highway Geometric Design: Topography and physical features, cross section elements like carriageway width, formation width, right of way, etc., friction, Light reflecting characteristics, roughness, camber, sight distances, horizontal alignment, design speed, super-elevation, transition curve, gradients.

Unit 2 (8 hours, 16 marks)

(a) Road Materials: Aggregates and their types, physical and engineering properties, Fillers, bitumen, characteristics, emulsions and cutbacks, basic tests on all materials, soil investigation, test on soil; CBR, plate load test.

(b) Construction of Roads: Stabilized earth, gravel roads, W.B.M. roads, high cost Roads: bituminous roads, cement concrete roads.

Highway Drainage: Surface and sub-surface drainage arrangements,

(c) Highway Pavements: Design of Flexible (G.I. method and CBR method using IRC recommendations) and rigid pavements (Westergaurd wheel load analysis), Maintenance and Strengthening of pavements.

Unit 3 (8 hours, 16 marks)

(a) Traffic Engineering: Road user characteristics, vehicular characteristics, traffic flow characteristics, speed, traffic volume studies, parking studies - definition, purpose, types, survey methods. Accident studies - purpose, types, causes, collision diagram, condition diagram, preventive measures

(b) Traffic control devices: pavement marking, signs, signals, Traffic management, various types of intersection and their design criteria, Traffic Simulation and it's advantages,

Roadside Developments: Arboriculture, street lighting.

(c) Advanced Urban Transport Technology: Classification, mass and rapid transit system, introduction to intelligent transportation System (ITS), electronic toll Collection.

Unit 4 (8 hours, 16 marks)

(a) Bridges: Site investigation, waterway calculations, scours depth, afflux, and economic span.

(b) Classification and suitability : Classification of superstructures with respect to Structural behavior and material used types of substructures, flooring joints, Movable bridges, and temporary bridges.

(c) Construction methods and Maintenance: Methods of erection of various types of bridges, testing and strengthening of bridges.

(d) Bridge Bearings and Foundation: Suitability for each type of bridges

Unit 5 (7 hours, 16 marks)

(a) Introduction to Tunneling: Need, classification, advantages and disadvantages of tunnels compared to open cuts, shape and size of tunnel shafts, pilot tunnels, Alignment of Tunnel.

(b) Tunneling in hard rock: Meaning of the term 'Faces of Attack', Mucking, methods of removal of muck, heading and benching method, drillingpatterns, blasting, tunnel lining(rock bolting and strata anchoring), methods of Ventilation, Lighting and aspects of drainage, Dust control, Safety in tunnel construction.

Tunneling in soft materials: mucking, forepoling and shield methods, needle beam method, modern tunneling methods.

CONTENTS

Unit - I

Chapter 1 : Highways Planning and Development	1.1-1.36
Chapter 2 : Field Surveys	2.2-2.18
Chapter 3 : Highway Alignment	3.1-3.4
Chapter 4 : Highway Geometric Design	4.1-4.58

Unit - II

Chapter 5 : Road Materials	5.1-5.58
Chapter 6 : Construction of Roads	6.1-6.28
Chapter 7 : Highway Drainage	7.1-7.10
Chapter 8 : Highway Pavement	8.1-8.46

Unit - III

Chapter 9 : Traffic Engineering	9.1-9.34
Chapter 10 : Traffic Control Devices	10.1-10.32
Chapter 11 : Roadside Developments	11.1-11.12
Chapter 12 : Advanced Urban Transport Technology	12.1-12.8

Unit - III

Chapter 13 : Bridges	13.1 – 13.16
Chapter 14 : Classification and Suitability of Bridge	14.1 – 14.30
Chapter 15 : Bridges Bearings and Foundation	15.1 – 15.24
Chapter 16 : Construction Methods and Maintenance of Bridge	16.1 – 16.8
Chapter 17 : Introduction to Tunneling	17.1 – 17.14

Unit - IV

Chapter 18 : Tunneling in Hard Rock	18.1 – 18.22
Chapter 19 : Tunneling in Soft Materials	19.1 – 19.10

Unit - I

CHAPTER 1
HIGHWAYS PLANNING AND DEVELOPMENT

1.1 INTRODUCTION

The man always tries to become superman. The whole effort of the individual is to make his life worth it's living. The development of new ideas and ways is the result of this thinking. The subject of Highway Engineering is no exception to this general rule. Throughout the ages, the man is making efforts to know how best roads could be made and sleek express ways and auto bahns of today could be built because of the past experience and knowledge which our fore-fathers have gathered in the art of Highway Making. To study what by gone generations know about roads, we shall trace the history of Highways.

1.2 HISTORY OF HIGHWAYS IN THE CONTINENT

Civilisation cannot exist without some means of communications. Even sparse human settlements have to communicate with each other and well trodden foot paths may be considered fore - runner of highways. In the Bible too, there is mention to the construction of road between *Egypt and Babylon* about 500 years before the christian era. Roman civilisation which is a founding father of European civilisation had good roads. These roads were primarily made for military conquest and subjugation of colonies. The important road called Via Appia connecting Rome with the Southern tip of Italy could be quoted in this context. These Roman roads were direct in alignment, well drained, well above the general ground level, and sufficiently thick and strong arch bridges spanned the water courses. The roads in the Roman cities were brick on edge pavements to sustain charriot loads. The decline of the Roman empire saw set back in road building in Europe.

Persians under the king Darius 1, are believed to have constructed a road from turkey to the Persian Gulf. This road, called Persian Royal Road was constructed when Persian empire was at it's Zenith.

After the Roman civilisation, the art of road building received a boost in Europe with the coming of Industrial Revolution. Wheeled coaches and animal drawn passenger coaches began to make their appearance in sixteenth century and this gave rise to a demand for good roads. A french gentleman, who was then the Inspector General of Roads in France, named Pierre Tresaguet, made the road profile slightly higher in the centre and lower towards the shoulder, what we recognise as camber today. He tried for proper maintenance and drainage of roads.

In United Kingdom, around eighteen century, a further development occurred. The art consisted of putting boulders on the ground, compact them and spread gravel as surface layer. For the soft ground, bundles of heather were used as sub-base. This improvement is generally ascribed to John Metcalf. In the early part of nineteenth century, Thomas Telford introduced a innovation in the road building. He used hand picked boulders as foundations for road bases. The original idea was of course due to Met calf but Telford popularised it and constructed many roads with this innovation. In India, many secondary and tertiary roads are constructed with boulder soling as base, the origin of which is Telford construction.

John Macadam, a Scottish engineer must be mentioned here. He propagated two important principles which are valid even now :

(1) All loads are finally carried by mother earth and if the earth on which the road pavement rests is in dry state, heavy loads can be carried without undue settlements.

(2) Instead of big boulder paving, advocated by Telford small angular pieces of aggregate compacted together are better bonded together and thus can provide better hard surface. The size of the stone advocated by Macadam to give practical utility to it, is that it should be possible for the engineer to put it in mouth. The contributions of John Macadam were important. It may be good idea to compare Telford and Macadam construction here.

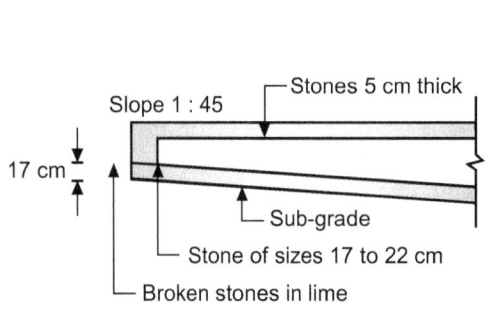
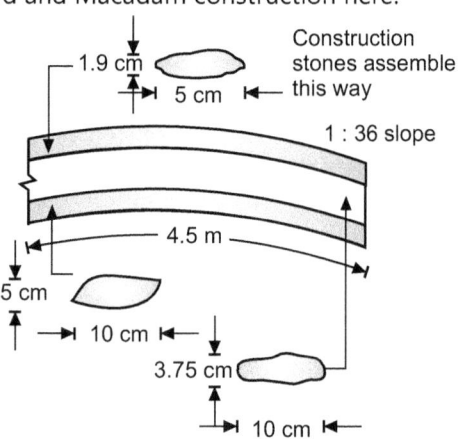

Fig. 1.1 (a): Telford construction   Fig. 1.1 (b): Macadam construction

Combination between Telford and Macadom Construction

Telford Construction	Macadam Construction
(1) Gentle slope	(1) Steep slope
(2) Bigger sizes of stones.	(2) Smaller sizes of stones.
(3) Typical assemblage of stones in the standing fashion.	(3) Assemblage in sitting fashion. Therefore better stress distribution.
(4) From the point of view of stress distribution, Telford is inferior.	(4) From the point of view of stress distribution, Macadam is superior.
(5) Requires less stones.	(5) Requires more stones.

The construction features of Roman Roads, Tresaguet, Telford and Macadam are indicated in Fig. 1.2.

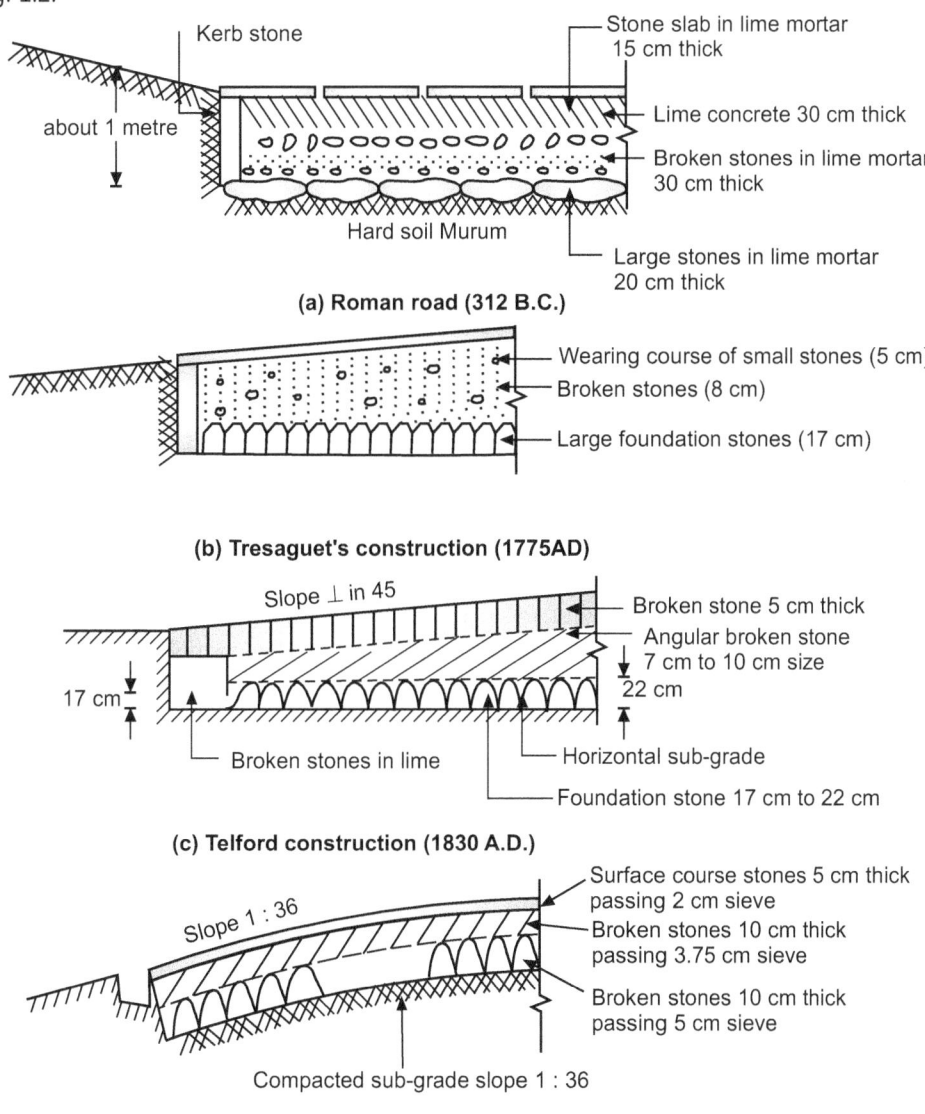

(a) Roman road (312 B.C.)

(b) Tresaguet's construction (1775AD)

(c) Telford construction (1830 A.D.)

(d) Macadam construction (1827 A.D.)

Fig. 1.2 : Early Roads

The use of steam road roller developed by Eveling and Bedford in nineteenth century and use of portland cement in construction in nineteenth century paved the way for modern road construction in Europe. In fact tars and asphalts were being used for road construction in 1830 s. But in fairness it must be said that the basic traffic on road was not much, that need was catered for by Railways. The invention of automobile with pneumatic tyred wheel is vastly responsible for the road development.

Though developed quite early, the automobile had a slow development in the nineteenth century but the first world war of 1914 -18 gave a fantastic boost to it's growth. With the growth in the number of automobiles, the traffic on the roads increased considerably and roads became a permanent and important feature of modern life in Europe. Now, the roads can almost be compared with arteries in human body, which do the basic work of transporting. Without good motorable roads the transportation of material will come to a standstill, and the place of roads is now no more a "stand by" to railways, as more than 40 % of freight is through road and roads have now come to stay as permanent feature of modern life.

1.3 THE HISTORY OF ROADS IN INDIA

Hindu Period in India : During the Aryan period or vedic period, there is no question that a good network of road work existed. Kautilya the great sage and the administrator had laid down standard widths of roads and Megas-thenes, the Greek Ambassador to the Court of Maurya mentions the prevelance of good roads. Patliputra was connected to all important towns by good roads, on which heavy charriots could ply. The roads were lined with trees and provided with wells and rest houses in between. Fa-hein the Chineese traveller had come to India during Gupta (3rd and 4th century) period and his writings indicate presence of good roads. Hiuen-Tsang who visited India during the regime of Harsha testifies it. All this literature tells us that a good trunk road existed connecting Patliputra to Takshashila touching Varanasi, Kausumbhi, Mathura. Indraprastha and Kurukshetra. The excavations carried out at Mohen-Jo-Daro has indicated that good intercity roads existed then - that is in pre-biblic time. However, the art of road making was not converted into a proper text and we can only make a guess as to the material composing the roads. Not only Mohen Jo Daro but recent excavations at Harappan site have also indicated existence of great cities. For example, excavation by the Archaeological Survey of India (ASI) at Dholavira in Gujarat's Kutch border district has unearthed a unique city, probably among the most important Harappan sites discovered yet.

Ever since the discovery of Dholavira in 1967-68 by Jagat Pati Joshi Director-General of ASI this site has aroused the curiosity of archaeologists the world over.

Now a nine-week operation under the direction of ASI superintending archaeologist Ravindra Singh Bisht has revealed part of a magnificant city, indicating earlier surface observations, an official spokesman has said.

The main city, spread over 48 hectares, or even more, was secured by massive mud brick defences. Within these walls, there is evidence of three principal divisions that have been named as the 'Citadel' 'Middle Town', and 'Lower Town', on the basis of their relative location and layout.

While the Citadel and Middle Town have separate but inter-connected fortification systems, the Lower Town has not yet shown any such provision. But all three are within the general fortification and present a perfect example of rectangular town planning.

As in the Harappan site of Kalibangan, the Citadel has two conjoined and fortified sub-divisions the taller of which (in the east) has been named as the 'Castle' and the lower (in the west) as 'Bailey'. The Castle had at least three gates opening in different directions. Of these, the north gate was possibly the grandest and probably used for ceremonial occasions, the excavations indicate.

The gates, at least in the later stage, were designed as ascending terraces with flights of steps, raised platforms, passageways and chambers, all in striking symmetry.

Exposed houses contain rooms, fire places, storage jars, simple or cut stone drains and sullage jars or pits, and some of the houses indicate such specialised craft activity as bead manufacturing or shellwork. The principal building material is rubble, hammer-dressed stone blocks pillars, standardised fire bricks and earth.

Apart from town planning, another unique contribution of Dholavira is the find of four members of a stone pillary consisting of an exquisite damru-like base and three pieces of the upward tapering shaft. This kind of pillar has not been found at any other Harappan site so far.

Other important finds include micro-drill bits made out of a hard stone, 13 complete or fragmented seals, eight seal impressions on clay and one bronze figurine of an animal. Seals bear short epigraphs in the Harappan script and many of them are engraved with unicorns.

Among the other finds are beads of semi-precious stones, gold, copper, shell, steatite, faience and clay, copper objects including a pin with two spiral heads, bangles of stone, shell and clay, terracotta models of wheels, animals, games-men and a variety of stone querns, grinders, rubbers, polishers, pestles and mortar used for domestic and manufacturing purposes.

The excavation work underway holds promise of adding new perspectives and colour to the Harappan personality according to archaeologists.

Dholavira is unique in that the striking perfection that underlies the city's layout and construction of gateways does not find a parallel anywhere. Further, the intricately carved pillar members are altogether new items of Harappan architecture. Smaller pillar-like members are also coming up during excavations and their real importance is under investigation.

The excavation may also throw up clues about the locational importance of Dholavira in the settlement network of the Harappans.

There is no question that such a fine city, described as above cannot function without good roads. We as Indians to whatever caste creed and religion we may belong have every reason to take pride in the fact that when most of the rest of the world was moving in sheep skin clothes, our fore-fathers had constructed such good cities and roads.

Islamic Period in India : In northern India, where the, Mughal, Turks, Aphaghan dynasties had a sway over a considerable time, the importance of good roads was immediately felt to subjugate this vast land, where rebellions were but a order of the day. Northern India was essentially a plain country and without the formation of reasonable roads, it was impossible to govern. In fact, one reason why these invaders, which later on became part and parcel of Indian Heritage, could not force their dynasties in the Deccan, Rajastan, the land of the Ahoms - i.e. the Asam, the Chambals, might be that they faced unhospitable country along with the populace. One name which shines in the Islamic period is the Afghan monarch Sher Shah Suri. He adorned the throne of Delhi for a considerable shorter span but he constructed the Grand Trunk Road, more or less on the pattern of the present National Highway from Delhi to Culcutta.

The grand trunk road made by him was paved with Kankar (limestone) and had a sound bed. In fact, he had constructed Sarais (Rest places) and planted trees alongside the road. However, it must be said, that the population in Islamic period was living in sort of ghettos and there was very little interaction between different social economic and ethnic groups, with the result that there must have been very less traffic on roads. With the present day ideas of expecting reasonable return from the road, the roads must have been a "luxury." All the same that the roads existed, may be for the military use, is important.

In general, there were less court historions at the court of Muslim Kings in the Deccan, and as such we have less evidence of recorded building activity, but the excavations at Hampi in Karnataka have indicated high rise wall constructed with two parallel walls along the foundations to remove the thrust of the wall on the main walls. The people whose thinking is so deep must have thought about roads. The ruins of Vijayanagaram clearly indicate that those times also, there was reasonable and efficient road system.

1.4 DEVELOPMENT OF ROADS IN INDIA DURING BRITISH PERIOD

The British when they came to India saw in existing road structure, the possibility of military manoeuvres. William Bentinck constructed the modern Grand Trunk Road from Calcutta to Delhi which was then extended to Peshawar. This particular road had permanent bridges and good stone or Kankar bed. The controversial Dalhousie created the provincial P.W.D. in place of military boards in 1885. Some Engineering Colleges were also started and in general by the end of nineteenth century, there was a good system of trunk roads.

Now, arose a competitor to road industry in the form of Railways. The first railway line was opened in 1853 in Bombay i.e. Mumbai and in the immediate decades to follow the railway network was rapidly extended throughout the length and the breadth of the country. The railways were useful to the British for carrying troops and also raw material and therefore in the British interests only feeder roads that led to and supported the system of railways were constructed. In general, roads received scant attention. The Government of India Act of 1919 made the roads a subject of provincial charge and the Central Government bothered with roads of strategic importance. The lag between the advent of railways and the appearance of motor vehicle in India was nearly fifty years or so and in this time, the road construction took a back seat. Though the development of automobile in Europe and America was faster, the beginning of the twentieth century saw the first motor vehicle on the road which gave impetus to road building as industry. Then came the First World War and partly as it's result, there was a tremendous growth in the number of the motor vehicles.

Jayakar Committee : As a result of this motor vehicle population, there was a demand for better roads, even in the Council of States, then existing. Government of India as a response to this demand, appointed a committee called the Road Development Committee consisting of members from both the houses of central legislature and Mr. M R. Jayakar was appointed chairman of the committee. This committee popularly known as Jayakar committee went into an exercise of finding out

- whether the existing road requires further development and if so
- how this development can be achieved and how finances could be arranged with reference to the distribution of functions between the Central and Provincial Governments in the forms existing then.

The findings of the Jayakar Committee could be summarised as follows :

- It came to the conclusion that the road system existing then was totally inadequate and that it must be developed further so that it can serve specific functions namely (a) as a complement and tributory to the existing railway network (b) for social and political progress of rural population so that they can partake the benefits of motor transport and (c) for better marketing of agricultural produce.
- The committee came to the conclusion that only the resources of state exchequer were not enough for road development and that the Central Government should bear some burden of this task.
- To raise the finances to meet the cost of road development, there should be additional taxation which should include (a) duty on motor spirit (b) vehicle taxation (c) license fee for vehicles plying on the road.

    The additional funds collected from motor spirit duty were to go to the central Revenue as Road Development fund, intended for road development.

- Committee did not consider it worth while to create additional authority in the form of Central Road Board but recommended appointment of road engineer instead.
- Jayakar Committee also recommended holding of periodic Road Conferences to discuss inter alia questions relating to road construction and road development.

Jayakar Committee was possibly the first attempt in the nineteenth century to go into the intricacies involved in the road development and hence is important.

The Government seriously considered the recommendations of the Jayakar Committee. Most of it's findings were accepted. The central road fund was created with the help of additional duty that was then levied on motor fuel i.e. petrol. Ten percent of this fund was detined by the Central Government and the remainder was then distributed amongst the provinces, then existing in the ratio of the consumption of the petrol in that province to the total consumption of India.

As a result of the recommendations of Jayakar Committee, the first conference of highway engineers took place in 1930. These conferences from 1930 – 1934 created greater awareness in the road development and construction and paved the way for establishment of Indian Roads Congress (IRC) in 1934.

1.5 ROAD CLASSIFICATION

1.5.1 Classification Based on the Weather Condition

The different types of road are classified into two categories, depending on whether they can be used during different seasons of the year.
1. All-weather roads
2. Fair-weather roads

1. All-Weather Roads : All-weather roads are those which are negotiable during weather, except at major river crossing where interruption to traffic is permissible upto a certain extent, the road pavement should be negotiable during all weather.

2. Fair-Weather Roads : Roads which are called fair-weather roads on these, the traffic may be interrupted during monsoon season at causeways where stream may overflow across the road.

1.5.2 Classification Based on the Road Pavement

Based on road pavement, roads are classified as paved roads and unpaved roads.
1. Paved road
2. Unpaved road

Pavement Roads : If they are provided with a hard pavement course which should be at least water bound macadam (WBM) layer.

Unpaved Roads : If they are not provided with a hard pavement course of at least a WBM layer. Thus, earth road and gravel road may be called unpaved roads.

1.5.3 Classification Based on the Pavement Surfacing

Based on the type of pavement surfacing providing, the roads are divided into two categories as:
1. Surfaced road
2. Unsurfaced road

1. **Surfaced Roads :** Surface roads which are provided with a bituminous or cement concrete surfacing.
2. **Unsurfaced Roads :** Unsurfaced roads which are not provided with bituminous or cement concreting.

1.5.4 Classification Based on the Road Plan

Classification of Rural Roads : (I.R.C-1980)

The road plan classified the roads in India based on location and function into following categories :

1. Expressways
2. National Highways (NH)
3. State Highways (SH)
4. Major District Roads (MDR)
5. Other District Roads (ODR)
6. Village Roads (VR)

1. **Expressways :** Expressways are a separate class of highways with superior facilities and design standards and are meant as through routes having very high volume of traffic. The expressways are to be provided with divided carriageways, controlled, grade separations at cross roads and fencing. These highways should permit only fast moving vehicles. Expressways may be owned by Central Government or a State Government, depending on whether the route is a National Highway or State Highway.
Example : Mumbai-Pune Expressway.

2. **National Highways (NH) :** National highways are highways running through the length and breadth of India, connecting major ports, foreign highways, capital of large states and large industrial and tourist centers including roads required for strategic movements for the defence of India.

3. **State Highways (SH) :** State highways are arterial roads of a state, connecting-up with the national highways of the adjacent states, district head quarters and important cities within the state and serving as the main arteries for traffic to and from district roads. The NH and SH have the same design speed and geometric design specifications.
Examples : State Highway in Maharashtra State

4. **Major District Roads (MDR) :** Major district roads are important roads within a district serving areas of production and markets and connecting those with each other or with the main highways of a district. The MDR has lower speed and geometric design specifications than NH/SH.

5. **Other District Roads (ODR) :** Other district roads are roads serving rural areas of production and providing them with outlet to market centres, taluka head quarters, block development head quarters or other main roads. These are of lower design specifications than MDR.

6. **Roads (VR) :** Village roads are roads connecting village or groups of villages with each other to the nearest road of a higher category.

1.5.5 Classification of Urban Roads (I.R.C. - 1977)

The road systems within urban areas are classified as Urban Roads and will form a separate category of roads to be taken care by the respective urban authorities. They are divided into following types.

1. Arterial roads
2. Sub-arterial roads
3. Collector streets and
4. Local streets

1. **Arterial Roads :** The city roads which are meant for through traffic usually on a continuous route are called arterial streets. Arterial streets are generally spaced at less than 15 km in developed business centres whereas in less important areas, these may be 8 km apart. Arterial roads are also divided highways with fully or partially controlled access. Parking, loading and unloading activities are carefully regulated. Pedestrians are permitted to cross them at intersections only.

2. **Sub-Arterial Roads :** The city roads which provide lower level of travel mobility than arterial streets are called as sub-arterial streets. Their spacing may vary from 0.5 km in central business districts to 3 to 5 km in sub-urban areas. Loading and unloading are usually restricted. Pedestrians are allowed to cross these highways at intersections.

3. **Collector Streets :** The city roads which are constructed for collecting and distributing the traffic to and from local streets, and also to provide an access to arterial and sub-arterial streets, are also called collector streets. These are located in residential, business and industrial areas. These roads are accessible from the building along them. Parking restrictions are few that too during peak hours.

4. **Local Streets :** The city roads which provide an access to residence, business and other building are called local streets. The traffic carried either originates or terminates along the local streets. Depending upon the importance of the adjoining areas, a local street may be residential, commercial or industrial. Along local streets, pedestrians may move freely and parking may be permitted without any restriction.

1.6 NAGPUR PLAN

The Nagpur Plan was at the initiative of the Central Government then existing in 1943. Then on slaught of Second World War has caused sufficient increase in the traffic and consequent deterioration of the pavements. The Chief Engineers of the then provinces therefore, met at Nagpur at the instance of Central Government to evolve road plan for the next twenty years and is now generally called as the Nagpur plan. The major recommendations of this conference were

- The roads should be divided into four categories viz.
(a) **National Highways :** Which would traverse the provinces and would be major arteries of communications and will be of national importance from strategic and other purposes.
(b) **Provincial or State Roads :** Which connect major towns in the state or province.
(c) **District Roads :** Which would connect important townships in the districts and therefore would take traffic from the national and state roads to the interior of the district. Depending upon the importance they could be further classed as major district roads or other district roads.
(d) **Village Roads :** Which would link important villages to the road network.
- National Highways should be the major frame work within which road system of the country should develop. Maintenance and construction of national highways should be liability of Central Government, financially.
- The national, state and major district roads should have durable hard pavement crust, but the other district road, village roads may have an earth surface, but further improvement in this earth surface such as soil-stabilization gravelling should be considered when necessity is felt.
- All national highways, provincial highways, and major district should have permanent bridges - preferably non-submersible bridges and causeways if at all provided should not cause detention of traffic of more than 12 hours at a time or more than six times a year.
- The committee felt that construction of other district road and village roads should not be left to the district boards then existing, and that this role should be assumed by state highway engineers.
- There should be a balanced development of all the roads i.e. all the roads should be developed more or less simultaneously.

1.6.1 Determination of Road Length by Nagpur Plan

The Nagpur plan proposed a formula for calculating the road length of different categories of road, taking into consideration the geographical, agricultural and population conditions. Length in km of National, State and Major District

$$\text{Roads} = \frac{A}{8} + \frac{B}{32} + 1.6\,N + 8\,T + DJ - R$$

where,
A = Agricultural Area in km².
B = Non-Agricultural Area in km².
N = Number of towns and villages with population range 2001 to 5000.
T = Number of towns and villages with population over 5000.
D = Development allowance, where value will be generally taken as 15 % for agricultural and industrial development.

R = Existing length of railway track in km.

$$J = \frac{A}{8} + \frac{B}{32} + 1.6\,N + 8\,T$$

The total length of secondary category roads for other district and village roads in km is given by the formula :

Mileage of such roads = 0.32 V + 0.8 Q + 1.6 P + 3.2 S + DJ

where,

V = Number of villages with population 500 or less.
Q = Number of villages with population range 501 – 1000
P = Number of villages with population range 1001 – 2000
S = Number of villages with population range 2001 – 5000

and D = Development allowance generally taken as 15 %.

J = 0.32 V + 0.8 Q + 1.6 P + 3.2 S.

The above formula is on the assumption of star and grid pattern of road network.

It must be brought out here that the Nagpur plan strategy gives cumulative lengths i.e. the total length of National highways and total length of secondary roads, but it is not possible to obtain individual road length of state highways or village roads etc. This is it's lacuna.

1.7 BOMBAY PLAN

By the end of second plan, the targets fixed by Nagpur plan were achieved but there was demand for more road to cater for the rapidly growing economy of the country. Estimates committee of the Parliament therefore recommended that draft plan be prepared for the nation's requirement for the next 25 – 30 years. A twenty year draft plan was prepared by the Roads wing of the Government of India and approved by the Chief Engineers in 1959 at Bombay. Hence, it is sometimes called as Bombay Plan.

The Objectives and Features of The Plan : The objectives of the draft plan were :

(1) Provision of good communication network in the rural areas will increase urbanisation and hence every village should be brought near the road. The guidelines were as follows:
- Every village in a developed area should be brought within 6.5 km (4 miles) of a metalled road and 2.4 km (1.5 miles) of any road.
- Every village in semideveloped area should be brought within 13 km (8 miles) of metalled road and 5 km (3 miles) of any road.
- Every village and human settlement in undeveloped and uncultivable area should be bought within 20 km (12 miles) of any road.

(2) The road length should be increased so as to give road density of 32 km per 100 sq. km (52 miles per 100 sq. miles) of area.

(3) There should be overall development road network. Places of pilgrimage, administrative head quarters, ports, railway junctions must be connected by roads and in addition strategic roads should be given due importance.

(4) Express ways should be considered where necessary. In fact the plan envisages 1600 km length of express ways.

(5) While calculating road length in hilly regions, an allowance upto 100 per cent may be made in arriving a road length. Hills with high altitudes above 2300 metres may be ignored in calculating the road length. This is a contradictory recommendation in view of the strategic importance of hill roads.

- The funds for road construction and maintenance should be derived not only from the direct beneficieries (motor vehicle taxation) but also from indirect beneficieries - such as land revenue, tax on diesel oil etc.
- Arterial roads should be bridged and preferably two lane wide.
- Maintenance of roads should be accorded high priority. It was expected that the maintenance expenditure would increase from 30 crores in 1961 to 130 crores in 1981 due to new construction of roads.
- Fresh entrants, who would work as Highway Engineers should be professionally trained.
- Each highway department should have a cell to deal with traffic engineering road standards.
- Some roads such as village roads, panchayat road, zilla parishad roads which are under the superintendence of these authorities, should get guidance from state highway authorities.

Road Way Length Targets

The road lengths for different categories of roads were fixed in miles since km as a unit was not in vogue in 1959. Converted to km these formulas were

(a) National Highway (km)

$$= \left[\frac{A}{64} + \frac{B}{80} + \frac{C}{96}\right] + 32K + 8M + D\left[\frac{A}{64} + \frac{B}{80} + \frac{C}{96} + 32K + 8M\right]$$

(b) National Highways + State Highways (km)

$$= \left[\frac{A}{20} + \frac{B}{24} + \frac{C}{32} + 48K + 24M + 11.2N + 1.6P\right] \times \left(\frac{100 + D}{100}\right)$$

(c) National Highways + State Highways + Major District Roads (km)

$$= \left[\frac{A}{8} + \frac{B}{16} + \frac{C}{24} + 48K + 24M + 11.2N + 9.6P + 6.4Q + 2.4R\right] \times \left(\frac{D + 100}{100}\right)$$

(d) National Highway + State Highways + Major District Roads + Other District Roads (km)

$$= \left[\frac{3A}{16} + \frac{3B}{32} + \frac{C}{16} + 48K + 24M + 11.2N + 9.6P + 12.8Q + 4R + 0.8S + 0.32T\right] \times \left(\frac{D+100}{100}\right)$$

(e) National Highways + State Highways + Major District Roads + Other District Roads + Village Roads

$$= \left[\frac{A}{4} + \frac{B}{8} + \frac{C}{12} + 48K + 24M + 11.2N + 9.6P + 12.8Q + 5.9R + 1.6S + 0.64T + 0.2V\right] \times \left(\frac{D+100}{100}\right)$$

where,

- A = Developed and Agricultural Area, km²
- B = Semideveloped Area, km²
- C = Undeveloped Area, km²
- K = Number of towns with population over 1 lakh
- M = Number of towns with population between 50000 to 1 lakh
- N = Number of towns with population between 20,000 to 50,000
- P = Number of towns with population between 10000 to 20000
- Q = Number of towns with population between 5000 to 10000
- R = Number of towns with population between 2000 to 5000
- S = Number of settlements with population between 1000 to 2000
- T = Number of settlements with population between 500 to 1000
- V = Number of towns with population less than 500
- D = Development allowance generally taken as 5 % for the 20 year draft plan period.

1.8 LUCKNOW PLAN

Considering the lessons understood from the first to seventh plan, the Chief Engineers of various states and the Indian Roads Congress formulated a long term plan for India for the period 1981 – 2001. This plan is called as Lucknow Plan. The goals and policies of this road plan are :

- Accessibility to all the villages with a population of above 500 should be provided by the turn of the century.

- Master plan should be prepared, for towns cities, district, state and national level and it should be remembered while making these master plans that the plan should generate employment and industrial growth.
- The national highway length should be so increased as to form square grid of 100 km side.
- Speedy travel may be facilitated by Expressways. The expressways should be constructed on major traffic corridors.
- Environmental standards must be maintained in the construction and maintenance of roads and energy conservation in the form of petrol saving must be given high priority and road safety measures should be undertaken to contain and bring down the accident rates.
- Major District Roads should serve and connect all towns and villages with a population of 1500 and above and other village roads should serve and connect villages with a population of 1000-1500.
- Expressways are recommended on major traffic corridors to promote speedy travel. As traffic develops the widening of roads should be taken-up but care should be taken to see while initial constructing the road that sufficient sideway margin is available for future widening from this point of view, ribbon development should be checked right from the beginning if required by suitable legislative measures.
- Resources crunch may make it difficult to make all rural roads all-weather roads. As a beginning, the roads may be made earthen roads or gravel roads.
- Computer-aided designs of highways and highway parameters, research and development activities and data based on traffic flows and connected fields should be strengthened.
- There should be modernization of road making machinery and strengthened highway contracting industry.
- Additional sources of highway finance such as toll roads and private sector financing should be explored. Where required for special problems, private consulting firms could be contacted without hesitation.
- The lengths of various categories of road as far as twenty year plan is concerned could be calculated as under :

    (a) National Highways, length in km $= \dfrac{\text{Area in sq. km}}{50}$

    (b) State Highways, length in km $= \dfrac{\text{Area in sq. km}}{25}$

or

State Highways, length in km $= 62.5 \times \text{Number of Towns} - \dfrac{\text{Area in sq. km}}{50}$

(c) Major District Roads, length in km = $\dfrac{\text{Area in sq. km}}{12.5}$

or

Major District Road length = 90 × Number of Towns

(d) Total Road length = 4.74 × Number of Villages and Towns

(e) Rural road length (ODR + Village roads) may be obtained by subtracting the length of SH NH and MDR from the total length. For calculating these road lengths, NH system is supposed to have a grid of 100 km side.

The idea of obtaining State Highway length is that it should be twice the National Highway length. Similarly, it is assumed in the above formula that NH and SH will pass through all towns with population more than 5000. On this basis, on the assumption of 3364 towns, the length of the square grid works out to be

$$\sqrt{\dfrac{\text{Area of the country}}{\text{Number of Towns}}} = \sqrt{\dfrac{3287782}{3364}}$$

= 31.25 km

As such length of NH and SH = 2 × 31.25 × Number of Towns

= 62.5 × Number of Towns

The idea behind the formula to work out length of MDR is that it should be twice the length of State Highways, whereas the another formula for MDR is empirical. The total road length in the nation is computed on the assumption that every town and village must be connected by road. Since, there are 583563 villages and towns, the average area per human settlement is

$$= \dfrac{\text{Area of Nation}}{\text{Number of Villages}}$$

$$= \dfrac{3287782}{583563}$$

= 5.64 sq. km

∴ Length of grid = $\sqrt{5.64}$ = 2.37 km

∴ Length of total road = 2 × 2.37 × Number of Villages and Towns

= 4.74 × Number of Villages and Towns

The above criteria results in a road density of 0.82 km/sq. km as against 0.46 in 1981.

- Requirement of funds as per 20 year plan (1981 – 2001) is estimated around 64000 crores. The present yearly revenue from the Central and State Governments from motor vehicles is around 5000 crores. Therefore, the expenditure is justified. The overall goal of 20 year plan is indicated in the table below.

Table 1.1

Category of Road	Existing Length km	Target Length km	Additional Length km	Cost in Crores
Express Highway	–	2000	2000	To be met from toll collection
National Highways	31737	66000	34263	16950
State Highways	95491	144000	48509	10664
Major Highways	153000	280000	145000	12759
Rural Roads	912684	2212000	1299316	24879
Total	1192912	2704000	1529088	129774

For calculating road length, formula based on area is preferred. Towns are defined as settlements having at least municipalities.

1.9 THE DEVELOPMENT OF ROADS IN INDEPENDENT INDIA

Speedy economic development and upliftment of masses can be undertaken in India only with efficient road network. The important aspects which road network is going to satisfy in modern India are :

- India with it's about 5,90,000 villages placed in different parts and extreme interior can be connected with good road network thus bringing social uplift health and education of the village population.
- India is a land of many marvels. On one hand we have hilly terrain in Jammu Kashmir, Himachal Pradesh, Sikkim, Assam, Meghalaya, Manipur, Mizoram, Tripura, Nagaland, Arunachal Pradesh, and hilly regions of U. P. and on the other hand we have deserts of Kutch, Rajputana and Swamps of Mand in Punjab. In such unhospitable terrain, only roads can serve as link of mass communication. The roads in such regions are not only serving as arteries of nation but these roads are of strategic importance and serve ideal frame for defence network.
- The roads handle 58 % of goods traffic and about 80 % of passenger traffic. For short hauls of 300 – 350 km cost advantage is with road traffic, high value commodities such as tea, raw cotton are generally transported even for longer hauls. For perishable commodities like fruit and livestock, road transport has an advantage upto about 450 km. Because of this economics, it is generally cheaper to bring agricultural goods to Mandis by road transport. The green revolution in the country owes not a little to roads. Punjab and Haryana which have connected all their villages by road are examples of agricultural prosperity brought by roads. The collection and processing of surplus milk generated in the villages is possible only because of the road and in that sense even the white revolution owes a lot to the good road network.

- The forest wealth of the country is being exploited mainly because of the roads penetrating into the jungles. Similarly, the development of fisheries along the coast line has been made possible because of the construction of link roads leading to the coast.
- Some of the ancient monuments, religious places, tourist spots are accessible only by roads. Indian tourism has received a big boost because of the motorable road network.
- Road construction in India is still labour intensive. Therefore, it is possible for the road transport sector to give gainful employment to more number of people in the construction, maintenance and in actual transport.
- Presently, India has the smallest ownership rate of car viz 6 per thousand persons as against 668 per thousand in U.S.A. and 320 per thousand in U.K. But India is developing and the growth rate of motor vehicle population is around 10 % per annum (compound). There were about 86 lakhs motor vehicles in India in 1985. Though the growth rate is somewhat smaller, the initial numbers of cars are large (of course due to large population) and therefore number of cars coming every year on road is large, requiring good network.
- This vast land of diverse climate and nature can be brought under one administrative umbrella by efficient network of roads. Law and order and dispensation of justice can not simply be achieved without road network in India. National integration and cohesion has been brought by roads. People go to different parts, understand them and there is a feeling of oneness. Roads have also helped in case of famine and flood operations.

1.10 DEVELOPMENTS OF ROADS IN FIVE YEAR PLANS

After independence, we declared ourselves as socialistic sovereign, state with more or less mixed economy. Systematic planning in public sector and directional planning in private sector started and therefore it is worth while to watch the progress in highways plan wise.

1.10.1 Pre-plan (Period 1943 – 1951)

During the pre-plan period of 1943 – 1951, the Nagpur plan was already there as a model for road development. However, due to partition of our country, there was paucity of fund and Nagpur plan expectations could not be fulfilled.

1.10.2 First Five Year Plan (Period 1951 – 1956)

In this particular plan period, 6.7 % of the total plan expenditure was incurred on roads and this expenditure was about 30.2 per cent of the expenditure on the transport sector. The salient features of road development in the first five year plan could be summarised below.
- **National Highways :** Through the National Highway Act, the national highways became the central subject and the Central Government statutorily took them over. The missing links on N. H. system to the tune of 2000 km were constructed. About 30 major bridges and improvements to nearly 10,000 km of national highway was taken-up. Expenditure to the

tune of about Rs. 27 crores was incurred. Some important inter-state reads such as Passi-Badarpur Road in Assam, Assam - Agartala Road connecting Assam with Tripura were taken up. The state sector roads also increased in length. The total road length increased from 399940 km to about 498340 km registering an increase of 25 %.

1.10.3 Second Five Year Plan

About 4.8 % of the total plan expenditure and 20 % of the total transport sector expenditure was incurred on roads. The Central Government sponsored Dhar-Udampur Road and construction of west coast road (Bombay - Kanyakumari Road) which was taken during the first plan was continued. About 40 major bridges were constructed. In line with the activities of the Central Government, the State Governments also formulated different schemes and completed them. As a result, there was an increase in road length from 498340 km to 7012120 km. i.e. about 42 % increase. Thirty three per cent of the roads by this time were surfaced roads.

1.10.4 Third Five Year Plan (Period 1961 – 1966)

The Bombay road plan served as a frame work for the third fourth and fifth five year plans. In fact this plan saw tremendous growth in highway construction activity. The significant developments that took place in this plan period.

- There was the most important and eye opening event of the epoc that is the Chinese external aggression. As a result of this aggression, Border Road Development Board was created under Transport Ministry to deal with problems concerning these roads. Most of these roads were hill roads or desert roads and as such development of hill roads got a boost.
- The system of National Highways was strengthened. Sixty six major bridges were constructed on the national highway system, which included Mahanadi Bridge at Cuttack and Sone Bridge in Bihar.
- In this particular period, there was a bottleneck in the coal transportation and the planners realised the shortcoming of railways as a means of communications. Therefore, they started looking towards road work as a means to transport coal, since coal as a source of energy is very important.
- In general, there was some shift from labour intensive road construction to somewhat mechanised road construction.
- Under the central aided scheme, the lateral road project on the foot - hills of Himalayas from Uttarpradesh to Assam was sanctioned and taken up for construction while the work on West Coast Road already started continued.
- In this plan period, Government of India received credit from the World Bank for construction of selected national highway. An expenditure of about Rs. 440 crores was incurred in this plan period which constituted 22 % of the expenditure on transport sector and 6 % of the overall plan expenditure. The total road length registered a rise of 49 % over the length at the end of the second plan.

1.10.5 The Fourth Plan (Period 1969 – 1974)

In between 1966 - 1969, there was plan holiday and the actual fourth plan commenced in 1969. The salient achievements of this plan were as follows :

(1) In June, 1971, certain new additions to the highway system were done. These were

    (a) Highway No. NH 44 - connecting Shillong, Passi, Badarpur and Agartala,

    (b) NH 21 Highway connecting Bilaspur, Kulu and Mandi with Chandigarh,

    (c) Highway NH 5A connecting Pardeep port to NH 5 at Haridaspur and

    (d) NH 4 A connecting Belgaum, Phonda and Panaji.

(2) One important happening in this period was that the Government set-up one - man commission with Mr. H. P. Sinha as chairman to study the condition and possible development of rural roads. This happened in 1967 and the report got published in 1968 just before the plan period. The recommendations of the committee were.

    (a) High-level rural board should be set-up in each state for planning and allocation of funds for the rural roads and there should be a post of chief engineer in the state to look after these roads. This recommendation was not followed.

    (b) It also envisaged that at least third of the rural road construction cost should come from the beneficiaries. In fact the committee made the proposal that if the third road cost is deposited by the people concerned, the state should come forward to spend the rest 2/3 and construct the road.

    (c) The chairman Mr. Sinha favoured a total length of at least 324000 km of village roads and 230,400 km of other district road. Of course the implication of the findings of the committee were felt in fifth plan period.

1.10.6 The Fifth Plan (Period 1974 – 1979)

The significant achievements of this plan period were

- The additions to National Highway network.
- As a part of Minimum Needs Programme (M.N.P.) it was proposed to construct all weather rods so that the villages with a population of more than 1500 are interconnected. This was not totally achieved.
- Expenditure in this plan period including the plan period 1979 - 1980 was around 31 % of the total transport sector and the road length increased from 1393930 km to about 1534200 km. This expenditure includes the cost that went for conversion of single lane widths to two lane widths for certain National Highways.

1.10.7 The Sixth Five Year Plan (Period 1980 – 1985)

Sixth Five Year Plan is characterised by the following achievements :

- Many highways to the tune 2500 km were constructed in the strategic North Eastern Zone.

- The minimum needs programme of the sixth plan was reinforced.
- In general, this plan could be said to be stock checking plan, the deficiencies in the previous plans were made-up, missing links provided, certain inter - state roads of economic importance and border roads were constructed. The sixth plan contained a provision of 3440 crores representing around 29 % of the outlay in the transport sector and around 3.5 % outlay in the total plan.

1.10.8 The Seventh Plan (Period 1985 – 1990)

The main objectives and the achievements of this plan are :
- Proposal to construct expressways i.e. Ahmedabad - Vadodara and Kolkata - Durgapur. These will be first expressways of the country.
- Continued rural road activity so that the minimum needs programme is completed. These rural roads will be constructed if required under Employment Gurantee Scheme or Rural Landless Employment Gurantee Programme (NLEGRP) or National Rural Employment Programme (NREP). Presently out of nearly 6,00,000 villages, about 2,60,000 villages only are connected by all-weather roads. The level of accessibility in respect of villages of 1500 population or above is 86 % and that of 1000 - 1500 is 63%.
- No National Highways as such were proposed and most of the expenditure went in consolidating the gains.
- The system of National Highway was strengthened. The expenditure that is to be in curred on National Highways in this plan as a comparison to other previous plans is indicated in the table 1.1.
- For the first time, provision of new generation of roads along high density corridors with divided carriageway facilities were proposed.
- The seventh plan makes an outlay of Rs. 892 crores for National Highways and Rs. 128 for other centrally sponsored schemes and Rs. 4180 crores for the state sector roads.

1.10.9 Eighth Five Year Plan Roads (Period 1990 - 1995)

- The existing deficiencies in national highways (NH) would require construction of missing links, four laning and two laning of various sections, construction of bridges and by-passes etc. The first priority will be given to complete the ongoing works. For systematic development of the NH system, different strategies will need to be adopted for low, medium and high volume traffic density routes. Capacity augmentation of high density traffic corridors carrying more than 15,000 passenger car units traffic per day, through four laning will need to be taken up during the Eighth Plan. For selected high density corridors, it may be necessary to consider expressway facility for rapid and safe movement of fast traffic. Levy of tolls may be considered for highway users. For national highways carrying medium traffic density, traffic upto 15000 PCUs, strengthening of pavement and widening to two-lanes including reconstruction of bridges, wherever

necessary, need to be taken-up. For low traffic density routes carrying traffic upto 5,000 PCUs, widening to two-lanes may be considered only on a selective basis, depending upon the resource availability. However, weak and narrow bridges have to be replaced.
- As regards additions to the National Highways system, it would be necessary to adopt a very selective approach in view of the resource constraints and the need to give priority to removal of deficiencies on the existing NH-system
- Constraints of resources may not permit removal of all the existing deficiencies in the State highways during the Plan period and a selective approach based on economic cost benefit analysis may have to be adopted.
- Rural roads are essential for achieving the objective of integrated rural development. The priority for rural road development in the Eighth Plan would be as under:-

   (a) Linking of all villages with a population of 1000 and above on the basis of 1981 census.

   (b) Special efforts to accelerate village connectivity in respect of backward regions and tribal areas.
- It would be appropriate to integrate rural road construction and maintenance under Minimum Needs Programme (MNP) with local area development planning. State Governments may pool the resources, made available under MNP and special employment programmes and undertake rural road construction under the respective local area development plan.

1.10.10 Ninth Five Year Plan (Period 1995 - 2000)

The following goals and objectives have been kept in view while framing the outline of the Ninth Plan :

- Phased removal of deficiencies in the existing NH network in the tune with traffic needs for 10-15 years with emphasis on high density corridors for four-laning.
- Bring in highway-user oriented project planning in identifying package of projects section-wise rather than isolated stretches.
- Greater attention to rehabilitation and reconstruction of weak/dilapidated bridges for the safety of the traffic.
- Modernization of road construction technology for speedy execution and quality assurance.
- Engineering measures to improve road safety and conservation of energy.
- Continued emphasis on research and development
- Integrating the development plans with Railways and other modes of transport.
- Providing employment opportunities to the labour force in rural areas.
- Special attention for development of roads in the North-Eastern Region.
- Encouraging private sector participation in development of roads.

1.10.11 Five Year Plan (Period 2001-05)

The following broad goals and objectives for road sector development have been set for the Tenth Plan :

- Balanced development of the total road network comprising three functional groups viz. the primary system (National Highways (NH) and expressways), secondary system (State Highways and Major District Roads) and rural roads.
- Development of roads to be considered an integral part of the total transport system supplementing other modes, integrating the development plans with railways and other modes of transport.
- Completion of the National Highways Development Project comprising the Golden Quadrilateral and the North-South and East-West corridors.
- Phased removal of deficiencies in the existing NH network in tune with traffic for the next 10-15 years with emphasis on four-laning of high-density corridors.
- To plan and take preliminary action for expressways to be built in future in those sections where these can be economically justified.
- To make long distance travel safer and faster so as to give a boost to the economy.
- Priority is to be accorded to areas like overloading of trucks, control of encroachments and unplanned ribbon development, energy conservation and environment protection.
- Greater attention to be paid to rehabilitation and reconstruction of weak/dilapidated bridges for traffic safety.
- Special attention is to be paid to the development of roads in the North-Eastern region.
- Particular emphasis needs to be given to the commercialisation of highways particularly the National Highways and State Highways and bringing in the concept of user-charges for sustainable financing of the road sector. Further steps must also be taken to encourage private sector participation in the highway sector. It is necessary to implement the policy of levying toll on all four-lane roads on the National Highway network. States must adopt a similar strategy in respect of State Highways etc.
- High-density corridors within the network of National and State Highways and Major District Roads should be identified. Such corridors and major inter-state roads should be developed on a priority basis.
- To improve the quality of life in rural areas and ensure balanced regional development by achieving the PMGSY target of providing connectivity through all-weather roads to all habitations with a population of over 500 persons (as per the 2001 Census).
- To encourage industry and export by providing sufficiently wide roads leading to industrial centres, ports, mining areas and power plants.
- To encourage tourism by improving roads leading to centres of tourist importance.
- To provide wayside amenities along highways.

- To reduce transportation costs by providing better riding surface and popularising the use of containers and multi-axle vehicles in the haulage of goods.
- Utmost attention to the proper upkeep and maintenance of the existing road network.
- To ensure road connectivity where rail link is not available or possible.
- Integrating the development plan with railways and other modes of transport and to:
  (a) Identify feeder roads to important railway routes and undertake needed improvement including periodic maintenance;
  (b) Link minor important ports with minimum two-lane NHs/SHs;
  (c) Link all Inland Container Depots/container freight stations with minimum two-lane NHs / SHs.
- Use of modern management techniques for scientific assessment of maintenance strategies/priorities.
- Development of a road data bank and computerized project monitoring system and promotion of the use of information technology in the highway sector.

1.10.12 Eleventh Five Year Plan (Period 2007-2012)

- The Tenth Plan stressed the need for improving mobility and easy accessibility. Accordingly, the National Highway Development Programme (NHDP) consisting of four laning of the Golden Quadrilateral (NHDP I) with a length of 5,846 km and the North-South and East-West Corridor (NHDP II) with a length of 7472 km coupled with Pradhan Mantri Gram Sadak Yojana (PMGSY) for rural roads were taken-up. The PMGSY programme has been recently expanded to achieve the Bharat Nigam target of connecting 1000 + habitation (500 + for hilly and tribal areas) by 2008-09 with all-weather roads. This programme will help bring India's villages into the market economy. It will also help us to tackle social sector problems like illiteracy, high IMR and MMR) which are dragging India down because while roads connect villages to markets, they also connect them to schools and hospitals. The "Special Accelerated Development Road Programme for the North Eastern Region (SARDP-NE)", will help in developing and integrating these regions with the rest of the country.
- The problems of development of our roads network are diverse and future requirements are formidable magnitude. Therefore, the strategy for development of roads would have to vary keeping in view the nature of problem and the development required. It is proposed to undertake an expanded programme for highway development going beyond NHDP I and II to include NHDP III to VII. This programme will involve substantial resources from public private partnership based on build, operate and transfer (BOT) model which has many advantages over the traditional contracts (See *Box* on PPPs). All contracts on provision of road services for high density corridors to be taken-up under NHDP III onwards would be awarded only on BOT basis, and the traditional construction contracts will be awarded only in specified exceptional cases. A

model concession agreement has been developed to facilitate speedy award of contracts. This is a very significant innovation in the areas of public-private partnership. This would leave a substantial part of National Highways network which would also require development during the Eleventh Plan period. These sections are characterised by low density of traffic. Some of these stretches fall in backward and inaccessible areas and others are of strategic importance. The development of these categories of National Highways would be carried out primarily through budgetary resources.

- The present traffic mix consisting of non-motorised and low-powered vehicles compels low speed Furthermore, most of the National Highways pass through habitations and ribbon development is a perennial problem. It is, therefore, necessary to establish a network of access controlled Expressways across the country for which advance planning would be undertaken during the Eleventh Plan. The actual construction (except for 1000 kms already taken-up) would be undertaken during the Twelth Plan period and would be prioritised according to the density of traffic.

- Vehicular traffic needs more than just the arterial routes to be of world class. Adequate attention has not been given in the past to other roadways, which are the responsibility of the state governments. Priority would be accorded for ensuring integrated development of road networks including State Highways, Major District Roads and Other District Roads. The increased emphasis on rural roads would also continue and a major proportion of the 1.72 lakh unconnected habitations would be connected with all weather roads under the PMGSY.

- The maintenance of roads has not been given adequate importance by the states mainly due to paucity of resources. This has resulted in poor riding quality of the road network which is highly uneconomic. A rupee spend on maintenance saves two to three rupees in vehicle operating costs, besides improving traffic flow. Therefore, there is a need to accord higher priority to the needs of maintenance by providing more allocation or considering it as a part of Plan. In fact, the 12th Finance Commission has recommended additional grants to the States, to the tune of Rs. 15,000 crore for maintenance of roads and bridges for the four-year period 2006-07 to 2009-10.

- The National Highway Authority of India (NHAI) has an enormous task before it to implement a road programme. The Authority is being restructured to give it greater professional skills combined with a measure of autonomy and accountability.

- Indian roads are considered very accident prone and claim a large number of casualties representing an enormous human and economic loss. This problem is compounded by the phenomenal growth in road transport fleet, particularly personalized vehicles and the consequent problems of increase in vehicular pollution and road safety. Steps need to be taken to improve the public transport system and safety of road transport operations.

1.11 THE INDIAN ROADS CONGRESS

Fifty years ago, in 1934, India was under the British rule; independence was 13 years away hidden in the mists of future. In the world, troubles were brewing and events were shaping themselves inexorably towards the misfortune of Second World War. Within the country, the call of independence was loud and clear. There were only about a hundred thousand motor vehicles including cars, buses, and Lorries in the whole country.

Fig. 1.3

The Railways were the main carriers of goods and passengers. Hardly any attention had been paid to the road system and surfaced roads were not much in evidence. Even though tar and asphalt surfacing, came to be known by 1922 or so, their actual application in the different provinces of the country was extremely limited. The total length of roads surfaced with tar, bitumen or asphalt was only about 6500 km. Paucity of funds was a major constraint as would be evident from the fact that application of surfaced treatment required sanction of the Legislature as an original work. The annual expenditure on the construction and upkeep of roads in all the eight provinces of British India together was only of the order of Rs 65 million. Road bridges consisted mainly of brick and stone masonry arches. Although, manufacture of portland cement within the country had started by about 1914, the first reinforced cement concrete slab bridges made their appearance only by about 1920 These were followed by a few R.C.C. slab and girder, arch and bowstring girder bridges.

It was into this milieu that was born the Indian Roads Congress. In December 1934, 73 Highway Engineers representing the various provinces, Indian States and Business Interests of the country met in New Delhi to consider and discuss questions relating to road construction and maintenance, thus heralding the birth of the Indian Roads Congress. The first meeting of the Indian Roads Congress was opened by Sir Frank Noyce, the then Member for Industries and Labour. The coming into being of the Indian Roads Congress gave the greatest fillip to the development of roads and transport in the country. Since then the Indian Roads Congress has grown steadily over the years and has now (2014) on its rolls more than 14,500 members representing Engineers of all ranks from Central and State

Governments, Engineering Services of the Army, Border Roads Organization, Road Research Institutes, Engineering Colleges, Local Bodies and Business Interests connected with roads and road transport.

The Indian Roads Congress (IRC) is the Apex Body of Highway Engineers in the country. The IRC was set up in December, 1934 on the recommendations of the Indian Road Development Committee best known as Jayakar Committee set up by the Govt. of India with the objective of Road Development in India. As the activities of the IRC expanded, it was formally registered as a Society in 1937 under the Societies Registration Act of 1860. Over the years Congress has burgeoned and grown into a multi dimensional many faceted organization, devoted to the cause of better roads & better bridges in the country.

The Congress provides a National forum for sharing of knowledge and pooling of experience on the entire range of subjects dealing with the construction & maintenance of roads and bridges, including technology, equipment, research, planning, finance, taxation, organisation and all connected policy issues. In more specific terms the objectives of the Congress are :

- To promote and encourage the science and practice of building and maintenance of roads;
- To provide a channel for the expression of collective opinion of its members on matters affecting roads;
- To promote the use of standard specifications and to propose specifications:
- To advise regarding education, experiment and research connected with roads;
- To hold periodical meetings to discuss technical questions regarding roads;
- To suggest legislation for the development, improvement and protection of roads;
- To suggest improved methods of administration, planning, design, construction, operation, use and maintenance of roads:
- To establish, furnish and maintain libraries and museums for furthering the science of road making; and
- To publish or arrange for the publication of proceedings, Journals, periodicals. and other literature for the promotion of the objectives of the Indian Roads Congress.

1.12 CENTRAL ROAD RESEARCH INSTITUTE (CRRI)

Central Road Research Institute (CRRI), a premier national laboratory established in 1952, a constituent of Council of Scientific and Industrial Research (CSIR) is engaged in carrying out research and development projects on design, construction and maintenance of roads and runways, traffic and transportation planning of mega and medium cities, management of roads in different terrains, improvement of marginal materials, utilization of industrial waste in road construction, landslide control, ground improvements environmental pollution, road traffic safety and analysis & design, wind, fatigue, corrosion studies, performance monitoring / evaluation, service life assessment and rehabilitation of highway and railway bridges.

Fig. 1.4

The institute provides technical and consultancy services to various user organizations in India and abroad. For capacity building of human resources in the area of highway engineering to undertake and execute roads and runway projects, Institute has the competence to organize National & International Training Programmes continuing education courses since 1962 to disseminate the R&D finding to the masses.

Services Offered by CRRI

Road agencies involved in development and maintenance of roads and road transport infrastructure, or city planning departments can avail the expertise and infrastructural facilities of the institute through contract/sponsored research and consultancy. Any agency (private, public and government) confronted with technical problems related to development and maintenance of roads and road transport infrastructure may contact CRRI for solution of their problems. Such specialized technical services of the Institute generally include the areas such as :

- Traffic engineering
- Geometric Design of Roads
- Design of Road Intersections
- Techno-economic analysis of projects
- Transport systems planning and analysis
- Subsoil investigations
- Ground improvement problems
- Use of geosynthetics in road works
- Landslide mitigation
- Zonation of hazardous regions
- Construction of roads on softer soils
- Utilization of waste & marginal materials
- Stabilization of expansive soils
- Rural road design and construction
- Axle road studies for pavement management

- Testing and design of concrete and bituminous mixes
- Design of Roads & Airfield Pavements
- Maintenance Management Aspects
- Evaluation of Rigid and Flexible Pavements
- Mastic Asphalt Construction
- Strengthening and Improvement of Distressed Pavements
- Alternate/Modified Binders
- Design of New Pavement System
- Rating of Existing Bridges
- Design of Composite Overlays
- Corrosion Problems
- Setting-up of Quality Control Laboratories
- Training of In-Service Highway Engineers
- Development of Software

1.13 NATIONAL HIGHWAY AUTHORITY OF INDIA (NHAI)

"The National Highways Authority of India was constituted by an act of Parliament, the National Highways Authority of India Act, 1988. It is responsible for the development, maintenance and management of National Highways entrusted to it and for matters connected or incidental thereto. The Authority was operationalized in February, 1995 with the appointment of full time Chairman and other Members. "

Vision of NHAI

"To meet the nation's need for the provision and maintenance of National Highways network to global standards and to meet user's expectations in the most time bound and cost effective manner, within the strategic policy framework set by the Government of India and thus promote economic well being and quality of life of the people."

National Highways Authority of India (NHAI) is mandated to implement National Highways Development Project (NHDP) which is

- India 's Largest ever highways project
- World class roads with uninterrupted traffic flow

The National Highways have a total length of 71,772 km to serve as the arterial network of the country. The development of National Highways is the responsibility of the Government of India. The Government of India has launched major initiatives to upgrade and strengthen National Highways through various phases of National Highways Development project (NHDP).

Fig. 1.5

The National Highways Development Project is a project to upgrade, rehabilitate and widen major highways in India to a higher standard. The project was implemented in 1998. "National Highways" account for only about 2% of the total length of roads, but carry about 40% of the total traffic across the length and breadth of the country. This project is managed by the National Highways Authority of India (NHAI) under the Ministry of Road, Transport and Highways. The NHAI has implemented US$ 71 billion for this project, as of 2006.

Phases OF NHDP

The project is composed of the following phases :

- **Phase 1 :** The Golden Quadrilateral (GQ; 5,846 km) connecting the four major cities of Delhi, Mumbai, Chennai and Kolkata. This project connecting four metro cities, would be 5,846 km Total cost of the project is Rs.300 billion funded largely by the government's special petroleum product tax revenues and government borrowing. In January 2012, India announced the four lane GQ highway network as complete.

- **Phase 2 :** North-South and East-West corridors comprising national highways connecting four extreme points of the country. The North-South and East-West Corridor (NS-EW; 7,300 km) connecting Srinagar in the north to Kanyakumari in the south, including spur from Salem to Kanyakumari (Via Coimbatore and Kochi) and Silchar in the east to Porbandar in the west. Total length of the network is 7,300 km). As of April 2012, 84.26% of the project had been completed and 15.7% of the project work is currently at progress. It also includes Port connectivity and other projects-1,157 km The final completion date to February 28, 2009 at a cost of Rs.350 billion with funding similar to Phase 1.

- **Phase 3 :** The government recently approved NHDP-3 to upgrade 12,109 km of national highways on a Build, Operate and Transfer (BOT) basis, which takes into account high-density traffic, connectivity of state capitals via NHDP Phase 1 and 2, and connectivity to centers of economic importance. contracts have been awarded for a 2,075 km

- **Phase 4 :** The government is considering widening 20,000 km of highway that were not part of Phase 1, 2, or 3. Phase 4 will convert existing single lane highways into two lanes with paved shoulders. The plan will soon be presented to the government for approval.

- **Phase 5 :** As road traffic increases over time, a number of four lane highways will need to be upgraded /expanded to six lanes. The current plan calls for upgrade of about 5,000 km of four-lane roads, although the government has not yet identified the stretches.
- **Phase 6 :** The government is working on constructing expressways that would connect major commercial and industrial townships. It has already identified 400 km of Vadodara (earlier Baroda)-Mumbai section that would connect to the existing Vadodara (earlier Baroda)-Ahmedabad section. The World Bank is studying this project. The project will be funded on BOT basis. The 334 km Expressway between Chennai-Bangalore and 277 km Expressway between Kolkata-Dhanbad has been identified and feasibility study and DPR contract has been awarded by NHAI.
- **Phase 7 :** This phase calls for improvements to city road networks by adding ring roads to enable easier connectivity with national highways to important cities. In addition, improvements will be made to stretches of national highways that require additional flyovers and bypasses given population and housing growth along the highways and increasing traffic. The government has not yet identified a firm investment plan for this phase. The 19 km long Chennai Port-Maduravoyal Elevated Expressway is being executed under this phase.

1.14 MAHARASHTRA STATE ROAD DEVELOPMENT CORPORATION (MSRDC)

MSRDC is a corporation established and fully owned by the Government of Maharashtra through a resolution on 9th July, 1996 and has been incorporated as a limited company under the Companies Act 1956 on 2nd August 1996.

MSRDC mainly deals with the properties and assets comprising movables and immovables including land, road projects, flyover projects, toll collection rights and works under construction which vested with the State Government and were under the control of the Public Works Department. These have been subsequently transferred to MSRDC.

Fig. 1.6

MSRDC - Vision

"Roads are arteries of a nation. Roads and bridges obliterate distance and connect people while they spur economic progress."

Major Functions of the Corporation are :
- To promote and operate - road projects
- To plan, investigate, design, construct and manage identified road projects and their area development
- To enter into a contract in respects of the works and any other matters transferred to the Corporation along with assets and liabilities
- To invite tenders, bids, offers and enter into contracts for the purposes of all the activities of the corporation.
- To promote participation of any person or body or association of individuals, whether incorporated or not, in planning, investigation, designing, construction and management of transport projects and area development.
- To undertake schemes or works, either jointly with other corporate bodies or institutions, or with Government or local authorities, or on agency basis in furtherance of the purposes for which the Corporation is established and all matters connected therewith.
- To undertake any other project and other activities entrusted by the State Government in furtherance of the objectives for which the Corporation is established.

MSRDC has been driven by a focused set of objectives as follows :
- To improve and develop integrated transport infrastructure such as roads, expressways, bridges, flyovers, MRTS, ports, rail projects, airports etc.
- To raise resources for the identified projects.
- To follow transparent and competitive bidding procedures to ensure quality works at the most economic cost.
- To encourage private sector participation in transport infrastructure.

MSRDC strives hard to deliver exceptional, strategic and integrated infrastructure services to the State of Maharashtra. MSRDC encourages the use of state of the art construction technology to reduce construction period. Decentralized decision-making, constructive co-ordination with the private sector, technical support from professional consultants and FIDIC system of contracts with work-specific amendments provide added advantage to MSRDC's lean organization structure. MSRDC envisions itself as the nation's chosen infrastructure expert and strategic advisor on transport-infrastructure.

1.15 FINANCING OF ROAD PROJECTS

An approximate estimation of the expenditure in the road sector in India, carried out for the coming ten years, amounts to Rs. 25,000 crore for expressways, Rs. 120,000 crore for National Highways and Rs. 70,000 crore for state highways The funding sources of this huge investment could be managed from the

- **Government Sector**
- **International Bank Loans**
- **Private Sectors etc.**

Fig. 1.7

The Golden Quadrilateral and North-South and East-West corridors, for example, will involve an approximate expenditure of Rs.58,000 crore. The funding of these projects has been arranged from various organizations – approximately Rs.20,000 crore from *cess* (from petrol and partially from diesel), Rs.20,000 crore from the *World Bank* and the *Asian Development Bank* loans, Rs.12,000 crore from market borrowing, and Rs.6,000 crore from the private sector. For the PMGSY project, it is decided that the finance will come from 50% of diesel *cess*, market borrowing, and external funding agencies

The government funding may come from various sources, like, budgetary allocation, special road development bonds, fund out of *cess* on diesel or petrol (Central Road Fund) etc. Toll revenue can be utilized for raising the debt finance, or, supporting the maintenance activities on that particular road stretch, and needs to be operated by government or private agency. The difficulty with the toll financing for debt realization is that the *plough back* time-period is long, and fluctuative. If at least the maintenance requirement of a particular stretch can be completely financed from toll, it can stay away from the competition with the requirements of the other roads in the network. Shadow tolling is another concept, where government pays the investor for each vehicle that enters the stretch. Shadow tolling works better than direct toll from vehicles.

Funding for transportation projects can as well be attracted from private organizations. The following policies have been adopted by the Government for encouraging participation of private organizations in highway construction projects :

- Declaration of the road sector as an industry.
- Provision of capital grants subsidy up to 40% of project cost on case-to-case basis.
- Duty-free import of certain identified high quality construction plants and equipment.
- 100% tax exemption for 5 years and 30% relief for next 5 years, which may be availed of in 20 years.

- Provision of encumbrance-free site for work, i.e. the Government shall meet all expenses relating to land and other pre-construction activities
- Foreign direct investment upto 100% in road sector
- Easier external commercial borrowing norms
- Higher concession period, up to 30 years
- Right to collect and retain toll

There could be various models of degree of involvement of private organizations in transportation project financing, like,

(1) Completely owned, financed and operated by private body

(2) Build, operate and transfer (BOT) approach

(3) Bbuild, transfer and operate (BTO) approach,

(4) Finance, build and lease approach etc.

Out of these models BOT is generally considered as the most effective form of privatization. Several variations of the BOT approach exist, like, build, own and operate (BOO), build, own, operate and sell (BOOS), built, operate, lease and transfer (BOLT), build, own, operate and transfer (BOOT) etc. Transportation project requires large outlay of investment; therefore, all the funding possibilities may have to be explored for successful implementation of a conceived project.

1.16 SAFETY AUDIT

It is the procedure of assessment of the safety measures employed for the road. It has the advantages like proper planning and decision from beforehand ensures minimization of future accidents, the long term cost associated with planning is also reduced and enables all kinds of users to perceive clearly how to use it safely. Safety audit takes place in five stages as suggested by Wrisberg and Nilsson, 1996. Five Stages of Safety Audit are :

1. **Feasibility Stage :** The starting point for the design is determined such as number and type of intersection, relationship of the new scheme to the existing road, the relevant design standards.

2. **Draft Stage :** In this stage horizontal and vertical alignment, junction layout are determined. After the completion of this stage decision about land acquisition is taken.

3. **Detailed Design Stage :** Signing, marking, lighting, other roadside equipment and landscaping are determined.

4. **Pre-opening Stage :** Before opening a new or modified road should be driven, walked or cycled. It should be done at different condition like bad weather, darkness.

5. **Monitoring of the Road in Use :** Assessment is done at the final stage after the road has been in operation for few months to determine whether the utilization is obtained as intended and whether any adjustment to the design are required in the light of the actual behavior of road users.

The safety benefits of RSAs have been documented primarily in international applications, which are summarized in chapter four. International assessments focus on the value added by proactively implementing the RSA find-ings. Several studies compared benefits of similar projects where RSAs were conducted with projects in which RSAs were not conducted. In the United States, where RSA tools have only recently been introduced, the quantitative benefits of RSAs have been difficult to document because the RSA is a proactive rather than a reactive safety tool. An analogy can be made to the medical field. It may be difficult to prove the benefits of preventive medicine, yet it is generally accepted that exercise, proper diet, and other measures can help reduce long-term medical costs.

Important Benefits Of Road Safety Audit

- Provide safety beyond established standards;
- Identify additional improvements that can be incorporated into the projects;
- Create consistency among all projects;
- Encourage personnel to think about safety in the course of their normal activities, throughout all stages of a project;
- Invite interdisciplinary input;
- Enhance the quality of field reviews;
- Provide learning experiences for the audit team and design team members;
- Provide feedback to highway designers that they can apply to other projects as appropriate;
- Provide feedback that helps to affirm actions taken and to work through outstanding issues; and
- Ensure that high quality is maintained throughout a project's life cycle.

REVIEW QUESTIONS

1. What is Nagpur plan? How the roads were classified as per this plan?
2. Write down classification of roads.
3. What factors are considered in finagling 20-year (1961-81) plan?

4. Briefly describe the historical development of roads in India
5. Write notes on:
6. Salient features of Bombay road development plan.
7. Salient features of Nagpur road development plan
8. Salient features of Lucknow road development plan
   (a) IRC
   (b) CRRI
   (c) NHAI
   (d) Financing of road project
   (e) Road safety audit
   (f) MSRDC
   (g) Highway planning in India
   (h) Road development in India

CHAPTER 2
FIELD SURVEYS

2.1 INTRODUCTION

Location of the highway alignment is done after carrying out survey of the area; these surveys are called Engineering Surveys. We have to locate an alignment which fulfills the basic requirements like the path must be short, safe, economic, easy and useful. To check all these basic requirements we can carry out the Engineering Surveys in the following phases :

2.2 SURVEYS TO BE CONDUCTED

While fixing the alignments, the following types of surveys are conducted.
- Reconnaissance survey.
- Preliminary survey.
- Determination of central line
- Final location survey.
- Traffic survey.
- Soil and material survey.
- Drainage studies.
- Preparation and presentation of Project documents.

Fig. 2.1

Map Study :

This is the first step of the Engineering survey, using a topographic map of the area under consideration, which can be availed from the Survey of India; we can propose different alternatives of the road alignment. This topographic map in general has a contour interval of around 30 m to 40 m. We can get the details of the natural and artificial features of the area using the topographic map, and accordingly we can suggest a numbers of alternatives for the road alignment. These routes are further studied in the Reconnaissance survey.

2.3 RECONNAISSANCE SURVEY

The main objective of Reconnaissance survey is to examine the general character of the area for the purpose of determining the most feasible route or routes for further detailed investigations. Naturally this type of survey is not required to be carried out where the work consists of improvement to an existing road unless bypasses are involved. The Reconnaissance survey may be conducted in following sequence.

Study of topographical survey sheets, geological and meteorological maps and photographs if available. Reconnaissance survey begins with the study of all available maps. In India, topographical sheets are available to the scale of one in fifty thousand. After study of the topographical features of the map, a number of alignments feasible in a general way are selected keeping in view the following points.

- Consideration of all control points, i.e. major cities and towns, having shortest length and most economical compatible with the requirements of gradients and curvature in a general way.
- Avoidance as far as possible of marshy ground, steep terrain, unstable hilly features, areas subject to flooding and inundation. Any bridging problems that might arise.
- Important towns and villages should be connected, at the same time, environment should be preserved and ecological balance must be maintained.
- After studying the topographical sheets if required, aerial photography may be arranged for further study in the interests of economy. These may be to a scale 1 : 20,000 or 1 : 50,000. If stereoscopic techniques are applied, these can yield quantitative data such as significant soil and sub-soil information.
- In addition to aerial topography, an aerial reconnaissance will provide a bird's eye view of the alignments under considerations along with surrounding area. This will help to identify the factors which call for rejection or modification of any of the alignments.

2.3.1 Ground Reconnaissance

The various alternatives located as a result of the map study are further examined in the field by ground reconnaissance. As such, this part of the survey is a very important link in the chain of activities leading to the selection of final route.

Points on which data may be collected during ground reconnaissance.

During ground reconnaissance, certain points should be remembered. These are :

- Topography of the area whether plain, rolling or steep.
- Length of the route along various alternatives and the number and the likely details of bridges on each alternative.
- Existing means of communication between the destinations - such as mule path, jeep, track etc. and right of way available, bringing out the constraints on account of built-up area, monuments and other structures.
- Terrain and the soil conditions and the likely geometrics, such as gradients, curves etc. likely to be met or arranged on each alternative.
- Geology of the area, nature of hill slopes, and the magnitude of the road length passing through different terrain - such as areas subjected to inundation and flooding, areas subjected to avalanches, snow drifts, rocky stretches, steep terrain, desert areas, areas of poor soil drainage, general elevation of the road, indicating maximum and minimum height negotiated by main ascents and descents in hill sections and the total number of ascents and descents in the hill section.

- Climatic conditions enroute such as monthly maximum and minimum temperature, average annual, peak intensity, and monthly distribution of rainfall data and the snowfall data if required, water table and it's variation between maximum and minimum, wind direction and velocities and extent of fog conditions.
- The facilities and the resources available for the proposed alignment : landing and dropping zones in the case of hilly areas, availability of labour, local contractor, water and the construction material. Value of land acquisition, period required for construction and cost of construction for various alternatives.
- Population that is served by the proposed alignment and the agricultural economic and marketing potential of the area served by the alignment, even future projects, such as dams, hydroelectric projects likely to be taken-up in the area.
- Proposed crossing with rail-lines or highways, necessity of bypasses that are required or that might be required in the future.
- Position of ancient monuments, religious structures etc. and the strategic importance of the route.

Bearing above points in the mind, ground Reconnaissance should be carried. It consists of general examination of the ground by walking or riding along the probable routes and collecting all available information necessary for evaluating the same. In the case of hilly sections, it is advantageous to start Reconnaissance from an obligation point situated close to the top. It is advisable to leave references to facilitate further survey operations. The instrument generally used during ground Reconnaissance will be compass, abeny-level. Pedometer, clinometer, ghat tracer etc. Walkie-Talkie sets are useful for communications. The above instruments are used to measure ground slopes maximum gradient, elevation of critical summits, stream crossings etc.

Based on the information collected during the Reconnaissance survey, a report should be prepared. The report will include a plan to the scale of 1:50000 showing the alternative alignments studied along with their general profiles and rough cost estimates. The information collected should be marked on the map and the different alternatives should be discussed for their merits or otherwise to help the selection of one or more alignments for detailed survey and investigation.

2.4 PRELIMINARY SURVEY

Preliminary survey stage is very important. It is a relatively large-scale instrument survey conducted for the purpose of collecting all the physical information which has the bearing on the proposed location of a new highway or on improvements in existing highway. In the case of new roads, it consists of running an accurate traverse lines along the route previously selected on the basis of Reconnaissance survey. In the case of existing routes where only improvements are proposed, the survey-line is run along the existing alignment. During this phase of survey, topographic features and other features like houses, monuments, places of worship, cremation or burial grounds, utility lines etc. are tied to the traverse line. Longitudinal sections throughout the alignment and cross-sections at regular intervals are taken and bench marks established. The data collected at this stage will form the basis for the determination of the final central line of the road. For this reason, it is essential that every precaution should be taken to maintain a high degree of accuracy. While running a traverse line the information should be collected regarding the following points :

(1) The character of the embankment foundations, particularly necessary in areas having deep cuts to achieve the grade.
(2) Any particular construction problem of the area such as high-level water storage across the alignment. Areas prone to land-slide, settlement of the slopes etc.
(3) The highest subsoil water level and the variation between the maximum and minimum, so also the maximum and minimum rainfall, it's duration and its spacing.
(4) Nature of the cut sections by ascertaining some trial pits or bore holes.

With the data collected it is generally possible to prepare cost estimates within reasonably, close limits for obtaining administrative approval and for planning further detailed survey and investigation.

- As stated earlier, the preliminary survey consists in running a traverse along the proposed alternative adhering as far as possible to the probable final central line of the road.
- The traverse should consist of a series of straight line, with their distance and intermediate angles measured very carefully.
- It is possible that in a difficult terrain the alignment may have to be negotiated through short chord. The traverse should be done with a **theodolite** and all angles measured with double reversal method.
- The distances along the traverse line should be measured with metallic tape or chain or tachometer. An accuracy of 1 : 2000 is desired in distance measurement.
- The directional changes in the alignment and visibility determine transit stations employed in the survey.
- In any case, these transit stations should be marked by means of stakes and numbered in sequences. They should be protected and preserved till the final location survey.
- Physical features such as building monuments, burial grounds, places of worship, posts, pipelines, existing roads and railwaylines, river crossing, cross drainage structure that are likely to affect the project proposal should be located by means of offsets measured from the traverse line.
- Where survey is for improving or upgrading an existing road, measurements should also be made for existing carriageway, roadway, and location and radius of horizontal curves.
- Generally, the survey should cover the entire right of way of road, with adequate allowance for possible shifting of central line from the traverse line.

Levelling work during the preliminary survey is to be kept to the minimum. Generally, fly level are taken along the traverse line at 50 metre intervals and at all intermediate breaks in the ground. The draw contours of the land survey, cross-sections should be taken at suitable intervals, generally 100 to 250 meters in plain terrain upto 50 meters in rolling terrain, and upto 30 meters in hilly terrain. This is a matter which is largely decided by the site engineer. To facilitate the levelling work, bench marks either temporary or permanent should be established at intervals of 250 to 500 meters.

Based on the Preliminary survey, now maps are to be drawn. Plans and longitudinal sections are referred to for detailed study to determine the final central line of the road. At critical locations like sharp curves, hair-pin bends, bridge crossings the plan should show contour at one to three metre intervals especially for roads in hilly terrain. The scales that are suggested for map preparation are 1 : 2500 for horizontal scale and 1 : 250 for vertical scale for plain and rolling terrain, and 1 : 1000 for horizontal scale and 1 : 100 for vertical scale for built-up area and stretches in hilly terrain.

2.5 Determination of Final Central Line in the Design Office

This step is actually a fore runner to the final location survey and involves the following operations :

- Making use of the map from the preliminary survey, few alternative alignments for the final Central line of the road are drawn and the one satisfying engineering, aesthetic, and economical requirement is tentatively selected.
- For the selected alignment a trial grade line is drawn, taking into considerations railways crossing, drainage crossings etc. In the case of improvements on existing road, the existing road levels should be kept in view.
- For the selected alignment, a study of the horizontal alignment in conjunction with the profile is carried out and adjustments made in both, for proper co-ordination.
- Horizontal curves are designed and the final central line marked on the map. The vertical curves are also designed and its profile determined. The design office's alignment could be cross checked in the field. Based on the final central line of the road, land acquisition proceedings can be started.

2.6 Final Location Survey

The purpose of the final location survey is to layout the final centre line of the road in the field based on the alignment selected in the design office. The two operations involved in the survey are the staking out of the final centre line of the road by means of a continuous theodolite survey and detailed levelling. The centre line of the road is then translated on the ground by the continuous survey, angles being measured with a transit theodolite measured with double reversal method. All the curve points namely the beginning of transition curve, beginning of circular curve, end of circular curve and the end of spiral transition should be fixed. The final centre line of the road should be fixed by stakes at 50 m intervals in plain and rolling terrain and 20 m intervals in hilly terrain. The stakes are intended only for short period for taking levels of the ground along the centre line and cross sections with reference there to. In the case of existing reference point, marks may be used instead of the stakes. Distance measurements along the final centre line should be continuous following the horizontal curves where these occur. At road crossing and railway crossings the angle with the intersecting road or railway should be measured by a theodolite.

- Suitable bench marks should be established at intervals of 250 m and at or near all drainages or underpass structures. The reference points for the point of vertical and horizontal intersection could also be used as bench marks.
- All the levels should be tied upto a G.T.S datum. Check level should be run over the entire line back to the first bench mark.
- For series of levels M km. in length the total error should not exceed $\sqrt{m} \times \sqrt{12}$ mm/km. Subject to the maximum error of 5 mm/km.
- Levels along the final centre line should be taken at all the staked stations and at all the breaks in the ground. Cross-section of the ground should be generally taken at 50 to 100 m interval in plan terrain and 50 to 75 m in rolling terrain depending, on the nature of work. Preferred distance for existing roads is around 50 m. The interval might be 20 m in hilly terrain.
- In addition, cross-section should be taken at points of beginning and end of spiral transition curves, and at the beginning, middle and end of circular curves, and at other critical locations.
- All the cross sections should be with reference to the final centre line. These extend normal upto the right of the way limit and show levels at every 2 to 5 m intervals and at all breaks in the profile.
- To connect grades at both ends, centre line profile is normally continued 200 m beyond the limit of the project. Profile along all intersecting roads should be measured upto a distance of 150 m.
- At railway level crossing the level on the top of the rail and in the case of sub-ways the level at the roof should be noted.
- The final location survey is complete when the designer is able to plot the final road profile and prepare the project drawings.
- Clear description of bench marks and reference points is a must so that at the time of construction the centre line and the bench marks could be located in the field without any difficulty at the time of execution. Construction lines will be set out and checked with reference to the final centre line established during the final location survey.
- It is therefore imperative that all the points referencing the centre line should be protected and preserved and so fixed at site that they are not disturbed and removed till the construction is completed.

2.7 TRAFFIC SURVEYS

Information about traffic is important since it forms the basis for the design of the pavement fixing the number of traffic lanes, economical appraisal of the project etc. The traffic survey may be in the nature of traffic counts. On rural highways, 7 days traffic counts once or twice a year for as many years as possible should be gathered. When road is being planned or extensive improvements are to be carried to an existing road, or a by-pass is under consideration it may become necessary to collect information about the origin and destination of traffic passing through the area in which the road is situated. If accident records are maintained they form a good basis for designing the improvements in accident prone locations. Most of this information is the domain of traffic engineering.

2.8 SOIL AND MATERIAL STUDIES

After selection of the final centre line of the road investigation for soil and other material required for constructions should start. This survey is required to ascertain the soil profile for design of embankment and pavements and proper method of handling the soils. If the embankment is to be constructed out of the soil from borrow pit, the borrow pits or borrow areas should be along the road land at intervals of 200 m. To assess the type of soil in the borrow area test pit 1.5 sq./m should be dug in the borrow area with the depth of the test pit not exceeding the depth of borrow pit by 15 cm. The soil from the test pit should be tested for gradation, liquid limit, plastic limit, optimum moisture content, and deleterious constituents. The results of the laboratory investigations may be summarised in a proforma.

The final selection of the borrow area could then be made in accordance to the norms recommended. For low embankment a soil having a liquid limit of about 40, a plasticity index of 10 and shrinkage limit of more than 10 % is okay. That is the murum soil or sandy soil or stabilized black cotton soil will be alright. However special investigation will be required for the design of high embankments which is dealt with elsewhere. For cut sections the soil properties should be ascertained along the central line of the road as in the case of low embankment. These tests would indicate the land-slide prone areas also. If there is a land-slide prone area, services of a geologist should be requisitioned.

One of the chief problems which the highway engineer has to address himself is the embankment over which the highway is to pass. Generally, problem of embankment construction and design can be divided into three categories :

(1) Routine cases : In which embankments of low to high heights are constructed over firm or reasonably firm ground, using sand, gravel and other suitable materials.

(2) Special cases : These cases are generally troublesome stretches of ground extending over limited length of road or the embankment material which is relatively unfavourable, such as silts and clays.

(3) Exceptional cases : In this category are the embankments that are routed over long distances on marine clays, tidal swamps, peats, creeks etc. where drainage conditions might

be critical in causing instability and post construction settlements might assume serious proportions. Whereas for embankments falling under the group routine category, not much vigilance is required in embankment design, when designing highway embankment over difficult foundation condition, the designer could choose one of the several alternatives that are available to him viz.
- Elevated viaduct.
- Embankment fill supported on piles.
- Excavations and replacement of sub soil.
- Sub-soil stabilization.
- Stage construction.
- Construction of embankments with berms.
- Relocation of alignment.
- Displacement of weak soil by surcharge weight or blasting.
- Use of light weight material such as cinder for embankment construction.

Once it is decided to construct the embankment from engineering and economic considerations, detailed calculations should be conducted for the design of embankment, whether the embankment is of low height, medium height, or high embankment. Failure of embankment generally takes place by one of the following modes viz.
- Slip circle failure through the slope or base.
- Block sliding over a weak soil strata in the foundation.
- Plastic squeezing and/or creep of foundation soils.
- Excessive and uneven settlement of embankment and foundation soil and
- Erosion of embankment. No design should be considered complete unless safety against failure by all the above modes is ensured.

Naturally, for a detailed discussion of embankment, the reader is referred to a book on "Soil Engineering."

2.9 DRAINAGE STUDIES

Drainage of highway refers to the disposal of surplus water. The water involved may be precipitation falling on the road, surface run-off from the adjacent land, seepage water moving through sub-surface channels, or moisture rising by capillary action. The main components of drainage study would be fixing the grade line of the road, design of the pavement, and design of the surface and sub-surface drainage system. The main components of the drainage investigation will be to determine highest flood level, pond water, depth of water table, range of tidal levels and amount of surface run-off. The road level should be above the H.F.L. The knowledge of the highest water table is necessary for fixing the sub-grade level, deciding the thickness of the pavement and taking other design measures such as provision of capillary cut-offs, or interceptor drains. The depth of the water table may be measured at open wells along the alignments or at holes specialled bored for this purpose. The observation should be taken at the time of the withdrawal of the monsoon when the water table is likely to be the highest. Such measurements are off course not needed in desert areas. In situations where water stagnates by the road sides for considerable period such as irrigated fields, information about the standing of water should be collected. In cut sections in rolling or hilly terrain, the water may saturate the road bay and it may become necessary to intercept the sub-surface seepage flow. There is generally no problem of surface run-off as for as highway is concerned since such run-off is ultimately laid away from the highway area to the natural drainage channels by means of longitudinal side drains.

The highway alignment is largely influenced by cross drainage works and it's location. This is a matter to be considered in greater detail for which a reference may be made to any book on bridges or aqueducts.

2.10 REALIGNMENT PROJECT

Most of the roads in India have been upgraded from preautomobile era. Naturally, they are lacking in geometric standards, length, widths etc. At least as far as national highways are concerned, it is thought necessary.

- To improve the horizontal alignment such as radius, superelevation, transition curve, site distances.
- To improve vertical alignment like steep gradients, humps and dips.
- Reconstruction of weak and narrow bridges, culverts and construction of over bridges and under bridges at suitable locations across a railway line, in place of level crossings.
- Raising the level of the road so that it is not flooded or water logged and the construction of a bye-pass to avoid the road running into a town or city have been realignment project. But the principles of new highway project and the realignment project are essentially the same, and it is largely a question of economy whether such realignment can be undertaken.

2.11 PREPARATION AND PRESENTATION OF PROJECT DOCUMENTS

The data collected during survey and investigations is to be presented in a proper form, so that the competent authority can take proper decision and funds can be allocated. This is known as complete project document and essentially consists of

- The project report,
- Estimate and
- Drawings.

The Project Report :

The project report should consist of the following :

(1) Preliminary preamble : Giving the name of the work, authority executing and planning it, the position of the work in the plan/non-plan period, present condition of the road in the case of improvement of road as project, topographical and geological features of the area, rainfall and temperature data such as annual average intensity and distribution during the year, range of temperatures during summer and winter months etc. comes under preliminary preamble.

(2) Road features : Here the merits and demerits of alternative routes investigated should be discussed and reasons for selecting the proposed route should be given. A tentative idea regarding the effect of the proposed route on the overall transportation pattern of the area should be given. The alignment of the proposed road section with reference to topographical and geological features and obligatory points should be given. Points such as high banks, heavy cuttings, nature of soil along the route should be clearly shown. Similarly, environmental factors, probable acquisition of structures along the roadway, carriageway width should be clearly emphasized and its economic aspect should be discussed. If traffic survey is conducted, the possible traffic that will be plying on new road and the possible future growth should be indicated. For existing roads, where the project is for the improvement, the accident data with special reference to accident prone locations should be given.

(3) Road design and specifications : This part should give fixation of grade line, H.F.L. water table level, proposed geometric standards, soil investigation data for the pavement design in a tabular form, deflection data for the existing roads, and tentative pavement design proposals with respective alternative routes, and the economic implications there of. If it is hilly road or high embankment requiring retaining wall, the design for the retaining wall should be given. If the road is having cross drainage works, may be culvert, hydrological details and the design details of the culverts should be given. The proposed drainage system of the road such as longitudinal side drains, catch water drains, blanket courses etc. should be discussed and relevant design calculations should be appended. This particular part of the project report should clearly bring out material, labour and equipment survey. Borrow area charts, quarry charts, type of equipment required for construction and it's procurement should be detailed. Availability of skilled and non-skilled labour should be given. This part of the project report should also give the schedule of rates that shall be adopted. The construction schedule either in the form of a bar chart or on the basis of critical path method should be developed if the project is big. Even the miscellaneous items, such as temporary worksheds, arrangement for water supply, road side plantations, facilities for tourists such as rest houses etc. should be included in this part of the project report.

Estimate :

This part of the project report is very relevant. The estimate part of the project report will be split-up in two major heads :

(a) General abstract of costs : This part gives the total cost of the scheme, with a general break-up under major heads. (with further sub-divisions as necessary) i.e. land acquisition, site clearance, earth work, sub-bases and bases, bituminous work/cement concrete pavement, cross drainage and other miscellaneous structures, percentage charges for contingencies, work charge establishment, quality control, and other miscellaneous items.

(b) Detailed estimates for each major head : This part of the project report should consist of abstract of cost, estimate of quantities analysis of rates for items not covered by the relevant schedule of rates and material source charts. Where a project work is proposed to be executed in stages, the estimate should be prepared for each stage separately.

2.12 DRAWINGS

The purpose of the drawing is to depict the proposed highway work in relation to the existing feature. It is recommended that the size of the drawing sheet may be 594 mm × 420 mm. On one sheet of this size it should be possible to accommodate the plan and L section of one km length of road, with sufficient overlap on either side, if drawn to the horizontal scale of 1 : 2500. A wider margin of 40 mm, is kept on the left hand side, so that the drawing sheets could be stitched into a folio. The type of drawings that constitute project report are :

(a) Locality map cum site plan : The locality map and the site plan could be either on the one sheet, if the length of the road section considered is reasonable. If the length of the section is substantial, the locality map is generally accommodated in one sheet and the site plan in a series of sheets that follow. The locality map also called as a key map is drawn to a scale 1 : 250,000. It shows the location of the road with respect to important towns, industrial centres etc. In short, it provides a bird's eye view of the project.

The site plan or the index plan shows the proposed project road, its immediate neighbourhood covering the important physical features such as rivers, hill tanks, railway lines etc. The key map shows the kilometrage from the beginning to end and is generally drawn to a scale of 1 : 50,000. The locality cum site plan should have a legend to explain the abbreviations and symbol used.

(b) Land acquisition plans : These maps are required for land acquisition proceedings. Generally, they are prepared on existing village maps, or settlement maps giving details of property and their survey number so that land acquisition proceedings could be smooth. A scale in the range of 1 : 2000 to 1 : 8000 depending on available maps will be suitable.

(c) Plan and longitudinal section : Plan and longitudinal section for one km length of the road should be shown on a single drawing sheet as far as possible. The plan should be drawn at the top and the longitudinal section at the bottom. The general scale for horizontal length is 1 : 2500 and for vertical distances 1 : 250. Naturally for hilly stretches, this scale could be changed. The plan will depict centre line of the road, right of way limits, existing structures, drainage ways intersecting road, and railway lines, electric and telephone cables, location of cross drainage structures, design details of horizontal curves, bench marks and location of cross-sections, contours etc. The longitudinal section should show the profile of the proposed road, and the general ground or the existing road whichever is applicable. It should incorporate details such as gradients, super elevation, details of horizontal alignments, location of drainage crossing and intersecting roads, location and set out data for vertical curves and continuous chainage.

(d) Typical cross-section sheet : In a general highway project, the elements of cross section like width of the carriage way and roadway side slopes, pavement cross fall i.e. camber is likely to remain constant for most of the road length. Therefore only typical cross sections need be drawn. At least one cross section each for road in fill, cut, and curve need be drawn.

(e) Detailed cross sections : The cross sections should be drawn serially along the continuous chainage. These cross sections should show existing road level / ground level, and the proposed road level, area of cut and fill involved and type and thickness of different pavement courses.

(f) Drawings for cross drainage structures : A highway is likely to cross many rivulets and streams requiring small and big cross drainage structures. For small cross drainage structures, Standard designs are adopted whereas for bigger cross drainage structures, separate designs are worked out. A separate drawing is given when there is typical and different design for the cross drainage structure. This is largely a part of "Bridge Engineering" for which reader is referred to a text book on "Bridge Engineering".

(g) Road junction drawings : A road junction drawing drawn at the initial stages solve many further problems that can crop up later on. The junction drawing should incorporate existing features of the intersecting roads, the proposed improvement and traffic control devices like signs, pavement markings etc. The scale to which these drawings are generally drawn is 1 : 500 or 1 : 600.

(h) Drawing for retaining walls and other structures : Particularly in hill roads, there are massive retaining walls. Drawings for the retaining wall should accompany the project report, and should show foundation condition and structural details as also the materials proposed to be used.

2.13 CHECK LIST FOR THE HIGHWAY PROJECT REPORT

The items that should be incorporated in complete project document are now summarised below and can form what is termed as check list for the complete project document. The complete project document should consist of

(1) Preliminaries consisting of :
- Name of the work and it's scope,
- Authority and plan provisions,
- History, Geography, Climate.

(2) Road features consisting of :
- Route selection,
- Alignment,

- Environmental factors,
- Cross-sectional elements,
- Traffic.

(3) Road design specifications consisting of :
- Road design,
- Pavement design,
- Masonry works,
- Specification.

(4) Drainage facilities including cross drainage structures consisting of :
- HFL, water table, seepage flows,
- Surface drainage, catch water drains, longitudinal side drains,
- Sub surface drainage blanket courses, sub drains and
- Cross drainage structures.

(5) Material labour and Equipment consisting of source and transport arrangement for equipment, material and labour.

(6) Rates that is schedule of rates and it's justification.

(7) Construction programming consisting of :
- Working season and
- Schedule of completing the work.

(8) Miscellaneous such as :
- Rest houses,
- Diversions,
- Road side plantations etc.

(9) Estimate consisting of :
- General abstract of work.
- Detailed estimate for each major head which will include abstract of costs, estimates of quantities, analysis of rates and material source charts.

(10) Project drawings consisting of :
- Locality cum site plan.
- Land acquisition plan.
- Plan and L section.
- Typical cross section sheet.
- Detailed cross section.
- Cross drainage drawings.
- Road junction drawings.
- Drawings for retaining wall and other structures.

2.14 AERIAL SURVEYS

Utilization of aerial surveys does not alter the long established sequence of transportation engineering work. Properly used, aerial surveys can result in better engineering, usually at a lower cost. The most efficient and effective procedures for using aerial surveys are within the following fundamental sequence of engineering stages :

1. **Planning :** The stage in which needs are determined and termini, standards, and priorities are established. Aerial surveys can be a useful tool to the planner.
   - Satellite imagery and very high flight height aerial photography reveal land use patterns useful in regional planning.
   - Periodic small scale photography of urban areas shows urban and suburban growth patterns.
   - Aerial photography is useful in traffic engineering, both to develop models for analyses and to study specific problems.
   - Periodic large scale photography can reveal parking patterns.
   - Large scale photography can be used to estimate distribution of population and of activities which generate traffic.

2. **Reconnaissance Survey of Area :** The stage in which all feasible route alternatives between the termini are determined. Aerial surveys provide the most complete and easiest way to perform this work.
   - Existing small scale photography is obtained or, where culture changes rapidly, new small scale photography is taken of a large area which includes the termini. Generally, the length of the area is at least 1.1 times, and the width is approximately 0.6 times the distance between the terminal or intermediate control points. The best available maps of the area are used to supplement the photography.
   - The photography is interpreted to determine the topography, geology, land use, soils, ecology, and other factors influencing route location.
   - Each feasible route alternative is determined and is then drawn, in stereoscopic correspondence, on the photographs. It may also be depicted on an existing topographic map, or the photographs may be assembled into a mosaic which serves as a map.
   - Where gradient governs location, available large scale topographic maps may be used, or the route may be placed in its best lo cation directly on the photographs by use of parallax measurements on stereoscopic pairs of the photographs.

3. **Reconnaissance Survey of Route Alternatives :** The stage in which each feasible route alternative is evaluated and one of them is chosen as the corridor within which the transportation facility will be located and designed. Each feasible route is evaluated for impact on the environment, service to the public, and economic advantage. Aerial surveys continue to be the best tool for this work, using, in most cases, the photography secured for the previous stage.

- Impact on the environment is assessed by interpretation of the photography or imagery.
- Where approximate construction costs are necessary to help in deciding between two alternatives, approximate earthwork quantities may be developed from parallax measurements on stereoscopic pairs of the photographs.
- To assign relative values to alternatives, it may be necessary, especially in urban areas, to secure medium scale photography, compile medium scale topographic maps, and make a tentative design in critical areas.

4. **Preliminary Survey of the selected Route Corridor :** The stage in which information essential for preparing the construction plans, specifications, and cost estimate is obtained. The source of much of this data is aerial surveys, which may usually proceed in the following sequence. Only where tall and dense vegetation obscures the ground and precludes accurate photogrammetric measurements is it necessary to secure by ground surveys enough data to establish limits for the clearing to be done before large scale photography can be taken to complete the survey by photogrammetric methods.

- The basic control survey determines accurately the horizontal and vertical position of monumented points along the corridor. This survey should be of first or second order accuracy and should start and end on high order geodetic points. The horizontal position of these points should be de scribed by coordinates in the State Plane Coordinate System, datum adjusted on an area or project basis.
- Photographic targets are placed on all basic control points within the area to be photographed. When supplemental control is by ground survey methods, targets may also be placed on supplemental control points.
  Since cadastral surveying and surveying of auxiliary points to be used during construction may be included in supplemental control surveys by photogrammetric methods, photographic targets may also be placed on property corners and on auxiliary points.
- Large scale photography of the corridor is taken using a cartographic camera.
- The supplemental control survey determines the position, to the needed accuracy, of enough additional points between the basic control points to fully control the photogrammetric mapping. Supplemental control may be by ground survey, by analog photogrammetric bridging, or by aerial analytical triangulation. A cadastral survey of the corridor may be included in a supplemental control survey by photogrammetric methods. The horizontal position of auxiliary points along the route, to be used during the construction survey, may also be included in a supplemental control survey by photogrammetric methods. The cadastral survey and the survey of auxiliary points benefit from the high accuracy of horizontal position inherent in analog photogrammetric bridging and aerial analytical triangulation.

- Detailed cadastral and topographic maps of the corridor are prepared, using the large scale photography in photogrammetric instruments of sufficient precision to com pile maps adequate for design, acquisition of right-of-way, and preparation of construction plans. Culture and cover may be shown graphically, or orthophotographs may be used as the base for the maps.

- The size of drainage structures needed depends on the cover, area, topography, and length of waterways of the drainage basin. All of this information may be secured easily and quickly from the photography; many small drainage areas show on the large scale photography taken for this stage, and most of the others show on the small scale photography secured for reconnaissance.

- The horizontal alignment and the vertical alignment of the facility are designed to fit the environment. The designer uses quantitative information derived from the topographic and cadastral maps and qualitative information derived from stereoscopic examination of the photography and interpretation of imagery to select the final alignments. When the horizontal alignment and the vertical alignment are satisfactory, a mathematical description of the horizontal alignment and its position on the map is computed. All instrument points on the centerline are defined by plane coordinates which can be used to draw the center line on the map manuscript and to stake the centerline on the ground.

- To aid in designing the alignment, in preparing the engineer's estimate of cost, and for payment during construction, cross sections are measured photogrammetrically to form a digital map for computing earthwork quantities.

5. **The Location Survey Delineates :** The ground for construction of the complete facility as designed, showing line, earthwork limits, rights-of-way and structure layouts. Unless preliminary clearing was necessary, this is the first staking of the facility on the ground. The location survey starts and ends on basic control survey points, and is staked using survey ties computed from the plane coordinates of the centerline instrument points and the basic control points.

6. **During the *Construction* of the facility, aerial surveys continue to be useful :**
   - The earthwork quantities determined photogrammetrically during the preliminary survey stage may be used for payment wherever the facility was constructed as designed. Where the vertical alignment or cross section was changed during construction, it is necessary to compute new quantities based on the previous photogrammetric measurements. Where horizontal alignment was changed, it is necessary to make photogrammetric measurements on the original photography along the new alignment. Where overbreak or underbreak occurred, or for borrow pits, photogrammetric measurements on new photography may be combined with measurements on the original photography to compute earthwork quantities.

- Sections of centerline needed to control construction operations may be reestablished accurately and quickly by utilizing survey ties between the centerline points and basic control points or the auxiliary points which were surveyed along with the supplemental control survey by photogrammetric methods.
- Aerial surveys may often be used to help solve special problems which arise during construction. Photography on hand from previous stages or new photography taken for the specific problem may be used to illustrate the problem when it is presented to others and to secure needed quantitative or qualitative information.

7. **Maintenance can utilize aerial surveys throughout the life of the facility :**
   - Vertical and oblique photography of the completed facility can supplement "as-built" plans.
   - Periodic photographic coverage of the entire right-of-way is useful for locating and assessing erosion damage, surface condition, authorized and unauthorized entrances, and encroachments.
   - Aerial surveys are helpful when special problems arise, just as they were during construction.

2.15 BRIDGE ALIGNMENT / LOCATION

Highway location determines bridge location, not the reverse. Only in cases where the bridges need to be skewed or foundation problems exist, the location of the bridge can be a factor in highway location due to higher costs associated with the above mentioned bridge conditions.

The location of centre line of a communication route to be carried by bridge at the selected site is called bridge alignment.

The following points should be considered while locating the alignment bridges :

- As far as possible centre line of bridge should be at right angle to the axis of river. Such an alignment is known as square alignment and the bridge so constructed is called square bridge. This type of alignment is always preferred because of square bridge is easy to construct and maintain.
- As far as possible, the alignment should not be skew since it is difficult to construct and maintain a skew bridge. Moreover it does not provide smooth entry and exit of water under the bridge.
- As far as possible, the alignment should not be curved since it is difficult to construct and maintain a curved bridge. Moreover, such a bridge is subjected to an additional force due to centrifugal action and there is a greater possibility of traffic accidents.

Despite disadvantages of a curved alignment a bridge may be aligned on a curve to smoothen entries and exists of water. In such a case it is always desirable to arrange piers parallel to the axis of river.

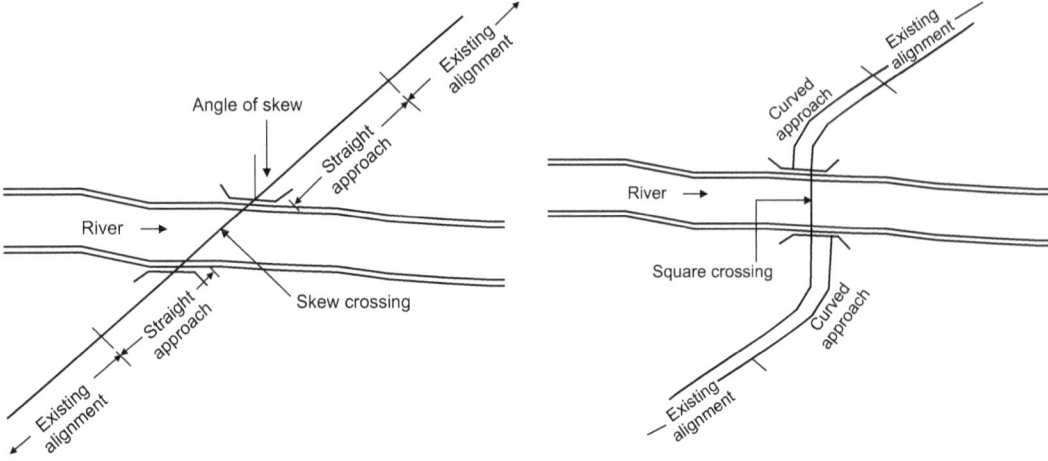

(a) Skew alignment skew crossing **(b) Skew alignment square crossing**

Fig. 2.2

Demerits of skew alignment of a bridge - when the centre line of the bridge is not at right angles to the axis of the river the alignment is called skew alignment and the bridge having such an alignment is known as skew bridge.

- The construction and maintenance of a skew bridge is difficult.
- The foundation of a skew bridge is more susceptible to scouring action.
- The piers of a skew bridge are subjected to excessive water pressure because the passage of water below the bridge superstructure is not smooth and whirls are formed.

REVIEW QUESTIONS

1. What is reconnaissance survey? Outline the steps in which the reconnaissance survey is carried out.
2. What points should be borne in mind in the fixation of route while studying maps?
3. What are the salient points to be remembered during ground reconnaissance?
4. How ground reconnaissance survey is actually carried out?
5. How the result of ground reconnaissance projected?
6. What is the importance of preliminary survey? How it is conducted?
7. When running a traverse line in the course of preliminary survey, what information should be collected?
8. What sort of levelling work is undertaken in the preliminary survey?
9. What type of maps is prepared in the preliminary survey work?
10. What are the types of drawings that constitute road project report?

CHAPTER 3
HIGHWAY ALIGNMENT

3.1 INTRODUCTION

Once we find that highway is necessary between the two cities or towns A and B, the next question which we should address ourselves is that what route should be taken between A and B, what sort of information should be collected in respect of traffic, soil, drainage etc. to find the most economic and highest return yielding route between A and B? How this information should be gathered and presented in the from of project report so that the authorities can easily come to the conclusion of best alternative? It will be the object of this chapter to know the method of collecting all such information and knowing the process of presenting such information in clear and concise form. The discussion is with reference to the relevant Indian Road Congress Specification.

Basic Requirements of an Ideal Alignment :

The basic requirements of an ideal alignment between two terminal stations are that it should be :

- Short.
- Easy.
- Safe and
- Economical.

Short : It is desirable to have a short alignment between two terminal stations. A straight alignment would be the shortest, though there may be several practical considerations which would cause deviations from the shortest path.

Easy : The alignment should be such that it is easy to construct and maintain the road with minimum problems. Also the alignment should be easy for the operation of vehicles with easy gradients and curves.

Safe : The alignment should be safe enough for the construction and maintenance from the view point of stability of natural hill slopes, embankment and cut slopes and foundation of embankments. Also it should be safe for the traffic operation with safe geometric fractures.

Economical : The road alignment could be considered economical only if the total cost including initial cost, maintenance cost and vehicle operation cost is lowest. All these factors should be given due consideration before working out the economical of each alignment.

The alignment should be such that it would offer maximum utility by serving maximum population and products. The utility of a road should be judged from its utility value per unit length of road.

3.2 GUIDING PRINCIPLES OF ROUTE SELECTION AND HIGHWAY LOCATION

The fundamental principle of route selection and highway location is to achieve the least overall cost of transportation which includes the cost of initial construction of highway facility, its periodic maintenance, and vehicle operation while at the same time satisfying environmental requirements. To achieve this objective it would be necessary to make a detailed investigation before the location is finally decided. The factors that should be kept in view while fixing the road alignment are listed below.

- The highway alignment should be as direct as possible between the towns to be linked resulting in economy in construction and maintenance. As the crow flies is possibly the best alignment, but this alignment should result in minimum interference to agriculture and established industries.
- The location of the highway should stay clear of obstructions, cementary burning ghats, places of worships, archeological and historical monument, public facilities like schools, hospitals playgrounds, fertile lands, and large industrial establishments. The highway can pass near such establishments but the location should be such that the shifting of these establishments is not required since it will involve large compensation.
- The present utility and services like overhead transmission lines, water supply lines should not as far as possible be shifted. The decision between changing the highway alignment or shifting the utility services should be based on relative economics and feasibility.
- The location should as far as possible facilitate easy grades and curvatures with frequent crossing and re-crossing of the railway line avoided.
- The site of the river crossing is an important obligatory point in selection of the route.
  If a particular bridge site is better, the highway alignment may be shifted to suit the bridge site, since shifting of the bridge site would generally cause more expenditure. The bridges should not in general be skew and submersible.
- The highway should as far as be located along the edges of properties rather than through their middle so as to cause least interference to cultivation and to avoid the need of frequent crossing of the highway.
- The highway location should be part and parcel of the surrounding landscape. There should be least adverse effects of highway construction on the environment. In this connection, it is better that the highway avoids wooded area so the constant destruction of forest is avoided. Where intrusion into such areas is unavoidable, the highway should be aligned on a curve so as to preserve an unbroken background.
- The location should be close to the sources of embankment and pavement materials so that haulage of these overlong distances is avoided and the cost minimised. An highway alignment if possible should permit balancing of the cost of cut and fill for the formation. This is illustrated in Fig. 3.1.

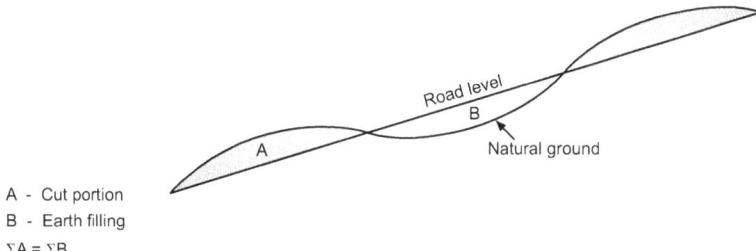

A - Cut portion
B - Earth filling
ΣA = ΣB

Fig. 3.1

- Marshy and low lying land areas having poor drainage and having very poor embankment material, areas liable to flooding, areas susceptible to subsidence due to mining operation should as far as possible be avoided and a preferred location is one which pass through areas having better type of soil. For example for the roads which passes through desert areas, location where sand is loose and unstable should be avoided, and the alignment selected along ridges having vegetation. For roads in desert areas preference should be given to areas having coarse sand against areas having fine wind blown sand. Similarly, in locating a road in this particular area, having longitudinal sand dunes, the best location is at the top of ridge or in the interdunal space. Location along the face of the longitudinal dunes should be avoided.
- Highway through villages and towns increase traffic hazard and cause delay and congestion. Where a serious problem of this nature is featured, it will be advisable to bypass the builtup area, staying clear of the limits upto which the town or village is anticipated to grow in the future. If the hill is to be surmounted for on highway alignment, there are special problems and considerations of location of highways in hilly areas, which should be looked into.

3.3 SPECIAL REQUIREMENTS FOR HILL ROADS

The main factors to be considered while deciding the alignment of hill roads are as discussed.

1. Length : The cost of construction of hill road per kilometer length is comparatively very high. It should therefore be ensured that length of the road connecting two stations should be minimum possible, adopting gradients along its most of the length.

2. Altitude of the Road : At lower altitudes, large numbers of cross drainage works are required to be constructed. Whereas at higher altitudes, the road pavement may witness snowfall during winter. This is why the alignment of hill roads should preferably be provided at an altitude between 900 m to 1500 m above M.S.L. At higher altitude, the alignment, if found necessary, should be provided on the hill slopes exposed to sun. The hill slopes which are subjected to high winds should never be selected unless and until there is no other alternative. In northern hemisphere, southern slopes of the hills are more suitable than northern slopes which remain in shades and are usually subjected to high winds. (See Fig. 3.2)

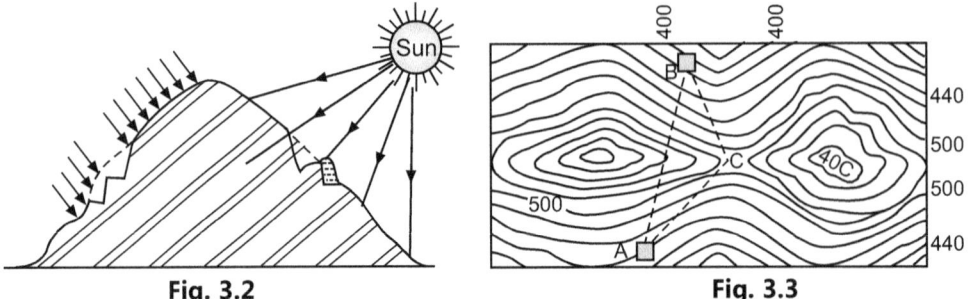

Fig. 3.2   **Fig. 3.3**

3. **Saddles or Passes :** While locating the counter gradient of the proposed alignment of a hill road on a contour map, it should cross the hill range through saddles. Though length of the road is increased, the heavy cost of cutting through rocks is avoided. Due to increased length, ruling gradients can be suitably adjusted. (See Fig. 3.3)

4. **Geology of Hill Slope :** Cutting through solid hard rocks is very expensive. The alignments of roads may be suitably deviated to avoid such areas.

5. **Tunnels :** Drilling of tunnels is very expensive. The long tunnels need ventilation as well as lighting arrangements. As far as possible, tunnels should be avoided and resorted to only if other suitable alternative is not possible.

6. **Valleys :** While deciding the alignment for crossing a river valley, due consideration should be given to avoid construction of a number of bridges on it's attributes.

7. **Geometric Standards :** The alignments of the hill roads should be selected on the hill slopes which easily provide recommended geometric standards i.e. gradients, curves, sight distance etc. Hairpin bends on roads should be avoided and if found necessary, these should be on gentle, stable and slopes. To have proper geometric standards, it might be necessary to change the alignment at number of places.

8. **Camping Sites :** At intermittent distance, the alignment of the hill road should pass through gentle slopes where suitable camping sites could be developed for military in case of necessity.

9. **Stability of Hill Slopes :** While deciding the alignment of hill roads, it should be ensured that the slopes are stable and not very steep. The area is not prone to land slides and settlements. This factor is of special importance in hills having sedimentary rocks.

REVIEW QUESTIONS

1. What guiding principles should be kept in mind while making a route selection for highway?
2. What are the preferential locations of highways in desert region?
3. Discuss the special care to be taken while aligning hill roads.
4. What are the basic requirements of an ideal alignment of highway?

CHAPTER 4
HIGHWAY GEOMETRIC DESIGN

4.1 INTRODUCTION

The first question that creeps up in the mind of the engineer is regarding meaning of the term geometry of highway. By geometry, we mean the physical proportion of highway, it's breadth, it's configuration on curves, it's cross-section, it's slope in cut and fill sections etc. This geometry of the highway regulates the capacity of the way - meaning thereby the number of road users that can safely and efficiently ply on the roads. For example, if we fix the breadth and cross-section of a highway in a level terrain, it will fix up the number of automobiles that use this way efficiently. It is a very common observation in India and to a certain extent in any developing country that the facility created is not generally adequate for the future. This is true of highways also. A highway which may be created for 100 vehicles/day may not have sufficient traffic to start with. It is possible that only 30 vehicles/day may pass on it. But as the time progresses and people realise the benefits that acquire from the roadway, they start using it. It is very natural that after 3 - 4 years, the highway may become inadequate for the traffic. Highway engineer must have therefore capacity to peep into the future and estimate the future traffic conditions.

4.2 PASSENGER CAR UNIT

In India, traffic is not, in general, segregated. For example, you will find a bullock cart plying on the same road, which is being used by automobile. Except for the future expressway, this scene is likely to continue for the forseeable future. If on the same road, four trucks, three bullock carts and one cycle rikshaw is plying, how do we fix-up the capacity of road. For this purpose, it is necessary to convert the heterogeneous traffic into standard passenger car unit. Indian Roads Congress has suggested for rural conditions the following P.C.U. factors.

Table 4.1

Sr. No.	Vehicle Type	P.C.U. Factor
1.	Passenger car, Auto rikshaw	1
2.	Cycle, Motor cycle or Scooter	0.5
3.	Truck, Bus or Agricultural tractor trailer unit	3.0
4.	Cycle Rikshaw	1.5
5.	Horse-drawn vehicle	4
6.	Bullock - cart	8

Now, if a particular road is being utilized by 50 cycle rikshaw, 10 cars, 2 trucks and 1 bullock cart per hour, then the equivalent passenger car unit which are plying on this road would be [1.5 × 50 + 1 × 10 + 8 × 2] i.e. 75 + 10 + 16 i.e. 101 passenger car units are plying on this road per hour.

Traffic on Indian Roads is of heterogeneous character. It consists of not only fast moving motorized vehicles but also of primitive modes such as animal drawn vehicle and human driven ones like cycle and cycle - rikshaw. On Indian roads, these vehicles share the same space without physical segregation creating traffic Examples. One way of accounting in configurations and characteristics of vehicles is to convert all vehicles into a common unit, and the most accepted unit for such purpose is passenger car unit (P.C.U.). Various agencies in India and abroad have recommended P.C.U. factors for different categories of vehicles. This is not very correct. For example, traffic stream with 10 bicycles may have more than 10 times detrimental effect on capacity than when there is only one bicycle. P.C.U. values should therefore depend upon factors like composition of traffic stream, total traffic volume on the road, the flow characteristics, etc. In India, IRC 106 - 1990 has provided P.C.U. factors for about 10 types of vehicles found on Indian Road, without considering these details. Chandrakumar and Sikdar have tried to study the effect of these traffic factors on P.C.U. and have tried to evolve a concept of dynamic P.C.U. It is seen that capacity of given facility is about 60 % overestimated with the use of static P.C.U. values as suggested by I.R.C. In a way it is a conservative approach. However, studies should be carried out to extend the concept of dynamic P.C.U. to roads so that some equation should result to calculate P.C.U. for a given vehicle in set of traffic conditions. Passenger car units/hour help us to determine width of road, number of lanes, traffic junctions, etc.

4.3 DESIGN VEHICLE

The next question that naturally will come up to anybody's mind is regarding standard design vehicle. The vehicles that ply on road are of various configurations and just as we had converted the haphazard vehicles into a typical passenger car unit, we might as well decide about standard design vehicle that should ply on the road. The design vehicle could be considered as a selected motor vehicle having standard specifications such as weight, dimensions, and operating conditions. These parameters would influence highway geometric aspects such as width of pavement, clearances, radii of curve, etc. The Indian Roads Congress vide IRC - 3-1984 have fixed up these dimensions as follows:

Table 4.2 (a) : Dimensions

Authority	Maximum Width	Maximum Height	Maximum Length		Semi Trailer	Truck Trailer	Single Unit Bus
			Passenger car	Single Unit Truck			
I.R.C. (1984)	2.5 metre	3.8 to 4.2	–	11.0 metre	16.0 metre	18.0 metre	12.0 metre

Table 4.2 (b): Weights

Authority	Single Axle	Double Axle
I.R.C. (1984)	10.2 metric tonnes	18.0 metric tonnes

There are two things to be remembered regarding design vehicles. The first thing is that choosing of design vehicle is dependent upon type and volume of traffic on the road. For example, super-express highway may have largest design vehicle. The second thing, that the concept of design vehicle is hypothetical in nature. Actual dimensions of vehicle may not tally with the configuration of design vehicle. It is a concept to determine pavement width radii of curve etc. Generally, the design vehicle is conservative in nature i.e. the parameter such as radii and width of pavements deduced on the basis of the concept of design vehicle are on safer side and hence the concept is accepted.

4.4 SPEED

The vehicles that ply on the road will have different speeds. Design speed is the maximum safe speed that can be maintained over a specified section of the highway when conditions are so favourable that the design features of the highway are the governing factors.

Table 4.3 : Suggested Design Speeds in India for Rural Highway (All values in K.P.H.)

Classification	Plain Terrain		Rolling Terrain		Mountainous Terrain		Steep Terrain	
	Ruling	Minimum	Ruling	Minimum	Ruling	Minimum	Ruling	Minimum
National Highways and State Highways	100	80	80	65	50	40	40	30
Major District Roads	80	65	65	50	40	30	30	20
Other District Roads	65	50	50	40	30	25	25	20
Village Roads	50	40	40	35	25	20	25	20

Table 4.4 : Suggested Design Speeds for Urban Roads as per I.R.C.

Classification of Roads	Speed in kilometer / hour
Arterial	80
Sub-arterial	60
Collector street	50
Local street	30

A design speed of 120 km/hour has been adopted for the expressway under construction between Ahmedabad and Vadodara. The design speed itself could be subdivided into two categories :

(a) Ruling Design Speed and

(b) Minimum Design Speed.

The word ruling has the same meaning as that of governing. It therefore denotes the maximum Speed within which the designer attempts to design the highway. It therefore shows the upper limit of speed for design purposes. The Indian Roads Congress has also suggested minimum design speed. This suggestion of I.R.C. in the opinion of the author of the book is redundant. If a highway can cater for the ruling design speed, it will automatically cater for minimum design speed for most of the cases. It is therefore un-necessary to suggest minimum design speed.

The design speed is a function of the grade or incline of the road and the type of pavement. Depending upon cross-slope, the terrain have been classified as follows :

Table 4.5

Terrain Name	Cross Slope of Ground in %
Plain	0 – 10
Rolling	10 – 25
Mountainous	25 – 60
Steep	> 60

Now, depending upon road classification which would generally determine the type of pavement surface and terrain classification, design speeds have been suggested for rural roads as follows:

Table 4.6 : Design Speed on Rural Highways

Road Classi-fication	Design Speed, km/hour for Different Terrain							
	Plain		Rolling		Mountainous		Steep	
	Ruling	Min.	Ruling	Min.	Ruling	Min.	Ruling	Min.
National and State highway	100	80	80	65	50	40	40	30
Major District Roads	80	65	65	50	40	30	30	20
Other District Roads	65	50	50	40	30	25	25	20
Village Roads	50	40	40	35	25	20	25	20

It has already been stated that fixing up of minimum design speed has no relevance if the road has already been designed for either maximum or ruling design speed.

4.5 GRADIENT

Gradient is the rise or fall given to the road pavement in it's longitudinal section. If two points A and B to be connected by road has a difference in elevation of say 100 metres and the distance between the two points A and B is say 10 km, then the road section between A and B should have a gradient of $\frac{100}{10 \times 1000} = \frac{1}{100}$. Depending upon the topography i.e. geographical features between points A and B, gradients have to be given so that this difference in elevation between points A and B is finally met. If the road between the points C and D is inclined to the horizontal by an angle α, then $\angle DCE = \alpha$. And then the gradient = $\tan \alpha = \frac{DE}{CE}$. This fraction $\frac{DE}{CE}$ could be expressed 1 in p i.e. $\frac{DE}{CE} = \frac{1}{p}$. It could also be expressed as n percentage, then $\frac{DE}{CE} = \frac{n}{100}$. Generally, ascending gradients are given positive sign and descending gradients are given negative sign. For example, the road CFE' between it's journey CF can have ascending gradient say + n_1 percentage and FE' can have descending gradient say $-n_1$ percentage. Then the deviation angle between the roads CF and FE' is angle $D\hat{F}E' = D\hat{C}E + \angle \hat{FE'}C = n_1 + n_2$ in a quantitative way.

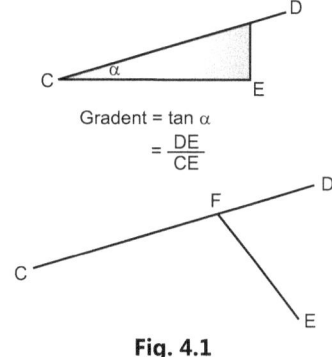

Fig. 4.1

Gradient which is a part of and parcel of vertical alignments can be classified as :
(1) Minimum gradient,
(2) Ruling gradient,
(3) Limiting gradient and
(4) Exceptional gradient.

(1) Minimum Gradient : Suppose there is no difference in elevation between the points A and B, then theoretically, the road should be laid between points A and B in a level stretch i.e. no gradient i.e. zero gradient should be given between the points A and B. But this is just theoretical. In practice, even for such a road, gradient has to be given from the point of view of drainage of the road.

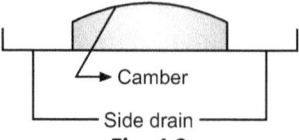

Fig. 4.2

If the road pavement has gradient in it's cross-section, it has camber, then the rain will be collected in side drains. If the road pavement has no gradient, and it's level road, then the rain water that is being collected in side drains have to be let off to natural drain such as nala etc. For this purpose, the side drain will have to be given longitudinal fall even though the road pavement has no longitudinal fall. In order that the water has perceptible velocity, this slope is estimated to be 1 in 300. That is in such case even though the road pavement has no gradient, downstream end of side drain will have to be deepened by 3 meters for every one km of road. This is not welcome from construction point of view and the desirable thing is that road pavement be given some longitudinal gradient so that the water that is collected in side drain shall have some initial force, and the slope to the side drain is gentle. Some sort of minimum ascending or descending gradient is always given to the road. This is called as minimum gradient. Naturally minimum gradient would depend upon rainfall run off, type of soil and other site conditions of side drains. The following table gives some guidance in this respect.

Table 4.7

Type of Side Drain	Minimum Gradient
Concrete drains or gutter	1 in 500
Inferior drains, brick drain, slate drains	1 in 200
Kutcha drains i.e soil drains	1 in 100

Grade Compensation: If the road is laid on horizontal curve that has gradient, then auto that plies on such road will have to exert tractive effort on two counts, (a) tractive effort on account of horizontal curve, (b) tractive effort on account of gradient. Sometimes this tractive effort is too much for the vehicle causing discomfort to the passengers. For the horizontal curves which are laid on sharp permissible gradient (ruling gradient), it is customary to reduce the gradient so that passengers do not feel discomfort. This is called as grade compensation. The grade compensation in percentage is given by $\frac{30 + R}{R}$ subjected to a maximum value 75/R, where R is the radius of curve in meters. According to Indian Roads Congress specifications, the grade compensation is not required for gradients flatter than 4 %.

(2) Ruling Gradient : Ruling gradient can also be called as design gradient, since it is defined as the maximum gradient that is available at the disposal of the highway designer for designing the vertical profile of the road. Theoretically, the ruling gradient is a function of automobile horse power. Suppose the vehicle is negotiating an upgrade with a design speed. Then the maximum grade that could be given on this stretch will be such that power developed by the engine is utilized to overcome the resistance generated due to grade. This then is the ruling gradient for this stretch. However, the Example is quite complex and not soluble mathematically in view of the diversity of the road vehicles, differing in tractive efforts, and I.R.C. has therefore recommended certain values.

(3) Limiting Gradient and Exceptional Gradient : If the topography is hilly and you want to adopt ruling gradients only, then this would involve large excavations and fills involving high cost. To prohibit this high cost we adopt gradients which are higher than ruling gradients. These are called as limiting gradients. In other words, these are ruling gradients for rolling terrain and hill roads. Such stretches of limiting gradient should be provided with level or easier grade before and after the start of such grade.

(4) Exceptional Gradient : In extra-ordinary circumstances, especially in hill roads, one can provide gradients steeper than the limiting gradients. These are called as exceptional gradients. However, exceptional gradients should be limited for a road length of 100 meter at a stretch. The guidelines for these gradients as suggested by I.R.C. are summarised below.

Table 4.8 : Guidelines for Gradients

	Terrain	Ruling Gradient	Limiting Gradient	Exceptional Gradient
(a)	Plain or rolling	3.3 % or 1 in 30	5 % or 1 in 20	6.7 % or 1 in 15
(b)	Mountainous or steep terrain at an elevation of 3000 meters and above the mean sea level	5 % or 1 in 20	6 % or 1 in 16.7	7 % or 1 in 14.3
(c)	Steep terrain upto 3000 m. height above mean sea level	6 % or 1 in 16.7	7 % or 1 in 14.3	8 % or 1 in 12.5

Critical Length of Grade : When a truck negotiates a grade, there is fall in speed. The reduction in speed by about 25 km/hour is considered as reasonable limit and the length of grade at which this reduction in speed occurs is critical length of grade. Naturally this length would depend upon initial speed at the start of grade, type of vehicle, it's B.H.P., it's tractive effort, minimum speed that the vehicle can have at the end of the grade so that this particular vehicle does not cause interference with the movement of the other vehicles at the end of grade. Many of these factors are not quantifiable, hence, there are no recommendations regarding critical length of grade by I.R.C.

4.6 CROSS-SLOPE OR CAMBER

Camber is the slope given to road pavement in cross-section. It's use is to drain out rainwater into side drains so that the pavement is free of water. Parabolic or elliptic shape is preferred for fast moving vehicles, since they are likely to cross the crown frequently in overtaking operations. The camber is generally left intact by pneumatic tyred vehicles. It is the animal drawn vehicles that cause serious damage to the camber. These vehicles do not have full and uniform contact with the pavement surface resulting in high stresses and subsequent denudation of pavement. Amount of camber is a function of type of pavement surface, which determines its draining capacity and the amount of rainfall in that region.

The following table recommended by the relevant Indian Roads Congress can be considered as a guide.

Table 4.9 : Recommended Values of Camber

Sr. No.	Type of Pavement	Range of Camber in Areas of Rainfall Range		
		Heavy	to	Light
1.	Cement concrete or high grade bituminous	1 in 50	to	1 in 60
2.	Thin bituminous	1 in 40	to	1 in 50
3.	Water bound Macadam	1 in 33	to	1 in 40
4.	Earth	1 in 25	to	1 in 33

The cross-slope of the shoulder could be 0.5 % steeper than the cross-slope of adjoining pavement subject to a minimum of 3.0 % (and a maximum value of 5.0 % for earth slopes).

Providing Camber in the Field :

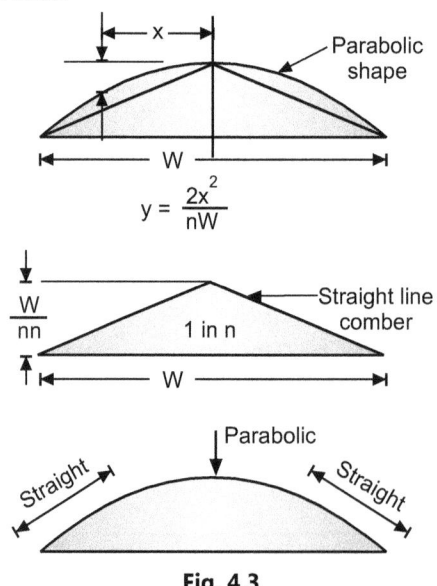

$$y = \frac{2x^2}{nW}$$

Fig. 4.3

As we know, camber is cross-slope. This cross-slope could be obtained by various curves. Some usual methods are indicated in Fig. 4.3.

The general method in construction to achieve camber is by preparing camber plate which are many times called as camber - boards to check the lateral profile of finished pavement. The camber can be achieved during construction by levelling operations also.

4.7 RIGHT OF WAY

As the name indicates, this is the land width over which highway engineers have authority. In fact, it is the area of land acquired for road construction and for it's future development. It is always better to have more land than the minimum specified by I.R.C. standards. Highway construction gives a fillip to the cost of land and land adjoining highway appreciates. It becomes difficult to acquire it then. This land width to be acquired depends on various factors such as :

- Category of highway, width of pavement and road margins.
- Height of embankment and depth of cutting and the side slopes of those.
- Dimensions of side drainage system.
- For horizontal curves, there is a widening of pavement and consequently more strip of load is to be acquired.
- Depending about spurt in the business that the highway is likely to bring, you have to reserve and acquire additional land in addition to above. The table below is indicative at right of way.

Table 4.10 : Recommended Land with for Rural Roads

Sr. No	Type of Road	Plain & Rolling Terrain				Steep & mountain Terrain			
		Open Area		Built-up Area		Open Area		Built-up Area	
		Normal	Range	Normal	Range	Normal	Range	Normal	Range
1.	National & State Highway	45	30 – 60	30	30 – 60	24	No ran-ge specified	20	No range specified
2.	Major District Roads	25	25 – 30	20	15 – 25	18		15	
3.	Other District Roads	15	15 – 25	15	15 – 20	15		12	
4.	Village Roads	12	12 – 18	10	10 – 15	9		9	

The another concept that must be understood at this juncture is the concept regarding building lines and control lines for urban roads. After the land width acquired as right of way, there is building line and no building activity is allowed in between the building line and right of way line as shown in Fig. 4.4. It should be remembered that, though no building activity is allowed in this zone, another activity say even farming, gardening can be allowed. It should be remembered that this space is not owned by the Government or Corporation. It only disallows building activity here. Beyond the building line, there is control line. For the space between control line and building line, the Government exercises control on the type of building to be constructed. For Government may disallow permit bar for reasons of discipline. This space is also not owned by the Government. It exercises control on type of building. Table below indicates recommended standards as per I.R.C.

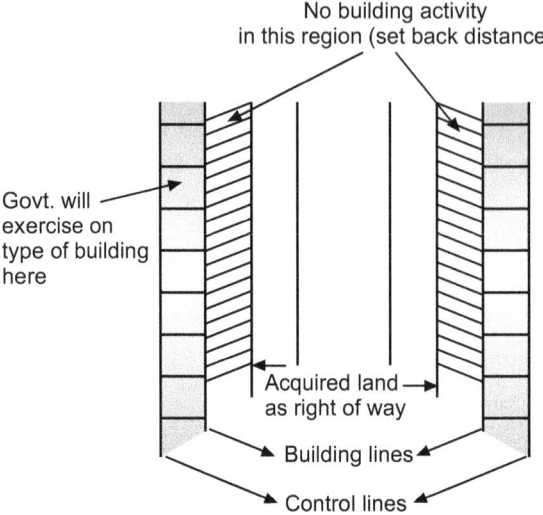

Fig. 4.4

Table 4.10 : Recommended Standards for Building Lines and Control Lines

Road Classification	Plain and Rolling Region			Steep & Hilly Region Distance between Building Line & Road Boundary (set back Distance) in m	
	Open Area		Built-up Area		
	Width Between Building Lines (m)	Width Between Control Lines (m)	Distance Between Building Line and Road Boundary (Set Back)	Open Area	Built-up Area
NH & SH	80	150	3 to 6	3 to 5	3 to 5
M. D. R.	50	100	3 to 5	3 to 5	3 to 5
O. D. R.	25 – 30	35	3 to 5	3 to 5	3 to 5
V. R.	25	30	3 to 5	3 to 5	3 to 5

It should be remembered that the above table is indicative practice but certain variations are possible. For urban road, recommended land widths as right of way are 50 to 60 m for arterial roads, 30 - 40 m for sub-arterial roads, 20 to 30 m for collector streets and 10 to 20 m for local streets. Again this is no hard and fast rule because the Example is essentially of land cost and acquisition cost.

4.8 WIDTH OF PAVEMENT OR CARRIAGEWAY

The carriageway for one line of traffic movement is called the traffic lane and width of pavement in this traffic lane is essentially a function of vehicle width and clearances between traffic streams. If side clearance is more, the pavement can accommodate more traffic, that is it's capacity is increased. IRC says that maximum width of vehicle would be 2.50 metres.

For this width, single and two lane pavement with requisite clearances is shown below in the figure. This pictorization is without consideration of kerbs or medians when no kerbs or traffic separators are provided. IRC recommendations in this respect are summarised below.

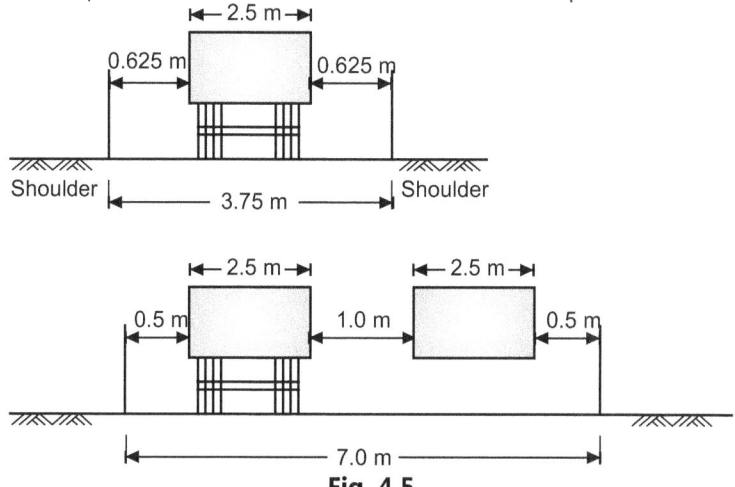

Fig. 4.5

Table 4.12 : Width of Carriageway

Sr. No.	Class of Road	Width of Carriageway	Remarks
(1)	Single lane	3.75 m	Single lane, village road could be 3.0 m
(2)	Two lanes without raised Kerbs	7.0 m	Single lane urban roads without Kerbs could be 3.5 m and access roads could be 3.0 m
(3)	Two lanes with raised Kerbs	7.5 m	
(4)	Intermediate carriageway	5.5 m	Minimum width for kerbed urban road is 5.5 m
(5)	Multilane pavement	3.5 m/lane	

4.9 TRAFFIC SEPARATORS AND KERBS

Traffic separators and Kerbs are shown in Fig. 4.6. Traffic separators also called as medians are provided to prevent head on collision of opposing moving traffic. Their job is to
(i) channelize the traffic;
(ii) segregate slow traffic and protect the pedestrians. In emergency, pedestrian can at least seek refuse on medians;
(iii) helping in turning the traffic. Traffic separators could have width of 8 to 15 m width. The I.R.C. recommends a minimum desirable width of 5.0 m for rural highways, which could be lessened to 3.0 m when land is costly, for urban roads. The minimum width of medians is 1.2 m and the desirable minimum width is 5.0 m for urban roads at intersection, the minimum width for pedestrian refuge is 1.2 m, 4.0 m and 7.5 m for protection of vehicles making right turn and 9.0 to 12.m for protection of vehicles crossing at grade. It should be

remembered that the recommendations are not obligatory in nature, since it is largely a question of cost of acquisition of land. The job of the kerbs is to keep the vehicle in it's own stream, but the kerb allow the driver to enter shoulder area in times of difficulty with less bother.

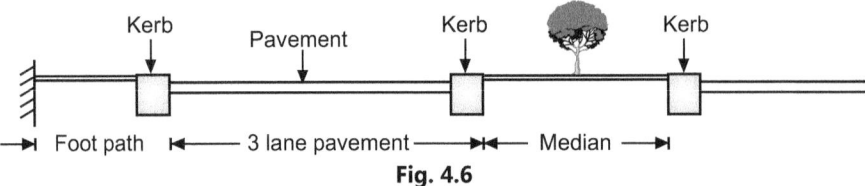

Fig. 4.6

Kerb can be :

(1) Low or Mountable Type : In this case, kerb is around 10 cm above the pavement edge with a batter for easy mounting of vehicles. Such kerbs are frequent for channelization of traffic scheme and useful for longitudinal drainage system.

(2) Semibarrier Type : This type has a height of some 15 cm, above pavement edge with a batter of 1: 1 on top 7.5 cm. This kerb prevents encroachment of parking vehicles and are therefore good when pedestrian traffic is dense.

(3) Barrier Type : Such kerb stone height is about 20 cm above pavement edge with a steep batter of 1.0 vertical to 0.25 horizontal. It protects pedestrian traffic and mounting of vehicles on shoulders is difficult.

4.10 ROAD MARGINS

Margins are traditionally provided in the right of way for specific purposes. For example, shoulders are provided along road edge so that, vehicles in times of emergency could use it. It is also a space provided as service lanes for vehicles that have broken down. The minimum width of shoulder as per I.R.C. is 2.5 m. Shoulders should have reserve bearing capacity to support truck load even in wet weather and the surface of the shoulder should be rough so that in general vehicles do not use it. Below is given the typical section with road margin.

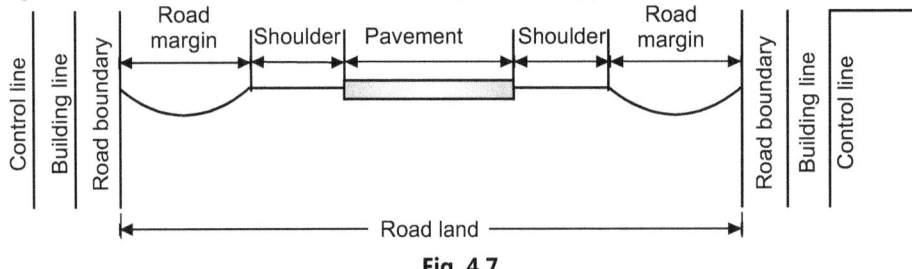

Fig. 4.7

Parking lanes : Whereas shoulders are to be provided for all roads, parking lanes are provided on urban roads for kerb parking. Parking should have width of 3.0 meter and should be marked.

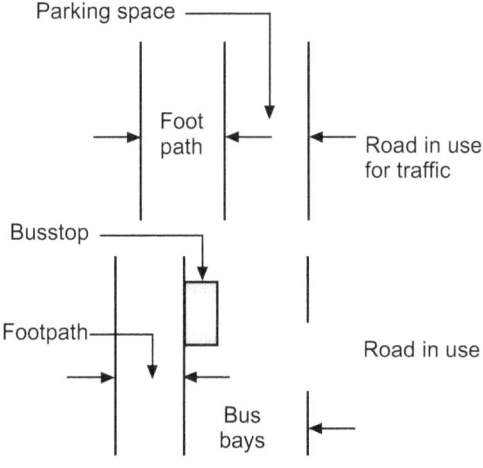

Fig. 4.8

Bus bays are provided to avoid conflict with moving traffic. It's positioning is shown in the figure. Foot-paths are spaces provided for pedestrians to walk whereas the width of foot path depends upon the pedestrian traffic. Slope given to the footpath should generally be 2 to 3 %. Fig. 4.9 shows the typical sections of divided highways on urban areas.

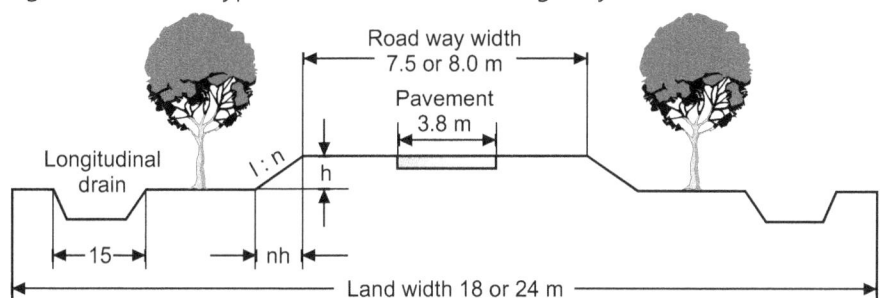

(a) Cross-section of VR or ODR in embankment

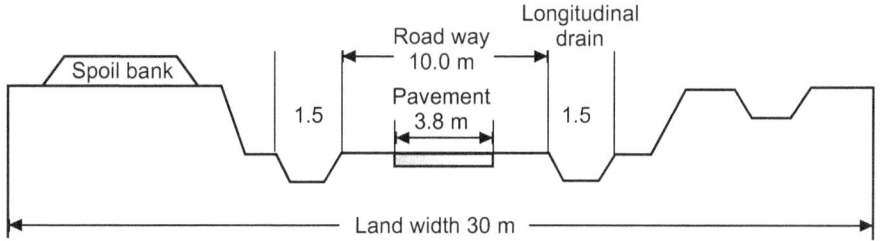

(a) Cross-section of major district road in cutting

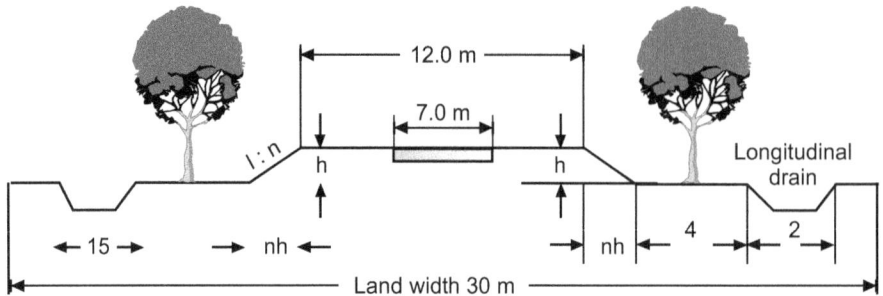

(c) Cross-section of national or S. H. in rural area

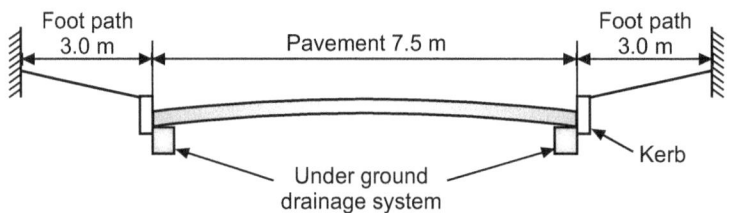

(d) Cross-section of two-line city road in built up area

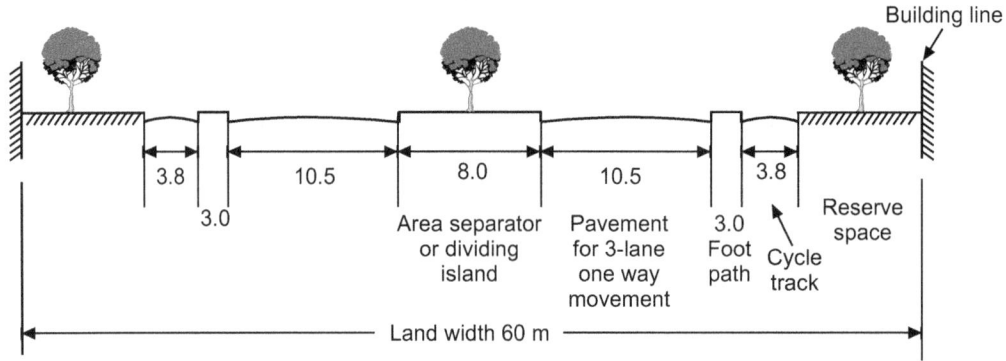

(e) Cross-section of divided highway urban area

Fig. 4.9 : Typical sections of divided highways on urban areas

4.11 CAPACITY OF THE ROADS

Capacity of highway has been defined as the safe number of vehicles that can be accommodated on a highway per hour per lane. Naturally, capacity would depend upon the type of vehicles plying on the roads. In the case of Indian Highways, where there is no segregation of traffic, capacity can not be that way determined. In case the road has only one kind of traffic,

$$\text{Capacity of roads } = C$$

$$C = \frac{1000\,V}{S}$$

where,
V = Speed in kilometer per hour.
S = Average spacing in meters between successive moving vehicles called headway.

The headway distance can be determined by actual observations. It could be called as distance travelled by vehicle when the driver of the vehicle sees the on-going vehicle in stream, sees the danger, applies the brake and the distance travelled by the vehicle during braking and the length of vehicle itself. Therefore,

S = Length of vehicle + Distance travelled in perception brake reaction time + Braking distance

Perception and Brake Reaction Time : Perception brake reaction time could be split up as summation of reaction time of the driver and brake reaction time. Reaction time of the driver is the time taken from the instant the object is visible to the driver to the instant the brakes are effectively applied. Whereas the perception time depends upon the psychology of the driver, his mental and physical condition and environmental conditions such as the light on road etc. The brake reaction time would depend on the skill of driver and the condition of the vehicle. The total reaction time could be split up into four parts :

(1) Perception Time : Which is the time required to perceive the object.
(2) Intellection Time : This is the time required by the brain to understand the situation.
(3) Emotion Time : After understanding the situation, the brain takes certain time to overcome certain human inadequacies such as fear, anger etc.
(4) Volution time : The brain takes certain time to arrive at a decision and then gives command which is called as volution time. Therefore, the total reaction time is the summation of these four types of times, and perceiving the total reaction time in this manner is petly called PIEV Theory. In any case, the total reaction time of an average driver may vary from 0.5 seconds to as much as 3 to 4 seconds for complex situations. If V is the design speed in m/sec and 't' the total reaction time in seconds, then the distance travelled by the vehicle during reaction time, which is often called as lag distance, is Vt meters. If V is expressed in kilometer per hour, then the lag distance is $V \times \frac{1000}{60 \times 60}\, t = 0.278\,V\,t$ metres

Braking Distance : Braking distance depends upon the fact whether the vehicle is plying a flat road or is ascending or descending. Let us suppose that the vehicle is plying ascending grade + n percentage. Then the component of gravity adds to the braking action and braking distance is decreased. In this case, component of gravity parallel to road is equal to $W \tan \alpha = \frac{Wn}{100}$ approximately, where n is percentage grade. If 'f' is the friction between road surface and vehicle and 'W' is the weight of vehicle, then 'fW' is the component of force due to the weight of vehicle parallel to road surface. Therefore, total force parallel to road surface is $\left(fW + \dfrac{Wn}{100}\right)$. If the braking distance is 'l', then work done is $\left(fW + \dfrac{Wn}{100}\right) \times l$. This should be equated to the kinetic energy of the vehicle during stopping. If 'V' is the speed, then corresponding kinetic energy is $\dfrac{1}{2} mV^2 = \dfrac{1}{2} \times \dfrac{W}{g} \times V^2$. Equating these,

$$\left(fW + \dfrac{Wn}{100}\right) \times l = \dfrac{1}{2} \dfrac{W}{g} \times V^2$$

$$\therefore \quad l = \dfrac{V^2}{2g\left(f + \dfrac{n}{100}\right)}$$

If 'V' is expressed in km/hr.

$$l = \dfrac{\left(\dfrac{V}{1000 \times 60 \times 60}\right)^2}{2g\left(f + \dfrac{n}{100}\right)}$$

$$= \dfrac{V^2}{254\,(f + 0.01\,n)}$$

Therefore,

Distance travelled during perception/ brake reaction time

$$= \dfrac{V^2}{254\,(f + 0.01\,n)}$$

Therefore,

S = Length of vehicle + Distance travelled in perception brake time + Braking distance.

$$= L + 0.278\,Vt + \dfrac{V^2}{254\,(f + 0.01\,n)} \quad \text{on ascending grade}$$

Obviously,

$$S = L + 0.278\,Vt + \dfrac{V^2}{254\,(f - 0.01\,n)} \quad \text{on descending grade}$$

$$S = L + 0.278\,Vt + \dfrac{V^2}{254\,f} \quad \text{on flat grade}$$

and

$$C = \dfrac{1000\,V}{S}$$

The fraction $0.278\,Vt + \dfrac{V^2}{254\,(f \pm 0.01n)}$ is actually the stopping sight distance. Therefore, one can say that

S = L + stopping sight distance in metres

This stopping sight distance which is the distance travelled during perception/brake reaction time theoretically is actually the stopping sight distance. The minimum stopping distance provided on curves, bends on roads is double this distance. The standards recommended by I.R.C. in this connection are as follows :

When there are two distant lanes one need not multiply by two, but when there is only one lane and two way traffic, multiplying by constant of two is essential. Many times the stopping sight distance is called as head light sight distance.

Table 4.12: Stopping Sight Distance

Design Speed, km/hr	20	25	30	40	50	60	65	80	100
Safe Stopping Sight Distance, m.	20	25	30	45	60	80	90	120	180

4.12 CONCEPT OF CAPACITY LEVEL OF SERVICE AND DESIGN VOLUME

The capacity of pavement essentially depends upon the speed. The ideal speed volume relationship is parabola having maximum volume at a value of speed equal to half the speed at free flow conditions (free speed). See the following figure.

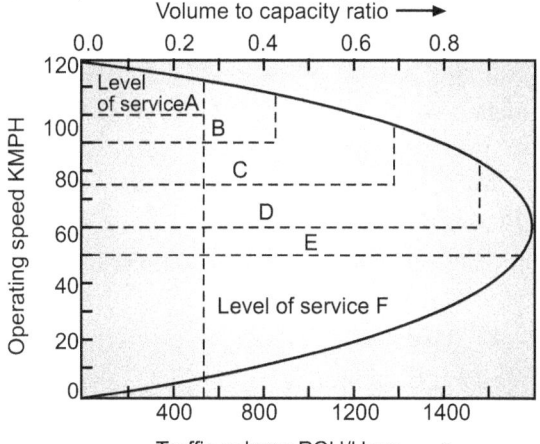

Fig. 4.10 : General concept of level of service

The American Highway Capacity manual recognises six levels of service A, B, C, D, E, F as shown in Fig. 4.10. For example, the level of service 'A' means that the volume of traffic to capacity of road is so low that majority of individual vehicles can travel at their design speed and can overtake the slower vehicles at their will. With increase in the volume, the operating speeds of faster vehicles and their opportunities to overtake slower vehicles decrease. In other words, the level of the service, which the highway is giving is decreasing. The Indian practice is to consider level of service B desirable for rural highways. At this level, the volume of traffic will be around 0.5 times the maximum capacity. This could be taken as the design service volume for purpose of determining road width in the design year. The design service volumes recommended by IRC for roads with various pavement widths in plain terrain are given in the table below.

The IRC guidelines give the design service volume for the design year. Thus, if a road is to be constructed, the design year traffic can be estimated knowing the present traffic and traffic growth rate. If the projected traffic is below the designed service volume, the pavement width provided is adequate. If not, higher pavement width is required. These guidelines can be used for determining the road section which have already reached the design service volume and need widening.

Table 4.14 : Suggested Design Service Volumes for Rural Highways in Plain Terrain as per IRC

Pavement Type	Pavement Definition	Design Service Volume PCU / day
Single lane	Narrowest pavement. Traffics in both directions. Width 3 to 3.75 m. Low volume traffic and less overtaking instances. To improve matters paved shoulders 0.75 - 1.0 m on either side could be provided.	1900 – 2000 pcu/day
Intermediate lane	Via media between single lane and two lane pavement 5 - 6 m width. To improve the function paved shoulders 0.75 - 1 m width can be provided. Not favoured on National Highway. In India, it is a common widening option from single lane.	5800 – 6000
Two lanes with earth shoulders	One lane of 7 m for each direction. Even our National Highways carrying 1/3 National traffic do not have this.	12500 – 15000
Two lanes with paved shoulder	Rare. Only urban roads.	14500 – 17250

Shortcomings of this Method

The limitations of the design service volume concept arise from the fact that it is based on an acceptable level of service with attendant speed and overtaking possibilities and not on any economic criteria such as losses suffered due to higher vehicle operating costs on narrow roads. The design service volume concept cannot provide basis for justifying investments on widening the pavements when costs are weighed against the benefits from widening. One such study conducted by Kadiyali shows (1994) that when you consider these parameters, widening is generally justified at values slightly lower than given by IRC guidelines. This study conducted on the basis of 1994 costs and certain other inputs such as cost of vehicles, cost of tyres, cost of petrol, grease etc. has to be modified on year to year basis but could be used as data base for the next 7 years or so. One of the side advantage of this study is the evolution of equation for determining Internal Rate of return (percentage) that can result from widening options. These equations are summarised in the table below.

Table 4.15

Sr. No.	Widening Option	Equation
1.	Widening single lane to intermediate lane	I. R. R. = $-1.97 - 0.32\,C + 0.014$ pcu $+ 0.116$ (pcu/C)
2.	Widening single lane to two lanes	I. R. R. = $5.42 - 0.167\,C + 0.0094$ pcu $+ 0.208$ (pcu/C)
3.	Widening Intermediate lane to two lanes	I. R. R. = $-2.15 - 0.117\,C + 133.98/C$ $+ 0.00648$ pcu $+ 0.08$ pcu/C
4.	Widening two lanes to four lanes	I. R. R. = $-4.08 - 0.04\,C + 0.0025$ pcu $- 3.93 \times 10^{-8}$ (pcu)^2 $+ 0.093$ (pcu/C)

Where, C = cost of widening in lakhs/km.

4.13 OVERTAKING SIGHT DISTANCE

The road pavement is occupied by slow and fast moving vehicle. It should be possible for fast moving vehicle to overtake the slow moving vehicle. The overtaking distance is therefore the distance which should be available to overtake another vehicle safely and comfortably without interfering the speed of incoming vehicle travelling at the design speed should it come into view after the overtaking manoeuvre is started. Overtaking sight distance can, of course theoretically calculated by making certain assumptions. In the opinion of the author, places should be provided as a bypass in the road architecture where overtaking should be allowed as shown in the adjoining figure. Overtaking is a Example when speed of vehicles plying the road is not very much. Generally, it is easy to overtake a very slow moving vehicle. Indian Roads Congress has recommended certain safe overtaking sight distances as below :

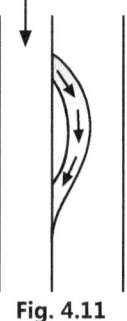

Fig. 4.11

Table 4.16 : Overtaking sight distance

Speed, km/hr	Safe overtaking sight distance (metres)
40	165
50	235
60	300
65	340
80	470
100	640

Sometimes instead of bypass as shown above, road pavement is widened where overtaking is permitted. See the adjoining figure. This is called as overtaking zone.

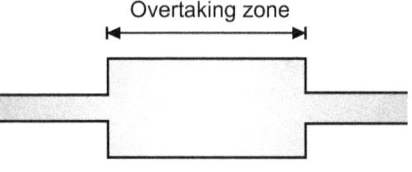

Fig. 4.12

Some of the important factors on which the minimum overtaking sight distance depends, are :

(a) speeds of the overtaking, overtaken and the vehicle coming from opposite direction.

(b) spacing between vehicles.

(c) skill and reaction time of the driver.

(d) rate of acceleration of overtaking vehicle.

(e) slope of the road.

Analysis of Overtaking Sight Distance

Fig. 4.13 shows the overtaking manoeuvre of vehicle A travelling at design speed, and another slow vehicle B on a two-lane road. Third vehicle C comes from the opposite direction. The overtaking manoeuvre may be split-up into three operations, thus dividing the overtaking sight distance into three parts d_1, d_2 and d_3.

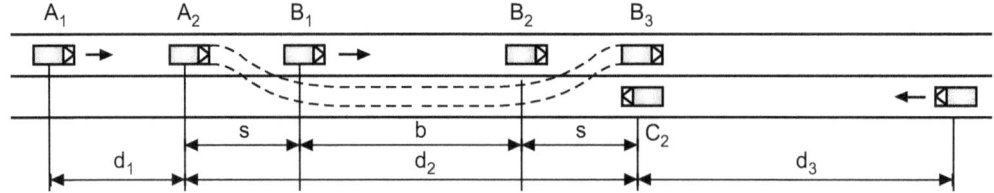

Fig. 4.13 : Overtaking manoeuvre

- d_1 is the distance travelled by overtaking vehicle A during the reaction time from position A_1 to A_2.

- d_2 is the distance travelled by the vehicle A from A_2 to A_3 during the actual overtaking operation.
- d_3 is the distance travelled by on-coming vehicle C from C_1 to C_2 during the overtaking operation of A.

Certain assumptions are made in order to calculate the values of d_1, d_2 and d_3. In Fig. 5.13, A is the overtaking vehicle originally travelling at design speed v m/sec or V kmph; B is the overtaken or slow moving vehicle moving with uniform speed or v_b m/sec or V_b kmph; C is a vehicle coming from opposite direction at the design speed v m/sec or V kmph. In a two-lane road, the opportunity to overtake depends on the frequency of vehicles from the opposite direction and the overtaking sight distance available at any instant.

- It may be assumed that the vehicle A is forced to reduce its speed to the speed of the slow vehicle B and moves behind it during the reaction time, till there is an opportunity for safe overtaking operation. The distance travelled by the vehicle A during this reaction time is d_1 and is between the positions A_1 and A_2. This distance will be equal to $v_b \times t$ metre, where, 't' is the reaction time of the driver in seconds. This reaction time 't' of the drivers may be taken as 2 seconds as an average value, as the aim of the driver is only to find an opportunity to overtake. Thus,

$$d_1 = v_b t = 2 v_b \text{ metres.}$$

- From position A_2, the vehicle A starts accelerating, shifts to the adjoining lane, overtakes the vehicle B, and shifts back to its original lane ahead of B in position A_3. The straight distance between positions A_2 and A_3 is taken as d_2. The minimum distance between positions A_2 and B_1 may be taken as the minimum spacing 's' of the two vehicles while moving with the speed v_b m/sec. The spacing between vehicles depends on their speed and is given by empirical formula :

$$s = (0.7 v_b + 6) \text{ metres.}$$

The minimum distance between B_3 and A_2 may also be assumed equal to s as mentioned above. Let the time taken by vehicle A for the overtaking operation from position A_2 to A_3 be T seconds. Then the distance covered by the slow vehicle B travelling at a speed of v_b m/sec in time T sec.

$$= b = v_b T \text{ metres}$$

Thus, the distance $d_2 = (b + 2s)$ metres.

Now, the time T depends on speed of overtaken vehicle B and the acceleration of overtaking vehicle A. This time T may be calculated by equating the distance d_2 to $\left(v_b T + \frac{1}{2} a T^2\right)$, using the general formula for the distance travelled by an uniformly accelerating body with initial speed v_b m/sec and 'a' is the acceleration in m/sec².

$$d_2 = (b + 2s) = \left(v_b T + \frac{aT^2}{2}\right)$$

Hence, $b = v_b \cdot T$, and therefore $2s = \frac{aT^2}{2}$

Therefore, $T = \sqrt{\frac{4s}{a}}$ secs, where, $s = (0.7 v_b + 6)$

Hence, $d_2 = (v_b \cdot T + 2s)$ metres

- The distance travelled by vehicle C moving at design speed v m/sec during the overtaking operation of vehicle A i.e., during time T is the distance d_3 between positions C_1 to C_2.

Hence, $d_3 = v \times T$

Thus, the overtaking sight distance,

$$OSD = (d_1 + d_2 + d_3)$$
$$= (v_b t + v_b T + 2s + vT)$$

In kmph units, above equation works out as:

$$OSD = 0.28 V_b t + 0.28 V_b T + 2s + 0.28 V T$$

Here, V_b = speed of overtaken vehicle, kmph

t = reaction time of driver = 2 secs

V = speed of overtaking vehicle or design speed, kmph

$$T = \sqrt{\frac{4 \times 3.6s}{A}}$$
$$= \sqrt{\frac{14.4s}{A}}$$

s = spacing of vehicles
$= (0.2 V_b + 6)$

A = acceleration, kmph/sec.

In case the speed of overtaken vehicle V_b is not given, the same may be assumed as $(V - 16)$ kmph, where V is the design speed in kmph or $v_b = (v - 4.5)$ m/sec and v is the design speed in m/sec.

The acceleration of the overtaking vehicle is to be specified. Usually this depends on the make of the vehicle, load and the speed. As a general guide, Table 5.16 may be used for finding the maximum acceleration of vehicles at different speeds. The average rate of acceleration during overtaking manoeuvre may be taken corresponding to the design speed.

Table 4.17 : Maximum Overtaking Acceleration at Different Speeds

Speed		Maximum Overtaking Acceleration	
V kmph	v m/sec	A kmph/sec	a m/sec^3
25	6.93	5.00	1.41
30	8.34	4.80	1.30
40	11.10	4.45	1.24
50	13.86	4.00	1.11
65	18.00	3.28	0.92
80	22.20	2.56	0.72
100	27.80	1.92	0.53

At overtaking sections, the minimum overtaking distance should be ($d_1 + d_2 + d_3$) when two-way traffic exists. On divided highway, the overtaking distance need be only ($d_1 + d_2$) as in one-way movement and no vehicle is expected from the opposite direction. On divided highways with four or more lanes, IRC suggests that it is not necessary to provide the usual OSD; however the sight distance in such highways should be more than the SSD.

Effect of Grade in Overtaking Sight Distance

Appreciable grades in the road, both the descending as well as ascending, increase the sight distance required for safe overtaking. In down grades though it is easier for the overtaking vehicles to accelerate and pass, the overtaking vehicle may also accelerate and cover a greater distance 'b' during the overtaking time.

On up grades, the acceleration of the overtaking vehicle will be less and hence passing will be difficult; but the overtaken vehicle like heavily loaded trucks may also decelerate in steep ascends and compensate to some extent the passing sight distance requirement. Therefore the OSD at both ascending and descending grades are taken as equal to that at level stretch. However, at grades the overtaking sight distance should be greater than the minimum overtaking distance required at level.

The IRC has specified the safe values of overtaking sight distance required for various design speeds between 40 and 100 kmph. These values have been suggested based on the observation that 9 to 14 seconds are required by the overtaking vehicle for the actual overtaking manoeuvre depending on the design speed. This overtaking time may be increased by about two-thirds to take into account the distance covered by the vehicle from the opposing direction in the case of two-way traffic road, during the overtaking operation.

Sight Distance at Intersection

Another important part of Highway Geometrics is sight distance that should be provided at intersection. Clear view should be available across the corners so as to avoid collision and properties should not be constructed in the sight triangle as shown in the adjoining figure. This is all the more important at unmanned intersections. The sight distance and the sides at sight triangle can again be theoretically calculated. The parameters that are taken into account for this purpose are reaction time for the driver, design speed, widths of road etc. However, I.R.C. has recommended a minimum visibility distance of 15 m along minor road and a distance of 220 meters, 180, 145 and 110 meters along the major road for corresponding design speeds of 100, 85, 65 and 50 km/hr.

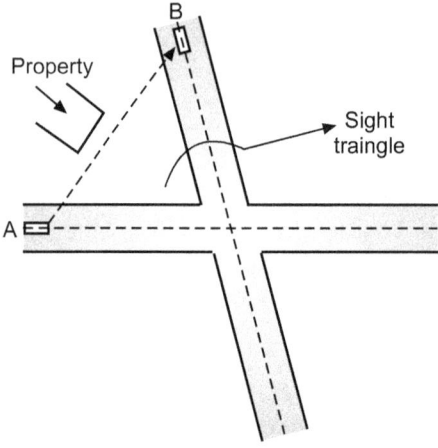

Fig. 4.14

4.14 HORIZONTAL ALIGNMENT

When there is a change of alignment as shown in Fig. 4.15, curves have to be introduced. When such curves are introduced, one shoulder of the pavement is to be raised as compared to the other shoulder. This is called as super-elevation. This is one part. The another part is that the curve cannot start at B'. Some sort of soothing curve has to be given at B' say FB' for the comfort of passengers. This curve is called as transition curve. We shall discuss these aspects now.

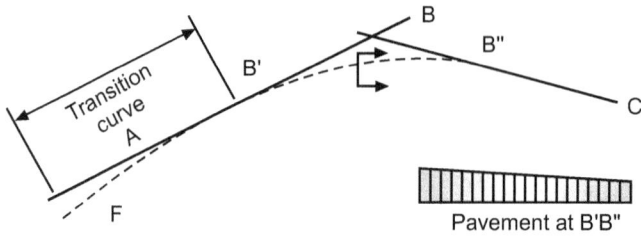

Fig. 4.15

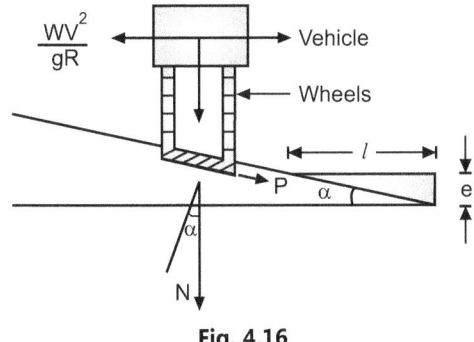

Fig. 4.16

Let,

- w = Weight of vehicle
- V = It's speed in m/sec
- R = Radius of curve
- γ = Side friction
- N = Normal force
- μ = Coefficient of lateral friction
- e = Super-elevation expressed as 1 in e
- α = Angle of super-elevation

When the vehicle is negotiating a curve, it experiences a centrifugal force. In order that vehicle body remains perpendicular to the road pavement for the passenger comfort, we have to raise one shoulder. Let that angle be α. For conditions of equilibrium,

$$\frac{W}{g}\frac{V^2}{R}\cos\alpha = W\sin\alpha + P$$

$$= W\sin\alpha + N\mu$$

But,

$$N = P = W\cos\alpha + \frac{W}{g}\frac{V^2}{R}\sin\alpha$$

Therefore,

$$\frac{W}{g}\frac{V^2}{R}\cos\alpha = W\sin\alpha + \mu\left(W\cos\alpha + \frac{W}{g}\frac{V^2}{R}\sin\alpha\right)$$

$$\frac{V^2}{gR} = \tan\alpha + \mu + \frac{\mu V^2}{gR}\tan\alpha$$

$\frac{V^2}{gR} \times \tan\alpha$ being very small, is neglected and

$$\frac{V^2}{gR} = \tan\alpha + \mu$$

If V is in km/hr, we have

$$\frac{V^2}{127\,R} = \tan\alpha + \mu$$

This is the basic equation which relates the speed of vehicle, radius of the curve, the super-elevation and coefficient of lateral friction. The value of coefficient of lateral friction depends upon many factors, the condition of tyres, the condition of the road, even wind etc. I.R.C. has recommended a uniform value of μ to be 0.15. Though super-elevation is a necessary evil, it is not asthetic. I.R.C. has therefore recommended certain maximum values of super-elevation that could be given. Super-elevation expressed as 1 in e is limited to 0.07 for hill roads when the area is snow bound. If the hill road area is not snow bound, one can adopt e = 0.1. In general, a value of 0.07 is considered maximum.

Minimum radii for curves

Since, $R = \dfrac{V^2}{127(e + \mu)}$

and maximum value of e is fixed, we get the minimum radii for curves as follows:

$R = 0.0357 V^2$ for plain and rolling terrain.

$R = 0.0315 V^2$ for hill roads that are snow bound.

$R = 0.0357 V^2$ for hill roads which are not snow bound.

In the above formula, V is design speed. But the current IRC gives two values of design speed (i.e. ruling and minimum). The above formulae would yield two values for radius, the ruling radius and the absolute minimum radius. One can of course calculate these values knowing V. Alternatively, recourse could be made to the table where these values have been tabulated by I.R.C. See Table 4.17.

The idea behind giving super-elevation is to counterpart of the centrifugal force, the remaining part being resisted by lateral friction. It also lessens skiding and unequal pressure on tyres. But super-elevation can be provided so that complete centrifugal force is catered for (In this case, μ is considered zero) or it can be provided to cater fixed proportion of centrifugal force. If we design that super-elevation is to take all the centrifugal force, it would result in sharp curves and high super-elevation (i.e. more than 1 in 15 also). But IRC has limited the values of super-elevation to 0.07 and 0.1. Therefore in that case, friction (i.e. lateral friction) would be called into play for very sharp curves. On the other hand, when the vehicle is negotiating a flat curve, friction would not be developed to the maximum. As a compromise, super-elevation should be such that moderate amount of friction should be developed in the case, of flat curves, but when negotiating sharp curves, very large friction should not be developed, since that is also not good for passenger comfort. This balance is struck by IRC by stating that super-elevation be calculated on the assumption that it should counteract the centrifugal force developed at three fourth the design speed. That is $e = \dfrac{(0.75 V)^2}{127 R} = \dfrac{V^2}{225 R}$. This super-elevation is now restricted to 0.07 and 0.1 as per IRC.

Radii for which no super-elevation required

The normal cambered section of the highway can be continued on the curve, where super-elevation calculated is less than the camber $e = \dfrac{V^2}{225 R}$ i.e. $R = \dfrac{V^2}{225 e}$.

If in this equation, e is substituted by allowed camber, we get the minimum radius beyond which no super-elevation is required. Though calculation may prove this point, IRC has prepared a table for the guidance of highway engineers. However, where the radii is more than the one given in the table, it would be desirable to remove the adverse crown in the outer half of the carriage way and super-elevate at the normal crown slope.

Table 4.18 : Minimum Radii of Horizontal Curve

Classification of Road	Plain Terrain		Rolling Terrain		Mountains Terrain				Steep Terrain			
					Areas not affected by snow		Snow bound area		Areas not affected by snow		Snow bound area	
	Ruling Min.	Abs. Min.	Ruling Min.	Abs. Min.	Ruling Min.	Abs. Min.	Ruling Min.	Abs. Min.	Ruling Min.	Abs. Min.	Ruling Min.	Abs. Min.
1. National Highways and State highways	360	230	230	155	80	50	90	60	50	30	60	33
2. Major District Roads	230	155	105	90	50	30	60	33	30	14	33	16
3. Other District Roads	155	90	98	60	30	20	23	23	20	14	23	15
4. Village Roads	90	60	60	45	20	14	23	15	20	14	23	15

Table 4.19 : Radii Beyond Which Super-Elevation is not Essential for Different Cambers and Speeds (Indian Practice)

Design Speed km/hr	Radius in Metres Beyond which no Super-Elevation is Required for Values of Camber				
	4 %	3 %	2.5 %	2 %	1.7 %
20	50	60	70	90	100
25	70	90	110	140	150
30	100	130	160	200	240
35	140	180	220	270	320
40	180	240	280	350	420
50	280	370	450	550	650
65	470	620	750	950	1100
80	700	960	1100	1400	1700
100	1100	1500	1800	2200	2600

Methods of Attaining Super-Elevation : Fig. 4.17 indicates the ways in which super-elevation can be attained. The figures are self explanatory.

- First stage attaining super-elevation by super-elevation equal to camber.
- The surface of the road is rotated about the inner edge, raising the centre and the outer edge.
- The surface of the road is rotated about the outer edge depressing the centre and the inner edge.

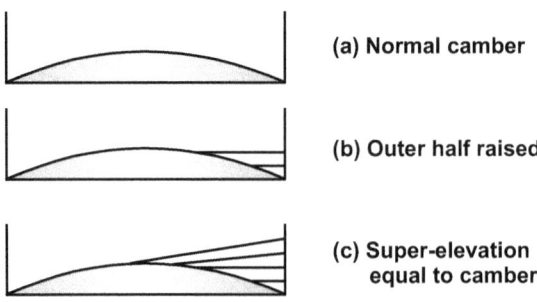

(a) Normal camber

(b) Outer half raised

(c) Super-elevation equal to camber

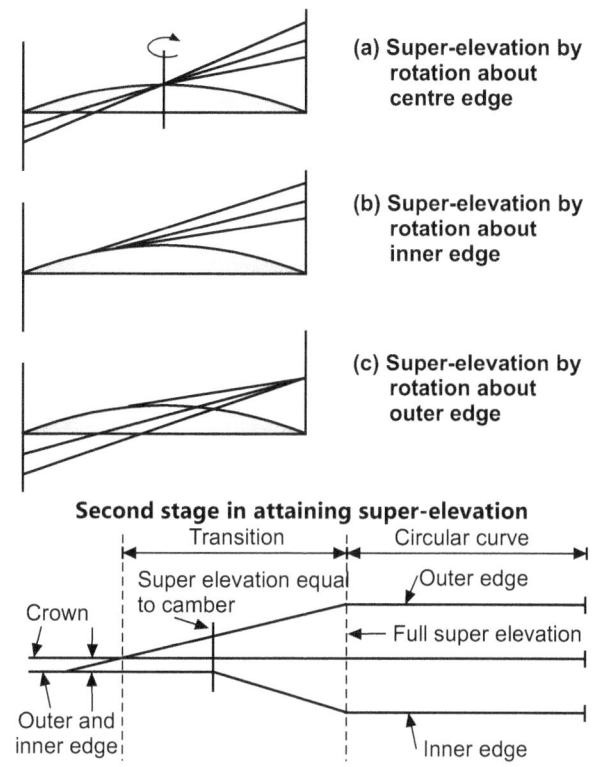

(a) Super-elevation by rotation about centre edge

(b) Super-elevation by rotation about inner edge

(c) Super-elevation by rotation about outer edge

Attaining super-elevation by revolving about the centre line

Fig. 4.17

4.15 TRANSITION CURVES

If a curve is given to a straight road, the vehicle is subjected to sudden centrifugal force causing discomfort to the passengers. This can be avoided by giving a curve such that its radius, where it meets straight section, is infinity and where it meets the designated circular curve, its radius is that of the circular curve. Such a curve is known as **transition curve**. It's function is :

(1) Gradual application of centrifugal force,

(2) Gradual application of super-elevation, and

(3) To ease the driving stress and cause comfort to the passengers.

The curve that could satisfy all such criteria, is ideal transition curve. One curve will not satisfy all the criteria. Many such transition curves are in vogue the most commonly used being spiral. As highway engineers we have already studied how to set out spiral in "Survey", we are only interested as highway engineers as how should we determine the length of this spiral. The length of transition curve is determined from two considerations.

(1) Rate of change of acceleration in negotiating a transition should be tolerable.

Let R be the radius of circular curve and V design speed. Then centrifugal acceleration encountered is $\dfrac{V^2}{R}$ as maximum. If L_s is the length of transition curve, then to transverse this transition curve, the time taken by vehicle is $\dfrac{L_s}{V}$, and rate of change of acceleration

$$= \dfrac{\text{Acceleration}}{\text{Time for this acceleration to take place}}$$

$$C = \dfrac{V^2}{R} \div \dfrac{L_s}{V} = \dfrac{V^3}{RL}$$

The comfortable rate of change of acceleration is $\dfrac{80}{75+V}$ (subject to a maximum of 0.8 and minimum of 0.5) as per IRC.

Therefore length of transition curve is determined by

$$C = \dfrac{80}{75+V} = \dfrac{V^3}{RL}$$

where, V is m/sec, R and L in metres. If V is in km/hr and R and L are in meters then

$$L = \dfrac{0.0215\, V^3}{CR}$$

(2) As the transition curve progresses, there is change in super-elevation. At point where it meets straight, super-elevation is zero and where it meets the circular curve, the super-elevation has the designated value. This rate of change of super-elevation should not cause higher gradient and unsightly appearance. Recommendations are 1 in 150 for roads in plain and rolling terrain and 1 in 60 for hilly terrain. Depending upon the way, the super-elevation is given (rotation about centre line, inner edge, outer edge) length of transition will alter. Widening of pavement at curves should be taken into account for calculation of length of transition. Higher of the values given by the above two methods should be adopted.

Widening on Curves

Curves are a necessary part of horizontal alignment and whenever, there is a curve laid out, the pavement has to be widened at that location. This is necessary since, (1) On curves vehicles are likely to occupy greater width. This is because rear wheels track inside the front wheel. (2) On curves, it becomes difficult for the drivers, psychologically to keep to the centreline of the lane. (3) Similarly, the driver has psychological inhibition to drive close to the edge of the pavement.

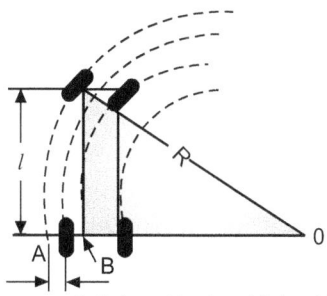

m = 2 Extra widening AB is widening
Fig. 4.18 : Widening on curves

From Fig. 4.18, and by simple geometry, we have
$$l^2 = AB \times (2\,AO - AB) = 2Rm - m^2.$$
Widening required being small, we may neglect, square of it. In that case,
$$m = \frac{l^2}{2R}$$

Most of the times, the wheel base is 6 metres and $m = \frac{18}{R}$ metres, if R is in metres.

If there are n lanes, then total widening $= nm = \frac{nl^2}{2R}$.

In addition to this widening, which is required because of vehicle geometry, we have to provide widening to cater for the psychology of the driver. This widening to cater for the psychology of the driver is $0.1\frac{V}{\sqrt{R}}$, where, V is speed in kilometer/hr and R is radius in metres.

Therefore, total widening $= n\frac{l^2}{2R} + 0.1\frac{V}{\sqrt{R}}$

Total widening for pavements where width is excess of 2 lanes is total widening
$$= n\frac{18}{R} + 0.1\frac{18}{\sqrt{R}}.$$

For single and two lane pavement, the widening that is recommended is given below.

Table 4.20 : Widening of Single Lane and Two Lane Pavement

Radius in Metres	upto 20	21 to 40	41 to 60	61 to 100	101 to 300	Above 300
Extra Width :						
Two Lane	1.5	1.5	1.2	0.9	0.6	Nil
Single Lane	0.9	0.6	0.6	Nil	Nil	Nil

As expected, when the curve becomes flatter, i.e. when it's radius is large, less and less widening is required.

4.16 GENERAL PRINCIPLES OF HORIZONTAL ALIGNMENT

We can now sum-up general principles of horizontal alignment involving curves. These are :
- Alignment should confirm topography and natural contours.
- It should be our attempt to limit the number of curves especially abrupt cuts. Short curves should be avoided. These locations are invitations to the accidents.
- Large radius curves should be preferred even when costly. For a deflection angle of 5°, curve radius should be minimum 150 metre and for every degree increase in deflection angle, curve radius may be increased by at least 30 metres.
- For high hills, sharp curves be avoided. If there are no shrubs and trees at the roadway perimeter, drivers find it difficult to estimate the extent of curvature. These should be planted.
- Curves in same direction but separated by short tangents called broken back curves should be avoided. These are not good asthetically.
- It is recommended that abrupt reversal in curvature be avoided. On hilly terrain, this is impossible. In that case long transitional curves should be inserted for super-elevation run-off.
- When single circular curve cannot be fit in, we may use compound curve as an exceptional measure. When such two curves are employed, the radius of the flater curve should not be disproportional to the radius of sharper curve. A ratio of 2 : 1 or preferably 1.5 : 1 may be adopted.

4.17 VERTICAL ALIGNMENT

Gradient is an important part of vertical alignment. Grade affects the speed of the vehicle and capacity of roads. In Indian context, where there is no segregation of traffic, the Example is more severe. Once the vertical profile is given, up-gradation is difficult since it will involve considerable investment. Therefore grade should be so selected so as to have uniform operation of most of the traffic. Table 5.20 gives Indian practice for maximum gradient.

Table 4.20 : Grades for Different Terrains

Sr. No.	Terrain	Ruling Gradient %	Limiting Gradient %	Exceptional Gradient %
1.	Plain	3.3 (1 in 30)	5 (1 in 20)	6.7 (1 in 15) For short distance not exceeding 100 m
2.	Rolling	3.3 (1 in 30)	4 (1 in 20)	6.7 (1 in 15) For short distance not exceeding 100 m
3.	Mountainous	5 (1 in 20)	6 (1 in 16.7)	7 (1 in 14.3) For a distance not more than 100 m at stretch
4.	Steep (a) Upto 3000 m above m.s.l.	5 (1 in 20)	6 (1 in 16.7)	7 (1 in 14.3) For a distance not more than 100 m
	(b) Above 3000 m (m.s.l.)	6 (1 in 16.7)	7 (1 in 14.3)	8 (1 in 12.5) For a distance not more than 100 m

To use this table, ruling gradient could be used as a matter of routine in the design. Limiting gradient is a gradient where the topography compels it to use it. That is, if one uses gentle gradient, heavy costs are involved, whereas the exceptional gradients are for exceptional circumstances. Even where these are used, these gradients should be separated by a minimum length of 100 meters of gentle gradient which may be even limiting gradient. When one uses exceptional gradients, rise in elevation over a length of 2 km should not exceed 100 metre for mountainous terrain and 120 metres in steep terrain.

Minimum Gradient for Drainage

Drainage of the pavement is affected by camber and longitudinal slope. We have noted that even in flat terrain, same longitudinal slope is necessary.

Grade Compensation in Curves

For horizontal curves on hill roads, the vehicle has to exert extra effort to negotiate the curve. In order to mitigate the suffering of the vehicle, it is usual to reduce the longitudinal gradient. This is known as grade compensation. Grade compensation in percentage is $\frac{30 + R}{R}$. Subject to a maximum of $\frac{75}{R}$, where R is the radius of the curve in metres.

Vertical Curves

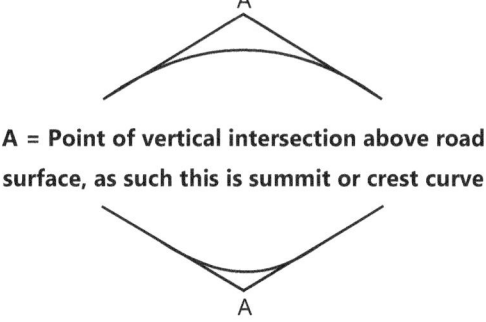

A = Point of vertical intersection above road surface, as such this is summit or crest curve

A = Point of intersection below road surface, as such this is sag curve

Fig. 4.19

Where there is change of grade, vertical curve is provided to see that change is not sudden. It can serve many purposes such as (1) The driver of the vehicle will undergo change of grade without discomfort, (2) For stopping and overtaking, visibility is assured and (3) humps and troughs are avoided. These curves are shown in the figure. If the total change of gradient does not exceed 0.5 %, one need not provide vertical curves. Road engineers have preferred parabola to be a preferred vertical curve. Though, when grade change is small, vertical curve, could be dispensed with, it is also a function of speed. That is for speedy vehicle you do require some curve. The minimum length of such vertical curves is given in Table 4.22.

Table 4.22 : Minimum Length of Vertical Curves (Sag or Summit)

Design Speed, km/hr.	Maximum Grade Change (Percentage) not Requiring a Vertical Curve	Minimum Length of Vertical Curve (meters)
upto 35	1.5	15
40	1.2	20
50	1.0	30
65	0.8	40
80	0.6	50
100	0.5	60

Length of vertical apex curve when sight distance 'S' is less than the length of curve 'L'.

To demonstrate this distance, assume h_1 and h_2 to be the height of drivers eye above the curve and height of object on the curve. Let S_1, S_2 be the horizontal distance between the driver and apex of the curve and S_2 be the horizontal distance between the object and the apex. Clearly $(S_1 + S_2)$ is 'S' the stopping sight distance. Let the grades $+ N_1$ and $- N_2$ intersect at point 'O'.

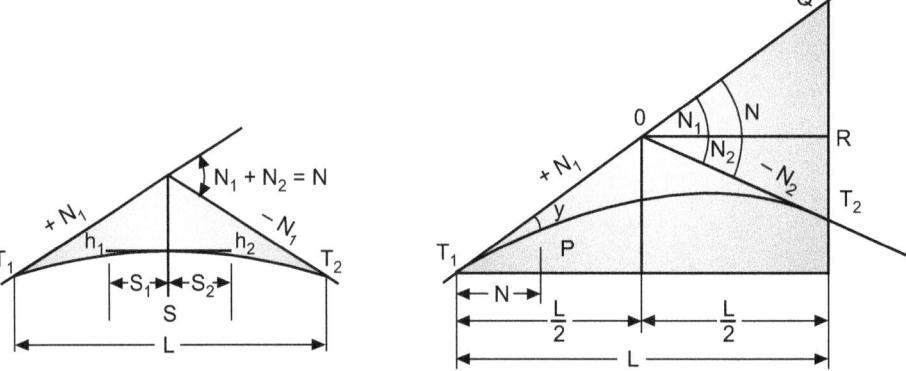

(a) Summit curve when S is less than L (b) Details of summit curve

Fig. 4.20

Then from Fig. 4.20, we have,

$$h_1 = \frac{S_1^2}{C} \qquad S_1^2 = \sqrt{Ch_1}$$

$$h_2 = \frac{S_2^2}{C} \qquad S_2^2 = \sqrt{Ch_2}$$

These equations assume the apex curve to be a parabola.

$$S = S_1 + S_2 = \sqrt{C}\left(\sqrt{h_1} + \sqrt{h_2}\right)$$

To get the value of 'C' we make recourse to the figure and find that for any point 'P' on the parabola,

$$y = \frac{x^2}{C}$$

And geometry demands,

$$QT_2 = QR + RT_2$$
$$= N_1 \frac{L}{2} + N_2 \frac{L}{2} = \frac{L}{2}(N_1 + N_2) = \frac{L}{2} N$$

At the end point of the curve i.e. at T_2,

$$y = \frac{LN}{2} \text{ and } x = L$$

$$\frac{LN}{2} = \frac{L^2}{C} \quad \therefore C = \frac{2L}{N}$$

Back substituting,

$$S = \sqrt{\frac{2L}{N}} \left(\sqrt{h_1} + \sqrt{h_2}\right)$$

$$= \sqrt{\frac{L}{N}} \left(\sqrt{2h_1} + \sqrt{2h_2}\right)$$

$$\therefore L = \frac{NS^2}{\left(\sqrt{2h_1} + \sqrt{2h_2}\right)^2}$$

General values of h_1 and h_2 are 1.2 m and 0.15 m as per I. R. C.

$$\therefore L = \frac{NS^2}{\left(\sqrt{2h_1} + \sqrt{2h_2}\right)^2} = \frac{NS^2}{4.4}$$

and if gradient is in percentage

$$L = \frac{NS^2}{440}$$

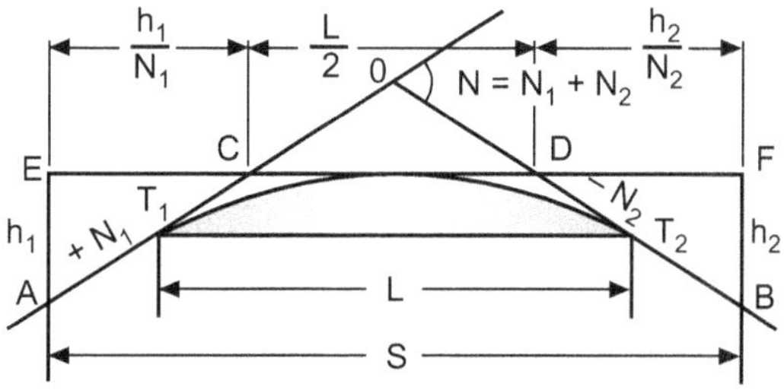

Fig. 4.21

For summit curve where S is greater than L, we take recourse to Fig. 4.21 and state that

$$S = CD + DF + EC = \frac{L}{2} + \frac{h_2}{N_2} + \frac{h_1}{N_1}$$

$$= \frac{L}{2} + \frac{h_1}{N_1} + \frac{h_2}{N - N_1}$$

For minimum S,

$$\frac{dS}{dN_1} = 0 = -\frac{h_1}{N_1} + \frac{h_2}{(N - N_1)^2}$$

$$\therefore \quad h_1 (N - N_1)^2 = h_2 N_1^2 \quad \text{or}$$

$$N_1^2 (h_2 - h_1) + 2 N N_1 h_1 - h_1 N^2 = 0$$

which is quadratic in N_1

$$N_1 = \frac{-Nh_1 + N\sqrt{h_1 h_2}}{(h_2 - h_1)}$$

When we substitute the above value of N_1 in equation for S, we get,

$$S = \frac{L}{2} + \frac{(\sqrt{h_1} + \sqrt{h_2})^2}{N}$$

and,

$$L = 2S - \frac{2(\sqrt{h_1} + \sqrt{h_2})^2}{N}$$

It should be noted that for brevity, intermediate steps are ommited. The students are however advised to perform these steps to gain confidence.

If we assume $h_1 = 1.2$ m and $h_2 = 0.15$ m we get

$$L = 2S - \frac{4.4}{N} \quad \text{and if N is expressed in percentage,} \quad L = 2S - \frac{440}{N}$$

Sometimes the values h_1 and h_2 are each taken to be 1.2 m. In that case, the equations are reduced to

$$L > S; \quad L = \frac{NS^2}{9.6}$$

$$L < S; \quad L = 2S - \frac{9.6}{N}$$

This case is sometimes referred as intermediate or overtaking sight distance case. In the case of summit curves, where there is ascending gradient on one side and descending gradient on the other side, effect of gradients on S i.e. stopping sight distance is neglected.

Sag Curves (Valley Curves)

Factors that determine length of valley curves are :

(1) Drainage control. i.e. water should not get stagnated at sag point.

(2) Vehicle head light sight distance. The driver of the vehicle should clearly detect the head light of the oncoming vehicle.
(3) Rider comfort I.R.C. has given more credance to the third factor, i.e. the rider comfort.

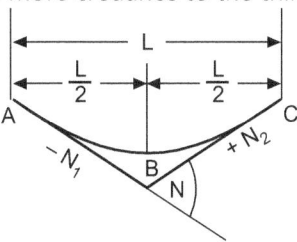

Fig. 4.22

Let L be the length of total valley curve. Here the assumption is that L is made-up of two transition curves i.e.

$$AC = AB + BC$$
$$= L_s + L_s$$

Vertical radial acceleration at A = 0

Vertical radial acceleration at B = $\dfrac{V^2}{R}$

This change in radial acceleration $\left(\dfrac{V^2}{R} - 0 = \dfrac{V^2}{R}\right)$ occurs in a distance L i.e. AB.

Time to travel $\quad AB = \dfrac{AB}{V} = \dfrac{L_s}{V}$

Rate of change of vertical radial acceleration

$$= \dfrac{V^2}{R} \div \dfrac{L_s}{V} = \dfrac{V^2}{R} \times \dfrac{V}{L_s} = \dfrac{V^3}{L_s R} = C$$

$L_s = \dfrac{V^3}{CR}$ where, C is recommended value of rate of vertical radical acceleration. I.R.C. says, C = 0.6 m/sec²

Value of R at $\quad L_s = \dfrac{L_s}{N} \quad$ where, N is deviation angle.

∴ $\quad L_s = \dfrac{V^3}{C \times \dfrac{L_s}{N}}$

∴ $\quad L_s^2 = \dfrac{NV^3}{C}$

∴ $\quad L_s = \left[\dfrac{NV^3}{C}\right]^{1/2}$

Therefore, length of sag curve = $L = 2L_s = 2\left[\dfrac{NV^3}{C}\right]^{1/2}$

But V km/hr = $\dfrac{V}{3.6}$ m/sec. $L_s = 0.19[NV^3]^{1/2}$

∴ $L = 0.38[NV^3]^{1/2}$ where N = Deviation angle in radian approximately equal to tangent of deviation angle.

Length of sag curve on the consideration of head light sight distance.

Two conditions arise

(1) length of curve more than stopping sight distance,
(2) length of curve less than stopping sight distance.

(a) L > S.S.D.

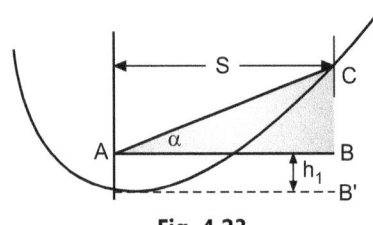

Fig. 4.23

Let head light be located at h_1 above road level and, it focus it's beam α angle upwards. The sight distance available is minimum when the vehicle is at sag point. Let sag curve be parabolic with an equation $y = aX^2$

∴ $y = B'C = BB' + BC$
$= h_1 + s \tan \alpha = aX^2$

If the sag curve is cubic parabola,

$y = h_1 + s \tan \alpha = aX^2 = \dfrac{N}{2L} \times S^2$

∴ $L = \dfrac{NS^2}{(2h_1 + 2s \tan \alpha)}$, where S is stopping sight distance

(b) L < S.S.D.

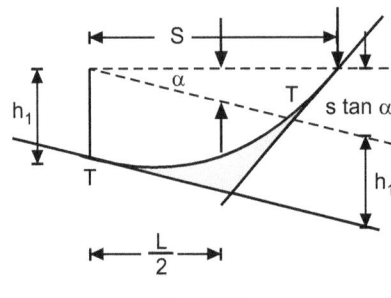

Fig. 4.24

In this case,

$h_1 + s \tan \alpha = \left(S - \dfrac{L}{2}\right) N$

∴ $L = 2S - \dfrac{(2h_1 + 2s \tan \alpha)}{N}$

The lowest point on sag curve will be on the bisector of grades if equal. If grades are unequal, this point is on a flatter grade at a distance $L\sqrt{N_1/2N}$. Generally the valley curve is given by $y = \dfrac{2W}{3L^2} X^3$ which is practically a spiral transition.

I.R.C. Practice : IRC practice is to take $h_1 = 0.75$ metres and beam angle $\alpha = 1°$ then two cases arise.

When L > SSD, $L = \dfrac{NS^2}{(2h_1 + 2s\tan\alpha)}$

$= \dfrac{NS^2}{(1.5 + 0.0355)}$ and

When L < SSD, $L = 2S - \dfrac{(2h_1 + 2s\tan\alpha)}{N}$

$= 2S - \dfrac{(1.5 + 0.0355)}{N}$

SOLVED EXAMPLES

Example 4.1 : For a hill road with a ruling gradient of 8 % with horizontal curve of 100 metres, what could be the compensation of gradient at this curve?

Solution :

Grade compensation $= \dfrac{30 + R}{R} = \dfrac{30 + 100}{100} = 1.3\%$

Max. limit of grade compensation

$= \dfrac{75}{R} = \dfrac{75}{100} = 0.75\%$

That is the grade compensation (max.) could be 0.75 % where the ruling gradient is 8 %. Therefore compensated gradient = 8 % – 0.75 % = 7.25 %.

That is the curve on this stretch shall have a gradient 7.25 % instead of 8 %.

Example 4.2 : For a hill road with ruling gradient 4 % with horizontal curves of 100 metres, what would be grade compensation?

Solution : Ruling gradient = 4 %.

Therefore no grade compensation. Gradient need not be eased beyond 4%.

Example 4.3 : What would be radius of horizontal curve, for which you would recommend no gradient i.e. laying of road on level ground?

Solution : In this case,

Grade compensation = Max. limit of grade compensation

$\dfrac{30 + R}{R} = \dfrac{75}{R}$

∴ $R = 75 - 30 = 45$.

That is for horizontal curves of 45 metres and below, they better be laid on flat ground. That is as far as possible.

Example 4.4 : Minimum sight distance between two approaching cars at 100 and 50 km/hr is wanted to avoid collision. One can assume reaction time of 3 seconds, coefficient of friction between road and vehicle 0.7 and brake efficiency of 0.8 and flat country. What should be the sight distance to avoid collision?

Solution : Stopping sight distance for the first car,

$$= 0.278 \, Vt + \frac{V^2}{254 \, f}$$

$$= 0.278 \times 100 \times 3 + \frac{(100)^2}{254 \times (0.5 \times 0.7)}$$

$$= 83.4 + 112.48 = 195.88 \text{ say } 196 \text{ meter}$$

We have halved, the coefficient of friction here for brake efficiency.

$$\text{S.S.D. for 2nd car} = 0.278 \times 50 \times 3 + \frac{(50)^2}{254 \times (0.5 \times 0.7)}$$

$$= 41.7 + 28.12 = 69.82 \text{ say } 70 \text{ meter}$$

Sight distance to avoid collision

$$= SD_1 + SD_2 = 196 + 70 = 266 \text{ metres.}$$

Example 4.5 : Stopping sight distance is 60 metres for two lane traffic. What would be stopping sight distance when there is only one lane and two way traffic?

Solution : Two way traffic and one lane, as such the stopping sight distance shall double the farmer i.e. $2 \times 60 = 120$ metres.

Example 4.6 : Calculate the grade at which the braking distance is infinite for a speed of 50 km/hr if coefficient of friction between road surface and vehicle is 0.6. Grade is descending.

Solution : Braking distance on grade $= \dfrac{V^2}{254 \, (f \pm 0.01 \, n)}$

For braking distance to be infinite

f − 0.01 n should be zero i.e $0.6 = 0.01 \, n$

$$n = \frac{0.6}{0.01} = \frac{6}{10} \times \frac{100}{1} = 60 \text{ percent}$$

That is if the grade is more than 60 % for this friction coefficient, it is difficult to stop the vehicle. The alternative is to reduce the descending grade.

Example 4.7 : Calculate the grade at which braking distance is zero. For a speed of 50 km/hr., if coefficient of friction between road surface and vehicle is 0.6 . Grade is ascending.

Solution : Braking distance on ascending grade

$$= \frac{V^2}{254 \, (f + 0.01 \, n)}$$

In order that this be zero, f + 0.01 n should be infinite or V should be zero. Both possibilities being improbable, braking distance cannot be zero.

Example 4.8 : Two major roads intersect at 90° and the design speed is 50 km/hr. If the sight distance at intersection allowed is 110 metres, sketch the triangle at intersection in which properties should not be constructed. Reaction time for the driver is 3 seconds.

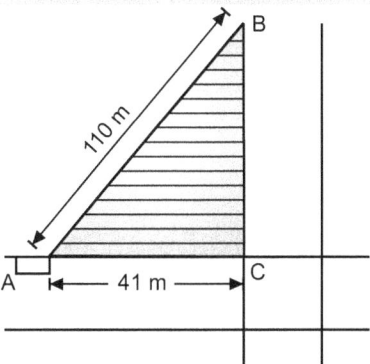

Fig. 4.25

Solution : Reaction distance = $3 \times \dfrac{50 \times 1000}{60 \times 60}$ = 41 metre

That is if the vehicle is A, distance AC must be 41 metres so that driver can take some action. Since sight distance allowed for this junction is 110 metres, AB is 110 metres and

$$BC = \sqrt{AB^2 - AC^2}.$$
$$BC = \sqrt{110^2 - 41^2} = \sqrt{12100 - 1681}$$
∴ $$BC = \sqrt{10419} = 102 \text{ met.}$$

Therefore, ΔABC sides 110, 41 and 102 metre at the intersection as shown, is the approximate area where properties should not be constructed.

Example 4.9 : For a vehicle traversing a curve of radius 100 metre with a design speed of 80 km/hr, indicate the amount of super-elevation that you would provide. Country is hilly and is non-snow bound.

Solution : $e = \dfrac{V^2}{225\,R} = \dfrac{(80)^2}{225 \times 100} = 0.28.$

But the max. value of super-elevation recommended is 0.1 and hence that should be given.

Example 4.10 : For plain terrain, and national highway, calculate ruling, minimum and absolute minimum radii.

Solution : Let us assume

    Design speed (Ruling) = 100 km/hr.
    Design speed (minimum) = 80 km/hr.
    Maximum super-elevation = 0.07   (as per IRC recommendations)
    Coefficient of lateral friction = μ = 0.15

$$R = \frac{V^2}{127(e+\mu)} = \frac{(100)^2}{127(0.07+0.15)} = 360 \text{ metres}$$

which is ruling radius.

Minimum design speed = 80

$$\therefore \quad R = \frac{(80)^2}{127(0.07+0.15)} = 230 \text{ m.}$$

which is absolute minimum radius.

Example 4.11 : Horizontal curve radius is 300 metres, design speed of 80 km/hr. and plain terrain. Find super-elevation. What could be coefficient of lateral friction mobilized if super-elevation is restricted to 0.07 ?

Solution : As per IRC practice,

$$e = \frac{(0.75V)^2}{127R} = \frac{V^2}{225R} = \frac{(80)^2}{225 \times 300} = 0.0999 = 0.1 \text{ say.}$$

As per IRC, maximum super-elevation = 0.07

Therefore balance centrifugal force will be catered by friction that is mobilized.

$$\therefore \quad (e+\mu) = 0.1, \ \mu = 0.1 - e = 0.1 - 0.07 = 0.03$$

which is below the recommended value of 0.15.

Example 4.12 : There is two lane pavement on national highway. Radius of curve is 300 metres. Ruling design speed is 100 km/hr. Maximum super-elevation is 0.07. Super-elevation is to be given by rotation about centre. Allowable rate of attainment of super-elevation is 1 in 150. Find length of transition curve if pavement is 7 metre.

Solution : Criterion A

Satisfactory rate of change of acceleration

$$= \frac{80}{75+V} = \frac{80}{75+100} = 0.46$$

Consider minimum of 0.5

$$L_s = \frac{V^3}{CR} = \frac{0.0215 \times (100)^3}{0.5 \times 300} = 145 \text{ metre}$$

Criterion B

Super-elevation allowed = $e = \frac{(0.75V)^2}{127 \times R} = \frac{(0.75 \times 100)^2}{127 \times 300}$

$$\therefore \quad e = 0.147$$

But this is high value and should be 0.07 only.

Since radius is 300 m, widening of pavement on curve is not necessary.

∴ Raising of pavement due to super-elevation

$$= 0.07 \times 7 = 0.49 \text{ m}$$

Assuming rotation of super-elevation about centre, raising of outer edge

$$= \frac{0.49}{2} = 0.245 \text{ metre.}$$

And length of transition = 0.245 × 150 = 36.8 m

Higher of the two values i.e. 145 metres is chosen.

Example 4.13 : For a curve of radius 50 metres, design speed is 40 km/hr. Determine length of transition curve on the following assumptions :

(1) Hilly terrain snow bound.
(2) Allowed super-elevation = 0.07
(3) Rate of attainment of super-elevation = 1 in 60
(4) $C = \frac{80}{75 + V}$ with maximum and minimum of 0.8 and 0.5
(5) Rotation about pavement centre.

Solution :

Criterion A

$$C = \frac{80}{75 + V} = \frac{80}{75 + 40} = 0.727$$

C is in the range of 0.8 and 0.5

$$L = \frac{0.0215 \, V^3}{CR}$$

$$= \frac{0.0215 \, (40)^3}{0.72 \times 50} = 38.2 \text{ metre}$$

Criterion B

$$e = \frac{(0.75 \, V)^2}{127 \, R} = \frac{(0.75 \times 40)^2}{127 \times 50}$$

= 0.141 high value.

Let e = 0.07
Extra-widening on curve

$$= n\frac{18}{R} + 0.1\frac{V}{\sqrt{R}} = 2 \times \frac{18}{50} + 0.1 \times \frac{40}{\sqrt{50}} = 0.72 + 0.56 = 1.28$$

Pavement width = 7 + 1.427 = 8.427 metres
Raising of pavement = 0.07 × 8.427 = 0.589 say 0.6 metre
Assuming rotation about centre line,

Length of transition = $\frac{0.6}{2} \times R = 0.3 \times 50 = 15.0$ metre

Higher of the two values i.e. 38.2 metres be adopted.

Example 4.14 : Radius of curve is 300 metre, super-elevation is 0.07. Is the curve as per standards for major district roads and plain terrain? If the super-elevation is to be provided by rotation about the crown, how much the pavement edge be raised or depressed? Assume pavement width of 7m.

Solution :

Allowable $\mu = 0.15$

$$\therefore \quad R = \frac{V^2}{127 (e + \mu)}$$

$$\therefore \quad V^2 = 127 (e + \mu) R = 127 (0.07 + 0.15) 300$$

$$\therefore \quad V = \sqrt{127 \times 0.22 \times 300} = 91.55 \text{ km/hour}$$

Ruling design speed for M.D.R. and plain terrain = 80 km/hr. and the absolute minimum design speed is 65 km/hr. These criterions are not met.

Total super-elevation = $0.07 \times 7 = 0.49$ m.

Half of this (0.245 m) to be provided by depressing the inner edge and balance (0.245 m) by raising the outer edge.

Example 4.15 : For a national highway, plain terrain and high bituminous road has a curve of radius 3000 metres. What should be super-elevation?

Solution : For this highway, design speed = 100 km/hr.

I.R.C. practice,

$$e = \frac{(0.75 V)^2}{127 R} = \frac{(0.75 \times 100)^2}{127 \times 3000} = 0.0147$$

i.e. 1 in 66.

Minimum camber for this type of highway is 1 in 50 to 1 in 60.

Better option would be to give camber of 1 in 66 or more and continue normal cambered section of highway.

Example 4.16 : Vehicle is negotiating a curve of radius 100 metres with a design speed of 70 km/hr. The wheel base is 8 metres and it is two lane pavement. Calculate the extra widening that is required.

Solution : Extra widening,

$$= n \frac{l^2}{2R} + 0.1 \frac{V}{\sqrt{R}}$$

$$= 2 \times \frac{(8)^2}{2 \times 100} + 0.1 \frac{70}{\sqrt{100}}$$

$$= 0.64 + 0.7 = 1.71 \text{ metres.}$$

Example 4.17 : Two grades one 1 in 200 and the other 1 in 200 are meeting at an apex. Stopping sight distance is 175 metre and height of driver and that of the object above roadway could be assumed to be 1.2 metre and 0.15 metre. Find length of apex curve.

Solution : Assume S < L

$$\therefore \quad L = \frac{NS^2}{440}$$

$$= \frac{(0.5 + 0.5) \times 175 \times 175}{440} = 69.60$$

Thus, S sight distance 175 metre is not less than L.

Let S > L,
$$L = 2S - \frac{440}{N}$$

$$= 2 \times 175 - \frac{440}{(0.5 + 0.5)} = -90$$

i.e. S is not greater than L.

Then the conclusion is grade change is too small and does not warrant designing a apex curve. Depending upon speed, length could be chosen. For example, if design speed is 65 km/hr, length of apex curve could be 40 meters as per IRC recommendations.

Example 4.18 : Two grades + 2 % and – 2.5 % meet at apex. Overtaking sight distance to be provided for is 600 metres, calculate L.

Solution :
$$L = \frac{NS^2}{9.6} \quad \text{when } L > S$$

$$L = 2S - \frac{9.6}{N} \quad \text{when } L < S$$

$$S = 600, \; L > S \text{ say}$$

$N_1 = + 2 \% = 1 \text{ in } 50, \; N_2 = - 2.5 \% = - 1 \text{ in } 40$

$$N = N_1 + N_2 = \frac{1}{50} + \frac{1}{40} = 0.045$$

$$L = \frac{NS^2}{9.6}$$

$$= \frac{0.045 \times 600 \times 600}{9.6} = 1687.5 > 600.$$

Assumption correct, provide L = 1687 metres.

Example 4.19 : Vertical grades +3 and –4 percent meet at sag point. Design speed is 80 km/hr. Perception brake time is 2.5 seconds. Friction coefficient between road surface and vehicle is 0.35. Find length of summit curve.

Solution : Assume S < L i.e. stopping sight distance < L

$$\text{S.S.D.} = 0.278\,Vt + \frac{V^2}{254\,f} \quad \text{on flat grade}$$

$$= 0.278 \times 80 \times 2.5 + \frac{80^2}{254 \times 0.35}$$

$$= 128 \text{ m.}$$

Deviation angle = N = 3 + 4 = 7 %

$$L = \frac{NS^2}{5.4}$$

$$= \frac{0.07 \times (128)^2}{4.4} = 260.6 \text{ metre}$$

260.6 > 128. Assumption is correct.

∴ Length of summit curve = 260.6 metre.

Example 4.20 : Two grades 1 in 100 and 1 in 125 meet at summit. Speed is 80 km/hr. The summit curve is to be designed for overtaking sight distance of 470 metres. Determine length.

Solution :

$$N = \frac{1}{100} + \frac{1}{125} = \frac{12.5 + 10}{1250} = \frac{22.5}{1250}$$

Assume L > overtaking sight distance

Then

$$L = \frac{NS^2}{9.6} = \frac{22.5}{1250} \times \frac{(470)^2}{9.6} = 414.18 \text{ metre}$$

That assumption proves incorrect. Therefore now assume L < S

$$L = 2S - \frac{9.6}{N} = 2 \times 470 - \frac{9.6 \times 1250}{22.5}$$

$$= 940 - 533.3 = 406.6 \text{ metre}$$

Assumption is correct. Therefore adopt this length.

Example 4.21 : Two grades $\frac{1}{50}$ and $\frac{1}{100}$ meet at summit. The stopping sight distance and overtaking sight distances are 200 and 650 metres. Calculate length of summit curve to fulfil both these requirements. On the assumption that topography demands length of summit curve as maximum 500 metres.

Solution :

$$N = \frac{1}{50} + \frac{1}{100} = \frac{3}{100}$$

S. S. D. = 200 metre

Let L > SSD,

$$L = \frac{NS^2}{4.4} = \frac{3}{100} \times \frac{(200)^2}{4.4} = 272.72$$

Assumption is correct in this case.

Now, let L > overtaking sight distance.

Then $L = \dfrac{NS^2}{9.6} = \dfrac{3}{100} \times \dfrac{(650)^2}{9.6} = 1320.3$ metre.

This assumption is correct in this case. That is we cannot provide curve which will cater for both the criterias i.e. stopping sight distance and overtaking sight distance, since 1320 > 500 metres. Let us provide therefore intermediate sight distance.

I. S. D. = 2 S. S. D. = 2 × 200 = 400 metre

If L > S.D. $\qquad L = \dfrac{NS^2}{9.6} = \dfrac{3}{100} \times \dfrac{(400)^2}{9.6} = 500$ metres.

Assumption is correct.

That is if we provide summit curve 500 metres, it will cater stopping sight distance and intermediate sight distance and will also be in limit of 500 m. So provide that.

Example 4.22 : Descending grade of 1 in 20 and ascending grade of 1 in 30 meet to form valley curve. Design speed is 80 km/hr. Design valley curve to fulfil comfort condition and head light sight distance if f = 0.35 and braking time = 2.5 sec.

Solution : $\qquad N = \dfrac{1}{20} + \dfrac{1}{30} = \dfrac{5}{60}$

$$V = 80 \text{ km/hr} = \dfrac{80}{3.6} \text{ m/sec} = 22.2 \text{ m/sec.}$$

From the point of view of comfort,

$L = 2\left[\dfrac{NV^3}{C}\right]^{1/2}$ $\qquad$ C = allowable rate of change of acceleration

$\qquad\qquad\qquad\qquad\qquad = 0.6$ m/sec³

$\qquad\qquad\qquad\qquad\qquad = 2\left[\dfrac{5}{60} \times \dfrac{(22.2)^3}{0.6}\right]^{1/2}$

$\qquad\qquad\qquad\qquad\qquad = 2 \times 38.98 = 77.96$ m.

From the point of view of head light sight distance, stopping sight distance.

$= Vt + \dfrac{V^2}{2gf} = 22.2 \times 2.5 + \dfrac{(22.2)^2}{2 \times 9.8 \times 0.35} = 127.5$ metres

Let us assume L > S. S. D., then $L = \dfrac{NS^2}{(1.5 + 0.035s)}$

$$L = \dfrac{\dfrac{5}{60} \times (127.5)^2}{(1.5 + 0.035 \times 127.5)}$$

$$= \dfrac{1354.08}{5.962} = 227.21 \text{ metre}$$

L > S. S. D. ∴ Assumption is correct.

Therefore we have the length of sag curves to be 77.96 metres and 227.21 metres from two different considerations. Provide higher value of 227.21 metres.

Example 4.23 : The traffic on a particular road as of today is 1000 p.cu/day. The traffic increase per year is 10 %. The present road width is 3 metres. Find when this road requires widening.

Solution : Present traffic =1000 p.cu/day

It is single lane. Let it reach saturation after n years of service. When the traffic will be 2000 p.cu/day,

$$2000 = 1000 (1 + 0.1)^n$$

When n = 7,   R.H.S. = 1000×1.9487

and when n = 8,   R.H.S. = 1000×2.143

That is the road will require widening between 7th and 8th year.

Example 4.24 : A single lane is to be widened to two lanes. Present traffic is 3000 p.cu/day. The cost of widening is Rs. 95 lakhs/km. Find internal rate of return.

Solution : We have here

$$IRR = 5.42 - 0.167 (95) + 0.0094 (3000) + 0.208 \left(\frac{3000}{95}\right)$$

$$= 5.42 - 15.87 + 28.20 + 6.57$$

$$= 24.32 \%$$

Example 4.25 : Calculate stopping sight distance on a highway at a descending grade of 2 % for design speed of 80 km/hr. Total reaction time is 2.5 seconds and coefficient of friction between road and tyre is 0.35.

Solution : Stopping sight distance

$$= 0.278 \, Vt + \frac{V^2}{254 \, (f \pm 0.01 \, n)}$$

$$= 0.278 \times 80 \times 2.5 + \frac{(80)^2}{254 \, (0.35 - 0.01 \times 2)}$$

$$= 130 \text{ metres.}$$

Example 4.26 : For an upward gradient of 2 % and speed 80 km/hr., calculate safe stopping distance if perception and brake reaction time total is 2.5 seconds, and the coefficient of friction varies from 0.40 at 20 kmph to 0.35 at 100 kmph.

Solution : Slope of f versus velocity curve

$$= \frac{0.4 - 0.35}{100 - 20} = \frac{0.05}{80}$$

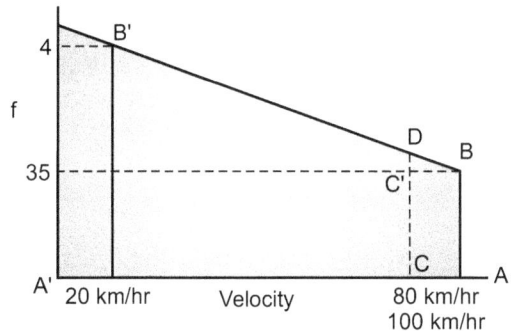

Fig. 4.26

f at 80 km/hr.
= CD = AB + C'D
= $0.035 + \frac{0.05}{80}(100 - 80)$
= 0.35 + 0.01 = 0.36

Stopping sight distance (safe)

$$= 0.278\,V\,t + \frac{V^2}{254\,(f + 0.01\,n)}$$

$$= 0.278 \times 80 \times 2.5 + \frac{(80)^2}{254\,(0.36 + 0.01 \times 2)}$$

$$= 55.6 + 66.3 = 122 \text{ metres approximately}$$

Example 4.27: Calculate the camber for the following cases: (1) Major district Road, light rainfall, and thin bituminous surface, pavement is 4 metre wide. (2) Heavy rainfall, W.B.M. pavement, pavement 3.8 wide.

Solution :

Case I : Camber of 1 in 50 is recommended

Rise of crown with respect to edges = $\frac{4}{2} \times \frac{1}{50}$ = 0.04 m

Case II : Camber of 1 in 33 is recommended

Rise of crown with respect to edges = $\frac{3.8}{2} \times \frac{1}{33}$ = 0.057 m.

Example 4.28 : A 400 metre radius curve is laid to effect change of direction of road. The distance between the centre line of the road and the centre line of the inside lane is 1 metre. If the sight distance on this horizontal curve is 300 metres, determine the set back distance.

Solution : Here, we have

$$\theta = \frac{S}{2(R-n)} \text{ radians} = \frac{300}{2(400-1)} = 0.375 \text{ radians}$$

$$= \frac{360 \times 0.375}{2\pi} \text{ in degrees} = 21.53°$$

m = R − (R − n) cos θ
= 400 − (400 − 1) cos 21.53 = 29 meters.

Example 4.29 : For the uncontrolled intersection at the confluence of major and minor road, the respective design speeds are 40 and 30 km/hr. The intersection is located on level ground, and the coefficient friction between tyre and road surface is 0.35. Sketch the line of sight and building restrictions, if road widths respectively are 4 and 3.5 metre.

Solution : Stopping sight distance for major road

$$= 0.278\,V + \frac{V^2}{254\left(f \pm \frac{n}{100}\right)}$$

$$= 0.278\,V + \frac{V^2}{254\,f} \quad ; n = 0 \text{ since level road}$$

$$= 0.278 \times 40 + \frac{V^2}{254 \times 0.35} = 0.278 \times 40 + \frac{(40)^2}{254 \times 0.35}$$

$$= 11.12 + 17.99 = 29.11 \text{ metre}$$

Stopping sight distance for minor road

$$= 0.278\,V + \frac{V^2}{254 \times f}$$

$$= 0.278 \times 30 + \frac{30^2}{254 \times 0.35} = 8.34 + 10.12$$

$$= 18.46 \text{ metre}$$

For intersection, the line of sight is shown in Fig. 4.27.

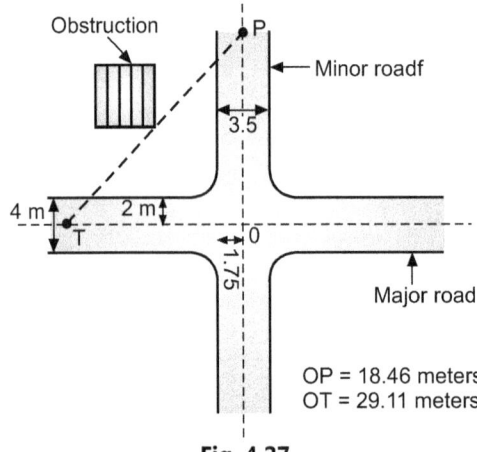

Fig. 4.27

OP = 18.46 meters
OT = 29.11 meters

Example 4.30 : Determine the capacity of mini round about, which is located at a crossing of two highways each two lane widths, each lane being of 3.7 metres. The area within the intersection line is 100.0 m². The efficiency coefficient is 65. Find approximate capacity of mini round about.

Solution : Here, $\sum W$ = sum of basic road width = 8 × 3.7
= 29.6 say 30 metres

a = area of junction widening = 100 m²

k = 65

q = pcu / hr capacity = $K (\sum W + a^{1/2})$

  = $65 (30 + \sqrt{100})$ = 40 × 65 = 2600

i.e. 2600 pcu per hour.

Example 4.31 : A particular highway is designed for 50 km/hr. as the speed. If the average spacing in metres of the moving vehicles is 0.5 metres, what would be capacity of the road?

Solution : Here S = 0.5 metre, V = 50 km/hr.

Therefore, capacity in vehicles/hr/lane = $\dfrac{1000 \, V}{S}$

$= \dfrac{1000 \times 50}{0.5}$ = 1 lakh vehicles/hr.

Example 4.32 : The highway is reserved for only cars and average length of cars is 3.2 metres. The perception time of the driver is one second and the friction factor is 0.5. The speed of car is 50 km/hr. and the acceleration due to gravity may be assumed to be usual value. What would be probable distance between cars that follow each other?

Solution : Here L = 3.2, V = 50 km/hr., t = 1 second,

g = 10 metre/sec² as such

$$S = L + \dfrac{t \, V \, 1000}{3600} + \left(\dfrac{V \times 1000}{3600}\right)^2 \times \dfrac{1}{2 \, gf}$$

$$= L + 0.278 \, Vt + \dfrac{V^2}{254 \, f}$$

$$= 3.2 + 0.278 \times 50 \times 1 + \dfrac{50 \times 50}{254 \times 0.5}$$

$$= 3.2 + 14.0 + \dfrac{50 \times 50}{127}$$

$$= 3.2 + 14 + 20$$

$$= 37.2 \text{ metres about}$$

V = 50 km/hr. = $\dfrac{50 \times 1000 \times 3.3}{60 \times 60}$

= 46 ft/sec about

∴ S = 21 + 1.1 V about

= 21 + 1.1 × 46 = 71 feet

= 22 metres about.

Example 4.33 : The width of weaving section of the rotary is 10 metres. The ratio of crossing stream traffic to the total traffic is 0.72. The average entry width is 7 metres and the length of weaving section between ends of channelising traffic in metres is 20. Find the capacity of weaving section.

Solution : Here, we have w = 10 metres, e = 7 metres, l = 20 metres, p = 0.72, therefore

$$Q_p = \frac{280 w \left(1 + \frac{e}{w}\right)\left(1 - \frac{p}{3}\right)}{1 + \frac{w}{l}}$$

$$= \frac{280 \times 10 \times \left(1 + \frac{7}{10}\right)\left(1 - \frac{0.72}{3}\right)}{1 + \frac{10}{20}} = \frac{2800 \times 1.7 \times 0.76}{1 + 0.5}$$

$$= 2380 \text{ vehicles at a time.}$$

Example 4.34 : For a particular case, the rolling gradient is 1 in 20 and if a horizontal curve of 125 metre radius is to be introduced on this gradient, find out the compensated gradient on this curve.

Solution :

$$\text{Ruling gradient} = 5.0\%$$

$$\text{Grade compensation} = \frac{30 + R}{R} = \frac{30 + 125}{125}$$

$$= 1.24\%$$

$$\text{Maximum limit of grade compensation} = \frac{75}{R} = \frac{75}{125} = 0.6\%$$

$$\therefore \quad \text{Compensated gradient} = 5 - 0.6 = 4.4\%$$

Example 4.35 : What is stopping Sight Distance? Find the non-passing sight distance on a highway at descending gradient of 2.5 percent for a design speed of 70 kmph. Assume other data suitably as per IRC recommendations only.

Solution : Total reaction time t may be taken as 2.5 secs. and design coefficient of friction as f = 0.35, V = 70 kmph, n = –0.025 (descending gradient), g = 9.8 m/sec^2.

$$V = \frac{70}{3.6} = 19.44 \text{ m/sec.}$$

$$SSD = Vt + \frac{V^2}{2g(f \pm n\%)}$$

$$= 19.44 \times 2.5 + \frac{(19.44)^2}{2 \times 9.8 (0.35 - 0.025)}$$

$$= 48.61 + \frac{377.91}{6.3765}$$

$$= 107.87 \text{ m} \approx 108 \text{ m}$$

$$\text{SSD} = 0.278\, Vt + \frac{V^2}{254\,(f \pm 0.01n)}$$

$$= 0.278 \times 70 \times 2.5 + \frac{70^2}{254\,(0.35 - 0.025)}$$

$$= 48.65 + \frac{4900}{82.55} = 108 \text{ m}$$

Example 4.36 : For a 2 lane road with design speed of 75 kmph, has a horizontal curve of radius 450 metre. Design the rate of superelevation for mixed traffic flow conditions. Also find the amount by which the outer edge of the pavement to be raised when the width of pavement is 7.50 metre for this 2 lane road.

Solution : For mixed traffic conditions, the superelevation should fully conteract the centrifugal force for 75% of design speed.

$$e = \frac{V^2}{225\,R} = \frac{70^2}{225 \times 450} = 0.048$$

Since this value is less than 0.07, the superelevation of 0.048 may be adopted.

The total width of pavement, B = 7.5 m.

Raising of outer edge with respect to centre

$$E = \frac{B \cdot e}{2}$$

$$= \frac{7.5}{2} \times 0.048 = 0.18 \text{ m}$$

Example 4.37 : Determine the safe O.S.D. for a design speed of 80 kmph for both one-way traffic and two-way traffic. You may assume the necessary data as per IRC recommendations only.

Solution :

$\qquad$ O.S.D. = $(d_1 + d_2)$ for one-way traffic

$\qquad$ V = 80 kmph

Assume $\quad V_b$ = V − 16 = 64 kmph and

$\qquad$ A = 3.28

(maximum overtaking acceleration at 64 kmph for IRS std)

$\qquad$ t = 2 secs

$\qquad d_1$ = 0.28 $V_b \cdot$ t

$\qquad\quad$ = 0.28 × 64 × 2 = 35.84 m

$\qquad d_2$ = 0.28 $V_b \cdot$ T + 2.S

$\qquad$ S = (0.2 V_b + 6) = 0.2 × 64 + 6 = 18.8 m

$$T = \sqrt{\frac{14.4S}{A}} = \sqrt{\frac{14.4 \times 18.8}{2.5}} = 10.4 \text{ sec}$$

$$d_2 = 0.28 \times 64 \times 10.4 + 2 \times 18.8$$
$$= 186.368 + 37.6$$
$$= 223.96$$
$$OSD = 35.84 + 223.96$$
$$= 259.80 \text{ m}$$

Example 4.38 : What do you mean by Grade compensation on horizontal curves? For a particular case, the ruling gradient is 1 in 20 and if a horizontal curve of 125 metre radius is to be introduced on this gradient, find out the compensated gradient on this curve.

Solution :

Ruling gradient = 5%.

$$\text{Grade compensation} = \frac{30 + R}{R} = \frac{30 + 125}{125}$$
$$= 1.25\%$$

$$\text{Maximum limit of grade compensation} = \frac{75}{R} = \frac{75}{125} = 0.6\%.$$

∴ Compensated gradient = 5 − 0.6 = 4.4%

Example 4.39 : Explain the terms (1) Stopping sight distance, (2) Total reaction time of a driver in brief, only. State the factors on which S.S.D. depend. And hence determine S.S.D. for a given speed of 80 kmph for a single lane two-way traffic roads. Assume t = 2.5 secs and f = 0.35.

Solution :

$$\text{Stopping sight distance} = 0.278 \, Vt + \frac{V^2}{254 \, (f \pm 0.01 n)}$$
$$= 0.278 \times 80 \times 2.5 + \frac{80^2}{254 \, (0.35 - 0.01 \times 2)}$$
$$= 130 \text{ metres}$$

Example 4.40 : Explain the terms in brief giving formulae for each:
(1) Radius of relative stiffness, (2) Equivalent radius of resisting section.
And hence, compute the radius of relative stiffness of 15 cm thick c.c. slab using the following data. E = 2,10,000 KSC, μ = 0.15 and K = 3 KSC per cm.

Solution :

$$K = 0.3$$
$$l = \left[\frac{Eh^3}{12 K (2 - \mu^2)}\right]^{1/4}$$
$$= \left[\frac{210000 \times 15^3}{12 \times 3 (2 - 0.15)^2}\right]^{1/4} = 67.0 \text{ cm}$$

Example 4.41 : What considerations you will have to take while designing the length of vertical valley curves? State clearly giving reasons. And hence design the length of valley curve for a design speed of 80 kmph when a valley curve is formed by a descending grade of 1 in 25 meeting an ascending grade of 1 in 30. Assume allowable rate of change of centrifugal acceleration C = 0.60 m/sec²/sec.

Solution :

$$N = -\frac{1}{25} - \frac{1}{30} = \frac{11}{150}$$

$$V = 80 \text{ kmph}, V = \frac{80}{3.6} = 22.2 \text{ m/sec}$$

(1) Comfort condition,

$$L = 2\left[\frac{NV^3}{C}\right]^{1/2} = 2\left[\frac{11}{150} \times \frac{(22.2)^3}{0.6}\right]^{1/2} = 73.1 \text{ m}$$

(2) Head light S.D. conditions t = 2.5 secs, f = 0.35

$$S.S.D. = Vt + \frac{V^2}{2gf}$$

$$= 22.2 \times 2.5 + \left(\frac{22.2^2}{2 \times 9.8 \times 0.35}\right) = 127.3 \text{ m}$$

If L > SSD,

$$L = \frac{NS^2}{(1.5 + 0.035 \, S)} = \frac{11 \times 127.3^2}{150 \, (1.5 + 0.035 \times 127.3)}$$

$$= 199.5 \text{ m} \approx 200 \text{ m}$$

Design value is 200 m.

Example 4.42 : The speed of overtaking and overtaken vehicles are 70 and 40 kmph respectively on two way traffic roads. If the acceleration of overtaking vehicle is 0.99 m/sec².
(1) Calculate safe overtaking sight distance.
(2) Mention the minimum length of overtaking zone assume t = 2 sec).

Solution : 1. Overtaking Sight Distance for Two-Way Traffic

$$= d_1 + d_2 + d_3$$

Assume the design speed as the speed of overtaking vehicle A.

$$v = 70 \text{ kmph}$$

$$v = \frac{70}{3.6} = 19.4 \text{ m/sec}$$

$$v_b = \frac{40}{3.6} = 11.1 \text{ m/sec}$$

Acceleration, a = 0.99 m/sec per sec.

$$d_1 = v_b \cdot t \text{ (Adopt t = 2 secs)}$$
$$= 11.1 \times 2 = 22.2 \text{ m}$$
$$d_2 = v_s \cdot T + 2 \cdot s$$
$$S = (0.7 v_b + 6)$$
$$= (0.7 \times 11.1 \times 6) = 13.6 \text{ m}$$
$$T = \sqrt{\frac{4 \cdot s}{a}} = \sqrt{\frac{4 \times 13.8}{0.99}} = 7.4 \text{ secs}$$
$$d_2 = 11.1 \times 7.47 + 2 \times 3.8 = 110.5 \text{ m}$$
$$d_3 = v \cdot T$$
$$= 19.4 \times 7.47$$
$$= 144.9 \text{ m}$$
$$\text{O.S.D.} = 22.2 + 110.5 + 144.9$$
$$= 277.6 \text{ m say 278 m}$$

2. **Mention the Minimum Length of Overtaking Zone = 3 (OSD)**

$$= 3 (d_1 + d_2 + d_3) \text{ for two-way traffic} = 3 \times 278$$
$$= 834 \text{ meters}$$

Desirable length of overtaking zone = 5 × (OSD)
$$= 5 \times 278 = 1390 \text{ m}$$

Example 4.43 : Calculate the extra widening required for a pavement within 7 m on a horizontal curve of radius 250 m if the longest wheel base of vehicle expected on be road is 7.0 m. Design speed is 60 kmph.

Solution : Extra widening required

$$W_e = \frac{nl^2}{2R} + \frac{V}{9.5\sqrt{R}}$$

n = 2 (two lines for pavement width of 7.0 m)
F = 250
V = 60 kmph

$$W_e = \frac{2 \times 7^2}{2 \times 250} + \frac{60}{9.5\sqrt{250}}$$

$$= 0.196 + 0.399$$
$$= 0.595 \text{ m say 0.6 m}$$

Extra widening required = **0.6 m**

REVIEW QUESTIONS

1. What constitutes "Geometric design" of highways?
2. What is critical length of grade? Are there any recommendations about it from IRC?
3. What are rotaries? How rotaries can function? What are the features of rotaries?
4. What are mini round abouts? Discuss their suitability.
5. Discuss the following types of intersections, their use and suitability: (a) Trumpet type interchange, (b) Four lagged interchange, (c) Clover-leaf, (d) Trumpet type interchange with toll plaza.
6. What are cycle tracks? Where these are provided? What purpose do they serve?
7. State IRC recommendations regarding summit and sag curves. What are the presuppositions in these recommendations?
8. Calculate stopping sight distance for a design speed of 100 km/hr on a level ground. Reaction time is 3 seconds and coefficient of friction is 0.4. Also calculate the stopping sight distance for an ascending grade of 1 in 50
   (**Ans.** Plain country 101.82 metres; Ascending grade 177.2 metres).
9. Write explanatory notes on (a) Shoulders, (b) Road Margins, (c) National highway in embankment, (d) Extra widening on curves, (e) Ideal transition curve.
10. Two lane pavement has a radius of 400 m. Design speed is 100 km/hr. Rate of change of centrifugal acceleration is max 0.8 and minimum 0.5. e = 0.07 maximum. Rate of attainment of super-elevation 1 in 150. Determine the length of transition curve. (**Ans.** 107.5 m)
11. Ascending grade of 1 in 50 and descending grade 1 in 30 form summit curve. Stopping sight distance is 180 metre. Determine length of summit curve.
    (**Ans.** 390 metre)
12. Valley curve is to be provided for descending grade of 1 in 30 and a level stretch from head light considerations. Stopping sight distance is 180 m. Determine the length. (**Ans.** 125 metre approximately)
13. What is meant by Single lane, Intermediate lane and Two lane pavement? What type of traffic plies on it?
14. Discuss the uses of (a) Kerbs, (b) Traffic separators with sketches.
15. What are road margins? Draw a sketch of road with road margins. Sketch a cross-section of a highway in urban area.
16. Outline the concept of "Capacity of road". On what factors does it depend? Derive expression for stopping sight distance.

17. What service road renders? Can it be measured and how?
18. Arrange the level of service in ascending or descending order with justification.
19. How road improvement decision can be based on the level of service?
20. Explain (a) Sight distance at intersection, (b) Safe overtaking sight distance, (c) PIEV concept.
21. Explain the concept of super-elevation. Why some curves may not require super-elevation? What part friction between tyre and road plays in determining super-elevation?
22. Why pavement is widened on curves?
23. State the general principles of horizontal and vertical alignment.
24. Present traffic on a particular road as of today is 5000 pcu/day. Traffic increase per year is 15 %. The present road width is 6 m. Find when this road would require widening. The maximum design service volume is 6000 pcu/day. **(Ans.** 2 years)
25. A two lane traffic road carrying 22500 pcu/day is to be widened to four lanes at a cost of Rs. 174 lakh/km. Find Internal rate of return. **(Ans.** 31.34 %)
26. What is meant by the term "Geometry of Highway"?
27. Describe the concept of passenger car unit. What are it's shortcomings?

    On a road 75 cycle rikshaw, 20 cars, and 1 bullock cart are plying per day. Determine the pcu per day of the road. **(Ans.** 1345 pcu/day)
28. Describe the concept of Design vehicle and design speed. Comment on the shortcomings of this concept.
29. What parameters determine the terrain as plain rolling or steep?
30. Comment on the concept of "Ruling Gradient" and limiting gradient. How are these fixed?
31. Why camber is given to the pavement?
32. Discuss the concept of Right of the way "building lines, control lines."

Unit - II

CHAPTER 5
ROAD MATERIALS

5.1 CLASSIFICATION OF ROADS

The civil engineering materials that are used for highway construction are :

(1) Soils, (2) Aggregate,
(3) Cement, (4) Bitumen,
(5) Sand, (6) Flyash,
(7) Certain stabilizing chemicals.

Whereas soil is essentially a part of subgrade, aggregate is used either as base course or as a part and parcel of cement concrete. Sand can be used in cement concrete or even bituminous surfacings. Flyash is used as replacement of cement, and stabilizing chemicals are used for stabilized bases. Materials that are used are no different from general civil engineering constituent materials, certain specific properties and performance are expected when they are used in highway construction. To assess these properties, certain tests have been developed. It is the object of this chapter to study these tests, understand their limitations and know, how the knowledge that is gathered from this testing can profitably be used. We shall first discuss the requirements of soil then aggregate and then bitumen the last. The test pertaining to other materials such as cement and sand are not specific. The tests regarding fly ash and stabilizing chemicals are discussed at the proper juncture.

Pavements are a conglomeration of materials. These materials, their associated properties, and their interactions determine the properties of the resultant pavement. Thus, a good understanding of these materials, how they are characterized, and how they perform is fundamental to understanding pavement. The materials which are used in the construction of highway are of intense interest to the highway engineer. This requires not only a thorough understanding of the soil and aggregate properties which affect pavement stability and durability, but also the binding materials which may be added to improve these pavement features.

Subgrade Soil : Soil is an accumulation or deposit of earth material, derived naturally from the disintegration of rocks or decay of vegetation that can be excavated readily with power equipment in the field or disintegrated by gentle mechanical means in the laboratory. The supporting soil beneath pavement and its special under courses is called subgrade. Undisturbed soil beneath the pavement is called natural subgrade. Compacted subgrade is the soil compacted by controlled movement of heavy compactors.

5.1.1 Desirable Properties

The desirable properties of subgrade soil as a highway material are :
- Stability.
- Incompressibility.
- Permanency of strength.
- Minimum changes in volume and stability under adverse conditions of weather and ground water.
- Good drainage.
- Ease of compaction.

5.1.2 Soil Types

The wide range of soil types available as highway construction materials have made it obligatory on the part of the highway engineer to identify and classify different soils. A survey of locally available materials and soil types conducted in India revealed wide variety of soil types, gravel, moorum and naturally occurring soft aggregates, which can be used in road construction. Broadly, the soil types can be categorized as Laterite soil, Moorum / red soil, Desert sands, Alluvial soil, Clay including Black cotton soil.

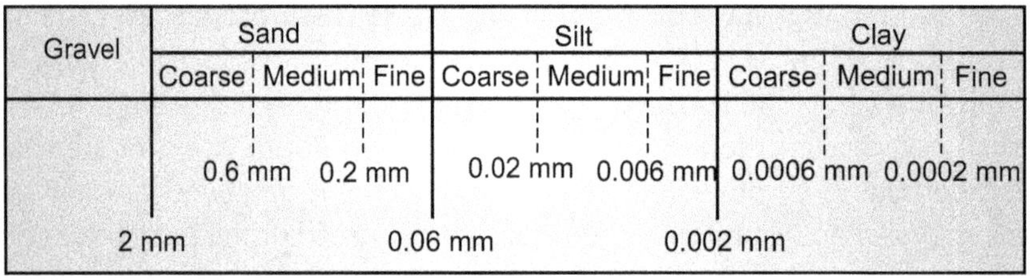

Gravel	Sand			Silt			Clay		
	Coarse	Medium	Fine	Coarse	Medium	Fine	Coarse	Medium	Fine
2 mm	0.6 mm	0.2 mm		0.02 mm	0.006 mm		0.0006 mm	0.0002 mm	
		0.06 mm			0.002 mm				

Fig. 5.1 : Indian standard grain size soil classification system

Gravel : These are coarse materials with particle size under 2.36 mm with little or no fines contributing to cohesion of materials.

Moorum : These are products of decomposition and weathering of the pavement rock. Visually these are similar to gravel except presence of higher content of fines.

Silts : These are finer than sand, brighter in colour as compared to clay, and exhibit little cohesion. When a lump of silty soil mixed with water, alternately squeezed and tapped a shiny surface makes its appearance, thus dilatancy is a specific property of such soil.

Clays : These are finer than silts. Clayey soils exhibit stickiness, high strength when dry, and show no dilatancy. Black cotton soil and other expansive clays exhibit swelling and shrinkage properties. Paste of clay with water when rubbed in between fingers leaves stain, which is not observed for silts.

5.1.3 Tests on Soil

Subgrade soil is an integral part of the road pavement structure as it provides the support to the pavement from beneath. The subgrade soil and its properties are important in the design of pavement structure. The main function of the subgrade is to give adequate support to the pavement and for this the subgrade should possess sufficient stability under adverse climatic and loading conditions. Therefore, it is very essential to evaluate the subgrade by conducting tests. The tests used to evaluate the strength properties of soils may be broadly divided into three groups :

- Shear tests.
- Bearing tests.
- Penetration tests.
- **Shear Tests** are usually carried out on relatively small soil samples in the laboratory. In order to find out the strength properties of soil, a number of representative samples from different locations are tested. Some of the commonly known shear tests are direct shear test, triaxial compression test, and unconfined compression test.
- **Bearing Tests** are loading tests carried out on sub grade soils in-situ with a load bearing area. The results of the bearing tests are influenced by variations in the soil properties within the stressed soil mass underneath and hence the overall stability of the part of the soil mass stressed could be studied.
- **Penetration Tests** may be considered as small scale bearing tests in which the size of the loaded area is relatively much smaller and ratio of the penetration to the size of the loaded area is much greater than the ratios in bearing tests. The penetration tests are carried out in the field or in the laboratory.

5.1.3.1 Plate Bearing Test

This test is useful in determining the modulus of subgrade reaction, whose value is used in the design of rigid pavements. Fig. 5.2 shows the arrangement for plate test.

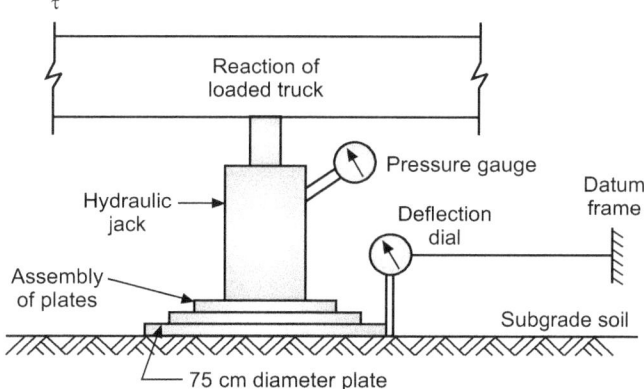

Fig. 5.2 : Plate bearing test

The plate used : Is generally 75 cm diameter of 25 mm thickness. Plate is located on the subgrade with sandwiched layer of sand in between for even distribution of load. In general, the load is applied through hydraulic jack. The deflection of the bearing plate is measured by dial gauges. Test naturally should be conducted on the subgrade when it is under worst moisture conditions, such as conditions of flooding. This may not always be possible. In such a case, artificial flooding should be resorted to, the initial seating load for the plate is 0.7 N/cm². For a 75 cm diameter plate, this load would work out to 310 kg. This seating load

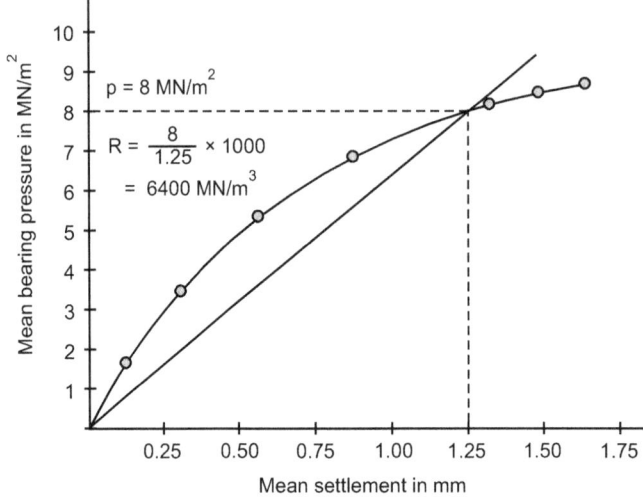

Fig. 5.3 : Load settlement curve for plate bearing test

should be applied, but then immediately released. The next increment of load should be such as to cause settlement of 0.25 mm approximately. When the load is acting on the plate, the rate of settlement decreases with time. Additional increment of load can be imposed when the rate of settlement is less than 0.025 mm/minute. This procedure should be repeated till a settlement of 1.75 mm results. A typical load settlement curve is shown in Fig. 5.3. If there is linear variation between stress and strain of the subgrade, the load settlement curve is straight line passing through the origin. Generally, this is not the case, and the load settlement line will be a curve. In such cases, the value of K, the modulus of subgrade reaction could be considered as the slope of the line passing through the origin and the point on the curve corresponding to settlement of 1.25 mm. For example, in the figure,

$$K = \frac{8}{1.25} \times 100 = 6400 \text{ MN/m}^3.$$

When the plate load test is conducted in the worst conditions of the ground, there is no correction required in the K value. But when the test is conducted at a moisture content other than the saturated condition, a correction is required to the K value. To assess this correction, a soil sample is compacted at density and moisture content corresponding to the density and moisture content available when plate load test is conducted and its CBR value is determined, let this CBR be CBR_1. Now the sample at this density and moisture content is prepared and then saturated and its CBR is determined. Let this CBR be CBR_2. Then the ratio $\frac{CBR_2}{CBR_1}$ is a multiplier with which obtained K value must be multiplied to get the K value when ground would be saturated.

If a small diameter plate (30 cm diameter) is used, the K value could be converted to the standard 75 cm diameter plate value by the experimentally obtained correction. $K_{75} = 0.5\ K_{30}$, where K_{75} represents K value with 75 cm diameter plate and K_{30} represents K value with 30 cm diameter plate. This formula of course overestimates the foundation strength and should be used with care.

5.1.3.2 California Bearing Ratio Test

California bearing ratio test abbreviated as CBR test is a very popular test with highway engineers. It was first devised by O. J. Procter of California Division of Highways and is now a basis for the design of flexible pavements. The test can be conducted on remoulded specimen in the laboratory, or undisturbed specimen brought in the laboratory or in-situ on the subgrade soil itself. The diagrammatic sketch of the test is shown in Fig. 5.4. The mould has internal dimensions of 150 mm diameter and 175 mm height and generally is of phospher - bronze. The mould also has a detachable perforated base. This perforated base can be fitted either at the top or bottom. When filling the mould with soil, a disc 50 mm deep and 152 mm diameter is kept at the bottom and then the compaction is commenced. This procedure gives a soil specimen exactly of 127 mm height. CBR is essentially a penetration test and the penetration is caused by a plunger 50 mm diameter, penetrating at the centre of specimen at constant rate of strain of 1.25 mm/minute. When the machine to cause constant rate of strain is not available, ordinary hydraulic testing machine can be used, with rate of penetration controlled by the stop watch.

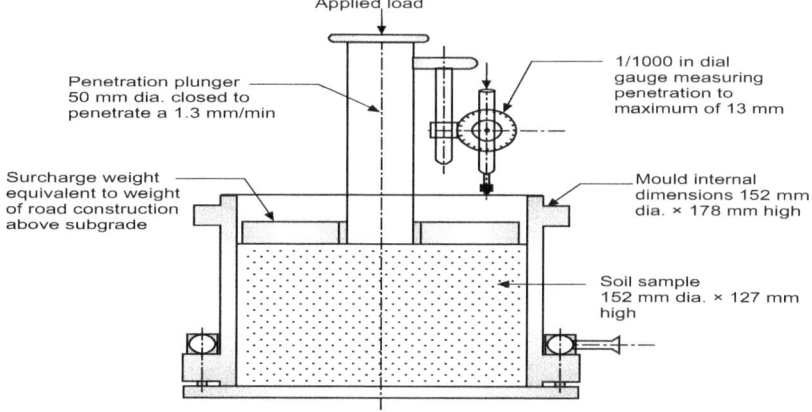

Fig. 5.4 : CBR test apparatus

For the in-situ test, loaded truck is used to provide the reaction and loading is through a screw jack. In actual field conditions, the subgrade is loaded by the weight of the pavement. To similiate these field conditions; surcharge weights are placed on the surface of the specimen. As a rough guide, 10 kg weight can be considered equal to 25 cm thick pavement. When conducting tests in the laboratory, the choice of the density and moisture content is very crucial. Naturally, the first choice is that the minimum state of compaction that might occur in the field. The design should be based on this CBR. Current standards in India suggest that subgrade should be compacted to at least 100 percent Proctor and hence this density could be used for test.

The recommended practice for new roads is to prepare the samples at optimum moisture content corresponding to Proctor compaction and get them soaked for four days and test them in this saturated condition. For existing roads, on which some modification is planned, the moisture content at which the testing should be done should be assessed just after the rains, in the field. In this particular case, the density of the specimen should be the field density, and not the maximum dry density. The water content and the field density should be determined at a distance of 0.6 to 1 meter from the pavement edge and directly below the pavement.

The procedure of soaking is dispensed within India, for :

(1) Roads in arid zones where the rainfall is less than 50 cms annually.

(2) Roads having a comparatively thick bituminous surfacing of impermeable nature and

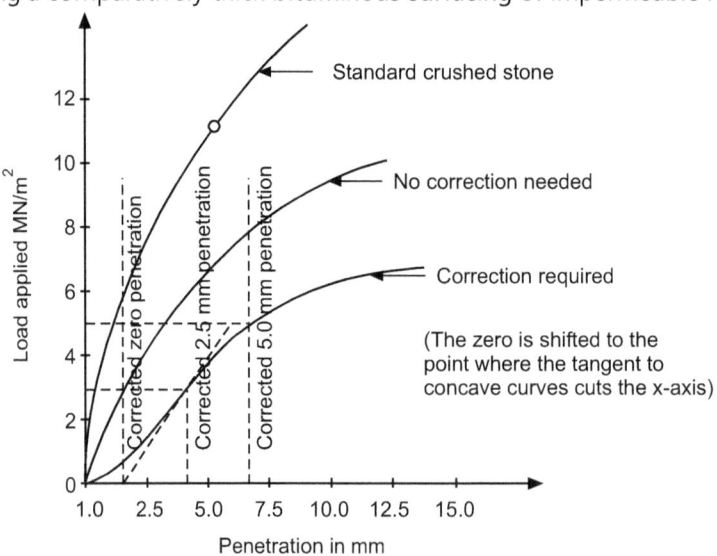

Fig. 5.5 : Load penetration curve

where the water table is too deep. To have an idea regarding the depth of water table, some sampling may be undertaken. Generally, if the water table is greater than one meter in sands, three meter in sandy clays, and six meter in heavy clays, the procedure of soaking may be dropped.

There is a school of thought that the CBR test should be conducted on samples, compacted at equilibrium moisture content. This school of thought has not received much backing in India.

After conducting the CBR test, the load penetration curve is drawn. A typical curve is shown in Fig. 5.5. Load penetration curve curving concave upwards, require correction. This correction is also shown in Fig. 5.5. The loads for penetration or 2.5 mm of 5 mm are noted. It has been seen that load of 6.895 MN/m² and 10.343 MN/m² cause the above penetrations in the case of standard crushed stones. The CBR value is expressed as a percentage of the actual load causing the penetrations of 2.5 mm or 5 mm to the standard loads just mentioned respectively. Thus,

$$CBR = \frac{\text{Load carried by specimen}}{\text{Load carried by standard crushed stone specimen}} \times 100$$

Two values of CBR can thus be obtained. The value at 2.5 mm is greater than that at 5 mm penetration, the former is adopted. If not, the test has to be repeated and if the new value of CBR at 5 mm penetration is still greater, this value of CBR will have to be used for design purposes. Some typical values of CBR of Indian soils are given in the table below.

Table 5.1

Type of Soil	Murum	Well Graded Sand	Sandy Clay	Silty Lay	Alluvial Silt	Black Cotton and Heavy Clays
CBR values	8 to 20	8 to 20	4 to 6	3 to 5	2 to 5	1 to 2

5.2 AGGREGATES

Introduction : Almost all the aggregates available in India and used for road construction are natural aggregates. The origin of all such aggregates could be igneous rocks, which are derived from the cooling of molten magma, or sedimentary rocks, which are formed due to action of water or ice, and metamorphic rocks which are end result of igneous or sedimentary rocks subjected to heat and pressure at deep depths of earth crust. Whereas the granite and basalt are both suitable for bituminous courses and cement concrete pavement, sedimentary rock such as quartzite which is reasonably hard and durable rock is good for bituminous courses and cement concrete pavement. It can also be used profitably for base courses. Limestone is good for base course but is not recommended for wearing course. Sandstone is good for road base. Laterites and Kankar are good for sub-base and base courses and their use as surface course is possible only in unimportant roads. In addition to the above terms designating the origin of the aggregate, some typical terms used in describing the aggregate are :

(1) Fine Aggregate : Aggregates mainly between 4.75 mm (5 mm) to 75 micron in size.

(2) Coarse Aggregate : Aggregate particles mainly larger than 5 mm in size.

(3) Crushed Rock : Aggregate obtained from the crushing of bedrock. All particles are angular.

(4) Screenings : The chips and dust or powder that are produced in the crushing of bedrock for aggregates.

5.2.1 Desirable Properties of Aggregates

Aggregate forms the major part of the pavement structure and it is the prime material used in pavement construction. Aggregates have to primarily bear load, stresses occurring on the roads and runways and have to resist wear due to abrasive action of traffic. Aggregate often serve as granular base-course underlying the superior pavements. Thus, properties of aggregates are of considerable significance.

Aggregates which are used in the surface course have to withstand the high magnitude of stresses, wear and tear due to abrasion. Such aggregates should have sufficiently high strength or resistance to crushing. These aggregates further need to be hard enough to resist the wear due to abrasive action of traffic. The specific gravity of stone is considered to be a measure for finding the suitability and strength characteristics of aggregates. Higher the specific gravity, better is the road aggregates. The presence of air voids or pores in stones is another property, which may indicate the suitability and strength characteristics of stones. More the voids, the strength is likely to be less, of course the specific gravity of such stones will also be lower.

The size of the aggregate is qualified by the size of square sieve opening through which the same may pass, and not the shape. Aggregates which happen to fall in a particular size range may have lesser strength and durability when compared with cubical, angular or rounded particles of the same stone. Hence too flaky and elongated aggregates should be avoided as far as possible. Rounded aggregates may be preferred in cement concrete mix due to better workability for the same proportion of cement paste and same water-cement ratio, whereas rounded particles are not preferred in granular base course and W.B.M. construction as the stability due to interlocking is lesser in these aggregates. In such construction, angular particles are preferred.

Heavy moving loads on the surface of flexible pavements may cause considerable deformation of the pavement layer resulting in possible relative movement and mutual rubbing of aggregate particles. This can cause wear on the points of contacts of the aggregates especially in the granular base course of flexible pavements. This action may not be of appreciable significance in bituminous concrete pavements. This Example is unlikely to exist in cement concrete roads as the pavement is rigid and no relative movement between the aggregate is possible before the pavement fails. The mutual rubbing action of the aggregates is termed as attrition and the resistance to wear due to attrition is considered as a desirable property for aggregates to be used in for W.B.M. construction, granular base, and surface course of flexible pavement.

Desirable properties of aggregates thus depend on type of pavement construction, traffic and climatic conditions. Above mentioned all properties need not necessarily be possessed by aggregates in a group for a particular construction. It is necessary, therefore, to carry out various tests on aggregates in order to ensure that not only are undesirable materials excluded from the pavements of highways, but also the best available aggregates are included.

5.3 TESTS ON AGGREGATES

The common tests on road aggregates in India are :
- Gradation and shape tests, consisting of, sieve analysis, flakiness index test and angularity number test.
- Specific gravity, porosity and water absorption.
- Estimation of deleterious materials such as clay lumps and soft particles.
- The strength test such as aggregate crushing.
- Hardness test such as Los-angeles abrasion.
- Aggregate impact.
- Aggregate polishing and stripping test. These are now discussed.

5.4 GRADATION TESTS

Introduction : This is the most common test performed on aggregates. Most specifications for concrete and asphalt mixes require a grain size distribution that will provide a dense, strong layer of aggregates.

A convenient system of expressing the gradation of aggregate is the one in which the consecutive sieve openings are doubled, such as 10 mm, 20 mm, 40 mm, etc. Under such a system, employing a logarithmic scale, lines can be spaced at equal intervals to represent the successive sizes. The aggregates used for making concrete are normally of the maximum size 80 mm, 40 mm, 20 mm, 10 mm, 4.75 mm, 2.36 mm, 600 micron, 300 micron and 150 micron. The aggregate fraction from 80 mm to 4.75 mm are termed as coarse aggregates and those from 4.75 mm to 150 micron are termed as fine aggregates.

From the sieve analysis, the particle size distribution in a sample of aggregate is found out. In this connection, a term known as "Fineness Modulus" is being used. Fineness modulus is a index of coarseness or fineness of the material. Fineness modulus is a factor obtained by adding the cumulative percentage of aggregate retained on each of the standard sieve ranging from 80 mm to 150 micron and dividing this sum by an arbitrary number 100. The larger the figure, the coarser is the material.

Experimental Procedure

(1) Apparatus

Table 5.2

Sr. No.	Type of Sieve	Sieve Designation
(1)	Square hole, perforated plates	80 mm, 63 mm, 50 mm, 40 mm, 31.5 mm, 25 mm, 20 mm,
(2)	Fine mesh, wire cloth	16 rag 12.5 mm, 10 mm, 6.3 mm, 4.75 mm, 3.35 mm, 2.36 mm, 1.18 mm, 600 micron, 300 micron, 150 micron, 75 micron

(2) Balance : The balance or scale shall be such that it is readable and accurate to 0.1 percent of the weight of the test sample.

Test Procedure : The sample shall be brought to an air-dry condition before weighing and sieving. This may be achieved either by drying at room temperature or by heating at a temperature of 100°C to 110°C. The air-dry sample shall be weighed and sieved successively on the appropriate sieves starting with the largest. Each sieve shall be shaken separately for not less than two minutes. Shaking shall be done with a varied motion, so that the material is kept moving over the sieve surface in frequently changing directions. Material shall not be forced through the sieve by hand pressure, but on sieves coarser than 20 mm, placing of particles is permitted.

On completion of sieving, the material retained on each sieve, together with any material cleaned from the mesh, shall be weighed. The results shall be calculated and reported as :

(a) The cumulative percentage by weight of the total sample passing each of the sieves, to the nearest whole number or

(b) The percentage by weight of the total sample passing one sieve, and retained on the next smaller sieve, to the nearest 0.1%.

5.5 SHAPE TESTS

Theory and Significance of Shape Tests : There are three mechanical measures of particle shape which may be included in the specification for road construction. These are the flakiness index, elongation index and angularity number. The flakiness index of an aggregate is the percentage by weight of particles whose least dimension (thickness) is less than three-fifth of their mean dimension; the mean dimension as used in each instance is the average of the two adjacent sieve aperture sizes between which the particles being measured is retained by sieving.

Elongation index of an aggregate is the percentage by weight of particles whose greatest length is greater than $1\frac{4}{5}$ ths times their mean dimension. The angularity number of an aggregate is the amount, to the nearest whole number, by which the percentage of voids exceeds 33 percent when aggregate is compacted in a specified manner in a standardized metal cylinder. Flat particles, thin particles, or long, needle shaped particles break more easily than cubical particles. Particles with rough, fractured faces allow a better bond with cements than the rounded, smooth gravel particles.

The standards for single-sized aggregates require that their flakiness indices should not be greater than 40 for 40 mm or larger size and 35 for aggregates which are 25 mm and smaller in sizes. Since other factors being equal, an aggregate composed of smooth rounded particles of a certain gradation will contain less voids than another aggregate of the same grading, but composed of angular particles, the angularity of an aggregate can be reflected in terms of the volume of contained voids when the aggregate is compacted. The angularity number may range from zero for a material composed of highly rounded beach-gravel particles to 10 or more for newly-crushed rock aggregates.

Apparatus : The apparatus shall consist of the following :

(a) Balance : The balance shall be of sufficient capacity and sensitivity and shall have an accuracy of 0.1% of the weight of the test sample.

(b) Metal Gauge or Thickness Gauge : The metal gauge shall be of pattern as shown in Fig. 5.6.

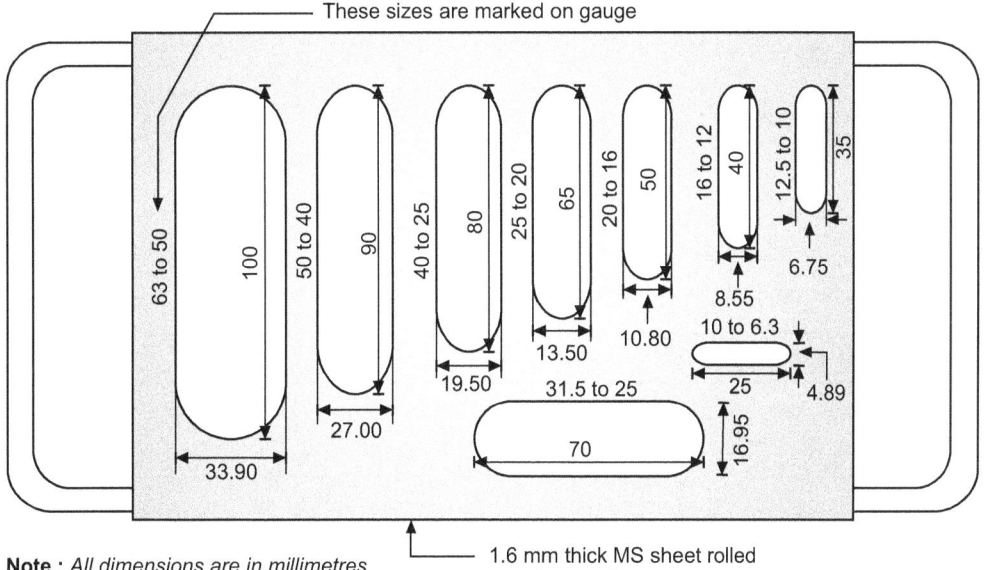

Note : *All dimensions are in millimetres*

Fig. 5.6 : Thickness gauge

(c) **Sieves :** Set of I.S. sieves.

Test Procedure : A sample of the aggregate to be tested is sieved through a set of sieves and separated into specified range as per the following table.

Table 5.3

Size of Aggregate		Thickness Gauge
Passing Through I.S. Sieve	Retained on I.S. Sieve	
63 mm	50 mm	33.90 mm
50 mm	40 mm	27.00 mm
40 mm	25 mm	19.50 mm
31.5 mm	25 mm	16.95 mm
25 mm	20 mm	13.50 mm
20 mm	16 mm	10.80 mm
16 mm	12.5 mm	8.55 mm
12.5 mm	10 mm	6.75 mm
10 mm	6.3 mm	4.89 mm

A quantity of aggregate shall be taken sufficient to provide a minimum two hundred number of pieces of any fraction to be tested.

Each fraction shall be gauged, in turn, for thickness on metal gauge as shown in Fig. 5.6. The width of slot used in the gauge shall be of dimension specified in the table for the appropriate size of material. Total amount passing the gauge shall be weighed to an accuracy of at least 0.1 percent of the weight of test sample.

Reporting of Result

$$\text{Flakiness index} = \frac{W_1}{W} \times 100$$

where, W_1 = Weight of flaky material from the whole sample.

W = Total weight of sample.

(Flakiness index is the percentage by weight of particles in it whose least dimension (thickness) is less than 3/5 ths of their mean dimension.)

5.6 ELONGATION INDEX

Definition : The elongation index of an aggregate is the percentage by weight of particles whose greatest dimension (length) is greater than one and four-fifth times their mean dimension.

Apparatus for Test : The apparatus shall consist of the following :

(a) **Balance**

(b) **Metal Gauge :** The metal gauge shall be of the pattern shown in Fig. 5.7.

(c) Sieves : A set of I.S. sieves.

The sample of aggregate to be tested shall be sieved through a set of sieves and separated into specified range as per the following table :

Table 5.4

Size of Aggregate		Length
Passing through I.S. Sieve (mm)	Retained on I.S. Sieve (mm)	Gauge
63	50	–
50	40	81
40	25	58.5
31.5	25	–
25	20	40.5
20	16	32.4
16	12.5	25.6
12.5	10	20.2
10	6.3	14.7

The sample shall be sieved first with the use of I.S. sieves. Each fraction shall be gauged individually for the length on the metal gauge of pattern shown in Fig. 5.7. The total amount retained by the length gauge shall be weighed to an accuracy of at least 0.1% of the weight of the test sample. The elongation index is the total weight of material retained on the various length gauges, expressed as the percentage of the total weight of the sample gauged.

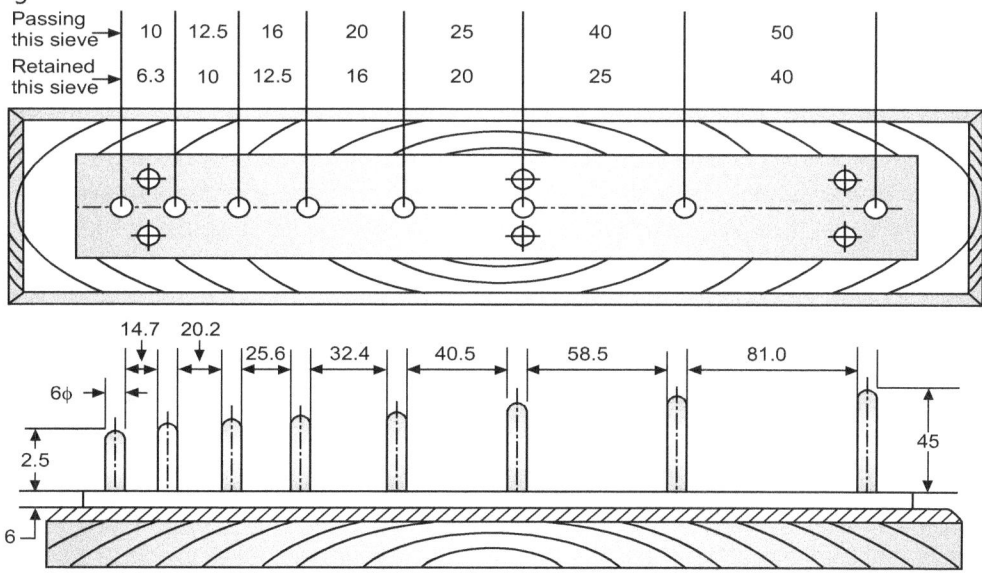

Fig. 5.7 : Length gauge

5.7 ANGULARITY NUMBER

The apparatus consists of :

(a) A metal cylinder closed at one end and of about 3 litre capacity, the diameter and height of it being approximately equal.

(b) Metal tamping rod of circular cross section 16 mm in diameter and 60 cm in length, rounded at one end.

(c) A metal scoop of about one litre heaped capacity of size 20 × 12 × 5 cm.

(d) A balance of capacity 10 kg to weigh upto 1 gm.

The cylinder is calibrated by determining the weight of water at 27°C required to fill it. The amount of aggregate available should be sufficient to provide, after separation on the appropriate pair of sieves, at least 10 kg of the predominant size as determined by the sieve analysis on the 26, 16, 12.5, 10, 6.3 and 4.75 mm I.S. sieves. The test sample should consist of aggregate retained between the appropriate pair of I.S. sieves having square holes from the following sets :

20 and 16 mm, 16 and 12.5 mm, 12.5 and l0 mm, 10.0 and 6.3 mm, 6.3 and 4.75 mm. In testing aggregates larger than 20 mm, the volume of the cylinder shall be greater than three litre capacity. The sample of aggregate is dried in an oven at a temperature 100° to 110°C for 24 hours, and cooled in an air-tight container prior to testing. The scoop is filled and heaped to overflowing with the aggregate, which is placed in the cylinder by allowing it slide gently off the scoop from the lowest possible height. The aggregate in the cylinder is subjected to 100 blows of the tamping rod at the rate of about 2 blows per second. Each blow is applied by holding the rod vertical with its rounded end 5 cm above the surface of aggregate and releasing it. So that it falls vertically and no force is applied to the rod. The 100 blows should be distributed evenly over the surface of the aggregate.

The process of filling and tamping is repeated exactly as described above with a second and third layer of aggregates. The third layer should contain only the aggregate required to just fill up the cylinder level before tamping. After the third layer is tamped, the cylinder is filled to overflowing, and the extra aggregate is struck off the level with the top using tamping rod as a straight edge. Individual pieces of aggregate are then added and rolled into the surface by rolling the tamping rod across the upper edge of the cylinder, and this finishing process is continued as long as the aggregates do not lift the rod off the edge of the cylinder on either side, during rolling. The aggregate should not be pushed in or forced down and no downward pressure should be applied to the tamping rod, which is only rolled in contact with the top of the cylinder, on both sides.

The aggregate in the cylinder is then weighed to the nearest 5 grams. Three separate determinations are made and the mean weight of the aggregate in the cylinder is calculated. If the results of any one of the determination differ from the mean by more than 25 gm, three additional determinations are immediately made on the same material and the mean of all the size determination calculated.

Reporting of Results : The angularity number is calculated from the following formula :

$$\text{Angularity number} = 67 - \frac{100 \times W}{C \times G_A}$$

where,
- W = Mean weight of aggregate in gram in the cylinder,
- C = Weight of water in gram required to fill the cylinder,

and
- G_A = Specific gravity of aggregate.

5.8 SPECIFIC GRAVITY AND WATER ABSORPTION TEST

Introduction : The specific gravity of an aggregate is considered to be a measure of strength or quality of material. Stones having low specific gravity are generally weaker than those with higher specific gravity values. The specific gravity test helps in the identification of stone. Water absorption gives an idea of strength of rock. Stones having more water absorption are generally considered unsuitable unless they are found to be acceptable based on strength and hardness test.

Specific gravity and water absorption of aggregates are important properties, especially in mix design for concrete and asphalt mixtures. With the aggregate for road works construction being proportioned by weight, as the usual practice, the specific gravity is of vital importance in determining the proper proportions of the resulting mixture.

Gradation specifications are valid only if the coarse and fine fractions have approximately the same specific gravities. If the value for the fine fraction is much greater than that for the coarse, the result is a mixture which, because of lack of fines, may be too harsh. On the other hand, if specific gravity of the coarse fraction is greater, a mixture which is too rich in fines may be obtained. When these conditions are encountered in practice, arbitrary gradation should not be used, but instead various gradation mixtures should be analysed carefully and evaluated on their own merits.

In reality, there are two specific gravities, depending on how measurement is made. As illustrated in Fig. 5.8 these are the bulk and apparent specific gravities. The bulk specific gravity is the ratio of the weight in air of a volume of aggregate (this includes voids which are permeable and impermeable) to the weight in air of an equal volume of distilled water. The apparent specific gravity is the ratio of the weight, in air of a volume of aggregate (including impermeable, but not permeable voids) to the weight in air of an equal volume of distilled water.

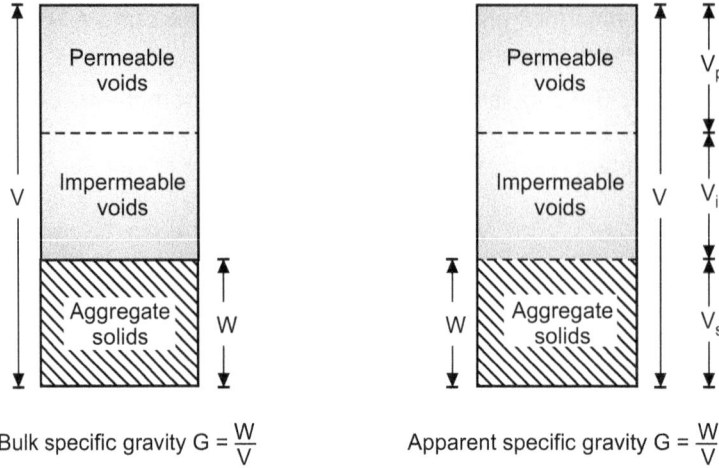

Fig. 5.8

Water absorption test is normally carried out in conjunction with the specific gravity test. Knowledge of the absorption properties of an aggregate is practically important in bituminous surfacing design, since the porosity of the aggregate affects the amount of binder required and additional binder material may have to be incorporated in the mixture to satisfy the absorption by the aggregate after the ingradients have been mixed. On the beneficial side, porous aggregates usually show better adhesion to the binder due to the mechanical interlock caused by the binder penetrating the particles.

The water absorption values allowed for road aggregates normally range from less than 0.1 percent to 2 percent for materials used in road surfacing, while values of upto 4 percent may be accepted in roadbases.

Apparatus for Test : The apparatus consists of following :

(a) A balance of capacity about 3 kg, to weigh accurate to 0.5 gm.
(b) A thermostatically controlled oven to maintain a temperature of 100°C to 110°C.
(c) A wire basket of not more than 6.3 mm mesh or a perforated container of convenient size with thin wire hangers for suspending it from the balance.
(d) A container for filling water and suspending the basket.
(e) An air-tight container of capacity similar to that of the basket.
(f) A shallow tray and two dry absorbent clothes, each not less than 75 × 45 cms.

Test Procedure : The weight of sample should not be less than 2000 gms. The sample shall be thoroughly washed first to remove finer particles and dust, drained and then placed in the wire basket and immersed in distilled water at a temperature between 22 to 32°C, with a cover of at least 5 cms of water above the top of basket. The entrapped air shall be removed from the basket by lifting it and then dropping. The basket and aggregate shall remain completely immersed during operation for the period of 24 ± 1/2 hours. Then take weight of basket plus aggregate in water, let it be A_1. Then remove the basket and the aggregate from water and allow them to drain for a few minutes, after which the aggregates shall be gently emptied from the basket on to one of the dry clothes and empty basket shall be returned to water and take its weight in water (A_2).

The aggregate placed on the dry cloth shall be gently, dried with the cloth, transferring it to second dry cloth when first will remove no further moisture. Then it is allowed to dry in absence of direct sunlight or heat, for not less than ten minutes. Take weight of dried aggregates (B). Then aggregates shall be placed in the oven in shallow tray, at a temperature of 100° to 110° C and maintained at this temperature for a period of 24 ± 1/2 hours. Remove it from oven and take its weight (weight C). This sample is oven dried and then crushed to smaller size (10 mm – 4.75 mm) and specific gravity test is carried out by use of pycnometer.

Procedure : A sample of about 1 kg for 10 mm to 4.75 mm or 500 gms of finer than 4.75 mm shall be placed in the bag and covered with distilled water at temperature of 22 to 32° C. Soon after immersion, air entrapped in or bubbles on the surface of the aggregates shall be removed by gentle agitation with the rod. The sample shall be immersed for 24 ± 1/2 hours. The water shall be carefully drained from the sample by decantation through filter papers, any material retained being returned to the sample. Then saturated and surface dried sample be weighed (weight A).

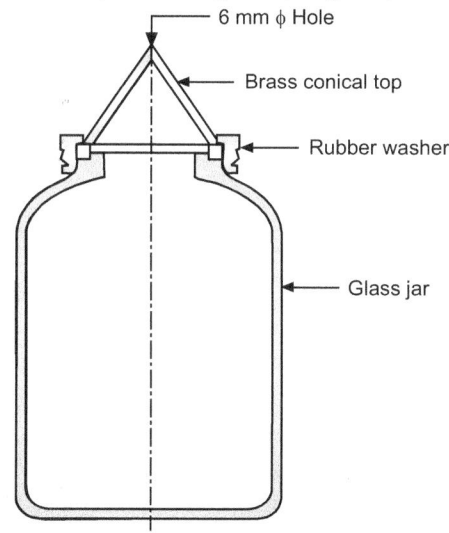

Fig. 5.9 : Pycnometer

Then aggregates shall be placed in the pycnometer which shall be filled with distilled water. Any trapped air shall be eliminated by rotating the pycnometer on its side, the hole in the apex of the cone being covered with finger. The pycnometer shall be trapped-up with distilled water to remove any froath from the surface. The pycnometer shall be dried on the outside and weighed (weight B).

Water shall be carefully drained from the sample by decantation through filter paper, and any material retained shall be returned to the sample. The sample shall be then ovendried to a temperature of 100° to 110°C for 24 ± 1/2 hrs., and then weighed (weight D).

Water shall be carefully drained from the sample by decantation through filter paper, and any material retained shall be returned to the sample. The sample shall be then ovendried to a temperature of 100° to 110°C for 24 ± 1/2 hrs., and then weighed (weight D).

Reporting of Results : Specific gravity, apparent specific gravity and water absorption shall be calculated as follows :

(1) For part I,

$$\text{Specific gravity} = \frac{C}{B - A}$$

$$\text{Apparent Specific gravity} = \frac{C}{C - A}$$

$$\text{Water absorption} = \frac{B - C}{C} \times 100$$

where, A = The weight in gm of saturated aggregate in water,
B = The weight in gm of the saturated surface - dry aggregate in air, and
C = The weight in gm of ovendried aggregate in air.

Use of Pycnometer

$$\text{Specific gravity} = \frac{D}{A - (B - C)}$$

$$\text{Apparent specific gravity} = \frac{D}{D - (B - C)}$$

$$\text{Water absorption} = \frac{(A - D)}{D} \times 100$$

where, A = Weight in gm of saturated surface dry sample
B = Weight in gm of pycnometer and sample and filled with distilled water
C = Weight in gm of pycnometer filled with distilled water only
D = Weight in gm of ovendried sample.

5.9 ESTIMATION OF DELETERIOUS MATERIALS

Deleterious substances are harmful or injurious materials. They include various types of weak or low-quality particles, and coatings that are found on the surface of the aggregate particles. Deleterious materials include organic coatings, dust, clay (lumps, shale, friable particles, easy to crumble), badly weathered particles, soft particles and particles which are dangerous to use because of their chemical composition. These substances may effect the bond between cement and aggregates or may break up during mixing or use. To find the deleterious materials, following tests are normally conducted :

(1) Dermination of clay lumps in the aggregate sample, and
(2) Determination of soft particles.

Determination of Clay Lumps

Object of Test : To determine clay lumps, present in the aggregate sample.

Apparatus for Test : The apparatus shall consist of the following :

(a) **Balance :** A balance or scale, sensitive to 0.1% of weight of the sample.

(b) **Containers.**

(c) **Sieves :** Sieves confirming to I.S. 460 -1962.

Test Procedure

Sample : Sample selected from material to be tested shall be first dried at a temperature not exceeding 110°C. Samples of fine aggregate shall consist of particles coarser than 1.18 mm I.S. sieves and shall weigh not less than 100 gms. Samples of coarse aggregate shall be separated into different sizes using 4.75 mm, 10 mm, 20 mm and 40 mm I.S. sieve. Total weight of different sizes shall not be less than the following table :

Table 5.5

Size of Particles Making-up the Sample	Weight of Sample (Minimum), gms
Over 4.75 mm to 10 mm	1000
Over 10 mm to 20 mm	2000
Over 20 mm to 40 mm	3000
Over 40 mm	5000

If the sample contains both fine and coarse aggregates, the material shall be separated into two sizes on 4.75 mm I.S. sieve, and sample of fine and coarse aggregate shall be prepared as per above table. Now, the sample shall be spread in a thin layer on the bottom of the container and examined for clay lumps. Any particles which can be broken into finely divided particles with fingers, shall be classified as clay lumps. After all discernible clay lumps have been broken, the residue from the clay lumps shall be removed by the use of sieves indicated below :

Table 5.6

Size of Particles Making-up the Sample	Size of Sieve for Sieving Residue of Clay
Fine aggregate (retained on 1.18 mm I.S. sieve)	850 micron
Over 4.75 mm to 10 mm	2.36 mm
Over 10 mm to 20 mm	4.75 mm
Over 20 mm to 40 mm	4.75 mm
Over 40 mm	4.75 mm

Reporting of Results : Particles of clay lumps shall be calculated to the nearest 0.1 percent in accordance with the following formula :

$$L = \frac{W - R}{W} \times 100$$

where
- W = Weight of sample.
- R = Weight of sample after removal of clay lumps.
- L = Percentage age of clay lumps.

5.10 Determination Of Soft Particles

The apparatus consists of a brass rod, having a rockwell hardness of 65 to 75 RHB. A brass rod of about 1.6 mm diameter and of poor hardness inserted into the wood of an ordinary lead pencil is a convenient tool for field or laboratory use.

Sample : Aggregate for the test shall consist of materials from which the sizes finer than the 10 mm I.S. sieve have been removed. The sample shall contain at least 10% or more of following sizes :

- 10 to 12.5 mm,   12.5 to 20 mm
- 20 to 40 mm   and   40 to 50 mm

Each particle of aggregate under test shall be scratched with the brass rod using only a small amount of pressure (about 1 kg). Particles are considered to be soft if during the scratching process, a groove is made in them without deposition of metal from the brass rod or if separate particles are detached from the rock mass.

The report shall include the following information :

(a) Weight and number of particle of each size of each sample tested with the brass rod.

(b) Weight and number of each size of each sample classified as soft in the test.

(c) Percentage of test sample classified as soft by weight and by number of particles.

(d) Weighed average percentage of soft particles calculated from percentage in item (c) and based on the grading of sample of aggregate received for examination or, preferably on the average grading of material from that portion of the supply of which the sample is representative. In these calculations, sizes finer than the 10 mm I.S. sieve shall not be included.

5.11 AGGREGATE CRUSHING VALUE

Theory : Scope and Significance : Aggregate used in road construction, should be strong enough to resist crushing under traffic wheel loads. If the aggregates are weak, the stability of the pavements structure is likely to be adversely affected. Thus, the aggregate must have a durable resistance to crushing. The strength of aggregate is assessed by aggregate crushing test. The aggregate crushing value provides a relative measure of resistance to crushing under a gradually applied compressive load. To achieve a high quality of pavements, aggregate possessing high aggregate crushing value should be preferred.

The aggregate crushing value should not be more than 45 percent for aggregate used for concrete other than wearing surfaces, and 30 percent for concrete used for wearing surfaces such as runways, roads and field pavements.

Apparatus for Test : See Fig. 5.10. The apparatus for the standard test consists of the following :

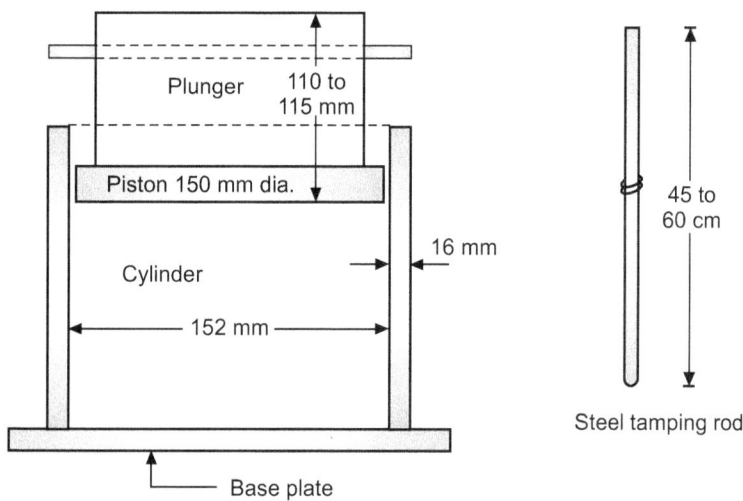

Fig. 5.10 : Crushing test apparatus

(1) Steel cylinder, with open ends and internal diameter 152 mm, square base plate, plunger having a piston diameter of 150 mm with a hole provided across the stem of the plunger so that rod could be inserted for lifting or placing the plunger in the cylinder.

(2) Cylindrical measure having internal diameter of 115 mm and height 180 mm.

(3) Steel tamping rod with one rounded end, having a diameter of 1.6 cm and length 45 to 60 cms.

(4) Balance of capacity 3 kg and accuracy upto 1 gm.

(5) Compression testing machine capable of applying load of 40 tonnes, at a uniform rate of loading of 4 tonnes per minute.

Test Procedure : The aggregate passing 12.5 mm I.S. sieve and retained on 10 mm I.S. sieve is selected for standard test. The aggregate should be in surface dry condition before testing. The aggregate may be dried by heating at a temperature 100° to 110°C for a period of 4 hours and tested after being cooled to room temperature. The cylindrical measure is filled by the test sample of aggregate in three layers of aproximately equal depth, each layer being tamped 25 times by the rounded end of tamping rod. After the third layer is tampad, the aggregate at the top of the cylindrical measure is leveled-off by using the tamping rod as a straight edge. About 6.5 kg of aggregate is required for preparing two test samples.

The test sample thus taken is then weighed. The same weight of the sample is taken in the repeat test. The cylinder of the test apparatus is placed in position on the base plate, one third of test sample is placed in this cylinder and tamped 25 times by the tamping rod. Similarly, two parts of the test specimen are added, each layer being subjected to 25 blows. The depth of material in the cylinder after tamping shall be 10 cm.

The surface of the aggregate is levelled and the plunger is inserted so that it rests on this surface in a level position. The cylinder with test sample and plunger in position is placed on compression testing machine. Load is then applied through the plunger at a uniform rate of 4 tonnes per minute until the total load is 40 tonnes. Aggregates including the crushed portion are removed from the cylinder and sieved on a 2.36 mm I.S. sieve. The material which possess this sieve is collected. The above crushing test is repeated on second sample of the same weight in accordance with above test procedure. Thus, two tests are made for the same specimen for taking average value.

Reporting of Results : Total weight of dry sample taken = W_1 gms – weight of the portion of crushed material, passing 2.36 I.S. sieve = W_2 gms.

$$\therefore \text{Aggregate crushing value} = \frac{W_2}{W_1} \times 100$$

The value is usually recorded correct to first decimal place.

5.12 AGGREGATE ABRASION VALUE

Significance of Test : Apart from testing aggregates with respect to its crushing value, impact resistance, testing the aggregate with respect to its resistance to wear is an important test for aggregate to be used for road construction, ware house floors and pavement construction.

Aggregates must be sufficiently hard to resist the abrasive effects of traffic over a long period of time. The abrasive tests, which are generally carried out, are basically accelerated tests. Whether the aggregate abrasion value test is a simulation of abrasion under actual traffic condition is, of course, very debatable. Numerous testings have shown, that the aggregates with abrasion values greater than 15 are too soft for use in the wearing course of a bituminuous surfacing. The accelerated polishing test might be considered more representative of tyre surfacing interaction on the road way. In any case, an extensive investigations carried out by the 'Road Research Laboratory' has shown that the state of polish of the aggregate at the end of the 6-hour test approximates the state of polish reached after several months on a heavily-trafficked road or several years on a road carrying light traffic. Results reported indicate that an aggregate with a polished-stone coefficient of greater than 0.8 is likely to remain rough under any traffic conditions, while one with a value of 0.3 or lower will become so highly polished as to give rise to a dangerously slippery road surface when either wet or dry.

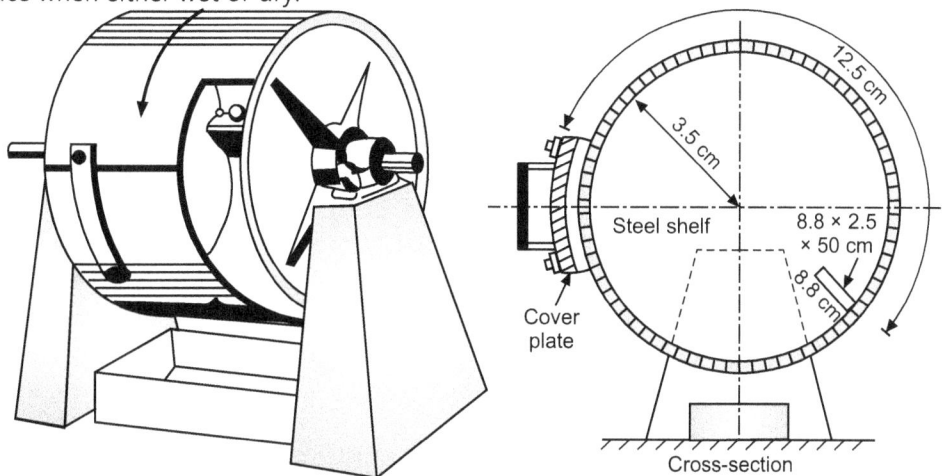

Fig. 5.11 : Los angeles abrasion testing machine

The Los Angeles abrasion test is actually an abrasion-cum-impact test due to the action of the steel balls in the drum as it is rotated. Normally, 'soft' limestones have Los Angeles values of over 50 percent, while very hard aggregates have values less than 20. Recommendations regarding the maximum percent wear given by the test vary, depending on the purpose for which the aggregate is to be used, the gradation, the testing procedures and the specifying authority. The abrasion value should not be more than 30 percent for wearing surfaces and not more than 50 percent for concrete other than wearing surface.

To determine abrasion value of aggregates by use of Los Angeles Abrasion testing machine, we require :

1. Los Angeles Abrasion testing machine. See Fig. 5.11.
2. Balance.
3. A set of I.S sieves
4. Abrasive charge, which consists of cast-iron spheres or steel spheres approximately 48 mm in diameter and each weighing between 390 to 445 gms.

Table 5.7 : Specified Abrasive Charge for Different Types of Gradings of Gggregates

Grading	Number of Spheres	Weight of Charge (gms)
A	12	5000 ± 25
B	11	4584 ± 25
C	8	3330 ± 20
D	6	2500 ± 15
E	12	5000 ± 25
F	12	5000 ± 25
G	12	5000 ± 25

Gradings of Test Samples

Table 5.8

Sieve Size		Weight in gm of Test Sample for Grade						
Passing, mm	Retained on mm	A	B	C	D	E	F	G
80	63	–	–	–	–	2500	–	–
63	50	–	–	–	–	2500	–	–
50	40	–	–	–	–	5000	5000	–
40	25	1250	–	–	–	–	5000	5000
25	20	1250	–	–	–	–	–	5000
20	12.5	1250	2500	–	–	–	–	–
12.5	10	1250	2500	–	–	–	–	–
10	6.3	–	–	2500	–	–	–	–
6.3	4.75	–	–	2500	–	–	–	–
4.75	2.36	–	–	–	5000	–	–	–

Test Procedure : The test sample consists of clean aggregate which has been dried in an oven at 105°C to 110°C and it should confirm to one of the gradings as shown in above table.

Test sample and abrasive charge is placed in the Los Angeles Abrasion testing machine and the machine is rotated at a speed of 20 to 33 revolutions per minute. For gradings A, B, C and D, the machine is rotated for 500 revolutions. For gradings E, F and G, it is rotated 1000 revolutions. At the completion of the above number of revolutions, the material is discharged from the machine and a preliminary separation of the sample made on a sieve coarser than 1.7 mm I.S. sieve. Finer portion is then sieved on a 1.7 mm I.S. sieve. The material coarser than 1.7 mm I.S. sieve is washed, dried in an oven at 105° to 110°C to a substantially constant weight and accurately weighed to the nearest gram.

Reporting of Results

$$\% \text{ Abrasion value} = \frac{\text{Material finer than 1.7 mm I.S. sieve}}{\text{Original weight of sample}} \times 100$$

5.13 METHOD OF TEST FOR DETERMINING AGGREGATES IMPACT VALUE COARSE AGGREGATES

This method covers the procedure for determining the aggregates impact value of soft and coarse aggregate used for bases and sub-bases of road pavements.

The apparatus shall consist of the following :

(1) The impact testing machine of the form shown in Fig. 5.12 and complying with the following :

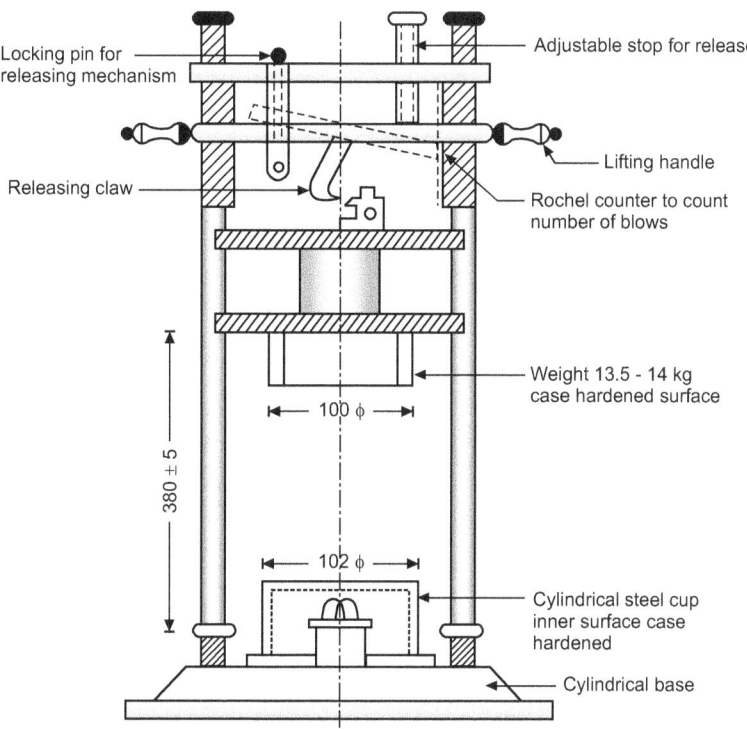

Fig. 5.12 : Aggregate impact testing machine

(a) Total weight neither more than 60 kg nor less than 45 kg.

(b) The machine shall have a metal base weighing between 22 and 30 kg with a plane lower surface of not less than 30 cm diameter, and shall be supported on a level concrete block or floor at least 45 cm thick. The machine shall be prevented from rocking either by fixing it to the block or floor or by supporting it on a level and plane metal plate cast into the surface of the block or floor.

(c) A cylindrical steel cup of the following internal dimensions and not less than 6.3 mm thick with its inner surface case-hardened, that can be rigidly fastened at the centre of the base and easily removed for emptying :

    Diameter   102 mm

    Depth   50 mm

(d) A metal hammer weighing 13.5 to 14.0 kg, the lower end of which shall be cylindrical in shape, 100 mm in diameter and 50 mm long, with a 2 mm chamfer at the lower edge, and case-hardened. The hammer shall slide freely between vertical guides so arranged that the lower (cylindrical) part of the hammer is above and concentric with the cup.

(e) Means for raising the hammer and allowing it to fall freely between the vertical guides from a height of 380 mm on to the test sample in the cup, and means for adjusting the height of fall within 5 mm.

(f) Means for supporting the hammer while fastening or removing the cup.

(2) Sieves : I.S. sieves of sizes 12.5 mm, 10 mm and 2.36 mm.

(3) Measure : A cylindrical metal measure, tared to the nearest gram, of sufficient rigidity to retain its form under rough usage, and of the following internal dimensions :

Diameter 75 mm.
Depth 50 mm.

(4) Tamping Rod : A straight metal tamping rod of circular cross-section 10 mm in diameter and 230 mm long, rounded at one end.

(5) Balance : Capacity not less than 500 g, readable and accurate to 0.1 g.

(6) Oven : A well-ventilated oven, thermostatically controlled to maintain a temperature of 100° to 110° C.

Preparation of Test Sample

(1) The test sample shall consist of aggregate the whole of which passes 12.5 mm I.S. sieve and is retained on a 10 mm I.S. sieve. The aggregate comprising the test sample shall be dried in an oven for a period of four hours till the time, the weight becomes constant at a temperature of 105° to 110°C and cooled.

(2) The measure shall be filled about one-third full with the aggregate and tamped with 25 strokes of the rounded end of the tamping rod. A further similar quantity of aggregate shall be added and a further tamping of 25 strokes given. The measure shall finally be filled to overflowing, tamped 25 times and the surplus aggregate struck-off, using the tamping rod as a straight-edge. The net weight of aggregate in the measure shall be determined to the nearest gram (weight of aggregate shall be used for the duplicate test on the same material).

(3) This oven-dried sample is immersed in water for three days.

(4) Wet sample after the immersion period is surface dried by suitable cloth.

Test Procedure

(1) The impact machine shall rest without wedging or packing upon the level plate, block or floor, so that it is rigid and the hammer guide columns are vertical.

(2) The cup shall be fixed firmly in position on the base of the machine and the whole of the test sample placed in it and compacted by a single tamping of 25 strokes of the tamping rod.

(3) The hammer shall be raised until its lower face is 380 mm above the upper surface of the aggregate in the cup, and allowed to fall freely on to the aggregate. The test sample shall be subjected to a total of 15 such blows each being delivered at an interval of not less than one second.

(4) The crushed aggregate shall then be removed from the cup and the whole of it sieved on the 2.36 mm I.S. sieve and washed with water till there is no further significant amount of loss. The fraction retained on the sieve shall be dried in an oven to the constant weight at 105 to 110 C and weighed to an accuracy of 0.1 g (weight B). The fraction retained on the sieve (weight B) shall be subtracted from the weight of the original oven-dried sample (weight A). The resultant weight (weight A – weight B) shall represent the fraction passing 2.36 mm I.S. sieve (weight C). Two tests shall be made.

Calculations

(1) The ratio of the weights of the fines formed to the total sample in each test shall be expressed as percentage of the oven dried, the result being recorded to the first decimal place :

$$\text{Aggregate impact value} = \frac{C}{A} \times 100$$

where, C = weight of the fines formed, and
A = weight of the ovendried sample.

Reporting of Results

(1) The mean of the two results shall be reported as aggregate impact value (wet) of the tested material. The detail result is as listed below.

According to above procedure, the Aggregate Impact Test was conducted on following three Aggregates : (1) Basalt, (2) Granite, (3) Marble. Results are listed.

Table 5.9

Sr. No.	Aggregate	Ovendried Weight A in kg.	Weight of Fraction Passing through 2.36 mm Sieve in kg.	Impact Value	Height of Specimen	Settlement
1.	Basalt	0.5	0.045	9%	4.8 mm	0.8
2.	Marble	0.5	0.052	10.4%	4.7 mm	1.05
3.	Granite	0.5	0.053	10.6%	4.8 mm	0.8

The chief advantage of the aggregate impact test is that it determines the resistance to the impact of stones. The test can be performed in a short time even at construction site or at stone quarry as the apparatus is simple and portable. Well-shaped conical stones provide higher resistance to impact, when compared with the flaky and elongated stones.

5.14 AGGREGATE POLISHING TEST

The aggregates should not get polished under traffic. To test polishing characteristics of aggregates, the aggregates are embedded in a curved mould in cement sand mortar and then subjected to increased polishing caused by a rotating pneumatic wheel. The size of each specimen is 45 mm wide × 90.5 mm long. Rubber wheel is 20 cm diameter, 5 cm broad, loaded with 40 kg load at a tyre pressure of 3.15 ± 0.15 kg/cm² sand and water are fed to the machine when it is rotated at an r.p.m. of 320 – 325 for 3 hours 15 minutes. The specimen are thereafter tested for their polishing characters on British Portable tester. The British Portable tester is essentially a rubber sliding shoe which is mounted at the end of the pendulum. The slider when released, brushes past the specimen and comes to a halt. The instrument directly measures the polishing value on a graduated scale. Limestones have poor p.s.v's ranging from 35 to 40. Granites have values in the range of 40 – 48 and sand stone has a high value of about 55.

5.15 STRIPPING TEST

It is necessary that aggregate should adhere to the bitumen film for good performance. The stripping test measures the adhesion of bitumen to aggregates. The aggregates are mixed with 5 percent binder at the specified temperature with regard to the bitumen used. The coated aggregates are then immersed in water and kept undisturbed at controlled temperature for about 24 hours. The percentage of area uncoated due to action of water is now usually assessed, which itself is the stripping value. The maximum stripping value could be 25 percent. There is possibility that when aggregates come into close contact with water, bond between bitumen and aggregates may get loosened. This reduction in bond is called stripping, which possibility exists in the case of open-graded mixtures and surface dressings. Stripping should be avoided as it will lead to collapse of base structure.

5.16 BITUMEN

Bitumen is manufactured from crude oil. Bitumen is obtained as the last residue in fractional distillation of crude petroleum. Crude petroleum is a mixture of hydrocarbons of different molecular weights. In the petroleum refineries the individual components like LPG, naphtha, Kerosene, Diesel etc. are separated through the process of fractional distillation. The heaviest material obtained from the fractional distillation process is further treated and blended to make different grades of paving grade bitumen. The actual bitumen output can be controlled not only by selecting the appropriate crude but also by adopting varying processes in the refinery. The choice of process would depend on the availability of suitable crude, demand of the end products and total commercial viability of the complete refining process.

Definition : Bitumen is defined as "A viscous liquid, or a solid, consisting essentially of hydrocarbons and their derivatives, which is soluble in trichloroethylene and is substantially nonvolatile and softens gradually when heated. It is black or brown in colour and possesses waterproofing and adhesive properties. It is obtained by refinery processes from petroleum, and is also found as a natural deposit or as a component of naturally occurring asphalt, in which it is associated with mineral matte.

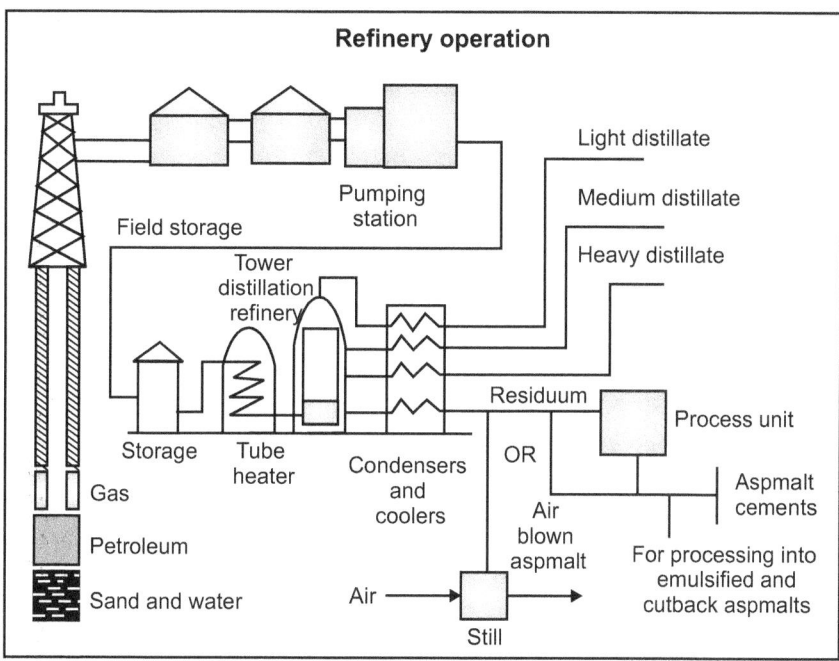

Fig. 5.13

5.16.1 Types of Bitumen

Bitumen or bituminous binder available in India is mainly of the following types :

- **Penetration Grade**

Bitumen 80/100 : The characteristics of this grade confirm to that of S 90 grade of IS-73-1992. This is the softest of all grades available in India. This is suitable for low volume roads and is still widely used in the country.

Bitumen 60/70 : This grade is harder than 80/100 and can withstand higher traffic loads. The characteristics of this grade confirm to that of S 65 grade of IS-73-1992. It is presently used mainly in construction of National Highways and State Highways.

Bitumen 30/40 : This is the hardest of all the grades and can withstand very heavy traffic loads. The characteristics of this grade confirm to that of S 35 grade of IS-73-1992. Bitumen 30/40 is used in specialized applications like airport runways and also in very heavy traffic volume roads in coastal cities in the country.

- **Industrial Grade Bitumen :** Industrial grade bitumen is also known as blown bitumen. This is obtained by blowing air into hot bitumen at high temperatures (normally beyond 180°C). Blowing hot air into bitumen at high temperatures results in structural changes in bitumen. Esters are formed in this process and these esters link up two different molecules and higher molecular weight material increases drastically. In the process the asphaltene content is increased which in turn results in higher softening points and very low penetration number. Industrial grade bitumen is used in industrial applications and in water proofing, tarfelting etc.
- **Cutback :** Cutback is a free flowing liquid at normal temperatures and is obtained by fluxing bitumen with suitable solvents. The viscosity of bitumen is reduced substantially by adding kerosene or any other solvent. Cutback has been used in tack coat applications.
- **Bitumen Emulsion :** Bitumen emulsion is a free flowing liquid at ambient temperatures. Bitumen emulsion is a stable dispersion of fine globules of bitumen in continuous water phase. Dispersion is obtained by processing bitumen and water under controlled conditions through a colloidal mill together with selected additives. The use of proper quality emulsifiers is essential to ensure that the emulsion has stability over time and also that it breaks and sets when applied on aggregates/road surface. It is chocolate brown free flowing liquid at room temperature. Bitumen Emulsions can be of two types cationic & anionic. Anionic bitumen emulsions are generally not used in road construction as generally siliceous aggregate is used in road construction. Anionic bitumen emulsions do not give good performance with siliceous whereas cationic bitumen emulsions give good performance with these aggregates. Therefore, cationic bitumen emulsions are far more popular than anionic bitumen emulsions.
- **Modified Bitumen :** Modified Bitumen are bitumen with additives. These additives help in further enhancing the properties of bituminous pavements. Pavements constructed with Modified Bitumen last longer which automatically translates into reduced overlays. Pavements constructed with Modified Bitumens can be economical if the overall lifecycle cost of the pavement is taken into consideration.

5.16.2 Properties of Bitumen

- **Bitumen – A Visco-Elastic Material :** The properties of Bitumen can be defined in terms analogous to the Modulus of Elasticity of solid materials. In case of solids, Modulus of Elasticity E is defined by Hooke's law Bitumen is a Visco-elastic material. At high temperatures it behaves like a liquid and hence liquid flow properties like Viscosity are exhibited. However, at low temperatures bitumen behaves like a solid and hence solid properties like stress and strain become relevant. Similarly, for shorter loading time bitumen behaves like a solid whereas for longer loading times bitumen behaves like a liquid. The properties that bitumen exhibits in the intermediate temperature range and loading time are of great relevance as this range is very long and bitumen is handled in this temperature range most of the times.

Fig. 5.14

Due to the visco-elastic nature of bitumen, there is always a phase lag in stress & strain in case of repetitive loadings. For purely elastic material the phase lag is 0^0 and for purely viscous material the phase lag is 90^0. In case of bitumen since it is neither a liquid nor a solid at most temperatures hence the phase lag is always between 0^0 to 90^0. The above theory is extremely useful in studying fatigue characteristics, properties of creep & also tensile strength of bitumen.

- **Adhesion Properties of Bitumen :** Bitumen has excellent adhesive qualities provided the conditions are favourable. However in presence of water the adhesion does create some Examples. Most of the aggregates used in road construction possess a weak negative charge on the surface. The bitumen aggregate bond is because of a weak dispersion force. Water is highly polar and hence it gets strongly attached to the aggregate displacing the bituminous coating. The factors influencing aggregate bitumen adhesion are plenty and some of the factors influencing this property are as below:

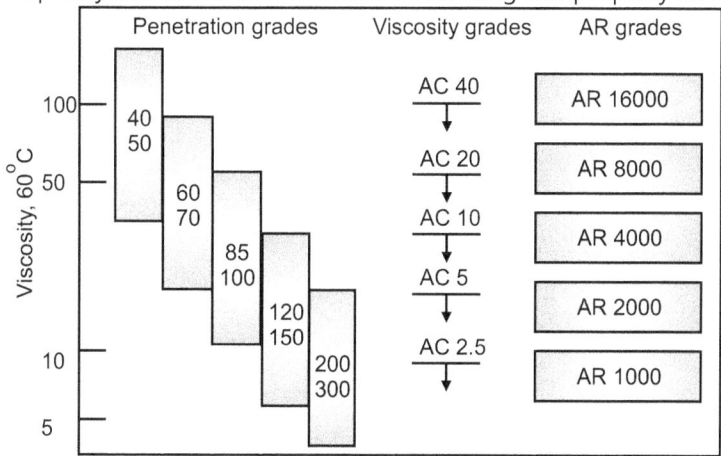

Fig. 5.15

- **External :** Rainfall, Humidity, Water pH, Presence of salts, Temperature, Temperature cycle, Traffic, Design, Workmanship, Drainage.

- **Aggregate :** Mineralogy, Surface texture, Porosity, Dirt, Durability, Surface area, Absorption, Moisture content, Shape, Weathering.
- **Bitumen :** Rheology, Constitution.
- **Mix :** Void content, Permeability, Bitumen content, Bitumen film thickness, Filler type, Aggregate grading, Mix type.

5.17 TESTS ON BITUMEN

Various tests are conducted to study the suitability of bitumen for various conditions. These tests are conducted as per present specification which contains some drawbacks. Although these specifications are supposed to bear relationship with those properties which directly govern the performance of mixes and bituminous pavements, these results are hardly used in the bituminous construction.

The present specifications which are used today to test the bitumen may have been specified to suit the conditions at the time, they were formulated but their usefulness is questionable today. As these tests are very simple and no elaborate equipment is required for conducting the tests, they continue to attract the attention of engineers. This does not mean that they should be completely abondoned but a more rational approach is needed to make them much more useful than what they are at present. Now a days, methods of design of pavements and techniques of construction are improving, hence more sophisticated tests are needed to meet the present requirements.

The present tests either need modification as in case of ductility test or complete replacement by a more reliable test, as they provide little or no information to the Engineer who is directly responsible for the service performance of bituminuous pavements or the manufacturers who play a pivotal role in the manufacture and supply of materials. This chapter deals with the Standard tests on Asphaltic Bitumen and their lacunas.

5.18 SOLUBILITY TEST

The pure bitumen is completely soluble in solvent like carbon disulphide and carbon tetrachloride. Hence any impurity in the form of inert materials, could be quantitatively analysed by dissolving the sample into those solvents. The standard procedure as per I.S. 1216 - 1978 is as follows :

Object : To determine the percentage of insoluble material in the bitumen.

Apparatus : Gooch crucible, conical glass flask of 20 ml capacity, carbon disulphide, carbon tetrachloride.

Procedure : Weight about 2 gm of the dry material correct to the nearest 0.001 gm into a 200 ml flask and add 10 ml of carbon disulphide or carbon tatrachloride. Stir the content of the flask and then allow it to stand loosely, cooled for a period of one hour, filter the content of the flask, through the flask, through the Gooch crucible prepared as per I.S. 1216 -1978. Moisten the asbestos pad with carbon disulphide before commencing the filtration and filter at a rate of not more than two drops per second at first. The filtrate shall be quite clear. Transfer the insoluble matter remaining in the flask to the crucible by washing out with steam of carbon disulphide from wash bottle. Wash the material retained in the crucible with successive small amounts of carbon disulphide until, the filtrate obtained is not discoloured. Allow the crucible to dry in air for 30 minutes, after which, place it in an oven at 110° C for one hour. Allow the crucible to cool in a desiccater and then weigh.

Matter soluble in carbon disulphide or carbon tetrachloride = A

We have, $$A = \frac{(W_1 - W_2)}{W_1} \times 100$$

where W_1 = Weight in gm of dry sample,

W_2 = Weight in gm of insoluble material remained in the Gooch crucible.

Precision : The test result shall not differ from mean by more than following.

Table 5.10

Matter Soluble in Carbon Disulphide	Repeatability	Reproducibility
Below 98%	0.5	1.0
98 to 100%	0.1	0.2

Comments on the Test : The purpose of this test is to determine the insoluble material in bitumen such as salt etc. In addition, bitumen also contains carbon with fraction, soluble in carbon disulphide but insoluble in carbon tetrachloride. Actually it should not increase 2% in most of the road bitumen. But its percentage is high in that bitumen which are subjected to excessive heating. The insoluble material should be preferably less than 1%. In solubility test with carbon tetrachloride, if carbonaceous residue is over 0.5%, the bitumen is considered to be cracked. The minimum portion of the bitumen soluble in carbon disulphide is specified as 99%. This test is useful not only to ensure due care in refinery operations and to detect the contaminations caused due to shipments in dirty tanks, but also to determine the colloidal instability or stability of materials.

5.19 Water Content Test

It is desirable that the bitumen contains maximum water content to prevent foaming of the bitumen when it is heated above the boiling point of water. The quantity of water present in the bituminous material is expressed as percentage by weight of the material.

- The standard procedure as per I.S. 1211 -1978 is as follows :

Object : To determine the water content of bituminous material.

Apparatus : Flask of capacity of 500 ml, condenser, receiver, a 100 ml graduated cylinder, heater, solvent (petroleum spirit with boiling range of 100° to 120°C).

Procedure : Place about 100 grams of sample, accurately weighed, in the flask and add 100 ml of solvent. Attach the flask to the condensing and collecting system and heat the flask at such rate that the condensate falls from the end of condenser at rate of two to five drops per second. Continue the distillation until the condensed water is no longer visible in any part of the apparatus except the bottom of the graduated tube and until the volume of water collected remains constant for period not less than five minutes.

Remove the ring of condensed water in the condensed tube, if any, by increasing the rate of distillation by few drops per second. Wash the droplet of water which adheres to the lower end of the condenser into the receiver with solvent using spray. Insert loose plug of cotton wool in the top of the condenser tube to prevent the condensation of atmospheric moisture in the condenser tube.

Allowable maximum water content = 0.2%.

Comments on the Test : Since percentage of water in the bitumen when heated above the boiling point of water is not to exceed 0.2% by weight. The specifications usually control the water content simply by stipulating that the material should not foam when heated to maximum road temperature. The weight of water condensed and collected is expressed by weight of original sample. The maximum water content of bitumen should not increase 0.2% by weight.

5.20 SPECIFIC GRAVITY

The density of bituminous binders is fundamental property frequently used as an aid in classifying the binder for use in paving jobs. The specific gravity value of bitumen is also useful in the bituminous mix design. The standard procedure as per I.S. 1209 -1978 is as follows. The ratio of the mass of an equal volume of substance and water, the temperature of both being specified. If the temperature of substance is t_1 °C and that of water is t_2 °C, the specific gravity is denoted by $S \times \frac{t_1}{t_2}$. The t_1 and t_2 shall be specified clearly.

Object : To find the specific gravity of the bituminous material (using specific gravity bottles.)

Apparatus : Specific gravity bottles of 50 ml capacity shall be used. One of the bottles shall be of 6 mm diameter neck and that of other having 25 mm diameter neck, constant temperature bath, thermometer.

Procedure : Clean, dry and weigh the specific gravity bottles together with the stopper (a).

Fill it with freshly boiled and cooled distilled water and insert the stopper firmly. Keep the bottle upto its neck for not less than half an hour in a beaker of distilled water maintaining at a temperature of 27°C or any other temperature at which specific gravity is to be determined. Wipe all surplus moisture from the surface with a clean dry cloth and weigh again (b). After weighing the bottle and water together (b), the bottle shall be dried again.

In case of solids and semisolids, bring small amount of the material to a fluid condition by gentle application of heat, care being taken to prevent loss by evaporation, when material is sufficiently fluid, pour a quantity into clean, dry specific gravity bottle mentioned above to fill atleast half. Slightly warm the bottle. Keep the material away from touching the sides above the final level of the bottle and avoid the inclusion of air bubbles. Weigh with the stopper (c).

Fill the specific gravity bottle containing the asphalt with freshly boiled distilled water placing the stopper loosely in the specific gravity bottle. Do not allow any air bubble to remain in the specific gravity bottle. Place the specific gravity bottle in the water bath and place the stopper in place. Allow the specific gravity bottle to remain in the water bath for period of not less than half an hour. Remove the bottle and wipe all the moisture and weigh it (d).

S = Specific gravity of bitumen

$$S = \frac{[c-a]}{(b-a)-(d-c)} = \frac{(c-a)}{(b-a)-(d-c)}$$

where,
- a = Mass of specific gravity bottle.
- b = Mass of specific gravity bottle filled with distilled water.
- c = Mass of specific gravity bottle about half filled with the material.
- d = Mass of specific gravity bottles about half filled with the material and rest with distilled water.

Comments on the Test : The density of bitumen binder is a fundamental property frequently used as an aid in classifying the binders for use in paving jobs. In most applications, the bitumen is weighed out finally when used with aggregate system. Specific gravity is not required except when weight-volume relationship is needed for filling and shipping purpose and for design of bituminous mixes. Increased amount of aromatic type compounds or mineral impurities cause an increase in the specific gravity.

Generally, specific gravity of pure bitumen is in the range of 1.01 to 1.03. The specific gravity of cut back bitumen may be lower depending on the type and proportion of dilution used. The tars have specific gravity ranging from 1.10 to 1.25.

5.21 FLASH AND FIRE POINT TEST

Bituminous material leaved out volatiles at high temperatures, depending upon their grade. These volatiles catch fire causing flash. This condition is very hazardous and it is therefore essential to qualify this temperature for each bitumen grade, so that paving engineer may restrict mixing and application temperature. This test is necessary to know the flash point and fire point of the bitumen. The flash point of the bitumen is the lowest temperature at which the application of test flame causes the vapours from the material momentarily given in the form of flash under specified condition. The flash point is the lowest temperature at which the application of test flame causes the material to ignite and burn at least for 5 seconds under specified condition of test. The standard procedure as per I.S. 1209 -1978 is as follows :

Apparatus : Pensky-Markens closed tester consisting of cup, lid, stirring device, cover proper, shutter, flame exposure device, stove, top plate, air bath, thermometer etc. See Fig. 5.16.

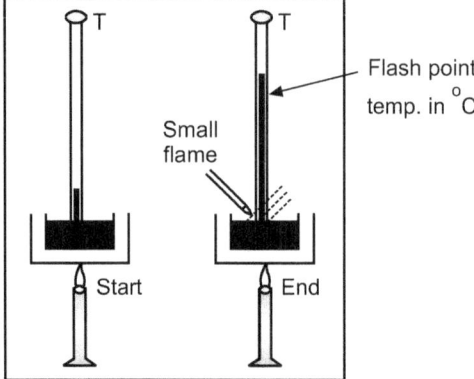

Fig. 5.16 : Flash point test

Procedure : Clean and dry all parts of the apparatus and its accessories thoroughly before the test is started. Take particular care to avoid the presence of any solvent used to clean the apparatus after previous test. Fill the cup with material to be tested upto the level indicated by the filling mark. Place the lid on the cup and set the latter on the stove. Take care that the locating devices are properly engaged. Insert the thermometer high on low range as required. Light and adjust the test flame such that it is of the size of a bed of 4 mm in diameter. Apply heat at such rate that the temperature recorded by the thermometer increases between 5° to 6°C.

Turn the stirrer at a rate of approximately 60 revolutions per minute. Apply the test flame at each temperature reading which is multiple of 1°C, upto 104°C. For temperature above 104°C, apply the test flame at each temperature reading which is multiple of 2°C. The first application of test flame being made at a temperature at least 17°C below the actual flash point. Apply the test flame by operating the device controlling the shutter road test flame burner so that the flame is lowered in 0.5 seconds, left in its lower position for one second and quickly raised to its high position. Discontinue the stirring during application of test flame.

Table 5.11

Sr. No.	Flash Point	Fire Point
1.	178°C	210°C
2.	182°C	208°C
3.	180°C	203°C

Comments on the Test : This test is essential for safety measures. This test is conducted to determine the temperature upto which the bitumen can be safely heated. The minimum specified flash point of bitumen used for pavement construction in Pensky- Markens closed type test is 175°C. The first application at test flame to be made below the actual flash point by an amount of 17°C.

5.22 Spot Test

This test is used for detecting overheated or cracked bitumen. This test is considered to be more sensitive than the solubility test for detection of cracking. About 2 gm of bitumen is dissolved in 10 ml of naphtha. A drop of this solution is taken out and placed on filter paper, one after one hour and second after 24 hours after the solution is prepared. If the stain of the spot on the paper is uniform in colour, the bitumen is accepted as uncracked. But if the spot forms dark brown or black circle in the centre with an angular ring of light colour surrounding it, the bitumen is considered to be overheated or cracked.

Comments on the Test : Although this test is not specified by Indian standard code, it is used in foreign countries like U.S.A., as this test is considered to measure homogeneous (colloidal stability) characteristic of asphalt. This test is again considered to be a controversal one due to the fact that it does not always detect the cracked materials in blend of cracked and normal materials.

5.23 Viscosity Test

It is a standard test as specified by I.S. 1206. **Viscosity** is the property of bitumen by which it resists flow due to internal friction. Viscosity is measured by Redwood viscometer. According to this method, viscosity is measured by determining the time taken by 50 ml of material to flow through specified orifice under standard temperature. The test is conducted at required temperature.

Apparatus : Tar viscometer, cup, valve, water bath, stirrer, thermometer, stop watch. See Fig. 5.17.

Procedure : Adjust the tar viscometer so that the top of tar cup is levelled. Heat the water in the water bath to the temperature specified for the test.

Clean the tar cup orifice of viscometer with suitable solvent and dry them roughly. Warm and stir the water under the temperature which is 20°C above the temperature specified for the test, pour the material into the cup. Place the thermometer in the material and stir it until temperature is exactly equal to specified temperature. The material is to be filled in the cup upto the index mark. The viscometer should be levelled before filling the material.

Lift the valve and suspend it on the valve support. Start the stop watch and determine the time required for collection of 50 ml of the material. Note the time in seconds.

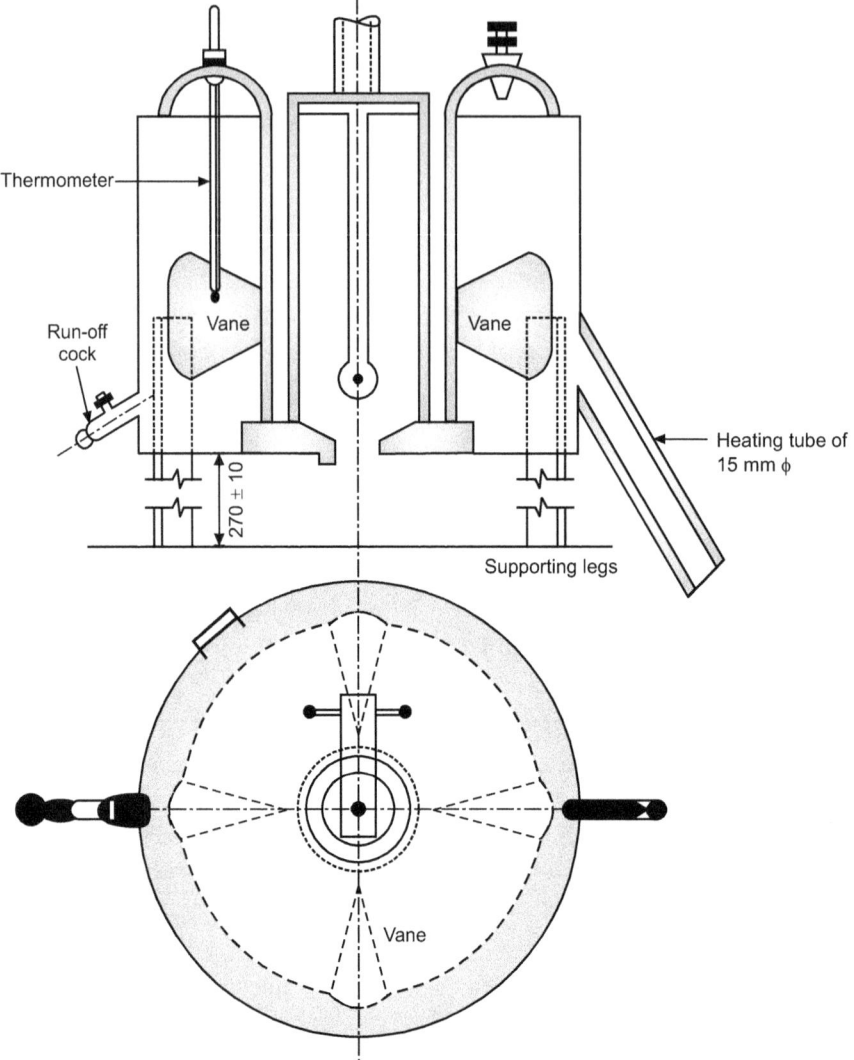

Fig. 5.17 : Tar viscometer

Precision : The result of repeat determinations on portions of same sample shall fall within ± 4% of the average of several readings.

Test Result : Test conducted with Redwood viscometer with 10 mm orifice.

        Road Tar of grade = R. T. 1

        Test temperature = 45°C

Table 5.12

Sr. No.	Viscosity	Mean	Precision
1.	24 sec.		− 21.3%
2.	28 sec.		− 8.2%
3.	33 sec.	30.5 sec.	+ 8.2%
4.	27 sec.		− 11.4%
5.	31 sec.		+ 1.64%
6.	34 sec.		+ 11.5%
7.	35 sec.		14.8%
8.	31 sec.		+ 1.64%
9.	21 sec.		− 4.92%
10.	33 sec.		+ 8.2%

As per I.S. 1206 -1978, precision allowed is ± 4% from the mean of several readings.

5.24 LOSS ON HEATING TEST

It is standard test as per I.S.1212 -1978. It is loss in weight (exclusive of water) of oil of a bituminous material when heated to a standard temperature and under specified conditions. The standard procedure as per I.S. code is as follows :

Apparatus : Oven, perforated metal shelf, container, thermometer etc.

Procedure : Stir and agitate thoroughly the material as received, warm it if necessary, to ensure a complete mixture before a portion is removed for the test. Heat the container in an oven at 100° to 110°C for 30 minutes, cool and weigh. Weigh into the container 50 gms at the material correct to the nearest 0.01 gm. Bring over to the temperature of 163°C and place the sample container in the oven. Close the oven and rotate the shelf during entire test at a rate of 5 to 6 revolutions per minute. The temperature being maintained at 163°C for 5 hours. The 5 hours period shall start when the temperature reaches 162°C and in no case shall the total time during which sample is in the oven, be more than 5 hours and 15 minutes. At the end of specified period, remove the container, cool to the room temperature and weigh it. When extreme accuracy is required, only one material, that is two containers shall be placed in the oven - at one time.

Precision : Result of duplicate shall not differ by following :

Table 5.13

Loss on Heating	Repeatability	Reproducibility
0 to 0.5%	0.1	0.2
0.5 to 1.0	0.2	0.4
1.0 to 2.0	0.3	0.6
Above 2.0	10% of mean	20% of mean

Test Result

Duration of heating = 5 hours
Grade of Bitumen = 80/100
Test temperature = 163° C

Table 5.14

Sr. No.	Wt. of Sample before Heating	Wt. of Sample After Heating	Percentage Loss
1.	50 gm	49.0 gm	2%
2.	50 gm	49.5 gm	1%
3.	50 gm	45.5 gm	3%
4.	50 gm	48.0 gm	4%
5.	50 gm	48.5 gm	3%
6.	50 gm	49.0 gm	2%
7.	50 gm	49.0 gm	2%
8.	50 gm	48.5 gm	3%
9.	50 gm	49.0 gm	2%
10.	50 gm	48.5 gm	3%

5.25 DUCTILITY TEST

Ductility test is standard test described in I.S. 1208 -1978. See Figs. 5.18 and 5.19. The **ductility** of bitumen is measured as the distance in centimeter to which a briquette specimen of bitumen will elongate before breaking, when the briquette is pulled apart at specified speed and temperature. The usual speed is 5 cm per minute and test temperature of water bath is 27°C. The ductility value signifies the property by which a bitumen can exist without breakings.

The standard procedure is as follows :

Object : To determine ductility of Bitumen.

Apparatus : Mould, Water bath, Testing machine, Thermometer etc.

Procedure : Unless otherwise specified, the test shall be conducted at 27°C and at rate of pull 50 mm/minute.

Completely melt the bituminous material to be tested to a temperature of 75° to 100°C above the approximately softening point until it becomes thoroughly fluid. Assemble the mould on the brass plate and in order to present the material under test from sticking, coat the surface of the sides of the mould with mixture of equal parts of glycerine and dextrine.

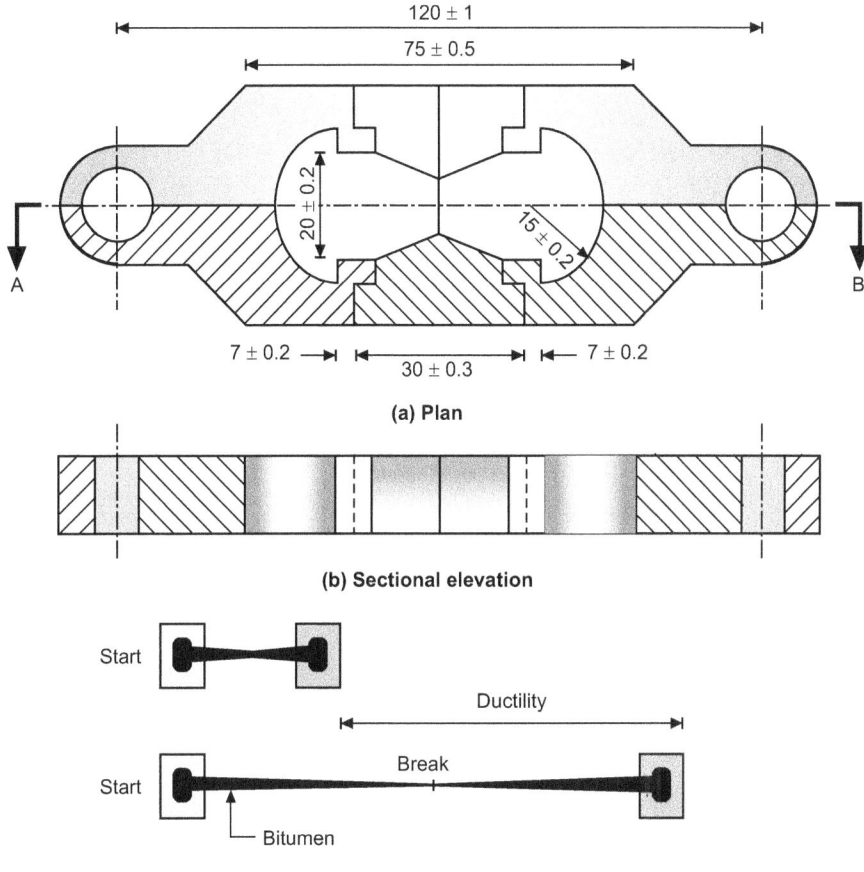

(a) Plan

(b) Sectional elevation

(c) Ductility test

Fig. 5.18 : Ductility test

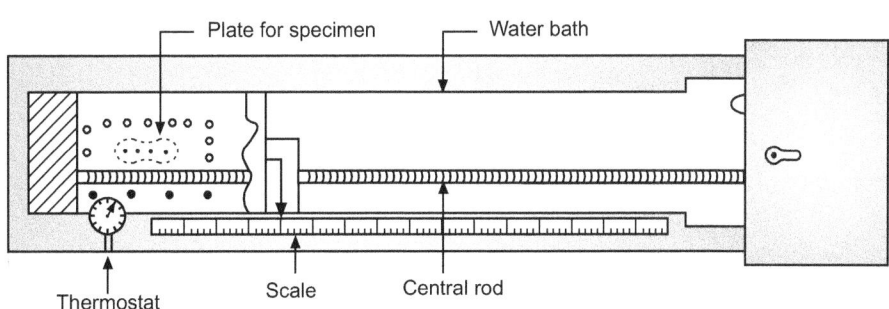

Fig. 5.19 : Ductility machine

Fill the material in the mould until it is more than level full. Leave it to cool at the room temperature for 30 to 40 minutes and then place in water bath maintained at 27°C for 30 minutes after which, cut off the excess bitumen by means of hot straight edged knife so that the mould shall be just level full. Place the briquette in the water bath. Remove the side pieces and test the specimen immediately.

Pull the two clips apart horizontally at a uniform speed of 50 mm/minute until the briquette ruptures. Measure the distance in centimeters through which the clips have been pulled, to produce rupture.

Precision : The test result shall not differ by the following :

Table 5.15

Repeatability	Reproducibility
10%	20%

Test Result

(1) Grade of bitumen = 80/100
Rate of Pull = 50 mm/minute
Test temperature = 27°C

Table 5.16

Sr. No.	Ductility (cm)	Mean Ductility (cm)
1.	45	
2.	41	43.4 cm
3.	42	
4.	46	
5.	43	

(2) Grade of bitumen = 60/70
Rate of pull = 50 mm/minute
Temperature = 27°C

Table 5.17

Sr. No.	Ductility (cm)	Mean Ductility (cm)
1.	41	
2.	38	39 cm
3.	40	
4.	39	
5.	37	

Lacunas in the Test : Test is conducted at 27°C but the maximum temperature on the road is normally more than 27°C and hence laboratory condition and practical condition are different. On roads, bituminous pavements are subjected to traffic loads but this test is conducted in the laboratory at uniform speed which is 50 mm/minute. Bituminous pavement contains aggregates along with bitumen, known as asphalt concrete which is subjected to traffic loads. But the laboratory sample is tested without aggregates.

The test is believed to measure the adhesiveness and plasticity of the bitumen. The bitumen may satisfy the ductility requirements. The materials with very high ductility are generally adhesive and have good cementing properties. High ductility is associated with high temperature susceptibility. The ductility value gets seriously affected by pouring temperature, dimensions of Briquette, level of Briquette in water bath, test temperature and rate of pulling.

Effect of temperature of water bath on ductility

(1)   Grade of bitumen = 80/100

        Rate of pull = 50 mm/min.

Table 5.18

Sr. No.	Temperature of Bath (°C)	Ductility (cm)
1.	27°C	43 cm
2.	32°C	39 cm
3.	46°C	33 cm
4.	51°C	29 cm
5.	55°C	25 cm

(2)   Grade of bitumen = 60/70

        Rate of pull = 50 mm/min.

Table 5.19

Sr. No.	Temperature of Water Bath (°C)	Ductility (cm)
1.	27°C	39 cm
2.	31°C	36 cm
3.	45°C	31 cm
4.	50°C	28 cm
5.	54°C	23 cm

The ductility gets affected by change in temperature of water bath. Ductility value gets reduced with increase in water bath temperature. The ductility value also gets reduced with increase in rate of pull. The ductility value when rate of pull was 50 mm/minute was less when the rate of pull was 10 mm/minute even though grade of bitumen was same. When ductility is calculated at strain controlled condition, it is found that the ductility value gets affected by size of aggregates. The ductility value gets reduced with increase in size of aggregates. Ductility value is also affected by load applied vertically downward. It gets reduced with increase in load. If ductility value by standard test is compared with ductility value by stress controlled test, it is found that later value is 0.65 times the standard value. The ductility values get affected by pouring temperature, dimensions of briquette, level of briquette in water bath, test temperature and rate of pulling. If the temperature of the bath is increased, the ductility gets reduced, to a significant extent but the rate of pull does not have significant effect on ductility. Even if the rate of pull is decreased to 10 mm/minute, ductility gets increased by hardly 5%.

In actual field conditions, the ductile property of the bitumen is in conjunction with aggregate. To test the ductility property of bitumen in conjunction with the aggregate, author devised a modified test. This method consisted of taking equal sized aggregates which are kept touching each other. The bitumen of specified grade is poured just enough to coat the aggregates and the two aggregates are then pulled apart in vertical direction with a fixed load and length of bitumen thread is measured at the point of breaking. The fixed load employed was 30 gm. The following table shows typical results obtained by us.

Table 5.20 : Grade of Bitumen - 80/100

Aggregate Size in mm	10	12	20	25	40
Ductility in cm	33	32	30	25	24

In general, the larger-sized particles reduce the ductility. The magnitude of the stretching load employed has also a pronounced effect on the ductility values. If the stretching load increases, the ductility gets reduced, the following table examplifies this point.

Table 5.21 : Grade 80/100 Temperature 28°C 40 mm Aggregate

Stretched Load (gm)	10	20	30	40	50
Ductility in cm	35	33	29	29	23

5.26 PENETRATION TEST

This is standard test as per I.S. 1203 -1978. The penetration test determines the hardness or softness of the bitumen by measuring the depth in tenth's of a millimetre to which standard loaded needle will penetrate vertically in five minutes. The penetration of bituminous material is the distance in tenths of a millimeter that a standard needle will penetrate vertically into a sample of the material under standard conditions of temperature, load and time. The standard procedure is as follows :

Object : To determine the penetration value of the bitumen.

Apparatus : Container, needle, water bath, transfer dish, Penetration apparatus (See Fig. 5.20), thermometer, time device etc.

Procedure : Soften the material to pouring temperature not more than 60°C for tars and not more than 90°C for bituminous materials above the approximate softening point and see that it is homogeneous and is free from air bubbles and water by stirring. Pour the material into the container to a depth at least 10 mm in excess of the expected penetration. Protect the sample and allow it to cool. Place it in the bath which is to be kept at 25° C. Unless otherwise specified, the test is carried out at 25°C.

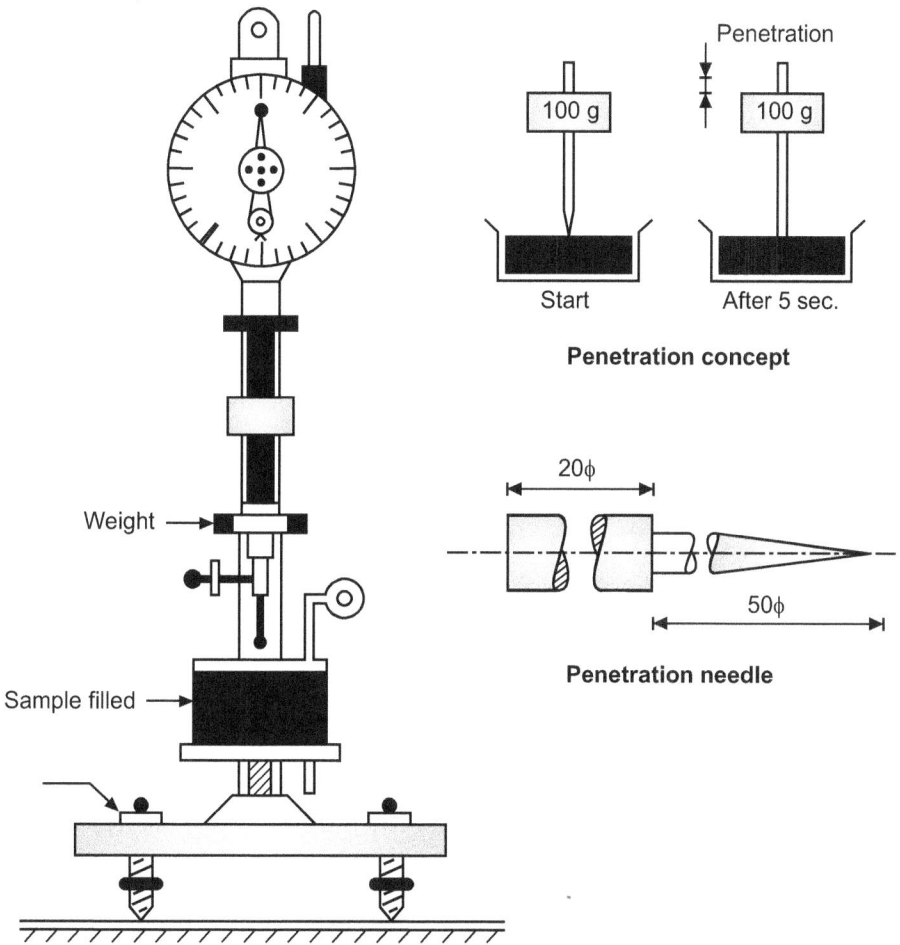

Fig. 5.20 : Penetrometer

Adjust the needle to make contact with the surface of the sample. Bring the pointer to zero. Release the needle and measure the distance penetrated. Make three determinations and express in one tenth of a millimeter.

Precision : The duplicate result shall not differ by following :

Table 5.22

Penetration	Repeatability	Reproducibility
Below 50	1 unit	4 units
Above 50	3% of their mean	8% of their mean

Test Result

Grade of bitumen = 80/100
Test temperature = 25°C

Table 5.23

Sr. No.	Penetration	Mean
1.	86	
2.	92	
3.	81	
4.	87	87
5.	82	
6.	89	
7.	88	
8.	93	
9.	85	
10.	87	

5.27 DETERMINATION OF SOFTENING POINT OF BITUMEN

Bitumen does not suddenly change from solid state to liquid state but as the temperature increases, it gradually becomes softer until it flows readily. All semi-solid state bitumen needs sufficient fluidity before they are used for application with the aggregate mix. For this purpose, bitumen is sometimes cut back with a solvent like kerosene. The common procedure however is to liquify the bitumen by heating. The **'softening point'** is the temperature at which the substance attains particular degree of softening under specified condition of test. For bitumen it is usually determined by 'Ring and Ball test'. A brass ring containing the test sample of bitumen is suspended in liquid like water or glycerine at a given temperature. A steel ball is placed upon the bitumen and the liquid medium is then heated at a specified rate. The temperature at which the softened bitumen touches the metal plate placed at a specified distance below the ring is recorded as the softening point of a particular bitumen. The apparatus and test procedure are standardized by ISI. It is obvious that harder grade bitumen possess higher softening point.

Apparatus required for performing the test is shown.

Apparatus : It consists of ring and ball apparatus.

(a) **Steel Balls :** They are two in number. Each has a diameter of 9.5 mm and weight 2.5 ± 0.05 g.

(b) **Brass Rings :** There are two rings of following dimensions.

Table 5.24

Sr. No.	Particular	Dimension
1.	Depth	6.4 mm
2.	Inside φ @ bottom	15.9 mm
3.	Inside φ @ top	17.5 mm
4.	Outside diameter	20.6 mm

(c) Support : The metallic support is used for placing a pair of rings. The upper surface of rings is adjusted to be 50 mm below the surface of water or liquid contained in bath. A distance of 25 mm between the bottom of rings and top surface of the bottom plate of support is provided. It has a housing for a suitable thermometer.

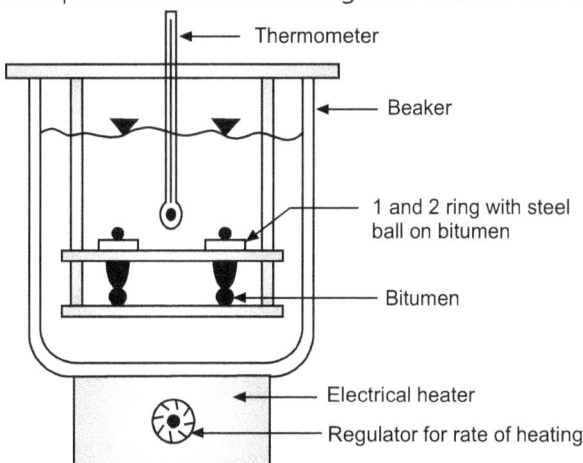

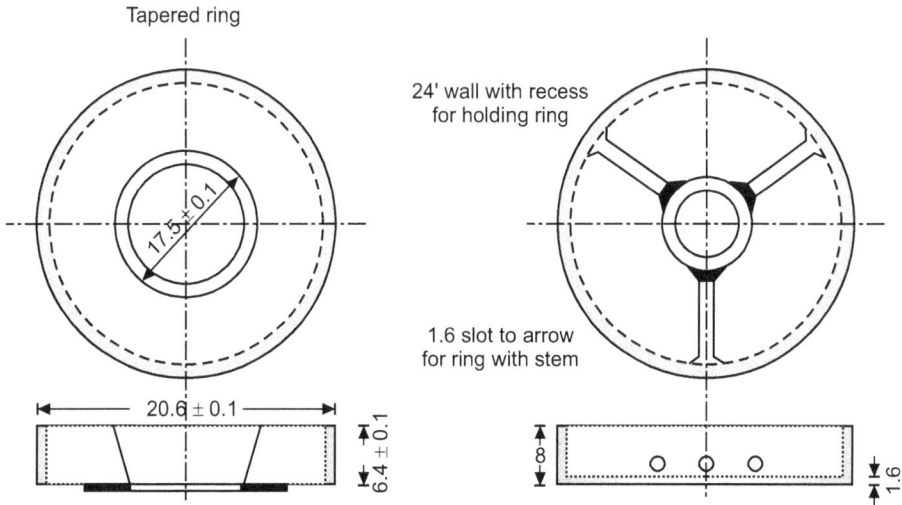

Fig. 5.21 : Softening point apparatus

(d) Bath and stirrer : A heat resistant glass container of 85 mm diameter and 120 mm depth is used. Bath liquid is water for materials having softening point below 80°C and glycerine for materials having softening point more than 80°C, mechanical stirrer is used for insuring uniform heat distribution at all times throughout the bath itself.

Procedure : Sample material is heated to a temperature between 75°C and 100°C above the approximate softening point until it is completely fluid and is poured and heated in rings. To avoid sticking of metal plates to bitumen, coating is done to this with a solution of glycerine and dextrine. After cooling the rings in air for about 30 minutes, the excess bitumen is trimmed and rings are placed in the supports as discussed in item (c) above. At this time, the distilled water is kept at 50°C. This temperature is maintained for 15 min. after which balls are placed in position. The temperature of water is raised at uniform rate of 5°C per minute with a controlled heating unit, until the bitumen softens and touches bottom plate by sinking the balls. At least two observations are made. For material whose softening point is above 80°C, glycerine is used as a heating medium and the starting temperature is 35°C.

Results : The temperature at instant when each of the ball and sample touches the bottom plate of support is recorded as softening point value. The mean determinations are noted. It is essential that the mean value of the softening point temperature does not differ from individual observations by more than following limits :

Table 5.25

Softening Points	Repeatability	Reproducibility
Below 30°C	2°C	4°C
30°C – 80°C	1°C	2°C
Above 80°C	2°C	4°C

Discussion : As in the other physical tests on bitumen, it is essential that the specifications discussed above are strictly observed. Particularly, any variation in the following points would affect the result considerably :

(1) Quality and type of liquid.

(2) Weight of balls.

(3) Distance between bottom ring and bottom plate.

(4) Rate of the heating.

Impurity in water or glycerine has been observed to affect the results considerably. It is logical to observe the lower softening point if the weight of the ball is excessive. On the other hand, the increased distance between the bottom of the ring and bottom base plate increases the softening point.

Applications of Softening Point Test : Softening point is essentially a temperature at which the bituminous binders have an equal viscosities. Softening point of tar therefore, is related to the equiviscous temperatures i.e. (e.v.t.). The softening point found by the ring and ball apparatus is approximate.

Observations

(1) Bitumen grade = 80/100

(2) Approximate softening point = 48.5° C

(3) Liquid used in bath water/glycerine = water

Table 5.26

Time in Minutes	Temperature		Time in Minutes	Temperature	
	Ball 1	Ball 2		Ball 1	Ball 2
0	5.0	5.0	11	24.0	24.0
1	7.0	7.0	12	26.5	26.5
2	7.5	8.0	13	30.0	30.0
3	9.0	9.5	14	32.5	32.5
4	10.0	11.0	15	36.5	36.5
5	13.0	12.0	16	39.0	39.0
6	14.0	13.0	17	42.0	42.0
7	15.0	14.0	18	46.0	46.0
8	17.0	16.0	18' 54"	48.0	–
9	18.5	18.0	19	–	48.0
10	20.5	21.5	19' 25"	–	49.0

Table 5.27

Test Property	Sample no. 1		Sample no. 2		Mean Value of Softening point
	Ball 1	Ball 2	Ball 1	Ball 2	
Temp. °C at which sample touches bottom	48°C	49°C	–	–	48.5°C
Repeatability	1°C	1°C	–	–	1°C
Reproducibility	2°C	2°C	–	–	2°C

Test Result : Grade of Bitumen 80/100

Table 5.28

Sr. No.	Ball No. 1 in °C	Ball No. 2 in °C	Softening point, °C
1.	39	40	39.5
2.	49	38	39
3.	42	40	41
4.	43	42	42.5
5.	40	41	40.5
6.	40	40	40
7.	42	43	42.5
8.	40	42	41

5.28 BITUMINOUS MATERIALS

While discussing the test, we have used the word "Bitumen". Bitumen is a petroleum product obtained by the specific distillation of petroleum crude. Bitumen can also be found in natural form but bulk of the supply of bitumen is through distillation of petroleum crude. Bitumen is completely soluble in carbon disulphide or carbon tetrachloride. The grades of bitumen used for the construction work of roads and air field pavements are called paving grades and those used for water proofing of structures and industrial floors are industrial grades. When the viscosity of bitumen is reduced by specific amount by a volatile dilutant, it is called cut back, on the other hand when the bitumen is suspended in a finely divided condition in aqueous medium and stabilized with an emulsifier, the material is known as emulsion. Similarly when bitumen contains some inert mineral, it is called as asphalt. Asphalt could be found naturally or artificially prepared. Compared to bitumen 'tar' is not derived from crude petroleum. It is obtained by the destructive distillation of coal or wood. Tar is soluble only in toluene. Tar in general has inferior weather resisting properties, change in viscosity of tar with temperature is considerable - not an asset from the point of road construction. Therefore, bitumen is generally preferred. As civil engineers, we are not interested in the production process of tar or bitumen.

5.29 BITUMEN MIXES

Bitumen along with aggregate can form tough paving surface. Aggregate should be sharp (not rounded). The maximum size of aggregate depends upon the thickness of the layer. For base course, maximum size of aggregate would be 2.5 to 5 cm. For surface course 1.25 to 1.87 cm size maximum aggregate may be O.K. The mix should be such that voids formed in the coarse aggregate should be filled by smaller-sized particles and bitumen should act as binder to all. As an example, the two recommended gradations for 40 mm thick bituminous surface are given in the table below.

Table 5.29

Sieve Size	Percent Passing by Weight	
mm	Grade 1	Grade 2
20	–	100
12.5	100	80 – 100
10.0	80 – 100	70 – 90
4.75	55 – 75	50 – 70
2.36	35 – 50	35 – 50
0.600	18 – 29	18 – 29
0.300	13 – 23	13 – 23
0.150	8 – 16	8 – 16
0.0075	4 – 10	4 – 10
Binder content, percent by weight of mix.		
	5 – 7.5	5 – 7.5

Since the bitumen aggregate mix consists of aggregate and bitumen, the usual Example is to find the properties of the mix knowing the properties of the individual i.e. the aggregate and the binder. This is easily done. For example, if W_1, W_2, W_3, W_4 are percent by weight of aggregates 1, 2, 3, 4 in a bituminous mix and G_1, G_2, G_3, G_4 are the specific gravities of the respective aggregates, then G_5, the specific gravity of blended aggregate mix will be,

$$G_S = \frac{100}{\frac{W_1}{G_1} + \frac{W_2}{G_2} + \frac{W_3}{G_3} + \frac{W_4}{G_4}}$$

The proportion G_1, G_2, G_3 etc. are to be so fixed that minimum voids should be left in the aggregate mix and dense matrix should result. This can be done by triangular chart method or Rothfuch's method. To this aggregate mix, let us assume W_b is percent by weight of bitumen is added, V_b percentage of bitumen by volume

$$G_T = \text{Maximum specific gravity of mix} = \frac{100}{\frac{100 - W_b}{G_a} + \frac{W_b}{G_b}}$$

This is the maximum specific gravity, provided bitumen occupies all the void volume. If this does not occur, and G is actual specific gravity of mix then percent air voids in the specimen would be given by,

$$V_v = \text{Percent air voids} = \frac{100(G_T - G)}{G_T}$$

and the percent voids filled with bitumen will be given by (VFB) V.F.B. $= \dfrac{100 V_b}{100 - \dfrac{G}{W_a}}$, where

W_a is aggregate content percent by weight. Actually the attempt should be such that all the void volume in the aggregate mix should be occupied by bitumen leaving no air voids. This is impracticable. Another criteria is that bitumen percentage in the bitumen-aggregate mix should be such that the mix should have requisite strength and flexibility. To assess this and thus aid in finding out the bitumen content, tests have been devised. There are Marshall stability, Hubbard field method and Hueom method. We shall discuss these.

Marshall Method : This method and test is applicable to the hot-mix design of bitumen and aggregate with aggregate maximum size of 2.5 cm. For paving jobs the test is suitable. Essentially it consists of testing a 10.16 cm diameter 6.35 height cylindrical bitumen aggregate specimens. The load is peripheral. The load is applied at the rate of 5 cm/minute i.e. strain controlled and the Marshall stability value is the maximum load in kg before failure and the flow value is the deformation of specimen in 0.25 mm. units upto maximum load. To the first trial aggregate mix. which is heated to 175°C to 195°C, bitumen which is heated to 120° to 145° C should be added (say 5.5 to 4% by weight of material aggregate) thoroughly mixed at the desired temperature and moulded. The moulds should be cooled and then weighed in air and under submergence. Prior to testing these moulds should be heated to 60° + 1° for about 30 to 40 minutes and then tested peripherally. The suitable equipments such as heaters, tamper should be available. Sometimes one cannot get the exact height of 63.5 mm. In such a case, the Marshall stability value, obtained from such a not upto the mark specimen, is to be corrected with the help of the following table :

Table 5.30 : Correction Factors for Marshall Stability Value

Volume of Specimen in CCs	Thickness of Specimen	Correction Factor
457 – 470	57.1	1.19
471 – 482	58.7	1.14
483 – 495	60.3	1.09
496 – 508	61.9	1.04
509 – 522	63.5	1.00
523 – 535	65.1	0.96
535 – 546	66.7	0.93
547 – 559	68.3	0.89
560 – 573	69.9	0.86

Maintaining the aggregate percentage, we have to go on increasing the bitumen content in increments of 0.5 percent upto about 7.5 or 8.0 percent bitumen by weight of total mix. The percent air voids in the specimen (V_V) could be computed by $V_V = \dfrac{G_T - G_m}{G_m} \times 100$, where, G_T is specific gravity of mixture and G_m bulk density of specimen. Bulk density of specimen could be obtained since we have weighed the specimen in air and under submergence. Now, the graphs are plotted. These graphs generally are

(1) Percent bitumen against Marshall stability value,

(2) Bitumen percent against flow value,

(3) Bitumen percentage against unit weight,

(4) Bitumen percent against percent voids in total mix (V_V) and

(5) Bitumen percentage against percent voids filled with bitumen VFB.

The purpose of Marshall test is to find out optimum bitumen content so that the mix has the requisite strength (Marshall stability No.) and flexibility (i.e. the flow value). The optimum bitumen content for the mix design is the average value of the following three bitumen contents found from the graphs of the test results :

(1) Bitumen content corresponding to maximum stability,

(2) Bitumen content corresponding to maximum unit weight,

(3) Bitumen content corresponding to the median of designed limits of percent air voids in total mix (4%). For type of pavement, certain Marshall stability value and flow value are recommended. One can check-up whether the optimum binder content found out from testing is more or less as per these recommendations or not. If so, the aggregate percentage mix and optimum binder mix so found out is O.K. As an example the following table is provided. However, many such tables are available.

Table 5.31 : Marshall Mix Design for Bituminous Concrete

Test Property	Recommended Value
Marshall stability (kg)	340 (minimum)
Flow value, 0.25 mm units	8 to 16
Air voids in total mix. V_V%	3 to 5
Voids filled with bitumen VFB%	75 to 85

Modified Hubbard : Field method of bituminous mix design. Though developed initially to design sheet asphalt mix, now it can be used with modifications to design bituminous mixes having coarse aggregate upto 19 mm size. The principle of the test is to prepare aggregate bitumen mould 15.24 cm diameter 6 to 87 cm height.

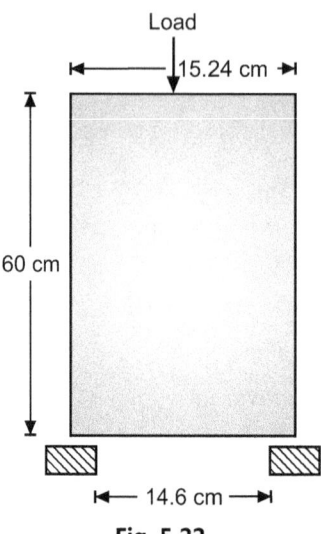

Fig. 5.22

This specimen is extruded through a ring of 14.6 cm diameter under load. The load that is required to do this is known as Hubbard - Field stability. The other graphs are same as in Marshall stability test. Test therefore would consist of :

(1) Preparation of Specimen : Aggregate in the desired proportions and the bituminous material are heated to the prescribed temperature and placed in preheated mould and tamped by 30 blows on each side. Static load of 4536 kg is applied for two minutes and specimen cooled to 37.8°C under same compressive load. Specimen is now removed, weighed and measured.

(2) Now the specimen is tested at 60° C under the rate of deformation of 6.1 cm/minute. It should be remembered that whereas one end of the specimen is loaded, the other end rests on ring of 14.6 cm. and the sample is getting extruded through this ring. The maximum load recorded is the stability value. The experiment is repeated with different bitumen content and the graphs that are plotted are : (i) Stability versus bitumen content, (ii) Unit weight versus bitumen content, (iii) Percent void in total mix versus the bitumen content, (iv) Percent aggregate voids versus bitumen content.

To determine optimum binder content the first step is to find bitumen content corresponding to 3 to 3.5 percent air voids in the total mix. For this bitumen content read the stability number from the graph. Certain values of stability number have been prescribed as shown in the table below :

Table 5.32 : Recommended Stability Number

Property	Medium and Light Traffic	Heavy and Very Heavy Traffic
Stability kg	545 – 910	7510
Voids, total mix.%	2 – 5	2 – 6

If the stability value is within specified limit, the mix is satisfactory. Otherwise change aggregate percentage and repeat the tests i.e. redesign. The final selection should depend upon economics and strength.

Comparison between Hubbard and Marshall Test : The most important aspect in Marshall test is peripheral load which is applied and flow value is recorded. Whereas in the Hubbard test cylinder is subjected to compressive load on flat end, the other end being resting on extrusion ring. Therefore, the sample is being extruded under compressive load. No flow value is observed. But there is large similarity in design methods since it is done through graphs.

Hueom Method of Bituminous Mix Design : This method consists of conducting two tests on bituminous mix : (1) stabilometer test and (2) cohesometer test. Stabilometer test is akin to triaxial test, whereas cohesometer test is akin to direct shear test. For stabilometer test, we have test specimen of 10 cm diameter and 6.25 cm height of specified mix. We generally prepare three specimen having same aggregate mix but binder content 0.5 to 1.0 percent above and 0.5 to 1.0 percent below the estimated binder content. The specimen are prepared at 110°C using kneading compactor. These specimens are now cooled at room temperature for one hour and placed in water pan for 24 hour for possible swell measurements. After the swell measurement the specimen is to be tested at 60°C in the stabilometer. The confining pressure applied is 0.35 kg/cm², vertical loads are then applied in the sequence of 227, 454 and in increments of 454 kg upto a maximum of 2722 kg. Due to application of vertical load, confining pressure may change, which is now reset to 0.35 kg/cm². The confining pressure is now increased to 7 kg/cm². The confining pressure is set by rotation of handle and number of turns of handle directly gives displacement of specimen. The specimen from the stabilometer test is now recovered and subjected to cohesiometer test. Of course before subjecting the sample to cohesometer test, it should be maintained at 60°C for two hours. Cohesometer test is direct shear test. The actuating load is being provided by lead shots. The stabilometer resistance value R and cohesometer value C can be computed by

$$C = \frac{L}{W(0.2H + 0.0176H^2)} \quad \text{and} \quad R = 100 - \frac{100}{\frac{2.5}{D_2}\left(\frac{P_v}{P_h} - 1\right) + 1}$$

where,

C = Cohesometer value.

L = Weight of shots (lead) in gms.

W = Diameter or width of specimen in cm.

H = Height of specimen in cm.

For stabilometer value R,

P_v = Vertical pressure applied.

P_h = Horizontal pressure transmitted at this P_h.

D_2 = Displacement of stabilometer fluid necessary to increase the fluid pressure from 0.7 to 7.0 kg/cm² measured in number of revolutions of calibrated pump handle.

For different types of traffic, the recommended values of these parameters are given below :

Table 5.33

Test Value	Criteria		
	High Traffic	Medium Traffic	Heavy Traffic
Stabilometer value R	> 30	> 35	> 37
Cohesometer value C	> 50	> 50	> 50
Swell mm	< 0.76	< 0.76	< 0.76
Air void present	> 4	> 4	> 4

SOLVED EXAMPLES

Example 5.1 : The following data refer to observation taken for angularity number

(1) Size of aggregate = 20 mm – 16 mm.

(Passing through 20 mm and retained on 16 mm)

(2) Specific gravity of aggregate = 2.856 = G_A.

(3) Weight of water required to fill the metal cylinder = 3000 gms = C.

(4) Weight of aggregate required to fill the cylinder = W = 3880 gms.

Find angularity number.

Solution :

$$\text{Angularity number} = 67 - \frac{100 \times W}{C \times G_A}$$

$$= 67 - \frac{100 \times 3880}{2.856 \times 3000}$$

$$= 67 - \frac{100 \times 3880}{2.856 \times 3000}$$

$$= 21.71 \qquad \ldots \text{Ans.}$$

Example 5.2 : For aggregate passing 40 mm and retained on 10 mm, following observations were taken

(i) Weight of basket = 110 gm.
(ii) Weight of basket + sample = 960 gm.
(iii) Weight of saturated surface dry sample = 1310 gm.
(iv) Weight of oven-dried sample = C = 1280 gm.

Find specific gravity, apparent specific gravity and water absorption.

Solution : Weight of sample in water = 960 − 110 = 850 gm

(1) Specific gravity $= \dfrac{1280}{1310 - 850}$

$= 2.78$ ... **Ans.**

(2) Apparent specific gravity $= \dfrac{1280}{1280 - 850} = 2.976$ ... **Ans.**

(3) Water absorption $= \dfrac{1310 - 1280}{1280} \times 100$

$= 2.34\%$ ... **Ans.**

Example 5.3 : From the following observations, determine water absorption, specific gravity and apparent specific gravity.

Size of aggregates 10 mm to 4.57 mm
(1) Weight of pycnometer + water = 1380 gm = C.
(2) Weight of pycnometer + water + sample = B = 1705 gm.
(3) Weight of pycnometer = 540 gm.
(4) Weight of ovendried sample = 495 gm = D.
(5) Weight of saturated surface-dried sample = 506 gm = A.

Solution :

(1) Applied specific gravity $= \dfrac{495}{495 - (1705 - 1380)}$

$= 2.911$ ... **Ans.**

Weight of saturated surface-dried sample = 506 gm

(2) Water absorption $= \dfrac{506 - 495}{495} \times 100$

$= 2.22\%$ ... **Ans.**

(3) Specific gravity $= \dfrac{495}{506 - (1705 - 1380)} = 2.734$ ... **Ans.**

Review Questions

1. Explain the procedure involved in aggregate crushing valve.
2. What are various test carried out on bitumen? Explain any one briefly?
3. What are various test carried out on soil? Explain any one briefly?
4. What are various test carried out on aggregates? Explain any one briefly?
5. Discuss various tests on aggregates for their stability.
6. Define terms (i) Flakiness Index (ii) Elongation Index, and also state the importance of that.
7. Write short notes on :
   (a) Bitumen and tar.
   (b) Impact test on aggregates.
   (c) CBR.
   (d) Plate load test.
   (e) Flakiness index test.
   (f) Angularity number test.
   (g) Specific gravity, porosity and water absorption.
   (h) Aggregate crushing value test.
   (i) Los-angeles abrasion.
   (j) Aggregate impact.
   (k) Aggregate polishing and stripping test.
   (l) Viscosity Test.
   (m) Fire and flash point test.

CHAPTER 6
CONSTRUCTION OF ROADS

6.1 SOIL STABILIZATION

Soil stabilization is a way of improving the weight bearing capabilities and performance of in-situ sub-soils, sands, and other waste materials in order to strengthen road surfaces. The prime objective of soil stabilization is to improve the California Bearing Ratio of in-situ soils by 4 to 6 times. The other prime objective of soil stabilization is to improve on-site materials to create a solid and strong sub-base and base courses. In certain regions of the world, typically developing countries and now more frequently in developed countries, soil stabilization is being used to construct the entire road

Earth road constructed will wear out very soon and will become unserviceable within no time. Constant repair of earth roads in villages is also not practicable. Hence to reduce the headache of maintenance and to keep the road in serviceable condition for the major part of the year, stabilized earth road should be constructed. Soil stabilization is defined as the process of treating a soil in such a manner so to improve or alter its physical conditions or properties so that it may become more stable and durable. The soil so stabilized may from the sub-grade or wearing layer of a road.

6.1.1 Objective of Stabilization

- To increase compressive strength irrespective of moisture content.
- To increase resistance to softening action of water.
- To reduce shrinkage due to withdrawal of moisture, and swelling due to wetting.
- To increase flexibility to take the wheel load without deformation and cracking
- To increase shear-strength and resistance to punching

6.1.2 Methods Of Soil Stabilization

Following are the different methods of soil stabilization :
1. Mechanical stabilization
2. Cement stabilization
3. Lime stabilization
4. Bituminous stabilization
5. Chemical stabilization
6. Grouting
7. Electrical stabilization
8. Complex stabilization

1. Mechanical Stabilization

Under this category, soil stabilization can be achieved through physical process by altering the physical nature of native soil particles by either induced vibration or compaction or by incorporating other physical properties such as barriers and nailing. Mechanical stabilization is not the main subject of this review and will not be further discussed.

2. Cement Stabilization

Cement is a binding material. When mixed with soil, if forms a sort of low strength concrete in which the soil acts as aggregate and cement as matrix. So the soil is excavated to a depth of nearly 15 cm and 8 to 12 % of cement is mixed. Sufficiently quantity of water is then added and the soil-cement mixture is compacted properly by road stabilizer. After it has been compacted it is then cured for about 7 to 8 days by similarly sprinkling water over it.

The Advantages of Cement Stabilization are Several

- Cement stabilization increases base material strength and stiffness, which reduces deflections due to traffic loads. This delays surface distress such as fatigue cracking and extends pavement structure life.
- Cement stabilization provides uniform, strong support, which results introduction stresses to the sub-grade. Testing indicates a thinner cement-stabilized layer can reduce stresses more effectively than a thicker un-stabilized layer of aggregate. This reduces sub-grade failure, pothole formation and rough pavement surfaces.
- Cement stabilized bases have greater moisture resistance to keep water out; this maintains higher strength for the structure.
- Cement stabilization reduces the potential for pumping of sub-grade fines.
- Cement stabilized base spreads loads and reduces sub-grade stress.
- The cement stabilization roads are water tight, require less maintenance and are very suitable for light traffic.

3. Lime Stabilization

In this case the process of stabilization is similar to that of cement stabilization. The soil is loosened, pulverized, sieved and mixed with 5 to 10 % by weight of hydrated lime. The two are thoroughly mixed. Sufficient quantity of water is added and the surface is compacted. The lime helps in reducing the shrinkage and swelling of soil. It is suitable for clay predominant soil.

4. Bitumen Stabilization

Soil stabilization with bitumen can be done with either of two additives. Depending upon project conditions, the choice is made between using an asphalt emulsion and using foamed bitumen as the additive. For example, extremely wet soil conditions might dictate the use of foamed bitumen rather than a standard asphalt emulsion to compensate for the high field moisture content. Emulsion might be chosen for projects where high-performance emulsions are readily available are practical considerations for stabilization with bitumen, just as with other construction activities.

5. Chemical Stabilization

Under this category, soil stabilization depends mainly on chemical reactions between stabilizer (cementations material) and soil minerals (pozzolanic materials) to achieve the desired effect. A chemical stabilization method is the fundamental of this review and, therefore, throughout the rest of this report, the term soil stabilization will mean *chemical stabilization*.

6.2 GRAVEL ROAD

A gravel road is a type of unpaved road surfaced with gravel that has been brought to the site from a quarry or stream bed. Gravel can be obtained from the river beds or by crushing the stone. The surface layer of gravel roads consists of 6 to 36 mm size gravel mixed with sand and clay. It works as binder. The function of binder is to fill up the voids and bind the particles of gravel.

The sub-grade is prepared and properly compacted. Proper camber and gradient is given to the sub-grade surface. The mixture of gravel, earth and sand is spread on the sub-grade, in a thickness which varies from 15 cm to 30 cm according to the requirement of the traffic. The layer of gravel is rolled by tandem rollers. During the process of rolling proper camber and gradient is maintained. The gravel is generally spread in two layers. During rolling some water is sprinkled on the surface. Gravel roads may be constructed either trench or father type as shown Fig 6.1 a and b

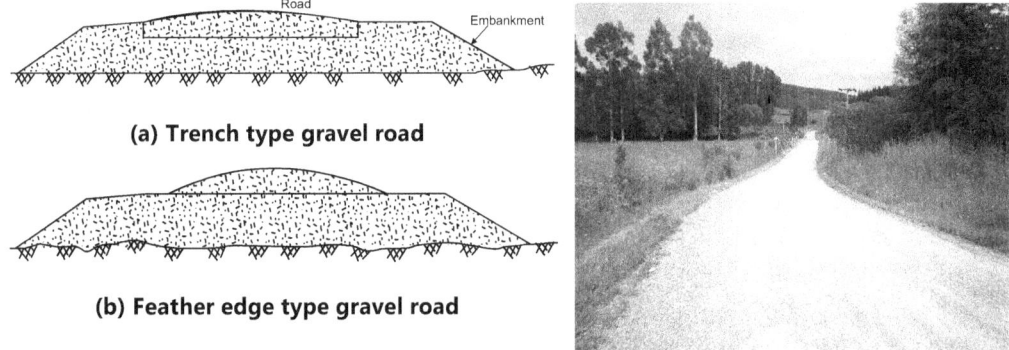

(a) Trench type gravel road

(b) Feather edge type gravel road

Fig. 6.1   Fig. 6.2

Trench type gravel roads are more common in India. In the feather type gravel roads, the gravel is spread on the formation directly without excavating a trench. The surface drainage in the gravel roads should be very efficient, so that the surface must not be worn out by water. Periodic repairs are necessary to maintain proper camber and gradient.

6.3 WATER BOUND MACADAM ROAD

These are very important roads in the Indian context. W.B.M. road as base was good, the total road structure would be good, and hence it's importance. Water bound macadam generally consists of clean crushed coarse aggregates mechanically interlocked by rolling and voids thereof filled with screening and binding material with the assistance of water (hence the name water bound) laid on prepared sub-grade, sub-base, base or even existing pavement as the case may be. Therefore, water bound macadam could be used as sub-base, base course or surfacing coarse. The crushed or broken stone that is to be embodied in W.B.M. should be hard durable, free from dirt and flat elongated soft particles. The properties of the aggregate for the type of construction are suggested in the table below.

Table 6.1 : Requirements of Coarse Aggregates for Water Bound Macadam

Type of Construction	Test and Test Method	Requirement	Remarks
1. Sub-base	Los-Angeles Abrasion or Aggregate impact value	Max 60 % Max 50 %	Aggregate should satisfy either of the two tests
2. Base course with bituminous surfacing	Loss Angeles Abrasion value Aggregate impact value Flakiness Index	Max 50 % Max 40 % Max 15 %	Aggregate like brick metal, Kankar and laterite should be wet tested for aggregate impact
3. Surface course	Los Angeles Abrasion value Aggregate impact value Flakiness Index	Max 40 % Max 30 % Max 15 %	

In addition or alternative to aggregate, one can use laterite, Kankar, overburnt bricks or crushed slag laterite rock aggregates. When used these should be hard compact, heavy and it's origin should not be light coloured sandy laterites. Kankar when used should be tough, free of clay and should have opalescent (blue-like) fracture if broken. Similarly, overburnt brick metal should be free from dust and other foreign matter. Crushed slag such as the air cooled blast furnace slag should not weigh less than 1120 kg/m^3 and percentage of glossy material in it should not be in excess of 20. Water absorption of the slag should not exceed ten percent. Slag having these parameters would generally be free from soft pieces, dirt and objectionable material. In India, the emphasis is on using aggregate derived from basalt or granite especially in southern India.

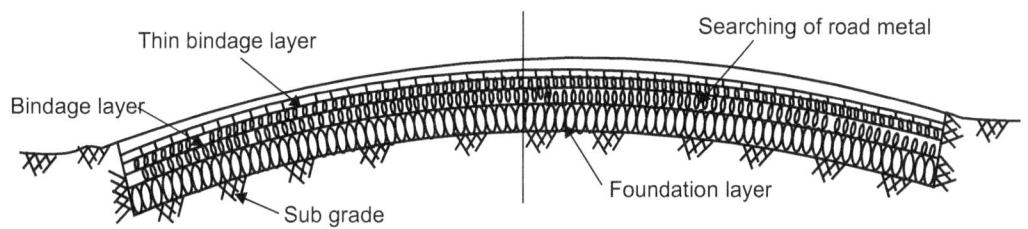

Fig. 6.3

Size and grading requirements of coarse aggregate. This is given in the table below with requisite remarks.

Table 6.2 : Size and Grading Requirements of Coarse Aggregates in W.B.M.

Grading No.	Size Range	The Actual Grading sieve no.	Percent by Weight Passing the Sieve	Remarks
1.	90 mm to 40 mm	100 mm	100	Suitable for sub-base course only and not tenable for compacted layer thickness less than 90 mm
		80 mm	65 – 85	
		63 mm	25 – 60	
		40 mm	0 – 15	
		20 mm	0 – 5	
2.	63 mm to 40 mm	80 mm	100	The grading no. 1, 2 and 3 are not strictly enforceable in case of brick, Kankar and laterite
		63 mm	90 – 100	
		50 mm	35 – 70	
		40 mm	0 – 15	
		20 mm	0 – 5	
3.	50 mm to 20 mm	63 mm	100	In that case, the grading should be as near to the grading specified
		50 mm	95 – 100	
		40 mm	35 – 70	
		20 mm	0 – 10	
		10 mm	0 – 5	

Screenings : Screenings should be derived from the same rock, from which aggregate is derived. If this is not possible, predominantly non-plastic material such as Kankar, murum, can also be utilized. The liquid limit and plasticity index of such material should be below 20 and 6 respectively and fraction passing 75 micron should not exceed 10 %. The grading requirement of screenings along with requisite remarks are given in the table below.

Table 6.3 : Grading Requirements of Screenings for W.B.M.

Grading No.	Size of Screenings	Sieve no.	Percent by Weight Passing	Remarks
A.	12.5 mm	12.5 mm	100	Screenings A should be used with grading No. 1 of coarse aggregate whereas B grading screening should be used with grading 2 of coarse aggregate. For murum gravel sceening, these gradings are not binding.
		10 mm	90 – 100	
		4.75 mm	10 – 30	
		150 micron	0 – 8	
B.	10 mm	10 mm	100	
		4.75 mm	85 – 100	
		150 micron	10 – 30	

Binding Material : Binding material should be fine grained material of plasticity index 4 to 9. When W.B.M. is base coarse with bituminous surfacing, limestone dust or Kankar nodules could be binding material. Binding material is not a 'must' when the screenings are of crushable material such as murum or gravel. However, when W.B.M. is a surface course and plasticity index of crushable screenings less than 4, one will be required to add binding material of P.I. 4 to 9 to it.

Quantities of Materials : For guidance of quantities of materials required for W.B.M. construction, the following tables are given

Table 6.4 : Quantities of Coarse Aggregate and Screenings Required for 100 mm Compacted Thickness of W.B.M. of 10 m²

Coarse Aggregate		Screenings			
		Stone Screenings		Crushable Screenings as Murum or Gravel	
Grading 1 90 ± 40 mm	Loose quantity 1.21 to 1.43 m³	Type A 12.5 mm	Loose quantity 0.4 to 0.44 m³	Not uniform	Loose quantity 0.44 to 0.47 m³

Coarse Aggregate and Screenings required for 75 mm compacted thickness of W.B.M. base/surface course for 10 m².

Table 6.5

Aggregate		Screenings				
		Stone screenings			Crushable Screenings as Moorum or Gravel	
Grading 2 Size 63 to 40 mm	Loose Quantity 0.91 to 1.07 m³	Type A 12.5 mm	W.B.M. Surface Course	W.B.M. Base Course	Non-uniform	All Cases
			0.14 to 0.17 m³	0.18 to 0.21 m³	do	0.33 to 0.35 m³

...Cont.

do	do	Type B 9 mm	0.24 to 0.26 m³	0.30 to 0.33 m³	do	do
Gradings 50 to 20 mm	do	Type B 9 mm	0.22 to 0.24 m³	0.27 to 0.30 m³	do	do

It is clear from the above table that larger quantities of binding material are recommended when W.B.M. is to act as surface course. The above table can be used as guide for estimation purposes.

Construction Procedure

- The layer that is sub-base, sub-grade, or base, which is to receive W.B.M. should be cleaned of all dirt, dust and any soft yielding spots that might be there should be rolled till firm.
- If W.B.M. is to be laid on existing unsurfaced road say earth road, the road surface should be scarified first and weak spots rolled. Where the existing road surface is black topped, 50 mm × 50 mm furrows shall be cut in the existing surface at 1 metre intervals at 45 degrees to the centre line of carriageway.
- After treating the layer which is to receive W.B.M. in the above said manner, this layer should be prepared to the required grade and camber.
- Now before we start W.B.M. construction by laying the coarse aggregate, necessary arrangements should be made for lateral confinement of aggregate.
- We can construct side shoulders in advance to a thickness corresponding to the compacted layer of W.B.M. The inside edges of such shoulders should be trimmed vertical and clean cut.
- However, the practice of constructing W.B.M. in a trench section excavated in the finished formation should be avoided.
- Now, the coarse aggregate could be spread uniformly and evenly in required quantities from the stock piles that are arranged on the sides or directly from the vehicles. Aggregate should not be dumped in heaps directly.
- By using templates about 6 metres apart, these aggregates should be spread to a proper profile. It is preferable to use mechanical devices rather than mannual methods.
- Compacted layers of W.B.M. should not be more than 75 mm. The spreading of the coarse aggregate at a stretch could be three days rolling work. Depending upon the type of coarse aggregate, one can choose, three wheel power roller for rolling.
- Rolling begins from the edges, with roller running forward and backward until the edges are compacted. The roller should then progress gradually from the edges towards the centre, parallel to the centre line of the road, uniformly lapping each preceeding rear wheel track by one half width.

- When partial compaction of aggregates with sufficient air voids is achieved, rolling is stopped for application of screenings.
- In case of crushable aggregate, where screenings are not applied, compaction could be continued until the aggregates are nicely keyed together with no creeping of stones ahead of the roller. One may add water for rolling.
- For superelevated portions of the road, rolling commences from the lower edge and progress gradually towards the upper edge of the pavement.
- When the sub-grade is soft, aggregates should be added right in the first so as to make it unyielding before we add main course of the coarse aggregate.
- If there are depressions in the sub-grade, these should be made-up by coarse aggregate and not by screenings.
- After the rolling of the coarse aggregate to grade and camber, we add screenings gradually to fill the interstices when screenings are spread, we dry roll, so that the jarring effect of roller causes screenings to settle into the voids of coarse aggregate.
- Screenings are to be applied in thin layers by spreading motion of hand shovels, mechanical spreaders or from trucks.
- Every application of screening (minimum 3) should be accompanied by rolling and brooming, spreading, rolling and brooming of screenings shall be taken-up on sections which can be completed, within one day operation. The object of rolling, brooming etc. is to fill the voids with screening. However, damp and wet screenings should not be used.
- After screenings are applied, the surface is copiously sprinkled with water, swept and rolled. Hand brooming operation is conducted on wet screenings so that these occupy the voids evenly. Sprinkling, sweeping and rolling to be continued and additional screenings applied until the coarse aggregate are well bound and firmly set and a grout of screenings and water form ahead of the wheels of the rollers. Water should be so added that there is no damage to shoulders. In sufficient or excess water is bad.
- Now the binding material, where necessary can be added at a uniform and slow rate in two or more successive thin layers. After each application of binding material, surface to be copiously sprinkled with water and resulting slurry swept by hand/mechanical brooms, so that it goes in voids and works as binding material.
- Now, 6 - 10 tonnes roller rolls the formations, water being applied to the wheels to wash down the binding material that may get struck to them. The spreading of binding material sprinkling of water, sweeping with brooms and rolling should continue until the slurry of binding material and water forms a wave a head of the wheels of moving roller.
- After these operations are over, the road should be allowed to cure overnight. The next day, the road should be inspected and weak spots filled with screenings or binding material.

6.4 BITUMINOUS ROADS

Bituminous pavements are composed of a mixture of bitumen and/or tar and mineral aggregates. Due to greater demand of cement in large number of projects in recent years, in India greater percentage of roads that exist today is Black Top. All the state P.W.D.'s, central P.W.D.'s and other agencies at present use mostly the bituminous materials for the surfacing of roads. Various types of bituminous pavements having thickness ranging between 0.75 cm to as high as 15 to 22 cm have been developed. When properly used and constructed, these pavements have long and economic lives. They serve the following main functions :

- Provide smooth and good riding surface;
- Provide high resistance to surface wear;
- Provide skid resistant surface;
- Protect the underlying layer and sub-grade from detrimental actions of water and other natural agencies i.e., it seals the ingress of rain water.

6.4.1 Types of Bituminous Pavements

Based on methods of construction, bituminous pavements can be classified under the following categories :

(1) Surface Treatments : They include :
- Prime coat,
- Tack coat,
- Surface dressing, and
- Seal coat.

(2) Grouted or Penetration Macadam : They include :
- Semi-grouted macadam, and
- Fully-grouted macadam.

(3) Road Mix Surfaces : They include :
- Open graded mixes,
- Dense graded mixes, and
- Sand asphalt.

(4) High Type Bituminous Pavements : They include hot premixed surfaces. For example,
- Bituminous macadam,
- Bituminous concrete or asphaltic concrete,
- Sheet asphalt or rolled asphalt,
- Sand asphalt,
- Mastic asphalt, and
- Tar concrete.

Bituminous pavements can also be classified on the basis of mixing and construction techniques. They are :

(1) Road mix, and

(2) Central plant mix.

Choice of binder type e.g. straight run bitumen, tar, cut back or emulsion depends upon the type of the pavement, availability of materials and equipments, climatic condition etc.

The specifications for Road and Bridge works issued by the M.O.T. (Roads Wing) Government of India and published by Indian Roads Congress gives detailed specifications for the Single Coat Surface Dressing, Double Coat Surface Dressing, 20 mm open Graded Premixed Carpet, Mixed Seal Surfacing, Built up Spray Grout Base Courses, Bituminous Bound Macadam base/binder Courses Semi-dense Carpet and Bituminous Concrete. These bituminous courses are roughly in ascending order of superiority for their use in road construction.

Fig. 6.4

Fig. 6.5

6.4.2 Surface Treatments

These are the works carried out to alter the qualities of a wearing surface. The different types of surface treatments are briefly described below :

Prime Coat : This consists of application of a low viscosity cut back e.g. RC-0, MC-1 or SC-1 as primers on an existing base of previous texture like WBM base. The various functions of a prime coat are:

- It plugs capillary voids and water proofs the existing base.
- It coats and blends dust and loose particles thereby hardening and toughening the surface.
- It provides adhesion between new and old surface.
- It serves as a table for road mix paving jobs.

Tack Coat : It is a treatment which is given to the under side of a surface or some other course to bind the previously prepared layer to the superimposed layer. It involves a simple single application of a bituminous binder for example, a bitumen emulsion, a cut back or a low viscosity tar to a previously prepared surface. They are commonly used when a new wearing surface is to be placed on an old bituminous surfacing, or on new or old concrete pavement, or on a brick, stone or black pavement, or on a primed granular base course.

The surface on which the tack coat is to be applied should be thoroughly swept and cleaned of dust and other foreign matters. The rate of spread of straight run bitumen may be 5 kg/10 m² area for an existing bitumen treated surface and 10 kg/10 m² area for an untreated WBM surface.

Surface Dressing : They normally consist of a layer of small aggregates such as chippings of stone, slag or gravel on a thin layer of binder which is freshly applied to an existing road surface. A surface dressing when provided on earth or gravel or WBM road, provides non-skid surface, improves night visibility, arrests disintegration and provides a clear demarcation between the carriage-way and the shoulders. It does not help in increasing the load carrying capacity but provides dust free and water proof surface normally, specifications suggested for use in surface dressing are single coat surface dressing, double coat surface dressing, and open graded premix carpet and mix-seal surfacing. Whereas, it is accepted that two coat surface dressing and 20 mm premixed carpet with seal coat are most commonly used specifications for light surfacing, the former consumes about 11 tonnes of bitumen for 1 km length of single lane road, the latter consumes about 13 tonnes of bitumen. Thus, a saving of nearly 15 % bitumen can be achieved if we go in for surface dressing rather than premixed carpet. For lighter traffic even one coat surface dressing may be sufficient, where suitably graded stone aggregates are available, mix-seal type of surfacing which requires some quantity of bitumen as two coat surface dressing should be preferred to 20 mm premixed carpet.

Construction Procedure : The surface dressing should consist of one or two coats, each consisting of a layer of bituminous binder sprayed on a prepared base followed by a cover of stone chippings. The surface dressing should be carried out only when the atmospheric temperature is above 16°C and the weather is dry and clear.

6.4.3 Materials

(1) Bitumen : The grade of the straight run bitumen is chosen depending upon the climatic conditions of the region in which surface dressing is to be constructed. In most parts of India 80/100 and 180/200 grade bitumen is used. Heavier grade cut backs, rapid setting emulsions or heavier grade tars may also be used. For single surface dressings on WBM base course, quantity of bitumen needed ranges from 17 to 195 kg per 10 m² area and 10 to 12 kg per 10 m² area in case of renewal of black top surfacing. For second coat of surface dressing, the quantity of bitumen needed ranges from 10 to 12 kg per 10 m² area.

Bulk bitumen lorries with tanks of capacity ranging from 5,000 to 15,000 litres are used to transport bulk bitumen.

(2) Aggregates : The stone chippings should consist of clean durable and uniform quality aggregates of following properties :

Table 6.6

Shape	Cubical
Los Angeles value	less than 35 %
Aggregate impact value	less than 30 %
Flakiness index value	less than 25 %
Water absorption	less than 1 %
Stripping	less than 25 %

The aggregates should also be free of elongated, flaky, soft pieces, salt, alkali vegetable matters and dust coatings. The quantity of aggregates used in first coat of surface dressing should be 0.15 m^3 per 10 m^2 area of 12 mm nominal size. On the other hand, the quantity of aggregate used in second coat of surface dressing should be 0.10 m^3 per 10 m^2 area and of 10 mm nominal size.

Preparation of Base : Before laying the surface dressing, it is essential to prepare the base in accordance with specified grade and cross-section. The prepared surface should also be thoroughly cleaned first with hard brushes, then with softer brushes and finally by blowing with gunny bags.

Application of Binder : Bitumen heated at 163 to 177°C is uniformly sprayed with the help of a mechanical sprayer or pouring can.

Application of Stone Chippings : Soon after the application of binder, the stone chippings are uniformly spread either by means of a mechanical gritter or manually with a twist of the basket containing the aggregates.

Rolling : Soon after the spreading of stone chippings, the entire surface should be rolled with a 8-10 tonne smooth wheeled roller. Rolling should start from the edges and progress towards the centre in such a way, so that each pass of the roller should uniformly overlap not less than one-third of the track made in the preceding pass. The rolling should continue till surface is firmly bedded.

Application of Second Coat : The second coat should be applied immediately after laying the first coat by method similar to the one as described above for single coat dressing. The surface should be checked with a 3 m straight edge for longitudinal profile and with a camber template for cross profile. The permitted tolerances of surface irregularities are 10 mm for longitudinal profile and 6 mm for cross profile. The road should not be open to traffic before 24 hrs.

Surface Dressing under Abnormal Conditions : Surface dressing can be laid even under abnormal conditions for example, cold and wet weather, steep grades and super elevations, etc. This involves additional expenditure and careful control. In hill roads, due to steep gradients abnormal shear stresses are created by gear changing while going upgrade and braking during down going. Binders of normal viscosity as used in plain regions will not be able to take these higher stresses. This necessitates using higher viscosity binders to hold the chippings on the hill roads.

The higher viscosity binder becomes viscous and will not allow proper penetration and wetting of aggregates. If lower viscosity binders like cut back with harder grade asphaltic cement is used, the binder flows down the grade when applied and will be in the form of a non-uniform film.

The various methods to overcome the above difficulties are :

(1) Using Heated Aggregates : In this method, the heated higher viscosity binder is spread, so that it can be applied in a thin film. As soon as it reaches the surface, it gets sufficiently hard to resist flow down the grade. To facilitate easy penetration and wetting of aggregates, pre-heated aggregates are spread on the binder film and lightly rolled. The heated aggregates will be able to soften the binder, penetrate and get coated easily.

(2) Use of Equipment : Equipment can be used for surface dressing on steep gradients, superelevation and cold weather conditions in most parts of the country under the prevailing cold weather conditions without deviating from the conventional method of construction.

(3) Use of Pre-coated Chippings : In this method, the pre-coated chippings with higher viscosity binder are spread on the surface and rolled when still warm. At high altitudes, when the air temperatures are very low, cut back bitumen may be used as the binding material.

(4) Use of Adhesive Agents : During wet weather, binder treated with adhesive agents for example, long chain amines or long chain aliphatic diamines or long chain amides should be used as a binding material for surface dressing.

Seal Coat : It is a final thin coat either over a previous bituminous pavement or over an existing worn out bituminous pavement. The main purposes of a seal coat are :
- To waterproof the surface.
- To provide a more desirable surface texture.
- To reduce slipperiness.
- To improve visibility.
- To build up pavement structure.

The seal coat can be of following two types :

Type I Seal Coat : It consists of an application of a layer of bituminous binder followed by a cover of stone chippings.

Type II Seal Coat : It consists of a premixed seal coat comprising of a thin application of aggregates premixed with bituminous binder.

Construction Procedure : In case of type I seal coat, the heated bitumen 9.8 kg per 10 m^2 area and 6 mm stone chippings 0.09 m^3 per 10 m^2 area are used in a manner similar to the one described for surface dressing. For the construction of type II seal coat, the preheated bitumen and aggregates mixed in a specified proportion are spread uniformly on the surface to be sealed. The quantity of aggregates (passing 1.7 mm sieve and retained on 180 micron sieve) to be utilized should be 0.06 m^3 per 10 m^2 area and bitumen 6.8 kg. per 10 m^3 area.

The mix after it has been spread uniformly on the bituminous surface to be sealed should be rolled with 6-9 tonne smooth-wheeled power rollers till a smooth uniform surface is obtained. The traffic may be allowed soon after final rolling, when the premixed material has cooled down to the surrounding temperature.

The quality control of work should be similar to the one described earlier for surface dressing.

6.4.4 Grouted or Penetration Macadam

This is a type of construction in which a bituminous binder is applied in a fluid state to partially compacted aggregate layer. When binder is allowed to penetrate to full depth, it is known as full grouted macadam and when it is allowed to penetrate half the depth, it is known as semi-grout macadam.

Full-grout macadam construction generally 5 to 8 cm thick is used in regions of very heavy rainfall. Semi-grout macadam construction generally 5 cm thick is used in regions of average rainfall and medium traffic.

Construction Procedure : Generally, grouted macadam consists of two layer composite construction of compacted crushed coarse aggregates with application of bituminous binder after each layer and key aggregates on the top of the second layer. This is also known built-up spray grout base course. This should be constructed only in dry weather when the atmospheric temperature is above 16°C.

Materials : The binder should be straight run bitumen of grade 80/100 or 60/70 or 30/40 of quantity 50 and 68 kg per 10 m^2 area for 5 cm and 7.5 cm compacted thickness respectively. Road tars i.e. RT-4 and cut backs can also be used.

Normally, the aggregates used are crushed stone or crushed gravel. They should be clean, cubical in shape, free of organic matters, hydrophobic and of low porosity. The various physical requirements of stone aggregates should be as follows :

Table 6.7

Shape	Cubical
Los Angeles value	Less than 50 %
Aggregate Impact value	Less than 40 %
Flakiness index value	Less than 25 %
Stripping value	Less than 25 %
Water absorption	Less than 1 %

The coarse aggregates and key aggregates required for 5 cm compacted thickness should be 0.60 m³ and 0.15 m³ per 10 m² area respectively. Their gradings should be as indicated in the table below :

Table 6.8

Sieve Size	Percent by Weight Passing the Sieve	
	Coarse Aggregate	Key Aggregate
50 mm	100	–
25 mm	35.70	–
20 mm	–	100
12.5 mm	0.15	35.70
4.75 mm	–	0.15
2.36 mm	0.5	0.5

The various construction operations for example, preparation of base, application of tack coat, spreading and rolling of aggregates for the first layer should be similar to the one as described earlier. Heated binder should be sprayed on aggregate layer at the rate of 12.5 kg/10 m² in a uniform manner with the help of mechanical sprayers. Soon after the first application of binder, the second layer of coarse aggregates should be spread and rolled. Again, the second aggregates layer should be given a binder spray at the rate of 12.5 kg/10 m² area. Immediately, after the application of binder, key aggregates should be spread uniformly at the rate of 0.13 m³/10 m². The surface should then be rolled with a 8 - 10 tonne smooth wheeled roller till the key aggregates are firmly in position. The road surface should be open to traffic after 24 hours.

6.4.5 Road Mix Surface

In this type of construction, the binder and aggregates are mixed on the top of an existing surface or a base. If the aggregates used are of uniform size, then the road mix is known as open graded mix. In dense graded mix, the aggregates used are well graded. In case of mix in place sand asphalt construction, the naturally occurring sand is mixed with liquid asphalt to form the wearing surface. The road mix surfaces are suitable for light to moderate traffic conditions, on old or new bases. These mixes have got following advantages over penetration macadam :

- Saving in quantity of bitumen,
- Better coating of aggregates, and
- Increased stability.

6.4.6 High Type Bituminous Pavements

These types of pavements use central plant mix for its construction. The various high type of bituminous pavements using premixed aggregates described in this chapter are bituminous macadam, bituminous concrete and mastic asphalt.

Bituminous Macadam or Bitumen Bound Macadam : This consists of a single construction 5 cm or 7.5 cm thick of compacted crushed aggregates premixed with a bituminous binder. This type of construction utilizes quite flexible gradation control and provides an economical and strong base course.

It has been established that a thinner section of bitumen bound macadam is equivalent to a thicker section of WBM or gravel base course section. This is because of the fact that the load distribution through the bitumen bound macadam is comparatively on a wider area and the surface is more resistant to deformation.

Bitumen bound macadam can be advantageously used in snow bound hilly terrain, regions of high ground water table and in areas where medium type of aggregates are available.

Construction Procedure: Bitumen bound macadam should be laid during dry weather only. Before actual construction, the base should be prepared, shaped and conditioned to a specified grade and cross-section. The prepared surface should be thoroughly cleaned and made free from dust.

Materials : The various binders used are : straight run bitumen, road tar, cut back or emulsion.

The straight run bitumen grade 30/40 or 60/70 or 80/100 is chosen depending upon the climatic conditions. The quantity of the bitumen needed depends upon the grading adopted in the design.

The crushed stone aggregates to be used should be clean strong, durable, cubical in shape, hydrophobic, low porosity and free from organic and other deleterious matters. The various physical requirements of aggregates should be as shown below :

Table 6.9

Shape	Cubical
Los Angeles Value	less than 35 %
Aggregate impact value	less than 30 %
Flakiness index value	less than 25 %
Stripping	less than 25 %
Water absorption	less than 1 %

The aggregate gradings both for 7.5 cm and 5 cm thick bitu-minous macadam should confirm to the followings.

The binder content for premixing generally varies from 3 to 4.5 % for grading I and grading II and 3.5 to 6 % for grading III. As per Asphalt Institute classification, 5 cm and 7.5 cm bitumen bound macadam falls under open mix type category. Marshall and Hubbard field methods of mix design are considered unsuitable for such type of mixes. Even though the Hveem's method is listed as doubtful by the Asphlt Institute for this type of mixture, this method of mix design is adopted for determination of optimum bitumen content to obtain the laboratory mix design.

Table 6.10 : Aggregate Grading for 50 cm Compacted Thickness of Bitumen Bound Macadam

Sieve Size	Percent by Weight Passing the Sieve		
	Grading I	Grading II	Grading III
63 mm	–	–	–
50 mm	100	100	–
40 mm	–	90 - 100	–
25 mm	37 - 70	50 - 80	100
20 mm	–	–	70 - 100
12.5 mm	0 - 15	10 - 30	–
10 mm	–	–	35 - 60
4.75 mm	–	–	15 - 35
2.36 mm	0 - 5	–	5 - 20
0.075 mm	0 - 3	0 - 5	0 - 4

Table 9.11 : Aggregate Grading for 7.5 cm Compacted Thickness of Bitumen Bound Macadam

Sieve Size	Percent by Weight Passing the Sieve		
	Grading I	Grading II	Grading III
63 mm	100	–	100
50 mm	90 - 100	–	100
40 mm	35 - 65	100	100
25 mm	20 - 40	70 - 100	70 - 100
20 mm	–	50 - 80	50 - 80
12.5 mm	5 - 20	–	–
10 mm	–	–	25 - 50
4.75 mm	–	10 - 30	10 - 30
2.36 mm	–	5 - 20	5 - 20
75 micron	0 - 5	0 - 5	–

It is essential to lay a tack coat over the base before laying bitumen bound macadam construction. The quantity of binder for tack coat should be 5.0 to 7.5 kg per 10 m^2 for bituminous base and 7.5 to 10 kg per 10 m^2 for untreated WBM layer.

Preparation of Mix : In a hot mix plant, the bitumen and aggregates are separately heated to a temperature in the range of 155 –163°C and 150 –177°C respectively. At no time the difference in temperature between the aggregates and bitumen should exceed 14 C. The mixing is so through, so that a homogeneous mixture is obtained in which all particles of the aggregates are coated uniformly. The mixture is carried to the site through vehicle or a wheel barrow. For small premix work and in places where mixing plant is not available hand operated drum mixer should be used.

List of Equipments for thin Premix Carpet and Bituminous Macadam :

(1) Drying and mixing unit.
(2) Bitumen boiler (preferably oil fired with pressure burner).
(3) Chain pulley arrangement for lifting of drums.
(4) Road roller (8-10 tonnes).
(5) Bitumen sprayer with spray-bar or spraying cans with 18 litres capacity.
(6) Buckets (G.I. sheets) 6 to 12 litres capacity.
(7) Spring balance (10 kg).
(8) Baskets (lined with gunny cloth).
(9) Wire brushes.
(10) Coir brushes.
(11) Gunny bags (old).
(12) Empty drums or G I. sheet tanks for storage of water (200 litres capacity).
(13) Spades.
(14) Rakes (big).
(15) Rakes (small) with long handles for levelling of mix.
(16) Templates.
(17) Camber board.
(18) Straight-edge (3 metres).
(19) Measuring Tape.
(20) Thermometers (dial type, mercury in steel, distant reading 0°C-250°C).
(21) Wheel barrow.
(22) Shovels.
(23) Gum boots.
(24) Hammer cutter for opening of bitumen drums.
(25) Angle iron or wooden strips of required dimensions for edges.
(26) Road barriers.
(27) Diversions boards.
(28) Red lamps.
(29) 30 and 15 litre capacity containers for checking quantity of aggregates.

Spreading : The mix should be spread immediately after mixing by means of a self-propelled mechanical paver with suitable screeds capable of spreading, tamping and finishing the mix. The temperature of the mix at the time of laying should be maintained in the range of 121-163°C.

Rolling : Soon after the spreading of the mix the rolling is done with 8 to 10 tonnes tandem roller. The rolling is commenced from the edges of the pavement and progressed towards the centre and uniform overlapping is provided. The roller wheels should be kept damp to avoid the bituminous material from sticking to the wheels The pavement surface should be checked and may be permitted 10 mm and 6 mm tolerances of surface regulating in longitudinal and cross profile respectively.

Built-up spray grout can be structurally equated to Bituminous Macadam (with an equivalency factor of 1 : 1.5. This implies that, whereas the quantity of bitumen required for a 50 mm thick. Bituminous Macadam Course is about 19 tonnes per 1 km length of a single lane road, the quantity of bitumen required for a structurally Equivalent layer of 75 mm built-up spray grout is only 13 tonnes involving a saving of bitumen of nearly 50 %.

Bituminous Concrete or Asphaltic Concrete : This is an intimate mixture of coarse aggregate, fine aggregates, mineral filler and bitumen. This hot mix, hot laid construction is probably the most stable and durable bituminous road mixture in India. This is also a dense, impervious, waterproof construction suitable for the most heavily travelled roads. It possesses considerable mechanical strength and this makes it to withstand high stresses without causing undue strain in the upper layer of the pavement structure. It has been found that unit thickness of bituminous concrete layer is Equivalent to three times thick crushed stone layer and four times thick sand-gravel layer. Bituminous concrete is normally used as the wearing course on the major roads- and very often also as base course.

As per Asphalt Institute, Maryland, USA. the bituminous concrete construction should be done in two layers i.e. binder course and wearing course. The different thickness requirement for various traffic conditions are given below :

Table 6.12

Traffic	Thickness Requirement		
	Binder Course	Wearing Course	Total
Light	–	5 cm	5 cm
Medium to heavy	4 to 5 cm	4 to 2.5 cm	8 cm
Very heavy	6 to 8 cm	4 to 2.5 cm	10 cm

Asphaltic concrete mix is designed on the basis of stability and durability considerations. The mix should meet the following requirements :

Table 6.13

Sr. No.	Description	Requirements
1.	Marshall stability, determined on Marshall specimens compacted by 50 compaction blows on each end.	227 kg
2.	Marshall flow value (0.1 mm units).	20 - 45
3.	Per cent voids in mix.	3 - 5
4.	Per cent voids in mineral aggregate filled with bitumen.	75 - 85
5.	Binder content per cent by weight of mix.	5 - 7.5

Construction Procedure : Bituminous concrete should be laid during dry weather conditions only.

Materials :

(1) **Binder :** The straight-run bitumen grade 30/40 or 60/70 or 80/100 is chosen depending upon the climatic conditions. The quantity of bitumen needed varies from 5.0 to 7.5 % by weight of mix.

(2) **Coarse Aggregates :** The crushed coarse aggregates to be used should be clean, strong, durable, cubical in shape, hydrophobic, of low porosity and free of organic or other deleterious matters. The physical requirements of the aggregates should conform to the one described for bitumen bound macadam.

(3) **Fine Aggregates :** The aggregates (passing 2.36 mm sieve and retained on 0.75 mm sieve) should be clean, hard, durable, uncoated, dry, and free from soft, or flaky pieces and organic or deleterious matters.

(4) **Filler :** The filler (passings 600 micron sieve) should be inert material for example, stone dust, cement, hydrated lime, fly-ash or other non-plastic matter.

(5) **Gradation of Aggregates :** The combined grading of mineral aggregates and filler should conform to any of the two gradings given below :

Table 6.14

Sieve Size	Per cent by Weight Passing the Sieve	
	Grading I	Grading II
20 mm	–	100
12.5 mm	100	80 - 100
10 mm	80 - 100	70 - 90
4.75 mm	55 - 75	50 - 70
2.36 mm	32 - 50	35 - 50
600 micron	18 - 29	18 - 29
300 micron	13 - 23	13 - 23
150 micron	8 - 16	8 - 16
75 micron	4 - 10	4 - 10

Generally, for compacted layer thickness of 25-40 mm any of the two gradings could be used but for layer thickness of 40-50 mm only grading No. 2 should be used. The permissible variations from the job mix formula should conform to the following limits :

Table 6.15

Description of Ingredient	Permissible Variation by Weight of Total Mix
Aggregate passing 4.75 mm sieve	± 5.0 per cent
Aggregate passing 2.36 mm sieve	± 4.0 per cent
Aggregate passing 600 micron sieve	± 3.0 per cent
Aggregate passing 75 micron sieve	± 1.0 per cent
Binder	± 3.0 per cent

Construction Operations : The various construction operations include preparation of base, application of tack coat, preparation of mix, spreading and rolling. During the preparation of base course all the irregularities including pot-holes or ruts are removed. It is desirable to lay a bituminous levelling course on an existing extremely wavy pavement. The construction operations like: application to tack coat, preparation of mix and spreading are similar to the one described for bitumen bound macadam construction.

Soon after the spreading of mix by paver the surface should be thoroughly compacted by rolling with all set of rollers moving at less than 5 kmph speed. It is always desirable that the initial rolling should be done with 8-12 tonne three wheel rollers. The surface finishing should be carried out by with 8-10 tonne tandem roller or pneumatic rollers. The rolling process is similar to the one described earlier. The rolling should be continued till the density achieved is at least 95 % of that of the laboratory Marshall specimen.

Field Controls : The various field controls include :
(a) Aggregates grading control,
(b) Binder grade control,
(c) Temperature control for aggregates, and
(d) Temperature control for mix during mixing and compaction.

It is recommended that at least one test for above field controls must be carried cut for every 100 tonnes of mix discharged by plant. The field density should also be checked once for every 1000 m² of compacted surface. The permitted tolerances of surface regularity are 8 mm and 4 mm for longitudinal and cross-profile respectively.

Mastic Asphalt : Mastic asphalt is superior to other types of surfacings because of its ability to take very heavy shear stresses without deformation. That is why mastic asphalt is recommended for very heavy traffic and in places where the braking and accelerating stresses are very heavy for example, bus-stops and round abouts. Mastic asphalt has not found any importance in our country due to :

(a) Non-availability of machinery required-to heat and mix at very high temperature.

(b) Non-availability of highly skilled labour to handle the mix in spreading at high temperature of 200°C.

(c) Non-availability of the grading of asphalt required.

(d) Very high cost due to large quantity of binder used.

6.5 CEMENT CONCRETE ROAD

Cast in place concrete is used in very diverse applications for the construction of road pavement because of numerous advantages i.e. :

- Great rigidity and consequently a good distribution of the loads on the foundation and excellent fatigue behaviour,
- Great resistance to wear and rutting and edges that do not erode;
- Not affected by oil, organic substances, chemicals;
- Bright colour, skid resistance and safety in winter;
- Environmentally friendly.

Concrete pavements last long too and require little maintenance, at least if they have been designed properly and executed professionally. If this is not the case, significant premature damage is liable to occur, resulting in high maintenance costs.

Following below, all aspects of the execution of monolithic pavements are discussed. This bulletin is intended to be a reference publication for people who are responsible for the execution of the works and for the supervision of construction. The evaluation of both older and recent concrete pavements demonstrates time and again how important the quality of the execution is. It requires special attention, both from the contractor executing the works and from the people ensuring that the specifications are complied with.

There are different types of monolithic pavements

(1) Plain Concrete (Short Pavement Slabs) :

This type of pavement consists of successive slabs whose length is limited to about 25 times the slab thickness. At present it is recommended that the paving slabs not be made longer than 5 m, even if the joints have dowels to transfer the loads. The movements as a result of fluctuations in temperature and humidity are concentrated in the joints. Normally, these joints are sealed to prevent water from penetrating the road structure. The width of the pavement slabs is limited to a maximum of 4.5 m.

(2) Reinforced Concrete

(a) Continuously Reinforced Concrete

Continuously reinforced concrete pavements are characterised by the absence of transverse joints and are equipped with longitudinal steel reinforcement. The diameter of the reinforcing bars is calculated in such a way that cracking can be controlled and that the cracks are uniformly distributed (spacing at 1 to 3 m). The crackwidth has to remain very small, i.e. less than 0.3 mm.

(b) Reinforced Pavement Slabs

Reinforced concrete pavement slabs are almost never used, except for inside or outside industrial floors that are subjected to large loads or if the number of contraction joints has to be limited.

(c) Steel Fibre Concrete

The use of steel fibre concrete pavements is mainly limited to industrial floors. However, in that sector they are used intensively. For road pavements steel fibre concrete can be used for thin or very thin paving slabs or for very specific applications.

Preparation of the Subgrade or the Base

The road subgrade has to be prepared carefully, in order to realize everywhere a pavement structure of an adequate and uniform thickness. This allows to provide a homogeneous bond between the concrete slab and its foundation which is important for the later behaviour of the pavement structure For roads with a base, drainage of the water must be provided. Mud, leaves, etc. have to be removed When the base is permeable, it should be sprayed with water in order to prevent the mixing water from being sucked out of the concrete.

However, if the base is impermeable (e.g. if the concrete is placed on a watertight asphalt concrete interlayer) it can be necessary under warm weather conditions to cool down this layer by spraying water on the surface.

The following points are important for roads without a foundation :

- Drainage of all surface water;
- Good compaction of the subgrade;
- Filling and compaction of any ruts caused by construction traffic;
- It is forbidden to level the subgrade by means of a course of sand. If the subgrade has to be levelled, it is advisable to do this by using a granular material: either slag or coarse aggregate e.g. with a grain size 0/20; provide an additional width of the subgrade for more lateral support.

It must always be avoided that water is sucked from the cement paste into the substructure or the base. This can be accomplished by either moderately moistening the subgrade, or by applying a plastic sheet on the substructure of the pavement. The latter work must be done with care, to prevent the sheet from tearing or being pulled loose by the wind.

6.5.1.1 Mixing and Transport of Concrete

Concrete Mixing Plant

The concrete mixing plant must have a sufficient capacity in order to be able to continuously supply concrete to the paving machines. The mix constituents and admixtures have to be dosed very accurately. The number of aggregate feed bins has to equal at least the number of different aggregate fractions. The bins shall have raised edges to prevent contamination of the aggregate fractions. The equipment for loading the materials shall be in good condition and shall have sufficient capacity to be able to continuously feed the bins. The bucket of the loaders shall not be wider than the bins. The content of the cement silos and the water tank are in proportion to the production rates. For small works, permanent concrete mixing plants are often called on.

In that case, mixing plants that are inspected and that can deliver BENOR (Belgian quality certification) concrete should be used. Furtermore it is useful and even essential to have a communication system between the concrete mixing plant and the construction site in order to coordinate the batching and paving operations.

6.5.1.2 Transport of the Concrete

Sufficient trucks must be available to continuously supply the paving machines. The number depends on the yield at the construction site, the loading capacity of the trucks and the cycle time (i.e. the transport time plus the time required to load and unload a truck). The loading capacity and the type of truck to be used depend on the nature of the work, the haul roads and the concrete paving machines. Usually, the specifications prescribe that the concrete has to be transported in dump trucks as paving concrete consists of a relatively dry mix having a consistency that makes transport and unloading in truck mixers difficult. Furthermore, dump trucks can discharge the concrete faster. For small works and in urban areas, the use of truck mixers is increasingly accepted. Under these circumstances an admixture (e.g. a superplastifier) can be mixed in just before discharging the concrete. The necessary measures have to be taken to prevent changes of the water content and temperature of the concrete during transport. To this end, the specifications prescribe to cover the dump trucks by means of a tarpaulin.

Fig. 6.6 : Preparation of the subgrade or the base

Fig. 6.7 : Placing of concrete

6.5.2 Fixed-form Concrete Paving

6.5.2.1 Setting up the Side Forms

In order to place the side forms properly the alignment of the road has to be staked out carefully. This is usually accomplished by driving iron rods firmly into the subgrade soil or the base at a spacing of maximum 5 m. After the elevations corresponding to the top of the forms have been marked on the rods, they are connected with a string line that represents the top of the forms. The form sections have to be properly supported on the base at all points. The inner surfaces of the forms shall be installed vertically and on line. In curved areas shorter or bent form sections are used, so as to better match the alignment of the curve. After the form sections have been properly aligned over a certain distance, they are secured by means of stakes. As the side forms serve as the reference for guiding the vibratory screed, the tolerances for the evenness shall not be exceeded. To accurately place the forms, a rigid template having the same width as the concrete pavement must be available on site, so that it can be checked at any time whether or not the form sections are set up parallel. The inside surface of the forms should be cleaned and oiled or coated with a form release product, to prevent spalling when the forms are stripped and to facilitate cleaning of the formwork elements before they are used again.

In urban areas, the formwork is often substituted by rows of paving bricks. These are placed on a bed of mortar or concrete with a cement content of at least 350 kg/m3. The rows of paving bricks divide the pavement surface into rectangular sections. They have to be placed a few days before the concrete is cast. If the surface of the stones is uneven, a thin plate is laid on top of them to make the sliding surface for the vibratory screed as smooth as possible.

6.5.2.2 Equipment

All equipment necessary for executing the paving must be present on site and has to function properly. This concerns primarily: manual needle vibrators and vibrating screed, equipment for floating the concrete surface, for applying the curing compound, for sawing the joints, etc. The profile of the finishing equipment has to be even, in order to obtain good final pavement smoothness. To check this, a gauge is placed at each end of the screed to be controlled. Subsequently, a string is tensioned between the two gauges and the distance between the string and the finishing surface of the screed is measured at various points. Another method consists of checking the evenness with a level and leveling rod. The consolidation equipment has to generate uniform vibrations with the right frequency and amplitude.

Fig. 6.8

Fig. 6.9

6.5.3 Slipform Concrete Paving

6.5.3.1 Preparation of the Track Runway

The quality of the runway for the tracks of the paving equipment is undoubtedly one of the most important factors that contribute to the realisation of a smooth pavement surface. In connection therewith, the following criteria have to be met:

- sufficient bearing capacity, so that the slipform paver can proceed without causing deformations;
- good skid resistance to prevent the tracks from slipping, especially when paving on a slope;
- good evenness to avoid that the self-levelling systems have to compensate for excessive differences in height. The track runway is a determining factor for the steering and consequently its surface has to at least as smooth as the concrete paving surface itself. The runway surface has to be permanently cleaned prior to the passage of the tracks. The track runway has to be wide enough taking into account:
- the greatest width of the paving machine plus an extra width (especially on embankments);
- the necessary space for placing the sensor lines.
- Furthermore, if the longitudinal slope is 4 % or more, the track runway has to be stabilised to prevent slipping. In addition to this the tracks can be equipped with plates or hooks or the paving can preferably progress ownhill.

6.5.4 Joints

Provisions of joints are necessitated due to:

1. Expansion, contraction and warping of concrete slabs resulting from temperature and moisture changes;
2. Facilitate a break in the construction at the end of day's work or for any unexpected interruption to work progress; and
3. Construction of pavements in lanes of convenient width.

6.5.4.1 Types of Joints

Transverse joints are of the following types:

(a) Expansion Joints

These provide for space in concrete to allow for expansion of slab. The practice with regard to spacing of expansion joints vary from 20 metres to a few hundred metres. Recent practice is to omit expansion joints and provide the same at junctions of roads with structure, like, bridges, etc.

(b) Contraction Joints

These joints are provided in concrete pavements to prevent stresses induced as a result of ambient temperature falling below the laying temperature. These are normally 3 to 5 mm, width and provided upto 1/3rd to l/4th the slab thickness. Spacing of contraction joints is generally 5 metres. For reinforced concrete pavements the maximum spacing varies from 7.5 m to 17.0 m depending upon thickness of slabs.

Fig. 6.10 : Expansion Joints

Fig. 6.11 : Construction Joints

(c) Construction Joints

These joints are provided at the end of a day's work or when the work is stopped unexpectedly due to interruption for more than 30 minutes. These are either contraction joints or expansion joints.

(d) Longitudinal Joints

These are required when the width of concrete pavement is more than 4 metres wide. These are intended to Provide for warping and even uneven settlement of subgrade. Generally, the joints are butt type dummy type joints are also used. These are saw cut joints for at least l/3rd of the depth of slab.

REVIEW QUESTIONS

1. Explain the details the construction procedures for WBM road
2. Explain the details the construction procedures for cement concrete roads.
3. Explain the details the construction procedures for bituminous road construction.
4. Enlist various equipment used for construction of various types for road. Explain any one detail.

5. Explain different types of joints in cement concrete pavements.

6. Write short note on :

   (a) Soil- stabilization for roads

   (b) Cement concrete road

   (c) Bituminous pavement

   (d) Gravel Road

CHAPTER 7
HIGHWAY DRAINAGE

7.1 INTRODUCTION

Appropriate drainage is important feature of good highway design in terms of ensuring required level of service and value for many are achieved. Highway drainage has two major objectives : Safety of the road user and longevity of the pavement. Speedy removal of surface water will help to ensure safe and comfortable conditions for the road user. Provision of effective sub-drainage will maximise longevity of the pavement and its associated earthworks. Highway drainage can therefore be broadly classified into two elements - surface run-off and sub-surface run-off : These two elements are not completely disparate in that some of the surface water may find its way into the road foundation through surfaces which are not completely impermeable, hence requiring removal by sub-drainage. Based on these fundamental principles, drainage methods in India are broadly divided into two categories :

(1) Combined systems, where the surface and sub-surface water are collected and transported in the same pipe, and
(2) Separate systems, where the two elements are collected and transported in separate pipes.

Within the broader definition of the two systems, there are a number of different drainage methods that are in use on Indian highways, some of them more common than others. Each method has its advantages and disadvantages and some may be more suitable in certain situations than the others. This paper describes some of the most common methods and provides an overview on their applications.

7.2 SIGNIFICANCE OF DRAINAGE

An increase in moisture content causes decrease in strength or stability of a soil mass; the variation in the soil strength with moisture content also depends on the soil type and mode of stress application. Highway drainage is important because of the following reasons :

- Excess moisture in soil sub-grade causes considerable lowering of its stability. The pavements are likely to fail due to sub-grade failure.
- Increase in moisture causes reduction in strength of many pavement materials like stabilized soil and water bound macadam.
- In some clayey soils, variation in moisture content causes considerable variation in volume of sugared. This sometimes contributes to pavement failure.
- One of the most important causes of pavement failure by the formation of waves and corrugations in flexible pavements is due to poor drainage.

- Sustained content of water with bituminous pavements causes failures due to stripping of bitumen from aggregates like loosening or detachments of some of the bituminous pavement layers and formation of pot holes.
- The prime cause of failures in rigid pavements by mud pumping is due to the presence of water in fine sub-grade soil.
- Excess water on shoulders and pavements edge causes considerable damages.
- Excess moisture causes increase in weight and thus increase in stress and simultaneous reduction in strength of the soil mass. This is one of the main reason of failure of earth slopes and embankment foundations.
- In places where freezing temperatures are prevalent in winter, the presence of water in the sub-grade and a continuous supply of water from the ground water can cause considerable damages to the pavement due in frost action.
- Erosion of soil from top of un-surfaced roads and slopes of embankments, cut and hill side is also due to surface water.

Requirements of Highway Drainage System
- The surface water from the carriageway and shoulder should effectively be drained off without allowing it to percolate to sub-grade.
- The surface water from the adjoining land should be prevented from entering the roadway.
- The side drain should have sufficient capacity and longitudinal slope to carry away all the surface water collected.
- Flow of surface water across the road and shoulders and along slopes should not cause formation of cross ruts or erosion.
- Seepage and other sources of underground water should be drained off by the sub-surface drainage system.
- Highest level of ground water table should be kept well below the level of sub-grade, preferably by at least 1.2 m.
- In waterlogged areas, special precautions should be taken, especially if detrimental salts are present or if flooding is likely to occur.

7.3 MECHANISM OF DAMAGE TO HIGHWAYS DUE TO FAULTY DRAINAGE

Lack of drainage affects the performance of highways in a number of ways. They are briefly discussed below :
- If the water falling on the pavement surface is not quickly drained away, it finds its way into the pavement layers through surface cracks, voids and joints (in cement concrete pavements). The water gets entrapped in the spaces between successive lifts of bituminous layers. The pavement is then in the "bathtub" condition, which may cause uplift pressures and result in reduced supporting power. Water may cause stripping of

bitumen from aggregates and lower the binding strength of the pavement. In cement concrete slabs, "pumping" is caused, which causes loss of fines in the soil and void space.

- A classic example of this phenomenon of entrapped water frequently met within India is the raising of pavements attempted by earthwork or granular bases over a black-topped surface, which is left intact. This interface acts as an impervious layer to entrap water and causes "bathtub" condition. In the bituminised road pavements, the development of 'potholes' is a common phenomenon mostly caused by the ingress of surface water, as illustrated in Fig. 7.1.
- The surface run-off or capillary water reaches the sub-grade soil, softens it and reduces its supporting power. Clayey soils are particularly affected by the ingress of moisture.
- Shoulders are rarely, if ever, surfaced. The bare earthen shoulders offer ready ingress of water. Lack of adequate outward slope presents longer opportunity for water to enter the sub-grade through the sides than if the shoulders were adequately sloped.

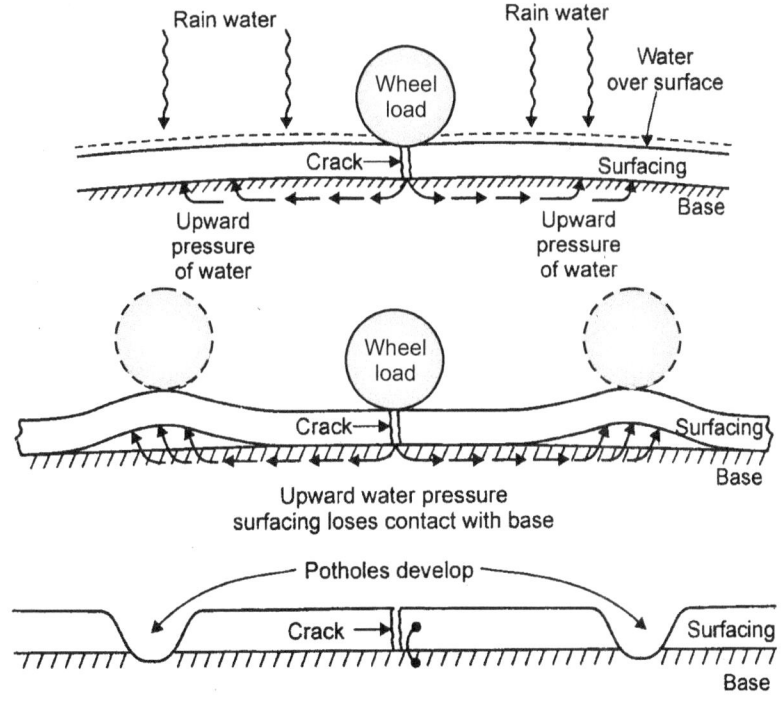

Fig. 7.1 : Development of potholes due to ingress of surface water

- In India, a commonly present road feature is the shoulders at a higher level than the road surface due to negligence of blading and dressing of the shoulders. During heavy downpour, water on the road surface does not get a free outlet and accumulates. Apart from finding its way through the cracks and voids in the pavement surface, the

pavement edge at its junction with the earthen shoulder provides a possible entry point to the water. The water thus enters the sub-grade from the sides of the pavement.
- Clayey soils, which are susceptible to high volume change when changes in moisture content take place, swell and shrink alternating with wet and dry spells. Deep cracks are formed in the sub-grade. Heaving-up and deterioration of the pavement follow. Black-cotton soils, frequently found in India, suffer this distress condition.
- In high embankments, stability of slopes is jeopardised when water enters the soil mass, causing an increase in its weight and at the same time reducing its shear strength properties.
- In cut sections, seepage water can build up sufficient pressure to cause the failure of slopes.
- Landslides and subsidences are caused by a general lack of drainage. The Himalayan hill region abounds in locations where serious landslides and subsidences are caused, totally disrupting road traffic. The National Highways to Srinagar and Gangtok are typical examples.
- Frost action, which takes place entirely due to water finding its way into the pores of the soil mass and the pavement layers, is a serious cause of pavement failure at high altitudes in cold season.
- Heavy downpour on the slopes of embankments and cuts can cause excessive soil erosion and lead to rain-cuts and slop failures.
- Unless water from the streams is safely led across the highway through adequate vents, the water can accumulate against the embankment, causing afflux, slope erosion and softening of the sub-grade.

7.4 PRINCIPLES OF GOOD DRAINAGE

Since water is, beyond doubt, one of the main culprits causing failure of highways, the designer should aim at keeping the water away from the road-bed. This can be achieved by following some principles of drainage design. They are outlined below :
- The surface run-off over the pavement surface and the shoulders should be drained away as quickly as possible preventing the water from finding entry into the pavement layers from the top and into the sub-grade from the top and sides.
- Precipitation over the open land adjoining the highway should be led away from the highway through natural drainage channels or artificial drains. Suitable cross-drainage channels should be provided to lead the water across the highway embankment which may be cutting cross to the natural drainage courses.
- Consideration should be given to deal with the precipitation on the embankment and cut slopes such that erosion is not caused.
- Seepage and sub-surface water is detrimental to the stability of cut slopes and bearing power of sub-grades. Similarly, it can be of great importance in preventing frost action. An effective system of sub-surface drainage is a guarantee against such failures.

- Landslide-prone zones deserve special investigations for improving drainage.
- Poor embankment soils can perform satisfactorily if drainage is considered in the design.
- Water-logged and flood-prone zones demand detailed consideration for improving the overall drainage pattern of the area through which the highway is aligned.

7.5 METHODS OF DRAINAGE SYSTEM

There are two methods of drainage system as follows :
1. Surface drainage system and
2. Sub-surface drainage.

7.5.1 Surface Drainage System

- During the rainy season, water gets controlled at road surface and percolated into the road surface and the sub-grade and thereby weakness the sub-grade. To prevent this percolation of water into the sub-grade from the surface of the pavement, the following remedies have been suggested :
- Providing a water-tight or impervious type of road surfacing at the top most layer. i.e. wearing surface.

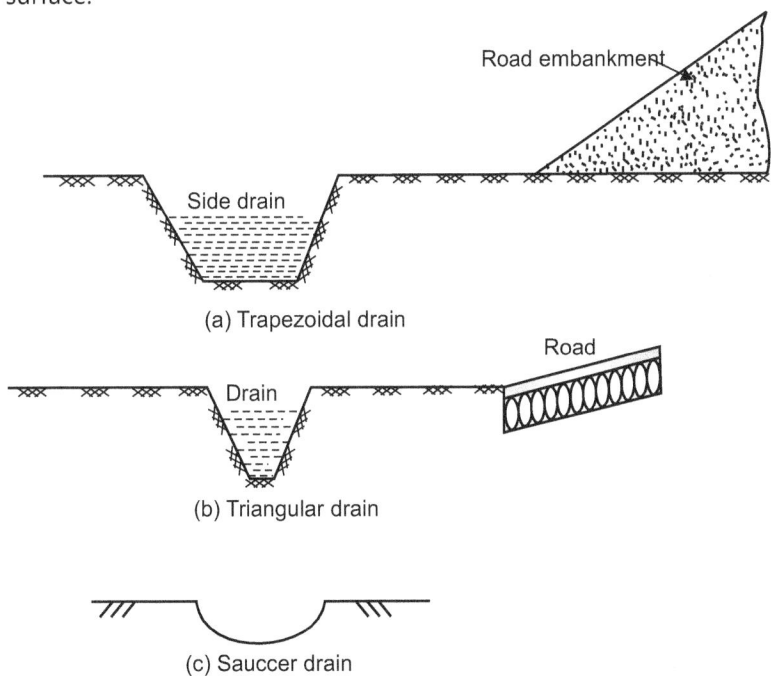

Fig. 7.2 : Surface drainage

- Providing sufficient cross and longitudinal slopes in the road surface.
- The top surface of the berms should be of an impervious material and should have proper slopes towards side drains.
- Providing side drains on both sides of the road. The drains should have a proper slope

or gradient so that the water from the road surface should be drained off easily. The side drains should not be less than 1.85m or 6ft from the edge of the formation of the road. In case of cutting, the surface drains should be just after the edge of formation.
- In these places where the rainfall is heavily, the side drains should be trapezoidal in section and in those places where there is less rainfall the section of the drain is triangular or sauccer as shown in Fig. 7.2.
- The height of the embankment should be nearly 60 cm or 2 ft. above the highest flood level of the area.

It is Suitable for
- Slowly permeable clay and shallow soil.
- Regions of high intensity rainfall.
- To fields where adequate out lets are not available.
- The land with less than 1.5 % slope.

It can be Made by
- Land smoothing.
- Making field ditches.

Advantages and Disadvantages of Surface Drains

Advantages
- Low initial cost.
- Easy for inspection.
- Effective in low water table.
- Effective in low Permeability area.

Disadvantages
- Low efficiency.
- Loss of cultivable land.
- Interference to cultural operation.
- High Maintenance cost.

7.5.2 Sub-Soil or Sub-Surface Drainage

Water which penetrates into the ground will continue to flow underground until it meets with some impermeable materials, then the flow ceases and the water accumulates. The top surface of this underground water is called water table. The ground above this level will remain unsaturated and below this level, saturated. The water table generally tends to be parallel to the ground level, but the depth of water table below the ground level may vary and it depends upon the geological conditions.

If this water table is very near to the sub-surface of the road, the consistency of the soil will changes from dry to plastic state and the bearing capacity will consequently decrease. Another adverse effect which results from the increased moisture content is the volumetric increase which will ultimately cause crakes in the road surfacing. Hence it is essential to drain off this water to prevent the sub-grade, which is the foundation of the road from these adverse effects of sub-soil moisture. The method of removal of the sub-soil moisture is called sub-soil drainage.

Following are the conditions under which sub-soil drainage should be provided :

- If the road is through flat country and water stagnates on adjacent lands which makes the road bed soft and unstable.
- When the road is in cutting and there is considerable seepage in the slopes.
- When the surface of the road has the normal underground water table sufficiently below the road crust even then due to capillary action moisture may rise to the surface of the road or the sub-surface.
- When the soil is subjected to the action of springs.
- When the road is at the foot of a hill and water there from flow on the road and it damages the road.

Types of sub surface drainage :

- Pile drainage.
- Mole drainage.
- Vertical drainage.
- Well drainage or Drainage wells.

Method of Providing Sub-Soil or Sub-Surface Drainage

Pipe Drains : This method of sub-soil drainage is suitable when a road runs in a flat country with low embankments and where the sub-soil water accumulates below the sub-grade. In this method pipe drains are placed. Below the surface of the ground in the permeable saturated stratum.

The pipes are usually made of vitrified clay and are placed on a bed of sand, crushed stone, or clay 15 cm thick, with open joints butting against each other. To prevent the earth from above entering the pipes, through open joints, a tarred paper is sometimes provided to cover the joints. These pipes are placed in the trench with proper slopes both cross and longitudinal. The pipes are 15 to 20 cm in diameter. Cross or transverse pipes which are 6 to 10 cm in diameter are also laid at a distance of 6 m to 20 m apart. The trench is then filled with hard porous materials as shown in Fig. 7.3.

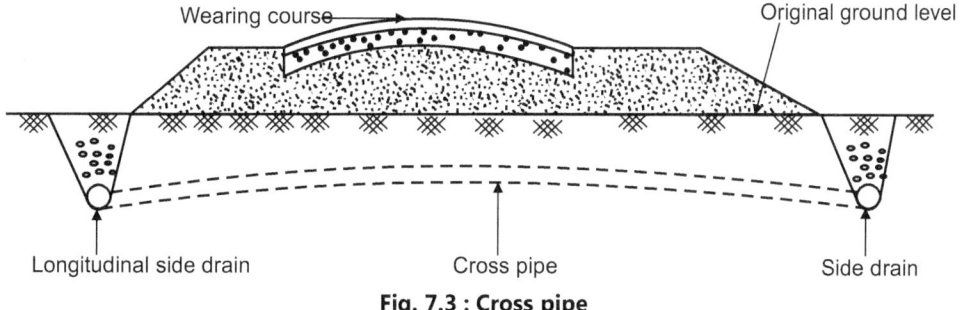

Fig. 7.3 : Cross pipe

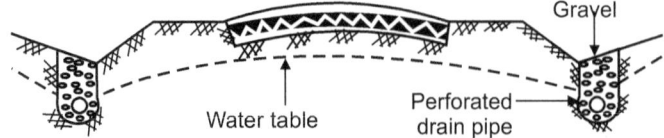

Fig. 7.4 : Longitudinal pipe of sides of roads

The main longitudinal pipes may be laid in the centre or on both sides of the road depending upon the moisture conditions. The main pipe discharge their water into the surface drain.

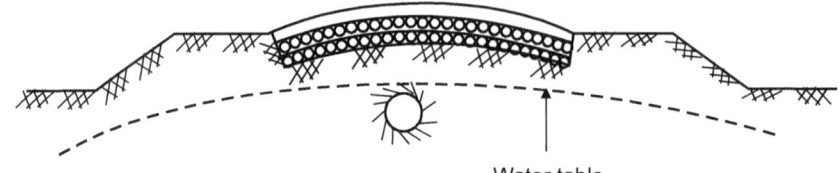

Fig. 7.5 : Longitudinal pipes in the centre of road

Kerb and Gullies

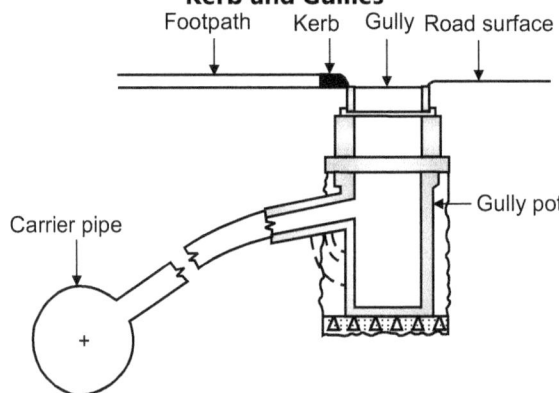

Fig. 7.6 : A typical scene of a kerb and gully drain and a layout of its construction

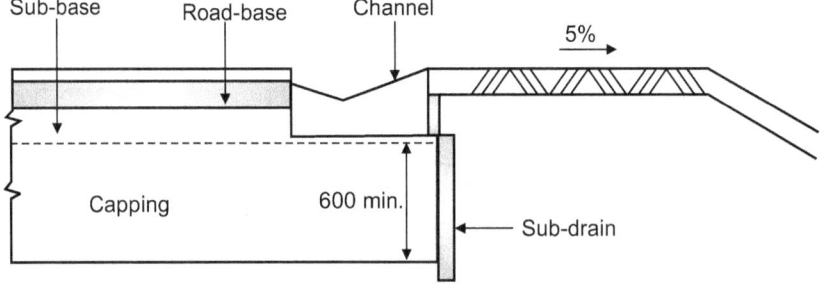

Fig. 7.7 : A typical scene of surface water channel drain and a layout of its construction

Surface water channels are normally of triangular/trapezoidal concrete section, usually slip-formed, set at the edge of hard strip or hard shoulder and flush with the road surface. They provide an economic alternative to edge channels and are the Agency's preferred edge-drain solution for rural locations (trunk roads and motorways). However, they may not be appropriate for roads with long stretches of zero longitudinal gradients. They provide a positive means of keeping the surface water on the surface for most of its journey thus avoiding the possibility of large quantities of water entering the road foundation and causing premature failures. Long length of channels, devoid of interruptions, can be constructed quickly and fairly inexpensively using slip-form techniques. They are capable of carrying large volumes of water over long distances and channel outlets can be located at appreciable spacing and to coincide with watercourses thus avoiding the need for a separate carrier pipe. They are easy to maintain and any long-term problems developing can be detected and monitored by simple visual inspection from the surface. Research suggests that properly designed channels pose no greater hazard than other common drainage features such as kerbs, embankments and ditches, and in most situations are potentially less hazardous.

7.6 TYPICAL DESIGNS OF SIDE DRAINS ON HILL ROADS

Some typical designs of side drains on hill roads are shown in Fig. 7.8.

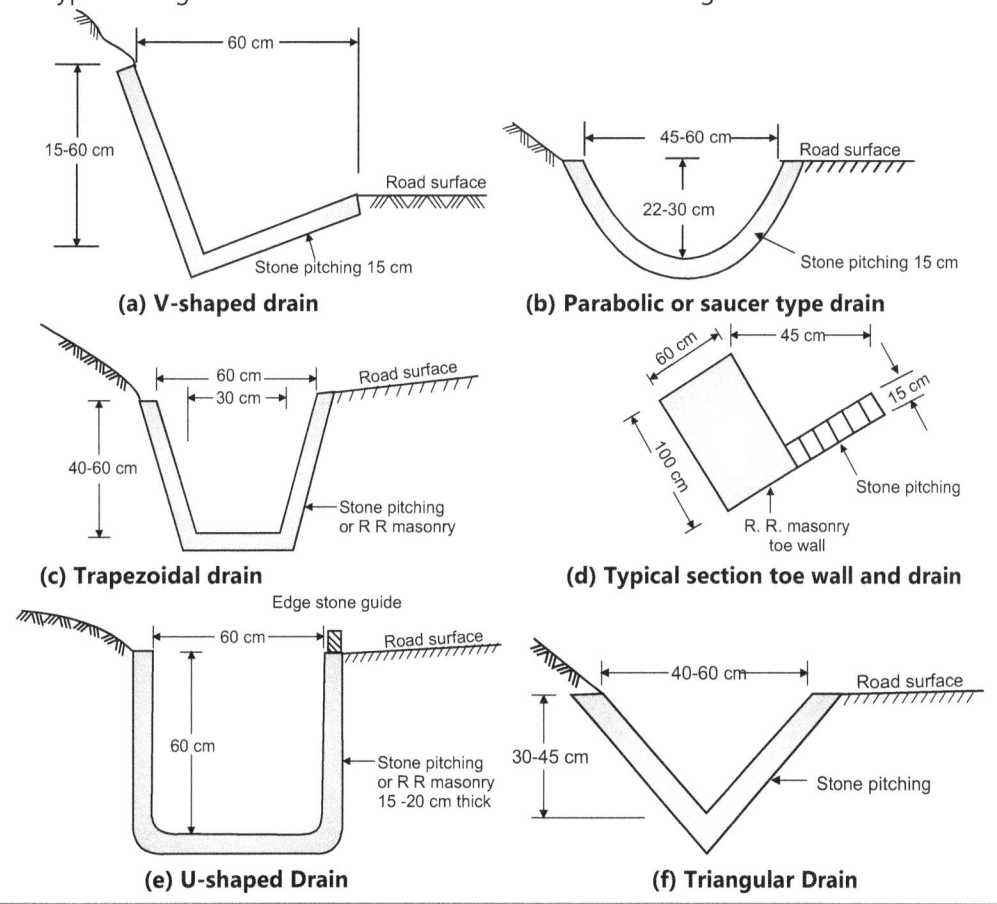

(a) V-shaped drain
(b) Parabolic or saucer type drain
(c) Trapezoidal drain
(d) Typical section toe wall and drain
(e) U-shaped Drain
(f) Triangular Drain

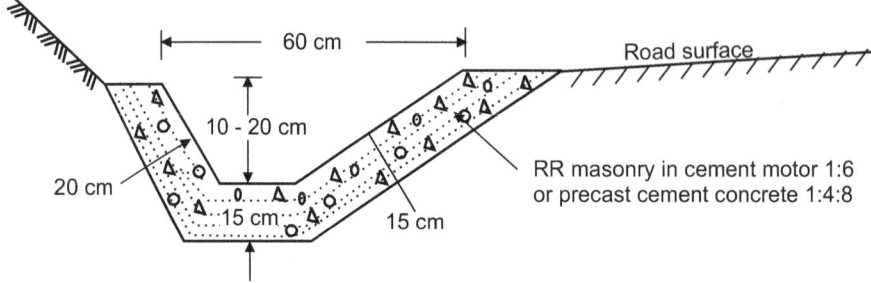

(g) Karb and channel drain

Fig. 7.8 : Typical designs of side chains on hill roads

REVIEW QUESTIONS

1. What is necessity of drainage ?
2. Explain the drainages problem in hill roads.
3. Discuss the following with neat sketches with respect to sub-surface drainage.
   (a) Lowering of water table.
   (b) Control of seepage flow.
4. Write short note on :
   (a) Importance of drainages.
   (b) Surface drainages.
   (c) Sub-surface drainage.
   (d) Typical Designs of Side Drains on Hill Roads.

CHAPTER 8
HIGHWAY PAVEMENT

8.1 OVERVIEW

A highway pavement is a structure consisting of superimposed layers of processed materials above the natural soil sub-grade, whose primary function is to distribute the applied vehicle loads to the sub-grade. The pavement structure should be able to provide a surface of acceptable riding quality, adequate skid resistance, favourable light reflecting characteristics and low noise pollution. The ultimate aim is to ensure that the transmitted stresses due to wheel load are sufficiently reduced, so that they will not exceed bearing capacity of the subgrade. Two types of pavements are generally recognized as serving this purpose, namely **flexible pavements** and **rigid pavements**. This chapter gives an overview of pavement types, layers and their functions and pavement failures. Improper design of pavements leads to early failure of pavements affecting the riding quality also.

8.2 REQUIREMENTS OF A PAVEMENT

The pavement should meet the following requirements :

- Sufficient thickness to distribute the wheel load stresses to a safe value on the sub-grade soil.
- Structurally strong to withstand all types of stresses imposed upon it.
- Adequate coefficient of friction to prevent skidding of vehicles.
- Smooth surface to provide comfort to road users even at high speed.
- Produce least noise from moving vehicles.
- Dust-proof surface so that traffic safety is not impaired by reducing visibility.
- Impervious surface, so that sub-grade soil is well protected.
- Long design life with low maintenance cost.

8.3 TYPES OF PAVEMENTS

The pavements can be classified based on the structural performance into two, flexible pavements and rigid pavements. In flexible pavements, wheel loads are transferred by grain-to-grain contact of the aggregate through the granular structure. The flexible pavement, having less flexural strength acts like a flexible sheet (For example, bituminous road). On the contrary, in rigid pavements, wheel loads are transferred to sub-grade soil by flexural strength of the pavement and the pavement acts like a rigid plate (For example cement concrete roads). In addition to these composite pavements are also available. A thin layer of flexible pavement over rigid pavement is an ideal pavement with most desirable characteristics. However, such pavements are rarely used in new construction because of high cost and complex analysis required.

8.3.1 Flexible Pavements

Flexible pavements will transmit wheel load stresses to the lower layers by grain-to-grain transfer through the points of contact in the granular structure (See Fig. 8.1).

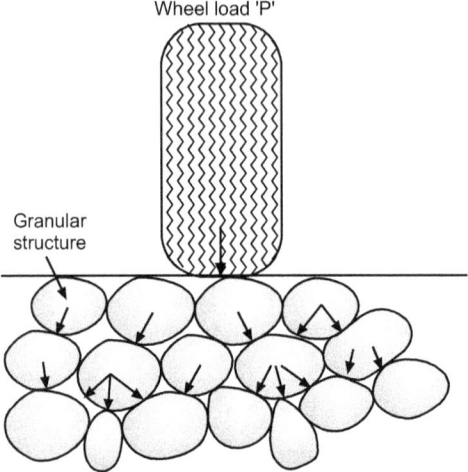

Fig. 8.1 : Load transfer in granular structure

8.3.1.1 Deflection on Flexible Pavement

The wheel load acting on the pavement will be distributed to a wider area and the stress decreases with the depth. Taking advantage of this stress distribution characteristic, flexible pavements normally has many layers. Hence, the design of flexible pavement uses the concept of layered system. Based on this, flexible pavement may be constructed in a number of layers and the top layer has to be of best quality to sustain maximum compressive stress, in addition to wear and tear. The lower layers will experience lesser magnitude of stress and less quality material can be used. Flexible pavements are constructed using bituminous materials. These can be either in the form of surface treatments (such as bituminous surface treatments generally found on low volume roads) or asphalt concrete surface courses (generally used on high volume roads such as national highways).

8.3.1.2 Types of Flexible Pavements

The following types of construction have been used in flexible pavement :

- Conventional layered flexible pavement,
- Full-depth asphalt pavement and
- Contained Rock Asphalt Mat (CRAM).

Conventional Flexible Pavements : are layered systems with high quality expensive materials placed at the top where stresses are high and low quality cheap materials are placed in lower layers. Full-depth asphalt pavements are constructed by placing bituminous layers directly on the soil sub-grade. This is more suitable when there is high traffic and local materials are not available.

Contained rock asphalt mats are constructed by placing dense/open-graded aggregate layers in between two asphalt layers. Modified dense graded asphalt concrete placed above the sub-grade will significantly reduce the vertical compressive strain on soil sub-grade and protect from surface water.

8.3.2 Typical Layers of a Flexible Pavement

Typical layers of a conventional flexible pavement include seal coat, surface course, tack coat, binder course, prime coat, base course, sub-base course, compacted subgrade and natural subgrade (See Fig. 8.2).

Seal Coat : Seal coat is a thin surface treatment used to water-proof the surface and to provide skid resistance.

Tack Coat : Tack coat is a very light application of asphalt, usually asphalt emulsion diluted with water. It provides proper bonding between two layer of binders course and must be thin, uniformly cover the entire surface and set very fast.

Prime Coat : Prime coat is an application of low viscous cutback bitumen to an absorbent surface like granular bases on which binder layer is placed. It provides bonding between two layers. Unlike tack coat, prime coat penetrates into the layer below, plugs the voids and forms a water- tight surface.

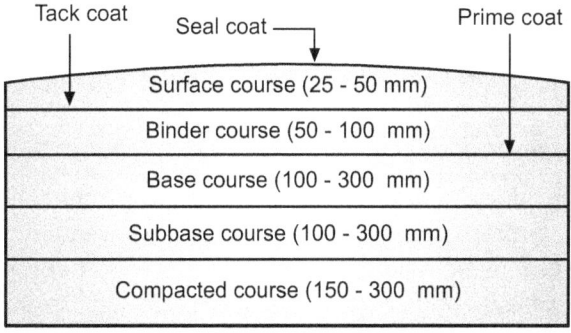

Fig. 8.2 : Typical cross-section of a flexible pavement

Surface Course : Surface course is the layer directly in contact with traffic loads and generally contains superior quality materials. They are usually constructed with dense graded asphalt concrete (AC). The functions and requirements of this layer are :

- It provides characteristics such as friction, smoothness, drainage etc. Also it will prevent the entrance of excessive quantities of surface water into the underlying base, sub-base and sub-grade.
- It must be tough to resist the distortion under traffic and provide a smooth and skid-resistant riding surface.
- It must be water proof to protect the entire base and sub-grade from the weakening effect of water.

Binder Course : This layer provides the bulk of the asphalt concrete structure. It's chief purpose is to distribute load to the base course. The binder course generally consists of aggregates having less asphalt and doesn't require quality as high as the surface course, so replacing a part of the surface course by the binder course results in more economical design.

Base Course : The base course is the layer of material immediately beneath the surface of binder course and it provides additional load distribution and contributes to the sub-surface drainage. It may be composed of crushed stone, crushed slag and other untreated or stabilized materials.

Sub-Base Course : The sub-base course is the layer of material beneath the base course and the primary functions are to provide structural support, improve drainage and reduce the intrusion of fines from the sub-grade in the pavement structure. If the base course is open graded, then the sub-base course with more fines can serve as a filler between sub-grade and the base course. A sub-base course is not always needed or used. For example, a pavement constructed over a high quality, stiff sub-grade may not need the additional features offered by a sub-base course. In such situations, sub-base course may not be provided.

Sub-grade : The top soil or sub-grade is a layer of natural soil prepared to receive the stresses from the layers above. It is essential that at no time, soil sub-grade is overstressed. It should be compacted to the desirable density, near the optimum moisture content.

8.4 RIGID PAVEMENTS

Rigid pavements have sufficient flexural strength to transmit the wheel load stresses to a wider area below. A typical cross-section of the rigid pavement is shown in Fig. 8.3. Compared to flexible pavement, rigid pavements are placed either directly on the prepared sub-grade or on a single layer of granular or stabilized material. Since there is only one layer of material between the concrete and the sub-grade, this layer can be called as base or sub-base course.

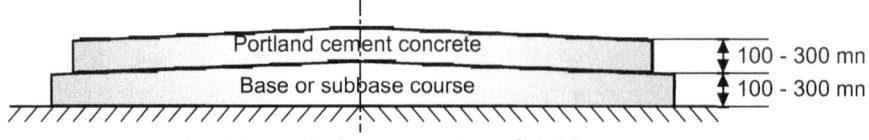

Fig. 8.3 : Typical cross-section of rigid pavement

In rigid pavement, load is distributed by the slab action and the pavement behaves like an elastic plate resting on a viscous medium (See Fig. 8.3). Rigid pavements are constructed by Portland Cement Concrete (PCC) and should be analyzed by plate theory instead of layer theory, assuming an elastic plate resting on viscous foundation. Plate theory is a simplified version of layer theory that assumes the concrete slab as a medium thick plate which is plane before loading and to remain plane after loading. Bending of the slab is due to wheel load and temperature variation and the resulting tensile and flexural stress.

8.4.1 Types of Rigid Pavements

Rigid pavements can be classified into four types :
- Jointed plain concrete pavement (JPCP),
- Jointed reinforced concrete pavement (JRCP),
- Continuous reinforced concrete pavement (CRCP) and
- Pre-stressed concrete pavement (PCP).

Jointed Plain Concrete Pavement : They are plain cement concrete pavements constructed with closely spaced contraction joints. Dowel bars or aggregate interlocks are normally used for load transfer across joints. They normally has a joint spacing of 5 to 10 m.

Jointed Reinforcement Concrete Pavement : Although reinforcements do not improve the structural capacity significantly, they can drastically increase the joint spacing to 10 to 30 m. Dowel bars are required for load transfer. Reinforcements help to keep the slab together even after cracks.

Continuous Reinforced Concrete Pavement : Complete elimination of joints are achieved by reinforcement.

8.4.2 Advantages of Rigid Pavement

- Rigid lasts much longer i.e 30+ years compared to 5-10 years of flexible pavements.
- In the long run it is about half the cost to install and maintain. But the initial costs are somewhat high.
- Rigid pavement has the ability to bridge small imperfections in the subgrade.
- Less Maintenance cost and Continuous Traffic and Flow.
- High efficiency in terms of functionality.

8.5 COMPARISON OF FLEXIBLE AND RIGID PAVEMENT

Sr. No.	Flexible Pavements	Rigid Pavements
1	Deformation in the sub grade is transferred to the upper layers.	Deformation in the subgrade is not transferred to subsequent layers.
2.	Design is based on load distributing characteristics of the component layers.	Design is based on flexural strength or slab action.
3.	Have low flexural strength.	Have high flexural strength.

...Cont.

4.	Load is transferred by grain to grain contact.	No such phenomenon of grain to grain load transfer exists.
5.	Have low completion cost but repairing cost is high.	Have low repairing cost but completion cost is high.
6.	Have low life span (High Maintenance Cost).	Life span is more as compare to flexible (Low Maintenance Cost).
7.	Surfacing cannot be laid directly on the sub grade but a sub base is needed.	Surfacing can be directly laid on the sub grade.
8.	No thermal stresses are induced as the pavement have the ability to contract and expand freely.	Thermal stresses are more vulnerable to be induced as the ability to contract and expand is very less in concrete.
9.	Thats why expansion joints are not needed	Thats why expansion joints are needed
10.	Strength of the road is highly dependent on the strength of the sub grade.	Strength of the road is less dependent on the strength of the sub grade.
11.	Rolling of the surfacing is needed.	Rolling of the surfacing in not needed.
12.	Road can be used for traffic within 24 hours.	Road cannot be used until 14 days of curing.
13.	Force of friction is less Deformation in the sub grade is not transferred to the upper layers.	Force of friction is high.
14.	Damaged by Oils and Certain Chemicals.	No Damage by Oils and Greases.

8.6 THE CONCEPT OF "EQUIVALENT WHEEL LOAD", "REIGIDITY FACTOR," REPEITION" AND "IMPACT"

Before we take up the actual design of pavements, we have to know certain concepts, these concepts are :

8.6.1 Equivalent Wheel Load

Most of the loads that pass on highways are not single wheels. For example, in the case of trucks we have axle loads. In such cases, two wheels are placed closely together. In such cases, pressure bulb created by these two wheels are likely to overlap. Most of the design methods are based on single wheel loading. Therefore, these dual wheels have to be replaced by single wheel called **equivalent wheel**. We have two criteria here. An equivalent single wheel load of wheel assembly based on equivalent deflection criterion will be defined as that, single wheel load having the same contact pressure which produces the value of maximum deflection at a given depth. On the other hand, equivalent single wheel load of tyre assembly based on equivalent stress criterion may be defined as that, single wheel load which produces the same value of maximum stress at the desired depth.

Equivalent deflection criterion is generally considered more suitable. According to the observations made by U.S. corps of Engineers, if we consider two wheel spaced 'd' from their inner faces, then at depths greater than $\frac{d}{2}$, stresses induced due to each load, start overlapping and at a depth '2s', where 's' is the distance between the centre lines of tyre, the dual wheel assembly acts as if it is a single unit carrying a load equal to double the each wheel load (i.e. $2 \times P$). In order to determine single wheel load at any depth, it is assumed that the value of equivalent single wheel load varies as the logarithm of the thickness of pavement between '$\frac{d}{2}$' and 2s. The equivalent single wheel load is first determined for an estimated design thickness of the pavement with the help of this assumption. This wheel load is then used in the design procedure and the thickness of the pavement is calculated. In case thickness so obtained is equal to the estimated thickness, then the equivalent single wheel load so considered is correct, otherwise more trials are to be made till the calculated thickness more or less equals the estimated thickness.

8.6.2 Rigidity Factor

Theoretically, if the tyre inflation pressure is p and the contact area is A, then the load that is actuating on the pavement is pA. This is on the assumption that the applied surface pressure is equal to tyre inflation pressure. Actually surface pressure is generally greater than tyre inflation pressure, when the tyre inflation pressure is less than 7 kg/cm^2. The contact surface pressure becomes less than tyre pressure for values of tyre pressure greater than 7 kg/cm^2. The ratio between the contact surface pressure to tyre inflation pressure is known as rigidity factor. The knowledge of stress-distribution from the principles of soil mechanics tells us that, effects of high tyre inflation pressure are more pronounced in the upper layers only and less effects at greater depths. Thus, the tyre inflation pressure will control the quality of material in the upper layer but not the total pavement thickness requirements. This is the reason, why in the case of iron tyred traffic, that is bullock carts, the stresses in the pavement surface are very high requiring strong material for surfacing courses.

8.6.3 Effect of Repetition of Loads

It is not the application of wheel load but the repetitive application of wheel load that causes deleterious effects on the highway. Elastic and plastic deformations are caused in the highway pavement due to repetition of wheel load. The repeated load application causes breaking down of base course aggregate material. The sucking and kneading action of the wheel load may cause working upwards of soil in the sub-grade. As per the findings of the A.A.S.H.O. road test, for a given axle load, the pavement thickness required to provide a given service is proportional to the logarithm of the number of repetition of the axle load.

As per Mcleod, a flexible highway pavement designed for one million coverages of the design load in 25 years requires 25 % of the design thickness only for one coverage. In the case of mixed traffic on highways, we can replace different wheel loads to an equivalent wheel load by using this concept. Suppose that P_1 is the wheel load which causes failure of the pavement in 'n_1' applications and P_2 is the wheel load which causes the same degree of failure in the same pavement, then Mcleod theorised that $P_1 n_1 = P_2 n_2$.

In order to determine equivalent load factors curves with 25%, designed thickness are plotted for various wheel loads on vertical axis against one application and total 100 % thickness on a vertical axis, drawn at one million repetitions. On the assumption that 25 cm thickness is required for highway pavement (generally flexible) on an ordinary sub-grade soil then for this 25 cm thickness of pavement respective repetitions could be read from this figure for different load applications and are shown in Table 8.1 below.

Table 8.1 : Load Repetitions for Failure

Wheel Load, kg	Load Repetitions for Failure
2268	1,05,000
2725	50,000
3170	22,500
3630	13,000
4080	6,500
4530	3,300
4990	1,700
5440	1,000

The table helps us in determining what is known as equivalent load factor. For example, a wheel load of 2268 kg when applied 1,05,000 fails the pavements, whereas 2720 kg wheel load requires 50,000 repetitions for failing the pavement. Therefore, 2720 kg wheel load may be considered equivalent to 1,05,000/50,000 i.e. 2.1 times the wheel load 2268 kg. That is equivalent wheel load factor for 2720 kg wheel is 2.1. These equivalent load factors were suggested by Liddle, on the basis of A.A.S.H.O. test to convert the vehicle to standard 8200 kg and are tabulated below. Equivalent load factor for any other standard weight axle could be had by assuming linear law.

Table 8.2 : Equivalent Factor

Axle Loads	Equivalent Factors	
	Single Axle	Tandom Axle Sets
910	0.0002	
1810	0.0025	
2720	0.01	0.0009
3630	0.04	0.0027
4540	0.08	0.01
5440	0.18	0.02
6350	0.34	0.03
7260	0.60	0.05
8160	1.00	0.08
9070	1.59	0.09
9980	2.43	0.11
10890	3.59	0.17
11790	5.15	0.24
12700	7.21	0.34
13610	9.88	0.47
14520	13.29	0.63
15430	17.57	0.82
16320	22.89	1.07
17320	29.40	1.38
18140	37.31	1.75
19070	46.82	2.19

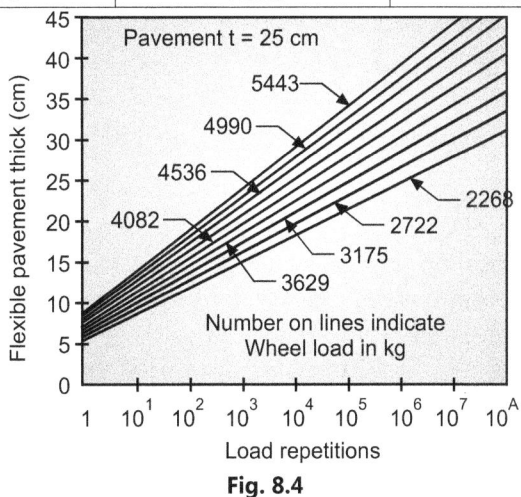

Fig. 8.4

The above table is based on the tests conducted by American Association of State Highways officials at Illinois and may vary from country to country. A general equation for equivalent factor can be stated as,

$$\text{Equivalent factor} = \left(\frac{W_i}{8200}\right)^A$$

The exponent A may vary from 2.5 to 4.6 depending upon the thickness of asphaltic pavement and its temperature. It should be noted, we in India have not been in a position to conduct such exhaustive tests such as A.A.S.H.O. due to monetary constraint. In the above equation, 8200 kg is considered standard wheel load.

Impact : As far as flexible pavements are considered, no impact allowance need be made. This is because of the fact that the traffic load comes rapidly and the strength of material tested rapidly is higher than when it is tested in a static condition. As the speed of the vehicle increases, stresses and deflections in the road surface decrease. For rigid pavements, joints do suffer due to impact. Generally, the impact allowance of 20 % is commonly used for the design of rigid pavements. But that is not a hard and fast rule.

8.7 METHODS OF DESIGNING FLEXIBLE PAVEMENTS

8.7.1 North Dakota Cone Test Method

This method was devised by North Dakota State Highway Department. The method essentially consists of pushing a cone in the sub-grade. The half angle of the cone is 7° 45'. The cone is pushed into the ground for successive weights of 5, 10, 20, 30, 40 kg and deflection under each load is obtained. Since, theoretically the penetration for 10 kg load should be half that of 40 kg load, the value of correction is C = Δ 40 − 2 Δ 10, where Δ 40 and Δ 10 are penetrations at 40 and 10 kg load. This correction is added to each of the observed deflection to get true penetration. Suppose for the load W, the true penetration is h, then the radius of the bearing area is $h \tan \frac{\theta}{2}$ and the bearing area is $\frac{\pi}{4}\left(2 h \tan \frac{\theta}{2}\right)^2$ or $\pi h^2 \tan^2 \frac{\theta}{2}$ and therefore, the bearing pressure for the load W is $\frac{W}{\pi h^2 \tan^2 \frac{\theta}{2}}$.

See Fig. 8.5 for each value of W i.e. 5 kg, 10 kg, 20 kg etc., we shall have different penetration and as such, we can get bearing pressures corresponding to different load. Averaging these bearing pressures, we can get bearing pressure for the ground. Boyd, has obtained the total thickness of the flexible pavement from this data as

$$h = \frac{72.45}{(\text{Bearing pressure})^{0.388}}$$

The discussed equation was obtained on the basis of cone bearing value data for many highways in Dakota U.S.A. It is also stated by Dakota Highway officials that, for cone bearing pressure of 28 kg/cm² or more, the minimum total thickness of 24 cm should be provided. This section may consist of 12.50 cm sub-base, 5 cm of stabilised aggregate base and 6.5 cm of asphaltic concrete wearing course.

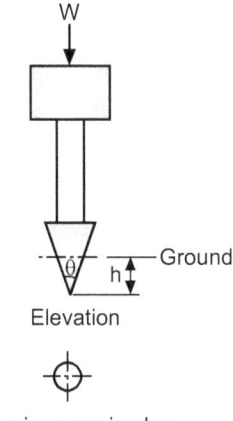

Fig. 8.5

When the cone bearing pressure is less than 28 kg/cm², additional sub-base is to be provided.

It is very clear that the method is useful for fine grained sub-grades, but when there are somewhat coarser particles in the sub-grade, one is likely to get eratic readings, and the method will fail in that case. The method is possibly very good for cement stabilized base coarse.

8.7.2 Methods Based on Plate Bearing Tests

The basis of these methods is to determine modulus of elasticity of sub-grade and from that, determine the pavement thickness. Originally this method was devised by U.S. Navy for air field pavements, but now is extensively used for highway pavements also. The method involves the following steps :

Step 1 :

A plate bearing test is conducted on the sub-grade. Preferably test should be conducted during the severest season. The circular plate is loaded in increments of 20 % of safe load for the final deflection of 6.25 mm. For a two layer system, modulus of elasticity of the sub-grade is given by

$$E_{sub} = \frac{1.18\, p_1\, a}{\Delta_1}$$

where, E_{sub} = Modulus of elasticity of sub-grade in kg/cm².

p_1 = Pressure on plate for Δ_1 deflection in cm in test on sub-grade.

a = Radius of plate.

Δ_1 = Deflection in cm.

Naturally, for each value of Δ and p, we can get E_{sub}, average value of observations may be taken for computation purposes. Now, base course of 15 to 30 cm thick is now constructed over the same area. The compacted density and moisture content of this constructed course should be the same as the base course to be constructed in the field. The base course constructed could be 4.5 m × 4.5 m or even upto 6 m × 6 m. At the centre of this course, the plate bearing test is now conducted as previously. Let p_2, Δ_2 be the pressure and deflection values in test 2. At this stage, we make use of Burmister analysis for two layer system.

8.7.3 Burmister Analysis for two Layer System

In the flexible pavement system, the system consists of layers of decreasing modulus of elasticity. Burmister considered an elastic slab of finite depth but of infinite horizontal extent placed on semi-infinite material of lower modulus of elasticity and the upper slab being loaded by a circular area. This more or less reflects the state of affairs in the flexible pavement. For a value of Poisson's ratio equal to 0.5 and for different ratios of modulus of elasticities of base and sub-grade, vertical stresses were computed by Burmister and shown in Fig. 8.6. The use of this figure is comparatively easy. Let us suppose that, plate that is loaded on the base is 0.5 meter radius and the intensity of loading is say 15 kg/cm². We require the state of stress at z = 1 meter. Then $\frac{z}{a} = \frac{1}{0.5} = 2$. Further, it is given that $\frac{E_{base\ course}}{E_{sub-grade}} = 5$, then vertical stress influence coefficient is 0.2 about and stress at this point is 15 × 0.2 = 3.0 kg/cm² about. Now suppose we want to know state of stress at z = 0.25 meter. Now $\frac{z}{a} = \frac{0.25}{0.5} = 0.5$.

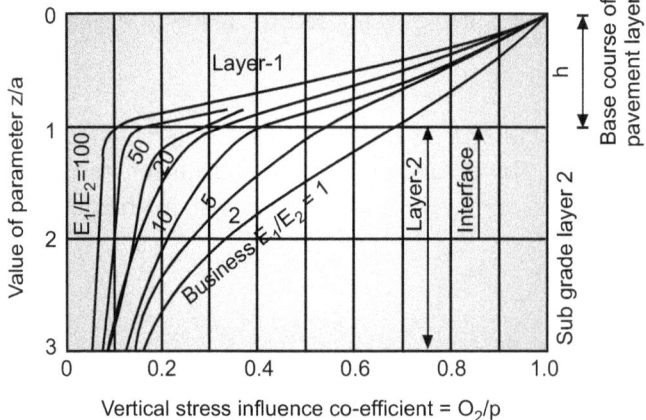

Fig. 8.6

For this value of $\frac{z}{a} = 0.5$ $\frac{E_{base}}{E_{sub}} = 5$, we have $\frac{6z}{p} = 0.9$ and the stress at this point is $0.9 \times 15 = 13.5$ kg/cm². When $\frac{E_{base}}{E_{sub}} = 1$, it is Boussinesque stress distribution. Since, all the curves for $\frac{E_{base}}{E_{sub}}$ lie to the left of the curve for $\frac{E_{base}}{E_{sub}} = 1$, it shows that, when we provide two layers, the stresses are reduced as compared to the case when we provide only one layer i.e. $\frac{E_1}{E_2} = \pm 1$. When $\frac{z}{a} > 3$, all the curves cluster towards each other showing that for $\frac{z}{a} > 3$, stresses in two layered medium and single layer medium are somewhat same. The same graph also shows that the clustering of the curves is occurring after $\frac{z}{a} = 2.5$. That is there is no point in increasing the thickness of the layer 2 beyond $\frac{z}{a} = 2.5$. Experiments in the field have also indicated that the capacity of granular materials to carry load per cm of its thickness decrease rapidly after reaching a maximum at a thickness approximately equal to the diameter of loaded area. The source of error in the graph and in general in using the Burmister theory for pavement thickness are :

- Elastic properties of the soil below a certain depth have very small effect on the stresses and displacements in the pavement and sub-grade. As far as stresses are concerned, the statement is O.K. but may not be alright as regards displacement.
- Burmister had assumed that Poisson's ratio will be 0.5 for all the layers while constructing the graph. This can cause error in the construction of the graph. On the assumption of rough interface between layer 1 and layer 2, irrespective of the ratio of $\frac{E_{base}}{E_{sub}}$ and the relative thickness of layer 1 and layer 2, the deflection of the two layer system was obtained as,

$$\Delta = 1.15 \frac{pa}{E_{sub}} F_W \text{ – for flexible plate}$$

and $$\Delta = 1.18 \frac{pa}{E_{sub}} F_W \text{ – for rigid plate}$$

F_W = displacement factor which is dimensionless and is a function of $\frac{E_1}{E_2}$ as well as the depth to radius ratio.

The curves of F_W against the thickness h in multiples of radius are shown in Fig. 8.7. Making use of this in Burmister analysis, we can now write

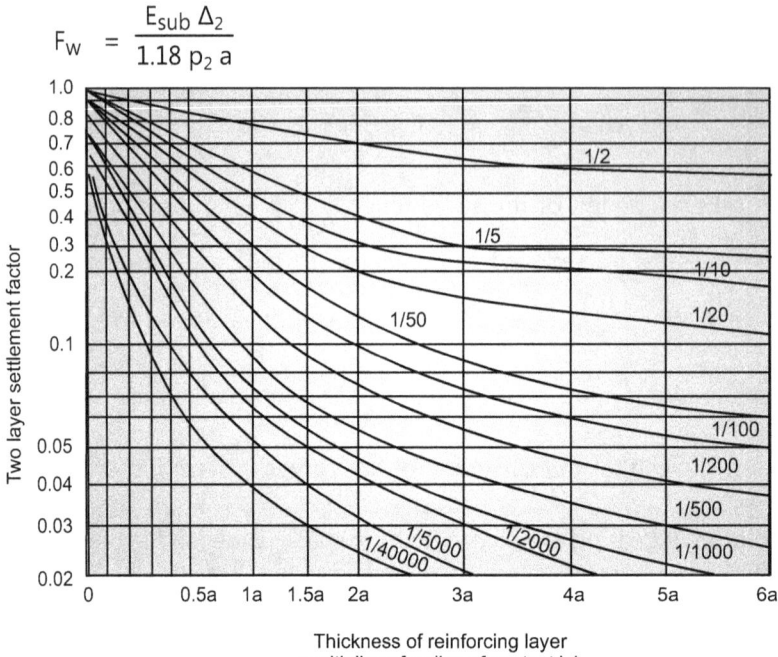

Fig. 8.7

In the case of flexible pavement design, we know h, the thickness of top bituminous layer a, the radius of bearing plate used for test, p_2 the bearing pressure for deflection Δ_2 and E_{sub} modulus of elasticity of sub-grade. The substitution of these factors in the above equation would yield F_w, the settlement factor. Now knowing the settlement factor F_w, h, a and using Fig. 8.7, we get the value $\dfrac{E_{base}}{E_{sub}}$, where E_{base} is modulus for the layer 1 that is the top layer or base course. We know the value E_{sub}, therefore we can get the value of modulus of elasticity for base course.

Let the wheel load be W and the tyre inflation pressure be pif, then approximate contact area will be $\dfrac{W}{pif}$. This is more or less on the assumption that supports furnished by side-walls of tyres is ignored. We may assume as U.S. Navy has done, that side wall support is ten percent and thus contact pressure may be assumed to be greater than tyre pressure by a factor equal to 1.1 and contact area is equal to wheel load divided by 1.1 × tyre pressure or $0.9 \times \dfrac{\text{wheel load}}{\text{tyre pressure}}$. We must remember here that, as far as plate bearing test is concerned, the plate can be considered as rigid but the wheel tyre can not be considered as rigid. In fact it is quite akin to a flexible plate. Therefore, we must make use of flexible plate equation to get settlement factor F_w. That is

$$\Delta_2 = \frac{1.5\, p_2\, a}{E_{base}}\, F_W$$

Here we assume $\Delta_2 = 0.5$ cm and get the corresponding value of p_2 from the actual test conducted and $F_W = \frac{0.5 \times E_{base}}{1.5\, p_2\, a} = \frac{E_{base}}{3\, p_2\, a}$. Thus we now know the settlement factor for flexible plate and $\frac{E_{base}}{E_{sub}}$. For this couplet, we can get the thickness h as a multiple of 'a' from Fig. 8.7. Thus, we have obtained the initial tentative thickness of base course.

Steps 2 and 3 :

This theoretical thickness is now to be verified. Let us suppose that the road is passing through fill section. Then on the actual alignment, we construct bases of varying thickness i.e. 0.5, 0.75, 1, 1.25, 1.5 times the theoretical thickness. Plate bearing test is conducted on each of this base. The plate has a radius corresponding to the effective contact area of radius 'a' and the load to be employed is a wheel load. Of course prior to the construction of the base course, the sub-grade should be in its weakest condition. All these tests should preferably be conducted in the severest season i.e. rainy season. If this is simply impossible, the sub-grade should be thoroughly saturated before constructing the base. Now in this plate load test, for a particular thickness of the base, we have the plate which has a radius corresponding to the effective contact radius and the load equal to wheel load. We thus, know the settlement for this combination. We plot this settlement against the thickness of the base. The thickness which produces the settlement of 5 mm is the required thickness.

In addition to base course, we have on it's top the bituminous surfacings. The added bituminous concrete surfacing is considered as additional and is not considered in arriving the thickness of the base. As a guide, the following table may be consulted for finding the thickness of bituminous concrete pavement. The table gives thickness depending upon wheel load.

Table 8.3 : Pavement Surface Thickness

Wheel Load (kg)	Thickness (cm)
6800 kg and soil cement or macadam base.	3.75
6800 kg or less other bases.	5.0
6800 to 11375 kg.	6.25
11375 to 22750 kg.	7.50
22750 kg and greater.	10.0

In general, the base course should have strength of 60 to 80 CBR for tyre pressure upto 10.5 kg/cm² or greater than 10.5 kg/cm².

8.7.4 Mcleod Method

Mcleod method is actually for the design of flexible pavement used in runways. This method was the result of extensive series of tests conducted on existing air fields in Canada. Surface, base and sub-grade of the runways were tested for plate load, CBR, triaxial compression etc. and the method evolved. This test data had indicated that, if the repetitive plate load test is carried on base/sub-grade the load at the surface is a direct function of sub-grade support for a fixed thickness of pavement. This relationship is shown in Fig. 8.8 and for a fixed deflection. This proposed deflection was 12.5 mm for runways and 9 mm for taxiways apron and turn around design. The analysis of the extensive data resulted in the following equation :

$$T_{base} = K \log_{10} \frac{P}{S}$$

where, T_{base} = Thickness of base.

P = Applied wheel load in kg at 12.5 mm deflection for runways and wheel load corresponding to 9 mm deflection for taxiways aprons and turn around designs for same contact area pertaining to P.

S = Support of sub-grade in kg for respective deflection and same contact area.

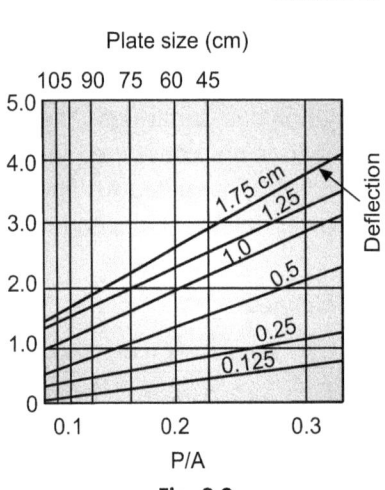
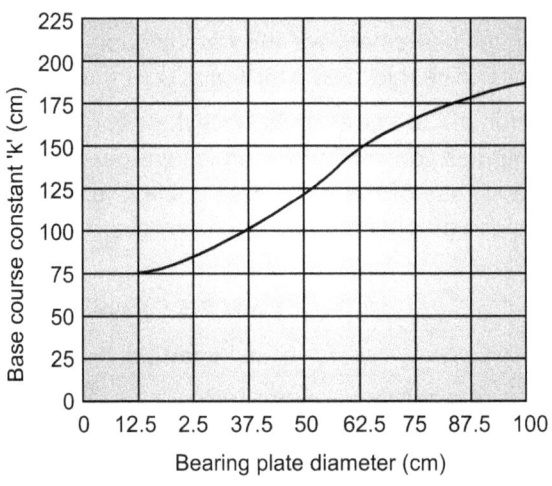

Fig. 8.8   **Fig. 8.9**

The base course constant K varies with the diameter of the plate employed and this variation is shown in Fig. 8.9. Though first evolved for air port runways, the method can be profitably used for highways also. It should be remembered that the thickness obtained is for crushed stone base. If stronger base is to be used, the thickness of crushed stone base should be divided by suitable conversion factor. The suitable conversion factors are given in Table 8.4.

Table 8.4

Base Material	Conversion Factor
High quality asphalt concrete.	2.0
Asphaltic pavement.	1.5
Water Bound Macadam Base.	1.5
Crushed stone.	1.0

The empirical relationship between sub-grade support for 75 cm diameter plate at 5 mm deflection and support at any other deflection is given in Fig. 8.9.

8.7.5 Effect of Lateral Confinement

The method discussed does not take into account the lateral confinement of the sub-grade. In actual practice, the base and the sub-grade is not that free for lateral expansion, that is, it is somewhat laterally confined. Mehdiratta, had tried to evaluate the effect of lateral confinement on pavement analysis. His studies has indicated that, by introducing vertical diaphragms of rigid material like stone slabs along the pavement edge, it is possible that reduced thickness of pavement could be used, thus lowering down the construction cost. Though the method holds promise, the author is of the opinion that, large scale field trials are required to justify this conclusion.

8.7.6 Application of Plate Load Method to Indian Conditions

In Indian conditions, water bound macadam road is first constructed between two destinations. When traffic increases, this water bound macadam road is to be black topped to cater for the increased traffic. In such case, the existent water bound macadam road which may be in denuded condition is levelled and made up. Since, this water bound macadam road is now the base course for the subsequent bituminous layer, the plate load tests have to be conducted on this W.B.M. The data will generally indicate that, the thickness of W.B.M. is not upto the expectation. In such additional aggregate is added to this W.B.M. course, so as to make-up its thickness to the desired and computed level.

8.8 IRC METHOD OF DESIGN OF FLEXIBLE PAVEMENTS

8.8.1 Overview

Indian roads congress has specified the design procedures for flexible pavements based on CBR values. The Pavement designs given in the previous edition IRC : 37-1984 were applicable to design traffic up to only 30 million standard axles (msa). The earlier code is empirical in nature which has limitations regarding applicability and extrapolation. This guideline follows analytical designs and developed new set of designs up to 150 msa.

Scope : These guidelines will apply to design of flexible pavements for Expressway, National Highways, State Highways, Major District Roads and other categories of roads. Flexible pavements are considered to include the pavements which have bituminous surfacing and granular base and sub-base courses conforming to IRC/ MOST standards. These guidelines apply to new pavements.

Design Criteria : The flexible pavements has been modeled as a three layer structure and stresses and strains at critical locations have been computed using the linear elastic model. To give proper consideration to the aspects of performance, the following three types of pavement distress resulting from repeated (cyclic) application of traffic loads are considered :

1. Vertical compressive strain at the top of the sub-grade which can cause sub-grade deformation resulting in permanent deformation at the pavement surface.
2. Horizontal tensile strain or stress at the bottom of the bituminous layer which can cause fracture of the bituminous layer.
3. Pavement deformation within the bituminous layer. While the permanent deformation within the bituminous layer can be controlled by meeting the mix design requirements, thickness of granular and bituminous layers are selected using the analytical design approach so that strains at the critical points are within the allowable limits. For calculating tensile strains at the bottom of the bituminous layer, the stiffness of Dense Bituminous Macadam (DBM) layer with 60/70 bitumen has been used in the analysis.

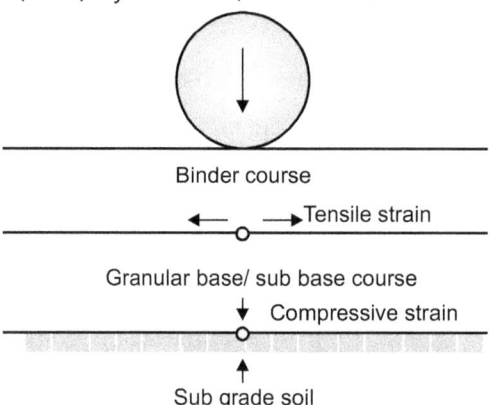

Fig. 8.10 : Critical locations in pavement

A and B are the critical locations for tensile strains (ε_t). Maximum value of the strain is adopted for design. C is the critical location for the vertical subgrade strain (ε_z) since the maximum value of the (ε_z) occurs mostly at C.

Fatigue Criteria : Bituminous surfacing of pavements display flexural fatigue cracking if the tensile strain at the bottom of the bituminous layer is beyond certain limit. The relation between the fatigue life of the pavement and the tensile strain in the bottom of the bituminous layer was obtained as :

$$N_1 = 2.21 \times 10^{-4} \times \left(\frac{1}{\varepsilon_t}\right)^{3.89} \times \left(\frac{1}{E}\right)^{0.854} \qquad \ldots(8.1)$$

In which N_1 is the allowable number of load repetitions to control fatigue cracking and E is the Elastic Modulus of bituminous layer. The use of equation 28.1 would resulting fatigue cracking of 20% of the total area.

Rutting Criteria : The allowable number of load repetitions to control permanent deformation can be expressed as :

$$N_1 = 4.1656 \times 10^{-8} \times \left(\frac{1}{\varepsilon_z}\right)^{4.5337} \qquad ...(8.2)$$

N_r is the number of cumulative standard axles to produce rutting of 20 mm.

Design Procedure : Based on the performance of existing designs and using analytical approach, simple design charts and a catalogue of pavement designs are added in the code. The pavement designs are given for subgrade CBR values ranging from 2 % to 10 % and design traffic ranging from 1 msa to 150 msa for an average annual pavement temperature of 35 C. The later thicknesses obtained from the analysis have been slightly modified to adapt the designs to stage construction. Using the following simple input arameters, appropriate designs could be chosen for the given traffic and soil strength :

- Design traffic in terms of cumulative number of standard axles; and
- CBR value of sub grade.

Design Traffic : The method considers traffic in terms of the cumulative number of standard axles (8160 kg) to be carried by the pavement during the design life. This requires the following information :

1. Initial traffic in terms of CVPD.
2. Traffic growth rate during the design life.
3. Design life in number of years.
4. Vehicle damage factor (VDF).
5. Distribution of commercial traffic over the carriage way.

(1) Initial Traffic : Initial traffic is determined in terms of commercial vehicles per day (CVPD). For the structural design of the pavement only commercial vehicles are considered assuming laden weight of three tonnes or more and their axle loading will be considered. Estimate of the initial daily average traffic flow for any road should normally be based on 7-day 24-hour classified traffic counts (ADT). In case of new roads, traffic estimates can be made on the basis of potential land use and traffic on existing routes in the area.

Traffic growth rate Traffic growth rates can be estimated (i) by studying the past trends of traffic growth and (ii) by establishing econometric models. If adequate data is not available, it is recommended that an average annual growth rate of 7.5 percent may be adopted.

(2) Design Life : For the purpose of the pavement design, the design life is defined in terms of the cumulative number of standard axles that can be carried before strengthening of the pavement is necessary. It is recommended that pavements for arterial roads like NH, SH should be designed for a life of 15 years, EH and urban roads for 20 years and other categories of roads for 10 to 15 years.

(3) Vehicle Damage Factor : The vehicle damage factor (VDF) is a multiplier for converting the number of commercial vehicles of different axle loads and axle configurations to the number of standard axle-load repetitions. It is defined as equivalent number of standard axles per commercial vehicle. The VDF varies with the axle configuration, axle loading, terrain, type of road, and from region to region. The axle load equivalency factors are used to convert different axle load repetitions into equivalent standard axle load repetitions. For these equivalency factors refer IRC : 37 2001. The exact VDF values are arrived after extensive field surveys.

(4) Vehicle Distribution : A realistic assessment of distribution of commercial traffic by direction and by lane is necessary as it directly affects the total equivalent standard axle load application used in the design. Until reliable data is available, the following distribution may be assumed. Single lane roads : Traffic tends to be more channelized on single roads than two lane roads and to allow for this concentration of wheel load repetitions, the design should be based on total number of commercial vehicles in both directions.

Two-lane single carriageway roads : The design should be based on 75 % of the commercial vehicles in both directions.

Four-lane single carriageway roads : The design should be based on 40 % of the total number of commercial vehicles in both directions.

Dual carriageway roads : For the design of dual two-lane carriageway roads should be based on 75 % of the number of commercial vehicles in each direction. For dual three-lane carriageway and dual four-lane carriageway the distribution factor will be 60 % and 45 % respectively.

(5) Pavement Thickness Design Charts : For the design of pavements to carry traffic in the range of 1 to 10 msa, use chart 1 and for traffic in the range 10 to 150 msa, use chart 2 of IRC : 37 2001. The design curves relate pavement thickness to the cumulative number of standard axles to be carried over the design life for different sub-grade CBR values ranging from 2 % to 10 %. The design charts will give the total thickness of the pavement for the above inputs. The total thickness consists of granular sub-base, granular base and bituminous surfacing. The individual layers are designed based on the recommendations given below and the subsequent tables.

8.8.2 Pavement Composition

Sub-Base : Sub-base materials comprise natural sand, gravel, laterite, brick metal, crushed stone or combinations there of meeting the prescribed grading and physical requirements. The sub-base material should have a minimum CBR of 20 % and 30 % for traffic upto 2 msa and traffic exceeding 2 msa respectively. Sub-base usually consist of granular or WBM and the thickness should not be less than 150 mm for design traffic less than 10 msa and 200 mm for design traffic of 1:0 msa and above.

Base : The recommended designs are for unbounded granular bases which comprise conventional Water Bound Macadam (WBM) or Wet Mix Macadam (WMM) or equivalent confirming to MOST specifications. The materials should be of good quality with minimum thickness of 225 mm for traffic up to 2 msa an 150 mm for traffic exceeding 2 msa.

Bituminous Surfacing : The surfacing consists of a wearing course or a binder course plus wearing course. The most commonly used wearing courses are surface dressing, open graded premix carpet, mix seal surfacing, semi-dense bituminous concrete and bituminous concrete. For binder course, MOST specifies, it is desirable to use Bituminous Macadam (BM) for traffic upto o 5 msa and Dense Bituminous Macadam (DBM) for traffic more than 5 msa.

SOLVED EXAMPLES

Example 8.1 : Design the pavement for construction of a new bypass with the following data :
1. Two lane carriage way.
2. Initial traffic in the year of completion of construction = 400 CVPD (sum of both directions).
3. Traffic growth rate = 7.5%.
4. Design life = 15 years.
5. Vehicle damage factor based on axle load survey = 2.5 standard axle per commercial vehicle.
6. Design CBR of subgrade soil = 4%.

Solution : (1) Distribution factor = 0.75.

(2) $N = \dfrac{365 \times [(1 + (0.075)^{15} - 1)]}{0.075} \times 400 \times 0.75 \times 2.5$

(3) Total pavement thickness for CBR 4% and traffic 7.2 msa from IRC : 37 2001 chart 1 = 660 mm.

(4) Pavement composition can be obtained by interpolation from Pavement Design Catalogue (IRC : 37 2001).
(a) Bituminous surfacing = 25 mm SDBC + 70 mm DBM.
(b) Road-base = 250 mm WBM.
(c) Sub-base = 315 mm granular material of CBR not less than 30%.

Example 8.2 : Design the pavement for construction of a new two lane carriageway for design life 15 years using IRC method. The initial traffic in the year of completion in each direction is 150 CVPD and growth rate is 5%. Vehicle damage factor based on axle load survey = 2.5 std axle per commercial vehicle. Design CBR of subgrade soil = 4%.

Solution :
(1) Distribution factor = 0.75

(2) $N = \dfrac{365 \times [(1 + (0.05)^{15} - 1)]}{0.05} \times 300 \times 0.75 \times 2.5$

　　= 4430348.837

　　= 4.4 msa

(3) Total pavement thickness for CBr 4 % and traffic 4.4. msa from IRC : 372001 chart 1 = 580mm

(4) Pavement composition can be obtained by interpolation from pavement Design Catalogue (IRC : 37 2001).
　　(a) Bituminous surfacing = 20mm PC + 50mm BM
　　(b) road-base = 250mm Granular base
　　(c) sub-base = 280mm granular material.

8.9 INTRODUCTION TO RIGID PAVEMENTS

Pavements could be classified as rigid or flexible. Bituminous pavements, Water Bound Macadam roads, stabilized bases etc. could be classed as flexible pavement whereas concrete pavements are rigid pavements.

8.9.1 Action of Rigid and Flexible Pavement

The flexible pavement layer transmits the stresses to the lower layer by grain to grain transfer. The vertical stress is maximum on the pavement surface and is equal to contact pressure. The stresses get decreased at lower layers in the shape of truncated cone. Therefore, the lower layer in the pavement structure could be of less strength and the topmost layer will have the highest strength. The top layer has also to cater for wearing action of wheel load. In general the strength and rigidity of flexible pavement is much less than that of the rigid pavement. Due to this the flexible pavement layers mirror the deformation of the lower layers on the surface of top layer, hence the name flexible. Since the layers are arranged one over the other in increasing strength order, stress distribution pattern is constrained. On the other hand rigid pavement possesses considerable flexural strength and rigidity. Most of the times, it is a concrete slab laid on sub-grade. Therefore stresses are not transferred from grain to grain to the lower layer. In fact due to slab action large amount sub-grade area takes-up stresses, therefore, it is the stresses generated in the concrete slab due to placement of wheel - load and temperature stresses generated that are the guiding factor. Due to it's rigidity, the rigid pavement does not get deformed to the shape of the lower surface as it can very easily bridge the minor variations of the lower layer. Cement concrete pavement surface is a good wearing surface, many a times it can be laid directly on the compacted sub-grade.

8.9.2 Methods of Pavement Design

Following methods of pavement design will be considered :

- Westergaard method,
- Goldbeck or Older's method,
- Spangler's Equation,
- Pickett's Equation,
- I.R.C. method.

(a) Westergaard Method : Westergaard in 1920 developed an equation for an elastic plate resting on subgrade. He assumed that :

- Cement concrete slab is homogeneous, isotropic elastic thin plane resting on the sub-grade below.
- Pavement slab is infinite in extent and the subgrade can be considered as if it is a dense liquid.
- The reaction of the subgrade is in vertical direction only and is proportional to the settlement of the slab, the coefficient of proportionality between them being the modulus of subgrade reaction.
- The slab has uniform thickness.
- In order to express deformation characteristics of the pavement, he coined the term, the radius of relative stiffness (l) which is,

$$l = \sqrt[4]{\frac{Eh^3}{12(1-\mu^2)k}}$$

where E, μ and h are respectively modulus of elasticity, Poisson's ratio and thickness of slab and k is modulus of subgrade reaction. He further defined equivalent radius of resisting section as $b = a$ for $\frac{a}{h} \geq 1.724$ and $b = \sqrt{1.6 a^2 + h^2} - 0.675$ for $\frac{a}{h} \leq 1.724$.

With these assumptions, he used theory of thin plates resting on elastic foundation along with Ritz method of successive approximation and the principle of maximum energy to determine tensile stresses at the edge corner and interior loading.

$$\text{Edge loading, tensile stress} = \frac{0.52 P}{h^2}\left[4 \log_{10}\left(\frac{l}{b} + 0.359\right)\right]$$

$$\text{Corner loading, tensile stress} = \frac{3P}{h^2}\left[1 - \left(\frac{a\sqrt{2}}{l}\right)^{0.6}\right]$$

$$\text{Interior loading, tensile stress} = \frac{0.3162 P}{h^2}\left[4 \log_{10}\frac{l}{b} + 1.069\right]$$

where, P is the wheel load and a radius of wheel load distribution. Corner loading is generally very severe. It develops negative bonding moment at the top of slab causing maximum tensile stress at the top surface parallel to the bisector of the corner angle. The maximum stress does not occur at the load point, but at a distance d along the corner bisector given by the relation $d = 2.38 \sqrt{al}$ where the terms a, and l are already described.

After computing stresses as per Westergaard, the thickness of pavement should be such that the stresses are within limit. The ideas propunded by Westergaard have been extensively used in I.R.C. method.

(b) Kelly Method : Teller and Southerland had carried out, what is now known as Arlington tests (1939). Kelly developed following equation based on these tests. The equation is valid for corner loading. Corner loading, tensile stress,

$$= \frac{3P}{h^2} \left[1 - \left(\frac{a\sqrt{2}}{l} \right)^{1.2} \right]$$

Kelly equation is incorporated in I.R.C. method. Kelly's equation for corner loading was simplified by Spangler (1942) and which is given below. Corner loading tensile stress

$$= \frac{3.2P}{h^2} \left(1 - \frac{a\sqrt{2}}{l} \right)$$

(c) Pickett Equation : Pickett (1951) proposed semi-empirical formulae both for protected and unprotected corners. These equations are

Unprotected corner, tensile stress

$$= \frac{4.2P}{h^2} \left[1 - \frac{\sqrt{a/l}}{0.925 + 0.22 \frac{a}{l}} \right]$$

For the protected corner,

$$\text{tensile stress} = \frac{3.36P}{h^2} \left(1 - \frac{\sqrt{a/l}}{0.925 + 0.22 \frac{a}{l}} \right)$$

(d) Goldbeck or Older's Method : When the circular loaded area occupies the corner of the pavement, pavement acts as a cantilever. By assuming that the bending moment acts on a plane diagonally across the corner and that it is distributed uniformly over the cross-section, Goldbeck obtained stress due to corner load as

$$\text{Corner load, tensile stress} = \frac{3P}{h^2}$$

8.9.3 Design of Rigid Pavements as per IRC

Design of rigid pavement based on the guidelines provided by IRC : 58 – 1988 proceeds on the basis of following lines.

Design Wheel Load : Axle loads of commercial vehicles have increased considerably. There is revision of legal limit on the maximum laden axle loads of commercial vehicles from 8160 kg to 10200 kg so that the maximum wheel load now is 5100 kg. For most of the commercial highway vehicles, the tyre inflation pressure could be taken from 5.3 to 7.3

kg/cm². Generally, the later value is taken so that maximum pressure is transmitted to the pavement.

Traffic Intensity : Repetitive loading caused due to traffic is a major devastating force for the highways. These effects may not be of much consequence in case of low traffic intensities because of considerable time lag between successive passes but has significant importance in the case of heavily trafficked pavements as the fatigue strength of concrete reduces with increase in the number of load repetitions. It is very clear that the maximum intensity of traffic will occur at the end of the design life of the road. It is considered adequate by I.R.C. to consider 20 years traffic for the rigid pavement. This traffic projection for main highways may be based on the following equation suggested by I.R.C.

$$T = P(1 + r)^{n + 20}$$

where, T = Design traffic intensity in terms of number of commercial vehicles (laden weight $\geq$ 3 tonnes) per day,

P = Traffic intensity at last traffic count,

r = Annual rate of increase of traffic intensity, and

n = Number of years since the last traffic count and commissioning the new concrete pavement.

The traffic intensity P should be based on seven days average based on 24 hours count, in exceptional cases three days count may be used. When data is not available, the value of r may be taken as 7.5 for rural roads and 10 for urban roads. Based on traffic intensity, the rigid pavement may be classed in the following categories for the purpose of design.

Table 8.5 : Traffic Classification for Rigid Pavement Design

Traffic Classification	Design Traffic Intensity Vehicles (Laden Weight > 3 Tonnes) Per Day at the End of Design Life
A	0 – 15
B	15 – 45
C	45 – 150
D	150 – 450
E	450 – 1500
F	1500 – 4500
G	> 4500 and all express ways

Environmental Parameters : The difference in temperature between the top and bottom surfaces of the concrete slab largely determines the thickness of the slab. Similarly, mean temperature cycles daily and annually of concrete pavement affect the maximum spacing of contraction and expansion joint in the pavement and for maximum safe spacing of expansion joint, this data is required. As far as the temperature differential between the top and bottom of slab is concerned, the following table prepared by Central Road Research Institute and incorporated in IRC 5.8 – 1988 may be used.

Table 8.6 : Temperature Differentials in Concrete Roads

Zone	States	10	15	20	25	30
I	Punjab, U.P., Rajastan, Gujrat, Haryana, North M.P., excluding Hilly regions and coastal area	10.2	12.5	20	25	30
II	Bihar, West Bengal, Assam, Eastern Orissa	14.4	15.6	16.4	16.6	16.8
III	Maharashtra, Karnataka, South M.P., Andhra Pradesh, Western Orissa, North Madras	14.75	17.3	19.0	20.3	21.0
IV	Kerala and South Madras	13.2	15.0	16.4	17.6	18.1
V	Coastal regions bounded by hills	12.8	14.6	15.8	16.2	17.0
VI	Coastal areas unbounded by hills	13.6	15.5	17.0	19.0	19.2
	For hilly regions, actual observations should be conducted					

As far as the second point regarding mean temperature cycle is concerned, extensive data is not available, and as such somewhat conservative recommendations have been made by I.R.C.

8.9.4 Foundation Strength and Surface Characters

Modulus of sub-grade reaction is the best way of expressing foundation strength. Limiting design deflection for concrete pavement is 1.25 mm and as such modulus of sub-grade reaction value (K value) should be at this deflection. Test should be run on 75 cm diameter plate and one test per km per lane as a minimum is recommended. Sometimes 30 cm plate is used for plate test and in this case the following equation could be used

$$K_{75} = 0.5 \, K_{30}$$

where, K_{75} and K_{30} are the K values obtained on 75 cm and 30 cm diameter plate. When the sub-grade is uniform, the equation is all right. For layered construction, the above equation over-estimates the sub-grade strength and should be used with caution. The plate test should be conducted on the sub-grade, when it is placed in the most unfavourable climatic condition. A test just after the monsoon is the best. When plate test is not carried, approximate K value can be calculated based on CBR value by making use of the following table.

Table 8.7 : Approximate K Value Corresponding to CBR Value for Homogeneous Sub-Grades

CBR Value % Soaked 4 Days	2	3	4	5	7	10	20	50	100
K value, kg/cm^3	2.08	2.77	3.46	4.16	4.84	5.54	6.92	13.85	22.16

If the K value of the subgrade is less than 5.5 kg/cm³, the subgrade should preferably be stabilized to attain higher value. For rocky sub-grades with K value more than 5.5 kg/cm³, the pavement can directly be laid on the subgrade after providing levelling course. These provisions do not apply to the clayey and expansive sub-grades which are dealt with separately.

Foundation Surface Characters : Smoothness or roughness of the foundation affects concrete slab movement and therefore joint spacing. The maximum safe spacing of joints increases with increase in surface roughness of the foundation in the case of expansion joints and decreases in the case of contraction joint. The following table classifies the foundation.

Table 8.8 : Types of Rigid Pavement Foundations According to their Surface Characters

Type of Foundation	Surface Characters
Compacted sand and gravel. Smooth foundation covered with water-proof paper	Very smooth
Compacted sand, gravel and clinker, stabilized soil, Rough foundation covered with water-proof paper	Smooth
Water bound macadam, soil gravel mix, Rolled lean concrete, lime pozzolona concrete etc.	Rough

The foundations adopted in our country are generally rough or smooth and these are considered by I.R.C.

Concrete Characteristics : Stresses induced in the concrete pavement i.e. rigid pavement are either due to bending or it's prevention and flexural strength of concrete is the governing criterion. This strength should not be less than 40 kg/cm² (40000 kN/m). This strength can be obtained from the concrete mix design strength by the following equation. Thus, if

- $\bar{S}$ = Structural design value for concrete strength to be considered for the design of concrete pavement.
- S = Mix design value of concrete strength.
- t = Tolerence factor for the desired confidence level.
- σ = Expected standard deviation of field test samples based on the knowledge of the type of the control. viz very good, good or fair then

$$\therefore \quad S = \bar{S} + t \cdot \sigma$$

That is the mix design strength should be slightly higher than the minimum flexural strength available in the field. To use the above equation, the values of t and σ for concrete compressive strength value of 280 kg/cm² (Table 8.9) are given in table below.

Table 8.9 : Quality Control and Values of t, σ to be Achieved

Quality Control	t	σ 1 kg/cm² = 100 kN/m²	Mix Design Strength, kg/cm² 1 kg cm² = 100 kN/m²
Very good	1.50	22 kg/cm²	315 kg/cm²
Good	1.50	33 kg/cm²	330 kg/cm²
Fair	1.50	52 kg/cm²	350 kg/cm²

8.9.5 The Quality Control

Very good, good, fair is described as follows :

Very good : Rigid and constant supervision of quality control team. Weigh batching use of graded aggregate with moisture determination of aggregates.

Good : Constant supervision of quality control team. Weigh batching. Use of graded aggregates with its moisture determination.

Fair : Control with volume batching for aggregates with occasional checking of quality control team for aggregate moisture and other things. The values given in the above table may vary plus or minus 7 %, 10 % and 15 % depending upon the quality control viz. very good, good or fair.

8.9.6 Modulus of Elasticity and Poisson's Ratio

The elastic modulus E of the concrete increases with increase in it's strength whereas the Poisson's ratio decreases with increase in value of E_o. Though experiments are best to ascertain these values for a concrete of flexural strength between 38 to 42 kg/cm², the value of E may be assumed to be 3×10^5 kg/cm² and the value μ to be 0.15.

8.9.7 Coefficient of Thermal Expansion

The coefficient of thermal expansion α of the concrete of the same mix proportion varies with the type of aggregate being high for siliceous aggregates, medium for igneous rocks and low for calcareous ones. For design purposes, a value of $\alpha = 10 \times 10^{-6}$/°C may be adopted.

8.10 DESIGN OF RIGID PAVEMENTS

Design of rigid pavement i.e. concrete pavement as per I.R.C. is split up in certain stages. These stages may be :

- Determination of slab thickness and spacing and layout of joints,
- Design of reinforcement at joints,
- Design of longitudinal reinforcement. These steps are now discussed.

Design of Rigid Pavement : The factors commonly considered for the design of pavement thickness are traffic loads and temperature variations as the two additives. The effects of moisture changes and shrinkage being generally opposed to temperature. These are of small magnitudes and would ordinarily relieve the temperature effects to some extent and as such are not normally considered relevant for the thickness design of pavement. We shall therefore consider the temperature and load effects only.

8.10.1 Temperature Effects

The top of the concrete slab is hotter than the bottom during the day and cooler during the night. The slab therefore warps upwards (top convex) during the day and downwards (top concave) during the night. The self weight of the slab tries to restraint this warping tendency, thus inducing stresses called temperature stress. These stresses are therefore flexural in nature being tensile at the bottom during the day at top and tensile at top during the night. Since resistance offered to warping at any section of the slab is a function of the weight of the slab upto that section, corners have very little resistance. The resistance or restraint is maximum in the slab interior and somewhat less at the edge. Therefore the temperature stresses induced in the pavement are negligible in the corner range and maximum at the interior.

8.10.2 Traffic Load Effects

Corner of the pavement slab is discontinuous in two directions, and maximum stress is caused here. The edge is discontinuous in one direction and as such has lower stress whereas traffic load causes least stress in the interior where the slab is continuous in all the directions. Furthermore, the corner of the slab tends to bend like a cantilever, thus inducing tension at top, interior, like a beam inducing tension at bottom. As far as edge is considered, main bending is along the edge, like a beam giving maximum tension at bottom.

8.10.3 The Combined Effect of Temperature and Load

The maximum combined tensile stresses in the three regions of the slab will thus be caused when the effects of temperature and loads are additive. This would occur during the day in the case of interior and edge region at the time of maximum temperature difference in the slab. In the corner region, the temperature stresses are negligible but the load stress is maximum at night when the corners of the slab exhibit tendency to lift updue to warping and loose partly the foundation support. Considering the total combined stress for the three regions viz corner edge and interior, it is therefore felt by IRC that both the corner and edge regions should be checked for total stresses and design of slab thickness based on the more critical conditions of the two. We therefore now set to calculate stresses in the regions as a prelude to design of pavement.

8.10.4 Calculation of Stresses

Edge Stresses : The edge stresses will be caused due to load and due to temperature. We shall consider these one by one.

Edge Stresses Due to Load : The load stress in the critical edge region may be obtained per Westergaard analysis and further modified by Teller and Sutherland. The following formula is suggested by I.R.C.

$$\sigma l e = 0.529 \frac{P}{h^2} (1 + 0.54 \mu) \left(4 \log_{10} \frac{l}{b} + \log_{10} b - 0.4048 \right)$$

where,
- $\sigma l e$ = load stress in the edge regions in kg/cm²
- P = design wheel load in kg
- h = pavement slab thickness in cm
- μ = Poisson's ratio for the concrete
- E = modulus of elasticity for concrete, kg/cm²
- K = reaction modulus of the pavement foundation, kg/cm³
- l = radius of relative stiffness = $\sqrt[4]{\dfrac{Eh^3}{12(1-\mu^2)K}}$
- b = radius of equivalent distribution of pressure area
  = a for $\dfrac{a}{h} \geq 1.724$
  = $\sqrt{1.6 a^2 + h^2} - 0.675 h$ for $\dfrac{a}{h} \leq 1.724$
- a = radius of contact area, contact area to be assumed circular

For ready reference, following tables may be consulted to ascertain the values of l and b directly. It should be noted that the formula suggested by IRC is in metric units and not in S.I. units.

Table 8.10 : The Values of Radius of Relative Stiffness for Different Values of Pavement Thickness and Foundation Reaction Modulus K, E for Concrete = 30×10^5 kg/cm²

h in cm	Radius of Relative Stiffness (cm) for Different Values of (kg/cm³)				
	K = 6	K = 8	K = 10	K = 15	K = 30
15	61.44	57.18	54.08	48.86	41.09
16	64.49	60.02	56.76	51.29	43.31
17	67.49	62.81	59.40	53.67	45.14
18	70.44	65.56	62.01	56.03	47.07
19	73.36	68.28	64.57	58.35	49.06
20	76.24	70.95	67.10	60.63	50.99
21	79.08	73.59	69.60	63.89	52.89
22	81.89	76.20	72.08	65.13	54.77
23	84.66	78.80	74.52	67.33	56.62
24	87.41	81.35	76.94	69.31	58.45
25	90.13	83.88	79.32	71.68	60.28

Table 8.11 : Radius of Equivalent Distribution of Pressure Section b, in Terms of Radius of Contact a and Slab Thickness 'h' i.e. Table of a/h Against b/h

a/h	b/h	a/h	b/h
0.0	0.325	1.0	0.937
0.1	0.333	1.1	1.039
0.2	0.357	1.2	1.143
0.3	0.387	1.3	1.250
0.4	0.446	1.4	1.358
0.5	0.508	1.5	1.470
0.6	0.580	1.6	1.582
0.7	0.661	1.7	1.695
0.8	0.747	1.724	1.724
0.9	0.840	> 1.1724	a/h

Edge Stresses Due to Temperature : Bradbury's coefficient along with Westergaard analysis may be employed in this case. The formula recommended by I.R.C. is

$$\sigma te = \frac{E \alpha \Delta t}{2} \cdot C,$$

where, σte = Temperature stress in the edge region.

Δt = Maximum temperature differential during day between top and bottom of the slab.

C = Bradbury's coefficient. This can be had from the charts, knowing the values of L/l and W/l.

L = Slab length, or spacing between consecutive contraction joints.

W = Slab width and

l = Radius of relative stiffness,

The Bradbury's coefficient may be obtained from table.

Table 8.12 : Values of Coefficient C Based on Bradbury's Chart

L/l or W/l	C
1.	0.000
2.	0.040
3.	0.175
4.	0.440
5.	0.720
6.	0.920
7.	1.030
8.	1.075
9.	1.080
10.	1.075
11.	1.050
12 and above	1.000

The intermediate values of C for the values of $\frac{L}{l}$ or $\frac{W}{l}$ may be incorporated and α is coefficient of thermal expansion for the concrete.

Design Charts : Fig. 8.11 and 8.12 give ready to use design charts for calculation of load stresses in the edge corner regions of rigid pavement slabs for the design wheel load of 5100 kg.

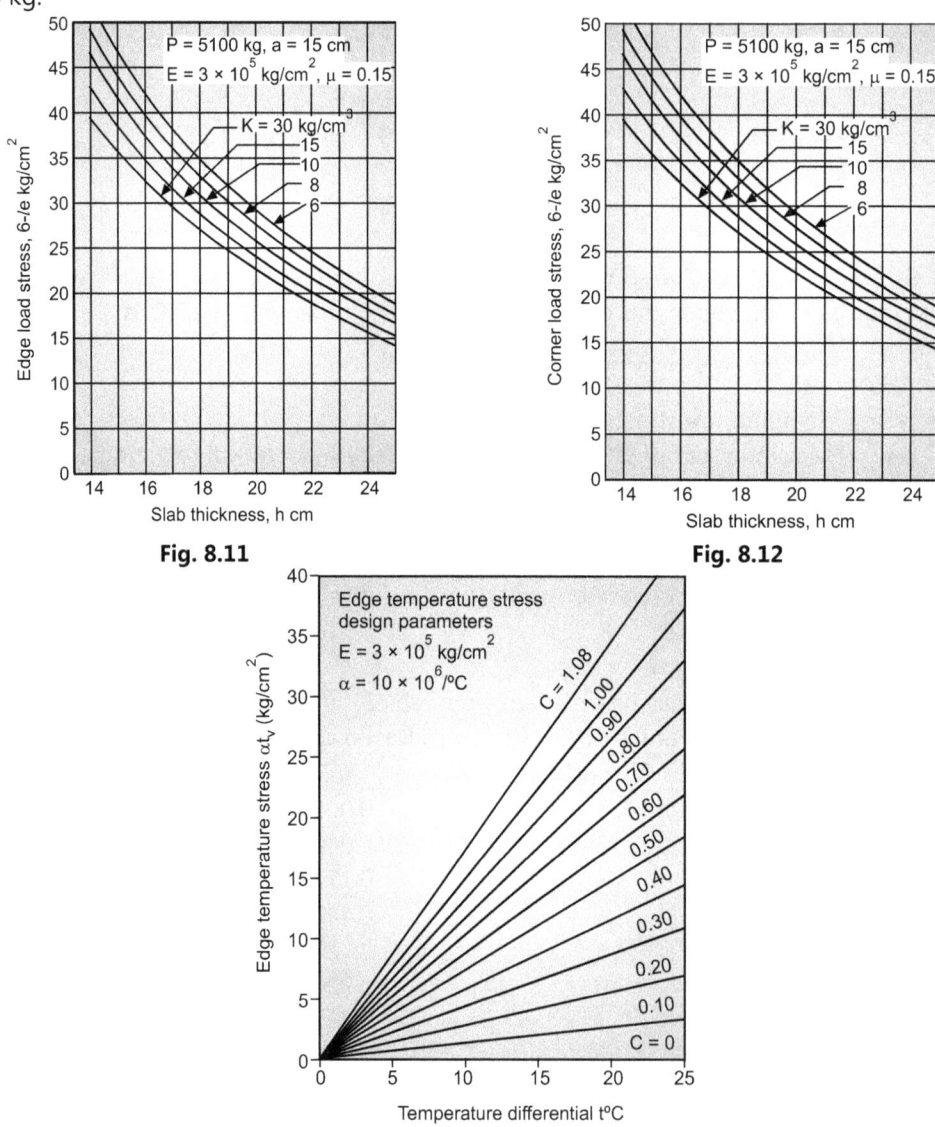

Fig. 8.11

Fig. 8.12

Fig. 8.13

Fig. 8.13 gives a design chart for calculation of temperature stresses in the edge region.

Having known the stresses at the different regions of the slab, we now set to design rigid pavement.

Determination of Slab Thickness and Spacing and Layout of Joints :

The table below recommended may be followed for spacing of joints.

Table 8.13 : Expansion Joint Spacing

Period of Construction	Degree of Roughness of Foundation	Maximum Expansion Joint Spacing Slab Thickness (cm)		
		15	20	25
Winter (oct. – march)	Smooth	50	50	60
	Rough	140	140	140
Summer (April – Sept.)	Smooth	90	90	120
	Rough	140	140	140

The degree of roughness is as specified previously. The above table is based on the study conducted by Central Road Research Institute. For contraction joint spacing, the following table may be followed.

Table 8.14 : Contraction Joint Spacing

Slab Thickness, cm	Maximum Contraction Joint Spacing, cm	Suggested Reinforcement in Welded Fabric in kg/m² for Reinforced Pavements
Unreinforced slabs		
10	4.5	
15	4.5	
20	4.5	
Reinforced slabs		
10	7.5	2.2
15	13.0	2.7
20	14.0	3.8

Having tentatively decided joint spacing, we can now design slab thickness in the following steps.

8.10.5 Design Procedure for Determination of Rigid Pavement Thickness

The following steps may be taken :
- Design values for the various parameters E, M are fixed.
- Joint spacing and lane width tentatively fixed.
- Maximum temperature stress for critical edge region determined by equation or figure. To do this tentative design, thickness of pavement slab will have to be assumed.

- Calculate residual available strength of concrete for supporting load.
- Calculate edge load stress from equation or figure and calculate factor of safety there on.
- If factor of safety is slightly more than one, the design is OK. If it is less than one or much more than 1, steps 3 to 5 to be repeated till the factor of safety is one or slightly more than one. Let this thickness be h_s.
- Depending upon the traffic intensity, the provided thickness may be obtained from the following equation :

$$h_p = h_s + h_t$$

The values of h_t may be obtained from the following table :

Table 8.15 : Values of h_t

Traffic Classification	A	B	C	D	E	F	G
h_t (cm)	− 5	− 5	− 2	− 2	+ 0	+ 0	+ 2

8.11 PROVISION OF REINFORCEMENT

The rigid pavement will have to be reinforced at the joints. In addition, suitable reinforcement will have to be given in the body of the pavement.

8.11.1 Reinforcement at Transverse Joint

Mild steel dowel bars are provided at transverse joint to relieve load stresses at the edge and corner regions. The load transfer capacity of a single dowel bar in shear, in bending and in bearing on concrete is given by the following equations as per Bradbury's analysis.

$$\overline{P_s} = 0.785\, d^2\, f_{s'}$$

$$\overline{P_{bn}} = \frac{2\, d^3\, f_c}{r + 8.8\, z} \quad \text{and}$$

$$\overline{P_{be}} = \frac{f_c\, r^2\, d}{12.5\, (r + 1.5\, z)} \quad \text{where,}$$

$\overline{P_s}$, $\overline{P_{bn}}$, $\overline{P_{be}}$ are the load transfer capacity of single dowel bar in shear, bending and bearing on the concrete, d, and r are the diameter and length of dowel bar, $f_{s'}$, f_s are respectively permissible shear and flexural stress in dowel bar and f_c is the permissible bearing stress in the concrete and z is the joint width. It is generally assumed that for balanced design, capacity of bar in bending and bearing should be equal which means we should equate these equations. When we do this, we get the following equations for known or assumed values of z and d.

$$r = 5d \left[\frac{f_s}{f_c} \times \frac{r + 1.5\, z}{r + 8.8\, z} \right]^{\frac{1}{2}}$$

For known values of z and d, r can be obtained by trial and then the equation for $\bar{P}_s$ or $\bar{P}_{bn}$ would give us load transfer capacity of single dowel bar. To calculate spacing of dowel bars, we first determine the required capacity factor from the following equation.

$$\text{Required capacity factor} = \frac{\text{Required load transfer capacity of system}}{\text{Load transfer capacity of single bar}}$$

The dowel bars are effective in load transfer on either side of load position upto 1.8 times the radius of relative stiffness. We may assume linear variation of capacity factor for a single dowel bar from L under the load to zero at a distance 1.8 l therefrom. For different spacings, the capacity factors could be calculated and the spacing which confirms to the required capacity factor may be selected for adoption. Dowel bars are not satisfactory for the thickness of slab less than 15 cm. There is an illustrated example at the end to high-light the points. It is to be noted that for dummy contraction joint, no dowel bars need be provided since aggregate interlock is sufficient in this case for load transfer. But the dowel bars are a must in the case of full depth construction joint. Typical tentative dowel bar arrangement for 20 mm wide expansion joint with 40 % load transfer are given in the table below.

Table 8.16 : Typical Dowel Bar Arrangement

Design Loading	Slab Thickness, cm	Dowel Bars		
		Diameter, mm	Length, mm	Spacing, mm
5100 kg	15	25	500	200
	20	25	500	250
	25	25	500	300

For working the above table, the values of design parameters assumed are f_s = 1400 kg/cm², f_c = 100 kg/cm², E_c = 3 × 10⁵ kg/cm², K_s = 8.3 kg/cm² joint width 20 mm and load transfer 40 per cent.

8.11.2 Reinforcement for Longitudinal Joints

Theoretically, no reinforcement is required for longitudinal joints. Practically these joints are required in service, for example in the case of heavy traffic, expansive sub-grades etc. The area of steel required per meter length of the joint may be computed by considering

    b = Distance between the joint in question and the nearest free joint or edge in metres.

    f = Coefficient of friction between pavement and the subgrade.

    W = Weight of slab in kg/m², and

    S = Allowable working stress in kg/m².

Therefore bW would represent the total weight of the slab and fbW would represent total frictional force between the pavement and the subgrade per metre length of slab. Assuming that this force is taken by steel, we have

A_s = Area of steel in cm² required per metre length of joint.

$$= \frac{fbW}{S}$$

To find length of this bar, it is assumed that the bond strength of the bar developed equals the working stress of the steel. If P is the perimeter of bar in cm and B is the bond stress in kg/cm², then the bond strength of the bar is LBP. The strength of steel bar is SA. Therefore,

$$LBP = SA \quad \text{and} \quad L = \frac{SA}{BP}$$

It is generally assumed that the length of any tie bar should be such it develops a bond strength twice that required that is the factor of safety should be two. Using this concept, we have

$$L = \frac{2SA}{BP}$$

The bond strength of plain and deformed tie bars may respectively be assumed as 17.5 kg/cm² and 24.6 kg/cm². To prevent warping at the joints and concentration of tensile stresses, the maximum diameter of the bar is limited to 20 mm and these should not be spaced more than 75 cm apart. The calculated length may be increased by 5 – 8 cm to account for inaccuracy of placement. As a guidance, for central longitudinal joint in double lane rigid pavements with lane width of 3.5 m, typical bar details are given below on the basis of f = 1.5, W = 24 kg/m²/cm of slab thickness and s = 1400 kg/cm².

Table 8.17 : Central Longitudinal Joint Two Lane Pavement

Slab Thickness	Tie Bar Details			
	Diameter mm	Maximum Spacing	Minimum Length (cm)	
			Plain Bars	Deformed Bars
15	8	38	40	30
	10	60	45	35
20	10	45	45	35
	12	64	55	40
25	10	30	45	35
	12	45	55	40
	14	62	65	46

8.12 JOINTS IN CEMENT CONCRETE PAVEMENTS

Introduction : Joints are the weakest link in the concrete pavement but it is also the necessary evil. Generally, all the deterioration of concrete pavement is in the vicinity of the joints and hence these are to be planned and constructed with due care. Joints are necessary in the concrete pavement due to following reasons :

- These allow concrete slab to expand and contract under the action of temperature and moisture changes, thus relieving the warping stresses due to temperature.
- These allow pavement to be laid in bays in lanes of convenient widths.
- These allow suitable measure for breaking at the end of days work. As far as possible, the number of joints should be kept minimum since laying of joints interferes with the progress of concreting and riding quality of a road is reduced if the joints are more in numbers. A good joint should have the following properties :

    (1) It must be waterproof and should not allow dirt or stone grit to enter it.

    (2) Free movement should be available at the joint.

    (3) It should not cause unnecessary hindrance in the concreting operations and should not be very weak so as to pose structural weakness and

    (4) It should not hamper the riding quality of the road to a significant extent.

Types of Joints : There are three general types of joints viz.

- Expansion joint,
- Contraction joint and
- Warping joint.

These are now discussed.

1. Expansion Joint : These joints provide the room for the expansion of the pavement. The compressive stresses that might be generated because of prevention of expansion are thus reduced and bulking of concrete slab is avoided.

2. Contraction Joint : These provide room for the contraction of the concrete slab, that might occur due to change in temperature, the tensile stresses are thus relieved, and warping is reduced.

3. Warping Joint : These joints relieve the stresses due to warping and are commonly used for longitudinal joints dividing the pavements into traffic lanes.

Construction Joints : These are provided whenever construction operations require them. These are generally full depth joints and may belong to any of the above types. All these joints can be located in the transverse way that is perpendicular to the direction of traffic on the road or in longitudinal way that is in the direction parallel to the direction of traffic on the road. The details of different joints are shown in Fig. 8.14.

Transverse Joints : These joints can be expansion, contraction or construction and should make a right angle with the centre line of the pavement. Contraction and expansion joints should be continuous from edge to edge of the pavement through all lanes, constructed at the same or different times.

8.12.1 Details of Joints

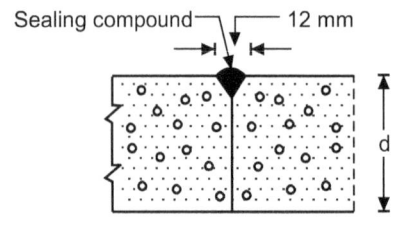

Plain butt joint (for longitudinal warping and construction joints)

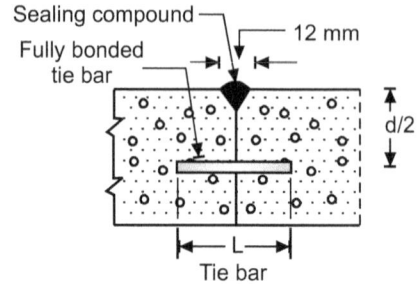

Butt joint with tie bar (for longitudinal warping joint)

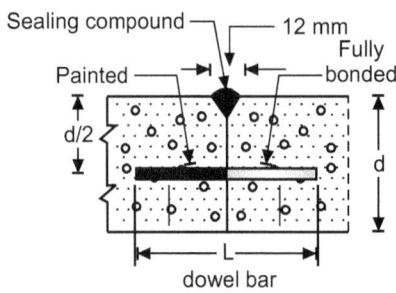

Butt joint with dowel bar (for construction joint)

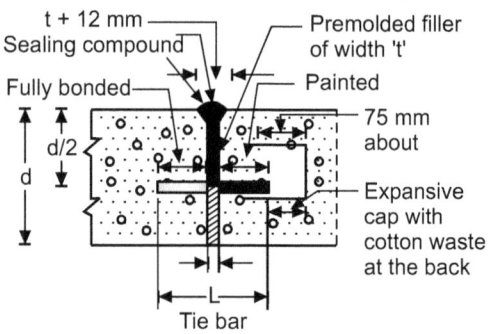

Expansion joint with dowel bar

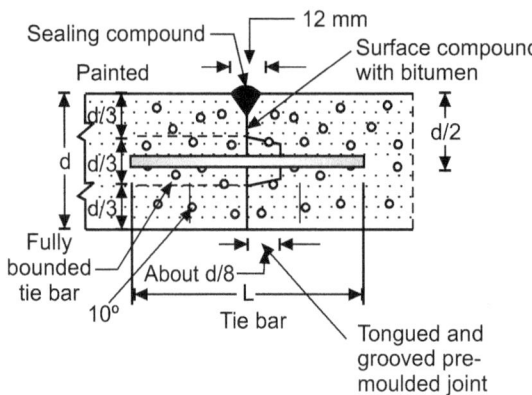

Keyed joint with tie bar (for longitudinal warping joint)

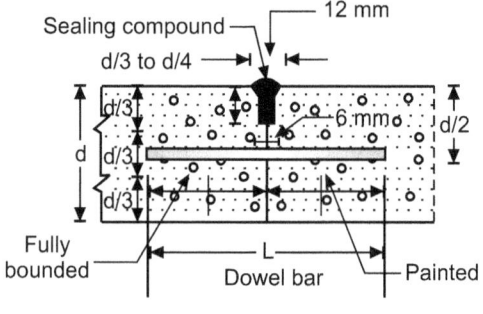

Dummy groove joint with dowel bar (for construction joints used with or without dowel)

Fig. 8.14

Note
   (a) Maximum radius for rounding of corners of slab-6 mm.
   (b) L = Length of dowel or tie bar.
   (c) d = Slab thickness.
   (d) t = Expansion joint width / premoulded filter board width.

Transverse Expansion Joint : These extend over the entire width of the pavement. Dowel bars are generally required at these joints to transfer the wheel load to the adjacent slab, however no dowel bars need be given for slabs less than 150 mm thickness. The gap between the adjacent slab is filled by premoulded expansion joint filler broad, confirming to I.S. 1838 - 1961. The top of the filler board should be 25 mm below the surface of the pavement. The dowel bar that is provided at the expansion joint is simply a load transfer device in the form of simple round steel bar, one half of which is anchored in either slab while the other half is free to move longitudinally within the adjacent slab. The free longitudinal movement of the dowel bar is ensured by coating the free half end of the dowel bar with a thin coating bitumen over it. An expansion cap is provided at the end to offer a space of about 2.5 cm for movements during expansion. These dowel bars should be placed parallel to each other and to the centre of line of the pavement.

Transverse expansion joints are essentially dummy groove type. These should be constructed by forming in the surface of the slab a slot not less than 6 mm wide and having a depth equal to one third to one fourth the depth of the pavement at the thinnest part of its section. The slot may be formed by pushing, into the concrete a flat bar or the wedge of a 'T' bar using a suitable vibratory device, removing the bar and keeping the slot open. 'T' bar is generally preferred. No spalling of the concrete should occur when the bar is being removed and the edge of the joint should be rounded with an edging tool before the concrete hardens.

Transverse Construction Joint : Transverse construction joint should be provided whenever placing of concrete is suspended for more than 30 minutes. It must be remembered that constructing activity should always be suspended (except in the case of emergency) at the regular site of expansion or contraction joint. If the concreting activity is stopped at the site of an expansion joint a regular expansion joint with dowel bars should be provided. If the concreting operation are stopped at the site of contraction joint or any such other place, the construction joint should be of butt type with dowels.

Longitudinal Joints : These should be of the plain butt type and formed by placing the concrete against the face of the slab concreted earlier. The face of the slab concreted earlier should be painted with bitumen with bitumen before placing of fresh concrete. Tie bars should be used at longitudinal joints and these should be supported so as not to be displaced during concreting operations. Tie bars should be bonded in the slabs across the longitudinal joints and while casting the first slab, these should be bent so that one end of them lies along the forms. After removal of the forms bars should be straightened so that they extend into the concrete placed on the other side of the joint.

Direction of Transverse Joints : All the transverse joints should be constructed in line across the full width of the pavement. It has been seen that where transverse joint has been staggered on either side to the longitudinal joint, cracking has often occurred in line with the joint in the adjacent slab, therefore staggered joints are not preferred. Similarly transverse joints should always be at right angles to the direction of traffic, any other angle that is the skew joint increases the risk of cracking at the acute angles and may also tend to make the slab move sideways. It follows from the above discussion that acute angled corners should also be avoided. Where these corners are unavoidable, as in the case of intersections, the corners should be strengthened by using adequate amount of reinforcement.

Spacing of joints, Reinforcement, Tie bars Dowels have been already discussed. Reinforcement in the concrete slab is not intended to contribute towards its flexural strength, therefore its position is not important. But general guidance is that the position of reinforcement should be such that it should be protected from corrosion. Since cracks starting with higher tensile stresses at the top surface are more critical to the riding characteristics of the pavement where they tend to open, the general preference is for the placing of the reinforcement about 50 mm below the surface. This is accomplished by striking-off the concrete such that the compacted layer is 50 mm below the final surface, placing the reinforcement and then placing the remainder of the concrete. Reinforcement is often continued across dummy groove joints to serve the same purpose as tie bars but at all full depth joints, the reinforcement is kept at least 50 mm away from the face of the joint or edge.

Sealing of Joints : After the curing period is over but before the pavement is opened to traffic, the transverse expansion, contraction, as well as longitudinal joint should be thoroughly cleaned and cleared of all the foreign material, if necessary by blowing the compressed air in it. All the contact faces of the joint should be cleaned by wire brush. The edge of the joint should be primed with thin bituminous paint, which should be allowed to dry out before the sealing compound is applied. The typical composition of the primer may be as follows

Table 8.18

Sr. No.	Primer	Percentage by Weight
1.	Bitumen (200 penetration grade)	66 (blended hot)
2.	Light Creosote Oil	14 (Blended hot or cold)
3.	Solvent Naphtha	20 (Blended cold)

The bitumen 200 penetration grade should be melted and fluxed with light creosote oil and when the mixture becomes cold, solvent naphtha should be added to form the ideal primer. In no case, bituminous emulsions be used as primers. There are many sealing compound, manufactured by many agencies. Generally, the sealing compound should not be heated above 200° C. Even a temperature of 180° C should not be continued for long periods.

Sealing compound should be powered into the joint opening only and as far as possible, it should not be allowed to spill on the concrete surface. Sometimes the exposed surface of the sealing compound is dusted with dry hydraulic lime to prevent tackiness. The line of separation between adjacent slabs of concrete should be cleaned and painted with 200 penetration grade bitumen.

Opening the Road to Traffic : The traffic should not be allowed to ply on concrete roads for 28 days after the formation of concrete, when ordinary portland cement, portland blast furnace slag cement, or portland pozzolona cement are used. Before the road is opened to traffic the joints must be properly sealed.

8.13 PAVEMENT FAILURE

Failures of bituminous pavements are caused due to many reasons or combination of reasons. Application of correction in the existing surface will enhance the life of maintenance works as well as that of strengthening layer. It has been seen that only 3 parameters i.e. unevenness index, pavement cracking and rutting are considered while other distresses have been omitted while going for maintenance operations. Along with the maintenance techniques there are various methods for pavement preservation which will help in enhancing the life of pavement and delaying of its failure.

8.13.1 Failure of Flexible Pavements

The major flexible pavement failures are fatigue cracking, rutting, and thermal cracking. The fatigue cracking of flexible pavement is due to horizontal tensile strain at the bottom of the asphaltic concrete. The failure criterion relates allowable number of load repetitions to tensile strain and this relation can be determined in the laboratory *fatigue test* on asphaltic concrete specimens. Rutting occurs only on flexible pavements as indicated by permanent deformation or rut depth along wheel load path. Two design methods have been used to control rutting: one to limit the vertical compressive strain on the top of subgrade and other to limit rutting to a tolerable amount (12 mm normally). Thermal cracking includes both low-temperature cracking and thermal fatigue cracking.

8.13.2 Common Flexible Pavement Distresses

- Cracking
- Deformation
- Deterioration
- Mat Examples
- Examples associated with seal coats
- **Longitudinal Cracking :** Cracks that are approximately parallel to pavement centerline and are not in the wheel path. Longitudinal cracks are non-load associated cracks. Location within the lane (wheel path versus non-wheel path) is significant. Longitudinal cracks in the wheel path are normally rated as Alligator 'A'cracking.

- **Fatigue Cracking :** Cracks in asphalt layers that are caused by repeated traffic loadings. The cracks indicate fatigue failure of the asphalt layer. When cracking is characterized by interconnected cracks, the cracking pattern resembles that of an alligator's skin or chicken wire. Therefore, it is also referred to as alligator cracking
- **Transverse Cracking :** Cracks that are predominately perpendicular to pavement centerline and are not located over port land cement concrete joints. Thermal cracking is typically in this category.
- **Reflection Cracking :** Cracks in HMA overlay surfaces that occur over joints in concrete or over cracks in HMA pavements.
- **Block Cracking :** Pattern of cracks that divides the pavement into approximately rectangular pieces. Rectangular blocks range in size from approximately 0.1 square yard to 12 square yards
- **Edge Cracking :** Crescent-shaped cracks or fairly continuous cracks that intersect the pavement edge and are located within 2 feet of the pavement edge, adjacent to the unpaved shoulder. Includes longitudinal cracks outside of the wheel path and within 2 feet of the pavement edge
- **Rutting :** Longitudinal surface depression that develops in the wheel paths of flexible pavement under traffic. It may have associated transverse displacement
- **Corrugtion :** Transverse undulations appear at regular intervals due to the unstable surface course caused by stop-and-go traffic
- **Shovinga :** longitudinal displacement of a localized area of the pavement surface. It is generally caused by braking or accelerating vehicles, and is usually located on hills or curves, or at intersections. It also may have vertical displacement
- **Depression : Small**, localized surface settlement that can cause a rough, even hazardous ride to motorists.
- **Overlay Bumps :** In newly overlaid pavements, bumps occur where cracks in old pavements were recently filled. This Example is most prevalent on thin overlays.
- **Delamination :** Loss of a large area of pavement surface. Usually there is a clear separation of the pavement surface from the layer below. Slippage cracking may often occur as a result of poor bonding or adhesion between layers.
- **Potholes :** Bowl-shaped holes of various sizes in the pavement surface. Minimum plan dimension is 150 mm.
- **Patching :** Portion of pavement surface, greater than 0.1 sq. meter, that has been removed and replaced or additional material applied to the pavement after original construction.
- **Raveling :** Wearing away of the pavement surface in high-quality hot mix asphalt concrete that may be caused by the dislodging of aggregate particles and loss of asphalt binder

- **Stripping :** The loss of the adhesive bond between asphalt cement and aggregate, most often caused by the presence of water in asphalt concrete, which may result in raveling, loss of stability, and load carrying capacity of the HMA pavement or treated base.
- **Polished Aggregate :** Surface binder worn away to expose coarse aggregate.
- **Pumping :** Seeping or ejection of water and fines from beneath the pavement through cracks.
- **Segregation :** Separation of coarse aggregate from fine aggregate as a result of mishandling of the mix at several points during mix production, hauling, and placing operations. Segregation leads to non-uniform surface texture and non-uniform density.
- **Checking :** Short transverse cracks, usually 1 to 3 inches in length and 1 to 3 inches apart, which occur in the surface of the HMA mat at some time during the compaction process. The cracks do not extend completely through the depth of the course, but are only about ½inch deep.
- **Bleeding/Flushing :** Excess bituminous binder occurring on the pavement surface. May create a shiny, glass-like, reflective surface that may be tacky to the touch. Usually found in the wheel paths.
- **Rock Loss :** Wearing away of the pavement surface in seal coats.
- **Bleeding / Fat Spots :** Excess binder occurring on the surface treated pavements. May create a shiny, glass-like, reflective appearance. Fat spots are localized bleeding.

8.13.3 Deficiencies in Cement Concrete Pavements

There may be many short comings in the concrete pavement caused due to variety of reasons. These are now listed :

(1) **Buckling blow up or tenting :** If there is insufficient joint space, there is localised upward buckling of the slab occurring at the transverse crack or joint which is called as tenting.

(2) **Pumping :** If for some reason, the water finds in road into the sub-grade, there is considerable loss of support in the sub-grade soil. Specifically at the juncture of joint, when the load is imposed on the slab, it is depressed on to the saturated sub-grade below. This results in squeezing the water and the fines in the sub-grade out through the joints and cracks from under the slab. This phenomenon is called as **pumping**

(3) **Scaling :** In the sub zero temperatures, freezing and thawing cycle, and the reaction from the de-icing materials, causes progressive disintegration and loss of wearing surface which is called as **scaling**.

(4) **Spalling :** Due to traffic load, pavement joint-edges generally break down, specifically if the slab is over finished at the joint. The visual appearance is that of cracks at slab edges directly over the reinforcing steel.

(5) **Joint Blast Damage :** Sometimes the joint material softens due to excessive heat. The fast moving traffic may blow this joint material out of the joint. In such a case, it is called as blast damage.

(6) Joint Failure : If the material used in joint scaling is incompressible, or if the incompressible material enters the joint, then slab expansion is prohibited and this results in broken or crushed slab edges due to traffic load. The joint has failed in this case.

(7) Joint Filler Extrusion : If there is insufficient adhesion between joint filler and the slab edges, or if there is too much material in the joint, or if the joint is narrow, the joint filler protrudes above joint edges. This defect is called as joint filler extrusion.

(8) Joint Stripping : The joint filler protruding above joint edges, when it comes out of the joint due to lack of adhesion to the joint edges, or contaminated joint edges, it is called as joint stripping.

(9) Curling or Bending or Warping : Due to uneven expansion or contraction of the top and bottom surfaces of the slab, the slab may bend curl or warp. The defect is more pronounced in unreinforced slabs.

(10) Faulting or Step : The defect is generally found at the junction of rigid and flexible pavement. In this defect, one slab settles more than the adjacent slab generally due to uneven road bed support under the slab. The visual appearance is that of "step" between the slabs.

(11) Corner Cracking : Due to over loading of the slab at or near the corners, coupled with unstable foundation, causes break in a pavement at the corner of the slab near the juncture of the transverse joint and longitudinal joint or slab edge.

(12) D Cracking : Series of fine hair line cracks usually parallel to the joint or major crack and usually curving across slab corner is called as D cracking. It is supposed that D cracking is due to freeze and thaw cycles.

(13) Longitudinal cracking : Due to lateral contraction and movement, cracks are caused parallel to the centre line of the pavement. This is called as longitudinal cracking.

(14) Random Cracking : This cracking has no established pattern. It is generally due to over loading of unreinforced slab.

(15) Transverse Cracking : Due to in sufficient contraction joint or overloading of an upward curled slab having inadequate road bed support, cracks are formed generally at right angles to the pavement centre line. This is called as **transverse** cracking.

(16) Crazing : Weak surface of the slab caused by excessive finishing or rich mortar in surfacing cause these cracks. These are fine hairline cracks extending only through the surface layer and tending to intersect at angle of approximately 120 degree forming a chicken mesh pattern. This is called as **crazing**.

(17) Shattering Blow-up : Excessive expansion of the slab with insufficient joint width causes shattering of the slab usually at a transverse crack or joint.

8.13.4 Strengthening of Exiting Pavement

It is essential to see for the successful maintenance of pavements that they are adequate to withstand the design traffic intensity and volume. If the pavements have to support increased wheel loads and loads repetitions, the pavements rapidly undergo the distress and no amount of periodic maintenance can help them. Due to unexpected economic developments in the given region, the loading conditions may become serve and the alternative would be either to divert the traffic on some adjacent route or to strengthening the existing pavements. i.e. to provide an overlay. If the existing pavements have completely deteriorated, then an overlay would be to remove the existing pavement structure and rebuild the same.

The maintenance engineers should therefore be vigilant and should take the decision in the for providing an overlay as and when needed.

8.13.5 Overlay Pavements

Normally, overlays of existing pavements are used to increase the load-carrying capacity of an existing pavement, or to correct a defective surface condition on the existing pavement. Of these reasons, the first requires a structural design procedure for determining the thickness of overlay, whereas the second requires only a thickness of overlay sufficient to correct the surface condition, and no increase in load-carrying capacity is considered. The design method for overlays included in this chapter determines the thickness required to increase load-carrying capacity. These methods have been developed from a series of full-scale accelerated traffic tests on various types of overlays and are therefore empirical. These methods determine the required thickness of overlay that, when placed on the existing pavement, will be equivalent in performance to the required design thickness of a new plain concrete pavement placed on subgrade.

Definitions for Overlay Pavement Design:

The following terms and symbols apply to the design of overlay pavements and are defined for the purpose of clarity.

- **Rigid base pavement :** An existing rigid pavement on which an overlay is to be placed.
- **Flexible base pavement :** Existing pavement to be overlaid is composed of bituminous concrete, base, and subbase courses.
- **Composite pavement :** Existing pavement to be overlaid with rigid pavement is composed of an all bituminous or flexible overlay on a rigid base pavement.
- **Overlay pavement :** A pavement constructed on an existing base pavement to increase load-carrying capacity.
- **Rigid overlay :** A rigid pavement used to strengthen an existing flexible or rigid pavement.
- **Flexible overlay :** A flexible pavement (either all-bituminous or bituminous with base course) used to strengthen an existing rigid or flexible pavement.

Types of overlay

Following combination exist :

	Existing pavement	Overlay
I	Cement concrete	Cement concrete
II	Cement concrete	Bituminous
III	Bituminous or flexible	Cement concrete
IV	Bituminous or flexible	Bituminous

The Main Objectives of the Overlay :

- Analyze the periodical performance data of selected highway pavements
- Prioritization of the selected project roads for maintenance based on traffic level and importance
- Evaluation of alternate maintenance strategies for different projects and selection of the best maintenance strategy considering life cycle cost analysis.

REVIEW QUESTIONS

1. Bring out the difference between rigid and flexible pavement.
2. Which loading is severe in Westergaard theory?
3. How do we calculate traffic intensity as per I.R.C. method of design of rigid pavements and how traffic is classified in it?
4. Discuss in brief methods for design of flexible pavements
5. Discuss the different type of consideration made in the design of rigid pavement as per IRC.
6. Outline the steps in the design of rigid pavement as per I.R.C.
7. What are the design criteria for the design of flexible pavements? Illucidate briefly.
8. What is maintenance and repair of highways? Also elucidate the importance of maintenance.
9. Write notes on
    (a) Strengthening of pavements
    (b) Overly method
    (c) CBR Method of pavement design
    (d) Westergaurd wheel load analysis
    (e) Maintenance of pavements

Unit - III

CHAPTER 9
TRAFFIC ENGINEERING

9.1 INTRODUCTION

Traffic engineering is comparatively a new science and it's advent is related to the speedy growth of motor vehicles on the road. Several shades of definition exist for Traffic Engineering. One may say that it is that branch of highway engineering which deals with planning, geometric design of streets and highways and the abutting lands, and with traffic operations thereon, so that convenient and economic transport of men and material can take place on highways.

In order to achieve the above objects, traffic engineering is generally split into further compartments such as :

(1) Traffic characteristics, (2) Traffic studies and analysis,
(3) Traffic operations, (4) Planning and analysis,
(5) Geometric Design, (6) Administration and management.

These compartments are made so that on one hand we can plan traffic and regulate the traffic generated and on the other hand frame by laws, so that highways are put to maximum efficient use.

9.2 TRAFFIC CHARACTERISTICS

To study the traffic characteristics, we have to know the attributes. i.e. the qualities of elements using the road. These are normally called as road user characteristics and these include the quality of roads also, since road user and the road have to be a contented couple.

Physical Characteristics : Physical characteristics may be related to road users. For example,

(1) Vision of the Road User : Field of clearest and acute vision is within a cone whose angle is about 3°. With eye movement, vision can be satisfactory upto 10° – 20° in horizontal plane. This vision element should be used in planning traffic signal.

(2) Hearing : It is a important phenomenon for pedestrian and cyclists but is not considered important for motorist in western countries. In India, honking by motorist and scooter owners is frequent and studies should be conducted in this domain.

(3) Strength : Lack of strength for the road can impede traffic flow, especially pot holes and weak spots can cause congestion in the traffic flow.

(4) Mental, Psychological and Environmental Factors : Mental and psychological factors relate to the condition of the mind of the driver: whether he is drunk, fatigued, responsivity of the driver, his anxiousness. These relate to the mind of the driver. To be upright, it should be possible to devise drivers worthiness tests just as air worthiness tests for the pilots, so that the wheel of the vehicle is in safe hands.

(5) Environmental Factors : These relate to the pattern of traffic flow whether it is mixed, heavy, one way, hilly etc. and the judgment of the driver to such environment. In a way,(4) and (5) are co-related.

9.3 VEHICLE CHARACTERISTICS

Road and the vehicle plying on the road could be considered as a consenting couple. However, a vista of vehicles ply on the road and the static and dynamic characteristics of these vehicles determine certain road elements. For example, the height of the vehicle affects the height of the overbridge. The height of driver seat affects the visibility distance and the height of head light determines the head light sight distance at the valley curve. The length of vehicle can affect the capacity and minimum turning radius. The dynamic characteristics of the vehicle generally refer to its engine weight, its B.H.P., suspension system etc. These factors to a large extent determine the riding comfort. Keeping these considerations in view, IRC has fixed up maximum dimensions of road vehicles and maximum permissible gross weights. These specifications are summarised in the table below :

Table 9.1 : Maximum Dimensions of Road Vehicles

Dimensions of Vehicle	Particulars	Maximum Dimensions in Meters (Excluding Front and Rear Bumpers)
Width	All vehicles	2.5
Height	(a) Single decked vehicle for normal application.	3.8
	(b) Double decked vehicle.	4.75
Length	(a) Single unit truck with two or more axles (Types 2, 3).	11.0
	(b) Single unit bus with two or more axles (Type 2, 3).	12.0
	(c) Semi-trailer tractor combination (Type 2s1, 2s2, 3s1, 3s2).	16.0
	(d) Tractor and trailer combination (Type 2–2, 3–2, 3–3).	18.0

No combination is allowed to be more than two units and no such combination loaded or otherwise should have overall length exceeding 18 m. The types of road transport vehicles are shown in Fig. 9.1.

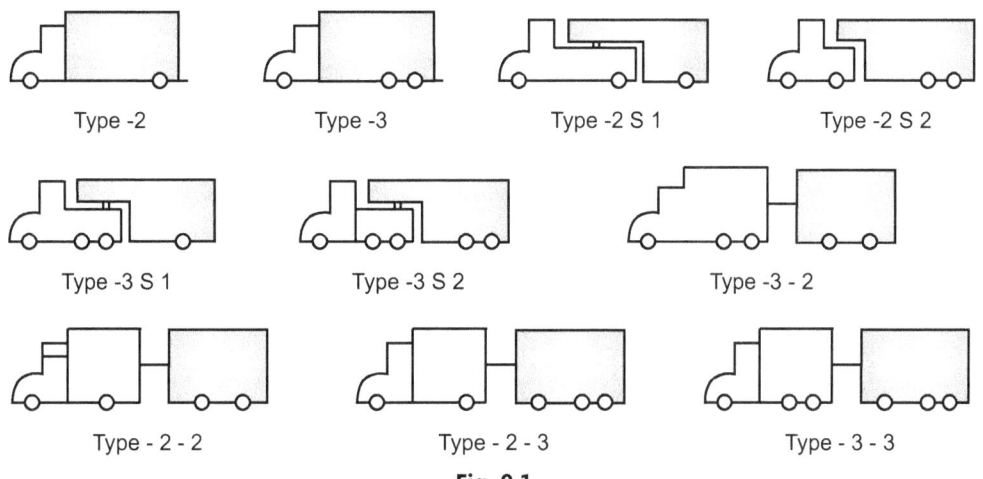

Fig. 9.1

The weights and other details of the vehicle are as shown in Table 9.2.

Table 9.2 : Maximum Permissible Gross Weight and Axle Weight of Transport Vehicles

Vehicle Type	Maximum Gross Weight	Maximum Axle Weight (Tonnes)			
		Truck / Tractor		Trailer	
		FAW	RAW	FAW	RAW
Type 2 (Both Axle single type)	12.0	6	6		
Type 2 (FA single type RA - Duel type)	16.2	6	10.2		
Type 3	24.0	6	18 (TA)	–	
Type 2 S – 1	26.4	6	10.2	–	10.2
Type 2 S – 2	34.2	6	10.2	–	18 TA
Type 3 S – 1	34.2	6	18 (TA)	–	10.2
Type 3 S – 2	42.0	6	18 (TA)	–	18 TA
Type 2 – 2	36.6	6	10.2	10.2	10.2
Type 3 – 2	44.4	6	18 (TA)	10.2	10.2
Type 2 – 3	44.4	6	10.2	10.2	18 TA
Type 3 – 3	52.2	6	18 (TA)	10.2	18 TA

- FAW – Weight on front axle; RAW – weight on rear axle;
- TA – Tandem axle fitted with 8 tyres.

Braking characteristics of motor vehicles are also very important especially in preventing accidents. Many times a braking test is conducted to assess the condition of braking system. To know whether the brakes are OK or not, a vehicle having initial speed of u m/sec is subjected to full braking for 't' seconds, if the vehicle is brought to stand still position in 'L' meters. Then clearly the braking distance L = $\dfrac{u^2}{2gf}$ on the assumption of the road being level. This equation can thus yield average skid resistance of the pavement surface.

9.4 TRAFFIC STUDIES

In order to determine the type of traffic which is being accommodated by the road, traffic studies are conducted. These studies are generally divided into :
- Traffic volume studies,
- Speed studies,
- Origin and destination study,
- Traffic flow characteristics,
- Traffic capacity study,
- Parking study and
- Accident studies.

9.4.1 Traffic Volume Study

This study involves the measurement of the number and the type of vehicles crossing a section of the road per unit time at a selected period. It is similar to determining discharge in a pipe line. To carry such study, naturally, you have to incur considerable cost. But such a study can be beneficial in many respects. For example :
- Higher the traffic volume, more important is the road. This will aid in not only judicious operation of existing facilities such as signals etc. but it may also tell us, whether road requires widening.
- Knowing the laden weight of vehicles and their numbers, it should be possible to know whether road cross-section is adequate from the point of view of strength.
- Traffic volume studies can help in planning regulatory measures such as one way streets intersections, signal timing, whereas pedestrian traffic volume study is used in planning side walks, subways etc.

To properly conduct traffic volume study, hourly traffic volume should be known with daily and seasonal variations. Traffic volume studies could be conducted by manual or mechanical counts. In manual methods, the number and type of vehicles passing a cross-section of the road are actually measured by individuals. Naturally this requires a large number of people to be employed for the purpose. And such studies are difficult to conduct for the whole day. In mechanical methods, the mechanical counter which is incorporated in the cross-section of the road records the number of vehicles (weightwise) crossing the section in the desired period. The advantage is one can take observations throughout the day, but the pedestrian traffic is difficult to measure by this method. The traffic volume data so collected in these studies could be expressed in various convenient ways. Some of the ways in which these studies could be expressed are :

(1) Annual Average Daily Traffic or Annual Daily Traffic : After collecting the data for the year this count can be calculated. Naturally the traffic consists of several type, such as motors, bullock carts, scooters etc. The concept of passenger car unit is employed to convert this traffic in a uniform pattern.

(2) Trend Charts : Trend charts could be prepared showing volume trends over a period of years. Similarly, variation charts showing hourly, daily or seasonal variations could be prepared.

(3) Traffic Flow Maps : In fact traffic flow maps along the routes could be prepared. To draw such maps the usual method is to consider the thickness of lines representing traffic volume to some derived scale.

(4) Traffic Flow Diagram : at any intersection could be prepared. These diagrams will give relative importance of roads and is useful in planning signal timings. A typical flow diagram at an intersection is shown below. Fig. 9.2 shows that though one arm of the intersection is balanced, the other arm is not balanced. That is the traffic coming in and out is not the same. There is stagnation and the junction requires remedial measures.

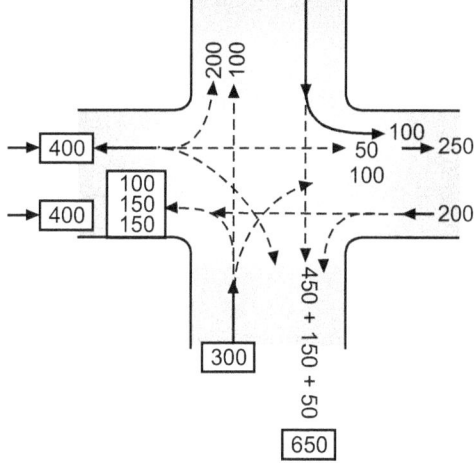

Fig. 9.2

(5) Thirtieth Highest Hourly Volume : This is defined as the 30th highest hourly volume that will be exceeded only 29 times in a year and all other hourly volumes of the year will be less than this value. This value is generally taken as the hourly volume for the design and will ensure that there will be congestion only during 29 hours in the year. This concept is not as yet popular in India, essentially since it requires amassing large traffic data.

30HV – 30th highest hourly volume of the year
30HV ≈ 0.15 ADT (for average rural roads)

30HV ≈ 0.10 ADT (for average urban areas)

The speed of the vehicle plying on the road can change instant to instant which is a function of geometry of the road and psycological factors related to the driver. The spot speed is the instantaneous speed of the vehicle at a specified location, whereas the average speed is the average of spot speeds of all vehicles passing a given point on the highway. Here again we have space-mean speed and time - mean speed, where the space-mean speed represents the average speed of the vehicle in a certain road of known length at given time, time-mean speed represents the speed distribution of vehicles at a point and it is the average of instantaneous speeds of observed vehicles at the spot. The following table brings out this point.

Table 9.3 : Average Instantaneous Speeds of Observed Vehicles

Space Mean Speed	Time Mean Speed
d = Length of road, in metres n = Number of individual vehicle observation t_1 = Travel time for i^{th} vehicle to travel distance 'd' in seconds then Space mean speed km/hr. $= \dfrac{3.6\, dn}{\sum_{i=1}^{n} t_1}$	V_i = Observed instantaneous speed of ith vehicles, km/hr. n = Number of vehicles observed, then Time mean speed $= \dfrac{\sum_{i=1}^{n} V_i}{n}$

Generally, space mean speed is slightly lower than time-mean speed especially on Indian rural roads. Running speed of the vehicle could be obtained by dividing the distance covered by the time during which vehicle was in motion, whereas the overall speed or travel speed is obtained by dividing the total distance between two destinations and time taken to travel between these destinations. Therefore this definition includes the delays and stoppages and the time consumed for them enroute. The speed studies could be further split-up into spot speed studies and speed and delay studies.

Spot speed refers to the speed of the vehicle at the instant. It could be affected by the geometry of the road, gradient, sight distance, the B.H.P. of vehicle etc. At a particular instant the speedometer of the vehicle gives the spot speed. This may be useful for the driver but is not of much use to traffic planner. The traffic planner can get resonably accurate value of spot speed by installing an observer on one side of the road and asking him to start the stop watch when the vehicle crosses him.

An enoscope which is just a mirror box supported on tripod is placed away from the observer (say 30 m), so that the image of the vehicle is seen by the observer when the vehicle crosses the section where the enoscope is placed and at that instant the stop-watch is stopped.

Thus we know the time required to traverse a particular length and therefore the speed. The method though simple, speedy observations are difficult to take, since spotting a particular vehicle in the stream of vehicles is somewhat cumbersome. There are other methods available such as graphic recorder, radar, photographic methods etc. However for a developing country like ours, these appear to be costly.

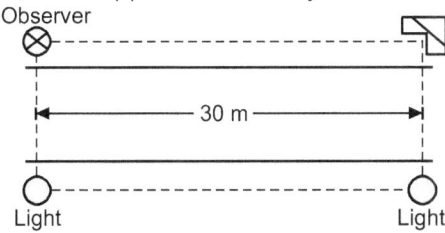

Fig. 9.3

The information from speed studies could be presented as :

- By arranging the data in groups covering various speed ranges and the number of vehicles in that range.

  Arithmatic mean then gives the average speed. Example 9.4 explains this concept.

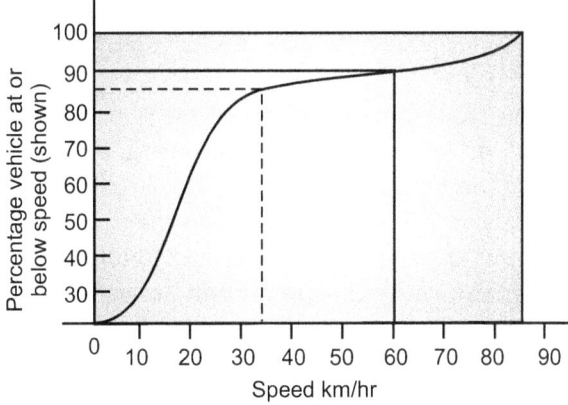

Fig. 9.4 : Cumulative speed distribution

- Average value of each speed group can be plotted on X-axis and cumulative percent of vehicles at or below the different speeds can be plotted on Y-axis to generate a graph as shown in Fig. 9.4. From this graph any percentile speed could be obtained.

  For example, 90th percentile speed is 60 km/hr. This means that only 10 percent of vehicles have speed more than 60 km/hr. Generally 85th percentile speed is considered to be speed limit for that zone. In Fig. 9.4, the 5th percentile speed is around 32 km/hr. For urban roads this is the safe speed limit. On Indian Roads, we do not lower speed limits to avoid congestion on the roads. In many countries, 15th percentile speed represents lower speed limit to avoid bottling of roads.

- Just as we have taken recourse to cumulative speed distribution to know about percentile speeds, we can plot frequency distribution of speeds. Here we plot speed of vehicles or average value of each speed group of vehicles on X-axis and percentage of vehicles in that group on Y-axis to yield speed distribution curve as shown. Such a curve will have a peak value of travel speed across the section, which is generally called as modal speed. The graph helps in determining the speed at which greatest proportion of vehicles move, which is given by modal speed.

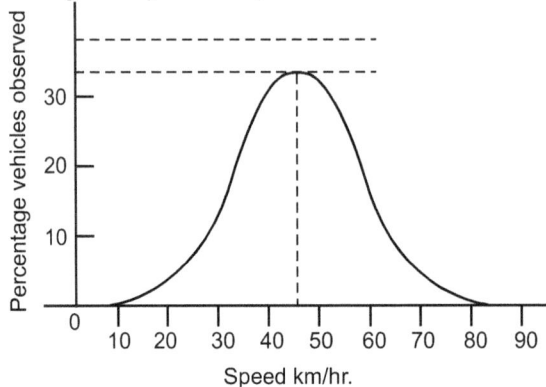

Fig. 9.5 : Frequency distribution for spot speeds

9.4.2 Speed and Delay Study

These studies can give the cause of delay between the two destinations A and B so that spots of congestion could be located and remedial measures undertaken. Travel time so determined can be used in the benefit cost analysis. It is usual to call delays as fixed delays which is due to traffic signals or level crossings whereas the operational delays are there due to traffic movements such as parking and turning, end turning of vehicles etc. Sometimes habitual operational delays can cause change in fixed delays i.e. change in signalling time. The speed and delay study as such can be undertaken by :

- Floating car or Riding check method.
- Licence plate or vehicle number method.
- Interview method.
- Elevated observations.
- Photographic technique.

The floating car method is generally followed in India. As the name suggests, here we have a car with four observers in it which is floating i.e. which is travelling at approximately the same speed as that of the traffic. The first observer equipped with two stop watches is an observer to record delays. At strategic locations, such as bridges, intersections, roads in vicinity of markets etc., he observes with the help of two stop watches the time required to negotiate these focal points, i.e. he observes the delay time. The second observer in the car notes the cause of this delay either in the tabular form or with vivid descriptions. It is the duty of the third observer seated in the car to find the number of vehicles that this floating car i.e. the test vehicle overtakes or is overtaken by other vehicles in specified time. The fourth observer in the car notes the number of vehicles travelling in opposite direction in each trip. It is possible that in the mixed traffic stream, these four observers are not enough to observe these things and more number of observers may be deployed.

The average journey time for all the vehicles in a traffic stream in the direction of flow q may be given by

$$\bar{t} = t_w - \frac{n_y}{q}, \text{ where } q = \frac{n_a + n_y}{t_a + t_w}$$

n_a = Average number of vehicles counted in the direction of stream when floating/test vehicle travels in the opposite direction.

n_y = Average number of vehicles overtaking the test vehicle minus the number of vehicles overtaken when the test is in the direction of flow 'q'.

t_w = Average journey time in minutes when the test vehicle is travelling with the stream 'q'.

t_a = Average journey time in minutes when floating / test vehicle is running against the stream.

- In the licence plate or vehicle number method, we have observers with synchronised stop watches placed at the entrance and exit of test section. A particular vehicle say MTA/3033 when entering the section, its time at entry is noted by one observer at entry point and its time at exit is noted by another observer at exit time. These two observations will therefore give journey time. Needless to say that for busy road, you require very large number of observers and of course, duration and reason for delay during journey time is not directly noted.
- In the interview method, the traffic department interviews the road users and from their experience tries to assess the cause of delay. The method though subjective in nature, sometimes gives very useful information.
- Elevated observations and photographic technique are excellent but can be used for short test sections such as intersections. The final object of all this study is to evaluate the efficiency and effectiveness of control devices such as signal system, rotary etc. and arrange remedial measures if required.

9.4.3 Origin and Destination Studies

Origin and destination study means to find out where and why the traffic originates and where and how it is destined.

There are many applications and use of such studies.

For example :

- In any existing highway network, we can know what routes are preferred by users and which are not preferred. We can know where there is congestion on these routes, so that proper one way regulations, bypasses or rescued routes can be introduced.

- To locate facilities such as bus terminals, bus stops, new bridges, widening of existing bridges, so that the commuters are benefitted to maximum use.
- Knowing the traffic density, we can check up whether the existing design standards of the road are adequate or otherwise.

The origin and destination study can be undertaken by various methods.

- **License Plate Method :** For an area, where origin and destination study is carried out, all the entry and exit points in this area are marked and observers are stationed at all these points and provided with synchronised time pieces. Now these observers note the registration number of the vehicle entering the specified area and the time at which it enters the specified area. Now simultaneously another set of observers may be noting down the registration number of the vehicle exiting this very specified area and the time at which it obtains this exit. Naturally data is collected for allotted time. All junctions have observers. Therefore for a particular vehicle having a given registration number, we can trace its trip direction and time for that trip. Field work is easy in this method but the office work is tedious. We also require large number of observers and hence limited area can be covered.

- **Return Post-Card Method :** It is a sort of modern marketing gimmick. Random road users are provided with reply paid post cards with questionnaire printed on it with a request to return the post-card to the mailbox with the questionnaire properly answered. When sufficient number of such cards are received, traffic planner can deduce proper conclusions from it. The shortcoming of this method is that with general apathy that is prevalent, one may not get sufficient feedback and the whole exercise will be futile. But the method has some promise where traffic density is heavy. In such case distributing points have to been carefully planned. These would be petrol pumps, or road intersections etc.

- **Tag on Car Method :** In this method, in a specified area, a precoded card is struck on the car with requisite information recorded on it. The usual information recorded, is time of entry, its speed etc. When the car leaves the specified area, exit time entry is recorded. The method has been found to be cumbersome to operate in India.

- **Home Interview Method :** In this method, 0.5 to 10 percent of population is first randomly selected. Now trained personnel would visit the residences of these persons and collect from them all the traffic data, which route an individual takes, how much time he takes, what is the cause of delay in his opinion, what are the timings when he uses the road, what suggestion would he likes to make ? etc. The data so collected can give valuable information, if analysed properly.

- **Work Spot Interview Method :** The only difference between home interview method and work spot interview method is that in this method the interviews are being conducted at workplaces, otherwise the method is same.

- **Road Side Interview Method :** In this method, the place of the interview is the road side. Help of administration is sometimes required so that traffic could be diverted to a side lane for interviewing purposes. The commuters may find this procedure irksome, since it might cause delay in going to the office. Very few surveys are undertaken by this method in India. It is true that the data can be collected in short duration and that too from the horse's mouth i.e. the feed back is direct, but the success of the method lies in the co-operation of the commuters which sometimes is not available.

Traffic Flow Characteristics

- The traffic study would indicate that there are types of traffic as shown in the Fig. 9.6 . In India, due to left hand drives, diverging on the left causes least traffic conflicts, but diverging to the right and also merging from the right can cause traffic conflicts to the traffic moving in the straight path. Naturally, this is due to typical British and Indian pattern of traffic where we stick to left.
- When the vehicle wants to change the traffic lane, naturally there would be merging and diverging. It is the crossing i.e. the traffic for the road intersection at level which cause greater Examples. In this case, vehicles on one road have to stop, thus allowing the crossing stream of vehicles to cross their path. Traffic capacity is thus greatly reduced at the intersection.
- Roads could cross at angles also in which case, there is an action of weaving. The most important parameter in the traffic flow is the transverse and longitudinal distribution of vehicles on the road way. As far the longitudinal distribution of vehicles of road way is concerned, the time-interval between the passage of successive vehicles moving in the same lane and measured from head to head as they pass a point on the roadway is termed as time headway.
- On the other hand the space headway determines the distance between successive vehicles moving in the same line measured from head at any instance. The number of headways per unit of time is a measure of traffic volume.
- When the vehicles gather speed, the minimum space-headway increases, whereas the minimum time headway would first decrease and after reaching a minimum value at optimum speed on the stream would then increase as shown in Fig. 9.7 for two lane highway. Naturally, maximum capacity would be obtained at this speed when time-headway is minimum.
- One of the important factors in the traffic flow is the Example of lane change. Demand for lane change will be more when the speed range of vehicles and traffic density is high.
- But the Example, as yet has not assumed that importance in India. All these traffic flow studies lead to traffic capacity studies.
- The traffic volume is the number of vehicles moving in a specified direction on a given lane that pass given cross-section during specified unit of time generally expressed as vehicles/hr or vehicles/day.

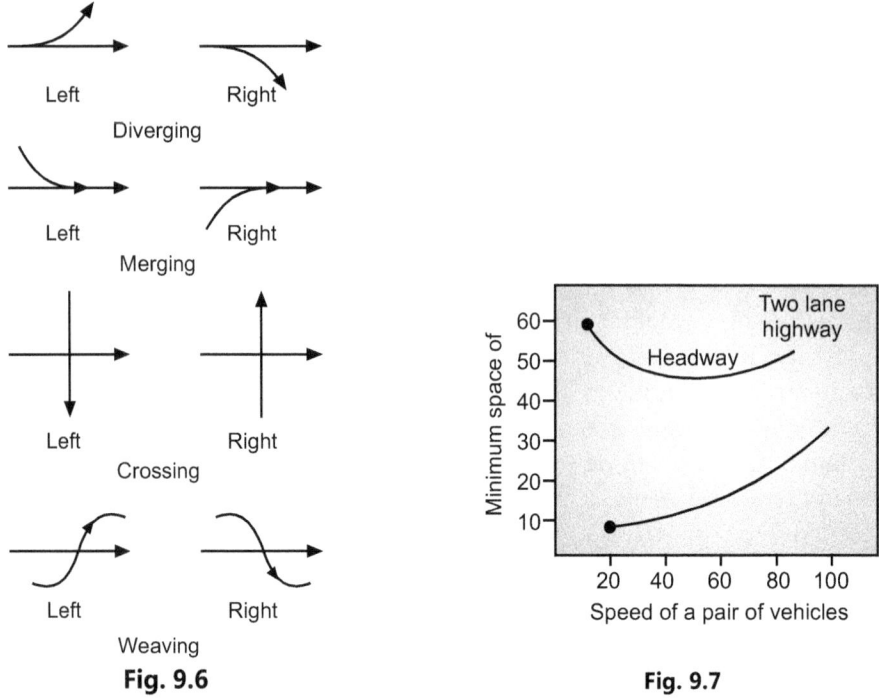

Fig. 9.6 **Fig. 9.7**

- Traffic density is the number of vehicles occupying a unit length of lane of roadway at a given instant generally expressed as vehicles/km.
- The third term in traffic flow Examples is the traffic capacity. We have already referred to this term. It may be said to be the ability of the roadway to accommodate traffic volume and expressed as the maximum number of vehicles in a lane that can pass a given point in unit time usually an hour.
- Capacity and traffic volume have the same units. But traffic volume is actual rate of flow and depending upon traffic demand it can vary.
- On the other hand, capacity indicates maximum rate of flow that can be accommodated with given service conditions. Thus capacity would depend upon existent roadway and traffic conditions.
- Again this capacity could be thought of as basic capacity, possible capacity and practical capacity, the last being more important. Basic capacity is the theoretical capacity, which we have derived. It refers to the maximum number of cars or vehicles (naturally same type) that can pass on roadway cross-section during one hour under ideal conditions.
- On the other hand, the possible capacity is maximum number of vehicles that can pass roadway cross-section during one hour under prevailing roadways condition. Naturally this is lower than the basic capacity and when there is congestion leading to stagnation of traffic, the possible capacity may even approach zero value.

- On the other hand for the ideal conditions of traffic the possible capacity itself will approach basic capacity. The another term is the practical capacity. It is the maximum number of vehicles that can pass cross-section on the lane or roadway during one hour without causing unreasonable delay, hazard, or accident etc. The practical capacity would depend upon many factors such as :

  (1) Lane Width : Decreasing lane, decreasing the capacity.

  (2) Lateral Clearances : Restricted lateral clearances, such as hedging, retaining walls, boundary walls etc. reduce the capacity.

  A minimum clearance of 1.85 m from the pavement edge to the obstruction is supposed to reflect capacity to its fullness. Reduction in this distance would decrease the practical capacity.

  (3) Commercial Vehicles : Large commercial vehicles such as buses, trucks, trucks with trailer moving with slow speed, occupy greater space and reduce the practical capacity.

  (4) Shoulder Widths : Narrow shoulder widths reduce the effective width of pavement. Vehicle parked on shoulders for some reason or the other would reduce the capacity of road.

  (5) Alignment : If the alignment and the corresponding stopping distances are not as per specifications, the full exploitation of road section cannot take place, thus telling on capacity.

  (6) Intersections : It is intersection which causes congestion. Intersection at a grade will have reduced capacity than the intersection on level ground. The best way is to have grade separated intersections.

  It is very clear from the above discussions, that the practical capacity depends upon many parameters, the definition is subjective in nature and theoretical formulation may be difficult. From this point of view, IRC has made certain recommendations about the practical capacity of roads.

Table 9.4 : Capacity of Roads in Rural Areas

Sr. No.	Type of Road	Practical Capacity Per Day (Both Directions) P.C.U.
1.	Single lane 3.75 m carriageway and earth shoulders.	1000 p.c.u.
2.	Single lane 3.75 m carriageway 1.0 m hard shoulders.	2500 p.c.u.
3.	Intermediate lanes of width 5.5 m and earth shoulders.	5000 p.c.u.
4.	Two lane roads 3.0 m carriageway and earth shoulders.	10,000 p.c.u.
5.	Four lane divided highway.	20,000 to 30,000 p.c.u.

Table 9.5 : Capacity of Urban Roads

No. of Traffic Lanes and Width	Traffic Flow	Capacity pcu/hr. for Different Traffic Roads		
		Roads, No Frontage Access, Very Little Cross Traffic And No Standing Cars	Roads, Frontage, Access, High Capacity Intersections But No Standing Cars	Roads With Free Frontage Access, Parked Vehicles And Heavy Cross-Traffic
Two lanes (7.0 – 7.5)	One way	2400	1500	1200
Two lanes (7.0 – 7.5)	Two way	1500	1200	750
Three lanes (10.5 m)	One way	3600	2500	2000
Four lanes (14.0 m)	One way	4800	3000	2400
Four lanes (14.0 m)	Two way	4000	2500	2000
Six lanes (21.0 m)	Two way	6000	4200	3600

The immediate conclusion, if the traffic density is more than the one specified above, then the widening of the road is required.

9.4.4 Origin Destination Study

Data Presentation : Origin destination data so collected is now to be considered along with existing traffic characteristics. The data could be presented in various forms.

- Desire lines could be plotted. Desire line is a straight line drawn on topo sheet or the map of the area connecting the origin and destination of a particular traffic, width of desire line is drawn proportional to the number of trips in both directions. The existing road pattern may not be always as per desire lines and therefore drawing of desire lines would indicate necessity of new road link, diversion, a bypass or may be a bridge. When desire lines are compared with existing flow pattern, it can tell you the spot of congestion. Therefore desire lines are very helpful.
- Pie charts can be drawn, diameter of circle being proportional to the number of trips.
- Simple tabular forms could be prepared showing trip generation and traffic density. By far, drawing desire lines appear to be a favourite of traffic planners.

9.4.5 Parking Studies

- In metropolitan cities, parking a vehicle is a great headache. Parked vehicle should cause minimum congestion and disturbance to the free traffic flow. In addition to this, parking facilities provided should be utilizable.

- The initiation of parking studies and for that matter any studies, is, first to assess the demand. One obvious method of knowing parking demand is to find out number of accumulated vehicles in a selected area during designated hour, preferably peak hour.

- Another method may be to find out the number of vehicles actually parked in a specified area in peak hours and duration of their parking time. This will involve large number of observers and field staff.

- Still another obvious method may be to interview the drivers and assess from them the parking demand. After making a reasonable estimate regarding parking demand, we should study existing parking characteristics.

- What are the present frequent places of parking. What is the percentage of two wheelers parked as compared to the four wheelers ? What is the length of parking lot and is the state of affair of kerb parking ? After knowing parking characteristics, we prepare what is known as parking space inventory. The map of specified area showing all places where kerb parking of off-street parking facilities can be provided to meet the parking demand is marked on this map.

- Knowing the parking demand and the existing parking facilities, the engineer has to strike a balance between parking capacity available and the parking demand. It is obvious that the Example is not mathematical but subjective in nature and some give and take is naturally understood.

- A parked vehicle is a necessary evil in an area. A vehicle-that is parked is going to offer some resistance to the traffic flow.

- On the other hand, people cannot transact business unless they park the vehicles. The usual method of parking in India is kerb parking, when you place your vehicle near the kerb, do business and get out. It has the advantage that your vehicle can be lodged near the place where you have work.

The kerb parking can be effected in various ways as shown in Fig. 9.8. For new township, not only wide roads should be provided but adequate parking facility, kerb or otherwise, should be left. For existing roads which are not as yet congested, it is prudent to forecast future traffic Examples and make objective provision for the future traffic demand in road with traffic parking etc. It is generally seen that once the road becomes congested, hundred percent solution cannot be found and any solution that is evolved can mitigate partial Examples. In order that parking facilities are not misused, these should be controlled by a policeman. It is healthy to collect a fee from the driver of the parked vehicle, so that facility provided is used in a optimum manner. Generally kerb parking is either angle parking or parallel parking. Angle parking is convenient for the motorist than the parallel parking. But this type of parking causes more obstruction to the traffic.

Even accidents have known to have occurred, due to angle parking. Generally 45° as the parking angle has been found to be convenient. In India, we have been preferring parallel parking. It is more effective when the road width and kerb parking space is limited. Parallel parking is difficult to manage, in the sense that for parking and unparking the vehicles, one is required to do forward and reverse movement of vehicle. The drivers generally do not like these movements. Parallel parking may be with equal spacing, facing the same direction or may be two vehicles placed closely with open interval between two car units. The number of scooters in India is also increasing continuously. It is now felt that for optimum use of road width, scooter parking, even when it is kerb parking should have a separate slot other than the car parking.

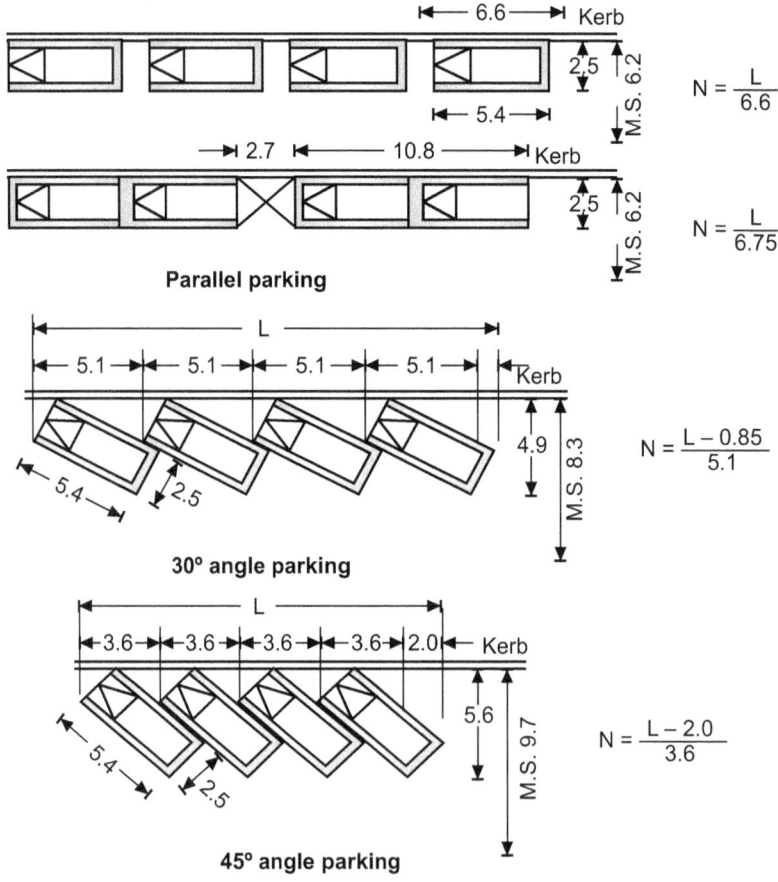

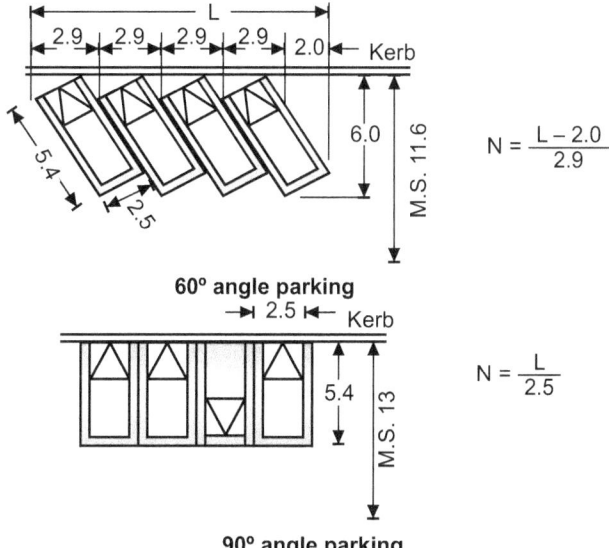

Fig. 9.8 : Patterns of kerb parking

- The present day, often talked about method of parking, is off-street parking, where the parking is provided at a separate place away from the kerb. This method relieves the traffic congestion but the user has to walk greater distances to do business.
- In the business centre, off-street parking cannot be provided at frequent intervals. Another advantage of off-street parking is that the owner of the vehicle is more certain about the safety of the vehicle in off-street parking than the kerb parking.
- Of course this may be called as mind-set. Off-street parking may be provided in the form of parking lots, when sufficient space is available at low cost.
- This parking lot system can be called as self parking system, when the owner or the driver himself parks the vehicle in the lot or it could be called as attendant parking system, when parking and delivering operations are conducted by the attendants of the parking lot. In both the cases, fees are usually charged for using the parking space.
- Attendant parking system is not much prevalent in India, though it has some advantages in the sense, that it might lead to optimum utilisation of parking space. If the parking is heavy and space costly, one can resort to multistoreyed parking garages.
- In such multistoreyed garages, it should be possible to provide interfloor travel facility for the vehicles either by elevators or ramps. Ramps need more space, elevators would take less space but would be susceptible to mechanical or power failure. Even multistoreyed parking garage would require some area at the entrance for acceptance and exist of vehicles.
- This space called reservoir area could depend upon arrival and departure rate of cars and the number of attendants for such facilities. In metropolitan cities of India, day is not far off, when multistoreyed parking garages would be required to be provided.

9.5 ACCIDENT STUDIES

The Example of accident is very acute in highway transportation due to complex flow patterns of vehicular traffic, presence of mixed traffic and pedestrians. Traffic accidents may involve property damage, personal injuries or even causalities. One of the main objectives of traffic engineering is to provide safe traffic movements. Road accidents cannot be totally prevented, but suitable traffic engineering and management measures can decrease the accident rate decreased considerably. Therefore, the traffic engineer has to carry out systematic accident studies to investigate the causes of accidents and to make preventive measure in terms of design and control. It is essential to analyse individual accident and to maintain zone-wise accident records. The statistical analysis of accidents carried out periodically at critical location or road stretches or zones will help to arrive at suitable measures to effectively decrease the accident rates.

9.5.1 Objectives of Accidental Studies

- To study the causes of accidents and to suggest corrective treatment at potential location.
- To evaluate existing design.
- To support proposed design.
- To carry out before and after studies and to demonstrate the improvement in the Example.
- To make commutations of financial loss.
- To give the economic justification for the improvements suggested by the traffic engineer.
- **Causes of Accidents :** There are four elements in a traffic accident :
  (1) Road users.
  (2) Vehicles.
  (3) Road and its condition, and
  (4) Environmental factors.

The road user responsible for the accidents may be the driver of one or more vehicles involved, pedestrians or the passengers.

- **Drivers :** Excessive speed and rash driving, carelessness, violation of rules and regulation, failure to see or understand the traffic situation, sign or signal, temporary effects due to fatigue, sleep or alcohol.
- **Pedestrians :** Violating regulation, carelessness in using the carriageway meant for vehicular traffic.
- **Passenger :** Alighting from or getting into moving vehicles. Vehicles involved in the accident may be defective.
- **Vehicle Defects :** Failure of breaks, steering system or lighting system, tyre burst and any other defect in the vehicles.

The conditions of road's surface and other existing geometric feature conditions of the road may not be upto the expectation causing an accident.

- **Road Condition :** Slippery or skidding road surface, potholes, ruts and other damaged conditions of the road surface.
- **Road Design :** Defective geometric design like inadequate sight distance, inadequate width of shoulders, improper curve design, improper curve design, improper lighting, and improper traffic control devices.

Environmental Condition : Any environmental conditions of the road may not be upto the expectation causing an accident. To sump-up, an accident may be caused due to a combination of several reasons and seldom due to one particular reason. Hence, it is often not possible to pin point a particular single cause of an accident.

- **Weather :** Unfavourable weather conditions like mist, fog, snow, smoke or heavy rainfall that restrict normal visibility and render driving unsafe.
- **Animals :** Stray animals on the road.
- **Other Causes :** Incorrect signs or signals, gate of level crossing not closed when required, ribbon development, badly located advertisement boards or services station etc.
- **Accident Studies and Records :** The various steps involved in traffic accident studies are collection of accident date, preparation of reports, location file and diagrams, and application of the above records for suggesting preventive measures.

(1) **Collection of Accident Data :** The collection accident data is the first step in the accident study. Standard forms for collecting the data are prepared, as suggested by the IRC. The details to be collected are briefly mentioned here :

   (a) **General :** Date, time, persons involved in the accident and their particular, classification of accident like fatal, serious, minor etc.

   (b) **Location :** Description and details of the location of accidents.

   (c) **Details of Vehicles Involved :** Registration number make and description of the vehicles, loading details, vehicular defects.

   (d) **Nature of Accidents :** Condition of vehicles involved, details of collision, and pedestrians or objects involved, damages, injuries, causality etc.

   (e) **Road and Traffic Conditions :** Details of road geometric, whether the road is straight or curved, surface characteristics such as dry, wet or slippery etc. Traffic condition-type of traffic, traffic density etc.

   (f) **Primary Causes of Accidents :** Various possible causes and the primary causes of the accidents.

   (g) **Accident Costs :** The total cost of the accidents compound in terms of rupees, of the various involvements like property damages, personal injuries and causalities.

(2) **Accident Report :** The accidents should be reported to police authorities that would take legal actions especially in more serious accidents involving injuries, causalities or

severe damages to property. Accident report of the individuals involved may be separately taken. The accidents data should be collected as given above and the report is prepared with all facts, which might be useful in subsequent analysis, claims for compensation.

(3) **Accident Records :** The accident records are maintained giving all particulars of the accidents, location and other details. The records may be maintained by means of location files, spot maps, collision diagrams and condition diagrams.

   (a) **Location Files :** These are useful to keep a check on the location of accident and to identify points of high accident incidences. Location fields should be maintained by each police station for the respective jurisdiction.

   (b) **Spot Maps :** Accident location spot maps show accidents by spots, pins or symbols on the map. A map of suitable scale say 1 cm = 40 to 60 meter, may be used for spotting urban accidents. The common legends used for spot maps.

   (c) **Conditional Diagram :** A conditional diagram is a drawing to a scale showing all important physical conditions of an accident's location to be studied. The important features generally to be shown in this diagram with suitable dimensions marked there in are roadway limits, curves, kerb lines, bridges, culverts, trees and all details of roadway condition, obstruction to vision, property lines, signs, signal etc. There are standard symbols used in showing various details. The condition and collision diagrams may be combined together in a single sketch, if necessary.

   (d) **Collision Diagram :** These are diagrams showing the approximate path of vehicles and pedestrians involved in the accidents. Collision diagrams are most useful to compare the accident pattern before and after the remedial measures have been taken. A typical collision diagram and symbol are shown in Fig. 9.9.

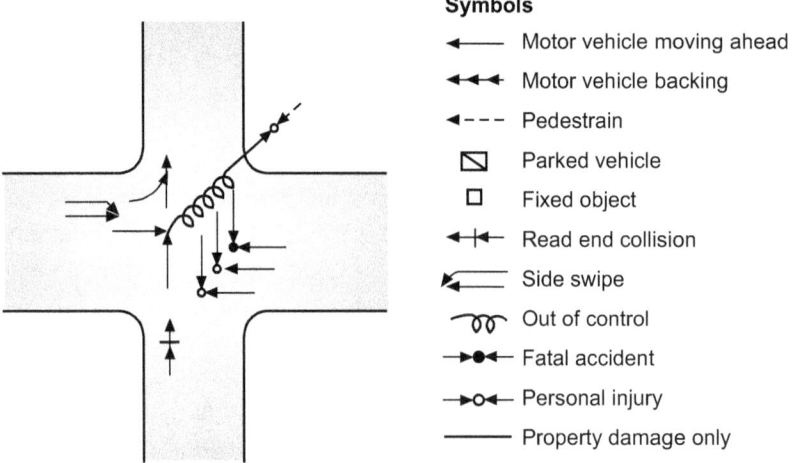

Fig. 9.9

Accident investigations and studies therefore may be carried out scientifically in the following three stages.
- Accident investigations.
- Analysis of Individual Accidents.
- Statistical Analysis of Accidents.

Type of accident	Fatal	Non-Fatal
Motor vehicle-pedestrian	•	•
Other motor vehicle traffic	•	•

The above figure shows legend for spot maps.

9.5.2 Measures for the Reduction in Accident Rates

The various measures to decrease the accident rates may be divided into three groups :
1. Engineering,
2. Enforcement,
3. Education

These three measures are generally termed "3-Es". The details of these measures are given below.

9.5.2.1 Engineering Measures

(a) **Road Design :** The geometric design features of the road such as sight distances, width of pavement, horizontal and vertical alignment design details and intersection design elements are checked and corrected if necessary. The pavement surface characteristics including the skid resistance values are checked and suitable maintenance steps taken to bring them upto the design standards. Where necessary by-passes may be constructed to separate through traffic from local traffic. To minimize delay and conflicts at the intersections, it may be essential to design and construct grade separated intersections or flyovers.

(b) **Preventive Maintenance of Vehicles :** The braking system, steering and lighting arrangements of vehicle plying on the roads may be checked at suitable intervals and heavy penalties levied on defective vehicles. These measures are particularly necessary for public carriers.

(c) **Before and After Studies :** The record of accidents and their patterns for different locations are maintained by means of collision and condition diagrams. After making the necessary improvements in design and enforcing regulation, it is again necessary to collect and maintain the record of accidents "before and after" the introduction of preventive measures to study their efficiency. A typical example of before and after study at an intersection is shown in Fig. 9.10 (a) and (b).

(d) Road Lighting : Proper road lighting can decrease the rate of accidents during night, due to poor visibility. Lighting is particularly desirable at intersections, bridge sites and at places where there are restrictions to traffic movements.

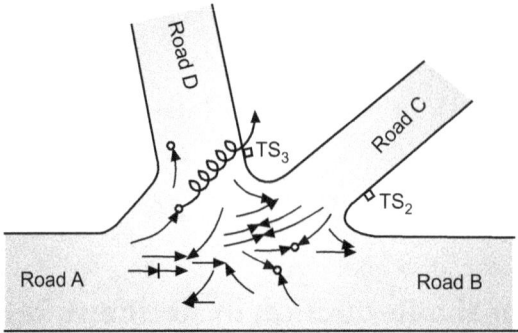

Fig. 9.10 (a) Uncontrolled movements of vehicles and pedestrians

Accident : Twelve in a period of two months

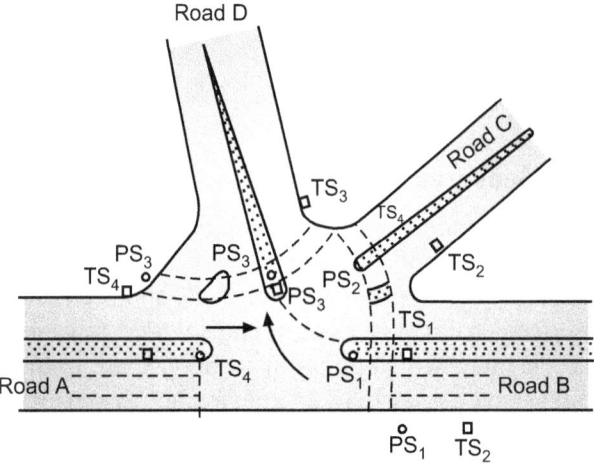

(i) Additional traffic signals (TS) installed and signal timings re-designed.

(ii) Pedestrian signals (PS) installed and pavement markings made for pedestrian crossings and control over other vehicular manoeuvers.

(iii) Divisional islands and channelizing islands provided by widening roads A-B

Accident : Only one in a period of two months.

Fig. 9.10 (b) : Typical case of before and after study

9.5.2.2 Enforcement Measures

The various measures of enforcement that may be useful to prevent accidents at spots prone to accident are enumerated here. The motor vehicle rules are revised from time to time to make them more comprehensive.

(a) **Speed Control :** To enable drivers of buses to develop correct speed habits, tachometers may be fitted so as to give record of speeds. Also surprise checks on spot speed of all fast moving vehicles should be done at selected locations and timings and legal actions on those who violate the speed limits should be taken.

(b) **Traffic Control Devices :** Signals may be designed or signal system be introduced if necessary. Similarly, proper traffic control devices like signs, marking or chennelizing islands may be installed wherever found necessary.

(c) **Training and Supervision :** The transport authorities should be strict in testing and issuing license to drivers of public service vehicles and taxis. Even the drivers who have passed the requisite tests should be kept under proper supervision and be trained in proper defensive driving.

(d) **Medical Check :** The drivers should be tested for vision and reaction time at prescribed intervals, say, once in three years.

(e) **Special Precautions for Commercial Vehicles :** It may be insisted on having a conductor or attendant to help and give proper direction to drivers of heavy commercial vehicles.

9.5.2.3 Educational Measures

(a) **Education of Road Users :** It is very essential to educate the road user for the various precautionary measures to use the road way facilities with safety. The passengers and measures and pedestrians should be taught the rules of the road, correct manner of crossing etc. This may be possible by introducing necessary instruction in the schools for the children. Posters exhibiting the serious results due to carelessness of road users may also be useful.

(b) **Safety Drives :** Imposing traffic safety week when the road users are properly directed with the help of traffic police and transport staff is a common means of training the public these days. Road users should be impressed on what should documentaries. Training courses may be conducted for drives. The IRC has been organizing Highway safety workshop in different regions of country.

9.5.3 Relationship Between Speed, Travel Time, Volume, Density and Capacity

Time and Speed : The travel time per unit length of road is inversely proportional to the speed. If T is travel time and V is the speed (kmph),

$$T \text{ (min/km)} = \frac{60}{V}$$

or $\quad T \text{ (sec./km)} = \dfrac{3600}{V}$

Fig. 9.11 shows the relationship between travel time and speed. It is seen that at higher speed, the rate of saving in travel time decreases.

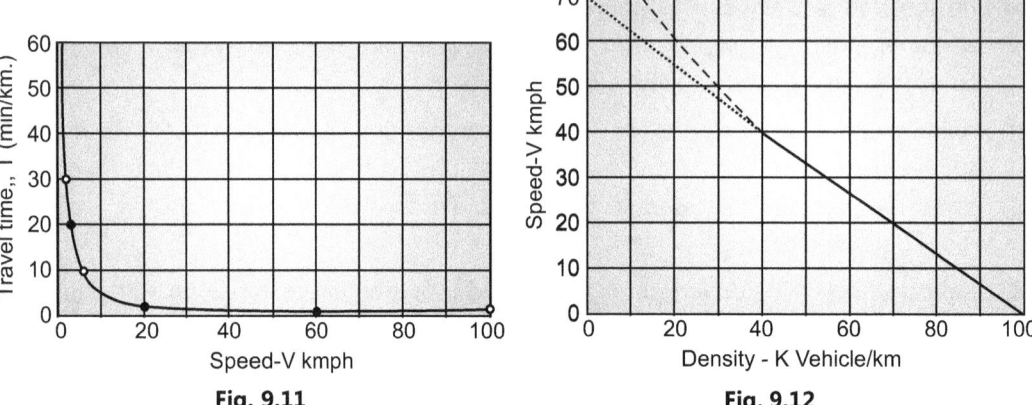

Fig. 9.11 Fig. 9.12

The fundamental relationship between traffic volume, density and speed may be given by the general equation of traffic flow:

$$q = K V_s$$

Where, q = The average volume of vehicles passing a point during a specified period of time (vehicle per hour).

K = The average density or number of vehicles occupying a unit length of roadway at a given instant.

V_s = Space-mean speed of vehicles in a unit roadway length (kmph).

With increase in speed of vehicles in a unit roadway length, the average density decreases. It is difficult to measure density directly, in practice. Hence the relationship between volume, density and speed is often used. The value of density K may be obtained by rewriting equation

$$K \text{ (vehicles/km)} = \dfrac{q}{V}$$

When the speed of the traffic flow decreases and becomes zero, the density attains the maximum value whereas, volume becomes zero. For increasing values of speeds, density decreases, whereas the volume increases upto a certain limit, as shown in Fig. 9.14. At high speeds, the volume starts decreasing and density keeps on further reducing. Eventually, if a hypothetical case is considered when volume approaches zero at very high speeds, the density also approaches zero, as shown in Fig. 9.15. Thus, there is a maximum flow in road corresponding to some optimum values of speed and density.

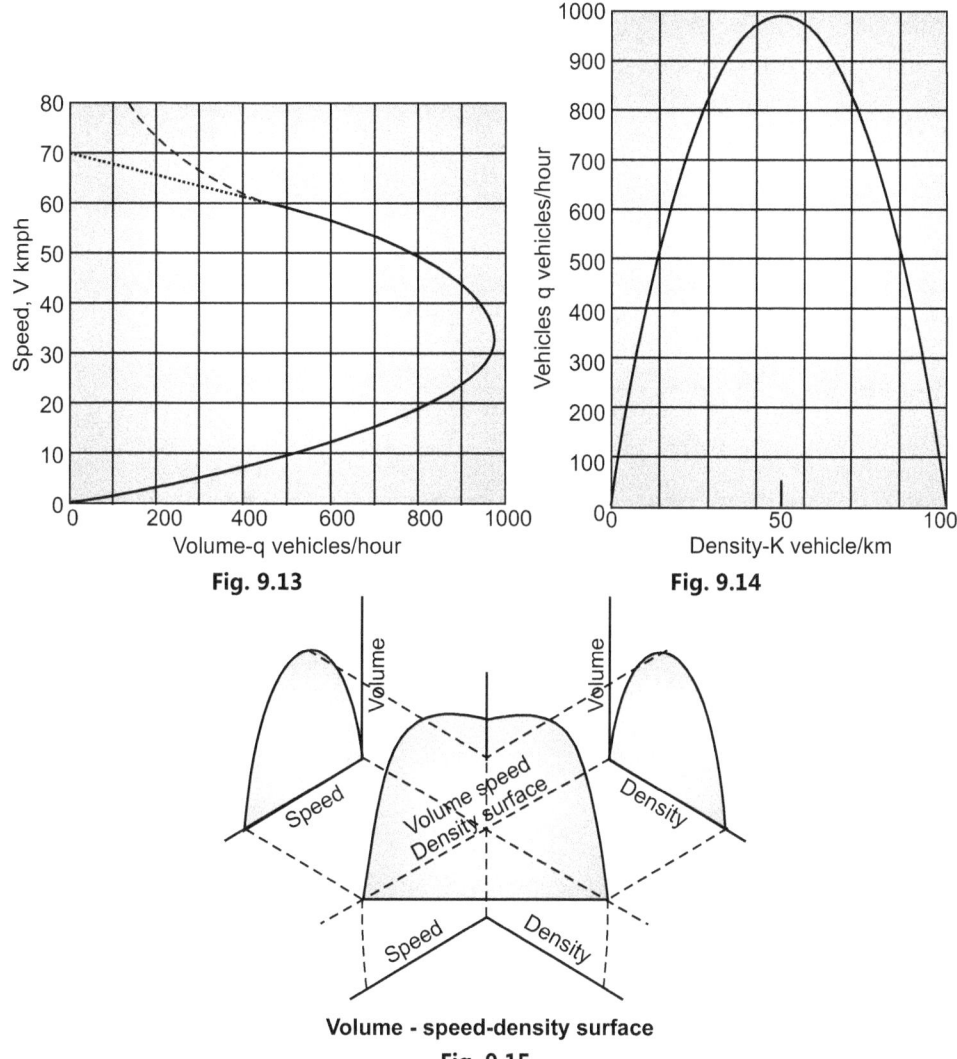

Fig. 9.13

Fig. 9.14

Volume - speed-density surface
Fig. 9.15

SOLVED EXAMPLES

Example 9.1 : A motor vehicle running at a speed of 30 km/hr was subjected to full loading and was stopped in 5.8 m length. Evaluate average skid resistance of pavement.

Solution : Initial speed $= \dfrac{30}{3.6} = 8.33$ m/sec

Since $\quad f = \dfrac{u^2}{2gL} = \dfrac{(8.33)^2}{2 \times 9.81 \times 5.8} = 0.61$

Example 9.2 : A motor vehicle running on level road with a speed of 40 km/hr was subjected to braking and the length of skid marks was 10.0 meter. Average skid resistance of the pavement is 0.70. What would be the braking efficiency of this vehicle ?

Solution :

Initial speed $= \dfrac{40}{3.6} = 11.11$ m/sec. $L = 10$ m

and $f = 0.70$

The developed skid resistance $= f = \dfrac{u^2}{2gL} = \dfrac{(11.11)^2}{2 \times 9.8 \times 10} = 0.629$

Braking efficiency $= \dfrac{\text{Developed skid resistance}}{\text{Resistance that could be developed}}$

$= \dfrac{0.629}{0.70} = 89.9\%$

Example 9.3 : Observations were recorded in a 100 meter stretch of the road. The travel time for vehicles to ply this section is as follows:

Table 9.6

Vehicles	Travel Time
10	12 seconds
30	15 seconds
7	3 seconds

What would be space mean speed ?

Solution : Space mean speed $= \dfrac{3.6\, dn}{\sum\limits_{i=1}^{n} t_1}$

where, d = length of section meter,
  n = number of vehicles under observation,
  t = corresponding travel time.

Table 9.7

Vehicle No.	Travel Time	$\dfrac{3.6\, dn}{t_1}$	Space Mean Speed for This Vehicle
1	2	$\dfrac{3.6 \times 10 \times 1}{2}$	$= 18$
2	3	$\dfrac{3.6 \times 10 \times 1}{3}$	$= 12$

Space mean speed for the traffic flow

$= \dfrac{3.6\, dn}{\sum\limits_{i=1}^{n} t_1} = \dfrac{3.6 \times 10 \times 2}{2+3} = 14.4$ km/h

Instantaneous speed for vehicle 1 = $\dfrac{3.6 \times 10}{2}$ = 18 km/hr.

Instantaneous speed for vehicle 2 = $\dfrac{3.6 \times 10}{3}$ = 12 km/hr.

∴ Time mean speed = $\dfrac{18 + 12}{2}$ = 15 km/hr.

It should be noted that space mean speed and instantaneous speed would be same if observations are taken for short stretch of road length,

∴ Space mean speed = $\dfrac{3.6\,[100 \times 10 + 100 \times 30 + 100 \times 7]}{12 \times 10 + 15 \times 30 + 3 \times 7}$

= $\dfrac{3.6\,[100]\,[47]}{120 + 450 + 21}$

= $\dfrac{16920}{591}$

= 28.62 km/hr.

Example 9.4 : Observations were recorded in 100 meter stretch and the observed instantaneous speed of the categories of the vehicles are as under.

Table 9.8

Vehicles	Speed
10	20 km/hr.
30	18 km/hr.
7	10 km/hr.

What would be time mean speed ?

Solution :

Time mean speed = $\dfrac{\text{Summation of instantaneous speeds}}{\text{Number of vehicles}}$

= $\dfrac{20 \times 10 + 18 \times 30 + 10 \times 7}{20 + 18 + 7}$

= $\dfrac{200 + 540 + 70}{45}$

= 18 km/hr.

Example 9.5 : From the following data, determine the average speed of vehicles on that road.

Table 9.9

Speed Range	No. of Vehicles
0 – 10 km/hr.	7
10 – 20 km/hr.	20
20 – 40 km/hr.	40
40 – 60 km/hr.	5

Solution :

Table 9.10

Vehicles	Average speed
7	5
20	15
40	30
5	50

Average speed on this track

$$= \frac{7 \times 5 + 20 \times 15 + 40 \times 30 + 5 \times 50}{7 + 20 + 40 + 5} = \frac{35 + 300 + 1200 + 250}{72}$$

= 24.79 say 25 km/hr.

Example 9.6 : For a certain section of highways, the speed data collected are shown.

Table 9.11

Speed Range, km/hr.	No. of Vehicles Observed	Speed Range, km/hr.	No. of Vehicles Observed
0 – 10	10	50 – 60	250
10 – 20	18	60 – 70	20
20 – 30	70	70 – 80	40
30 – 40	90	80 – 90	30
40 – 50	200	90 – 100	10

Determine : (i) Upper and lower values of speed limit for mixed traffic flow, (ii) Design speed.

Solution : We have to prepare cumulative speed distribution table. Total number of vehicles observed

= 10 + 18 + 70 + 90 + 200 + 250 + 20 + 40 + 30 + 10

= 738

∴ Total frequency of vehicles = 738

Plot the graph between speed and cumulative number of vehicles i.e. frequency. Speed corresponding to 85th cumulative frequency i.e. 85th percentile speed is the upper speed limit regulation.

The student is advised to plot this graph. He will find this speed limit around 55 km/hr which is the upper speed limit regulation.

The lower speed limit regulation to avoid congestion i.e. 15th percentile speed will be around 27th km/hr.

For designing geometrical elements, it is traditional to consider 98th percentile speed which is around 85 km/hr.

Table 9.12

Speed Range km/hr.	Mid Speed km/hr.	No. of Vehicles or Frequency	Frequency Percentage	Cumulative Frequency
0 – 10	$\frac{0+10}{2} = 5$	10	$\frac{10}{738} = 1.355\%$	1.355
10 – 20	$\frac{10+20}{2} = 15$	18	$\frac{18}{738} = 2.439\%$	1.355 + 2.439 = 3.794 %
20 – 30	25	70	$\frac{70}{738} = 9.485\%$	9.485 + 3.794 = 13.27 %
30 – 40	35	90	$\frac{90}{738} = 12.19\%$	13.27 + 12.19 = 25.46 %
40 – 50	45	200	$\frac{200}{738} = 27.10\%$	27.10 + 25.46 = 52.56 %
50 – 60	55	250	$\frac{250}{738} = 33.87\%$	52.56 + 33.87 = 86.43 %
60 – 70	65	20	$\frac{20}{738} = 2.60\%$	2.6 + 86.43 = 89.03 %
70 – 80	75	40	$\frac{40}{738} = 5.2\%$	5.2 + 89.03 = 94.2 %
80 – 90	85	30	$\frac{30}{738} = 4.05\%$	4.05 + 94.2 = 98.25 %
90 – 100	95	10	$\frac{10}{738} = 1.35$	1.35 + 98.25 = 100 %

Example 9.7 : Spot speed studies data is given below for a section of the road. Determine the most preferred speed at which maximum proportion of vehicles are travelling.

Table 9.13

Speed Range, km/hr.	No. of Vehicles Observed	Speed Range, km/hr.	No. of Vehicles Observed
0 – 10	0	50 – 60	225
10 – 20	12	60 – 70	70
20 – 30	40	70 – 80	25
30 – 40	100	80 – 90	0
40 – 50	250		

Solution : We need to prepare speed versus percentage of vehicles observed graph i.e. frequency distribution curve for solution of this Example.

Total frequency i.e. total vehicles

$$= 0 + 12 + 40 + 100 + 250 + 225 + 70 + 25 + 0 = 722$$

Table 9.14

Speed Range, km/hr.	Mean Speed	No. of Vehicles Observed or Frequency	Percent Frequency
0 – 10	5	0	$\frac{0}{722} = 0\%$
10 – 20	15	12	$\frac{12}{722} = 1.66\%$
20 – 30	25	40	$\frac{40}{722} = 5.54\%$
30 – 40	35	100	$\frac{100}{722} = 13.85\%$
40 – 50	45	250	$\frac{250}{722} = 34.62\%$
50 – 60	55	225	$\frac{225}{722} = 31.16\%$
60 – 70	65	70	$\frac{70}{722} = 9.69\%$
70 – 80	75	25	$\frac{25}{722} = 3.46\%$
80 – 90	85	0	$\frac{0}{722} = 0\%$
			100 %

The modal speed corresponding to the maximum value of percentage frequency when plotted on the graph is 45 km/hr. This is the most preferred speed at which maximum proportion of vehicles would travel.

Example 9.8 : Speed and delay studies are conducted on a stretch of road measuring 4 km in north-south direction. From this data, determine journey speed, running speed of traffic stream in either direction. Determine average values of volume too.

Table 9.15

Trip No.	Direction	Journey Time		Delay Time		Vehicles Overtaking	Vehicles Overtaken	Vehicles from Opposite Direction
		Min.	Sec.	Min.	Sec.			
1	N – S	6	35	1	30	5	7	250
2	S – N	7	00	1	40	6	3	180
3	N – S	6	50	1	30	5	3	280
4	S – N	7	50	1	30	2	1	200
5	N – S	6	00	1	00	3	4	230
6	S – N	8	15	2	20	2	2	150
7	N – S	6	25	1	30	2	5	300
8	S – N	7	30	1	40	3	2	160

Solution : We first prepare table for speed and delay data.

Table 9.16

Trip No.	Direction	Journey Time		Delay Time		Vehicles Overtaking	Vehicles Overtaken	Vehicles from Opposite Direction
		Min.	Sec.	Min.	Sec.			
	N – S	6	35	1	30	5	7	250
		6	50	1	30	5	3	280
		6	00	1	00	3	4	230
		6	25	1	30	2	5	300
Total		25	50	5	30	15	20	1060
mean		6.4	min	1.37	min	7.5	9.75	530
	S – N	7	00	1	40	6	3	180
		7	50	1	30	2	1	200
		8	15	2	20	2	2	150
		7	30	1	40	3	2	160
Total		30.58	min	7.16	min	13	8	690
mean		7.64	min	1.79	min	3.29	2	172.5

We have

(1) North - South Direction

n_y = Average no. of vehicles overtaking – overtaken
       = 7.5 – 9.75 = – 2.25

n_a = Average no. of vehicles in opposite direction i.e. SN = 172.5

t_w = Average journey time = 6.45 minutes = 6 mt 27 seconds

t_a = Average journey time in the trip against the stream i.e. SN = 7.64 m = 7 mt 38 sec.

q = Average volume $= \dfrac{n_a + n_y}{t_a + t_w} = \dfrac{172.5 + (-2.25)}{6.45 + 7.64}$

= 12.083 veh./min

i = Average journey time $= t_w - \dfrac{n_y}{q} = 6.45 - \dfrac{-2.25}{12.083}$ = 6.63 minutes

Average journey speed $= \dfrac{\text{Journey length}}{\text{Average journey time}} = \dfrac{4}{6.63}$ km/min

$= \dfrac{4 \times 60}{6.63}$ km/hr. = 36.19 km/hr.

Average delay = 1.37 minutes,

Average running time = Average journey time – Average delay
= 6.63 – 1.37 = 5.26 minutes

Average running speed $= \dfrac{4 \times 60}{5.26}$ km/hr. = 45.62 km/hr.

(2) South - North Direction

Now, $n_y = 3.25 - 2 = 1.25$, $n_a = 530$, $t_w = 7.64$ minutes, $t_a = 6.45$ minutes

$$q = \frac{n_a + n_y}{t_a + t_w} = \frac{530 + 1.25}{7.64 + 6.45}$$

$$= 37.704 \text{ veh./minute}$$

$$i = t_w - \frac{n_y}{q} = 7.64 - \frac{1.25}{37.70} = 7.606 \text{ minutes}$$

Average journey speed $= \dfrac{4}{7.606}$ km/min.

$$= \frac{4 \times 60}{7.606} = 31.55 \text{ km/hr.}$$

Average delay $= 1.79$ minutes

Average running time $= 7.606 - 1.79$

$= 5.81$ min

Average running speed $= \dfrac{4 \times 60}{5.81}$ km/hr. $= 41.3$ km/hr

REVIEW QUESTIONS

1. What are the traffic characteristics that should be considered while traffic planning ?
2. What are the vehicle characteristics that should be known for traffic planning?
3. What are traffic volume studies? How can you find out whether there is congestion at junction?
4. Write notes on thirtieth highest hourly volume.
5. What is space-mean speed and time-mean speed? What are special conditions for a vehicle when their speeds are same numerically?
6. Calculate - space mean speed for

Table 9.17

Vehicle	Road Stretch	Travel Time
30	100	15
40	100	12
10	100	8

(**Ans.** 12.47 km/hr)

7. For the above data calculate time - mean speed. (**Ans.** 29 – 62 km/hr.)
8. Distinguish between running speed and travel speed.
9. What is percentile speed ? How is it used to determine safe speed limit ?
10. From the following, determine average speed of vehicles on the track.

Table 9.18

Speed Range	No. of Vehicles
0 – 10	5
10 – 20	10
20 – 30	30
30 – 40	10

(**Ans.** 24 km/hr.)

11. On the basis of data for spot studies given below, upper and lower speed limit regulation as well as speed for design is to be calculated.

Table 9.19

Speed Range	No. of vehicles Observed	Speed Range	No. of Vehicles Observed
0 – 10	12	50 – 60	255
10 – 20	18	60 – 70	20
20 – 30	68	70 – 80	43
30 – 40	89	80 – 90	33
40 – 50	205	90 – 100	9

(**Ans.** Upper speed limit for regulation 60 km/hr.
Lower speed limit for regulation 30 km/hr.
Speed for design = 84 km/hr.)

12. How origin and destination can be defined ?
13. What are the uses of origin destination study ?
14. Describe how origin destination study can be conducted by "License plate method". What are the uses and limitations of this method ?
15. Fill in the blank and justify the reason for it. In India, diverging on the left would cause Examples than diverging to the right.

16. When maximum capacity for a particular speed is obtained on the highway ?
17. Distinguish between traffic volume and traffic capacity.
18. What is possible capacity and when it can approach zero level ?
19. What are desire lines ? What is the exact use for these lines ?
20. Describe the steps that need be taken for parking studies.
21. Describe what is meant by parallel parking and inclined parting. Discuss their merits and demerits.
22. Discuss the need for off-street parting. How it can be arranged ? What are the relative merits and demerits of this system ?

CHAPTER 10
TRAFFIC CONTROL DEVICES

10.1 TRAFFIC OPERATIONS

Traffic operations mean, how do we regulate and control the traffic on highways. In order to control flow, regulations have to be exercised. These controls may be :

(1) Driver Controls : Issuing driver's license only after adequate checks and issuing the license in such a way that in case of unforseen circumstances, driver should be traced. In the case of accident, driver has to suffer penal liability and owner civil liability.

(2) Vehicle Controls : This is a job of Regional Transport Office. Inspecting the vehicle for it's driving worthyness on regular basis for passing. Checking the vehicle for it's brake system etc. Motor vehicle act of 1939 generally covers this aspect such as ownership of vehicle, it's lawful transfer to other parties, insurance, vehicle dimensions etc.

(3) Traffic and General Controls : Traffic can be controlled by various signs. There are many signs. For example, the adjoining figure illustrates some signs. What is most important about traffic signs, is the awareness and urgency in the general public to follow these signs. Heavy penalty (financial) should be levied for the drivers who do not abide by these signs. In urban area one of the effective way to control traffic is through traffic signals. At intersections, where two or more roads cross each other the old practice was to post police. He used to show stop signs alternatively at the cross-roads so that one of the traffic streams may be allowed to move, while the cross-traffic is stopped. This used to put extra pressure on traffic police. The present procedure on urban roads is to install automatic signalling and the posting of the traffic police is for the purpose of catching the offenders. Properly designed traffic signals have many advantages. For example,

- There is orderly movement of traffic and increased capacity of intersections along with smooth heavy traffic flow. The pedestrians can cross the road safely.
- Accidents, in our country right angled collisions are reduced.
- Properly co-ordinated signalling system ensures a certain reasonable speed on major roads, but at the same time, traffic plying on minor roads can safely pass the main stream at regular and reasonable interval of time.

Fig. 10.1

- Near the intersection, fitted with signalling, most of the vehicles will move at approximately the same speed, similar to the movement of platoons and thus reducing rate of accidents. That way in final analysis, signalling installation, though costly to start with would prove economical in the longer run. The above discussion may lead to false impression that there are absolutely no shortcomings of signalling as a system. It is not so. Intersections with signalling have tended to increase rear end collisions. Improper design of signalling can increase congestion on that road. Intersections where signalling have been provided, the commuters get used to it. So much so, that electric power failure at such intersections, when it occurs, simply criple such intersections. Such is the force of habit.

In India, traffic control signals have three coloured light glows facing each direction of traffic flow. Whereas the red light signifies stop motion, the green light indicates 'Go' and the amber or yellow light indicates the clearance time for the vehicles which enter the intersection area by the end of green time to clear off. It might be necessary to provide additional green lights for separate movement of turning traffic where necessary. The period of time required for one complete sequence of signal indications is called the cycle. That part of the signal cycle where traffic movement is allowed is known as phase and any of the division of signal cycle during which signal indications (i.e. colour) do not change is called as interval.

- In India, we have various types of signal procedures. Fixed-time signals or pre-timed signals are set to repeat regularly a cycle of red, amber and green. The timing of each phase of cycle, i.e. duration of time during signal will be red or green or amber is predetermined and managed automatically by electric operation.
- Very simple to install, the only drawback, sometimes when traffic on one road is very heavy and the traffic on the other road almost nil such eventuality cannot be catered by this system. It will continue at predetermined times.
- Traffic actuated signals are those in which signalling time can be changed as per traffic demand. On the other hand, with semiactuated traffic signals, we have detectors installed at the approaches, so that normal green light can be extended for few seconds more, so that few more vehicles approaching closely can be cleared.
- In fully actuated traffic signals, there are detectors and coupled computer which assigns the right of way for various traffic movements on the basis of demand.
- This alternative is somewhat costly and typical, but effective Indian alternative is to assign traffic police at such intersection. It is the job of police, now to assess traffic demand and vary the timing of phase and cycle. This method has proved well.
- When there are series of signals on city road at each intersection with cross-road, signalling system should preferably be operated by one controller. In such road pattern, it should be seen that vehicle moving along main road at normal speed is not required to stop at every signalized intersection at a stretch. Where there are zebra crossing i.e.

pathway across the road which can be utilized by the pedestrians for crossing the road, these crossings can also be controlled by proper signaling.

The traffic signal system can be operated in various ways; for example :

(1) Simultaneous System : In a typical system of this type, all signals along a given roadway would show the same colour (indication) at the same time. Thus division of cycle at all intersections is now bound to be same. In general, this system is not preferred.

(2) Alternate System : This system is better than the previous. The principle is alternate signals or group of signals show opposite indications in a route, but at the same time. By reversing the red and green indicator connections at successive signal system, single controller can operate two successive intersections.

(3) Simple Progressive System : In this system each signal unit works as a fixed time signal with equal signal cycle length, but the phase and interval at each signal installation may be different. This allows continuous operation of group of vehicles along the main road at moderate reasonable speed. Thus there is predetermined time schedule for "Go" indications along this road.

(4) Flexible Progressive System : This is a computerised system and length of cycle, cycle division, time schedule can be altered as per requirements. In addition to these one can use flashing beacons to be carried by traffic police. On seeing this the drivers would stop before entering the nearest cross-walk or at any line which is marked.

Where Traffic Signals should be Installed : Each and every intersection need not and should not have traffic signals. Such general installation of traffic signals infact would cause congestion. Traffic engineering data should justify this installation. The standard recommendations are :

(1) There should be minimum vehicular traffic. The average traffic volume for eight hours on both approaches should be at least 650 motor vehicles per hour on major street with single lane and 850 vehicles on the streets with two or more lanes. In addition, motor vehicles approaching the intersection on minor street (for one direction only) should be at least 200 vehicles per hour on single lane street and 250 vehicles per hour when there are two or more lanes. The stated requirement could be decreased to 70%, when 85th percentile speed or average approach speed on major roads exceeds 60 kmph. Even when the intersection lies within the built-up area, the vehicular volume could be decreased to 70%.

(2) Minimum pedestrian traffic of 150 or more per hour should cross the major street with over 600 vehicles per hour on both approaches (1000 vehicles per hour in the case of Main Street with raised median). Again here also when average approach speed or the 85th percentile speed exceeds 60 kmph, 70 % of the stated requirement could be adopted.

(3) If there is interruption of continuous traffic flow on the major road which carries 1000 to 1200 vehicles per hour or when there is undue delay or hazard to traffic of 100 to 150 vehicles per hour in one direction only during any eight hours on average day, it is a fit case of signalized intersection.

(4) If there are accidents at the intersections, even 5 or more minor accidents in a year, signalling might help, if designed properly so as not to cause disruption of traffic. Public octroy and public demand are the main cause of installation of signalling in many cases.

10.2 SIGNALIZED INTERSECTION DESIGN

Intersection design objective is to cut short delays and ques and handle high volume of traffic. General principles of design could be listed :

(1) Red phase of the signal is the sum of either go and clearance intervals or it could be sum of green and amber phases of cross flow. i.e. $G_2 + A_2$ at two phase signal. If turning movements are not permitted, pedestrian crossing time may also be incorporated for the road.

(2) Towards the end time of red phase, there could be short duration when amber light are put on along with red signal which indicates get set go position. During this red-amber time, vehicles are not supposed to cross the stop line.

(3) Just after the green but before red, amber phase is provided for the clearance of traffic. This preposition satisfies two requirements (a) It provides stopping time for approaching vehicle to stop at cross line. This is essential when signal changes from green to amber and not to cross the line by the time signal changes to red phase. (b) It can also provide clearance time, which can be utilized by an approaching vehicle travelling at design speed to cross the intersection area. For such a vehicle, it is difficult to stop before the stop line at this stage. For such an operation, 2 to 4 seconds of amber phase is O.K.

(4) Traffic volume during peak hour and the length of que of vehicles would decide green that is 'go' time.

To design isolated fixed time signal we can resort to trial cycle method, approximate method, Webster's method and I.R.C. method. These methods are now discussed and illustrated in Examples 10.11, 10.12 etc. Two phase traffic signals with no turning are considered.

Trial Cycle Method

Let us suppose that two roads 1 and 2 are crossing each other. Vehicle that ply on these roads during peak hour are n_1 and n_2 during time 't' minutes. Assume first trial cycle of 'C' seconds. Number of cycles in 't' minutes are then $\dfrac{t \times 60}{C}$. Assume time headway be h_1

seconds then green period time = $\dfrac{n_1 \times \text{Time headway}}{\text{No. of cycles in 't' minutes}}$. Amber periods A_1, A_2 could be assumed to be 3 to 4 seconds and cycle length is $(G_1 + G_2 + A_1 + A_2)$ seconds. If the calculated and the assumed cycle length are closer, the exercise is adequate otherwise repeat, till there is reasonable convergence. The method is illustrated in Example 10.11.

Approximate Method : Cross-roads along with pedestrian signals can be designed this way also. Steps are :

(1) Amber period could be assumed as 2, 3, 4 seconds for low medium and fast approach speeds.

(2) Clearance for pedestrian time could be considered on the walking speed of 1.2 m/second.

(3) Pedestrian clearance time plus initial interval for pedestrians to start crossing could be minimum red time. This red time should be equal to minimum green time plus amber time for the cross-road.

(4) Minimum green time is calculated on the same principle as red time. This minimum green time is equal to red time for cross-roads minus amber period for the cross-road with the provison that (a) Walk period should not be less than 7 seconds, (b) Even when there is no pedestrian signal as such, the walk period of 5 seconds must be left.

(5) Actual green times may then be increased. For this, one of the green time is considered O.K. and the other increased, with the help of formula

$$\dfrac{\text{Green time road A}}{\text{Green time road B}} = \dfrac{\text{Heaviest vol./hr. on road A per lane}}{\text{Heaviest vol./hr on road B per lane}}$$

The cycle length so obtained is adjusted for the next higher 5 second intervals. Extra time so granted could be distributed to green timings in proportion to the approaching volumes of traffic.

These principles are illustrated in Example 10.12.

Webster's Method

For application of Webster's method we should know:

(1) Saturation flow per unit time on each approach of the intersection.

(2) Normal flow on each approach during design hour.

In case, there is mixed flow, it is to be expressed in terms of passenger car units. Saturation flow should be determined by field studies. In the absence of the data one may assume 160 passenger car units per 0.3 meter width of the approach to be saturation flow. Normal flow has to be determined by field studies conducted during peak or off peak hours. The optimum signal cycle is then $\dfrac{1.5 L + 5}{1 - Y}$ = Co.

where, L = Total lost time per cycle = 2n + R.

n = Number of phase.

R = All red time.

y = y₁ + y₂

$$= \frac{\text{Normal flow on road 1}}{\text{Saturation flow on road 1}} + \frac{\text{Normal flow on road 2}}{\text{Saturation flow on road 2}}$$

$$G_1 = \frac{y_1}{y}(C_o - L) \quad \text{and} \quad G_2 = \frac{y_2}{y}(C_o - L)$$

Design Method as per I.R.C. Guidelines

I.R.C. has formulated certain guidelines based on which signalling can be designed. These guidelines are :

(1) The green time for pedestrians for major and minor roads to be calculated on the basis of walking speed of 1.2 m/sec and initial walking time of 7.0 seconds. These are considered as minimum green time for vehicular traffic on major and minor roads.

(2) This minimum green time required for vehicular traffic on the major road is increased in proportion to the traffic on the two approach roads.

(3) The cycle time is calculated after allowing amber time of 2.0 seconds each. These three steps are similar to the approximate method.

(4) The minimum green time for the vehicular traffic to clear on any of the approach is 16 seconds. The first vehicle takes 6 seconds to clear and the subsequent vehicles (p.c.u.) in the que are cleared at the rate of 2.0 seconds each.

(5) The optimum signal time is computed by using Webster formula. For road widths (Kerb to median or centre line) of 3.0, 3.5, 4.0, 4.5, 5.0, 5.5 meter the saturation flows may be considered as 1850, 1890, 1950, 2250, 2550, 2990 pcu/hour. For width more than 5.5 meter, saturation flows could be taken as 525 pcu per hour per metre width in addition to above. The lost time is to be calculated from the amber time, intergreen time and initial delay of 4.0 seconds for the first vehicle on each leg. The signal cycle time and phases so calculated could be revised keeping in view the optimum cycle length and green time required for clearing the vehicles. The IRC method is compromise between Webster and approximate method. The method is illustrated in Example 10.14.

10.3 PAVEMENT MARKINGS

- In order to regulate the traffic, pavement is sometimes marked by light reflecting paints. Longitudinal line when used as pavement marking should be at least 10 cm thick. Centre lines are the general longitudinal lines. These are used to separate the opposing streams of traffic on undivided two-way roads.

- On national and state highways having two or three lanes, there could be single broken lines of width 0.1 m and length 4.5 segments repeated by 7.5 meter. For horizontal curve and approaches, the gap between the lines could be 3.0 m and 6.0 m respectively.
- For four and six lane highway, two solid continuous parallel lines of 0.1 m width with 0.1 m space in between can be painted. On urban roads upto four traffic lanes, the centre line consists of white broken lines of width 0.10 to 0.15 m, length of segment 3.0 m, and length of gap 4.5 m, to be reduced to 3.0 m, at curves and approaches to intersections.
- For urban undivided roads, where there are two traffic lanes for each direction of traffic flow, the centre line marking should consist of two solid continuous lines.
- Just as we have centre line, we have other lines which indicate the use to which the pavement should be put to.
- There are no passing zone markings to show restriction on overtaking, turn marking which are painted near intersections so that proper lateral placement of vehicles take place turning to the different directions, stop lines which are meant for signalling the drivers to stop near the pedestrian crossing, cross walk lines also called zebra crossing, are places where pedestrians are directed to cross the pavement.
- The width of zebra crossing may be 2.0 to 4.0 m depending upon pedestrian traffic. In addition to these usual lines we have marking for bus-stop.
- The length of kerb or the pavement which is reserved for buses to stop are marked by continuous yellow lines. In this space parking is prohibited. It is better to widen the pavement at the bus-stop point, since later on bus-stop is likely to become focal point of traffic congestion.
- The length and width of pavement reserved for parking should also be marked. Edges of rural roads which have no kerb stones along the edges should be marked by border or edge lines. Route direction arrows should be marked by one or more arrows to guide effectively the traffic lines into correct lanes. Kerb marking could be marking on the kerb and edges of island are marked with alternate black and white lines.
- Similarly obstructions in the pavement way, such as supports for bridge, level crossing gates, culvert head walls should be properly painted. In addition to these markings, to facilitate night driving, we have roadway indicators, hazard markers, and object markers. Roadway indicators are guide posts 0.8 to 1.0 m high painted with black and white strips, preferably reflecting type, to mark the edges of the roadway.
- Hazard markers are about 1.2 m high plates standing on posts either with three red reflectors or markers with black and yellow strips at 45° towards the side of the obstruction.
- This is meant to define obstructions. Object markers are circular red reflectors arranged on triangular or rectangular panels and are used to indicate hazard and obstruction within the path of vehicles like the channelizing islands placed close to the intersections.

10.4 Traffic Planning

In India, there is a mixed reaction to traffic planning. The question of traffic planning is very important in urban areas. In India, we have two types of cities. The cities which have been developed and planned such as New Mumbai, New Delhi, Chandigarh etc. In this case the principles of traffic planning can be applied. Since it is a planned city, we know the population present and future which is likely to inhabit particular area, its expanse in sq. km. Shopping arcade, business districts etc. are all fixed, in fact we know the present and approximate future number of cars, therefore traffic planning can be easily done. The Example is acute in existent cities such old Pune, Old Delhi, where population, number of vehicles, pedestrians etc. have increased, whereas the road network is essentially the old one. In this case the Example to be faced is mitigating as far as possible the griefs of the vehicle owners and commuters. The first step in such a case is to estimate trip generation. It means that we have to estimate the trips produced in or attracted to a given zone. Actually the trip has been defined as the one-way movement having single purpose and mode of travel between the point of origin and point of destination. If one can choose zones having less population and estimate the trips, it shall give idea about the type of road network that is required. Knowing the existing network, we can think of measures to better this network. The first step in this case is to develop linear equation connecting total number of trips and the population in the zone. The usual form of equation that is assumed for elementary analysis is

$$y = b_0 + b_1 x_1$$

where,
- y = Total number of trips in hundred per zone.
- x_1 = Population of zone in thousands.
- b_0 = Regression constant, and
- b_1 = Regression coefficient.

The equation is supplemented by

$$b_1 = \frac{n \sum xy - \sum x \sum y}{n \sum x^2 - (\sum x)^2} \quad \text{and}$$

r = correlation coefficient

$$= b_1 \left[\frac{n\sum x^2 - (\sum x)^2}{n\sum y^2 - (\sum y)^2} \right]^{1/2}$$

where, x and y refer respectively to the population of the zone and trips generated in it as a known data. The principle is explained in Example 10.15.

After knowing the generation of trip in a particular zone, we are interested in knowing trips generated between the two zones. For this purpose we use what is known as gravity model.

It is based on the principle that the trips generated between any two zones i and j are directly proportional to the number of trips generated in the zone i, the number of trips attracted to zone J and are inversely proportional to some function of distance between the zones or

$$T_{ij} = \frac{G_i A_J F_{ij}}{\sum_{J=1}^{n} A_J F_{iJ}}$$

where, T_{ij} = Number of trips from zone i to zone j.

G_i = Trips generated in zone i.

A_J = Trips attracted to zone J.

F_{iJ} = Friction factor calculated on area-wise basis.

n = Number of zones in the urban area.

Friction factor can be initially assumed and the existing data analysed. If there is discrepancy, friction factor is now modified and the data reworked till tolerance limit is reached. Actual method is beyond the scope of this book. Having known total trips between the zones we can know the trips that are made by cars and how many trips are made by buses. General method to achieve this, between two points, time and cost of travel by car and bus are determined. Then with the help of diversion curves the number of bus trips or car trips, between these two origin destination points can be assessed. This is known as model split. After the work of model split, we can assign the various trips between any two origin-destination pair on different highway routes. This is known as traffic assignment. This is also beyond the graduate studies. The object of traffic planning is to estimate demand so that road network can be planned.

10.5 GEOMETRY OF THE ROAD FOR TRAFFIC PURPOSES

When the traffic on the road increases, we have to construct the "Road Geometry" in a peculiar fashion so that traffic congestion is eased. These are rotaries, round abouts, intersections, etc. We shall now discuss these.

10.5.1 Rotary

See Fig. 10.2. Capacity of the rotary is a function of capacity of weaving section and the capacity of weaving section is a function of percentage of weaving traffic, geometric layout, etc. Without going into intricacies of these details, we may use the following formula recommended by the Transport and Road Research Lab (U.K.).

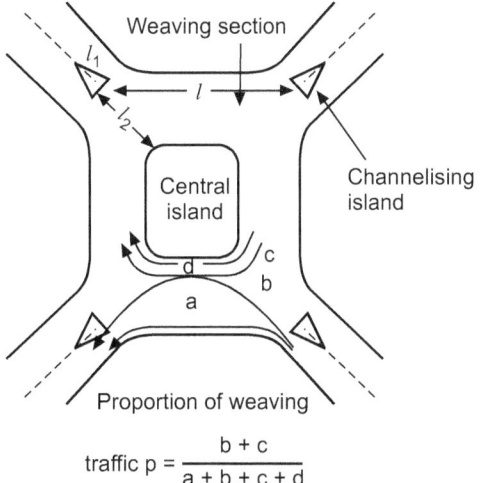

traffic $p = \dfrac{b+c}{a+b+c+d}$

Fig. 10.2 : Relevant dimensions of weaving section and proportion of weaving traffic for use in capacity formula for rotaries

$$Q_p = \dfrac{280\,w\left(1+\dfrac{e}{w}\right)\left(1-\dfrac{p}{3}\right)}{1+\dfrac{w}{l}}$$

where, Q_p = Capacity of weaving section of rotary.

w = Width of weaving section in metres (limited from 6 to 18 metres).

e = Average entry width = $\dfrac{l_1 + l_2}{2}$

l = Length of weaving sections between ends of channelising islands in metres.

p = Proportion of the weaving traffic i.e. ratio of sum of crossing streams to the total traffic on the weaving section = $\dfrac{b+c}{a+b+c+d}$

Fig. 10.2 shows the meaning of the symbols. The equivalency factor for passenger car units as recommended by IRC and TRRL are given in Table 10.1.

Table 10.1

Vehicle Type	P.C.U. Equivalent
Cars, light commercial vehicles, and 3 wheelers, Buses and medium heavy commercial vehicles	1.8
Motor cycles, scooters	0.75
Bicycles	0.5
Animal drawn vehicles	4 to 6

The formula is valid under following condition: (1) No parking vehicles on the approaches, level site and approach gradient not more than 1 in 15. (2) The value of $\frac{l}{w}$ is between 0.4 to 1.0 and $\frac{w}{l}$ should be between 0.12 and 0.40. (3) p should be between 0.4 and 1.0 and l should be between 18 to 90 meters.

In the above formula, some modifications can be made to cater for geometric layout. These are (a) Where the entry angle is between 0° to 15°, deduct 5 percent from the capacity of the weaving section, and when the entry angle is between 15° and 30°, deduct 2.5 per cent from the capacity of the section. (b) For an exit angle between 60° and 75° and above deduct five percent from the capacity of the weaving section. (c) When the internal angle is greater than 95°, deduct 5 percent from the capacity of weaving section. (d) When the pedestrians cross an exit at the rate equal to or more than 300/hr, deduct 16.7 percent from the capacity of weaving section.

The above recommendations and the design is based on U. K. experience. In India and U. K., traffic pattern is to keep left and hence above recommendation are acceptable.

Miscellaneous Features : Rotary should be located on flat ground, having a slope flatter than 1 in 50. For central islands, and channelising islands, mountable type of kerbs whereas for outer edges of the rotary, a barrier type of kerb may be provided. The later discourages the pedestrians from crossing over.

Increasing the Efficiency of Rotary : By adopting traffic signals on the approaches and strictly enforcing "give way to traffic on right" rule, capacity and efficiency of rotary can be increased.

10.5.2 Mini Round Abouts

The rotary, as discussed, suffer from the drawback that once the traffic gets locked into it, the rotary gets jammed and then the police help is required to clear up the traffic. To put it in words, it becomes the case of entering the "Chakravuha" but not finding way out of it. Therefore rotary or round about is not always self regulatary. In U.K., where rotaries are very popular, they introduced "Priority from the right rule" in 1966. This rule reduced weaving and there was a possibility of the central island being cut to size. This rotary with a reduced central island where right rule is strictly followed is called as mini round about. A typical mini round about is shown in Fig. 10.3.

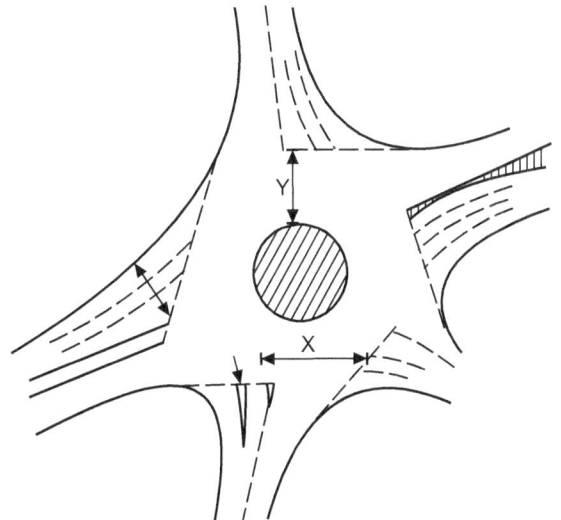

Fig. 10.3 : Typical mini round about as per U. K. practice

The basic principles of design of mini round about are (1) A hypothetical circle inscribed within the outer carriage way boundries is drawn. A central island of a diameter $\frac{1}{3}$ of this hypothetical circle can be provided. (2) At the "give way line" i.e. the location where the priority from the right rule is to be enforced, there is additional lane created. (3) A minimum stopping distance between the "give way line" and opposing vehicle from the left is to be provided. This distance is called x in Fig. 10.14 and is generally about 25 meters. The distance between the traffic island and the central island shown x should be equal to or more than the total lane width at the entry (i.e. the distance z). The entry taper (about 1:6) should be twice sharp as the exit taper (1 : 12). (4) A deflection island shown as B should be installed as as to block straight through movements. (5) The capacity of mini round abouts can be maintained by tapering a single lane approach to three lanes at the junction and two lane approach to four lanes. At the exit, the merge could be from four lanes to two lanes. It is clear that mini round about will work well where there is traffic discipline and priority from the right rule is followed voluntarily and by every person. Given a small percentage of road user not following the rule will result in chaos worse than the chaos when a rotory is blocked. The capacity of a mini round about could be determined by the following formula

$$q = k (\sum W + a^{1/2})$$

where,

    q   = Total entry volume in pcu per hour.

    $\sum W$ = Sum of the basic road width (not half widths) used by traffic in both directions to and from the intersection in meters.

a = Area of the junction widening i.e. area within the intersection outline, including the islands which lies outside the area of the basic cross roads in square meters.

k = Efficiency coefficient, whose value would depend upon the number of junctions.

For a three way and four way junctions, the value is 80 and 70 respectively, whereas for 5 and more route junctions, the value is 65. The practical capacity of a mini round about will be 80 % of the theoretical value. The above formula given by Blackmore is applicable to Indian conditions.

Merits and Demerits of Round About : Where law can be strictly enforced mini round about can accommodate higher volume of traffic, sometimes even higher than the signalized junctions. There is a likelyhood of reduced rate of accidents. The demerits are, the success of the round about revolves around the strict enforcement of priority from the right rule. Similarly a very high standard of pavement markings, great care in the installations of the kerbs, and adequate visibility of approaching drives is necessary. The driver must be in a position to see the approaching drives and then only he can give way to the traffic on the right.

10.5.3 Grade Separated Intersections

Grade separated intersection can very effectively achieve channelization of traffic. The essential principle is that the two intercepting highways or routes are to be provided at different elevations i.e. grades, so that there is no conflict between the crossing streams. In India, provision of grade separated intersections at the railway crossings, specifically in urban area can go a long way in curtailing the accident rates and removing the traffic conjestion. The current Indian practice requires grade separation across streets and highways to be provided based on certain criteria. These criterias are :

(1) Grade separation should be provided if the estimated traffic value in the next 5 years is more than the capacity of the intersection. This state of affair requires immediate construction of grade separated intersections, but when traffic estimates show that the traffic in next 20 years is not likely to exceed the capacity of present intersection, grade separated intersection need not be constructed immediately.

(2) Intersections of divided rural highways may be provided if the average daily traffic (fast vehicle only) on the cross roads within the next 5 years, exceeds 5 thousand. When there is possibility that this figure is likely to reach with next 20 years, grade separation should be left to the planning stage. The most important grade separation is of course, across the railway lines. IRC recommended that grade separation across the existing railway line should be provided if the product of ADT (fast vehicles only) and the number of trains per day exceeds 50 thousand within the next 5 years. When the facility is planned to relieve the traffic conjestion such as bypasses, grade separation should be provided even when the product of ADT and number of trains per day does not exceed 25 thousands.

10.5.3.1 Types of Grade Separated Intersections

Basically, there are two types of grade separated intersections :

(1) Grade separated intersection with interchange: Which is an facility of over-bridge, underpass, or flyover, whereby the traffic at different level ply separately without any interchange between them.

(2) In a facility with interchange, though routes at different grades are there, there is a possibility of interchange between them. These facilities can also be classified depending upon the routes involved - such as three leg interchange, four leg interchange etc., and can then be subdivided.

The general classification is therefore :

(1) Three leg interchange which can be in the form of
  (a) T interchange,
  (b) Y interchange or
  (c) Partial rotary interchange.

(2) Four leg interchange, which can be in the form of
  (a) Diamond interchange,
  (b) Half clover leaf interchange,
  (c) Clover leaf interchange,
  (d) Rotary interchange and
  (e) Directional interchange.

(3) Multi-leg interchange which is generally a rotary interchange.

Types :

The types of interchange mentioned above are now discussed.

Three Leg Interchange

Fig. 10.4 shows a 'T' interchange, generally called as trumpet, due to it's shape. Junctions of major streets with expressways are suitable locations for this interchange. The drawback is vehicles leaving the major road such as at a in the figure have to negotiate small radius.

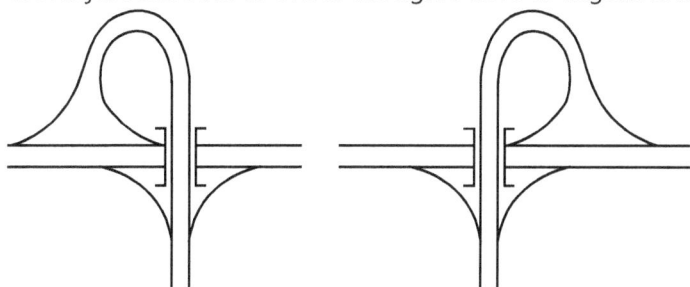

Fig. 10.4 : Trumpet interchange

Fig. 10.5 shows Y shaped interchanges which will allow only restricted movements.

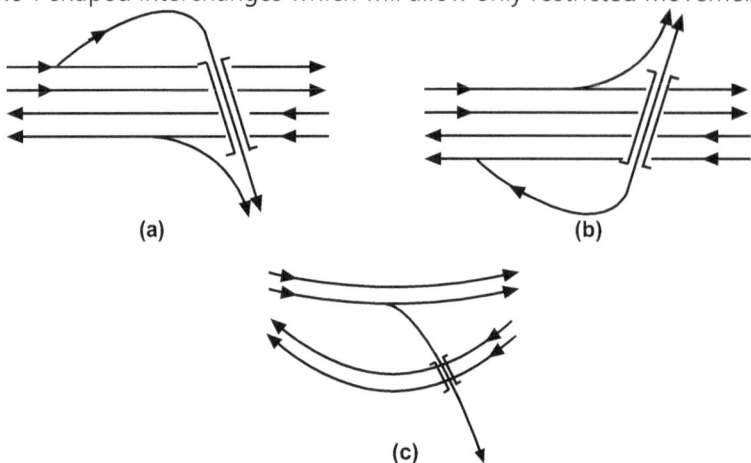

Fig. 10.5 : Y - shaped interchanges

Fig. 10.6 is also a three-leg interchange of the Y type. But this can be converted to a full cloverleaf at future date when traffic so demands.

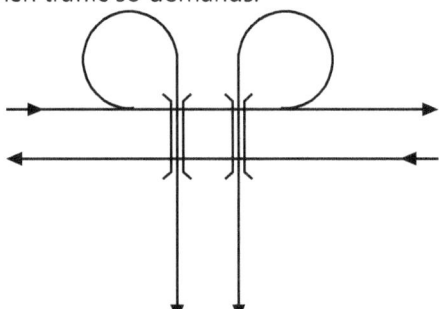

Fig. 10.6 : Three-leg interchange which can be converted to a cloverleaf

A partial bridge rotary intersection is shown in Fig. 10.7. It is clear from these figures that overbridge is necessary to work interchange.

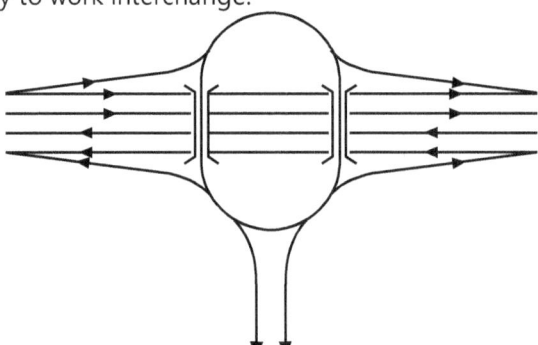

Fig. 10.7 : Partial bridged intersection

Four Leg Interchange

In this the diamond interchange is shown in Fig. 10.8. This is a popular type of interchange for urban sites, for crossing of major and minor roads. The diamond interchange can be of split variety shown in Fig. 10.9, where two parallel cross streets are available as connections to the main road. The half cloverleaf interchange is shown in Fig. 10.9. This interchange is suitable when a major road crosses a minor road with not more than 3 lanes.

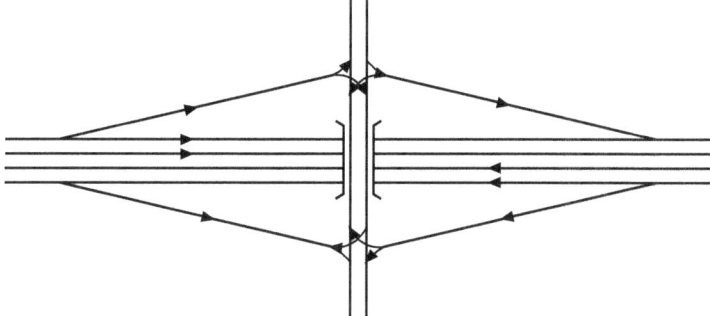

Fig. 10.8 : Diamond interchange

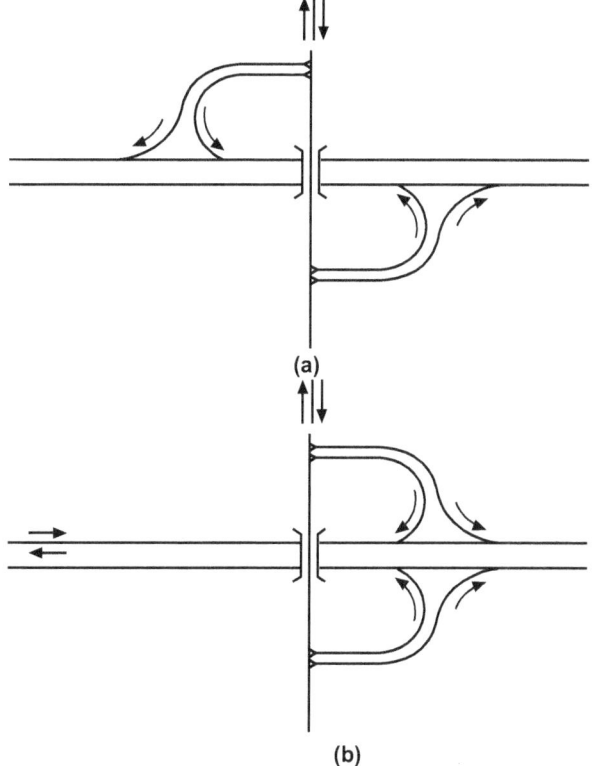

Fig. 10.9 : Partial cloverleaf for major - minor road crossing

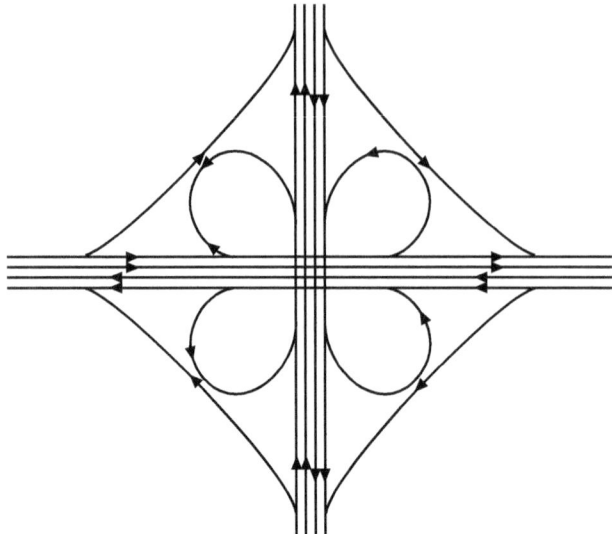

Fig. 10.10 : Cloverleaf interchange

Cloverleaf interchange is a four-leg interchange with a single unitary structure. This facility is becoming very popular these days, and is very useful when high volume, high speed vehicle routes such as expressways cross each other. The advantages of the cloverleaf construction are:

(1) There is only one unitary structure and left turning traffic has a direct path.

(2) There is no impediment to the traffic and it does not confuse the drivers.

The disadvantages are:

(1) Compared to the rotary intersection, higher carriageway width and more total area is required.

(2) The U-turns are long and operationally difficult.

(3) The loop design in case you want higher speeds requires very large area is to be acquired.

(4) And lastly it is costly to construct the cloverleaf. A typical sketch of cloverleaf interchange is shown in Fig. 10.11.

The rotary interchange is shown in Fig. 10.11. It accommodates rotary and the grade intersection. The advantages are:

(1) it requires less area and less carriageway widths.

(2) U-turns are comparatively easy. The disadvantages are that the capacity of the rotary interchange is dependant on the capacity of the round about itself. Just as the sketch shows directional interchange with rotary with two levels, 3 level rotary interchange can also be

arranged. Directional interchanges are generally complicated structures, but these can give direct or semi-direct connections for the major right turning movements. The trumpet type of interchange can be very useful for expressways with toll plazas. The toll plazas planned on Indian highways are thought somewhat different than toll plazas on bridges. At the entry, the expressway user will only collect the card and pay the toll at the exist. A typical trumpet type interchange with toll plaza is shown in Fig. 10.11.

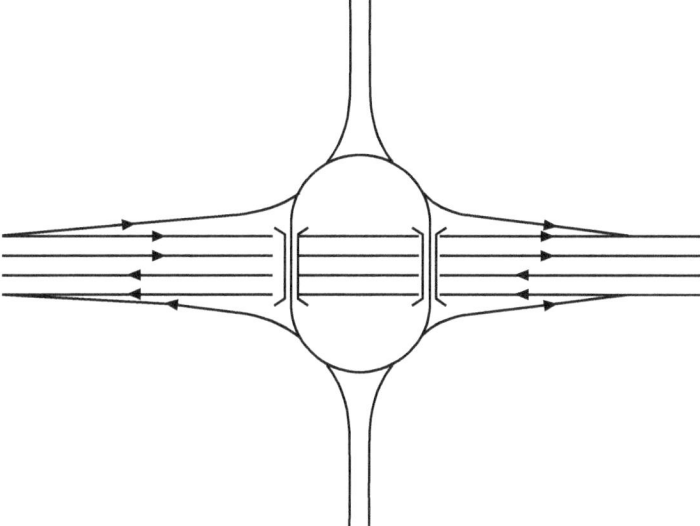

Fig. 10.11 : Grade separated interchange

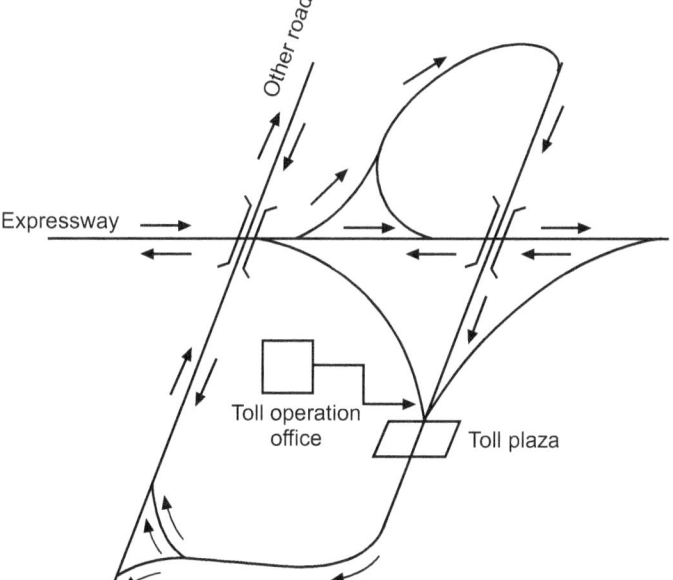

Fig. 10.12 : Trumpet type interchange with toll plaza

10.6 CHANNELIZATION OF TRAFFIC BY CYCLE TRACKS

As discussed earlier, the cycle tracks can also effectively provide channelisation of traffic, if the cycle traffic is significant. They are generally on both sides of the road but separated from the main carriageway by a berm or verge about 1.0 metre wide. These are clear ways for the cyclists. With approximate design speed of 30 km/hr, the design criteria for cycle tracks are laid down by IRC.

Generally, the cycle track may be provided when the peak hour cycle traffic is 400 or more on routes with a traffic of 100 motor vehicles or more but not more than 200 per hour. When the number of motor vehicles using the route is more than 200 per hour, separate cycle tracks could be justified even if the cycle traffic is only 100 per hour. As a general rule the capacity of cycle track may be taken as given in Table 10.2.

Table 10.2

Width of Cycle Track	Capacity in cycles / Day	
	One-Way Traffic	**Two-Way Traffic**
Two lane	2000 to 5000	500 to 2000
Three lane	Over 5000	2000 to 5000
Four lane	–	Over 5000

Cycle track could be classified as

(1) **Adjoining Cycle Tracks :** which completely fit in with the carriageway and are adjacent to and on the same level with it.

(2) **Raised Cycle Track :** These are adjoining the carriageway but are at a higher level.

(3) **Free Cycle Track :** These are separated from the carriageway by a verge and may be at the same level as the carriageway or at a different level.

10.7 HIGHWAY LIGHTING

Highway lighting is a very important subject. In view of the fact that most of the accidents have occurred during night times, the subject occupies special importance. Lighting on rural roads has not attained importance due to cost and rather poor percentage of slow traffic that uses rural road during nights. Even on rural roads, lighting has been found to increase safety of travel. On urban roads, intersections, bridge sites, level crossings, places where there is congestion of traffic, proper highway lighting, for obvious reasons is a "must." Driving, with only head light on is not sufficient safe. One common term used by highway engineers is silhoutte. When the brightness of the object is less than that of the background (i.e. highway), the object will appear darker than the road surface, and we have silhoutte effect. When the brightness of the object is more than that of the background, which should be the desired case, the objects above the pavement surface can be better seen by process of reverse silhoutte. Thus night visibility on concrete and other light coloured pavements is better than black top surface. Rough textured surface is the best. Mirror like black top surface, shining wet surfaces are not useful in identifying the objects above the highway pavement. You require more intense highway lighting in these cases. Actually night visibility is a function of many factors which could be

(1) Size and brightness of the object on the pavement,
(2) Amount and distribution of light flux from highway lighting,
(3) Psychology of the driver, time available to him to see the object, his response to glare and
(4) Reflecting characteristics of pavement surface. The objective discussion of these parameters is not required at this level. On the other hand, design principle that could govern highway lighting could be listed as

(1) Lamps,
(2) Distribution of light,
(3) Spacing of lighting units,
(4) Height and overhang,
(5) Lateral placement and
(6) Lighting layout.

Lamps and Distribution of Light from Them : The various types of lamps that could be used are filament, fluorescent, sodium or mercury vapour lamps in the ascending order of preference. It is economical to use large lamp size, thus providing sufficient uniformity of pavement brightness. Lamps should be so provided with covers that high percentage of lamp light is utilized in illuminating the pavement and the adjacent areas. The illumination should preferably cover 3 meter to 5 meter beyond the pavement edge. Average level of illumination on road side could be 20 to 30 lux for important urban roads carrying fast traffic and about 15 lux for main roads carrying mixed and arterial traffic. The Indian standards recommends an average level of illumination of 30 lux on important roads carrying fast traffic and 15 lux on other main roads. The ratio of minimum to average illumination suggested is 0.4.

Spacing, Height and Overhang of Lighting Units : Many times the horizontal spacing of mounting units is not independent. It is a function of electrical distribution poles, road layout, property lines etc. Electrical distribution of pole points is generally the points where highway lighting is arranged. For intersections, bridges, special attention has to be paid. For height and overhang of the mounting the consideration is that of glare. The power of the lamp (i.e. wattage) increases the glare and increased height of mounting decreases the glare. Illumination on the road would increase with the power of the lamp, as such requirements are conflicting with each other. Here the overhang could play an important role.

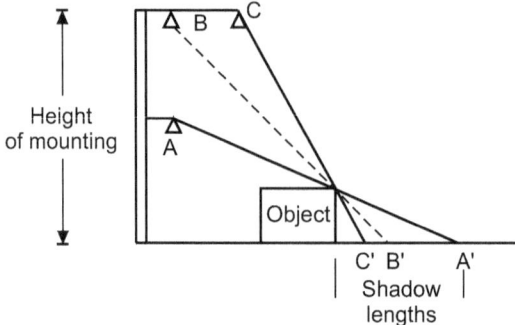

Fig. 10.13

The above figure clearly shows that increased height of mounting and long overhang would decrease shadow lengths, which is good from the point of view of prevention of accidents. It should be interesting to know that minimum vertical clearance for electrical power lines upto 650 volts above the pavement surface is 6 m as per I.R.C. Keeping this in view, usual mounting heights are from 6 metres to 10 metres and the length of overhang is generally the width of foot path on minimum basis. Lateral placement of lighting poles as recommended by I.R.C. is given below.

Table 10.3

Road Specification	Clearance
1. For roads with raised kerbs (as in urban roads).	1. Minimum 0.3 metre and desirable 0.6 m from the edge of raised kerb.
2. Roads without raised kerbs as for rural roads.	2. Minimum 1.5 m from the edge of carriageway subject to minimum of 5.0 m from the centre line of carriageway.

The clearance mentioned in the table above would also apply to poles carrying electric power and telecommunication lines too. In addition to the above specifications, as a general precaution, poles should not be installed, close to the pavement edge, so that traffic is not obstructed.

Lighting Layouts : Three types of lighting layouts are recognised (1) Single, (2) Staggered, (3) Central. These are shown in the adjoining figure and are self-explanatory. On curves the spacing between light poles is closer and the lights are on the outer side of the curves for better visibility. At vertical summit curves, summit lights have closer intervals. At road intersections, naturally you require more illumination for avoiding conflict of vehicles. For urban area intersection, the illumination could equal to the sum of illumination values for two roads, forming the intersection on a minimum scale. As a rule, lighting unit must be posted near the pedestrian crossing, channeling islands and signs.

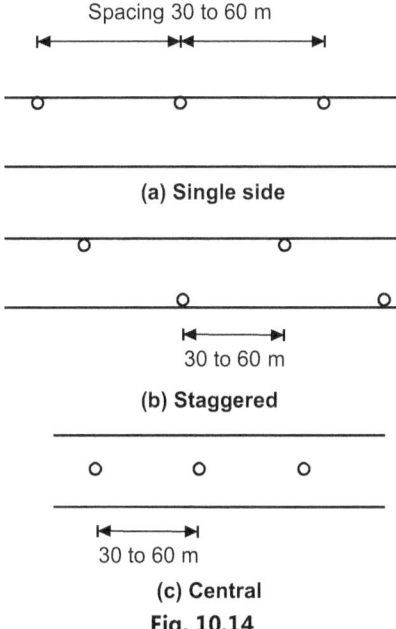

Fig. 10.14

Design of Highway Lighting System

For approximate design of highway lighting system, you require utilization coefficient chart for determination of average intensity over the pavement surface, when lamp, paved area characteristics and spacing is known. A typical such graph is shown in the adjoining figure which would be used for Indian condition. For computation of spacings, we have,

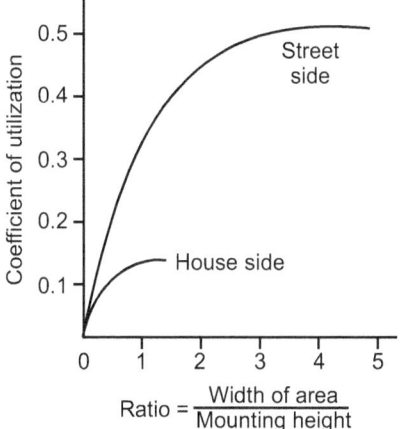

Fig. 10.15 : Coefficient of utilization

$$\text{Spacings} = \frac{\text{Lamp lumen} \times \text{Coeff. of utilization} \times \text{Maintenance factor}}{\text{Average lux} \times \text{Width of road}}$$

Maintenance factor is based on the experience..

10.8 TRAFFIC SIMULATION MODELLING

A simulation is the imitation of the operation of real-world process or system over time.
- Generation of artificial history and observation of that observation history
- A *model* construct a conceptual framework that describes a system
- The behavior of a system that evolves over time is studied by developing a simulation model.
- The model takes a set of expressed assumptions:
  Mathematical, logical
  Symbolic relationship between the *entities*

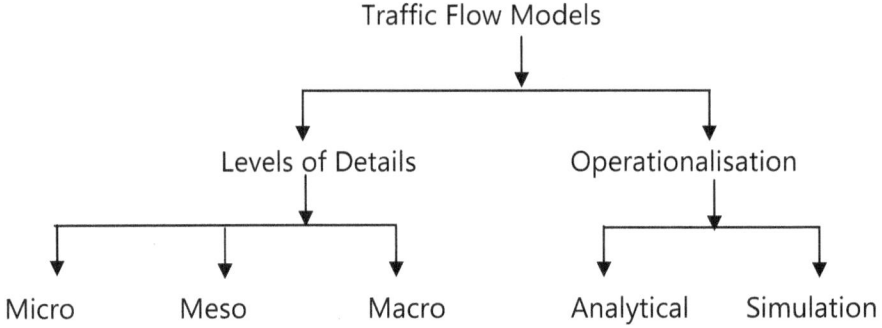

Fig. 10.16

Main Factors of Traffic Simulation
1. Advanced research in traffic theory
2. Advancement in computer hardware technology
3. Advancement in computer software technology
4. Development in information, communication infrastructure
5. Increased importance of traffic and transportation in the society

Advantages of Traffic Simulation
1. Simulation is cheaper than many forms of field experimentation and analytical modelling, in terms of time, resources and cost.
2. Simulation is a powerful tool for comparing the consequences' of a number of alternative strategies and improvement plans.
3. The task of developing the logic of various events and their occurrences involves the collection of pertinent data. The engineer gains an insight into the traffic characteristics and the way traffic interaction takes place during the process of collection of data and modelling. This may ultimately lead to a better formation of an analytical model.
4. In real life situations, it is extremely difficult to obtain conditions in the field which are needed for building a better analytical formulation.
5. Simulation techniques can be employed to check uncertain analytical solutions.

6. Simulation techniques provide opportunity for controlled experimentation, altering one variable at a time or specific variables simultaneously, and the final effect can be observed. Traffic systems in particular, are highly complex systems, with many variables, interactions and sub-systems.
7. In the case of many analytical models certain assumptions have to be made to simplify the task. Often these assumptions are of a doubtful nature. Simulation models can overcome such deficiencies.
8. Simulation models are "transparent," in the sense that anyone who wishes to know how they work can see through the model.

Limitations of Traffic Simulations

Simulations are resource limited
- Resolution : Level of detail
- Fidelity: Degree of realism
- System size: The network size to be covered
- Simulation speed: Speed of simulation compared to real time
- Resources: Computational resources, programming time

Steps in Simulation

Certain sequential operations are involved in any Example wherein Simulation techniques are adopted.

These are :
1. Definition of the Example.
2. Field studies to determine inputs needed for model formula.
3. Development of Logic.
4. Development of Computer Simulation Programme
5. Calibration of Model
6. Validation of Model

SOLVED EXAMPLES

Example 10.1 : Street lighting system is required to be designed when street width is 15 m and the mounting height is 7.5 m and the lamp size is 7000 lumen. Calculate the spacing between lighting units to produce average lux of 6.0.

Solution : $\dfrac{\text{Pavement width}}{\text{Mounting height}} = \dfrac{15}{7.5} = 2$

From figure, coefficient of utilisation is 0.44.

Maintenance factor relates to the maintenance of system. Let us assume it to be 0.8.

$\text{Spacing} = \dfrac{\text{Lamp lumen} \times \text{Coeff. of utilization} \times \text{Maintenance factor}}{\text{Average lux} \times \text{Width of road}} = \dfrac{7000 \times 0.44 \times 0.8}{6.0 \times 15}$

= 27.7 meters say 27 meters

Example 10.2 : We observed 15 minute traffic counts on roads 1 and 2, during peak hours to be 180 and 150 vehicles per lane approaching the intersection. Based on approach speeds on roads 1 and 2, the amber time requirement is 3 and 2 seconds respectively. If the time headway is 2.5 seconds, what is total cycle length ?

Solution : Let

C = Assumed trial cycle time = 50 seconds

t = Duration of traffic count = 15 minutes

n_1 = No. of cycles = $\dfrac{t \times 60}{C} = \dfrac{15 \times 60}{50} = 18$

G_1 = Green time for road 1 = $\dfrac{n_1 \times \text{Time headway}}{\text{No. of cycles in 't' minutes}}$

$= \dfrac{2.5 \times 180}{18} = 25$ seconds

G_2 = Green time for road 2 = $\dfrac{150 \times 2.5}{18} = 20.8$ seconds

Amber times A_1 and A_2 are 3 and 2 seconds.

Therefore, cycle length = 25 + 20.8 + 3 + 2 = 50.8

This is quite close to the assumed value of 50 seconds. Therefore adopt 50 seconds. Adopt $G_1 = 25$, $G_2 = 20$, $A_1 = 3$ and $A_2 = 2$ seconds respectively. Phase diagram is shown below.

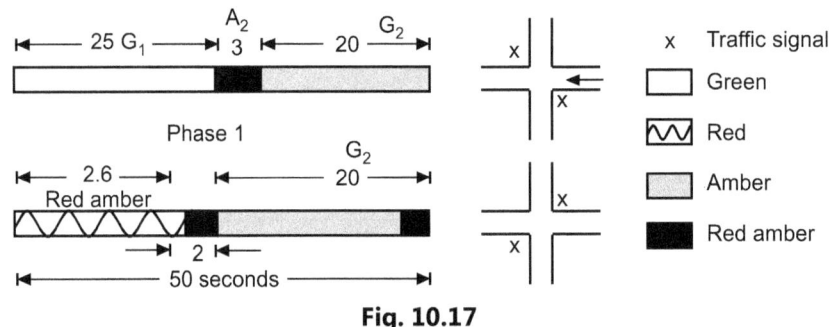

Fig. 10.17

Example 10.3 : Road A 18 m wide and road B 12 m wide cross each other at right angles. The heaviest volume per hour for each lane of A and B are 300 and 250 respectively. Design pedestrian signal and timings of traffic if approach speeds are 60 and 40 km/hr.

Solution :

The attack starts with assumption of amber time. Road A has fast approach speed. Road B has medium approach speed. Let us assume amber 4 and 3 seconds for these roads.

Pedestrian time for road A = $\dfrac{\text{Road width}}{\text{Walking speed}} = \dfrac{18}{1.2} = 15$ seconds

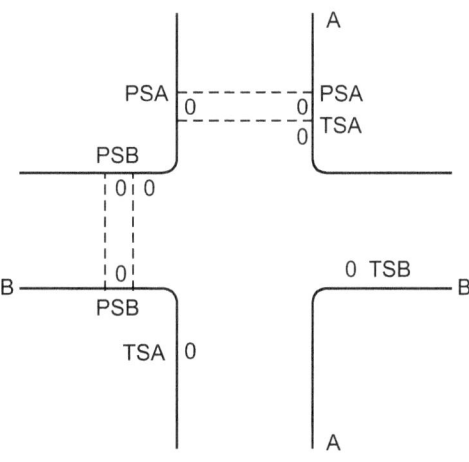

Fig. 10.18

For road B, the pedestrian time = $\frac{12}{1.2}$ = 10 seconds.

Walk period (min) = 7 seconds

Pedestrian time for road A = 15 + 7 = 22 seconds

= Minimum red time for A

Pedestrian time for road B = 10 + 7 = 17 seconds

= Minimum red time for B

Minimum green time for road A = Red time for B − amber time (B)

= (10 + 7) − 4 = 13 seconds

Minimum green time for road B = (15 + 7) − 3 = 19 seconds

Assume green time for road B = 19 seconds to be alright. Now

$$\frac{\text{Green time for road A}}{\text{Green time for road B}} = \frac{\text{Heaviest vol./hr/lane of A}}{\text{Heaviest vol./hr./lane of B}}$$

$\frac{GA}{GB} = \frac{300}{250} = 1.2$ ∴ GA = 1.2 GB = 1.2 × 19

= 22.8 seconds

Total cycle length = GA + Amber times for A and B + GB

= 22.8 + 4 + 3 + 19 = 48.8 seconds

Next 5 seconds to be adopted. Adopt 50 seconds.

Additional period 50 − 48.8 = 1.2 second is distributed to green timings in proportion to approach traffic volume.

Ratio of traffic volume = $\frac{300}{250}$ = 1.2. Let increments in GA and GB be GA' and GB'.

$$\frac{GA'}{GB'} = \frac{1.2}{1} \text{ and } GA' + GB' = 1.2$$

$$1.2 \, GB' + GB' = 1.2$$

∴ $\quad GB' = \frac{1.2}{2.2} = 0.54$ second and

$\quad GA' = 1.2 - 0.54 = 0.68$ seconds

∴ Actual GA = 22.8 + 0.68 = 23.48

GB = 19 + 0.54 = 19.54 seconds

Red amber time RA = GB + AB = 19.54 + 3 = 22.54 seconds

Red amber time RB = GA + AB = 23.48 + 4 = 27.48 seconds

Pedestrian signals

PSA (Don't walk period) = Red amber time for B = 27.48 seconds

PSB (Don't walk period) = Red amber time for A = 22.54 seconds

Pedestrian clearance interval have been calculated to be 15 and 10 seconds respectively

For PSA walk time (WA) = Cycle length − (PSA + Pedestrian clearance time for A)

= 50 − (27.48 + 15) = 7.52 seconds

For PSB walk time = 50 − (22.54 + 10) = 17.46 seconds

Phase diagram can suitably be drawn.

Example 10.4 : Average normal flow on roads A and B are 400 and 300 pcu per hour. Saturation flow values on these roads are 1250 and 1000 pcu/hour. The all-red time required for pedestrian crossing is 12 seconds. Using Webster method, design traffic signal on the basis of two phase traffic signal.

Solution :

$$y_a = \frac{\text{Normal flow on road A}}{\text{Saturation flow on road A}} = \frac{400}{1250} = 0.32$$

$$y_b = \frac{\text{Normal flow on road B}}{\text{Saturation flow on road B}} = \frac{300}{1000} = 0.30$$

$$y = y_a + y_b = 0.32 + 0.30 = 0.62$$

$$L = 2n + R = 2 \times 2 + 12 = 16 \text{ seconds}$$

$$C_o = \frac{1.5 \, L + 5}{1 - y} = \frac{1.5 \times 16 + 5}{1 - (0.32 + 0.30)}$$

$$= \frac{29}{0.38} = 76.31 \text{ seconds}$$

$$GA = \frac{y_a}{y}(C_o - L)$$

$$= \frac{0.32}{0.62}(76.31 - 16) = 31.12 \text{ seconds}$$

$$GB = \frac{y_b}{y}(C_o - L)$$

$$= \frac{0.30}{0.62}(76.31 - 16) = 29.18 \text{ seconds}$$

All-red time for pedestrian crossing = 12 seconds

Total cycle time = GA + GB + All-red time + Amber time

= 31.12 + 29.18 + 12 + 2 ∞ (2) = 76.3 seconds

Two roads, these 2 × Amber time of 2 seconds.

Example 10.5 : Road 1 and road 2 are crossing each other at right angles. Road 1 has four lanes and two approaches, has a total width of 12 meters and road 2 having two lanes has total width of 6.6 m. The volume of traffic approaching the intersection during design hour are 900 and 700 pcu/hour on the two approaches of road 1 and 275 and 180 pcu/hour on the two approaches of road 2. Design signal timings as per IRC guidelines.

Solution :

Design traffic on road 1 = higher of the two approach volume

$$= \frac{900}{2} = 450 \text{ pcu/hour}$$

Design traffic on road 2 $= \frac{275}{2} = 137$ pcu/hour say.

(A) Pedestrian green time for road 1 $= \frac{12.0}{1.2} + 7 = 17$ seconds

Pedestrian green time for road 2 $= \frac{6.6}{1.2} + 7 = 12.5$ seconds

Therefore green time for vehicles on road 2 = 17 seconds

Green time for road 1 $= 17 \times \frac{450}{275} = 27.81$ seconds

(B) Let us add 2.0 seconds each towards clearance amber and 2 seconds intergreen period for each phase, therefore total cycle time required = (2 + 17 + 2) + (2 + 27.81 + 2) = 52.81.

Since the signal cycle time should be conveniently set in multiples of five seconds, so let us choose the next 5 second phase as such, let the cycle time be 55 seconds. The extra (55 − 52.81 = 2.19 seconds) per cycle may be diverted to the green times of roads 1 and 2. As such, let us make G_1 = 27.81 + 1.2 to be 28 seconds and

$$G_2 = 17 + 1 = 18 \text{ seconds.}$$

(C) Vehicle arrivals per lane cycle on road 1 = $\dfrac{450}{55}$ = 8.2 p.c.u.

Minimum green time for clearing vehicles on road 1

$$= 6 + (8.2 − 1.0)\,2 = 20.4 \text{ seconds}$$

Vehicle arrivals per cycle on road 2 = $\dfrac{275}{55}$ = 5 pcu

Minimum green time for clearing vehicles on road 2

$$= 6 + (5 − 2)\,2 = 14 \text{ seconds}$$

Green time provided is more than these values as such above design values are O.K.

(D) Lost time per cycle = (amber time + intergreen time

+ time for initial delay of first vehicle) for two phases

$$= (2 + 2 + 4) \times 2 = 16 \text{ seconds} = L$$

Saturation flow for road 1 = 525 × 6 = 3150 pcu/hr.
Saturation flow for road 2 = 1850 pcu/hr. approximately

$$y_1 = \dfrac{900}{3150} = 0.286 \text{ and } y_2 = \dfrac{275}{1850} = 0.148$$

$$y = y_1 + y_2 = 0.286 + 0.148 = 0.434$$

$$\text{Optimum cycle time} = \dfrac{1.5\,L + 5}{1 − y} = \dfrac{1.5 \times 16 + 5}{1 − 0.434}$$

$$= 51.2 \text{ seconds}$$

Therefore the cycle time of 55 seconds designed earlier is O.K. Cycle time may be shown in the table below.

Table 10.4

Road	Green	Amber	Red	Cycle
1	28	2	23 + 2	55
2	18	2	33 + 2	55

Example 10.6 : Results of transportation survey conducted in a town are given below.

Table 10.5

Traffic zone No.	Population in thousands	Total trips in hundreds
1	25	12
2	28	10
3	30	18
4	35	16
5	20	10
6	30	16
7	20	9
8	25	10

If the population of a particular zone increases to say 50,000, trip generation from that zone is required to be predicted.

Solution : We first prepare the table.

Table 10.6

Zone	x	y	xy	x^2	y^2
1	25	12	300	625	144
2	28	10	280	784	100
3	30	18	540	900	324
4	35	16	560	1225	256
5	20	10	200	400	100
6	30	16	480	900	256
7	20	9	180	400	81
8	25	10	250	625	100
n = 8	$\Sigma x = 213$	$\Sigma y = 101$	$\Sigma xy = 2790$	$\Sigma x^2 = 5859$	$\Sigma y^2 = 1361$

$$b_1 = \frac{n\Sigma xy - \Sigma x \Sigma y}{n\Sigma x^2 - (\Sigma x)^2} = \frac{8 \times 2790 - 101 \times 213}{8 \times 5859 - (213)^2}$$

$$= \frac{807}{0.503} = 0.536$$

$$b_0 = y - b_1 x_1 = \frac{\Sigma y - b \Sigma x_1}{n}$$

$$= \frac{101 - 0.536 \times 213}{8} = \frac{101 - 114.16}{8} = -1.64$$

Trip model is $\quad y = -1.64 + 0.536 x_1 = 0.536 x_1 - 1.64$

and $\quad r = b_1 \left[\dfrac{n\sum x^2 - (\sum x)^2}{n\sum y^2 - (\sum y)^2} \right]^{1/2} = \left[\dfrac{8 \times 5859 - 213 \times 213}{8 \times 1361 - 101 \times 101} \right]^{1/2} = 1.47$

model is $y = 0.536 x_1 - 1.64$

Future population of the zone 50,000

$y = 0.536 \infty 50 - 1.64 = 25.16$ in hundreds

So total trips generated would be 2516.

REVIEW QUESTIONS

1. Explain the significance of following pavement markings zebra crossing, bus-stop-point, hazard markers, and stop lines.
2. What is the use of estimation of trips? How it is done?
3. How many types of road junctions are there? Describe with sketches.
4. Why are the main advantages of road signals?
5. Why are traffic island provided? What are the different kinds of traffic inland, which are generally provided?
6. How briefly signalized intersection can be designed?
7. What are different traffic signal systems? Explain simple progressive system.
8. What the I.R.C. recommendation that tells you the necessity of traffic signals?
9. What are the principles of highway lighting?

CHAPTER 11
ROADSIDE DEVELOPMENTS

11.1 INTRODUCTION

Arboriculture science can contribute knowledge about trees and roadside environments in ways that improve forest health and human health alike. There needs to be better collaboration between urban foresters and the transportation officials to find better solutions for tree planting along city streets. The transportation industry is generally less aware of recent advances in roadside vegetation management, and engineers haven't yet acknowledged that there are professional and scientific groups.

11.2 LAND SCAPING AND ROAD SIDE ARBORICULTURE

The highways should be so planned that they should appear part and parcel of the surroundings. Some of the principles of highway landscaping may be

- The alignment of the road should follow the natural terrain and harmoniously blend with it and it should preserve aesthetically valuable features, such as rock outcrops, waterfalls, architectural monuments etc. For example, for alignment between Satana and Khajuraho, the road while passing through the wooded area near Khajuraho passes near the Rajagarh Palace built by Chandelas. Road alignment in this part of the highway, is such that this palace is directly seen by the commuters plying on the road kindling in him the desire to see this off beat tourist attraction.
- Ugly scars due to cutting existing slope should be made good by vegetation, flatter slopes of embankments should be closely blended with the natural ground and vegetation should be grown on it to prevent erosion.
- All rotary islands and medians should be provided with flowering shrubs and borrow areas should be so treated that they do not leave ugly spot.
- The Architecture of bridges and culverts should be given careful thought.

11.3 ROAD SIDE ARBORICULTURE

The road side arboriculture refers to the road side trees and nursaries that are developed. It has the following purposes.
- The trees afford shade, provide effective screen for unsightly views as slums, junks yard, storage depots etc.
- They yield fruits, wood, sometimes oil such as eucalyptus oil, making it a profitable proposition.

- Trees act as deterrent to auto-exhaust and pollution due to it and to some extent prevent rain and wind erosion. Walking through boulevards is an experience. Many artists have drawn an inspiration from the trees that line the roads. For many writers tree - line pathways have symbolized tranquility that is conducive to creative thinking. It should be noted that not only the highway department but also the railways are thinking of permanent way side plantations. In fact the Railway Board conducted a special study in December 1981 with the objective of evolving a plan of action of tree plantation along the track and the target has been set for 10 crores of trees in the next fifteen years. Time is not far off when not only our highways but even the rail-tracks will be tree lined.

11.4 THE PRINCIPLES TO BE FOLLOWED IN ARBORICULTURE

The principles that should be followed in road side development could now be discussed.

- In urban areas, road side plantation has aesthetic value. On wide urban roads, besides road plantation on road sides, medians or separator should be provided with shrubs, which reduce the head light glare during night driving. A typical arrangement is shown in Fig. 11.1. Wide crowned trees are not preferred. These obstruct the day light and are unsafe for night driving, therefore arrangement such as shown in Fig. 11.2 is not preferable but arrangement shown in Fig. 11.3 is preferable, in which carriageway is clear to the sky. Generally, trees are 12 metres away from the centre of the road. The general plan may be as shown in Fig. 11.1.

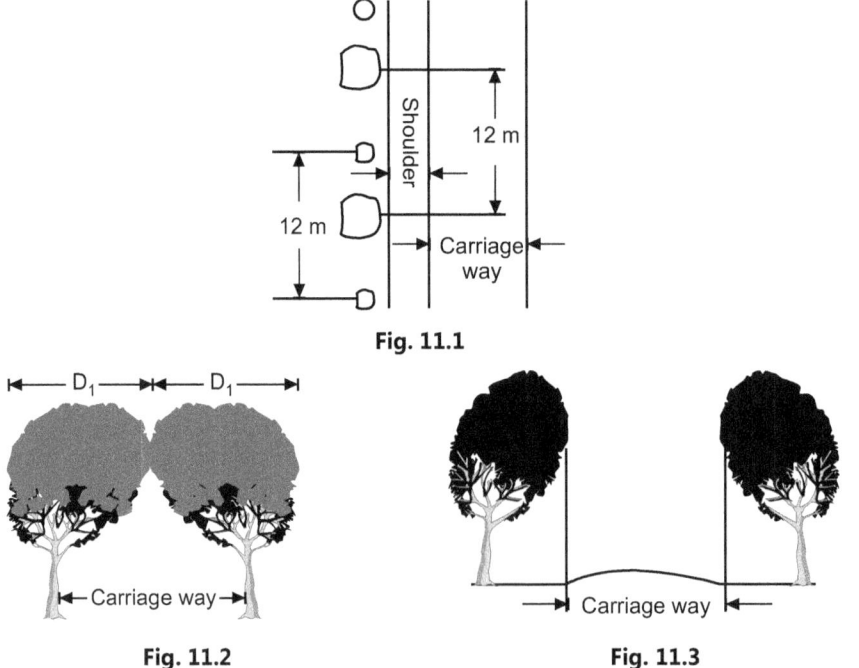

Fig. 11.1

Fig. 11.2

Fig. 11.3

- Plantation of the trees should be done on the advice of horticulturist. The species should be so selected that these are suitable for the existing soil type, and climate. The species should be fast developing, should be strong to resist heavy wind, if the road is passing through desert. In sub zero climate, proper trees should be chosen. The trees planted should be protected by either Iron guard, brick work or used bitumen drum, or a trench as shown in Fig. 11.4. The use of trench is of course recommended in rural areas.

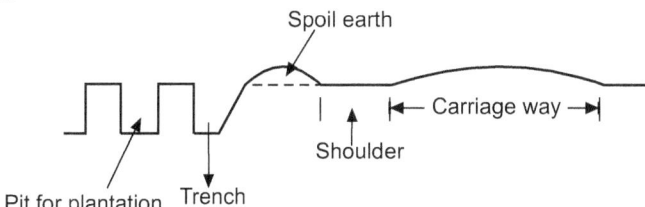

Fig. 11.4

- Nursary should be developed on the roadside so that there is a regular supply of plants. A typical layout of nursary is shown in Fig. 11.5. A nursary should be established 2 to 3 years in advance for transplantation. It is generally felt that new avenues would require about 180 and old avenues would require about 100 plants per km of road length for which nursary should be capable of supplying 270 plants for new avenues and 150 for old avenues, since seedling may die during the early growth.

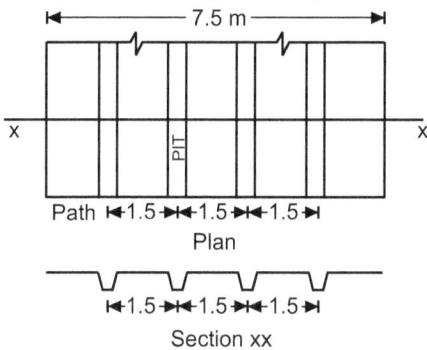

Fig. 11.5

- During the life time of the trees, these must be properly cared for with such operations such as deforking, lopping and felting. It must be stressed that growing healthy trees is a job of horticulturist and therefore he must be consulted at all stages. The civil engineer can make finances and skilled labour available to him and the job must be done under his supervision.
- If the road is located on embankment, providing turf on the side slopes, cuts and side drains give pleasing appearance. However, turf shoulders are generally not preferred as the grass grown on these shoulders can not resist traffic. The rain water that passes on

road has in general more velocity due to smooth riding surface and it can cause erosion, hence in addition to road side plantation, woody plants or shrubs less than a metre high grown at sides can contain soil erosion effectively.

- As an example, how the trees can be provided to roadside, we give here the example of Amravati Bypass. The alignment of Amravati National Highway No. 6 Bye Pass of 17.8 km outside the Amravati Town is approved by ministry of transport. An amount of Rs. 25 lakhs was sanctioned in 1987 and the work was got done through specilised agency on regular contract of three years with the object of desired growth and survival of plants. The selection of tree species was declared on the basis of soil, rainfall, humidity, subsoil water, foliage, root depth fruition etc. with the help of experts. The entire proposed road was fenced on both sides. The tender documents for this work were such that the contractor has to grow specified trees upto specified height and growth with 90 % survival. The responsibility of giving proper watering agrochemicals, nutrients, pesticides etc. rested completely on the contractor.

Mr. Danjay Dhavad and Mr. A. K. Deo were the officers in charge and such a type of arboriculture was first taken-up on such a large scale in Maharashtra State devising somewhat new tender documents.

11.5 SERVICE ROADS

The concept of service roads or frontage roads in limiting the access on main highway, while simultaneously meeting the demand of abutting land owners for ingress and egress, has a lot of relevance. Such service roads prevent congestion on the main way, reduce number of intersections, lessen the number of accidents and it is recommended that service roads should be insisted upon on highways where ribbon development has taken place, so also along new bypasses where it is feared in near future.

11.5.1 Removal of Road Side Encroachment and Control of Roadside Developments

The ribbon development always starts as an insignificant temporary structure along the highways and slowly develops into unsightly ribbon. Laws are existing in our country to evict these and what is required is a long term political will, non-corrupt organisation to nip such evil in the bud. Ribbon development and road side advertisements are twin evil that thrives on each other. In our country the roadside advertisement is generally controlled by municipal law, and they should be strictly enforced.

11.5.2 The state of Laws to Control Ribbon Development

There have been some state laws such as the Bombay Highways act 1955, The Punjab Scheduled Road and controlled areas Restriction unregulated development Act 1963, The

United Provinces Road side Land Control Act 1945, The Mysore Highway Act 1964. The Mysore Public premises land (eviction rent recovery act 1972) which is in force in their respective territories. The deficiency of some of these acts is, they do not relate to National Highways. What is required is the unified approach throughout the nation, for which a model Highway Bill has been proposed by IRC, but it is not as yet accepted as legislation.

11.6 ROAD TRAFFIC NOISE

The road traffic noise can be controlled by variety of measures. Trucks, buses, and motor cycles are a major source of noise pollution. It is possible to control the noise level pollution by making the vehicles less noisy through legislation, but replacement of existing lorries and buses by new generation of quiet vehicles will take long time. Another misconceived notion in India for motorcycle riders is frequent use of horns and making noise by unnecessary acceleration, which must be curbed.

If we avoid existing residential area by diverting commercial through traffic away from the city streets, noticeable improvements in noise level can be obtained. Traffic management measures such as reducing the number of stopping, making one way streets; ban on Lorries can also reduce noise levels

11.6.1 Good Engineering Designs

Good engineering designs such as proper alignment, lesser grades, fewer stops at intersections, smoother road surface textures, and providing physical noise screens can reduce traffic noise considerably. Barriers are especially effective for elevated roads near low rise houses and if they are a part of the original design, they can be made visually acceptable. The usual tolerance level in residential area is around 70 dB (A). It has been found that an 11 feet concrete wall can provide good shield for noise. The eleven feet wall may not provide good appearance but a combination of five feet earth mond, topped by 6 feet wall can be pleasing and functional. The earth monds are better as they can both block and absorbs energy. Porous cinder block or expanded shale block, with the side away from the highway coated with stucco is advantageous. It has been proved beyond doubt that trees and plants do not serve any useful purpose they are porous to air flow vibrate easily and lack density and hence do not provide any sound benefit. There merit is to improve appearance and provide psychological shielding. The problem of noise on Indian roads is not as yet well taken care of.

11.7 STREET LIGHTING

- Improved street lighting can contribute towards increasing safety. It can prevent road traffic crashes, injuries and fatalities. Street lighting not only reduces the risk of traffic accidents, but also their severity.

- Lighting needs of pedestrians are different from those of vehicular traffic and therefore need to be designed and integrated within the overall lighting strategy for the street. This would aid the safety of pedestrians on pavements after dark.

- The street lights should be placed in the MUZ, clear of pedestrian walkways. It can be coordinated with other street elements such as trees, hoardings etc., so that they do not obstruct illumination. Up lighting is not recommended to prevent spillage of light and wastage of energy.

- The height of light poles on all streets other than at major arterial intersections can be restricted to not more than 12m to avoid undesirable illumination of private properties. For pedestrian scale lighting, 3-5m high light poles are recommended to illuminate the footpath adequately and avoid tree shadows. Wherever possible, street light and pedestrian lights can be combined.

- Spacing should be based on the intensity of light, height of the fixture and clearances from tree canopies. White lighting at 25-40 lux for footpaths is recommended. It is recommended that colour contrast be maintained from the road surface.

- Lighting engineers should be consulted for design calculations including pole heights, type of luminaries, etc. for achieving appropriate lighting levels in all parts of the street. (Source- IRC 103- 2012 Guidelines for Pedestrian Facilities and UTTIPEC)

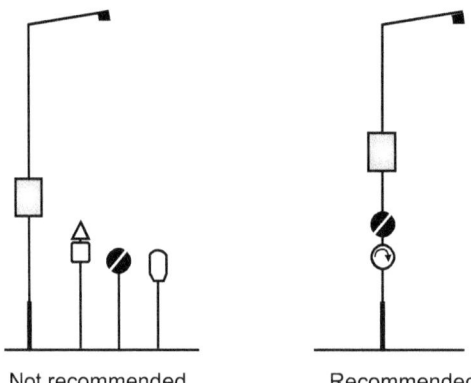

Not recommended   Recommended

Fig. 11.6

11.7.1 Factors Affecting Street Lighting

For efficient and proper street lighting the following factors should be kept in mind :

- The electric posts poles should be located at proper places.
- The light from the sources should illuminate the entire road surface uniformly.
- The posts should be spaced uniformly.

- The light should not produce glare.
- The height of lamps should be adjusted in such a way that it should produce such a shadow which may not darken the entire line.

11.7.2 Lighting has an Important Role to Play

- Reducing risks of night time accidents;
- Assisting in the protection of property;
- Discouraging crime and vandalism;
- Making residents feel secure; and
- Enhancing the appearance of the area after dark.

11.7.3 Factors Affecting Night Visibility

- Amount and distribution of light.
- Size of object.
- Brightness of object.
- Brightness of background.
- Reflection characteristics of pavement.
- Glare on eye.
- Time available to see an object.

11.7.4 Design Factors for Highway Lighting

- Contrast.
- Glare.
- Lamps
- Luminaire distribution of light.
- Lateral placement of lighting poles.
- Brightness of background.
- Height and overhang of mounting.
- Spacing of lighting units.
- Lighting layouts

1. Contrast is the difference in luminance and/or color that makes an object (or its representation in an image or display) distinguishable

Discrimination of differences of brightness between an object and its background.

Silhoutte Brightness of object is less than that of background.

Reverse Silhoutte Brightness of an object is more than that of the immediate background, discrement is by reverse silhoutte.

2. **Glare :** Disturbing influence when viewing a difficult visual task under low brightness is known as glare. Glare is the main source of accidents and in the greatest cause of wastage of illumination contract lighting arrangement reduces glare.

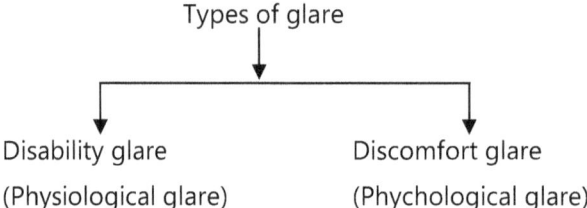

3. **Lamps :** Source, power and type of light greatly effect the visibility on the road. lighting on modern highways can be as;

- Filament lamp
- Sodium vapour lamp
- Fluorescent lamps.
- Mercury vapour lamp.

Filament lamps are commonly used for ordinary roads for street lighting as they are cheap and easily available. Sodium vapour lamps produce distinctive yellow light are most suitable for hazardous localities. Mercury vapour lamps are being increasingly used on account of their long life and light efficiently. Fluorescent lamps are particularly used for overhead lighting.

4. **Luminaire Distribution of Light**

An acceptable level of street lighting is c5lux, although DfT (Inclusive Mobility, 2005) recommend that at locations where people gather, for example bus stops, 10lux is appropriate. In providing inclusive streetscapes, continuity of lighting levels is important, with sudden changes in lighting level being particularly problematic for partially sighted people. The shading effect of street trees should also be considered in determining their species, location and management.

Purposes

- Cover total width of pavement including kerb.
- Lighting on traffic signs
- Lighting beyond the pavement edge (3 to 5 mt)
- Uniform distribution of light

5. **Lateral Placement of Lighting Poles**

Not closed to pavement edge, decrease capacity.

IRC Recommendations

Table 11.1

Sr. No.	Location	Distance Form the Edge of Pavement
(a)	For road with raised kerbs (as in urban road)	Min. 0.3 mt desirable 0.6 mt
(b)	For road with raised kerbs (as in rural road)	Min 5 mt from edge
		Min 5 mt from center line

6. Height and Overhang of Mounting

Distribution of light, shadow, and glare depends on mounting height.(Ht. 6 to 10 m)

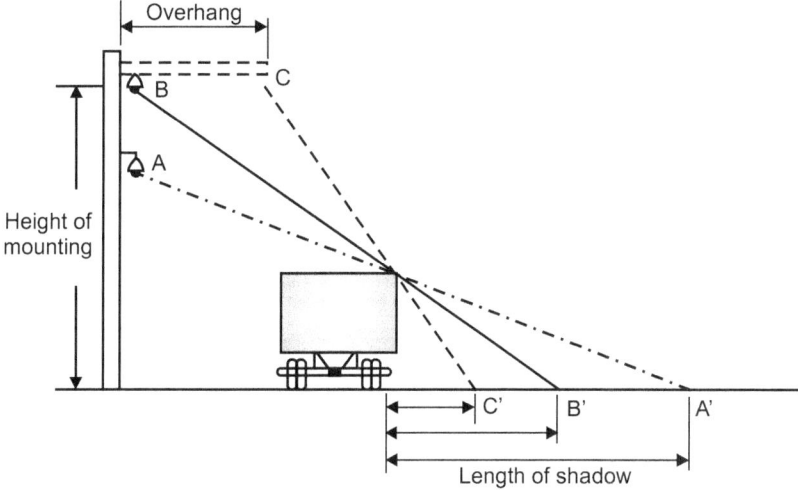

Fig. 11.7

7. Spacing of Lighting Units :

On straight road spacing = 3 to 5 times the mounting height. The spacing of the light poles is reduced on the curves, bridges, level crossings etc. for better light requirements.

8. Lighting Layouts : (30 to 60 mt)

- Single side
- Both side-staggered
- Both side- opposite.
- Central lighting

The side mounted lamp posts can be arranged opposite to each other on both sides of the road or arranged staggered. The staggered arrangement is more efficient.

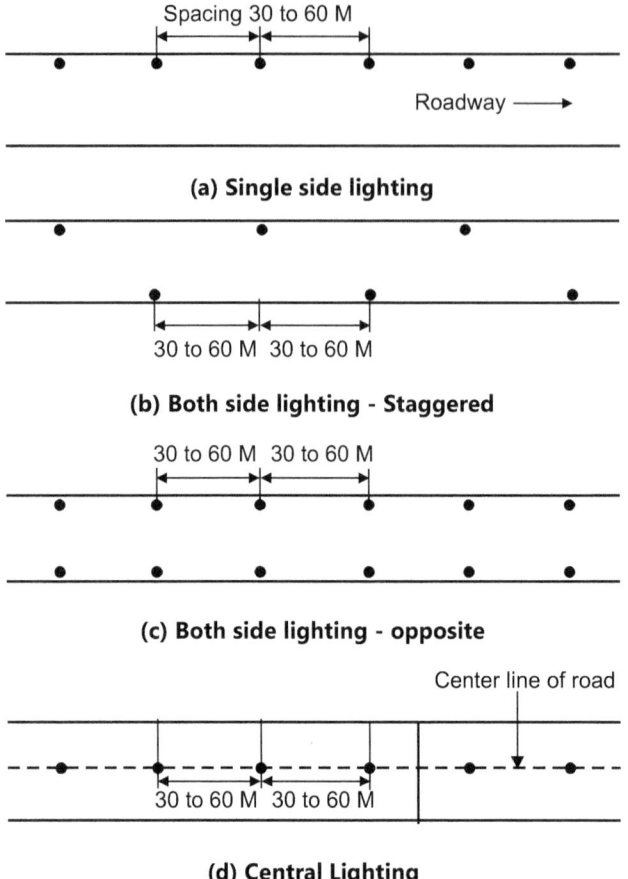

Fig. 11.8

Location Effect

- On horizontal curve
- At intersection

At all the road junctions and roundabouts, it is most importance for safety to ensure that sources of light are so placed that a driver cannot only see from some distance away that he is approaching a junction but he can also see the route, he has to follow. At the small roundabouts upto 18 m diameter, a si8ngale light centrally mounted at a height of 9 to 10.6 m above the carriageway will be suitable. For bigger roundabouts, the light should be provided along its circumference.

At the mouth of crossing, a bright patch must be provided. On the intersection of two roads, four light lamps at more 12 m along each road should be provided.

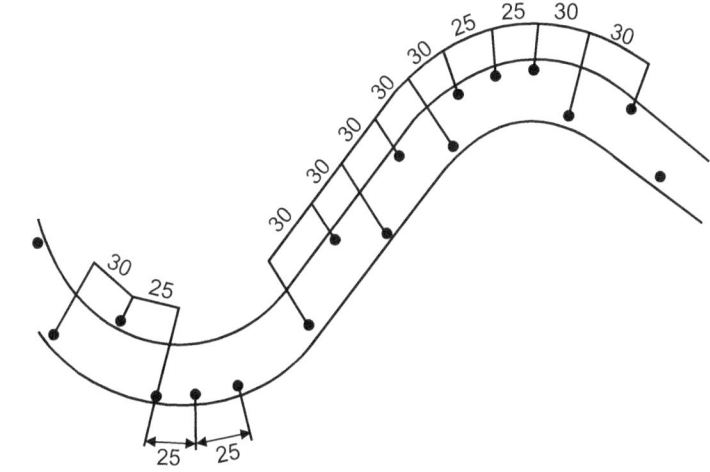

Fig. 11.9 : Lighting layout on horizontal curves

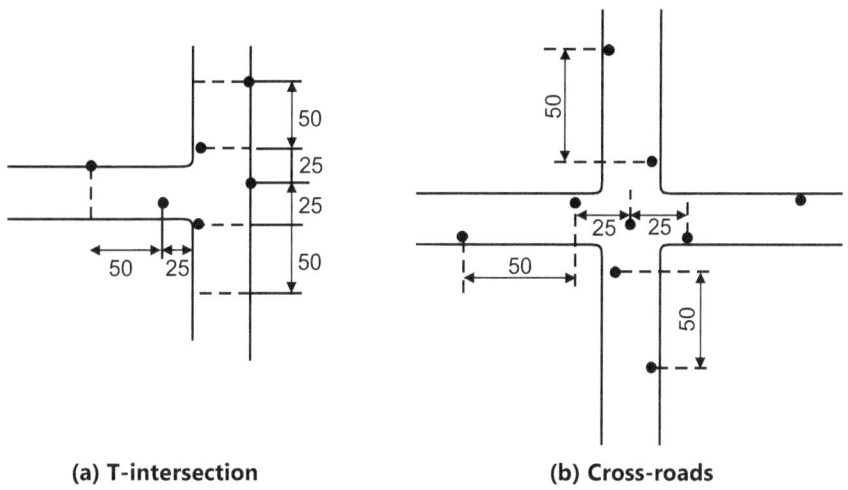

(a) T-intersection (b) Cross-roads

Fig. 11.10

11.7.5 Benefits of Highway lighting

- Better police control
- Increase business
- Beautification
- Reduction in accident
- Pleasant atmosphere.
- Safety

REVIEW QUESTIONS

1. What is Arboriculture? What role does it play in highway environment? Discuss any specific case.
2. What principles should be kept in view, while designing landscaping and road side arboriculture?
3. What are the benefits derived from road side arboriculture?
4. What principles should be kept in view, while designing street lighting?
5. What are the benefits derived from road side lighting?
6. Write note on
   (a) Roadside Developments
   (b) Arboriculture
   (c) Street lighting

CHAPTER 12
ADVANCED URBAN TRANSPORT TECHNOLOGY

12.1 What Are Rapid Transit Systems

There is no single and unambiguous definition of a Rapid Transit System, but the term often refers to systems that are called Metro, Subway or Underground. Whereas the words Subway and Underground indicate that the system is sub-surface, the terms Metro and Rapid Transit typically also include systems that are elevated or at surface level. A popular definition of metro is urban, electric passenger transportation system with high capacity and high frequency of service, which is totally independent from other traffic, road or pedestrians. The dividing line between rapid transit and other modes of public transport, such as light rail and commuter rail, is not always clear.

A common way to distinguish rapid transit systems from light rail is by their separation from other traffic. While light rail systems may share roads or have level crossings, a rapid transit system runs on a grade-separated exclusive right-of-way, with no access for pedestrians and other traffic. Rapid transit systems are primarily used for transport within a city and have higher service frequency. Furthermore, these systems do not share tracks with freight trains or inter-city rail services. The First Rapid Transit System was the London Underground, which opened in 1863. The technology quickly spread to other cities in Europe and then to the United States, where a number of elevated systems were built. Since then the largest growth has been in Asia and with driverless systems. More than 160 cities have rapid transit systems, totaling more than 8,000 km (4,900 miles) of track and 7,000 stations. Twenty-five cities have systems under construction.

12.1.1 Introduction

The urban population of the world as a whole has been expanding at the rate of nearly 3% per year, presumably faster than the existing world population growth rate. Roughly half of the global population lives in the cities (Peterson, J., 1984). Presently approx. 30% of India's population lives in urban areas. The current trends of urbanization inspired by the better quality of life are posing multiple stresses on our environment. Coupled with rapid urbanization each city consists of a no. of supporting systems. Transport or Rapid Transit Systems are one of them, which provide mobility, flexibility and accessibility to urban people.

12.1.2 Need of Mass Rapid Transit System

Transport demand in most Indian cities has increased substantially, due to increase in population as a result of both natural growth and migration from rural areas and smaller towns. Availability of motorized transport, increases in household income and increases in commercial and industrial activities have further added to transport demand. In many cases the demand has outstripped the road capacities. As the cities grow in size, the no. of circular trips on road system goes up. Individual cities cannot afford to cater only to private modes of transportation as cars and scooters or bikes. This necessitates a pragmatic policy to discourage private modes and encourage public or mass transit modes once the traffic along any travel corridor in one direction exceeds 20000 persons/hr. Thus the introduction of Mass Rapid Transit Systems is called for. MRTS are capital intensive and have a long gestation period. It has been observed that in developed countries, planning of for mass rapid transit system starts when the city population exceeds 1 million, the system is in position by the time the population reaches 2 to 3 million and once the population exceeds 4 million or so, planned extensions to the MRTS is vigorously taken up. But on the other hand, in developing countries including India, because of paucity of funds planning and implementation MRTS has been lagging behind the requirement. MRTS has been a victim of ignorance, neglectand confusion. As far as MRTS in Indian cities is concerned, dedicated city Bus Services are known to operate in 17 cities only and Rail Based Transit Systems in less than 10 cities out of all the cities with population in excess of 1 million.

12.1.3 Mass Transit System

Mass transit system refers to public shared transportation, such as trains, buses, ferries etc that can commute a larger number of passengers from origin to destination on a no-reserved basis and in lesser time. It can also be termed as Public Transport.

Rapid transit is an important form of mass transit such as subways and surface light rail systems, designed for commuting inter-city or intra-city. Mass transit may be based on fixed route system such as subway trains, metros or non-fixed route system such as buses. It is potentially more economical, eco-friendly and less time consuming. In addition it is the most competent way of reducing the ever growing traffic congestion of the developing city. Mass transit has the advantage of smaller rights of way and developing lesser amount of infrastructure required for highways and roads. The drawback of the system is the necessity to travel on a fixed rather than an individually selected schedule and to enter and disembark from the system only at certain designated locations. Mass transit can be of two types : heavy rail or light rail. Heavy rails are one of the better forms of mass transit as :
- They are fast
- They will not interfere with the other traffic as they require separate underground infrastructure.

But the initial cost of heavy rail is very high. It works best at places where a larger number of people will ride them such as in the center of big and densely populated cities.

12.1.4 Impacts - Advantages of Mass Transit

Environmental Impacts

Mass transit is believed to be more environmental friendly than other public transport facilities. Private vehicles emit about twice as much carbon monoxide and other volatile organic compounds than public vehicles. Mass transit reduces the number of cars on the road which in turn reduces the pollution caused by individual cars.

Impacts - Advantages of Mass Transit
Environmental Impacts
Mass transit is believed to be more environmental friendly than other public transport facilities. Private vehicles emit about twice as much carbon monoxide and other volatile organic compounds than public vehicles. Mass transit reduces the number of cars on the road which in turn reduces the pollution caused by individual cars.

Social Impacts of Mass Transit
All members of the society irrespective of their financial status, religion or cast are able to travel which enhances the social integrity of the country. The necessity of a driving license is also eliminated. It is a blessing for those individuals who are unable to drive.

Economic Impacts of Mass Transit
Mass transit development can both improve the usefulness and efficiency of the public transit system as well as result in increased business for commercial developments and thus serves to improve the economy of the country. Transit systems also have an indirect positive effect on other businesses. Mass transit systems offer considerable savings in labor, materials, and energy over private transit systems. Also mass transit allows a higher amount of load to be transported to far away destinations in lesser time because of its reasonable capacity than private vehicles. Because of their larger capacity offering them to carry high efficient engines they also help in saving fuels.

Negative Impacts of the Project
- Change in Land Use Pattern at he Station Areas and neighborhood.
- Impact on green Cover and Felling of Trees.
- Barricading of Sites.
- Traffic Diversions during Construction Phase.
- Soil Erosion and Health Risks at Construction Sites.
- Accidental Hazards during Construction Phase.
- Noise and Vibrations due to Construction activities.
- Impact on Water Quality due to runoff from construction sites.
- Oil Spillage during project operation.
- Station Refuse.

12.2 INTELLIGENT TRANSPORTATION SYSTEMS (ITS)

Intelligent Transportation Systems (ITS) is the application of computer, electronics, and communication technologies and management strategies in an integrated manner to provide traveler information to increase the safety and efficiency of the surface transportation systems. These systems involve vehicles, drivers, passengers, road operators, and managers all interacting with each other and the environment, and linking with the complex infrastructure systems to improve the safety and capacity of road systems.

As reported by Commission for Global Road Safety(June 2006), the global road deaths were between 750,000 to 880,000 in the year 1999 and estimated about 1.25 million deaths per year and the toll is increasing further. World health organization report (1999), showed that in the year 1990 road accidents as a cause of death or disability were the ninth most significant cause of death or disability and predicted that by 2020 this will move to sixth place. Without significant changes to the road transport systems these dreadful figures are likely to increase significantly.

Traditional driver training, infrastructure and safety improvements, may contribute to certain extent to reduce the number of accidents but not enough to combat this menace. Intelligent Transport Systems are the best solution to the problem. Safety is one of the principal driving forces behind the evolution, development, standardization, and implementation of ITS systems. ITS improves transportation safety and mobility and enhances global connectivity by means of productivity improvements achieved through the integration of advanced communications technologies into the transportation infrastructure and in vehicles. Intelligent transportation systems encompass a broad range of wireless and wire line communication based information and electronics technologies to better manage traffic and maximize the utilization of the existing transportation infrastructure. It improves driving experience, safety and capacity of road systems, reduces risks in transportation, relieves traffic congestion, improves transportation efficiency and reduces pollution.

12.2.1 ITS User Services

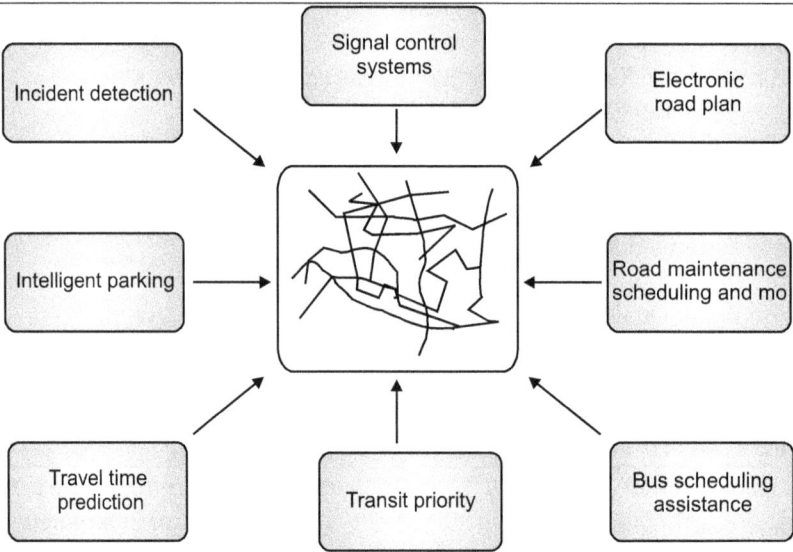

Fig. 12.1 : ITS user services

In order to deploy ITS, a framework is developed highlighting various services the ITS can offer to the users. A list of 33 user services has been provided in the National ITS Program Plan. The number of user services, keep changing over time when a new service is added. All the above services are divided in eight groups. The division of these services is based on the perspective of the organization and sharing of common technical functions. Some of the

user services offered by ITS are shown in Fig. 12:1. The eight groups are described as follows :
- Travel and traffic management
- Public transportation operations
- Electronic payment
- Commercial vehicle operations
- Advance vehicle control and safety systems
- Emergency management
- Information management
- Maintenance and construction management

12.2.2 It's Architecture

The ITS Architecture provides a common framework for planning, defining, and integrating intelligent transportation systems. It specifies how the different ITS components would interact with each other to help solving transportation problems.

It provides the transportation professionals to address their needs with wide variety of options. It identifies and describes various functions and assigns responsibilities to various stake-holders of ITS. The ITS architecture should be common and of specified standards throughout the state or region so that it can address solution to several problems while interacting with various agencies.

- **Interoperability :** The ITS architecture should be such that the information collected, function implemented or any equipment installed be interoperable by various agencies in different state and regions.
- **Capable of sharing and exchanging information :** The information by traffic operations may be useful to the emergency services.
- **Resource sharing :** regional communication towers constructed by various private agencies are required to be shared by ITS operations.

12.3 ELECTRONIC TOLL COLLECTION (ETC)

Electronic toll collection (ETC) is a technology enabling the electronic collection of toll payments. It has been used in various highways, bridges, and tunnels requiring such a process. This system is capable of determining if the car is registered or not, and then informing the authorities of toll payment violations, debits, and participating accounts. The most obvious advantage of this technology is the opportunity to eliminate congestion in tollbooths, especially during festive seasons when traffic tends to be heavier than normal. It is also a method by which to curb complaints from motorists regarding the inconveniences involved in manually making payments at the tollbooths. Other than this obvious advantage, applying ETC could also benefit the toll operators.

The benefits for the motorists include :
- Fewer or shorter queues at toll plazas by increasing toll booth service turnaround rates;
- Faster and more efficient service (no exchanging toll fees by hand);

- The ability to make payments by keeping a balance on the card itself or by loading a registered credit card; and
- The use of postpaid toll statements (no need to request for receipts).
  Other general advantages for the motorists include fuel savings and reduced mobile emissions by reducing or eliminating deceleration, waiting time, and acceleration.

Meanwhile, for the toll operators, the benefits include :
- Lowered toll collection costs;
- Better audit control by centralized user accounts; and
- Expanded capacity without building more infrastructures.

12.3.1 Toll collection by Radio Car Tag

Toll collection, transit fare payment, and parking payment are linked through a multi-modal multi-use electronic system. With an integrated payment system a traveller driving on a toll road, using parking lot would be able to use the same electronic device to pay toll, parking price and the transit fare. Fig. 12.2 shows the electronic payment facility by radio car tag.

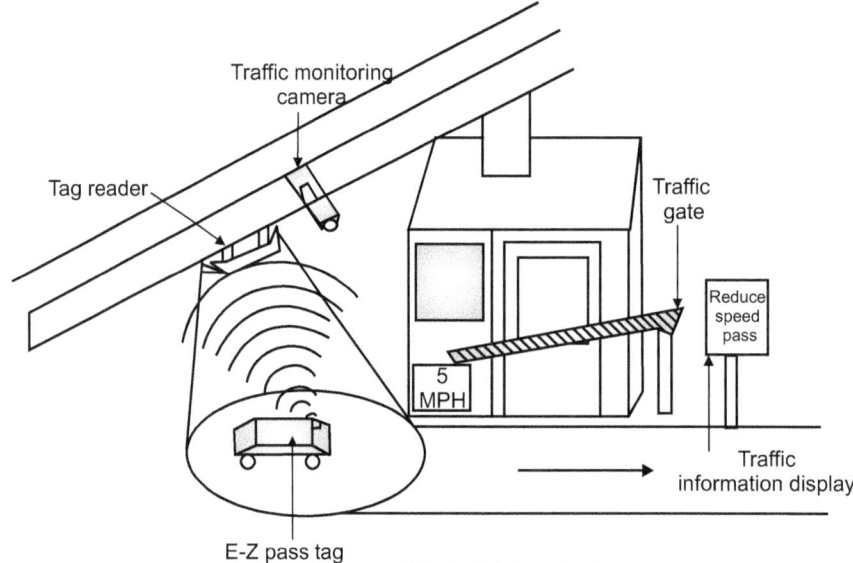

The E-Z pass process

Fig. 12.2 : Electronic payment facility

Thus, the ETC system is a win-win situation for both the motorists and toll operators, which is why it is now being extensively used throughout the world. .

12.3.2 Toll collection by Radio Frequency Identification system

An ETC system commonly utilizes radio frequency identification (RFID) technology. RFID is a generic term used to identify technologies utilizing radio waves to automatically identify people or objects. RFID technology was first introduced in 1948 when Harry Stockman wrote a paper exploring RFID technology entitled, "Communication by Means of Reflected Power".

RFID technology has evolved since then, and has been implemented in various applications, such as in warehouse management, library system, attendance system, theft prevention, and so on. In general, RFID is used for tracking, tracing, and identifying objects.

A complete RFID system consists of a transponder (tag), reader/writer, antenna, and computer host. The transponder, better known as the tag, is a microchip combined with an antenna system in a compact package. The microchip contains memory and logic circuits to receive and send data back to the reader. These tags are classified as either active or passive tags. Active tags have internal batteries that allow a longer reading range, while passive tags are powered by the signal from its reader and thus have shorter reading range.

Tags could also be classified based on the content and format of information. The classifications range from Class 0 to Class 5. These classes have been determined by the Electronic Product Code (EPC) Global Standard. In the table below, classes refer to a tag's basic functionality (i.e., it either has a memory or an on-board power), while generation refers to the tag specification's major release or version number. The class structure for the tags is shown in the table below.

Table 12.1 : Class Structure for Tags

EPC Class	Definition	Programming
Class-0 Gen-1	Read only Passive tags	Programmed by the factory
Class-1 Gen-1	Write once, Read many passive tags	Programmed by the user and then locked
Class-1 Gen-2	Write-many read-many passive tags	Programmed by the user and then locked
Class 2	Rewritable passive tags with extra functionality, including encryption and emulation	Can be re-programmed
Class 3	Semi-passive tags that support broadband communication	
Class 4	Active tags that can communicate with other peers	
Class 5	Readers, they can power other tags of class 1, 2 and 3 can communicate with class 4 wirelessly	Not applicable

A reader contains an antenna to transmit and receive data from the tag. The reader also contains a decoder and an RF module. It could be mounted or built as a portable handheld device. The computer host acts as an interface to an IT platform for exchanging information between the RFID system and the end-user. This host system then converts the information obtained from the RFID system into useful information for the end-user.

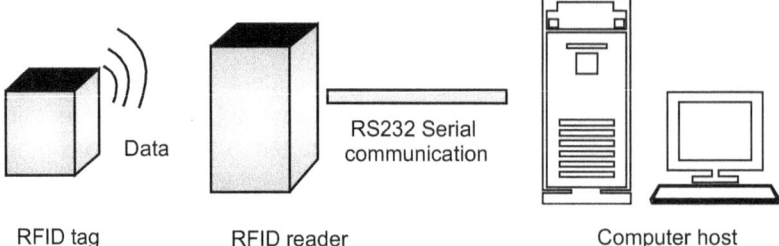

Fig. 12.3

REVIEW QUESTIONS

1. What are rapid transit systems? What the impact of MRTS?
2. What the advantage of intelligent transportation system?
3. Explain in details electronic toll collection system?
4. Write short notes on :
   (i) Mass and rapid transit system
   (ii) Introduction to intelligent transportation system (its)
   (iii) Electronic toll collection.

Unit - IV

CHAPTER 13
BRIDGES

13.1 INTRODUCTION

A bridge is an arrangement made to cross obstacle in the form of a low ground or a stream or a river or over a gap without closing the way beneath. The bridges are required for the passages of railways, roadways and footpaths, and even for the carriages of fluids. In short, a bridge is a structure built to span physical obstacles such as a body of water, valley, or road, for the purpose of providing passage over the obstacle. Designs of bridges vary depending on the function of the bridge, the nature of the terrain where the bridge is constructed, the material used to make it and the funds available to build it.

Bridge is a structure having a total length of above 6 m between the inner faces of the dirt walls for carrying traffic or other moving loads over a depression or obstruction such as channel, road or railway. These bridges are classified as :

Small Bridge - Overall length of the bridge between the inner faces of dirt walls is upto 30m and where individual span is not more than 10m

Minor bridge - Total length upto 60m

Major bridge - Total length greater than 60m

13.2 SITE INVESTIGATION

The aim of the investigation is to be select a suitable site at which a bridge can be built economically. Moreover it should satisfy the demands of traffic, the stream, safety etc. before a bridge can be built at a particular site, it is essential to consider many factors, such as need for a bridge stream characteristics, the present and future traffic, sub-soil conditions, cost, alternative sites etc.

Objectives of Site Investigation

The principal objectives for a bridge Site Investigation are as follows :

- **Suitability :** Are the site and surroundings suitable for the bridge site?
- **Design :** Obtain all the design parameters necessary for the works.
- **Construction :** Are there any potential ground or ground water conditions that would affect the construction?
- **Materials :** Are there any materials available on site, what quantity and quality?

- **Effect of Changes :** How will the design affect adjacent properties and the ground water?
- **Identify Alternatives :** Is this the best location?

13.1.1 Field Reconnaissance Survey

For most bridge investigations access and environmental constraints have major influences on cost. It is therefore necessary for a field reconnaissance survey to be conducted as the first stage of a geotechnical investigation. This may be undertaken by concern department or by a consultant specifically engaged for this survey. Information on the following should result :

- Legal and physical aspects of access to site and bridge alignment – both riverbed and adjoining properties.
- Availability of any services or supplies of water, electricity, earthworks plant.
- Buried or overhead services.
- Photographs of surface conditions.
- Traffic control requirements.
- The possible effects of alternative investigation techniques on the environment (for example, ground disturbance, vegetation removal, water discharge, noise etc).
- On-ground survey details.
- Tide, river level or other natural constraints.
- Notes on any exposed geology, for example the presence of boulders, bedrock exposure, swamps etc.
- The physical relationship of the proposed construction to the immediate natural surroundings and any existing developments.

The field reconnaissance survey must be diligently prepared and conducted to allow for reliable cost estimates to be prepared. Experienced and suitably qualified personnel should perform the survey. Further stages of the investigation should be held until the field reconnaissance survey has been completed and reported to department. Cost estimates for the major part of the investigation will be based partly on this reconnaissance survey.

13.1.2 Desk Top Study

Every site investigation should commence with a desk study directed towards collecting, collating and reviewing the following :

- Design drawings from any previous structure at the site.
- Previous site investigation reports, borehole logs, penetrometer results and construction experience e.g. piling records.
- Geological and Topographical maps, survey data and records.
- Hydrological data.

- Aerial photographs.
- Regional seismicity data.
- Survey records, local knowledge and resources.

The collection and collation of the above information, where possible, could be undertaken during the field reconnaissance survey stage. However, further work to fully explore the extent of information available may be required. During the desk study stage, an overview of complexity and risks associated with each geotechnical design should be clearly identified.

13.1.3 Sampling and Testing

This stage of the Geotechnical Investigation is involved with the exploration of subsurface conditions and retrieval of test data for generating geotechnical parameters and geotechnical profiles.

13.1.4 Laboratory Testing

In conducting laboratory testing, procedures to be applied shall be in accordance with Indian Standards, or American Standards (ASTM) and other relevant registered procedures

13.2 SITE SELECTION

The selection of site for a bridge is usually governed by engineering, economic, social and aesthetic considerations. In order to select a least objectionable site, the bridge engineer should consider the following characteristics of an ideal bridge site :

- A well defined and narrow channel.
- A straight reach.
- Good foundation bed at a short depth.
- Suitable high banks.
- Angle of crossing, the axis of steam at bridge site should be crossing at right angles to the centre line of the communication route as far as possible.
- Absence of scouring and silting - It should be free from whirls and cross-currents.
- Location of river tributaries.
- Minimum obstruction to waterway.
- Sound, economical and straight approaches.
- Absence of costly river training work.
- Minimum construction work inside water.
- Proximity to the alignment of communication route.
- Availability of sufficient free board.
- Availability of labour and construction materials.

- Advent of materials / new materials.
- Advances in other branches of science.
- Improvements in constructional methods.

An ideal bridge site is never possible because some ideal conditions are always lacking. Therefore, a least objectionable site is always selected. The best compromise at the time of making selection of a bridge site is a matter of judgement which depends upon the experience of the concerned engineer.

13.3 BRIDGE ALIGNMENT

The location of centre line of a communication route to be carried by bridge at the selected site is called bridge alignment.

The following points should be considered while locating the alignment bridges :

- As far as possible centre line of bridge should be at right angle to the axis of river. Such an alignment is known as square alignment and the bridge so constructed is called square bridge. This type of alignment is always preferred because of square bridge is easy to construct and maintain.
- As far as possible, the alignment should not be skew since it is difficult to construct and maintain a skew bridge. Moreover it does not provide smooth entry and exit of water under the bridge.
- As far as possible, the alignment should not be curved since it is difficult to construct and maintain a curved bridge. Moreover, such a bridge is subjected to an additional force due to centrifugal action and there is a greater possibility of traffic accidents.

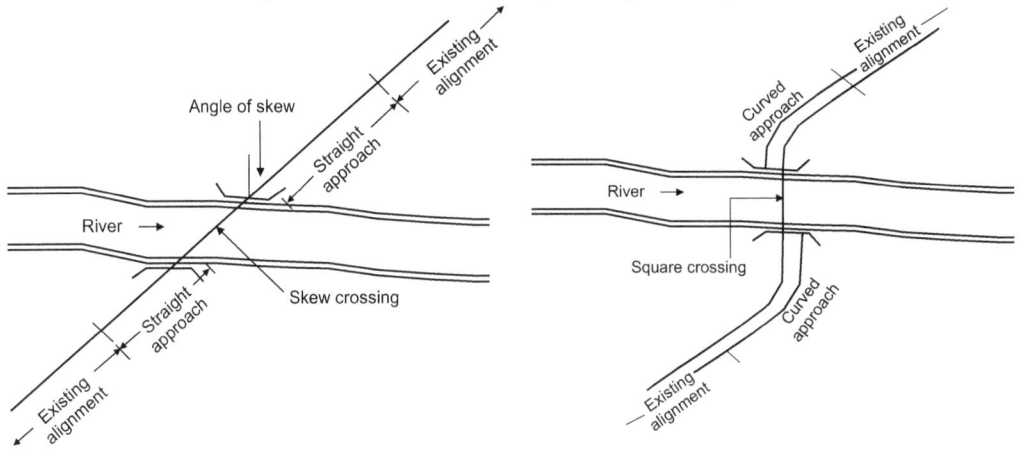

(a) Skew alignment – skew crossing (b) Skew alignment – square crossing

Fig. 13.1 : Skew and square crossing

Despite disadvantages of a curved alignment a bridge may be aligned on a curve to smoothen entries and exists of water. In such a case it is always desirable to arrange piers parallel to the axis of river.

Demerits of skew alignment of a bridge - when the centre line of the bridge is not at right angles to the axis of the river the alignment is called skew alignment and the bridge having such an alignment is known as skew bridge.

(a) The construction and maintenance of a skew bridge is difficult.

(b) The foundation of a skew bridge is more susceptible to scouring action.

(c) The piers of a skew bridge are subjected to excessive water pressure because the passage of water below the bridge superstructure is not smooth and whirls are formed.

13.3.1 Collection of Design Data for a Bridge

1. General data :
   (a) Index map
   (b) Contour survey map
   (c) Site plan
   (d) Cross-section
   (e) Longitudinal section
2. Alternative bridge sites and their typical cross-sections.
3. Hydraulic data for the particular selected bridge site.
4. Geological data.
5. Climatic data.
6. Loading and other data.

13.3.2 Determination of Design Discharge

1. From the record available, if any of the discharge observed on the stream at the selected bridge site or at any other nearby site.
2. From the rainfall and other characteristics of the catchment area by any one of the following methods :
   (a) By an empirical formula method.
   (b) By a rational method.
   (c) By the area velocity method.
   (d) By unit hydrograph method.

13.3.2.1 Empirical Method

This is an indirect method of determining the maximum flood discharge. in this method, the maximum flood discharge is determined by an empirical formula in which the area of the catchment or basin is mainly considered.

1. **Dickens Formula :** This formula is used almost throughout India.

   According to this formula

   $$Q = CM^{3/4}$$

   where, Q = Discharge in m³/sec, M = Area of catchment is sq. km the value of 'c' in Dickens formula for different regions is given below

   Table 13.1

Region	Value of 'c'
In area where the annual rainfall is 60 to 120 cm	11 to 14
M.P.	14 to 19
Western ghats	32

2. **Ryve's Formula :** Southern India.

   $$Q = CM^{2/3}$$

   where, C = 6.8 for area within 25 km from coast
   = 3.5 within 25 to 160 km
   = 10.1 for limited hilly areas

3. **Inglis Formula :** This formula is used in Maharashtra state only.

   $$Q = \frac{4350\, m}{\sqrt{m + 1.04}}$$

   where, m = Catchment area in sq. km.

13.3.2.2 Rational Method

Indirect Method : This method is applicable for determination of flood discharge for small culverts only.

The runoff, $Q = 0.028\, P.F.A.I_c$

where, Q = Discharge or runoff in m³/sec
F = Co-efficient
A = Catchment area in hectares
I_c = Critical intensity of rainfall in cm/hour
P = % coefficient of run-off

13.3.2.3 Area Velocity Method

This is direct and an accurate method in determining the maximum flood discharge at the proposed site of a bridge by direct observation. The procedure for determining velocity of flow of a steam water by direct observation is described below :

1. Two cables are stretched across the stream at 15 to 30 m apart.

2. Then width of stream is divided into suitable number of compartments by hanging pendants as shown in Fig. 13.2.

3. After this, the mean velocity of flow of stream water is determined by using any one of the following devices :

    (a) A surface float or sub-surface in case of a small river.

    (b) A velocity rod or current meter in case of a large river.

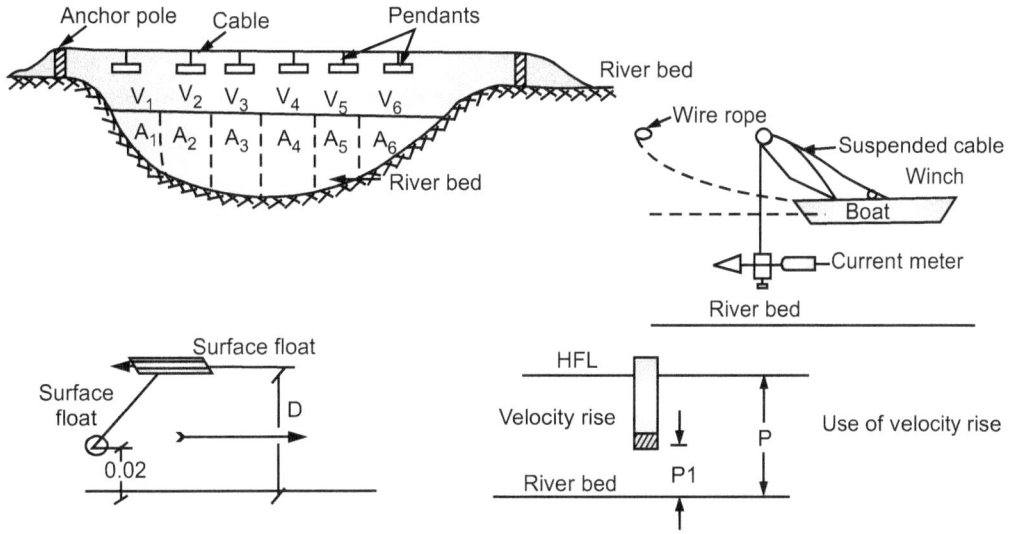

Fig. 13.2

The surface float, sub-surface float or the velocity rod to be used for determining the velocity of flow is allowed to travel from one section to the other in the centre of each compartment and the time taken to cover this distance is noted. Thus, a mean value of the velocity is obtained by taking the average of all the velocities observed in different compartments.

Thus, mean velocity, $v = \dfrac{V_1 + V_2 + V_3 + V_4 + V_5 + V_6}{6}$

All these devices of measuring velocity of flow of stream water are shown above.

In this case, when surface floats are used, the surface velocity so obtained should be multiplied by a suitable constant to determine the mean velocity of flow as detailed below.

$$\text{Mean velocity} = 4/5 \times \text{Surface velocity}$$

[If surface velocity is less than 0.9 m/sec.]

No correction is required when sub-surface float or velocity rod is used for determining the velocity of flow of stream water.

For determining the velocity of flow by a current meter it is lowered in water from a boat, anchored at the centre of the compartment. Normally, the current meter is kept at a depth of about 0.60 times the depth of water. Then the mean velocity of flow is worked out by the formula supplied by the manufacturer of the meter.

Thus, the maximum flood discharge can be determined from the following relation :

Maximum flood discharge, Q = A.v.

where, A = mean cross-sectional area of the steam upto the highest flood level

v = mean velocity of flow of stream water as determined by any of above method

13.3.2.4 By Unit Hydrograph Method

In this method, the continuous discharge of a stream on time base is represented graphically with the aid of a hydrograph.

13.4 CRITERIA FOR FIXING DESIGN DISCHARGE

For fixing design discharge, flood discharge may be determined by as many methods as possible. Then the highest of these values should be taken as the design discharge provided it does not exceed the next highest discharge by more than 50%.

13.5 DETERMINATION OF WATERWAY

The area through which water flows under a bridge structure is known as **waterway.**

While fixing the waterway of a bridge, the following guiding principles must be kept in mind to ensure safety of the bridge structures :

- The increased velocity due to obstructed waterway should not exceed the permissible velocity under the bridge.
- The free board for high level bridges should not be less than 600 mm.
- Sufficient clearance should be allowed according to the navigation requirements.

If 'Q' is maximum flood discharge (design discharge) and 'V' is the permissible velocity of flow under the bridge, then

$$\text{waterway, a} = \frac{Q}{V}$$

The maximum permissible velocity of flow (V) depends upon the nature of the river bed as given in Table 13.2. The velocity of flow of stream or river water should not be more than the values mentioned in this table.

Table 13.2

Sr. No.	Types of Soil	Permissible Velocity
1.	Clay	2.10
2.	Sandy clay	1.50
3.	Very fine sand	0.60 to 1.50
4.	Find sand	0.90 to 1.50
5.	Fine gravel	1.50 to 1.80
6.	Rocky soil	3.00
7.	Rock	4.20 to 6.00

13.6 SCOURING

The process of cutting or deeping of river bed due to action of water is called **scouring**.

When the velocity of stream water exceeds the limiting velocity it causes vertical cutting of the river bed, which is known as scouring. It differs from errosions which causes horizontal widening of the river bed.

Determination of Normal Scour Depth

The normal scour depth is the depth of water in the middle of stream when it is carrying the maximum flood discharge.

1. **Scour Depth of Alluvial Streams**

Case – I : When linear waterway of the bridge is equal to the regime width : In this case, the normal scour depth is equal to the regime depth given by the following Lacey regime equation.

$$D = 0.473 \left(\frac{Q}{F}\right)^{1/3}$$

where,
D = Normal scour depth below H.F.L. for regime section of the channel in m.
Q = The maximum design discharge in m^3/sec
f = Lacey's silt factor which varies from 0.5 to 1.5

Case – II : When linear waterway is less than the regime width :

$$D' = D \left(\frac{W}{L}\right)^{0.61}$$

where, D' = The normal scour depth with constructed waterway in m.

D = The normal scour depth in m when L = W as calculated in the first case

L = Linear waterway provided under the bridge in m

W = The regime width of the stream in m, which can be equal to wetted verimeter $P = 4.8\,(Q)^{1/2}$

2. Scour Depth for Quasi Alluvial Streams :

In quasi-alluvial streams having rigid banks and erodable beds the normal scour depth, when the stream width is large as compared to depth, can be determined as follows :

Case – I : When velocity is known, we may use the equation

$$D = \frac{Q}{W.V}$$

where, W = The regime or fixed width of the stream in m

V = Velocity of flow

Case – II : When slope is known : We may use the equation

$$Q = 1/n\, W\, S^{1/2}\, D^{5/3}$$

where, n = Manning's coefficient

S = Bed slope

W = The regime or fixed width of the stream in m.

Case – III : When both velocity and slope factors are not known : We may use the equations

$$D = \frac{1.21\, Q^{0.63}}{F^{0.33} \times W^{0.60}}$$

where, F = Silt factor

Normal scour depth in case of quasi-alluvial streams for constructed waterway can be determined by this equation.

13.6.1 Determination of Maximum Scour Depth

Maximum scour depth is the depth of water at the round obstruction to the flow of water when the river carries maximum flood discharge.

It usually occurs at bends, pier noses and on the understream noses of guide banks provided for a bridge. Therefore, for the safety of the bridge foundations it becomes essential to estimate the maximum scour depth correctly and design the bridge foundations accordingly.

As per I.P.C. recommendations, the maximum depth of scour may be taken as follows :

- In case of a bridge on a straight reach of the stream having single span, the maximum depth of scour should be taken as 1.5 times the normal scour depth of water.
- For bridge sites on curves or where cross current exists or when the bridge is a multi-span structure, the maximum depth of scour should be taken as 2 times the normal depth of scour.
- In case of bridge causing construction, the maximum scour depth should not be less than the value obtained by the following equations

$$D_m = D \left(\frac{W}{L}\right)^{1.56}$$

where,
D_m = Maximum scour depth in m
W = Regime width of stream in m
D = Normal scour depth in m
L = Linear waterway in m

13.6.1.2 Prevention of Scouring

1. The site of the bridge should have stream line flow.
2. At the site of bridge, the river bed soil should be such as to resist the maximum velocity of water.
3. Sufficient waterway should be provided under the bridge so that velocity of water may not exceed the limit after which scouring occurs.
4. The shape of the piers should be designed in such a way that it may not cause eddies and currents in water.
5. The river bed on upstream side, downstream side and the portion under the bridge should be properly pitched with beams and long stones.
6. In the case of sandy beds, sheet piling may be done on understream and downstream sides of the bridge to prevent scouring.
7. Piles may also be driven in river bed, where scouring is likely to occur.

13.7 DETERMINATION OF LINEAR WATERWAY

The linear waterway is the linear measurement of the area way along the bridge. It is equal to the sum of all the clear spans of the bridge.

In the case of large alluvial streams with underlined banks the linear waterway may be determined by the following Lacey's formula i.e.

$$L = C\sqrt{Q}$$

where, L = The linear waterway in metres of regime surface width in m
Q = The maximum design discharge in m³/sec
C = A constant which is generally taken as 4.8 but for regime channels, it may vary from 4.5 to 6.3 according to the local conditions.

If 'Q' is the design discharge, 'h' is the head or water causing flow and 'ha' is the afflux, then the linear waterway can also be determined from the following relation.

$$\text{Linear waterway, } L = \frac{Q}{\text{Depth of water} \times \sqrt{2g(h + ha)}}$$

The linear waterway thus calculated is divided into a number of spans, keeping in view the economy of the bridge.

13.8 DETERMINATION OF AFFLUX

The phenomenon of heading up of water on the upstream site of the bridge is called **afflux.** When a bridge is constructed, its components like abutments and piers, cause the reduction of the natural waterway. Due to this reduction in natural waterway, the velocity under bridge increases so as to carry the maximum flood discharge. This increased velocity gives rise to a sudden heading up of water on the upstream site of the stream or river. The phenomenon of this heading up water is known as afflux. Thus, greater the afflux greater will be velocity under down stream side of the bridge and greater will be the depth of scour and consequently greater will be the depth of foundation required. Hence, determination of afflux is necessary for the safe design of the bridge.

In view of the above mentioned facts, the afflux should be kept as low as possible due to the following reasons.

- It result in providing shallow foundation of the bridge because lower the afflux, lower will be the velocity under the down stream side of the bridge and lower will be the depth of the scour and thus shallow will be depth of foundation required.

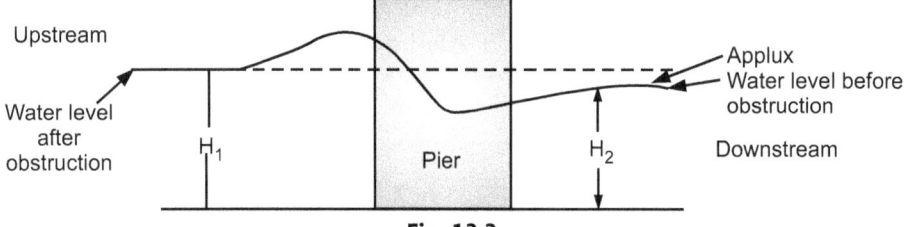

Fig. 13.3

- It helps in deciding the top levels and lengths of guide banks, and flood protection bunds conveniently and economically.
- It facilitates the provision of the bridge at lower level with sufficient free board.

Afflux is determined by using any one of the following two equations :

1. **Marriman's equations.**
2. **Molesworth's equations**

1. **Marriman's Equation :** This equation is generally used for determining the values of afflux. According to this equations

$$ha = \frac{V_a^2}{2g}\left\{\left(\frac{A}{C \cdot A_c}\right)^2 - \left(\frac{A}{A_1}\right)\right\}$$

where
- ha = Afflux in metres
- V_a = Velocity of approach in m/sec
- A = Natural waterway area at this bridge site in m
- A_c = Constructed area in m^2
- A_1 = The enlarged area upstream of the bridge in m^2
- C = Coefficient of discharge which is

$$= 0.75 + 0.35\left(\frac{A_c}{A}\right) - 0.1\left(\frac{A_c}{A}\right)^2$$ approximately, which may be taken 0.7 for sharp and 0.9 for bell mounted entry.

2. **Molesworth's Equations :** According to this equation

$$ha = \left[\frac{V_a^2}{17.9} + 0.015\right]\left[\left(\frac{A}{A_c}\right)^2 - 1\right]$$

where V_a, A and A_c have the same meanings as used in the Marriman's equation.

Determination of Length of Bridge :

After determining waterway and economic span the length of bridge can be determined by the following relation

$$L = Nl + (N - 1)b$$

where
- L = Length of the bridge
- N = Number of economic span
- l = Length of each economic span
- b = Thickness of each pier

Example 13.1 : A bridge has a liner waterway of 150 m constructed across a stream, whose natural liner waterway is 220 m. If the average floods discharge is 1200 m^3/sec, and average flood depth is 3 m, find Afflux under the bridge.

Solution :

The natural waterway are at the site = A = 220 x 3 = 660m^2
Contracted waterway area = A_c = 150 x 3 = 450 m^2
The Velocity of approach = V_a = Q/A
Here, Q = Flood discharge = 1200 m^2/sec
V = 1200/660 = 1.818 m/sec
Using **Molesworth's Equations,** the afflux can be given by

$$ha = \left[\frac{V_a^2}{17.9} + 0.015\right]\left[\left(\frac{A}{A_c}\right)^2 - 1\right]$$

$$ha = [(0.184 + 0.015)(660/450)^2 - 1]$$

ha = 0.199 x 1.15
ha = 0.229m

Afflux Under the Bridge = 0.229 m

13.9 DETERMINATION OF ECONOMIC SPAN

The economic span is the span for which the overall cost of a bridge will be minimum.

The overall cost of a bridge includes the cost of its substructrure as well as superstructure. The cost of superstructure increases and that of substructure decreases with an increase in span length and vice versa.

Thus, the most economic span length is that for which the cost of the superstructure is equal to that of substructure.

The derivation for economic span can be established on the basis of the following assumptions :

- The bridge has equal span lengths.
- Cost of the supporting system of superstructure varies as the square of the span length.
- Cost of flooring and parapets varies directly as the span.
- Cost of one pier and its foundation is constant.
- Cost of one abutment and its foundation is also constant.

Let,
L = Total linear waterway
l = Economic span length
N = The total number of spans = $\frac{L}{l}$
C_p = Cost of one pier and its foundation
C_{ap} = Cost of one approach, railing etc.
C_{ab} = Cost of one abutment and its foundation
T_c = Overall cost of the bridge

Now there are (N − 1) number of piers, two abutments and two approaches providing/provided in the proposed bridge.

According to assumptions (2) and (3) cost of one span of superstructure = $(a_1 l^2 + a_2 l)$.

Where a_1 and a_2 are constant of variation for supporting system of superstructure and for flooring and parapets respectively.

Thus, the overall cost of the bridge = Cost of supporting system of the superstructure and that of flooring and parapets for all span + Cost of (N − 1) piers + Cost of two abutments + Cost of two approaches, railings etc.

or
$$T_C = N(a_1 l^2 + a_2 l) + (N-1) C_p + 2C_{ab} + 2C_{ap}$$
$$= \frac{L}{l}(a_1 l^2 + a_2 l) + \left(\frac{L}{l} - 1\right) C_p + 2C_{ab} + 2C_{ap} \qquad \left[\because N = \frac{L}{l}\right]$$

$$T_C = a_1Ll + a_2L + \frac{C_pL}{l} - C_p + 2C_{ab} + 2C_{ap} \qquad \ldots (13.1)$$

Differentiating equation (13.1) on w.r.t. l we get

$$\frac{dT_C}{dl} = a_1L + 0 - \frac{C_pL}{l^2} - 0 + 0 + 0 = a_1L - \frac{C_pL}{l^2}$$

Now, for T_C to be minimum $\frac{dT_C}{dl} = 0$

$$\therefore \quad a_1L = \frac{C_pL}{l^2}$$

$$\therefore \quad C_p = a_1 l^2$$

or Economic span, $l = \sqrt{\dfrac{C_p}{a_1}}$

Hence, for total cost of the bridge to be minimum, the cost of one pier and its foundation should be equal to the cost of supporting system of the superstructure. In other words, for each economical span the cost of substructure is equal to the cost of superstructure.

This equation is suitable for steel girder bridges, truss bridges and arch bridges.

As per I.R.C. recommendation the values of economic span (l) for small culverts and road bridges are as follows :

- For R.C.C. slab bridges $l = 1.5\,H$
- For masonry arch type bridges $l = 2\,H$
- For steel girder bridges $l = 1.75\,H$
- For steel truss bridges $l = 3\,H$

Example 13.2 : Following are the costs involved in a uniform multiple span bridge construction

Table 13.3

SPAN (m)	5	8	11	14	17
Cost of Girder Rs	2,000	6,000	15,000	22,000	40,000
Cost of Girder Pier and Foundation Rs.	15,000	20,000	25,000	35,000	42,000

Calculate the Economic Span

Solution :

Assuming that the costs of superstructure span various as the square of the span, the constant of variation, a_1 for various values of span is as under :

$$a_1 = \frac{C_p}{l^2}$$

For 5 m span, $\quad a_1 = \dfrac{2000}{25} = 80.00$

For 8 m span, $a_1 = \dfrac{6000}{64} = 93.75$

For 11 m span, $a_1 = \dfrac{15000}{121} = 123.96$

For 14 m span, $a_1 = \dfrac{22000}{196} = 112.24$

For 17 m span, $a_1 = \dfrac{40000}{289} = 138.40$

An average valve of a_1 = 80.00 +93.75 + 123.96 + 112.24 + 138.40 = 109.67.

The average cost of sub-structure unit, = 15000+20000+25000+35000+42000=27400

$$\text{Economic span, } l = \sqrt{\dfrac{C_p}{a_1}}$$

Economic span, $l = \sqrt{27400/109.67}$ Economic span, $l = 15.80$ m

REVIEW QUESTIONS

1. Define the following : Waterway, Effective linear waterway, Afflux, HFL, Scour depth.
2. Discuss how the design flood discharge can be estimated by direct method.
3. What are different methods of determining flood discharge?
4. What are preliminary data required for investigation of site for bridges.
5. What is height of afflux? State also its importance and hence calculate the height of afflux from the following particulars.
6. Derive the expression for economical span and the factor affecting on it.
7. Preventive measures to minimize the effect of scour.
8. What is height of afflux? State also its importance and hence calculate the height of afflux from the following particulars.
   (i) Normal velocity of flow in a river is 1.50 m/sec.
   (ii) The normal and artificial waterway under the bridge and enlarged area upstream of the bridge are respectively 8000 m^2, 7000 m^2 and 10,000 m^2. Assume g = 9.81 m/sec^2. Use Merriman's formula. Also find increase in velocity.
9. Following are the costs involved in a uniform multiple span bridge construction

Table 13.4

SPAN (m)	5	10	15	20
Cost of Girder Rs	4000	13000	26000	45000
Cost of Girder Pier and Foundation Rs.	16000	18000	22000	250000

Calculate the Economic Span

CHAPTER 14
CLASSIFICATION AND SUITABILITY OF BRIDGE

14.1 INTRODUCTION

A bridge is an arrangement made to cross obstacle in the form of a low ground or a stream or a river or over a gap without closing the way beneath. The bridges are required for the passages of railways, roadways and footpaths, and even for the carriages of fluids. In short, a bridge is a structure built to span physical obstacles such as a body of water, valley, or road, for the purpose of providing passage over the obstacle. Designs of bridges vary depending on the function of the bridge, the nature of the terrain where the bridge is constructed, the material used to make it and the funds available to build it.

Components of Bridges

The two basic components of a bridge are :

Substructure : It includes the piers, the abutments and the foundations.

Abutments are the end supports of the superstructure. They also retain the earth of the banks on their back and protect it from falling. Piers are the intermediate supports of the superstructure. They transfer the load from the superstructure to subsoil through the foundations. They divide the length of the bridge into suitable spans, leading to economy in the design and construction. They, however, obstruct the water, if any, flowing in the vally and cause the heading up of the same.

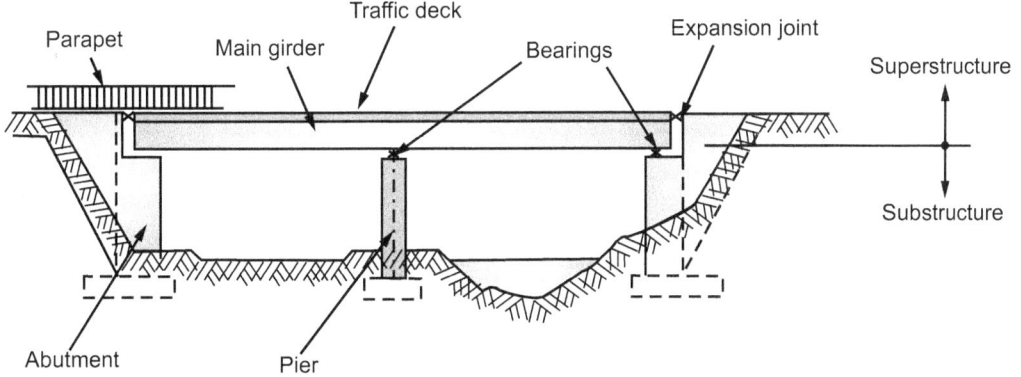

Fig. 14.1 : Elevation of typical girder bridge

Superstructure : It consists of the deck structure itself, which supports the direct loads due to traffic and all the other permanent and variable leads to which the structure is subjected.

The connection between the substructure and the superstructure is usually bearings, however, rigid connections between the pier (and sometimes the abutments) may be adopted, particularly in frame bridges with tall (flexible) piers.

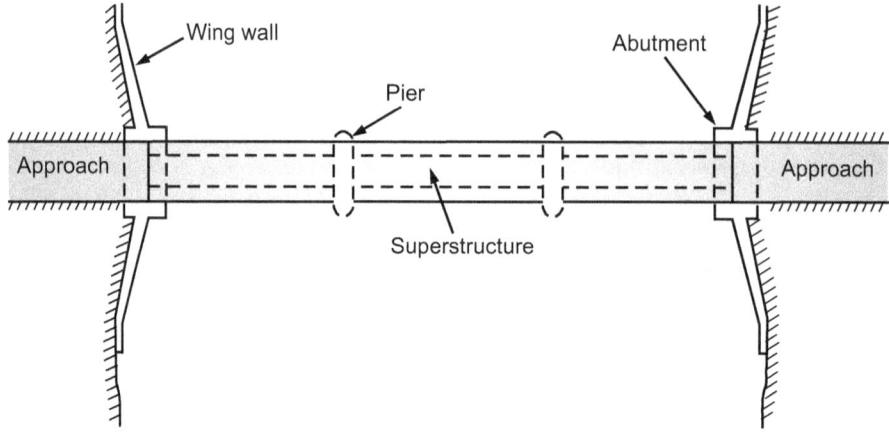

Fig. 14.2 : Typical plan of bridge

Location of Piers and Abutments

Principles to locate piers and abutments :

- The best use of the foundation conditions available;
- The navigational or aesthetic requirements;
- The minimal number of spans;
- An odd number of spans preferable to even ones;
- Ratio of span to pier or abutment height.

A small bridge with open foundations and solid masonry piers and abutments, the economical span is approximately 1.5 times the total height of the pier or abutments. The span for masonry arch bridges is about 2.0 times the height of the keystone above the foundation. For major bridges with more elaborate foundations, the question has to be examined in greater detail.

14.2 CLASSIFICATION OF BRIDGES

1. **According to Life**
   (a) Temporary bridges
   (b) Permanent bridges
2. **According to Loading**
   (a) Class 'AA' bridges
   (b) Class 'A' bridges
   (c) Class 'B' bridges

3. **According to Span Lengths**
   (a) Culverts
   (b) Minor bridges
   (c) Major bridges
   (d) Long-span bridges

4. **According to Purpose**
   (a) Aqueducts
   (b) Viaducts
   (c) Grade separations
   (d) Foot bridges
   (e) Highway bridges
   (f) Railway bridges

5. **According to Materials Used for Constructions**
   (a) Timber bridges
   (b) Masonry bridges
   (c) Iron and steel bridges
   (d) R.C.C. bridges
   (e) Prestressed concrete bridges

6. **According to Structural Form**
   (a) Beam type bridges
   (b) Arch type bridges
   (c) Suspension type bridges

7. **According to Alignment**
   (a) Straight bridges
   (b) Skew bridges

8. **According to Level of Bridge Floor**
   (a) Deek bridges
   (b) Semi-through bridges
   (c) Through bridges

9. **According to Position of High Flood Level**
   (a) Submersible bridges
   (b) Non-submersible bridges

10. **According to Movement of Bridges**
    (a) Swing bridges
    (b) Traverses bridges
    (c) Bascule bridge
    (d) Transporter bridges
    (e) Lift bridges
    (f) Flying bridges
    (g) Cut boat bridges

11. **According to Span Length of Bridges**
    (a) Small bridge - Overall length of the bridge between the inner faces of dirt walls is upto 30m and where individual span is not more than 10m
    (b) Minor bridge - Total length upto 60m
    (c) Major bridge - Total length greater than 60m

12. According to Type of Connection

Under these types the steel bridges can be classified as pinned connected, riveted or welded bridges.

14.3 SUBSTRUCTURES

14.3.1 Abutments

Abutment of bridge is one of the important and vital structural parts. An abutment is the substructure on which rests one end of the superstructure of the bridge. The abutment has following purposes to serve :

- Supporting one end of the bridge.
- Laterally supporting the embankment which serves as an approach to the bridge.
- Protecting embankment from scour.
- Withstanding lateral pressure of the backfill.
- The abutments establish the connection between the bridge superstructure and the embankments.
- They are designed to support the loads due to the superstructure which are transmitted through the bearings and to the pressures of the soil contained by the abutment.

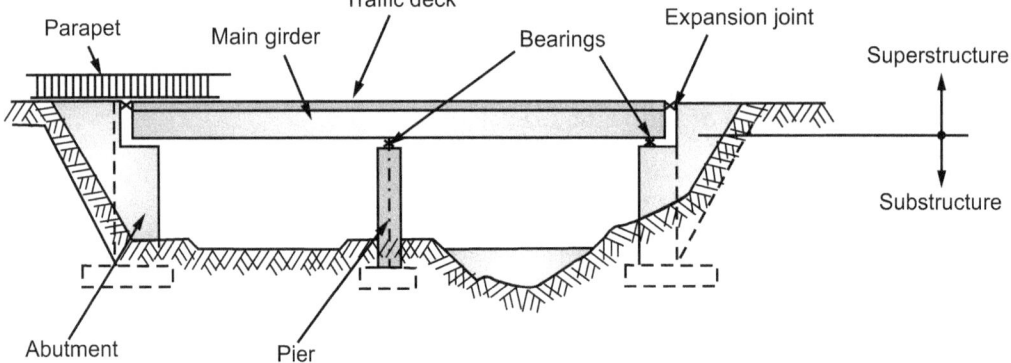

Fig. 14.3

A two spanned bridge has two abutments and one pier and four-spanned bridge has two abutments and three piers. For a bridge or culvert with more than one span, there are intermediate supports which called pier. The function of the abutment is to transmit the load from the bridge superstructure to foundation, to give final formation to the bridge and to retain the earthwork of the embankment of the approaches. The abutment serves both as pier and as a retaining wall. Abutments can be of brick masonry, stone masonry, and concrete or of pre-cast concrete blocks. An abutment consists of the breast, which supports dead load and live load of the superstructure, wings and extension of breast and furnish no support for the superstructure but act as retaining walls for the material deposited behind the abutment and back or parapet wall which prevents the material in back of the abutment from flowing onto the bridge. It is necessary to provide weep holes in abutment and wing walls of the height of the course and two inches wide packed with spalls for draining the embankment.

Types of Abutments

1. **Stub or Straight without Wings :** The earth fill flows around the ends of abutment and flow water may wash the fill away and the banks are damaged.

2. **Abutment with Straight Wing Wall :** Suitable for a railway bridge over a roadway or a street crossing another street at a lower level. Not suitable over a water way as water may flow immediately behind the wing wall and damage the embankment.

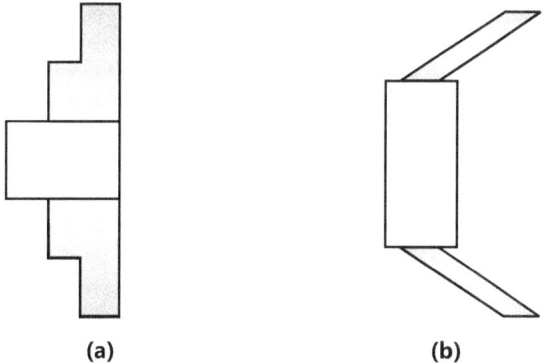

Fig. 14.4

3. **Abutment with Splayed Wing Walls :** The wing walls are straight but splayed at an angle of 45° to 35° with the face of the abutment.

4. **Abutment with Wings Shaped Convex or Concave Facing the Flow of Water :** The latter type form eddies; the former is preferred for the smooth flow of water although the latter is more.

5. **Abutment with Wing Walls at Right Angle to it i.e. U Abutment :** The wings are tied together by old rails. The wing walls run back into fill, which flows down infront of the wings; the wings are parallel to the roadway, suitable where rock slopes make it possible to step up the wing wall footing.

6. **T Abutment :** The head of T supports the bridge and the stem carries the roadway. Was widely used in early rail road construction. The stem carried the railway track and had to be wide enough. The quantity of masonry in its construction is larger than in any other type.

7. **Pulpit Abutment :** It is a variation of U abutment, the arms of U being made short; adopted for high abutments. The returned wings are only of sufficient length to prevent the retaining material from flowing on bridge seat.

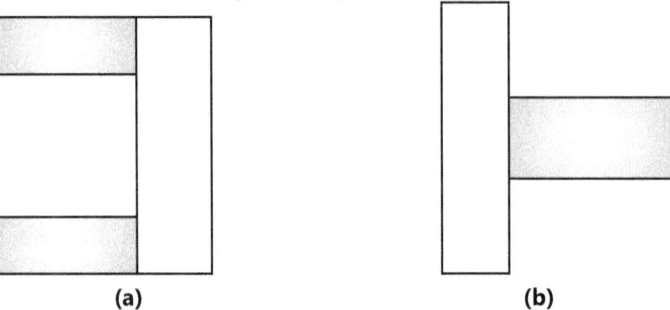

Fig. 14.5

8. **Buried Abutment :** Instead of placing the abutment at the edge of the stream, it is set back in the embankment and the latter spills out in front of the bridge seat. Here the earth pressure at the back is balanced by that in the front and so less massive abutment is required, but this involves greater length for the superstructure. Sometimes a pier is placed at the toe embankment.

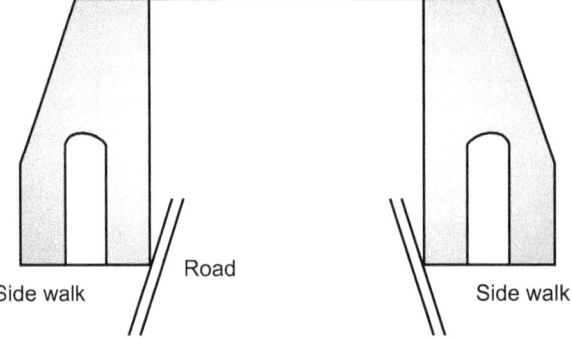

Fig. 14.6

9. **Hollow or Arch Abutment or Box Type Abutment :** This abutment is adopted where a rail road crosses a highway having sidewalks.
10. **Abutment with Flying Wing Walls :** The wings extend a sufficient depth into the embankment to prevent spewing out beneath them.

There are two types of abutments :
- Gravity type abutments
- Counter-fort type abutments

Comparison between Counter-Fort Type Abutment and Gravity Type Abutment

Though counter-fort requires complicated design and skilled labours, still it has advantages over the gravity type in many aspects. Counterfort requires less labour, material, time for construction and therefore is economical in comparison with the gravity type abutment.

In the gravity abutment, there may exist few limitations such as the height increases, there is a variable and drastic increase in cost, which is undesirable. The gravity type abutment is advantageous in some aspects such as the design procedures are simple and hence easily approachable. The construction work requires less skilled labours, i.e. more unskilled labour force can be utilized. The counterfort type is uneconomical upto the height of abutment upto 7 metre, so gravity type is preferred.

The counterfort type also has higher material availability. As it uses hi-technology, reliability is higher as compared to the gravity type abutment. It is always advantageous to use ready formwork of the other structural member making no major alteration in it. Therefore versatility and ready use of formwork helps in saving cost and thus counterfort is preferred to gravity type abutment.

From the including design and estimation one can easily conclude that, counterfort type abutment is much more preferable to gravity type abutment.

14.3.2 Piers

1) Piers for Girder Bridges

The piers may be of solid or open type. One type piers are composed of beams, columns and bracings. Solid piers have a solid section in elevation, plan or end views.

(a) Solid Piers

They are classified as follows :

- Masonry piers.
- R.C.C. piers.

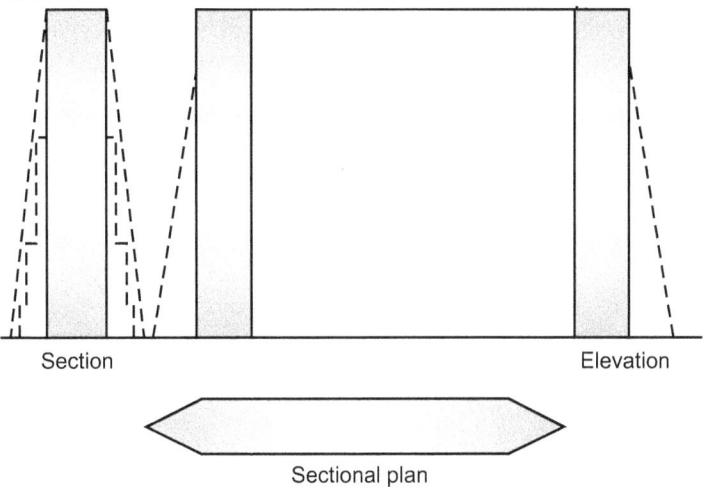

Fig. 14.7 : A masonry pier

Masonry piers may be constructed of brick, stone, plain cement concrete or plum concrete. Plain cement concrete may be used cast-in-situ or pre-cast in blocks. Sometimes, hollow cells of masonry are filled with moorum, sand etc. to form a solid pier.

- **Masonry Piers**

The cross-section of a masonry pier is shown in Fig. 14.7. Its top is in level and may carry a cement concrete block of a richer mix, called the bed block. Sometimes, for small spans, a stone slab may also serve the purpose. The sides of a masonry pier may be vertical, uniformly or varyingly battered or stepped. The alternative treatments are shown in the Fig. 14.7 by dotted lines. In elevation, the pier has its ends vertical or slightly battered. In plan, the ends are given any of the shapes shown in Fig. 14.8. The end on the upstream side is known as the cutwater and that on the downstream side is known as the easewater. They are shaped for easy passage of water. Both ends may be similarly or differently shaped according to the design. The cutwaters are usually triangular in shape, making an angle of 30° to 60°. The easewaters are generally semi-circular or consist of two parabolic arches.

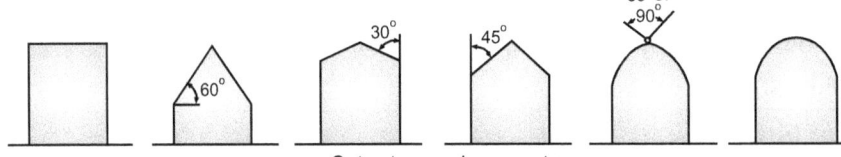

Cutwaters and easewaters
Fig. 14.8 : Cutwaters and easewaters

- **R.C.C. Piers**

They are generally rectangular in cross-section. They too are provided with easewaters and cutwaters. They do not need bed blocks. The main reinforcement is vertical and secondary reinforcement is provided horizontally along the length, binding the main reinforcement.

Dumbbell Pier is a special type of R.C.C. pier. It consists of R.C.C. columns connected by thin reinforced concrete web, all along their height, in a direction transverse to the bridge (See Fig. 14.9). The columns here may have a variety of shapes and may be stepped, if exceptionally high.

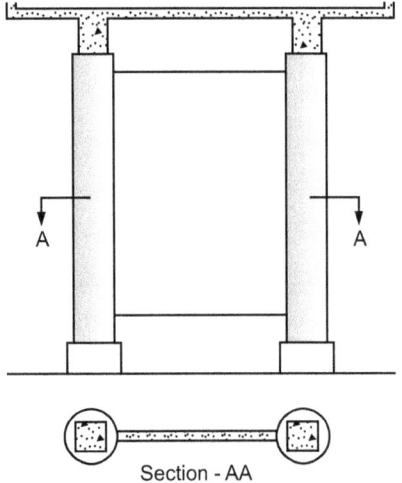

Section - AA
Fig. 14.9 : R.C.C. Dumbbell pier

(b) Open Piers

They are classified as follows :
- Cylindrical piers.
- Pile bents.
- Column bents.
- Trestle bents.

- **Cylindrical Piers**

Here, mild steel cylinders, filled with concrete, are constructed to support the main girders. They are connected by steel frame work. They are many times, extended below ground level and are connected to steel cylinder caisson.

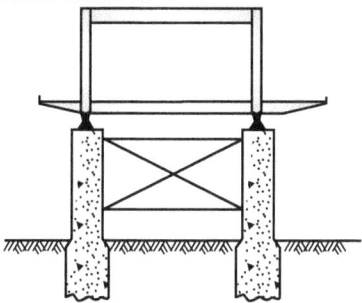

Fig. 14.10 : A cylindrical pier

- **Column Bents**

Here, two or more columns are constructed to support the main girders and are connected laterally by beams and braces or short diaphragms. Fig. 14.10 shows an R.C.C. column bent of two R.C.C. pillars with a beam, brace and a diaphragm, to connect them. The columns may be uniform in cross-section or may have varying section.

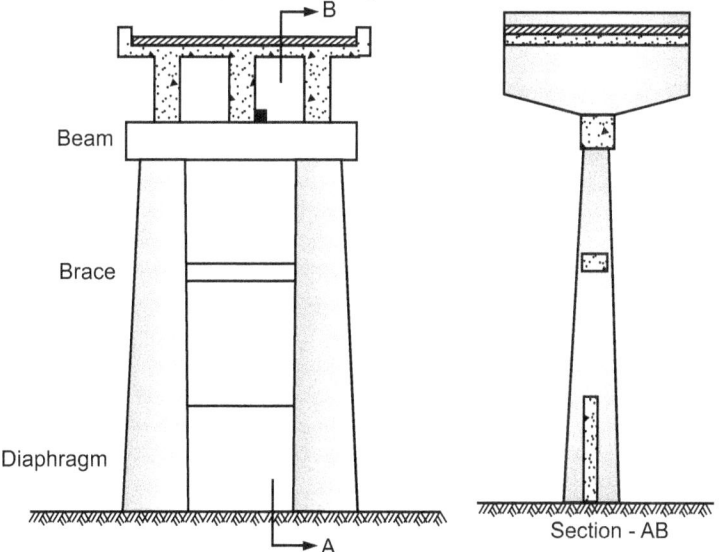

Fig. 14.11 : An R.C.C. column bent

- **Pile Bents**

The piles may be used to support the main girders over their caps. They are laterally connected by frames of steel or R.C.C. The piles may be R.C.C. or steel or screw or disc type. They extend below the bed level to form the foundation. Wooden piles will not be used for substructure of a permanent bridge.

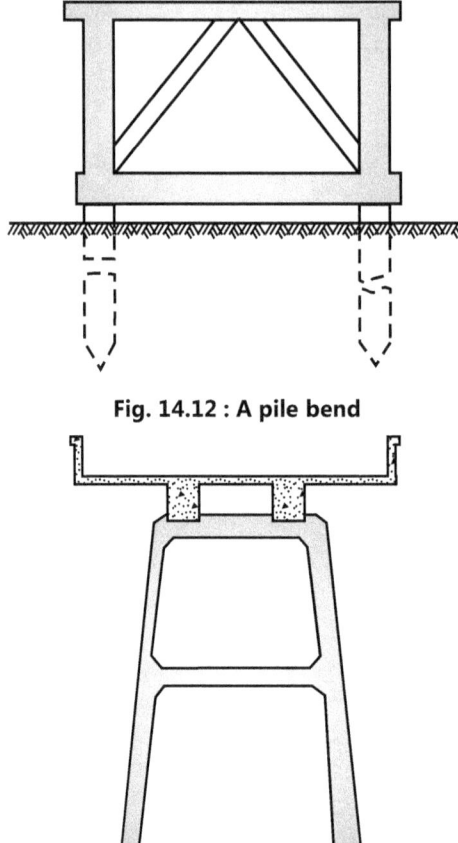

Fig. 14.12 : A pile bend

Fig. 14.13 : An R.C.C. trestle bent

- **Trestle Bents**

An R.C.C. trestle bent is shown in Fig. 14.13 and a steel trestle bent is shown in Fig. 14.14.

All the members are square or rectangular in section. A steel trestle may have bracings of the type shown in Fig. 14.14. The connections of the steel trestle bent may be riveted or welded.

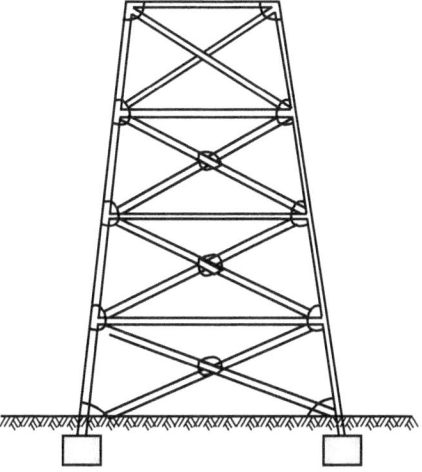

Fig. 14.14 : A steel trestle bent

2) Piers for Arch Bridges

The piers or abutment piers for an arch bridge are always solid. In cross-section, at the top their sides are splayed to receive the arch rings or their bearings normally (see Fig. 14.15). Other details are similar to those of solid piers of girder bridges.

If the bridge consists of a number of arches, every fourth or fifth pier is made of thicker cross-section and strong enough to resist the horizontal thrust of the arch on each side. Such abutment piers reduce the cost of centering because the arches ay then be constructed in set between abutment piers. They also localize damage caused by failure of an arch under adverse conditions.

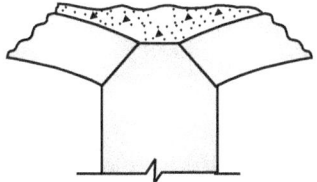

Fig. 14.15 : A pier of an arch bridge

3) Piers for Suspension Bridges :

Piers for big suspension bridges are sometimes, called towers. They are either of masonry or more generally, of steel. If masonry is used, the pier may consist of shafts springing from a solid common base below the flooring. These shafts are connected together at the top by arches. If steel is used, the pier consists of two pier legs braced together by cross girders and bracings or by arched portals. Steel pier columns are made of built-up sections.

For high piers, individual legs may be made of braced construction, each leg consisting of four columns spreading apart towards the base and cross braced.

4) Piers for Rigid Frame Bridges :

Here a pier is not provided as a separate structural pait, but the intermediate legs of the frames may be loosely called piers.

14.3.3 Wing Wall

The abutment can be either buried or its front face can be left exposed. In the latter case, the walls constructed on either side of an abutment to support and protect the embankment are known as the wing walls.

Functions of Wing Walls

A wing wall has mainly to perform the following two function :

1. To provide a smooth entry into the bridge site; and
2. To support and protect the embankment.

Types of Wings Walls

According to their functions there are three types of wing walls

1. Straight wing walls
2. Splayed wing walls
3. Return wing walls

According to their materials used for construction there are two types of wing walls

1. Masonry wing walls
2. R.C.C. wing walls

Temporary Bridge / Superstructures

The temporary bridge superstructure does not necessarily mean low cost structures or short duration life span structures. Temporary bridge superstructure means that the bridge has been erected for a specific purpose and after that purpose is served it is possible, to dismantle the bridge in short time and the material used elsewhere. The necessity of constructing temporary bridges arises when :

1. In military campaigns, when in short time you want to construct the bridge for the passage of foot soldiers, tanks, armored vehicles etc. and once this material is transported, you want to unwind the bridge so that material can be reused.
2. There is shortage of funds and time.
3. There is shortage of resource and skill.
4. Repairs are to be carried out to the permanent bridge.
5. Due to requirement of another bridge to facilitate the construction of permanent bridge.
6. Due to requirement of some sort of arrangement to span the river during the construction of permanent bridge, i.e. Diversion Bridge.
7. Due to requirement of soundings in the river.

Advantages of Temporary Bridges
- These bridges are easy in construction
- They are cheap in construction
- Their structural from is simple, therefore be easily designed
- Less skill labour is required
- Cost of repair and maintenance is less
- Require less time for construction
- Temporary bridges are most suitable in case of emergency.

Disadvantages of Temporary Bridges
- Temporary bridges are not suitable for heavy traffic
- Useful life of these bridges is less up to 10 years
- Not suitable for every purposes

14.3.4 Classification of Temporary Bridges

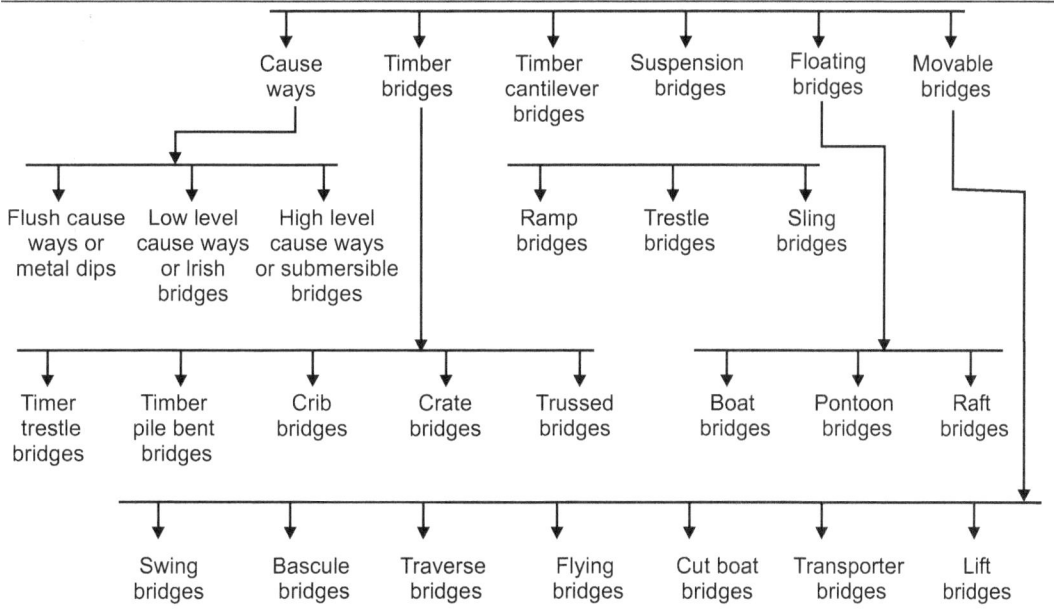

Fig. 14.16

Introduction of Military Bridges

During the military campaign, the army engineers, the army engineers have to erect structures to bridge either river or dry gaps or may be glaciers so that movement of troop and material is facilitated. During large religious gathering such "Kumbha Mela" also these types of bridges are constructed since these can be constructed at a short notice and are sufficiently strong.

The Types of Military Bridges

The types of military bridges are (1) fixed bridges for narrow streams and dry gaps. (2) floating bridges where a roadway is laid on floating supports, here we many have boat bridge, pontoon bridge or raft bridge.

(A) Fixed Type Bridges

This bride essentially consists of light prefabricated modular units which are to be transported at the site of works and then assembled so that full bridge designed by Sir Donald Bailey and extensively used in World War II. The typical details are shown in Fig. 14.17 (a), (b). It consists of standard truss panel, bracing frames, transforms, stringers, bearings, slinks and pin. The roadway consists of wooden chases laid over stringers which rest on transforms supported on trusses on the two sides of the roadway. Each truss composes of a number of panels pined together. The Bailey Bridge can be assembled by man power alone, can carry upto 100 t overspans of 9 to 67 meters. Depending upon span length and load the bridge may have one or more trusses and one or more storeys of panels.

Generally the bridge is constructed by cantilever launching with the aid of launching nose. Framework of panels is corrected on rollers on the near bank for suitable length of nose and the first bay is added. After constructing additional bays, the entire bridge is pushed forward on rollers across the gap. When leading end of nose reaches the far bank, it is to be guided on rollers on that bank. When the first bay comes and settles on the other bank, the launching nose can be dismantled and end posts are attached. The bridge is to be jacked off the rollers one end and one roller at a time and lowered on to the stable bearing. The bridge can be opened to the military traffic by adding end ramps. The military bridge class is denoted by number 8, 9, 40, 70 etc. i.e., 70 class carry 70 ton vehicle i.e., a centurian tank with trailer. Army engineers and their research organizations are now trying to use light, strong durable alloys for Bailey bridges, so that weight is lessenced and assembling can occur in short time.

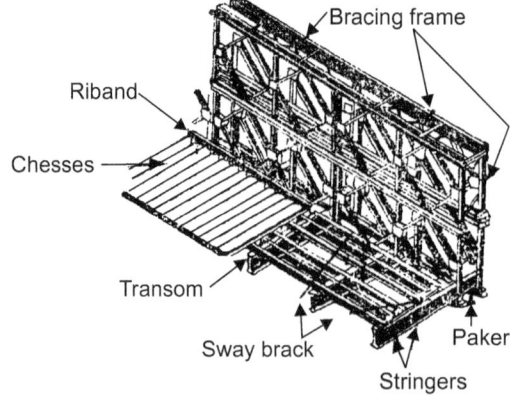

Fig. 14.17 (a) : Out away view showing components

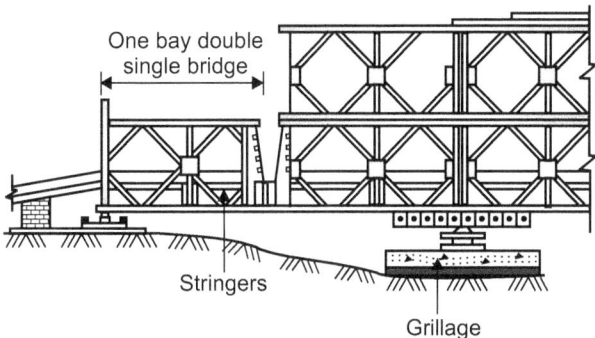
Fig. 14.17 (b) : Elevation at bank end

(B) Floating Bridges

Foating bridges i.e., the boat bridge or pantoon bridge or the raft bridges have been used in wars in historical times and even now. Alxeander has been credited to pass the mighty Sindhu with the help of boat bride during night. The major advantages over the fixed bridge are

1. Quicker to construct.
2. Capital can be constructed where firm ground for locating the rollers of Bailery is not available for example marshy ground.

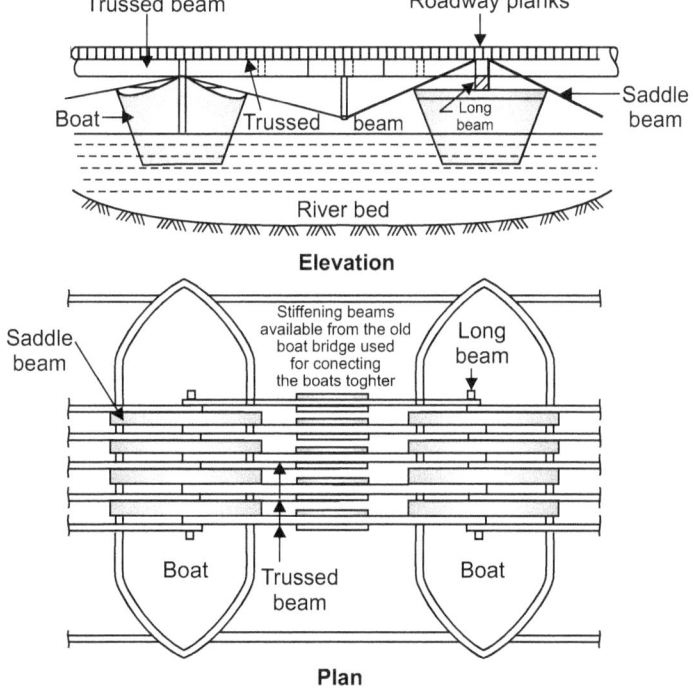
Fig. 14.18 : Boat bridge

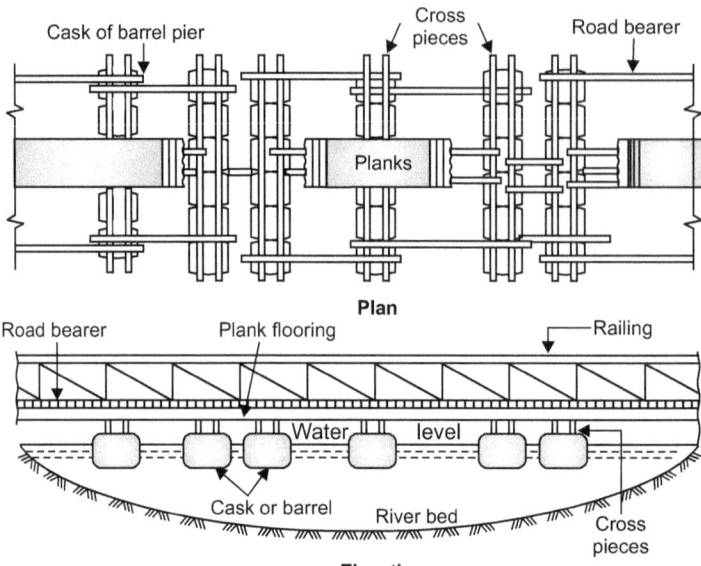

Fig. 14.19 : Raft bridge

3. They can be constructed and used during night and after use dismantled before sun rise such that enemy may not spot it. A schematic diagram of a boat bridge is shown in Fig. 14.18 and the pantoon bridge is shown in Fig. 14.20 whereas the raft bridge is shown in Fig. 14.19.

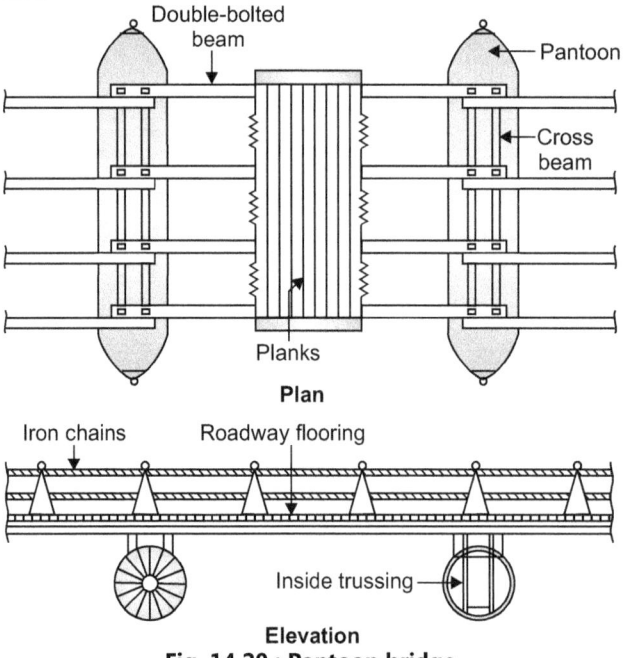

Fig. 14.20 : Pantoon bridge

The floating bridge consists of floating pantoons/boats main axis parallel to current of river. The pantoons/boat may be flat bottomed, decked large or pneumatic, pneumatic ones are now preferred. In between superstructure and the float, saddle is placed for seating purposes. Float has number of air pockets, so that damage to one or few air pockets due to enemy fire will not cause distress to the bridge. The superstructure could be that of Bailey bridge, the superstructure is designed as one continuous member, so that load on one span will be carried by a number of pantoons on either side. This facilitates the design of pantoons. The spacing of pantoons is such that floating matter in the river should pass without causing damage, wider spacing of boats or pantoons make the bridge superstructure heavy and difficult to assemble. The pantoons or the boats must be anchored together so that alignment is maintained. Throughout the world army engineers are now opting for Krup-man brides made out of aluminium alloy section for transporting heavy fighting military equipment. A defense establishment at Ambazhari in Maharashtra is scheduled to manufacture these components.

Cause Ways

Bridges constructed with their decks flush or little above the bed of river are known as **causeways**, i.e. arish bridges or metal dips. These can be made in R.C.C. masonary and can carry light traffic even small amount of flood passes over the deck since its level is slightly above the bed stream. When the traffic on the communication route increases these have to be replaced by permanent bridges.

Circumstances for Causeways : These are :

1. Unimportant road and the crossing carrying practically no or little water for major part of year.
2. The floods if and when they occur are of small duration (3 days in a year).
3. Pauncity of funds.
4. Hilly region when many small streams have to be crossed.
5. Natural width of stream considerable.

Classification of Causeways : These are classified as :

1. High level causeway or vented causeway.
2. Low level causeway or Irish bridges.
3. Flush causeway or metal dips.

Whereas the high level causeway is a sort of permanent bridge the later two falls in the category of temporary bridges due to this comparative short life.

Flush Causeway

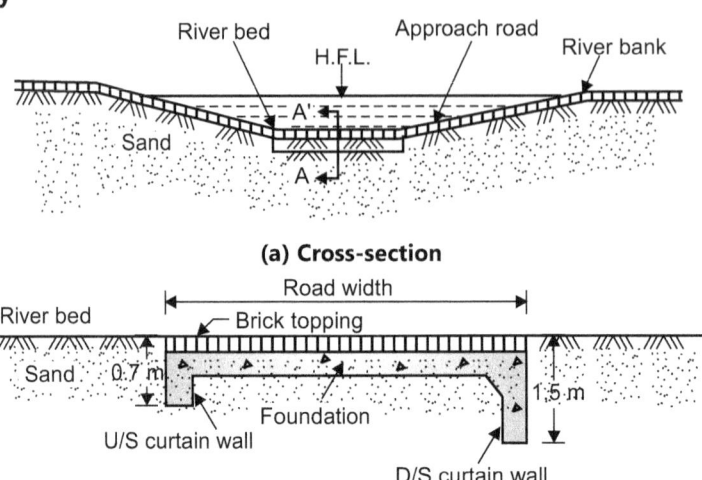

(a) Cross-section

(b) Enlareged section at A-A'

Fig. 14.21 : Flush causeways

In these structure, the bank of the stream is tailored to a gentle slope, and stream is paved for sufficient width on both sides of the causeway. The floor is flush with bed of the stream with no vents. In the most crude form it may be in the form of bundles of grass held in position by stakes across the sandy bed. When the floor is metallied, it is known as the metal dip. Sometimes R.C.C. slab may be provided in the stream bed for providing smooth surface Fig. 14.21 shows pictorial view of flush causeway. Many times curtain walls are constructed to prevent distress of causeway slab due to scour. Downstream side curtain wall may be 0.8 m deep than that u/s curtain wall which may be 0.7 m deep. The metal dips are good for non-perenial streams in hilly roads where flood duration is short and the river or stream water level in food is about 1.7 m.

See Fig. 14.22. low level causeway the those in which one or two vents are provided under the roadway slab so that small discharge may pass in dry reason and road deck is free of water. These causeway are called as Irish bridges. The level of the roadway near the stream bed is raised and 30-40 cm vents provided below roadway slab. During moderate discharge traffic is therefore undisturbed by flood of course high flood cannot be catered by Irish brides. Socur can be prevented by u/s and D/s curtain walls and an apron on D/s. Road pavement leading to Irish bridges are required to the made stable if bank to river bed slope is steep and approaches long. In such case cross dwarf walls are provided as shown. The low level causeways are good for shallow perennial rivers having a discharge depth of 30 to 45 cm depth for major part of the year and heavy discharge for only rainy season for a few hours only.

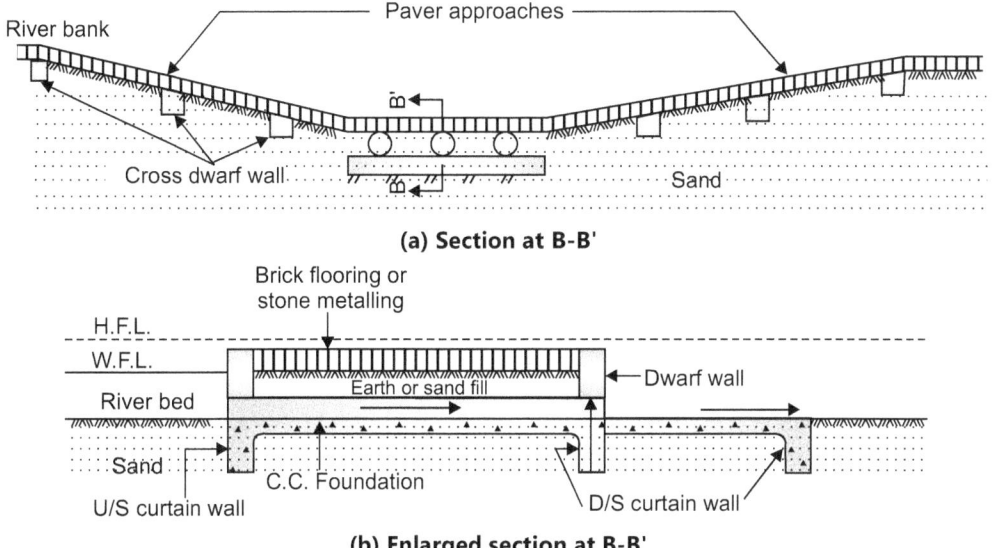

(a) Section at B-B'

(b) Enlarged section at B-B'

Fig. 14.22 : Low level causeway or Irish bridge

14.4 TIMBER BRIDGES

When the substructure and superstructure of a bridge made out of timber it may be called timber brides. Life of timber bridge may be 10-15 years even when painted.

14.4.1 Suitability and Limitations

In hilly areas where timber is plentry and cheap timber bridges may be adopted as a short term measure. During the time of constructing permanent bridge it may be used as diversion. At the most it can be used for B loading with no impact. Evidently these brides are not popular. Reasons are :

1. The present high cost of timber.
2. Ease with which timber can catch fire.
3. Non-uniform strength of timber.
4. Effect of environment on timber and the decay and disintegration caused by it and as such the short life associated with it.

14.4.2 Superstructure of Timber Bridges

The typical superstructure of the timber bridge is shown in Fig. 14.23. The floating would be 30 cm wide planks on longitudinal beams called bearers. If the span is more than 6 m, we have to use wood trusses in place of bearers. The details of wooden truss is also shown in the Fig.

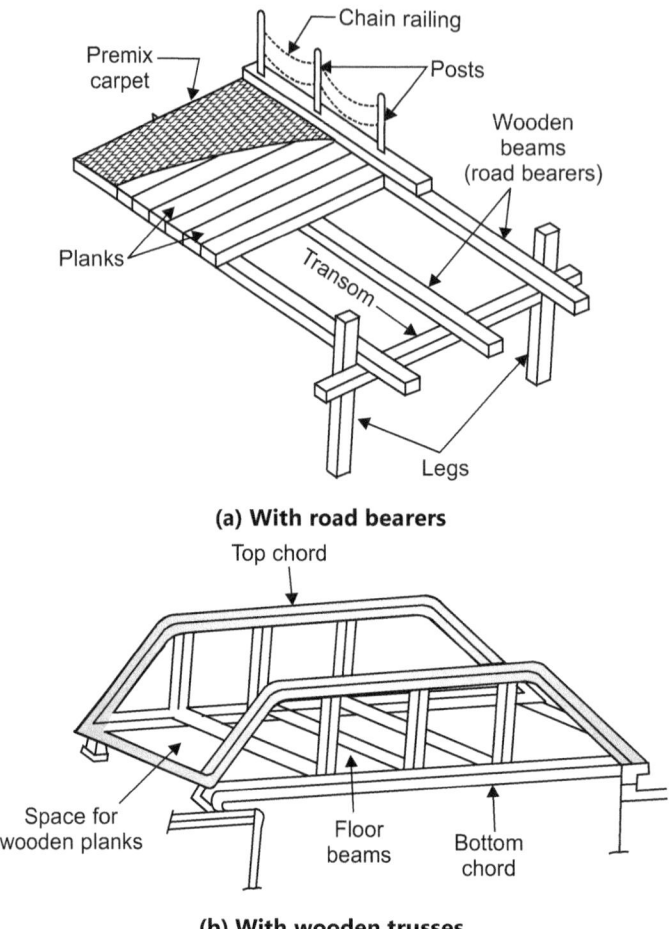

(a) With road bearers

(b) With wooden trusses

Fig. 14.23 : Superstructure of a timber

14.4.3 Substructure of Timber Bridges

In timber bridges the pairs and abutments also to be made out of timber. The piers and abutments could be timber pile-bent, timber crib or timber crate. The bridges are named accordingly.

(a) Timber Trestle Bridge

These trestles are shown in Fig. 14.24. They could be of square or round sections the spikes and nails being used to bind square section and ropes and steel wires being used to bind round sections. Two legged, three legged and four legged trestle are shown in Fig. 14.24.

When trestles an be used when the stream bed is hard and the velocity of water is not much.

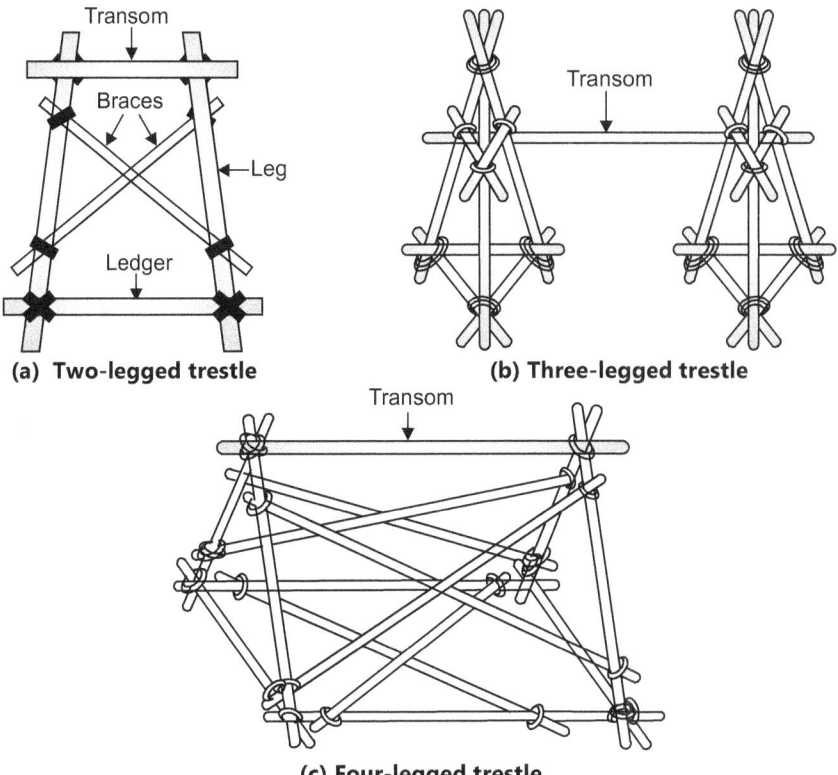

(a) Two-legged trestle   (b) Three-legged trestle

(c) Four-legged trestle

Fig. 14.24 : Different types of timber trestles

(b) Pile Bents

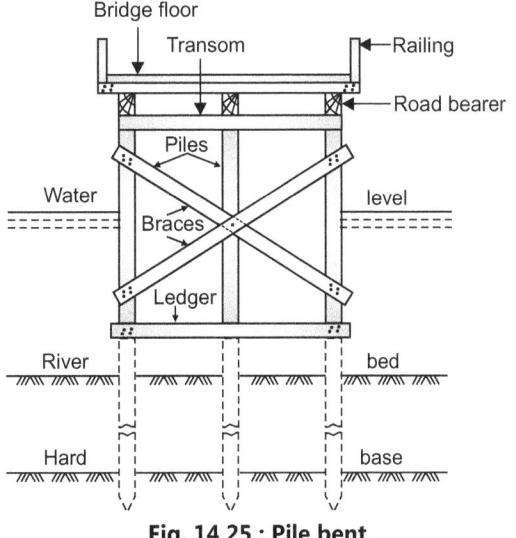

Fig. 14.25 : Pile bent

In this case two or three wood piles are driven vertically in a line about 1.2 meters away parallel to the axis of the stream. Piles are connected together at top by horizontal member called transom or capsill and braced together by diagonal members called braces. Pile may be kept in position by connecting their lower portion by a member called ledger. Older bridges had these pile bents. A typical bent is shown in Fig. 14.25. The bents may used for muddy streams.

(c) Cribs

Wooden sleepers placed in transverse direction alternatively in layers fastened together with ropes and bikes constitute crib. Different wood sections as are available at site may be used. Crib is construcuted on bank tower to the site and sunk by filling stones in the interior places, such that it is sufficiently heavy so as not to be washed away by running water. A typical crib is shown in Fig. 14.26. These could be used as piers and abutments.

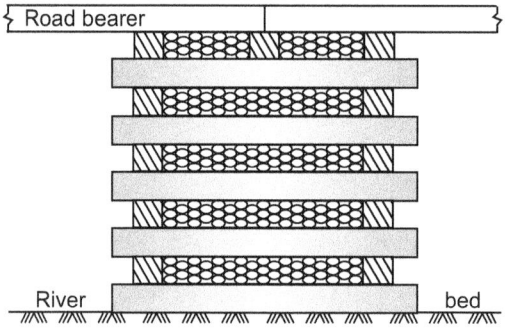

Fig. 14.26 : Crib pier

(d) Crates

Crates are generally used for piers. Each pier would consist of four vertical stout wood members called uprights connected to top and bottom as shown in the Fig. The bottom is generally planked for ease of towing. We may add an inclined pole to form cutwater. Fig. 14.27 shows the general arrangement. Crate is prepared on the bank towed to site of pier and sunk by filling the inter space by brushwood and stones. Crates an take heavy load.

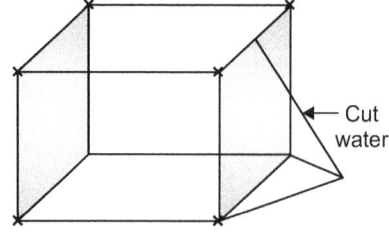

Fig. 14.27 : Crate pier

14.4.4 Timber Cantilever Bridges

These bridges generally are made of timber logs laid in layers projecting beyond the underlying layer from each bank. Fig. 14.28 illustrates these bridges. Each timber section projects around 1.5 m to 3 m beyond the underlying layer. The middle gap of about 4-6 meter is bridged by the road bearer and then the flooring is completed. All timber sections are anchored together by spikes and buried in dry stone masonary of the abutment. Wire stays can be provided to this bridge to carry moderate traffic. The bridge is suitable when foundation condition of the river bed is poor so that testle bents can not be erected. These bridges are O.K. when velocity of running water is high since there is no obstruction to the river flow in these of bridges. In hilly regions where timber logs are somewhat spans upto 50 m have bridged by this type of bridges.

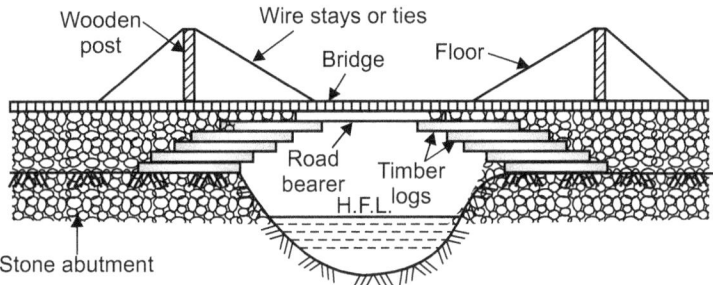

Fig. 14.28 : Cantilever bridge

14.4.5 Suspension Bridges

When two or more cables hang in space and support the roadway it is a suspension bridge. The suspension bridge could be of the following types :

(a) Trestle Suspension Bridge

See Fig. 14.29. In this case, the roadway is supported on trestles which in turn in supported by cable which are well anchored. Compared to the sway of suspension bridge, this type less sway, but it is very heavy and costly.

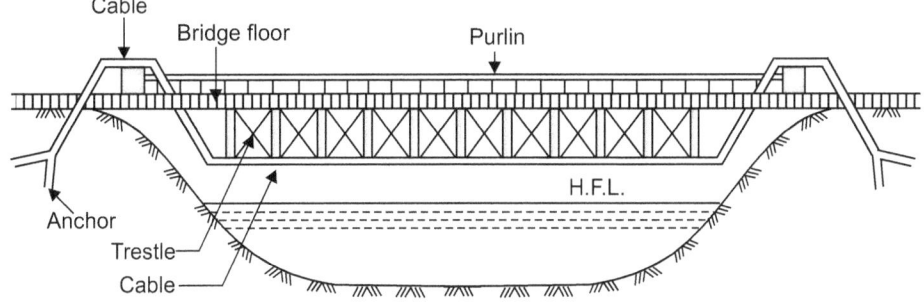

Fig. 14.29 : Trestle suspension bridge

(b) Sling Bridge

See Fig. 14.30. It consists of two sets of cables which carry the roadway through suspenders known as slings.

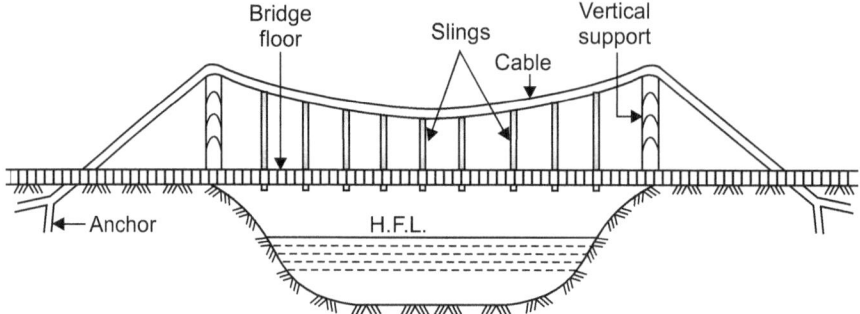

Fig. 14.30 : Sling type suspension bridge

The roadway may be wooden planks connected at ends to the wooden transom beams hung by suspenders from the cables or ropes. The cables generally pass over the vertical towers and then these are safely anchored in the bed.

(c) Ramp Bridge

See Fig. 14.31. This bridge requires less quantity of material and can be constructed in short duration. Here the roadway would be generally wooden planks directly laid on rectangular pattern of cables. The longitudinal cable is supported on two vertical posts erected on each bank. Naturally with the movement of traffic the roadway is distorted and suffers sway.

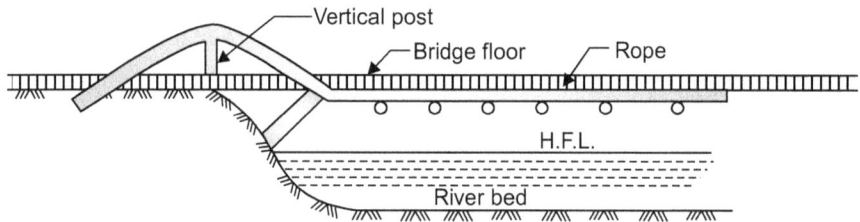

Fig. 14.31 : Ramp suspension bridge

14.5 MOVABLE BRIDGE

Movable bridges are those which can be somehow change position or moved so as to open a clear passage for ships or boats. There are many different kind of movable bridges- grouped according to the manner in which they open. It may be a swing bridge, double swing span bridge or others are bascule and vertical lift type. Another useful movable bridge is Pontoon, a floating bridge form. These are generally in military use and an essential part of army equipment. Movable bridges are operated by electrical and mechanical machinery, so its responsibility of bridge engineer to oversee the design of mechanical equipment along with bridge design.

14.6 MOVABLE STEEL BRIDGES

It is not always possible to construct the bridge superstructure at such a level that navigational ships can pass below bridge superstructure during high floods. On such rivers, bridge might the designed so that one or two spans of the superstructure can be moved out of position whenever required for passage of ships, steamers or boats. Movable steel bridges can be classified as temporary bridges, because these can be put out of use whenever required. But it must be remembered that the life span of movable steel bridge is considerable. These bridges may be

14.6.1 Swing Bridges

In this type of bridge superstructure, it can be rotated in a horizontal plane on vertical axis. It is generally a balanced girder carrying the flooring supported at its ends on abutment tops, and in the centre on an intermediate pier, provided usually with disc bearing. The schematic diagram is in Fig. 14.32. When the steamer wants to navigate the river, the superstructure is rotated through an angle of 90° by means of mechanical or electrical power which is provided on the intermediate pier, where the disc bearing is located. When the ship has passed, the bridge is brought back to its original position to allow the traffic to pass on it.

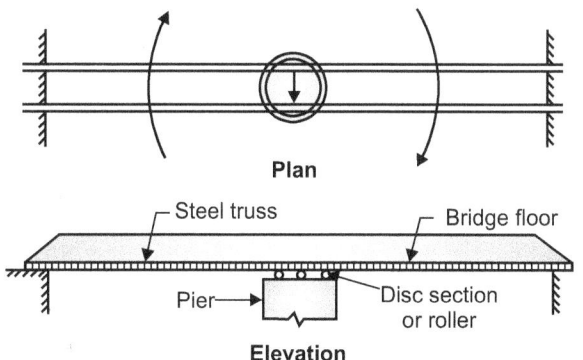 

Fig. 14.32 : Swing bridge

14.6.2 Traverser Bridge (See Fig. 14.45)

In this type the superstructure is a balanced framework in the form of steel truss which carries the bridge floor on its bottom chord. The superstructure can be rolled back wards and forwards a cross the opening so that sufficient gap can be created for the ship to pass unobstructed. Rollers are provided under the bridge superstructure on one of the banks for this purpose. The movement of the bridge is by manual means of electrical power.

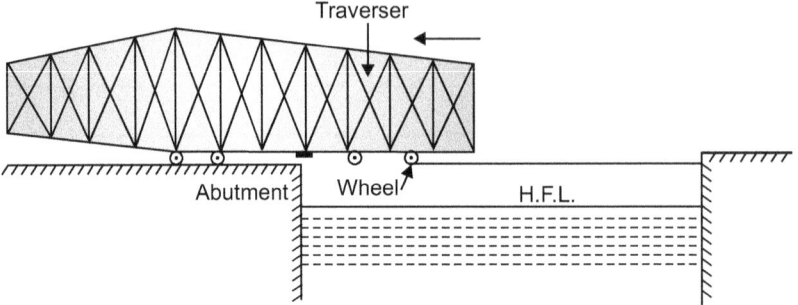

Fig. 14.33 : Traverser bridge

14.6.3 Transporter Bridge

Here we have solid or open type steel girder resting on top of two high towers which are provided on each bank. The girder supports the travelling cage or cradle through suspension cables as shown. The travelling cage can move from one bank to the other generally through the use of electrical power. This type of bridge is for transportation of materials rather than men since the capacity of cage has to be limited.

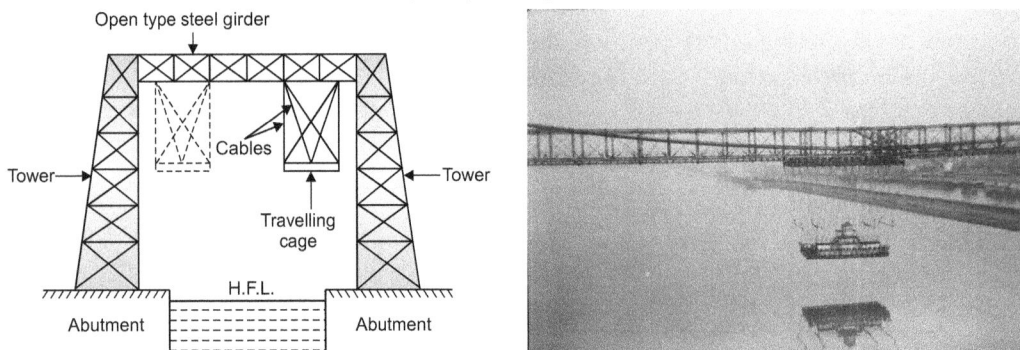

Fig. 14.34 : Transporter bridge

14.6.4 Bascule Bridge

In this type, the superstructure can be moved vertically on a horizontal hinge. See Fig. 14.35. The hinge is provided on the abutment. The bridge could be called single leaf or double leaf, according to the span of the bridge. For short span of the bridge. For short span single leaf bridge and for long spans double leaf bascule Leaf Bridge is commended. The arrangement may be such that the bridge can be countered weighted at ends and raised or lowered by rack and pinion arrangement shown in Fig. 14.35. When the bridge is lowered, the counter weights provided lowers into the pit called bascule chamber.

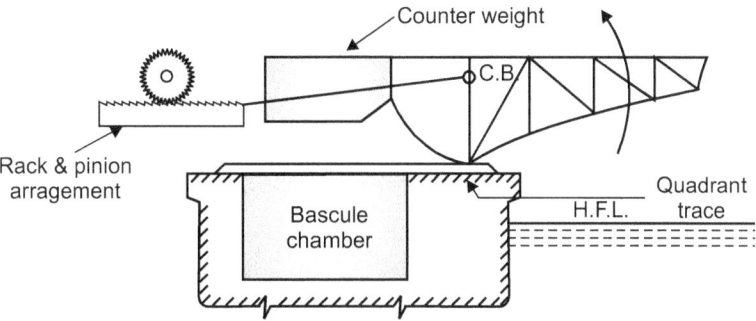

(a) Single leaf Bascule Bridge

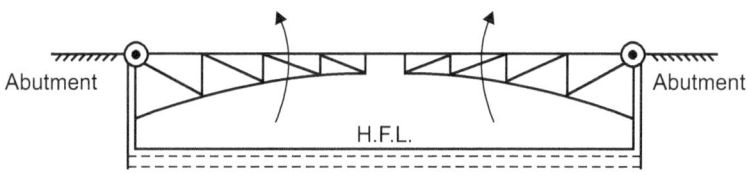

(b) Double leaf bascule bridge

Fig. 14.35 : Types of bascule bridge

Fig. 14.36 : Single leaf bascule bridge

Fig. 14.37 : Double leaf bascule bridge

14.6.5 Life Bridge

There are two towers on each bank. The tops of towers are connected by overhead span. This gives more rigidity to the structure. In between the two towers a main span carrying the bridge floor is provided. This main span can be lifted by means of cables which pass over sheaves fixed on the towers, when the ship is to be passed across. Lift bridge is generally not recommended.

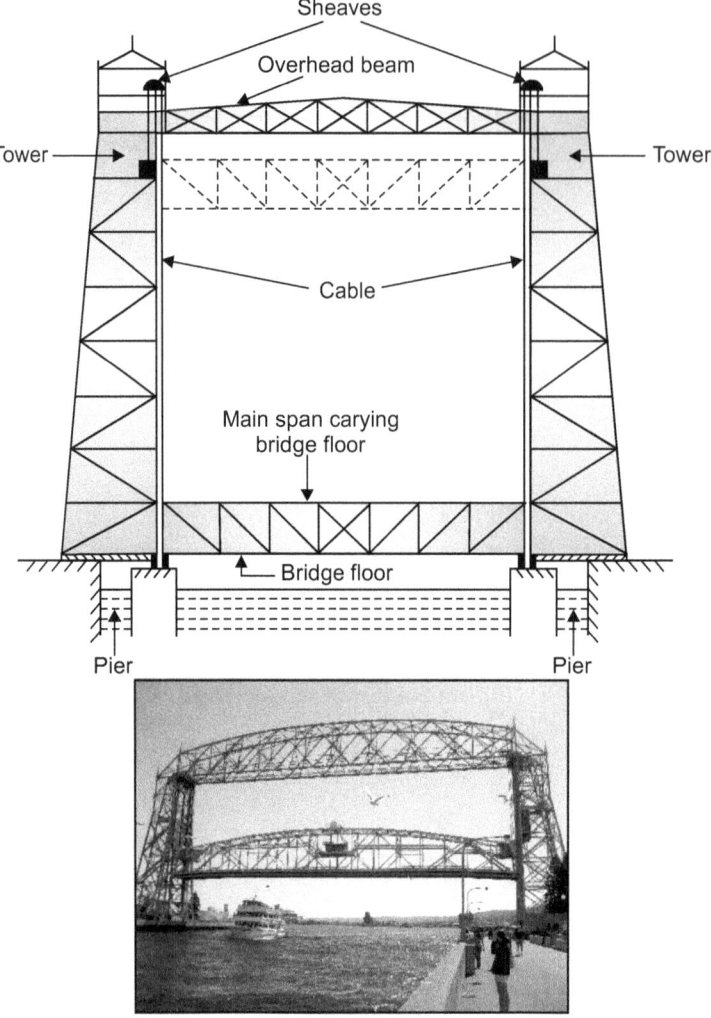

Fig. 14.38 : Lift bridge

14.7 OTHER TEMPORARY BRIDGE SUPERSTRUCTURES/BRIDGES

It is not only the army which is required to construct temporary bridges. This may be due to paucity of funds or as a short term measure. We have over here the following types.

(A) Flying Bridges

In this case a boat or a raft is used as a ferry. The ferry boats which either rowed or pulled across are termed as flying bridges. We can guide the ferry by the following three methods.

1. Suspension Cable

Here a cable is suspended on the river. Cable is supported on two vertical towers tone on each bank such that cable will be above H.F.L. Cable carries a traveler which in term is attached to a boat by two cables. The length of these two cables is such that the boat makes an angle of 45° to the river current. the traveler is to be pulled by which or manpower from either bank thus transporting the ferry from one bank to the other. See Fig. 14.39.

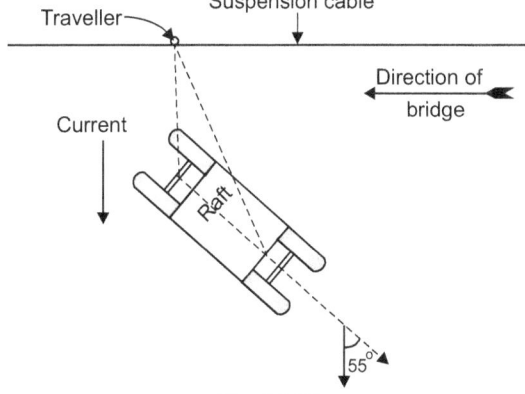

Fig. 14.39

2. Using Anchors and Switching Cables

In this case a cable in the centre of bridge and along the river line is laid. One end of the cable is supported on a float or casks and is anchored to the river bed. The other end is connected to the ferry in such a way that ferry always makes an angle of 45° to the river current. The cable is slack between ferry and the anchorage and is about $1\frac{1}{2}$ times the breadth of river. In this method the men in the boat actually row the boat from one bank to the other and the use of cable is to keep the angle around 55° and give extra support. See Fig. 14.40.

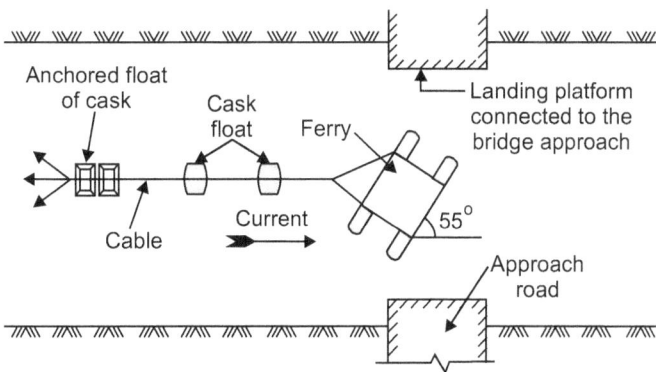

Fig. 14.40 : Drying bridge with anchors and swinging cables

3. Using a Warp or Cable with Rollers

In this method cable is erected on two vertical towers one on each bank. Instead of the traveler in the first method we have here rollers fixed on the raft and the cable moves through the rollers. By moving the roller from the bank to the other, transportation is achieved.

(B) Cut-Boat Bridges

The cut-boat is also a type of floating bridge. It is employed when you want some portion of river navigable, to allow the boat traffic to pass. Therefore, one or more bays of the floating bridge are made movable. The movable bays are to be constructed into an independent raft which is allowed to float downstream during the time river is used for navigation purposes. See Fig. 14.41.

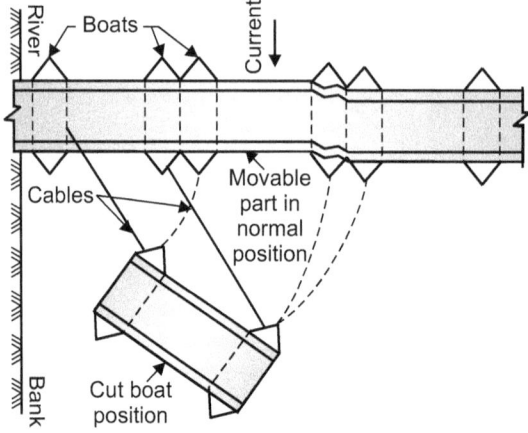

Fig. 14.41 : Cut-boat bridge

REVIEW QUESTIONS

1. Give detail classification of bridges stating clearly on which these depend?
2. Discuss the various forces coming over bridge pier and also state the conditions of stability.
3. Sketch the different types of abutments.
4. Sketch the different types of wing walls.
5. Sketch the different types of piers.
6. Describe the various types of foundations to piers and abutments.
7. Mention the different types of wing walls and explain them with neat sketches.
8. What are the advantages and disadvantage of Temporary Bridges?
9. Enlist various classifications of Temporary Bridges.
10. Write notes on
    - (a) Superstructure of Bridges
    - (b) Sub-Structures of Bridges
    - (c) Temporary Bridges
    - (d) Movable Bridges
    - (e) causeways
    - (f) timber bridges
    - (g) suspension bridges
    - (h) Floating bridges
    - (i) Movable bridges

CHAPTER 15
BRIDGES BEARINGS AND FOUNDATION

15.1 INTRODUCTION

The devices which are provided over the supports of bridge to accommodate the changes in the main girders due to deflection, temperature, vertical movement due to sinking of the supports, shrinkage, prestressing creep etc. and to transmit the load from the superstructure to the substructure are within permissible limits are known as the bearings. Thus, the bearings are provided for the distribution of the load evenly over the substructure material which may not have sufficient bearing strength to bear or take-up the load of superstructure directly.

In this chapter, some of the salient features of this important component of the bridge structure will be discussed.

15.2 FUNCTIONS OF BEARINGS

- To allow for the longitudinal movement of the bridge deck and the girder due to variation in temperature. This movement takes place in steel R.C.C. or prestressed bridges and it is the job of bearings to allow for it.
- Rotation at supports due to breaking. The knowledge of applied mechanism tells us that under the action of load, the bridge girder deflects and this results in angular movement over the supports. The bearings which are provided at the end must also rotates so that there is uniform distribution of bearing pressure.
- Transference of horizontal forces. The application of breaking force induces a horizontal force which can be transmitted to the substructure by the use of bearings.
- To allow some vertical movement due to sinking of foundations.

15.2.1 Purposes of Bearings

Following are the purposes or objects of providing bearings in a bridge :
- To absorb movements of girder,
- To allow for angular movements of girder due to deflection under the load,
- To allow for longitudinal expansion or contraction due to changes in the temperature,
- To distribute the load on a large area,
- To keep the compressive stress within safe limits,
- To make movements of girder harmless,
- To rotate at supports to accommodate the deflection of a simply supported girder under load,
- To simplify the procedure in design.

- To take up the vertical movement due to sinking of the support,
- To transfer horizontal forces developed due to application of brakes to the vehicles etc.

15.2.2 Importance of Bearings

It should be remembered that the successful functioning of a bridge primarily depends on the design of its bearings. It is observed that faulty design or improper working of the bearings in the main cause of failure of many bridges that have collapsed. The design of bearing to be adopted for a particular bridge will mainly depend on the type of supports, length of the span and the type of superstructure.

The bearings form an important component of a bridge and hence, extreme care and skill should be exercised in its design, execution and maintenance. For major bridges, the cost of bearings roughly works out to about 10 to 15 per cent of the total cost of the bridge. Hence, there is ample scope of achieving economy by designing the bearings properly and carefully.

15.3 WHY ONE BEARINGS IS FIXED AND THE OTHER FREE

Generally for each span, one end of the supporting girder is kept fixed and the other free. The reason is the free end of the girder allows movement in the longitudinal direction. This movement may be due to temperature, tractive force etc. If this is not done internal excessive stresses will be generated in the girder.

15.4 BEARING FOR STEEL GIRDER BRIDGES

These are
(1) Fixed bearing
(2) Expansion bearings.

15.5 FIXED BEARINGS

Here we have :

(a) **Shallow or Fixed Plate Bearing :** Her in between the lower flange of the girder and the pier or abutment we have flat rectangular steel plate which is anchored to the girder on one hand and to the bridge pier on another hand through two anchor bolts. See Fig. 15.1 (a). Suitable upto 12 m span.

(b) **Deep Cast Base Bearing :** Here instead of shallow plate, we have deep cast base on one hand attached to the bridge girder and on other hand anchored to pier. Because of the depth of bearing, stress concentration is less and suitable for 12 to 16 m span. See Fig. 15.1 (b).

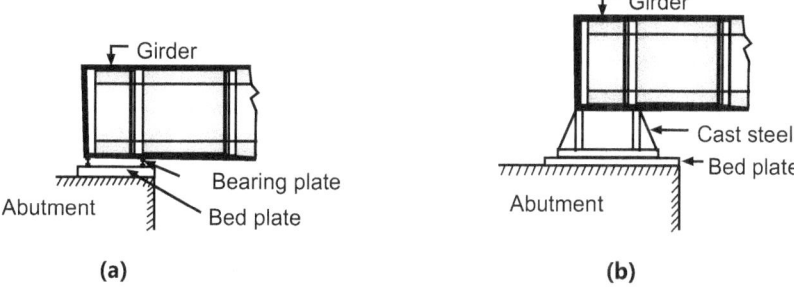

Fig. 15.1

(c) **Rocker Bearing :** Here the steel girder had a top inverted shoe and the abutment or pier has a depression shoe. In between these, rocker pin is inserted, with the deflection of the girder, the top inverted, shoe rotates, over the pin and this allows free angular movement of girder. See Fig. 15.2 (a).

(d) **Knuckle Bearing :** In this case, there is no rocker pin. The bottom shoe which is anchored to the pier or abutment is formed in the shape of hemisphere on which top shoe can rotates. Thus there is no rocker pin. Bearing is good for 20 m to 30 m. See Fig. 15.2 (b).

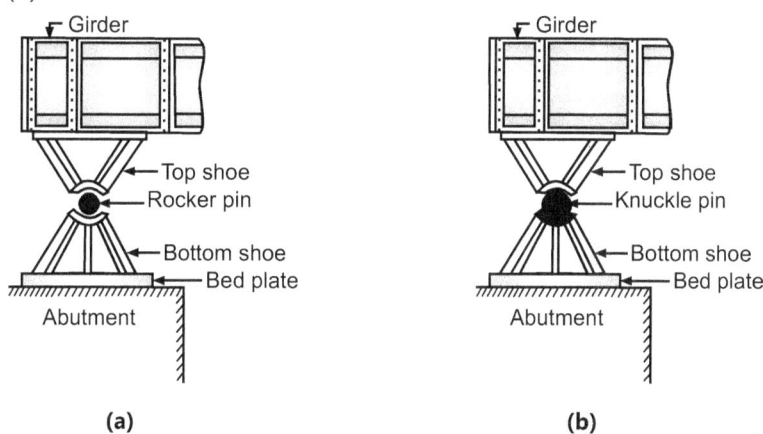

Fig. 15.2

15.6 EXPANSION BEARINGS

These bearings allow longitudinal movement of the bridge girder and hence are called as expansion or free bearing. The general practice is to give one fixed bearing at one end of the bridge, the other end of the bridge girder being provided with expansion bearing so that the expansion or the contraction of the bridge girder due to variations in temperatures in allowed for. These bearings could be

(a) Sliding plate bearing.

(b) Deep cast base curved plate bearing.

(c) Rocker bearing with curved base.

(d) Rocker and roller bearing.

(a) **Sliding Plate Bearing :** In this case, there is a slotted plate which is attached to underside of the girder. The slotted plate rests on bed plate which is anchored to the pier or abutment. The joint between bed plate and slotted plate is through iron bolts which are well anchored to the bed plate and go through the slots of sliding slotted plate. Because of the gap thus provided by slots the horizontal movement of girder is possible. Suitable for 12 to 20 m span. See Fig. 15.3 (a).

(b) **Deep Cast Base with Curved Plate Bearing :** In this case, deep case base with curved bed plate is anchored to the bridge pier/abutment as shown. The sole plate which is anchored to the underside of the girder rests on this deep cast base curved base plate. Because of the spherical shape of the curved bed plate, the girder is allowed some longitudinal and some rotational movement. See Fig. 15.3 (b). The bearing may be O.K. for 12 to 20 m.

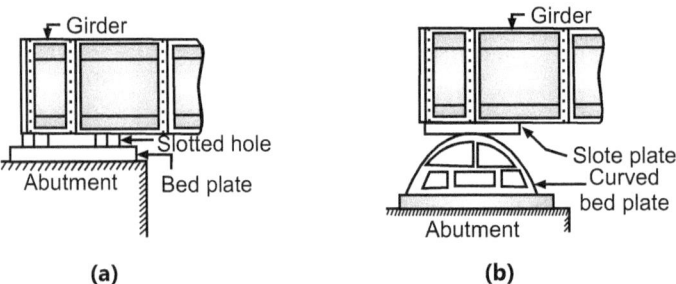

Fig. 15.3

(c) **Rocker Bearing with curved Bottom Base :** See Fig. 15.4 (a). In this case the bottom shoe is provided with curved bottom. Thus offering lessened resistance to the longitudinal movement of the girder. The horizontal force generated because of the restraint put on this movement is thus lessened. Suitable for 12 to 20 m span.

(d) **Rocker and Roller Bearing :** See Fig. 15.4 (b). This is essentially a rocker bearing with bottom shoe resting on number of steel rollers which in turn roll on honey combed bed plate (i.e. bed plate which is not very smooth). This bed plate is anchored to pier to abutment. Free longitudinal and rotational movement is thus allowed for. The general practice is to install rocker bearing one end and rocker and roller bearing on the other end of the bridge girder. In such case the bearing can be used for spans more than 20 m.

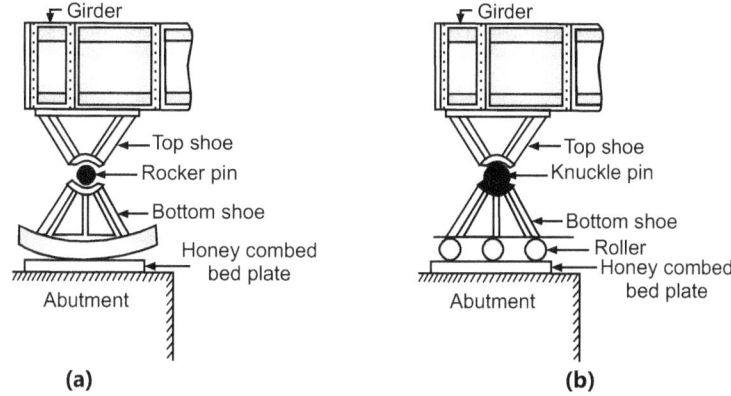

Fig. 15.4

(e) **Bearings for Each and Suspension Bridge :** Arch and suspension bridge require inclined bearings. These are illustrated in (Fig. 15.5).

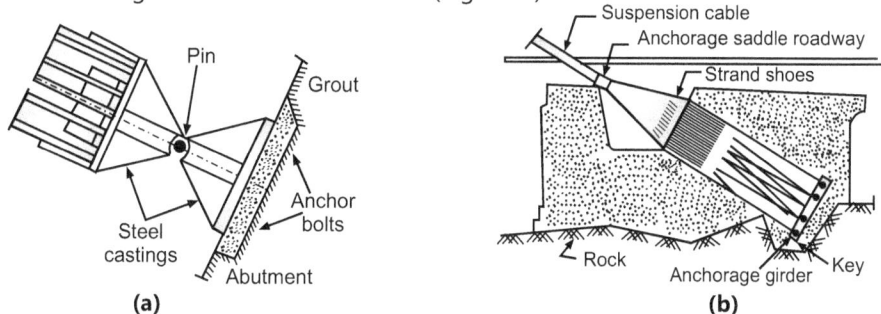

Fig. 15.5

15.7 EMPLOYMENT OF METALLIC BEARINGS

For different span lengths, different bearings are generally recommended for steel bridges. The following guidelines may be followed in such a case.
- Simply supported spans less than 8 m, only a bituminous layer or paper (which should be impregnated with tar and bitumen) may be interposed between the supporting member and the superstructure.
- Simply supported spans 8 to 16 m and for floating spans resting on abutments/piers, sliding plate bearing at free end and fixed plate bearing with curvature in the top plate could be recommended.
- Simply supported span 16 to 24 m and for suspended units of balanced cantilever construction of spans not more than 16 m, rocker roller bearing and free end and fixed plate bearing with curvature in the top plate at the fixed support.
- Simply supported spans more than 24 m and suspended units of balanced cantilever construction spans more than 16 m, rocker roller bearings at the expansion support (free end) and rocker or knuckle bearings at the fixed support.

15.8 BEARINGS FOR CONCRETE BRIDGES

Here we have the following types of bearings :

15.8.1 Bearings for Slab Bridges

See (15.6). Here we have several layers of tar paper placed between bridge slab and the capping slab of pier or abutment. The provision of paper is to prevent bending between abutment and slab. The abutment or pier or the capping slab of the abutment or pier is rounded so that slight rotational movement of bridge girder is possible. For spans upto 8 m the bearings function nicely. For such bridges, one support of the slab has to be dowelled and the other end is to be kept free. For single span, slab bridges, downelling has to be dowelled at abutments, but for pipe no dowelling need be done. While the case of multispan bridge dowelling be done to abutment and alternate piers and bearings on the remaining piers be kept undowelled.

Fig. 15.6

The bearings for the slab may be classed as fixed end and free end bearing. These details are shown in Fig. 15.7 (a) and (b). The bearings which restrain expansion but permit rotation are fixed end bearings. These are shown in Fig. 15.7 (a). Here we provide a lead sheet of 3 mm thickness. Due to deformation of lead sheet, rotation movement is possible but not free expansion. For concrete bridges more than 8 m span, there is considerable rotational movement and these bearings are good for such cases. Free end bearing allow for free movement, these are shown in Fig. 15.7 (b) and suitable upto 8 m span.

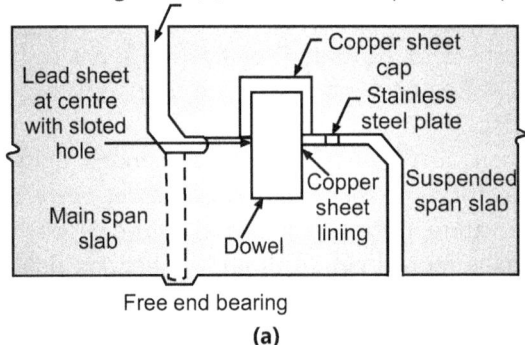

Free end bearing
(a)

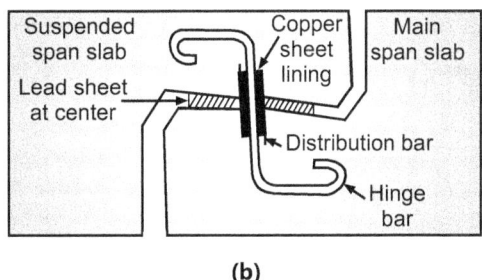

(b)

Fig. 15.7

15.8.2 Bearings for Concrete Girder Bridge

Here we have

(a) Fixed Plate Bearing : See Fig. 15.8 (a). Here we have two mild steel plates bearing on one another with flat machined surfaces, the top plate being anchored to the girder and the bottom plate being anchored to the pier through capping slab. Generally a few mild steel rods are provided as shown for dowelling the girder to the capping slab after cutting through top mild steel plate. There may be lead sheet between two m.s. plaes which equalize the bearing pressure and allows may be slight rotation. For spans of 8 to 16 m, these bearings can transmit to the substructure the lateral force that might be induced due to variation in temperature and the tractive force.

(b) Sliding Plate Bearing : See (Fig. 15.8 (b)). These are essentially expansion bearings. Here we have the slope plate attached to the underside of the girder which can slide over another plate which is well anchored to the capping slab of abutment or pier. A thin lead sheet can be provided in between the two m.s. plate to improve the efficiency of bearing. These bearings allow free expansion or contraction of girders due to temperature variation and can also allow slight rotation, good for spans of 8 m to 16 m.

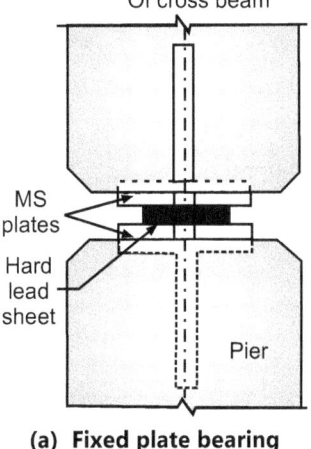

(a) Fixed plate bearing

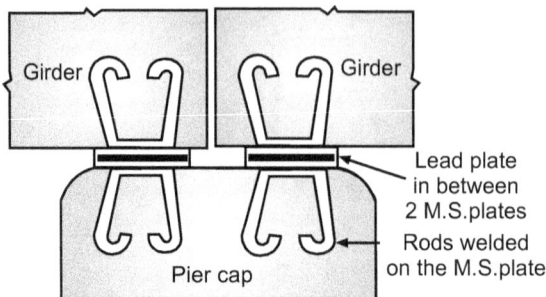

(b) Sliding plate bearing
Fig. 15.8

(c) **Sliding Plate Bearing with Curved Top Plate :** Here we have curved sole plate attached to the underside plate to allow longitudinal and rotational movement. The constructional details are same as sliding plate bearing as above. Good for 8 m to 20 m span.

(d) **Free Bearings :** These are essentially roller bearing with a Kunckle pin or a rocker pin as discussed for steel bridges. Instead of steel girder we have concrete girder here. Rollers could be case or mild steel the latter is preferable. Good for span of 20 to 27 m.

15.9 BEARINGS FOR SUBMERSIBLE BRIDGES

In case of bearings provided in the submersible bridges, these bearing get submerged when the river is in spate. There is also a possibility that due to the velocity of flowing water, or due to the impact of objects floating in the river, the bridge may slide, specially since bridge slab weight is not very heavy.

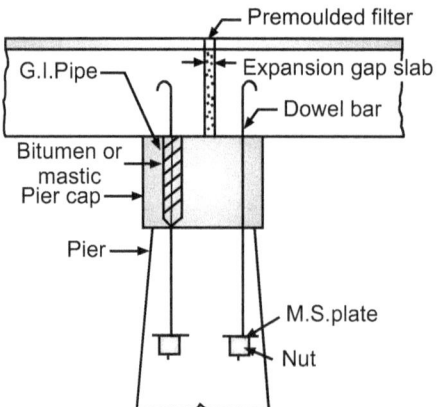

Fig. 15.9 : Bearing for a submersible bridge

Therefore, in the case of submerisible bridges which are generally minor bridges of small span the slab should be anchored to the sub-structure below. For such provision, when the slab is anchored, the longitudinal expansion or contraction of the bridge slab due to temperature variation should be catered for by inserting a dowel bar through a pipe filled with bitumen or mastic as shown in the Fig. 15.9.

For small submerisible bridges, two plate sliding bearing at the free end and two plate bearing at the fixed end be provided. In order that rusting should not take place, the material of the bearing should be copper alloy or stainless steel.

15.10 Bearings for Continuous Span Bridges

When the total length of continuous span does not increase 14 m no bearings need to given. Between the supporting members i.e. pier and the superstructure several leavers of tar paper or a laver of bearing may be as in Fig. 15.10. For this arrangement AC is the span which is maximum affected by temperature charge. The following guidelines may help in installing bearing for continuous bridges.

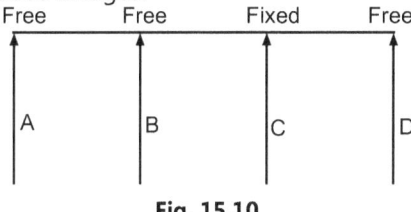

Fig. 15.10

1. **Continuous Span 7 to 26 m :** Sliding plate bearing on free support and fixed plate bearing with curvature in the top plate at the fixed support.
2. **16 m to 24 m Continuous Spans :** Metallic roller bearings over the free supports and fixed plate bearings with curvature in the top plate at fixed supports.
3. **Spans More than 24 m :** Metallic roller bearings at free support and metallic rocker bearings at the fixed support.

15.11 The I.R.C. Provisions for Bearings

The bridges code classifies the bearings as metallic and elastomeric.

15.12 Metallic Bearings

These could be :
1. **Sliding Bearing :** A type of bearing where sliding movement is permitted between two surfaces. Fig. 15.11.
2. **Rocker Bearing :** A type of bearing where no sliding movement is permitted but which allows rotational movement. Fig. 15.12.

3. **Sliding-Cum Rocker Bearing :** A type of bearing where, in addition to the sliding movement either the top or bottom plate is provided with suitable curvature to permit rotation.
4. **Roller Cum-Rocker Bearing :** A type of bearing which permits longitudinal movement by rolling and simultaneously allows rotational movement. See Figs. 15.13 and 15.14.

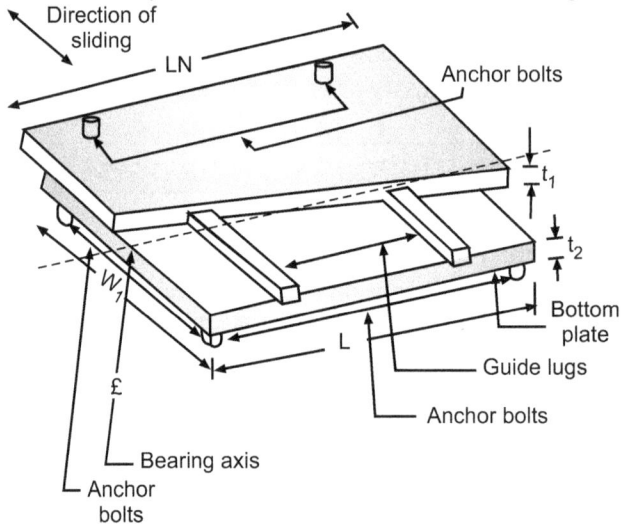

Fig. 15.11 : Sliding bearing

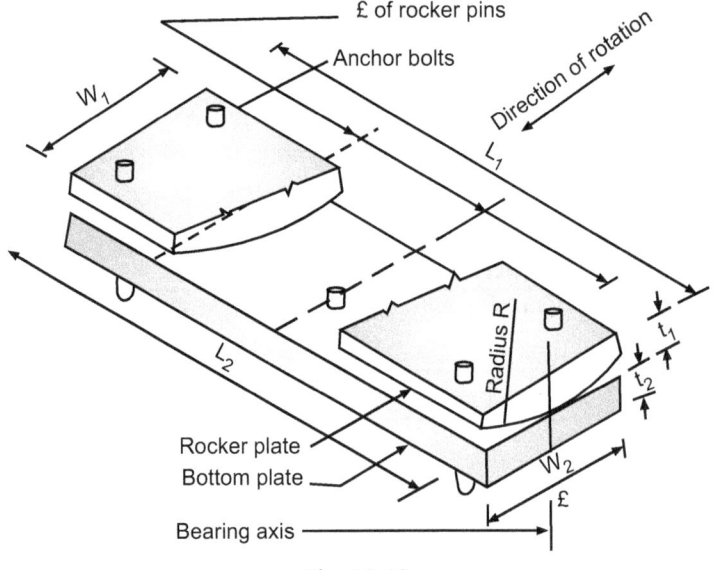

Fig. 15.12

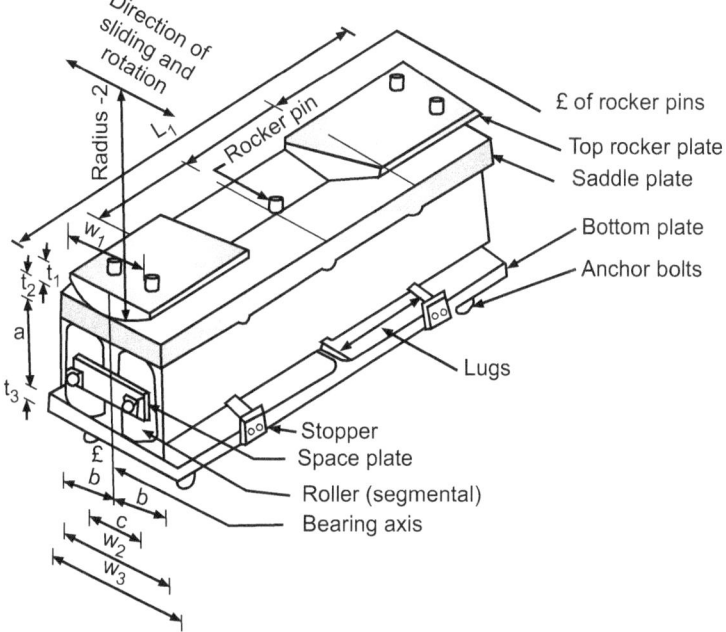

Fig. 15.13 : Roller rocker bearing (with segmental roller)

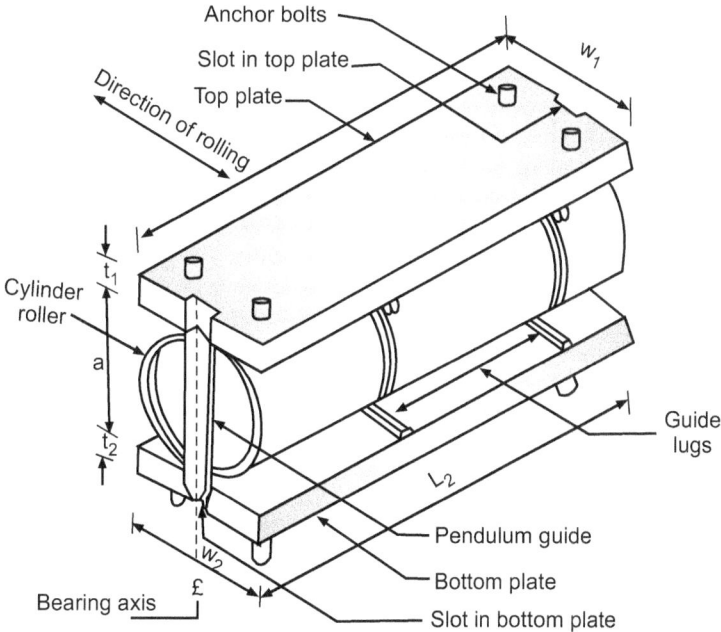

Fig. 15.14 : Roller-cum-rocker bearing with slots to guide movement of roller

15.13 PARTS OF METALLIC BEARING

These are :

1. **Top Plate :** A plate which is attached to the underside of the structure and which transmits all the forces from it to the other members of the bearing.

2. **Saddle Plate :** A plate which is positioned between the top plate and the rollers.

3. **Roller :** A part of bearing which rolls between a top plate and a bottom plate or between a saddle plate and a bottom plate. The roller may either cylinder or segmental.

4. **Bottom Plate :** A plate which rests on the supporting structure and transmits forces from the baring to the supporting structure.

5. **Kunckle Pin :** A cylindrical pin provided between recesses of the top and bottom parts of a bearing for arresting relative sliding movement of the top and bottom parts without restriction rotational movement.

6. **Knuckle :** A recess in the surface of the bottom/saddle plate or top plate housing a knuckle pin preventing relative movement between two plates without restricting rotational movement.

7. **Rocker Pin :** A lug on the surface of the bottom plate or saddle plate which fit into corresponding clear recess made in the top plate to prevent relative movement of the two plates without restricting rotational movement. Fig. 15.13.

8. **Guide :** A projection on the surface of bottom plate, top plate or saddle plate, which fits into a corresponding clear recess made in the rollers, to maintain their alignment.

9. **Stopper :** A projection provided in the bottom plate, to arrest the roller from moving beyond the bottom plate.

10. **Anchor Bolts :** A rag bolt or ordinary bolt anchoring the top and bottom plates to the structure.

11. **Spacer Bar :** A bar loosely fixed at each end of a roller assembly for connecting the individual rollers in a nest and to facilitate movement of rollers in unison.

12. **Free Support/Free Bearings :** A support/bearing which permits the free relative movement of the parts of the structure.

13. **Fixed Support/Fixed Bearing :** A support/bearing which prevents the translational movement of the relative parts of the structure.

14. **Bearing Axis :** The symmetrical axis of the bearing.

15. Effective Displacement : The total relative movement between the structures in contact with the bearing.

15.14 ROCKER AND ROLLER-CUM-ROCKER BEARINGS

- **Top, Saddle and Bottom Plates** be symmetrical to the bearing axis.

- The width of plates shall not be less than either of the following :

  (i) 100 mm or

  (ii) The distance between the centre to centre distance of outermost rollers (where applicable) plus twice the effective displacement during service or twice the thickness of the plate plus 10 mm as margin for error in sitting. (The centre to centre distance of outermost rollers if these is two or more. For single roller bearing shall be taken as zero). See Fig. 15.15.

- The thickness of the plate shall not be less than (i) 20 mm or (ii) $1/4^{th}$ the distance between consecutive lines of contact, whichever is higher.

- The thickness of the plate shall also be checked, based on the contact stresses arrived at accounting for the actual width of the plate provided, to satisfy the requirements of structural design and permissible stresses as laid down in code.

- **Rollers :** The minimum diameter of roller shall be 75 mm.

- The ratio of the length of the roller to its diameter shall normally not be more than 6 but not more than 10 m any case.

- The effective contact length with the plate shall be used for arriving at the length of the rollers to be used in the formula given.

- The gap between the rollers shall not be less than 5 mm in case of multiple full rollers.

- Preferably cylindrical rollers shall be used. In case segmental rollers are used, diameter for such rollers shall exceed 250 mm.

- The width of segmental rollers shall be at least half the diameter of the roller or four times the effective displacement of the bearings, whichever is more.

- The gap between the segmental rollers shall not be less than 0.1 d, where 'd' is the diameter of the roller.

- Wherever single segmental roller is used, it shall be provided with vertical guide plate. When two or more segmental rollers are used, necessary shall be made to ensure positive.

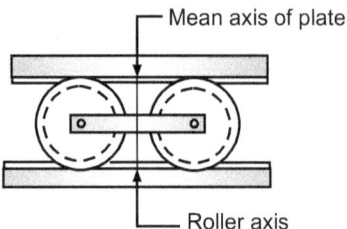

Fig. 15.15

15.15 SLIDING BEARINGS

- Sliding plate bearings along with their components shall be composed of one metal or a combination of different metals which are not likely to result in electrolytic action. However sliding bearings with mild steel contact shall be avoided.
- The top plates shall project on all sides over the bottom plate by at least 10 mm for any extreme position of the bearing.
- The thickness of the plate shall satisfy the requirements of structural design and permissible stresses laid down in but shall not be less than 12 mm.

15.16 ELASTOMERIC BEARINGS

Now-a-days there is more emphasis to provide elastomeric bearings. These do not rust.

Laminated rectangular free elastomeric bearings as shown in Fig. 15.16 are in common use in road bridges. These should satisfy the following requirements.

- Internal layers of elastomer should be of equal thickness having elastomer cover on top, bottom and sides and the entire bearing vulcanized as single homogeneous block.
- Top and bottom of elastomer should bear directly on structure face. There should be no adhesive or other external and choring device in between.
- No dowel holes in elastomer and laminate be provided including those filled in subsequently.
- In general, special elastomeric bearings to be used for subzero temperature.

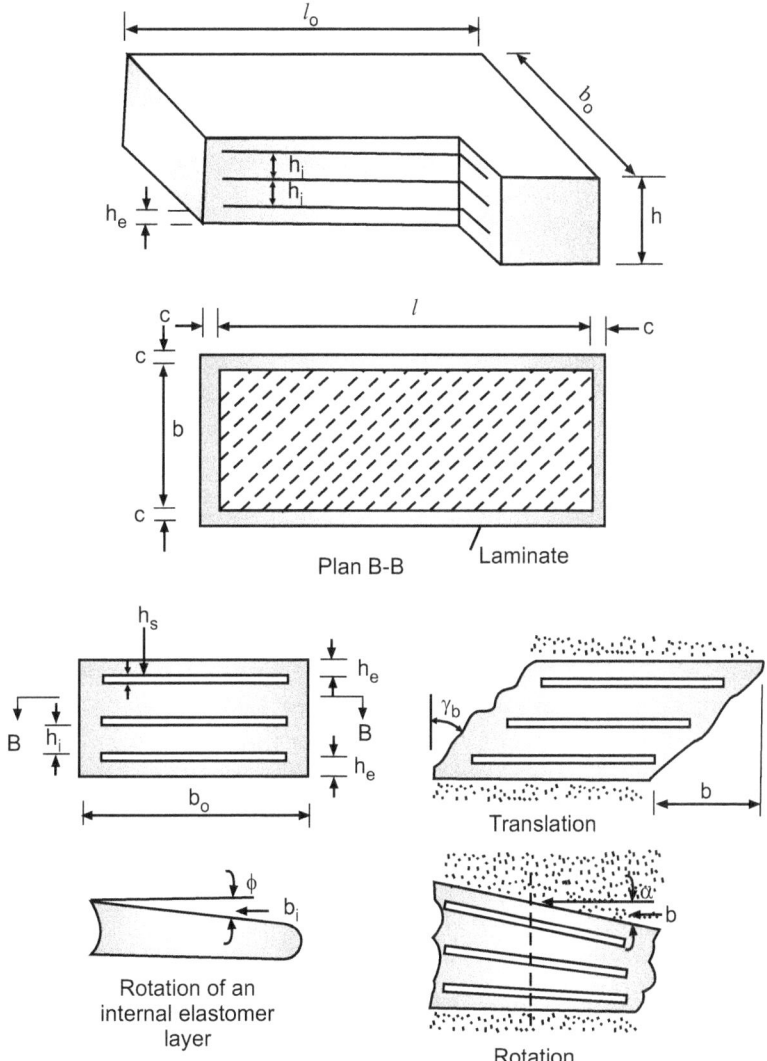

Fig. 15.16 : Elastomeric bearing general features

15.17 MAINTENANCE OF BEARINGS

- The bearings shall be subjected to planned maintenance care.
- The exposed bearing surface shall be maintained clean and free iron contamination with grease or oil etc.
- Annual routine maintenance inspection or special maintenance inspection of all bearings shall be made to check for any surface cracking or signs of damage, deterioration or distress.

- Damaged bearings shall be replaced immediately. To avoid differences in stiffness all adjacent bearings on the same lines of support shall also be replaced.
- Arrangement for insertion of jacks to lift the bridge deck shall be made in detailing of the structure.

The lifting of a cast-in-place post-tensioned bridge deck for relieving time dependent deformation shortly after installation of bearings should be avoided. In case such lifting is unavoidable, the lifting arrangement, proper seating of the girder on the bearing etc. shall be rigidly controlled to avoid any risk of misalignment.

15.18 Defects in the Bearings

In a bridge, bearings are provided between the superstructure and the substructure to cater for movements resulting from elongation of shortening, bending of the deck. The superstructure system is subjected to two types of movements viz (i) expansion and contraction this may be due to change in temperature of the area from time to time are due to creep and shrinkage in concrete etc. (ii) rotational movement at the support due to deflection in the girder on account of its own weight or due to superimposed load etc.

As per IRC Bridge Code for concrete structures, provision shall be made for movements resulting from variations in temperature of ± 17°C for moderate climate and ± 25°C for extreme climate. Collection of climate data giving the variation in temperature for different areas is an essential prerequisite in the temperature variation to be catered for it with reference to the normal temperature. Calculations for the initial set of the bearings should take into considerations the normal temperature, the temperature at the time of placement of bearing, time dependent deformations the creep and shrinkage in concrete etc.

Some instances have come to notice where metallic bridge bearings of road bridges have tilted excessively resulting in the girder ends jamming and hitting against the dirt walls. Some of the possible causes for such a phenomenon are.

- Inaccurate alignment and positioning of bearings at the time of construction due to lack of proper supervision.
- Wrong initial set of rollers.
- Rotation of the foundation and substructure even by a fraction of a degree.

In case suitable measures are not taken to prevent excessive movement or to reset the bearings in time when excessive movement occurs, the bridge may be put out of commission.

15.19 Measures to Avoid Excessive Movement in Bearings

- IRC Bridge Code Section V(RC-24-1967) specifies that in seismic areas where seismic coefficient exceeding G/20 is taken, segmental rollers shall not be permitted. Even in other areas, it is suggested that cut rollers should be avoided both in respect to large spans where excessive movement is expected and also in respect of cases where

settlement and or tilting of abutment is anticipated due to poor soil supporting the abutment or in cases where high abutment are provided.
- Where cut rollers are provided, the width of the cut roller should be such that even with the maximum anticipated movement, 50 per cent of the rolling margin is still left. The top and bottom plates should also be made larger.
- In order to cater for any possible relative undue movement between the superstructure and the dirt wall over the abutment resulting in the girder ends jamming and hitting against the dirt walls, a bigger gap (say 150 mm) could be provided between the girder end and the dirt wall.
- The back filling upto the abutment cap level should be done before the superstructure is constructed so that most of the tilting of the abutment, if any, due to the earth pressure can take place before the superstructure is in position, thus facilitating the placing of the bearings in their correct positions.
- Adequate soil investigations should be carried out for the foundations so that cut rollers can be avoided in cases where soil is likely to yield.
- Regarding back filling of the abutments, the specifications for material and construction of backfill laid down should be fully complied with. It should be ensured that heavy rolling is not resorted to behind the abutments.
- Initial reverse tilt to be given for the cast in situ prestressed concrete bridges should be very carefully worked out. It may even to desirable to reset the bearings after completion of prestressing and back filling particularly for long spans (greater than 30 m). The temperature at the time of erection shall be taken into account in placing the rocker/rollers and the top bearing plates. The rocker or rollers shall be adjusted (or set) at the time of placement in such a way that if any computed or anticipated movement of the bridge seat (due to creep, strinkage and temporary effects) takes place after they have been set, the line of the bearing will be centred on the bearing plates at the normal temperature adopted in the design.
- The bearings shall be protected while concreting the decking in-situ that there is no flow of mortar or any other such matter into the bearing assembly and particularly on to the bearing surfaces. The protection shall be such that it can be dismantled after the construction is over without disturbing the bearing assembly.
- Special attention should be given to the temporary fixtures to be provided for the bearings during the concreting of superstructure in order to ensure that they do not get displaced during the initial installation itself.
- The behaviour of the bearings right from the time of installation should be watched at regular intervals and observations recorded in a systematic way so that corrective action could be taken in time. In particular there should be a thorough examination of the bearings just before the expiry of the defect liability period so that the excessive

movement if any, could be got rectified through the contractor who has constructed the bridge.
- Provision should be made for jacking up to superstructure, so as to facilitate resetting of bearings in case abnormal movement is noticed in spite of the above precautions.
- Adequate investigations, design expertise and competent supervision all go a long way to avoid the problem.

15.20 BRIDGE FOUNDATION

FOUNDATIONS

Depth of Foundations

The foundation shall be taken to such depth that they are safe against scour, or protected from it. Apart from this, the depth should also be sufficient from consideration of bearing capacity, settlement, stability and suitability of strata at the founding level and at sufficient depth below it.

(A) Depth of Foundations in Soil (Erodible Strata)

(a) **Depth of Shallow Foundations :** Foundations may be taken down to a comparatively shallow depth below the bed surface provided a good bearing stratum is available and the foundation is protected against scour.

R.L. of foundation = Designed H.F.L.(Tallied H.F.L.)
- Maximum scour depth
- Depth of Embedment (D.E.)

Where   Depth of Embedment = Minimum 2.0 m for piers and abutments with arches.
= Minimum 1.2 m for pier and abutments, supporting other type of superstructure.

(b) **Depth of Deep Foundations (in Erodible Strata)**

R.L. of foundation = Designed H.F.L. (Tallied H.F.L.)- 1.33 * Maximum scour depth.

(B) Depth of Foundations in Rock

Foundation R.L. in case of Hard Rock = R.L. of strata of Hard Rock - 0.60 m

Foundation R.L. in soft rock / exposed rock = foundation R.L. in soft rock / Exposed rock - 1.50 m. (Scourable rock strata is not considered while taking R.L. of rock top)

Selection of a particular type of foundation is a very important job as it affects the entire proposal for the bridge. e.g. if the rock is not available at shallow depth, the tendency may be to adopt well foundation and as well foundations are costly the situation may lead to adoption of bigger spans, with P.S.C. structures. On the other hand if scour depth is less and flood depth is also reasonably small the raft foundation could be the choice. This will result in smaller spans, less height of bridge, may be a submersible bridge with permissible interruptions is felt sufficient.

Presence of soft/hard rock within 5m would attract open foundation depending upon the scour depth, the type of bridge and height of the bridge above and below the bed level. Situation with 5m depth of foundation below bed and 2m to 3m height of pier above bed may not sound good. Alternative should be thought of in such cases. So look for the strata where foundation can rest. Start with open foundation. If the depth of strata is deeper than 6m to 7m think of wells or piles. Simultaneously study scour depth and height of the bridge above bed level. If the scour depth is within 3.0 m and there is no problem of standing water, consider the possibility of raft foundations.

Important Points

The following points are to be noted while preparing bridge proposal.
- Span to height ratio for
  - Raft foundation be kept as 1.00 to 1.25
  - Open foundation be kept as 1.25 to 1.50
  - Pile foundation be kept as 1.25 to 1.75
  - Well foundations it should be 1.50 to 2.00

The height of pier is measured from foundation to top of pier i.e. up to pier cap top.
- The dimensions of pier, abutment and well foundation to be taken from type designs or from the latest I.R.C. Codes.
- Proper uniform sitting of well foundation could be ensured by taking the foundation into rock by about 15 cm.
- The raft foundation details be taken from the type designs as applicable.
- Other similar designs prepared and approved by the Designs Circle should also be studied and referred to.
- Open foundations are comparatively easy to decide about.
- Anchorage of open foundation into the rock shall be as per IRC-78 i.e. minimum 0.60m into hard rock and 1.50 m into soft rock excluding scourable layers.
- Levelling course and annular filling should be proposed for open foundation. Annular filling should be done with M 15 concrete upto rock level.
- Stability of foundation should be worked out. The beginner should obtain the standard calculation sheets from office, and do the calculations manually to gain confidence. Further trials could be on computer. Software is available for checking the stability of the foundation.
- Area under tension as per IRC:78-2000 clause 706.3.3.2 is allowed up to 33 % for load combinations including seismic or impact of Barge and 20 % for other load combinations.

Function of Foundation

The Following are the Functions of Foundations :

- To distribute the load of the structure over a large area of the sub soil, so that the of the intensity of pressure may not cross the safe bearing capacity of the soil.
- To prevent tilting and overturning of the piers and abutments.
- To prevent the lateral escape of the supporting material of the river bed, so that piers may not sink and cause the failure of the bridge.
- To provide a leveled base for the construction of piers and abutments.
- To prevents unequal settlement of sub-soil and super-structure, by transferring the load uniformly over the sub-soil.

Foundation Types

Generally two types of foundations are adopted for bridge structures.

- Shallow foundations   - Open foundations
                          - Raft foundations
- Deep foundations   - Pile foundations
                          - Well foundations   1. Box caissons
                                                2. Open caissons
                                                3. Pneumatic caissons

15.20.1 Open

Open foundations are preferred over any type. These are to be provided when good-founding strata is available at shallow depth and there is not much problem of dewatering. R. C. C. footing are preferred over P. C. C. footing in case of RCC piers.

15.20.2 Well

The shape of well can be, Single Circular, Double D-Type, Dumbell Type, Twin Circular as shown in Fig. 15.17. The various methods of starting well foundations and typical components of well are shown in Fig. 15.18 and Fig. 15.19.

Some important points to be noted regarding well foundations are as follows –

- If the external diameter of single circular wells exceeds 12 m relevant provisions of clause 708.1.2 of IRC : 78-2000 shall apply.
- The steining thickness of well shall not be less than 500 mm and shall satisfy the following relationship

$$h = kd\sqrt{L}$$

Where h = minimum thickness of steining in m

d = external diameter of circular well in m

L = depth of wells in m below top of well cap or LWL whichever is more

K = constant(for well in cement concrete 0.03 brick masonry 0.05 and twin D wells 0.39 (For details refer to clause 708.2.3 of IRC : 78-2000).

- In case of PCC wells the concrete shall not be learner than M-15. In case of conditions of severe exposure, steining shall not be leaner than M-20. The horizontal annular section of well steining shall be checked for ovalisation moments taking account of side earth pressure.
- M.S. cutting edge shall not be less than 40 kg/m to facilitate sinking through all types of strata. In case of well curb the internal angle should be kept at about 30° to 37°. Well curb shall not be leaner than RCC M-25.
- The bottom plug provided should be such that the top is kept lower than 300 mm in the centre above the top of the curb sump to be provided below the level of cutting edge. Well filling above the bottom plug shall be done generally with sand. Top plug of 300 mm in M-15 shall be provided over filling.

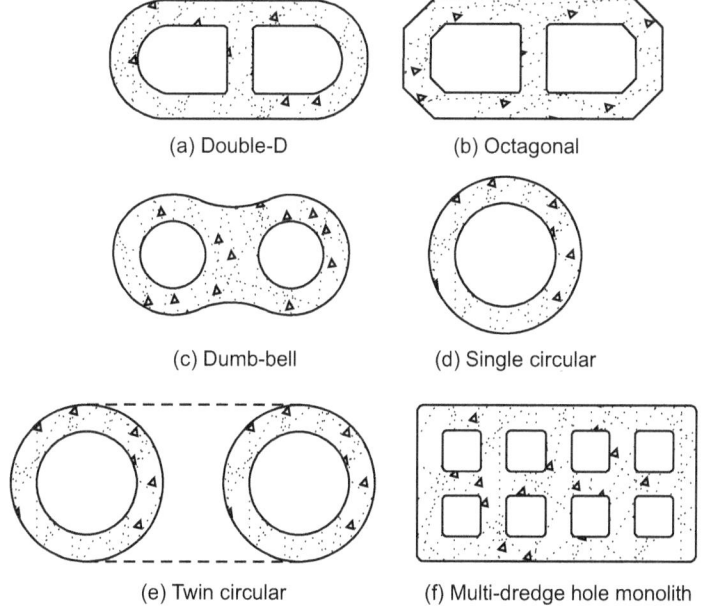

(a) Double-D   (b) Octagonal

(c) Dumb-bell   (d) Single circular

(e) Twin circular   (f) Multi-dredge hole monolith

Fig. 15.17 : Various shapes of wells

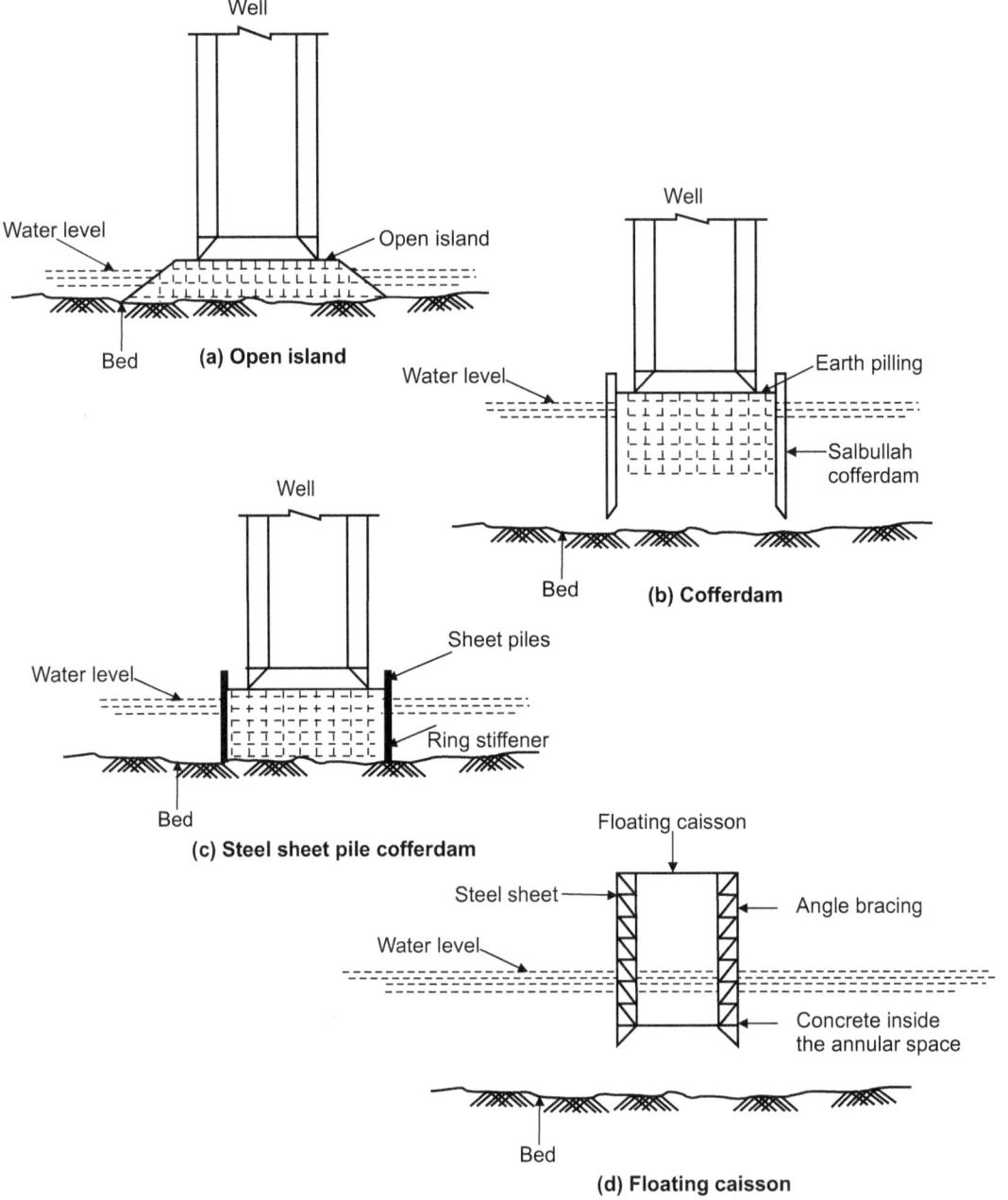

Fig. 15.18 : Various methods of starting well foundations

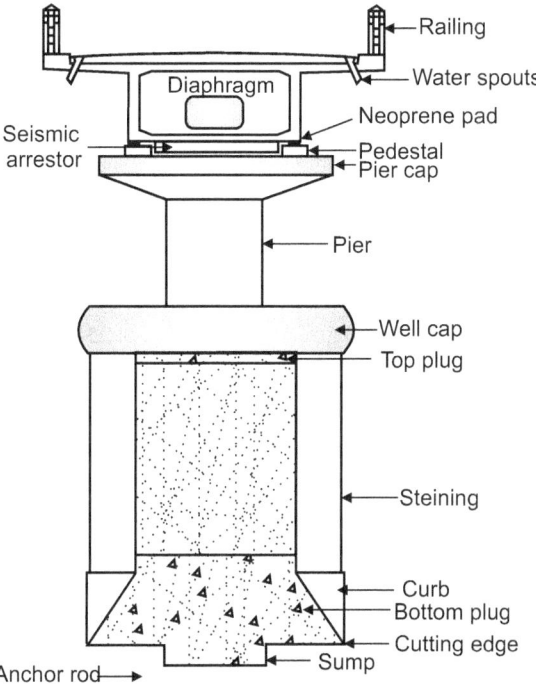

Fig. 15.19 : Typical section of well

15.20.3 Piles

Although piles can be designed as end bearing or friction piles. Only end bearing bored cast-in-situ piles drilled with rotary rig be preferred. Design with single row of piles per substructure and annular piles filled or not filled should not generally be preferred.

Table 15.1

Type of Strata	Minimum Embedment	S.B.C. in T/m^2
Hard rock	1.5 × dia. of pile	400
	1.0 × dia. of pile	300
Soft rock	3.0 × dia. of pile	250
	2.0 × dia. of pile	200
	1.5 × dia. of pile	150

(B) Selection of Type of Foundation

Raft foundation is, however, not recommended when
- Spans more that 10m raft being uneconomical.
- Bridge foundation that can not be inspected during the service life.
- Serious problem of dewatering due to large in flow of water/standing water.
- Where open foundation are feasible.

In other cases of small span bridge on weak soils, the raft foundations may be a most practicable solution.

(C) Types of Raft Foundation

The raft foundation in vogue can be broadly classified in three categories.
- R.C.C. solid slab raft.
- R.C.C. Channel raft.
- Raft for box bridges.

Solid slab type raft is nothing but a slab resting on elastic bed, designed as one way (if cut off walls are detached) or two way if cut off walls are attached to the raft. The channel type raft is a monolithic unit designed and constructed as a channel cross-section. The third one for box bridges is unique type, since it is a past of the closed box with piers and superstructure. This can rightly be considered as a slod slab type raft, as the cut off walls should be detached from the raft, if not considered in analysis.

(d) Important Aspects of Design of Raft

The raft foundation is designed with the assumption that it rests, on elastic bed. The analysis is based on Hetenyi's theory of beams on elastic foundations. The analysis considers the deflection pattern of the raft resting on elastic bed. Thus under the self weight of the bridge and the moving loads, the bending moments and shear forces are worked out at the desired sections in the raft.

REVIEW QUESTIONS

1. What are bridge bearings? Explain the procedure of design of elastomeric bearing.
2. State various functions of bearings for bridges.
3. Explain various part of metallic bearing.
4. What are bridge bearings? Explain with the neat sketches.
5. Write a detail note on maintenance of bridge bearings.
6. Draw a neat sketch of the following and label the parts.
   (a) Knuckle bearing
   (b) Roller cum rocker bearing
   (c) Elastomeric bearing.
   (d) Open caisson foundation
   (e) Well foundation
7. Differentiates between :
   (a) Rocker and Roller bearing and Expansion bearing.
   (b) Fixed bearing and free bearing.
8. What are functions of bridge foundation?
9. What are various foundations used in bridge construction. Explain any one foundation in details.

CHAPTER 16
CONSTRUCTION METHODS AND MAINTENANCE OF BRIDGE

16.1 Bridge Erection

The method selected depends very much on the type of bridge construction, span, height above ground or water etc.

Commonly used methods for the erection of bridges :

- **In-situ :** assembly of bridge components on temporary falsework.
- **Lifting :** e.g. (a) beams and trusses - placing of individual beams or a complete deck by crane (b) suspension bridges - lifting of pre-fabricated deck modules which are then hung from the deck hangers connected to the previously installed main cables, slung between the main towers and anchorages.
- **Launching :** sequential construction (on rollers or tracks) of a continuous deck at one end of the bridge. As each new section is added the whole deck is pushed or pulled out (usually over multiple spans).
- **Sliding or Rolling :** construction of a complete new bridge (usually alongside a busy existing bridge) which is then jacked into place over a few hours or days, to replace the existing structure.
- **Cantilevering :** (a) for arches - successive construction from the two springing points which is temporarily tied back until the two halves can be joined at midspan (b) for cable-stayed bridges - successive cantilevering out from the pylons of deck units suspended from the stay cables.

16.2 Factors to be Considered While Erecting a Bridge

The following factors should be considered while making the choice between methods of bridge construction :

- The site conditions.
- Type of the bridge structure to be constructed.
- Depth and current of the river water at the site.
- Standards of material and layout available.
- The equipment available.
- Type of foundation bed available at the site.
- Scheduled period of construction.
- Sequence of construction.

16.2.1 Problems During Erection of Bridge

- Passing of existing traffic during construction of the bridge.
- Transportation of the materials and machinery required for construction of the bridge.
- Storage of the material.
- Space required for placing equipment and machinery.
- Diversion of the river course.
- Time pattern in which the bridge is to be completed.

16.2.2 Erection of Steel Girder Bridges

- Erection by assembling the girders on the river bed.
- Erection by use of staging.
- Erection by floating the girders.
- Erection by rolling out girders.
- Erection by launching of single girder span.

16.2.3 Erection of Suspension Bridges

The bridge is generally constructed in the following order :

- Erection of tower.
- Erection of suspension.
- Erection of stiffening trusses.
- Erection of flooring system.
- **Erection of Tower :** The main towers of a suspension bridge are erected first with the help of floating crane or derrick. The successive towers are erected with the help of a creeper traveler.
- **Erection of Catwalk :** Catwalk are working platforms which help in the over ropes placed concentric with the main cables. A tramway system is then installed from anchorage to anchorage along the catwalk for pulling the bridge wire. At each anchorage a wheel called spinning wheel is attached to the tramway system.

    The bridge wire ends are fastened to anchorage end and then looped over the spinning wheels. The wheels are then pulled along the catwalk and over the towers to the opposite anchorage, the wires are attached to the anchorage and the procedure is repeated.

- **Erection of Suspender :** Cable bands are placed around the cable to grip it at each-point of suspension of the roadway. Suspenders are attached to the cable bands to receive the roadway.
- **Erection of Flooring System :** The flooring system is provided over the stiffening trusses and the roadway surface is placed over it.

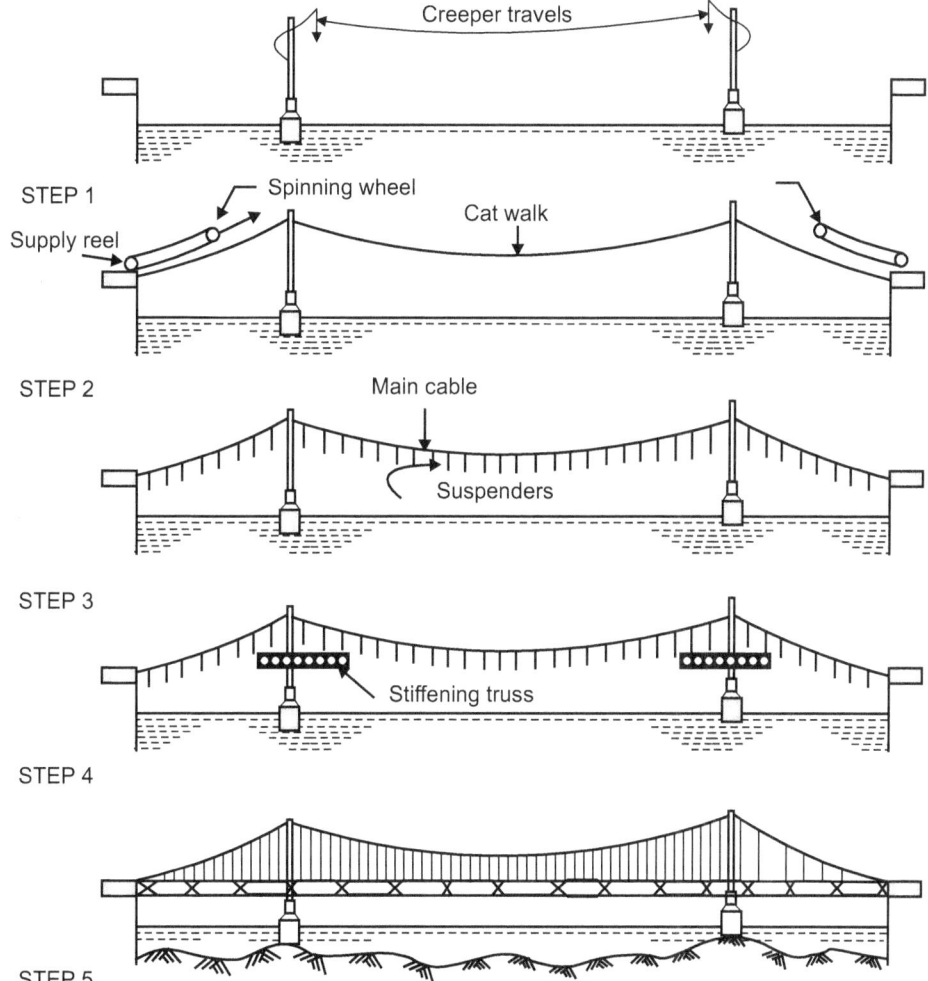

Fig. 16.1 : Erection of suspension bridge (parallel wire type)

16.2.4 R.C.C. and Prestressed Concrete Bridges

In these types of bridges the main work is Form work and placing of steel reinforcement in-position. Normally the work is done cast in-situ.

After completing form work and placing reinforcement, the concrete (1 : 2 : 4) is poured. Then curing is done. After 21 days generally form work is removed.

The construction of prestressed concrete super-structure is carried out in the following stages :

- Casting of beams in casting yard.
- Transport of the beams from the casting yard to the nearest abutment.
- Transporting beam to the span where it is to be placed.
- Casting of the deck and other details.

Note : For transporting the beams from casting yard to the abutments a rail-track is laid. Two trolleys one caring the rear and the other the front end of the girder are used to move on this track. Placing is done by using a block of rollers under the beam and a polley-block.

16.3 MAINTENANCE OF BRIDGES

The maintenance details vary with the materials of construction. Steel must be painted at regular intervals. R.C.C. works must be inspected for the cracks and if any cracks are found, they should be sealed as soon as possible. Masonry works must be kept well-plastered or pointed.

The regular inspection of bridges is a matter of great importance, since the early detection of trouble and the prompt attention may well obviate costly repairs which may be needed, if defects are allowed to develop too far.

The matters required regular attention are as follows :

- The proper functioning of weep holes and other drainage devices.
- The free action of expansion joints and drainage.
- Examination of bridge superstructures and sub-structures.
- Clearing of obstructions in channels tending to cause scour.
- Detection and tracing of water leakage through decks.
- Maintenance of water-proofing coats.
- Signs of movement of foundations, especially on clay, as evidenced by cracks in the structure or the road surface over it.
- The careful examination of steel structures for corrosion, especially in parts where moist or polluted air may be partially trapped.

It is well to systematize inspection and to record the results so that a full history of each bridge, including any trouble which may have been encountered during construction, is readily available.

16.4 STRENGTHENING OF BRIDGES

In the past, live load carried by a bridge was very light as compared to the dead load. There has been a tremendous increase in the carrying capacities of our transport vehicles. The road system however, has not sufficiently developed to cater for such increase in payloads. There is a dire need for improvement of the old and out of service bridges on our roads.

Strengthening of Bridge Substructure : The substructure is strengthened in following different ways :

1. **Masonry Substructure :** In case of old masonry substructure showing signs of disintegrations, the entire loose material all around the structure is removed to find out the defect. If it is found that masonry has large cavities, then they should be filled with cement concrete. Later a wire netting should be stretched around the entire masonry and fastened there to with spikes. Finally a coat of cement mortar is forced by a gun.

2. **Strengthening of Bridge Pier :**
- In order to strengthen an old pier a cofferdam is constructed around the piers. A thick concrete casing is provided all around the pier after pumping out the water.
- In case of foundation showing unequal settlements it is necessary to underpin the base of pier in deep and running water. This is done by sinking a pneumatic caisson near the pier.

16.5 STRENGTHENING OF BRIDGE SUPERSTRUCTURE

Method of strengthening a bridge superstructure depends upon the type of the bridge. The following methods for different types of bridge are in vogue :
- To fill large voids in honey combed concrete by cement grouting so that quality of concrete is improved and cover to reinforcement is obtained.
- Sealing of cracks and voids by epoxy grouting.
- To impact extra shear strength to girders when shear cracks appear on the girder, by providing shear plates.
- Providing I-beams on sides.

(a) Grouting : High pressure grouts are not useful for strengthening of R.C.C. bridges. Therefore grouting should be done by hand operated pump with low pressure operations for cracks more than 0.25 mm in any bad concrete, we may employ solid suspension grout such as cement water or cement sand water with water cement ratio 0.47 to 0.52. For finer cracks, we may employ chemical grout as epoxy grout.

For thin cracks and pressure, epoxy should be used under pressure.

(b) I-Beams : R.C.C. beam and slab bridge - In this type, the beams are strengthened by providing steel I-beam on each side of the existing beams. In case of longer spans the load from the existing beams are directly taken away by steel cross girders supported on steel built-up girders.

If an existing bridge in sound condition is proposed to be widened by adding additional beams. It is preferable to do the entire widening on one side, from considerations of lateral stability provided the geometrics of the road alignments permits it.

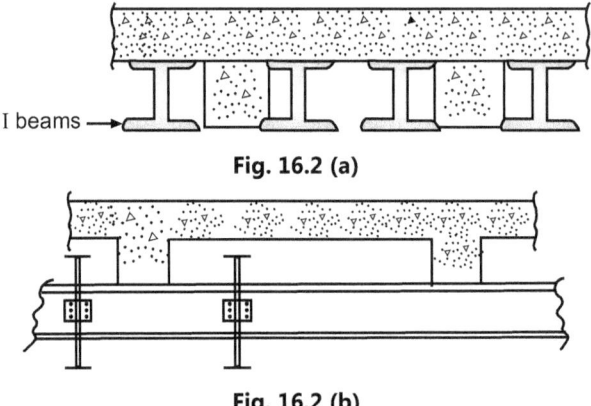

Fig. 16.2 (a)

Fig. 16.2 (b)

(c) Masonry Arch Bridges : They are usually strengthened by first removing the filling above the arch and then casting R.C.C. arch slab on the top of the roughened extrudes. the slab is securely keyed into the abutments.

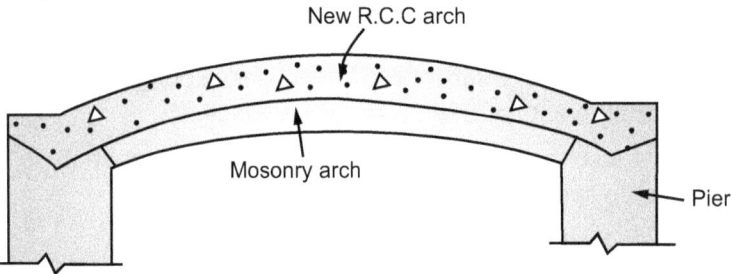

Fig. 16.3 (a)

When the arch is too weak to hear loud more than its own weight, then a new R.C.C. arch must be built several centimeters above existing extrudes with the help of removable shuttering.

(d) Continuous Bridge : They are strengthened by methods similar to that of single span care should be taken that when a span is being strengthened the adjacent span is not weakened.

(e) Steel Bridge : They are strengthened by providing extra steel plates or angles or concrete encasements.

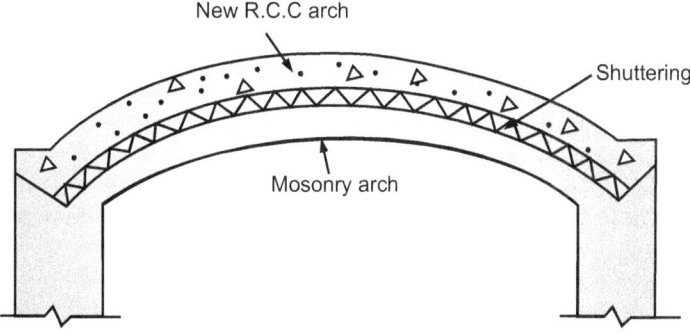

Fig. 16.3 (b)

(f) Suspension Bridge : They are usually strengthened by providing additional cables with fasteners.

(g) Shear Plates : When girder shows shear cracks, external shear reinforcement in the form of shear plate could be provided in end portion of girder where generally, these cracks are observed. These plates are to be bounded to the sides of ribs by cutting groove and bounding them with epoxy. Edges of plate are to be sealed with epoxy. Mortar and epoxy injected through inlets to achieve good bond with concrete proper anchorage with bond plate is necessary. For this, mild steel bars in the inverted U fashion are welded to bond plate and embedded in the concrete.

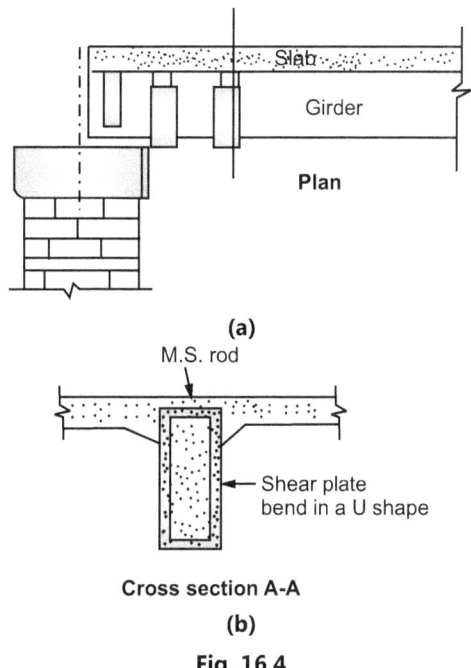

Fig. 16.4

REVIEW QUESTIONS

1. What are different techniques of erecting of bridge superstructures?
2. Why maintenance of bridges required.
3. What important items you will keep in view while inspecting a bridge?
4. Describe the various repairs those are carried out to a bridge during maintenance.
5. Describe the method of erection of suspension bridges.

Unit - V

CHAPTER 17
INTRODUCTION TO TUNNELING

17.1 INTRODUCTION

A tunnel is a closed or roofed structure carrying a road through, or under an obstacle. This obstacle may be anything in the path of a preferred road alignment such as a mountain, a body of water, a building or a complete development. It is also defined as" an engineering structure, artificial gallery, passage or roadway beneath the ground, under bed of a stream or through a hill or mountain"

These are constructed for the transportation of passengers, freight, water, gas sewage etc.

Tunneling is an art known to man since Stone Age, because, he used to take shelter under natural or artificial caves. Tunnels required for mining various metals, tombs, temples and mining of various metals like copper, gold etc. were made in Greek and Egypt around 3000 to 1000 B.C.

The oldest caves in the world are found to be at Bhimbeta, about 45 km from Bhopal (M.P.), where about 1000 rock shelters have been discovered. 29 caves of Ajanta are in a curve of a gorge and date from 200 AD to 650 AD and at Ellora. There are 34 caves at Ellora (which is about 30 km from Aurangabad) amongst which sheer size of cave 16 [Kailash temple] is overwhelming. It covers twice the area the Parthenon in Athens and $1\frac{1}{2}$ times as high. This gigantic structure was cut out of solid rock. Carving out Kailash temple alone entailed removing of 2,00,000 tons of rock. The temples were cut from top down, so that, it was not necessary to provide any scaffolding.

The underground excavation can be used in a variety of ways such as shorter routes for railways, highways, transport of water, sewage, gas, tube railways in metropolitan cities, swimming pools, parking areas, sports clubs, storage of military weapons/radioactive materials etc.

In 19th and 20th century, the art of tunneling has taken a quantum leap with respect to speed of construction, ability to cope up in a variety of underground strata, accuracy, safety etc.

Tunneling activity in India has also improved substantially.

Developments in Tunneling Techniques

In the early stages, excavation in soft soil/rock was done with the help of sharp stones, horns of animals, by dislodging rock through natural or artificial planes of weakness.

Artificial planes of weakness were created by heating rock, which on cooling resulted in cracks. By use of wedges, sledge hammer, crowbars, rock was dislodged. Naturally the speed of progress was slow, and excavation in hard rock was difficult.

Significant progress in tunneling has been possible due to :

- Pneumatically and hydraulically operated drilling equipment as against manually operated equipment.
- Significant improvement in tunneling is achieved due to improvement in various types of powerful explosives, electric and non-electric delay detonators have helped in achieving smooth and efficient blasting with desired fragmentation of muck.
- Support improvements :
    (a) Advances in various fields has lead to effective support of roof by means of rock bolting, shotcreting.
    (b) Improved ground control by pressure grouting.
    (c) Improved precast R.C. linings, C.I. linings.
    (d) Use of tunnel shield and tunnel boring machine (TBM).

17.2 NEED OF TUNNELS

- To avoid longer surface route of road or railway track for reaching the other side of a hill.
- to avoid more depth of open cut for reaching the other side of a hill. as depth of open cut larger than 20 m is difficult to construct and maintain.
- To connect two terminal stations separated by a mountain.
- To carry road or railway traffic or pipe line under the river bed when the provision of a bridge across the river is inconvenient and costlier.
- To avoid acquisition of valuable land and property for a road or railway project.
- To provide rapid transportation system in big cities and to avoid holding of traffic, for long periods due to traffic congestion.
- To protect railway track or road at high altitudes fro blockages due to landslides or snow fall.
- To economically carry public amenities like water, oil, gas etc. Across a stream or mountain.
- To avoid damage to transportation system of strategic importance and for safety of traffic during aerial war.

17.3 CLASSIFICATION, FUNCTIONS, REQUIREMENT AND SHAPE OF TUNNELS

17.3.1 Classification of Tunnels

Tunnels can be classified in the following ways :

Classification based on

(a) Purpose of tunnel

(b) Type of strata encountered

(c) Position or alignment of tunnel

17.3.1.1 Classification based on Purpose of Tunnel

(a) Transportation : This includes

- Transportation of people and goods through railways, highways, metros, pedestrian tunnels.
- Transportation of water for supply of drinking water to cities, supply of water to hydroelectric power station, irrigation, canals, cooling towers etc.
- Transportation of sewage, industrial waste water.
- Cables and piped services.

(b) Storage plant, public amenities.

These include :

- Car parks, underground sports complexes, swimming pools, etc.,
- Storage of oil, liquid, wine etc.,
- Underground power stations,
- Disposal of radioactive wastes and
- Storage of military weapons.

(c) Protection to people during war and secret escape routes.

17.3.1.2 Classification based on Strata

The classification based on strata encountered can be classified as :
- Tunnels in hard rock,
- Tunnels in soft rock,
- Tunnels in soft soil,
- Tunnels in quick sand, and
- Tunnels below bed of river.

17.3.1.3 Classification Based on Position of Tunnels

(a) Saddle Tunnel

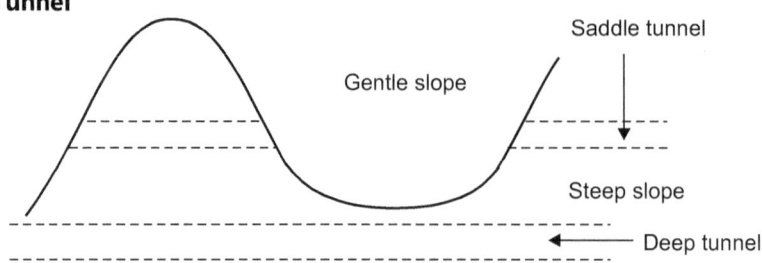

Fig. 17.1 : Saddle tunnel

When tunnel is to pass through valleys, then in the valley portion where steep gradient exists, tunnel is provided and in the portion, where gradient is gentle, vehicles/railways are allowed to travel along the ground surface. By such arrangement, length of tunnel is reduced. Such arrangement is justified if expected volume of traffic in long run is less. However, if in the course of time, volume of traffic is expected to be high, it is advisable to provide longer tunnel at lower elevation.

(b) Spiral Tunnel : In narrow valley, tunnel of gentle gradient is to be provided, for a fixed drop in height, it becomes essential to increase the length of tunnel. This can be attained by providing a spiral tunnel of minimum permissible radius and suitable gradient.

(c) Off Spur Tunnel : This type of tunnel is provided to avoid local obstruction. This is achieved by providing small detour with short tunnel.

17.3.2 Shapes of Tunnels

The following shapes are generally used for tunnel cross-section :

(1) Circular section

(2) D shaped section

(3) Horse-shoe section and Modified horse-shoe section

(4) Egg shaped section and Egglipse section.

(5) Rectangular section.

(1) Circular Shape

- Tunnels with circular shape are the best for resisting external as well as internal pressure, hence are used for tunnels carrying water under pressure.
- These tunnels can be easily constructed in soft soil and soft rocks.
- For constant perimeter, of all the shapes, circular shape offers maximum cross-sectional area.

Invert portion of the tunnel (i.e. bottom portion of circular tunnel) is required to be filled to obtain a level surface, as such, a portion of tunnel is not utilized. The wastage is quite appreciable, especially when tunnel for more than two traffic lanes is to be provided. Under such circumstances, rectangular section becomes more economical.

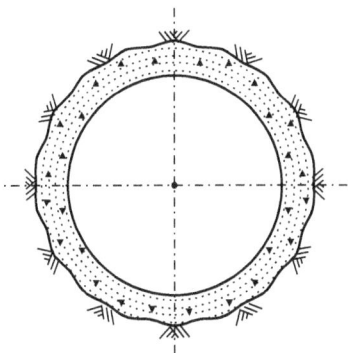

Fig. 17.2 : Circular section

(2) D Shaped Tunnel : Here, the width and height of tunnel is sufficient to accommodate operation equipment. Roof consists of semi-circular or segmental arch. Side walls are vertical. Rock bolts are provided in roof and side walls to increase stability. This section is suitable when firm to hard rock is encountered.

D Section : D section would be found suitable in tunnels located in massive igneous, hard, compacted, metamorphic and good quality sedimentary rocks where the external pressure due to water or unsound strata upon the lining is light and also where the lining is not required to be designed against internal pressure. The principal advantages of the section section over horse-shoe section are the added width of the invert which gives more working floor space in the heading during driving and the flatter invert which helps to eliminate the tendency of wet concrete to slump and draw away from the tunnel sides after it has been spread.

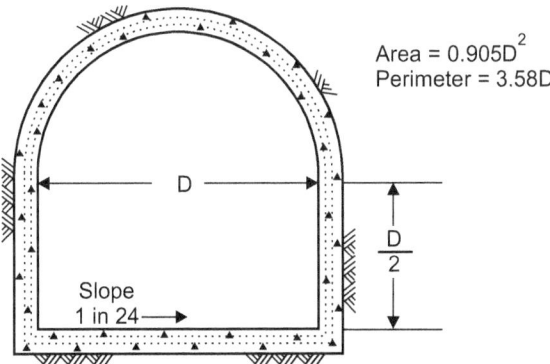

Area = $0.905D^2$
Perimeter = $3.58D$

Fig. 17.3 : D section

(3) Horse-Shoe and Modified Horse-Shoe Section : Horse-shoe shape tunnels have semi-circular shape in crown roof portion, curved surface, curved portion in side walls/below springing level and nearly flat portion in the invert/bottom portion. The curved portion in the roof and sides help in resisting internal and external pressure, whereas bottom portion provides nearly level surface required for railway and highway tunnels. This section is also adopted in tunnels conveying water through hard soils and soft rock.

These sections are a compromise between circular and D sections. These sections are strong in their resistance to external pressures. Quality of rock and adequate rock cover in terms of the internal pressure to which the tunnel is subjected govern the use of these sections. Modified horse-shoe section offers the advantage of flat base for constructional ease and change over to circular section with minimum additional expenditure in reaches of inadequate rock cover and poor rock formations.

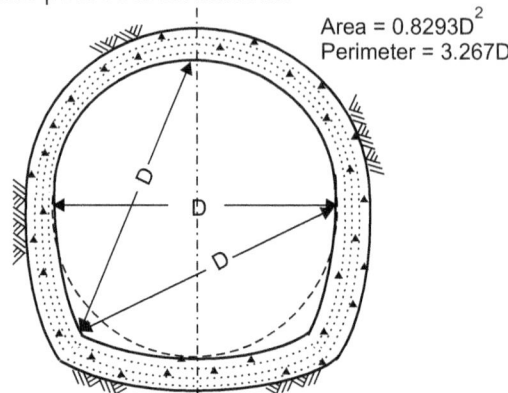

Area = $0.8293D^2$
Perimeter = $3.267D$

Fig. 17.4 : Horse-shoe section

where,
R = Radius of hydraulically equivalent circle
Area of section = $3.253\,572\,r^2$
Perimeter of section = $6.426\,334\,r$
Hydraulic radius = $0.506\,287\,r$
A = $0.780\,776\,r$
B = $1.561\,553\,r$
θ = 31° 22' 01"

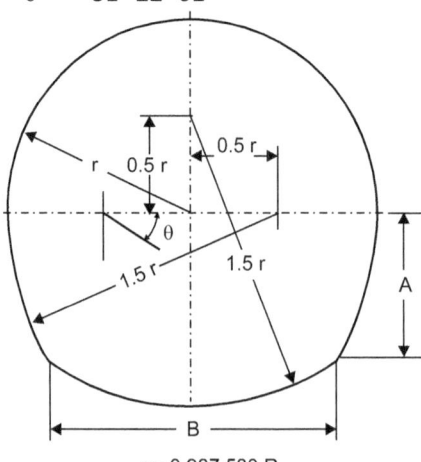

r = 0.987 580 R
Fig. 17.5 : Modified horse-shoe section

(4) Egg Shaped and Egglipse Section

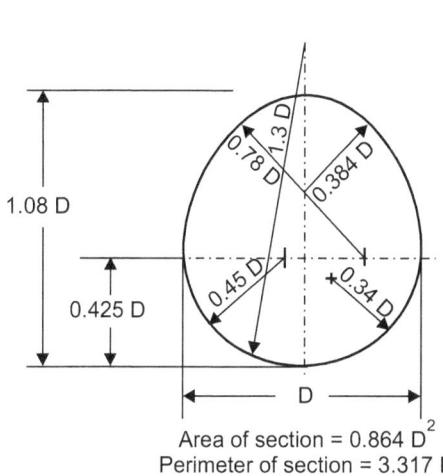
Area of section = 0.864 D^2
Perimeter of section = 3.317 D

Fig. 17.6 : Egg shaped section

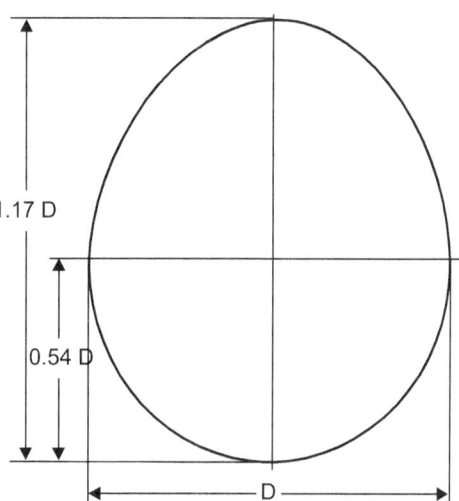

Fig. 17.7 : Typical egglipse section

Where the rock is stratified, soft and very closely laminated (as laminated sand stones, micaceous schists, etc.) and where the external pressure and tensile forces in the crown are likely to be high so as to cause serious rock falls, egg shaped and egglipse sections should be considered. In the case of these sections there is not much velocity reduction with reduction in discharge. Therefore, these sections afford advantage in case of sewage tunnels and tunnels carrying sediments. Egglipse has advantage over egg shaped section as it has a smoother curvature and is hydraulically more efficient.

(5) Rectangular or Box Type Tunnels : The rectangular tunnels are small in depth and full use of cross-section can be made.

Small rectangular tunnels are provided to house instrument to observe performance of main tunnel with reference to settlement, pressure etc.

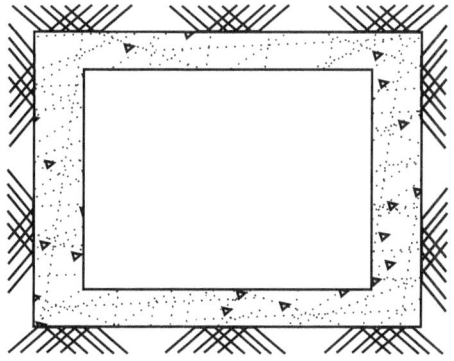

Fig. 17.8 : Rectangular or Box type tunnels

When tunnel is to be designed for more than two traffic lanes, then providing circular tunnel becomes uneconomical, since unnecessarily a very large volume of earth is required to be removed. This increases cost of excavation etc. substantially.

17.4 ADVANTAGES AND DISADVANTAGES OF TUNNELS COMPARED TO OPEN CUTS

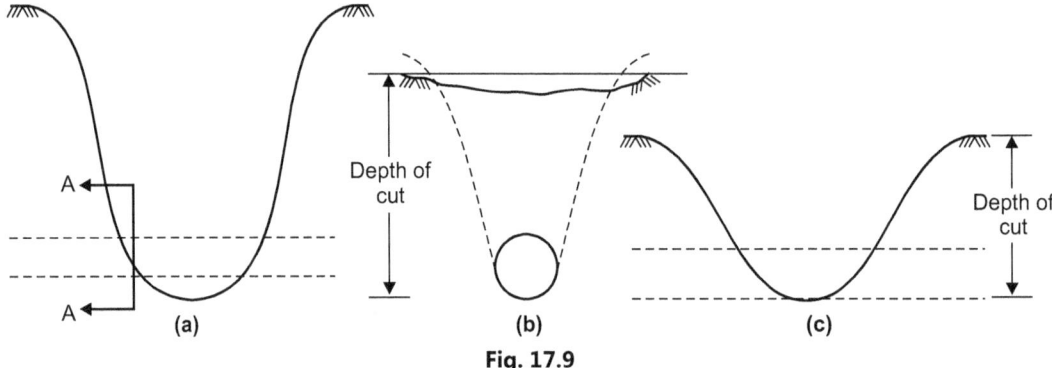

Fig. 17.9

- From Fig. 17.9 (a) and (b), it will be clear that, if open cut excavation upto ground level is carried out, volume of earth to be removed, will be quite large. In such case, it is advisable to provide tunnel, so as to reduce volume of excavation. On the other hand, if depth of tunnel from ground level is less as in Fig. 17.9 (c), open cut excavation will prove to be economical, instead of providing tunnel.

- Open cut excavation is comparatively easy, does not require skilled labour and costly equipment. The special equipment may not be easily available. Further, unless works which will involve repeated use of such costly equipment are not available, the equipment may remain idle and will prove to be uneconomical.

  On the other hand, equipment required for open cut excavation, can be used for variety of works, hence can be continuously used. As a result, open cut may prove to be economical.

- In case of tunnel works, detailed exploration of soil strata is essential, since based on the information, plan of execution of project can be decided. Usually detailed exploration for open cut is not considered essential.

- It is possible to provide tunnel below water such as below creek, across river etc., whereas this is not possible in respect of open cut.

- In case of long tunnel, special arrangement is required to be made to provide ventilation/fresh air to workers. No such arrangement is required in respect of open cut excavation.

- Open cuts are subjected to deformations due to forces of rain, snow etc. and require maintenance. Very less maintenance is required in respect of tunnels.
- During war tunnels can be used for taking shelter or for storage of materials etc.
- As compared to tunnels, works of open cuts can be completed early. Work of open cut can be commenced at many places. For early completion, shafts are to be provided, but require additional expenditure.
- Problems associated with acquisition of land can be avoided by providing tunnels. In case of open cuts, not only problems associated with land acquisition but also damage to environment is required to be taken into account.

17.5 TWIN TUNNELS

When volume of traffic to be handled is large, it becomes essential to provide more traffic lanes. This can be done, either providing one single tunnel housing all lanes or by providing two tunnels one tunnel to handle traffic in one direction and the other tunnel for traffic in opposite direction. Providing two separate tunnels have following advantages :

- As more faces are available for construction, work can be speeded up.
- In case, work or traffic is held up in one tunnel due to unusual incident like flooding of tunnel due to seepage or collapse of roof, fire, major accident etc. use of other tunnel can be made.
- As the size of tunnel increases, cost of measures to support the roof increases, since thicker lining, deeper/closer rock both are required to be provided. As such providing two separate tunnels finds to be economical.

Note :
- "Channel Tunnel" which links UK and France, not only twin tunnels are provided, but one more tunnel of smaller diameter, in between the two tunnels, with cross connection to twin tunnels is provided. This smaller tunnel helps in carrying service equipment or to have an access to main tunnel in case of fire, accident, collapse of roof etc.
- Similar such arrangement is made, for 54 km long tunnel in Japan.

17.6 PILLOT TUNNEL (REFER FIG. 17.10)

When the diameter of tunnel is large say 8 to 9 m, adopting full face excavation posses many problems. Instead, if a small size say 2.5 to 3 m diameter tunnel called as pilot tunnel is driven, as it allows many advantages :

- Pilot tunnel serves as exploratory tunnel and gives information regarding the strata likely to be encountered; so that proper strategy can be planned and likely problems tackled.
- It provides an access for ground treatment.

- In a large face, the effects of relaxation of stress penetrate further ahead and larger volume of ground is involved over longer period, resulting in much stronger support. This is more important in case of soft ground than in rock or stiff clay.
- With increase in the size of tunnel, more than proportionate thrust is required due to decrease in arching action. If d and p represent diameter of pilot tunnel and ground pressure and if 2d is the diameter of main tunnel, then ground pressure increases to 1.5 p load to be carried increases six times $1.5 p \left(\frac{2d}{d}\right)^2$ = 6p and bending moment increases to 12 times.
- In larger tunnel, time required for removal of large volume of muck increases. As a result, excavated face remains unsupported for a long time and danger of falling of large volume is muck from top, thereby probability of serious accidents increases.
- Pilot tunnels help in improving drainage and ventilation.
- By providing cross-cuts from pilot tunnel to main tunnel, work can be carried out simultaneously in various stretches of tunnel, thereby increasing speed of work.

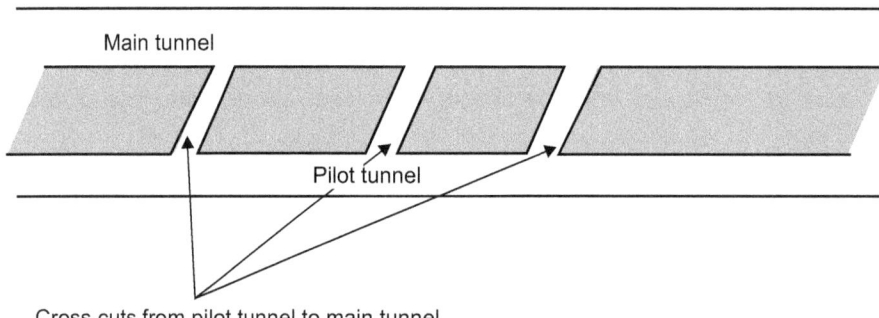

Fig. 17.10 : Pilot tunnel

17.7 PORTAL

It is the portion of the tunnel, which is located at the entrance or exit of the tunnel. This portion of the tunnel is continuously subjected to action of weathering and therefore, while designing of portal, following points are required to be considered :

Just as entrance door of a house is aimed at to be strong and attractive, portal is designed to be massive, strong enough to resist destructive/destabilizing forces. The measures adopted may include the following :

- Providing gentle slopes.
- Strengthening strata around by grouting/shorting/by providing gabbion walls etc.

- Providing massive masonry structure or cast in situ concrete or precast lining or steel frame work.
- Marking entrance attractive.
- Vibrations and seepage water leads to exertion of heavy earth pressure. Hence arrangements are made to provide drainable soil for backfilling and to carry draining water far off.

17.8 SHAFTS

Shafts are intermediate vertical or inclined openings usually provided along the centre line of tunnel, to serve as an access to the main tunnel. Each shaft provides two additional faces to work, thereby help in speedy completion of work. This is achieved by providing shaft.

- Shaft also helps to improve ventilation in tunnel, especially when shaft is vertical and along tunnel alignment.
- It also helps to some extent in knowing the strata likely to be encountered.
- Shafts help in pumping water from sub-aqueous tunnels.
- In hydroelectric projects, "surge shaft" is provided to reduce adverse effects of water hammer pressure.
- In hydroelectric power project, small diameter shafts are provided for the passage of power cable and control cable to transformer yard.

17.8.1 Requirements of Shaft

- The ground, where shaft is to be provided, should be level, available from the inception of the project and should have easy access for transport of materials.
- Sufficient space should be available to accommodate construction material for stock piling of excavated material and to carry out survey work without any obstruction.

17.8.2 Classification of Shaft

Depending upon the position, the shafts are classified as follows :

1. Vertical Shafts
2. Inclined Shafts
3. Permanent Shafts
4. Temporary Shafts
    - The shafts which shaft is constructed in the plumb are called vertical shafts.
    - The shafts which are inclined and not in plumb are known as inclined shafts.

- The shafts which are left open after construction of the tunnel and used for various purposes such as ventilation, etc are called vertical shafts.
- The shafts which are closed by filling excavated materials in them after the completion of the construction of the main shafts are called temporary shafts.

17.8.3 Size of Shafts

The size of the shaft mainly depends on the following factors :

- Depending upon purpose of tunnel
- Method of tunnel construction
- System used for hoisting
- Size of the muck car
- Quantity of the muck to be lifted
- Space requirement for working arrangements
- Size and type of construction equipment to be used
- Number of the workers to be work inside the shafts
- Water harvesting and reuse.
- Escape uses
- launch and receival shafts for pipe jacking applications
- Storage overflow and pump stations (sewerage)

17.8.4 Shapes of the Shafts

Shafts can be rounding, elliptical, square, or rectangular. Both subsurface conditions including soils and groundwater and the tunneling method will dictate construction methods. For example, trench boxes may be suitable for small conventional tunneling through stiff clay above the water table, whereas watertight steel sheeting may be required for the same tunnel setup in sand below the groundwater table. Micro tunneling shafts typically require water-tight excavation support regardless of subsurface conditions (except rock) to prevent "blow-back" of the pressurized slurry.

Following two main shapes of the shafts are in common practice :

1. Rectangular shafts
2. Circular shafts

1. Rectangular Shafts

When the shafts are of temporary nature and are to be filled later on, this shape may be provided. The rectangular shafts are usually strutted with timber from all sides to prevent the falling of timber and preventing accidents.

2. Circular Shafts

This is most common shape of the shaft which is generally used. These shafts are lined with pressed steel liner plates or concrete. This shape is adopted for the construction of the permanent shafts.

Fig. 17.11

17.9 ALIGNMENT OF TUNNEL

Alignment of Tunnel and Allied Construction

For connecting two given points normally a tunnel follows a straight alignment. Curves are some times introduced in tunnel alignment to avoid difficult tunneling zones. Route survey is done with precision survey instruments.

When the ground which is to be tunneled is accessible from surface, the centre line of tunnel can be set on the surface. In such cases tunnel driving can be aided by digging vertical shafts along the path of tunnel. (Fig. 17.12) The vertical shafts provide extra working faces and ventilation to be tunnel. Centre line from of plumb bobs. Two plumb bobs 3 meters apart are suspended from a steel wire into the shaft t0 indicate centre line of tunnel.

In line with the help of transit theodolite. (Fig. 17.13)

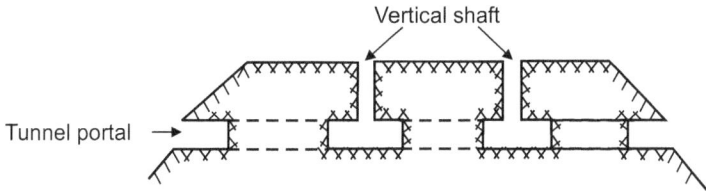

Fig. 17.12 : Tunnel driving with help of vertical shafts

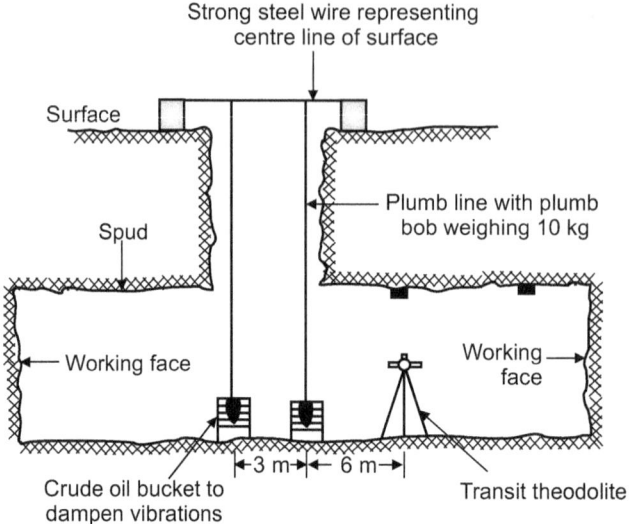

Fig. 17.13 : Transfer of allegement from surface to tunnel

REVIEW QUESTIONS

1. Define : Tunnel and open cut.
2. What are the advantages of tunnels over open cuts ?
3. Write short notes on :
   (a) Circular shape tunnel.
   (b) D-shape tunnel.
   (c) Egg shaped tunnel.
   (d) Twin tunnel.
   (e) Portal.
   (f) Pilot tunnel.
4. What are the advantages of tunnel?
5. What are the advantages of pilot tunnel?
6. Explain necessity and advantages of shaft.
7. What are the various factors which influence size and shape of tunnel shaft? Describe any one briefly?
8. Write short notes on :
   (a) Alignment of tunnel.
   (b) Tunnel shafts

CHAPTER 18
TUNNELING IN HARD ROCK

18.1 Driving Tunnels in Hard Ground

18.1.1 Sequence of Operations of Tunneling

- Surveying and giving layout for drilling.
- Drilling holes, cleaning holes. Drilling holes according to most suitable drilling pattern, so as to get tunnel of desired size and shape and to cause least disturbance to adjoining rock.
- **Loading and Charging :** Placing explosives in the form of cartigues, increasing the density of explosives by tamping, providing necessary detonating fuse.
- **Blasting :** Connecting detonating fuses as per designed pattern and then passing direct electric current of high voltage connecting various delay detonators in desired fashion.
- **Defuming :** Poisonous gases produced by explosives during blasting are removed by exhaust fans and forcing fresh air inside.
- **Scaling :** After explosion, examining the excavated rock surface and dislodging / removal of loose rock by lightly tamping by hammer and or by crow bar, so that, falling of loose rock and accidents arising out of it can be avoided.
- Removal and disposal of excavated rock by suitable machines.
- Providing suitable rock support in the form of shotcreting, rock bolting, steel supports etc.
- Providing concrete lining using either cast in situ lining or by providing precast lining. Lining to tunnel is provided (1) to have smooth surface, which will enable free flow of water, (2) to prevent leakage of water, (3) to prevent ingress of aggressive chemicals etc.

Smooth Blasting

In tunneling it is desirable to remove rock only upto desired extent, without the disturbance to the rock beyond the excavated surface. If more than adequate explosive is detonated near the desired shape of tunnel, excessive rock will be removed, resulting

- Disturbance to rock in adjoining area.
- More explosive, more removal of rock, more quantity of filling and grouting beyond lining, hence more expensive operations.

Smooth Blasting is Achieved by

- Drilling a number of closely spaced parallel bore holes along the final excavation surface.

- Placing explosive of low density.
- Use of decoupled charge, which consists of providing slightly smaller diameter gelatine cartridge in a large diameter bore hole. Air in the annular space between bore hole and gelatine acts as a cushion and absorbs some of the initial explosive energy.
- **Use of Delay Detonators :** Instead of detonating al explosives simultaneously.

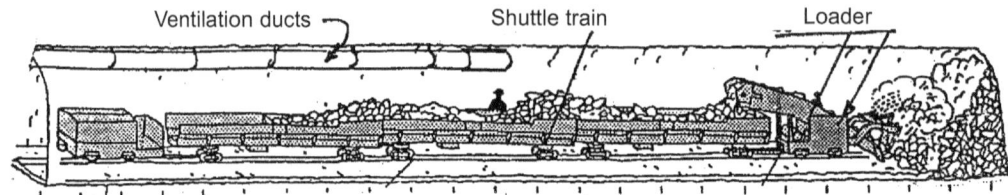

(a) Shows drilling operation using three boom jumbo, three holes can be drilled simultaneously. This reduces time required for drilling

(b) Shows that, while drilling operation is in progress, various other supplementary operations like fixing of rock bolt, extending track line, fixing of ventilation pipes are being carried out

(c) After drilling, blasting and defuming, excavated rock is removed, with the help of loader and filled in shuttle train

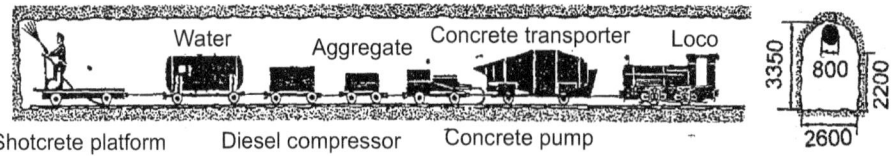

(d) The operation of shotcreting is in progress

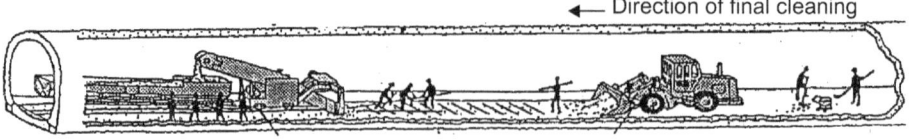

(e) Concreting in invert portion i.e. at the bottom is in progress

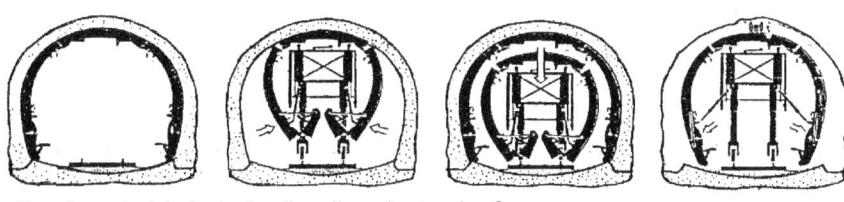

Function principle for hydraulic collapsel extension form

(f) Various stages of rail mounted tunnel form work for cast in situ concrete linings are shown

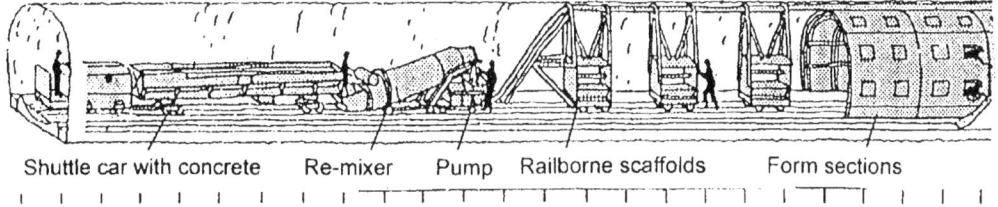

Shuttle car with concrete   Re-mixer   Pump   Railborne scaffolds   Form sections

(g) Instead of cast in situ lining, precast lining is being provided

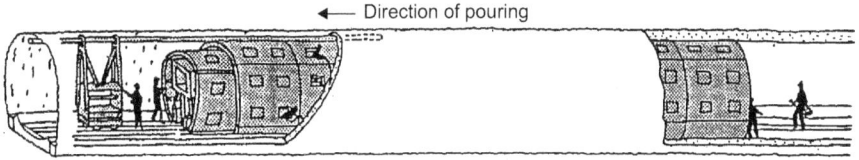

← Direction of pouring

Fig. 18.1 (h): Sequence of operations of tunneling

18.1.2 Factors Affecting Methods of Tunneling

The following factors are to be considered while deciding methods of tunneling.

(1) Ground Condition : The strata through which a tunnel has to pass may be or may not be homogeneous and may vary from soft silt to hard rock, implying a very wide range of behaviour in excavation. Ingress of water during excavation increases difficulties greatly.

Ground condition influences shape of tunnel, materials of construction to be used, method of construction. In short, this is the most influencing factor and as such thorough site investigation is absolutely essential.

(2) Structural Form / Shape of Tunnel : Structural form may be circular, horse shoe, egg shape, D shape or rectangular incorporating cast iron, concrete, brickwork, sprayed concrete etc. to carry loads.

(3) Construction Method : Construction method may be :

    (a) Boring by drilling and blasting (in hard and soft rock).
    (b) Tunneling with or without shield.
    (c) Using tunneling machine.
    (d) Adopting cut and cover method.

(e) Using prefabricated submerged tubes.

The choice of construction method is governed by ground condition, situation of the tunnel and economically available equipments and resources.

(4) Dimensions of the Finished Tunnel : These include length, width, height, gradient and curves of the finished tunnel. The requirements may impose narrow limits or may offer wide range of possibilities. Dimensions of the equipment to be used during construction and operation of tunnel are also to be considered. Various amenities required like ventilation, lighting, space for repairs and maintenance, requirements during breakdown, emergency, rescue operations are also required to be considered.

(5) Location of Tunnel : Tunnel situated in mountain and hills relatively effect saving in time and energy, when compared to tunnel below river, creek, lake or under city streets as they are not very complicated.

After drilling and before blasting the drilling rig together with rails are moved away to a safer distance. After blasting rails are relaid so as to bring the loading equipment near excavated muck. Loading is done with the help of vail-bound digging arm ladder which transfers excavated train comprising of 3 shuttle cars. (In trackless method, the loader transfer the excavated rock into dumpers.)

Whether a bridge of tunnel should be provided across a river, channel or creek depend upon economics of

- Unobstructed width and height required for navigation purpose.
- Favourable or unfavourable foundations for the bridge at moderate spans.

Tunneling permits construction in stages e.g. a six lane river crossing can be constructed in series of two lane tunnels as needed. Such advantage is not available, if a bridge is to be constructed for the same conditions.

It must be born in mind that, the factors mentioned above are mutually interdependent.

The size of tunnel chiefly depends upon the end use of the tunnel, whereas the shape tunnel is dictated by the requirements of end use and strata conditions.

As stated earlier, while considering the size of tunnel, following factors are required to be considered :

- Requirements of tunnel while it is in operation, including various equipments, machineries that will be operated, maintained and required inside the tunnel.
- Requirements of ventilation, drainage, safe clearances between tracks and side clearance.
- Requirements for regular maintenance of tunnel, emergency provisions, to enter rescue team, equipments etc. must be considered and due provision made.
- It is not possible to drill tunnel of exact size, due to possibility of over breaking. As a result, reasonable allowance for the same has to be allowed. Usually an allowance of 15 to 30 cm from finished tunnel surface is made.

18.2 METHOD OF TUNNELLING

The various method of tunnelling
1. Full Face Method
2. Heading and Bench Method
3. Drift Method
4. Drill and Blast Method for Rock Tunnelling

1. Full Face Method

In this method, the whole tunnel face is blasted at the same time. The advantages of this method are that it allows tunnelling in one operation and is efficient. However, large mechanical equipment is required for large tunnels and this method is not suitable for unstable rock where large opening will induce significant stress on the rock mass.

- Adopted for tunnels of small C/s area - diameter < 6 m and face areas < 19 m^2 - through stable and self supporting rocks
- Full face is opened out once for all and driven
- Extra units of tunneling equipment necessary
- TBMs –well suited for full face excavation
- Mucking truck can be positioned once and for further mucking the position in shafted in according to the progress of the work.
- Total ground disturbances and settlement is minimum in full face method

2. Heading and Benching Method

In large tunnels and when the quality of the rock is not satisfactory, heading and benching method is often used. This method involves the driving the top portion of the tunnel in advance of the bottom portion. The lining of roof arch can then be constructed first by using the bottom bench as temporary supports. Another advantage of this method is that when cutting the bottom bench, the blasting becomes more effective by using vertical blast holes behind the tunnel face and less explosives can be used.

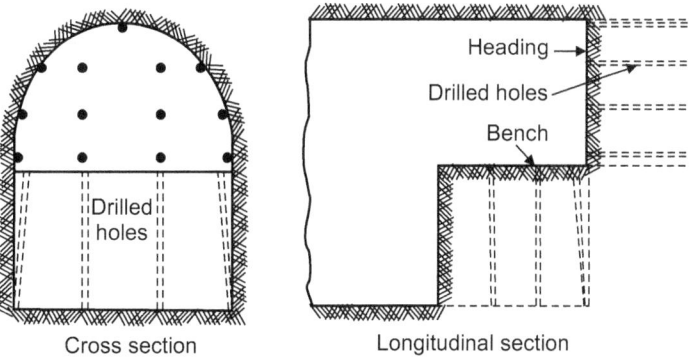

Fig. 18.2 : Heading and benching method

3. Drift Method

In very large tunnel or weak rock, the attacking of the tunnel face can be further subdivided into several stages. Similar to heading and benching, tunnelling is carried out in smaller section first and then widened subsequently. Drift method can be further classified into centre drift, side drift, top drift and bottom drift.

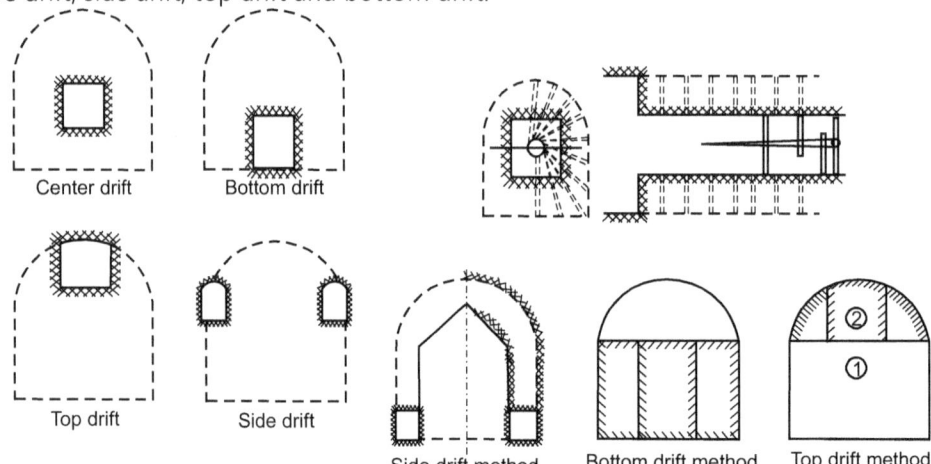

Fig. 18.3 : Drift methods

Advantages of Drift Method

- Any zone of bad rock or excessive water will be discovered prior to driving the full bore, thus permitting corrective steps to be taken away.
- The drift will assist in ventilating the tunnel during later operations.
- The scale of each blasting is smaller hence vibration and damage are reduced.
- Top and side drifts may facilitate the installation of support to the roof, especially for a tunnel driven through broken rock.

4. Drill and Blast Method for Rock Tunneling

This method is suitable in medium to strong rock. By jack hammers, blast holes are drilled on the tunnel face. Explosives are loaded in the blast holes and then blasting is taken place. R.C. tunnel lining can be cast by using travelling formwork, or more often, the tunnel lining is formed by sprayed concrete.

Fig. 18.4 : Rock drilling by Jack Hammer

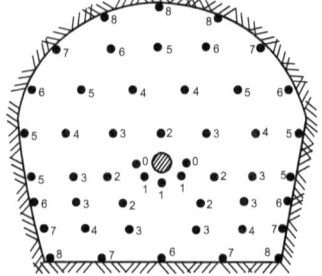

Fig. 18.5 : Drill and Blast Method

There are various methods of attacking the rock face. The choice depends on the size and shape of tunnel and the available equipment.

18.3 MUCKING AND DISPOSAL

"Muck" is the industry term for excavated material produced during the advancement of the tunnel. All tunnel mining produces muck. This excavated material must be removed from the working face of the tunnel so that the next advance can be made. Tunneling is a series of individual steps, each of which must be completed before the next can start. Once the muck is produced it must be removed from the tunnel and finally disposed of in a legal manner or used as fill for some portion of the tunnel project or other project where it could have a beneficial use.

Muck is actually a broken down state of the insitu material through which the tunnel is driven. Because the natural material is disturbed by either blasting, cutting with a TBM, road header or cut out with a bucket excavator the volume of muck removed actually is larger than the natural bank material. This swell is usually approximated as 70% to 100% more in rock and 25% to 40% for soil.

The material that is excavated must be removed from the tunnel. The method chosen to remove this material depends on many factors such as the diameter or size of the excavation, the length of the tunnel excavated from any given heading, the material being moved, the grade of the tunnel being driven and whether the material is going to a shaft for removal or a portal. Horizontal conveyor belts are commonly used for large excavated tunnels that are longer than a few thousand feet and are excavated by a TBM (Fig. 18.3). Conveyors can move a large quantity of material quickly. Conveyors require that the excavated material be of relatively uniform small size so that it will sit in the belt during the transfer to the shaft or portal. Conveyors can sometimes be used with a drill and blast excavation method if the contractor employs a crusher to make the drill and blast rock a more even and smaller consistency. This crushing is necessary to ensure that the material sits nicely on the belt, is small enough that when it is loaded onto the belt it does not damage or rip the belt material. Conveyors are usually limited to a grade (or slope) less than 18 degrees to successfully transport muck, but this is never an issue in road tunnels. Conveyors can transport rock or soil. The soil must not be too wet or it will not transport well. Conveyors can also be used in tunnels where there are curves in the alignment but this requires some special care and equipment.

Material that is too wet to carry on a conveyor belt can sometimes be pumped out of the tunnel through a pipeline from the TBM to the shaft or portal. This method is successfully used on soft ground tunnels where the material is clay like or where sufficient water (and often, conditioners) is mixed with the excavated material to make it slurry like.

For smaller tunnels excavated by a TBM, contractors often choose to load the excavated muck into rail cars and haul it out of the tunnel using locomotives. Rail haulage also has some limitations such as the grades are usually limited to less than 4%, a great amount of rolling stock is required and great care must be paid to maintaining the track.

Fig. 18.6 : Horizontal muck conveyor

Once the muck arrives at the shaft or portal it must be off loaded and then disposed of. Fig.18.7 shows a muck train dumping at a tunnel portal. A shaft is a vertical hole through which all excavated material must be lifted and removed and through which all material required for the tunneling operations must be lowered to the tunnel level. In addition all personnel working on or inspecting the tunnel must come in and out of this shaft. In other words it is a busy place. There are many ways to transport the muck up the shaft. Muck cars can be lifted one by one up the shaft, dumped in a pile on the surface and lowered back down to the tunnel. Muck cars can be dumped into a hopper at the bottom of the shaft and then loaded into a bucket that is hoisted to the top and dumped or the muck from the hopper could be loaded onto a vertical conveyor and conveyed to the top of the shaft and dumped onto a pile or hopper. Similarly the muck can be pumped to the surface and deposited on a horizontal conveyor, a stockpile or run through a processing plant to remove the water and the residual dumped on a pile or into hoppers.

Fig. 18.7 : Muck train dumping at portal

Portals provide easier access to a tunnel since they eliminate the bottleneck that the shaft imposes. Muck is easier to remove at a portal since track can be paced on the ground or on an elevated trestle so that muck cars can be pulled outside to dump their loads onto a muck pile.

The really important thing to remember is that tunneling is a series of steps that must be done and complete before the cycle can start again. This means that any disruption in the muck removal operation will delay the start of the next round or the next advance. If you cannot get rid of the muck you cannot produce more! This is also true once the muck reaches the surface. There should be a place to store the muck that is brought out of the tunnel until it can be loaded into trucks or rail cars and hauled away. Without this storage capability on the surface (Fig. 18.8), all muck brought out of the tunnel must immediately be loaded into surface trucks or rail cars for disposal. If there is a holdup in the surface trucking or rail cars then no more muck can be brought out and the tunnel advance must stop. This situation is called being "muck bound" and must be avoided at all costs. The more muck storage that is available the more unlikely it will be for a project to become muck bound. Work sites must be large enough to provide this storage cushion, the larger a worksite the bigger the cushion. It is increasingly more difficult to find available land in and around cities to provide a suitably large worksite. Typically urban sites are small and therefore special care must be taken to ensure a steady stream of vehicles to remove the muck as it is produced, and to deliver workers and materials as needed. Thought must also be given to the hours of operation allowed in urban tunnel projects. If the hours of operation for surface work are restricted, i.e., surface work is not allowed after 10 PM at night, then in order to operate the tunnel 24 hours per day, there must be some place to store muck underground that is produced on the shift where no surface work is allowed, and construction noises must be kept below a threshold based on local ordinances and/or certain realistic decibel levels

Fig. 18.8 : Surface muck storage area

Methods of Mucking based on Equipment Available
- Battery operated or electrically operated mucking system.
  Methods explained in (a) above come in this category.

- Use of dumpers : In place of railway track, use of dumpers is made. However, this has two disadvantages :
  (a) Lot of diesel gas is emitted while plying of dumpers and proper ventilation is required to be arranged.
  (b) There is lot of wear and tear of tyres plying on rock and suitable protective arrangement has to be made.
  (c) For turning of trucks through 180°, suitable space/enlargement is required to be made.
- **Use of Conveyor Belts :** Excavated muck is placed over conveyor belt, to carry muck, upto suitable place in tunnel, wherefrom it is hauled to dumping yard. This method is suitable is tunnel of small diameter, full of various types of pipelines etc. However, as tunnel progresses, suitable changes in conveyor belt has to be made.

18.4 DRILLING PATTERNS

The different types of drilling patterns generally used are
- Wedge cut
- Parallel holes
- Burn cut method
- Pyramidal cut pattern
- Centre cut method

The main features of this pattern are :

Holes are inclined inwards from the face.

These are closely assisted immediately by the 'erasers' or relievers (2) spaces in between. Further from those are lifers at the bottom and jack holes at the top (3) both of which are called rim holes. On the sides, the side holes, (4) assist the break. The numbers started above indicate the sequence of firing. The interval between these firing is however a few second only.

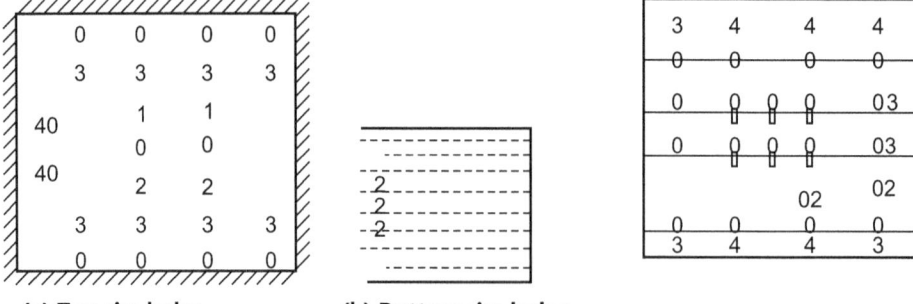

(a) Top rim holes   (b) Bottom rim holes

Fig. 18.9 : Pyramidal cut method   Fig. 18.10 : Centre cut method

18.5 BLASTING

Three factors have, by and large, influenced developments in blasting technology, namely safer handling, a reduction in toxicity and rapid and straight forward charging of the boreholes.

The quantity of explosives required for blasting rocks for tunneling depends on :
- Kind of explosive
- Method of tunneling
- Hardness of ground
- Profile f tunnel
- Depth of lift

Mainly the quantity of explosive is calculated on the basis of the previous experience of tunneling. In soft rocks about 2 kg of explosive is required for on cubic meter of solid rock, whereas it is about 5.7 kg in case of hard rocks.

Explosive : There is a wide range of explosive common explosives in basting are :
- Ammonia dynamite
- Blasting gelatin
- Semi-gelatin
- Special gelatin

Now a day pumpable emulsion explosive are used due to their higher safety, lower toxicity and speeded up charging phase. The tamping rod is introduced manually. The two emulsion components are mixed in the borehole by automatic means via radio remote control, volumetrically controlled, a as result of which the degree of fill and the explosive effect can be altered.

Detonators

Two types of detonators used in blasting operations re
- Ordinary
- Electric

The electric detonators are further divided into

(a) Instantaneous

(b) Delay

(c) Short delay

(d) Long delay

The advantages of the electric ignition system with regard to the controllability of the resistance is compensated for by the straightforwardness and robustness of the pyrotechnic tube ignition system when it is used in combination with electronic detonators in the contour. These electronic detonators guarantee paramount safety and at the same time, an accurate firing sequence of the individual stages. This facilities a considerable improvement in low vibration accurate blasting. Owing to their high individual costs, electronic detonators are used in combination with the tube ignition system. In conjunction with the electronic detonators in the contour zone, high cross-sectional accuracy is arrived at by achieving a clean break in the contour as a result of simultaneous ignition. The combination of various firing materials with pumpable emulsion explosives enhances the economy of drill and blast.

18.6 TUNNEL LINING

Introduction

Tunnel construction is a highly complex process. It includes considerations of various natures such as geology, geo-technique, organisation of the works, and economy. Above all, the safety of the workers and the users must be warranted as well as the serviceability of the tunnel on the long .Lining methods, which are the permanent support methods for the tunnel, play the main role for keeping tunnel from collapse and provide safe. There are different lining methods for tunnels. Selecting the efficient lining method should be in the context of the whole methods used for tunnel construction to achieve a harmonized tunnel construction system. Technical and nontechnical factors control the selection of the efficient tunnel lining methods.

The technical factors are : "Tunnel function", "Tunnel cross sectional profile", "Groundwater conditions" and "Ground conditions".

The main two non-technical factors are cost and time, they are very important factors and they can be the main factors for taking a decision of selecting the lining method.

Requirement of Permanent Lining

- Easy to maintain
- Economical
- Durable
- Simple toco0nstruct
- Stable

Purpose of Lining

The purposes of providing permanent tunnel lining are as follows :

- Withstands soil pressure when driven in soft strata
- Reduces losses by friction and erosive action.
- Rocks prone to air slaking receive a good protective covering
- Provides correct designed section to the tunnel.
- Supports large slabs of loose rock which might have loosened during blasting
- Prevents chemical action of water with certain types of rock

- Keeps inside of tunnel free from water percolation
- Reduces friction against flow and thereby ensures stream line flow of water.
- Lining increase appearance and neatness of the tunnel.

Types of Lining
- Timber lining
- Iron lining
- Cast steel lining
- Pressed steel liner plates
- Brick lining
- Stone masonry lining
- Concrete and R.C.C. lining
- Shotcrete lining
- Precast concrete segments
- Cast-in-place concrete,
- Pipe in tunnel

Tunnel Lining Materials

Permanent linings are required in most tunnels, always in soft ground and frequently in rock. They are required for two purposes : structurally to retain the earth and water pressure, and operationally to provide an internal surface appropriate to the function of the tunnel. The principal materials for permanent lining of bored tunnels are :

Brickwork, Blockwork and Masonry

Brickwork, blockwork and masonry had been used for tunnel lining but now they are obsolete.

Insitu Concrete

Insitu concrete lining is frequently in rock tunnelling where the roof is able to stay unsupported temporary. Specially designed travelling formwork is used for casting the concrete.

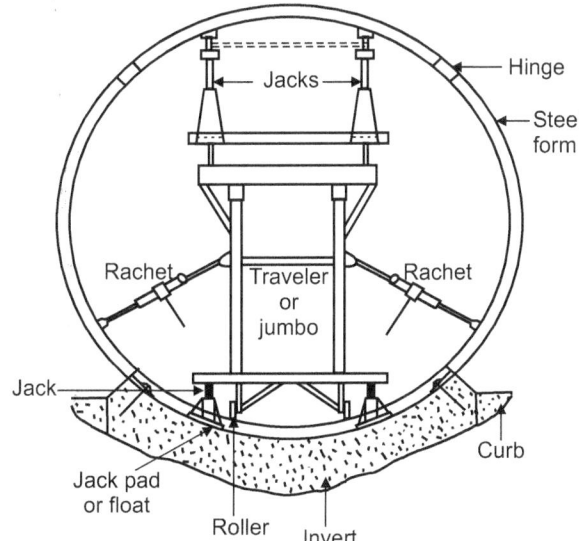

Fig. 18.11 : Taveling form for tunnel lining construction

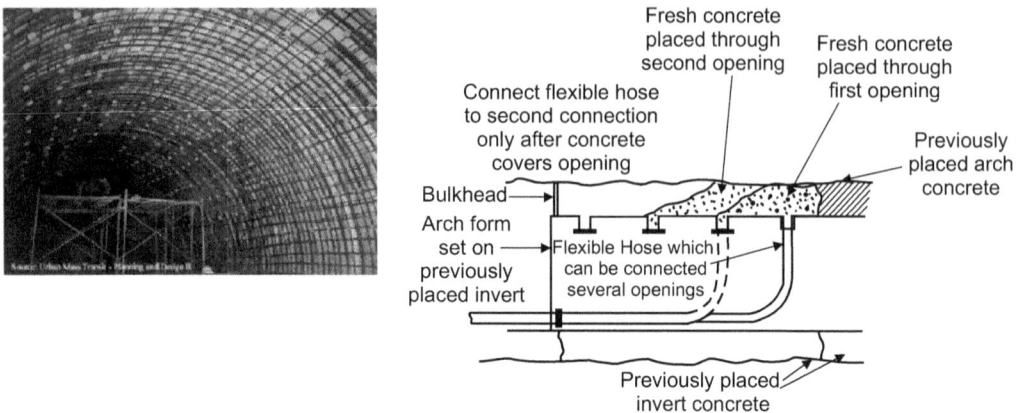

Fig. 18.12 : Tunnel lining reinforcement   Fig. 18.13 : Concreting for tunnel lining

Preformed Segments

Preformed segments may be made of cast iron, steel or normal reinforced concrete. This type of lining usually comes with TBM or shield tunneling methods. The segments are jointed together by bolting and the joints are sealed with neoprene gasket. Sometimes the joints are also caulked with rubberized bituminous strips. Voids behind the preformed segments are filled by bentonite cement grout.

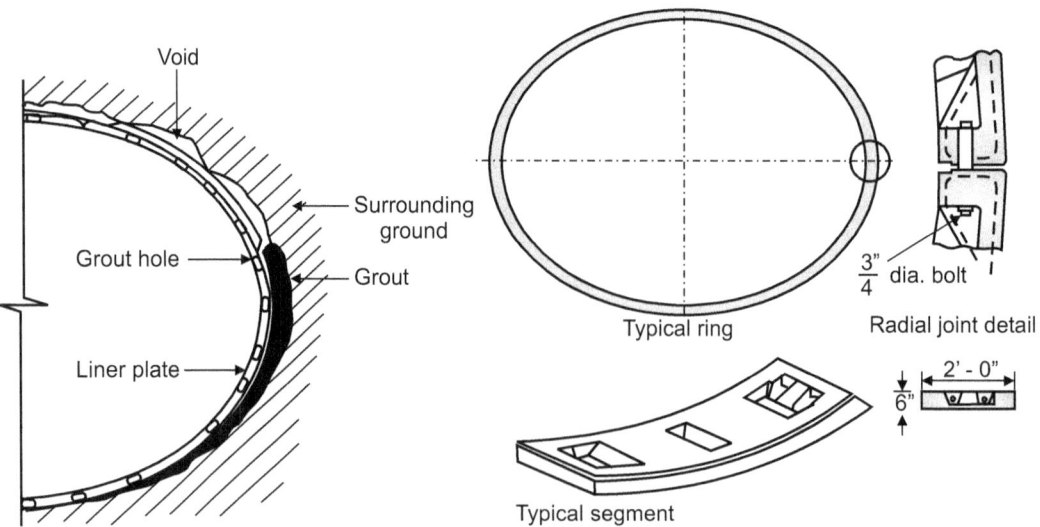

Fig. 18.14 : Grouting the void behind the lining   Fig. 18.15 : Typical segment

18.7 METHODS OF VENTILATION, LIGHTING AND DUST CONTROL

Ventilation :

Removal of foul gases produced during construction and in use of tunnels such as fumes from blasting, diesel gases, decomposition of organic matter, dust produced during drilling and mucking etc. and providing about 6 to 14 m^3 of fresh air per person per minute etc. is necessary, failing which efficiency of operators, workers will reduce. **IS : 5878-Part-II/Sec II-1971** code has, therefore, been formulated & to lay down the lighting requirement for tunneling

Methods of Ventilation

Ventilation can be either natural ventilation or mechanical.

Natural Ventilation

This can be achieved by

- Providing a small diameter tunnel for the entire length of tunnel, which can also serve as pilot tunnel.

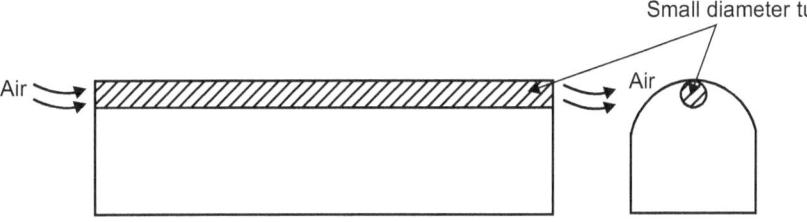

Fig. 18.16

- When diameter of tunnel is large, but is of a short length then no special provision is required.
- By providing/orienting tunnel in the direction of wind.

Mechanical Ventilation

This is achieved by blowing fresh air or by exhausting dust and foul air by proving fans of suitable capacity.

(a) Blowing in Air : Fresh air is blown by blower fans, through ventilation ducts. The ventilation ducts are made of suitable thin G.I. pipes, which are hung from roof.

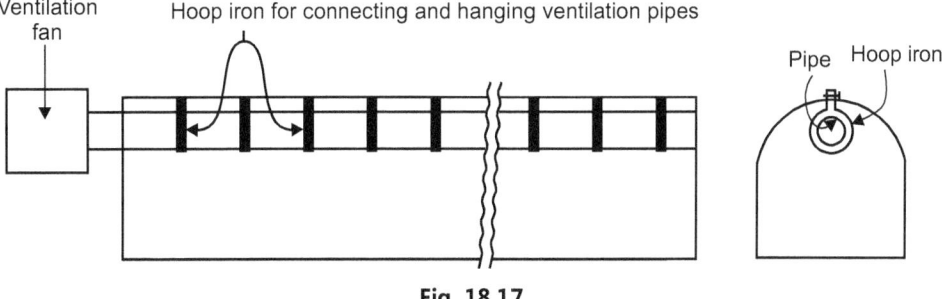

Fig. 18.17

In order to reduce friction and leakages, very smooth GI or plastic pipes with lesser joints are provided.

(b) Exhausting Fans : Arrangement is made to exhaust foul gases and due to difference in pressure, fresh air from outside enters into tunnel. There is no necessity to blow fresh air.

(c) Blowing in and Exhausting out : The same fan and the same ducts are alternately used to exhaust foul gases and by changing direction of rotation of fan, fresh air is forced inside the tunnel.

Table 18.1

Ventilation System		Merits	Demerits
Face Concentration	Air exhaust	1. Only air pipes to be extended 2. Easy maintenance 3. Little leakage	1. Gas flown to face 2. Only hard ventilation pipe available 3. Capacity of fan to be changed at portal 4. Local fan necessary at face
	Air supply	Above mentioned	1. Passage of dirty air in tunnel 2. Hard ventilation pipes to be used 3. Capacity iof fan to be changed at portal
Series Concentration	Continuous (Air exhaust / Air supply)	1. Economical due to small fan	1. Leakage at joints 2. Hard ventilation pipe to be used 3. One fan to be affected by trouble of another
	Continuous (Air exhaust / Air supply)	Above mentioned	1. Big leakage 2. One fan to be affected by trouble of another.

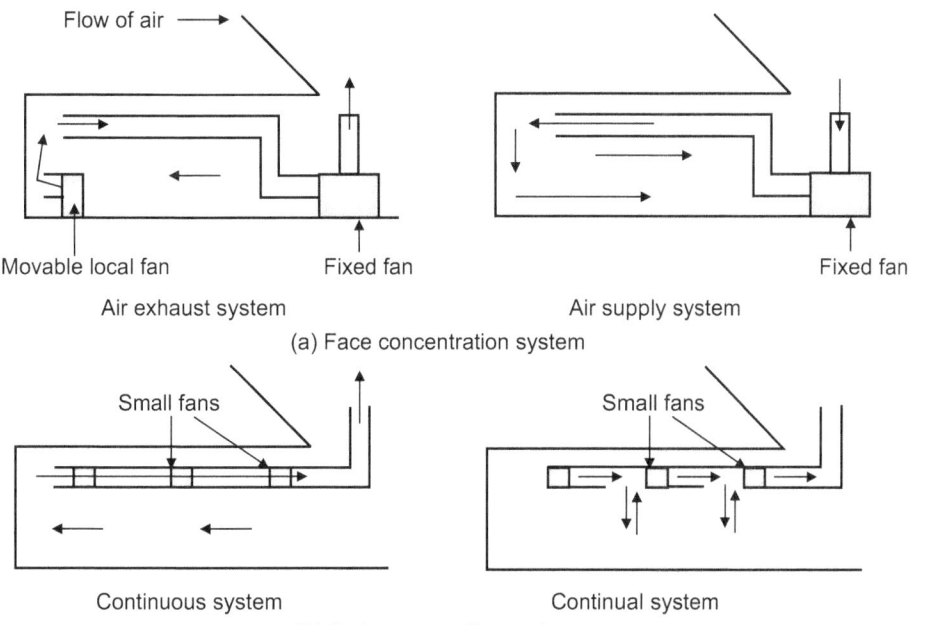

Fig. 18.18 : Ventilation systems

Lighting in Tunnels

If adequate light is not provided, efficiency of work is drastically reduced, due to fear and possibility of accident.

In large diameter/size tunnels, require more light or light at closer spacing is required than that for small diameter tunnel.

Except when it is not possible to provide electric lamps, battery operated lamps are provided. Intensity of light in working area of intensity of 260 lumens/m^2 should be provided.

Fig. 18.19

Electric lights are commonly used for following reasons :

- Does not consume oxygen as in case of lanterns for which oil is to be burnt.
- Connection can be easily extended or removed.
- Light of suitable intensity can be adjusted.

IS : 5878-Part-II/Sec II-1971 code has, therefore, been formulated & to lay down the lighting requirement for tunneling.

18.8 DRAINAGE OF TUNNELING

Drainage system is provided in tunnels to collect and remove water entering the tunnel during and after construction. After construction water and other liquids may enter a tunnel from various sources such as :

- Rainfall runoff from portal areas;
- Rainwater carried in by vehicles;
- Groundwater infiltration;
- Wastewater effluent from wash-down activities;
- Accidental spillage of fuel from damaged vehicles and the wash-down of such products;
- Operation of fire suppression systems; and
- Accidental rupture of a fire main or hydrant.

Necessity of Drainage

- For the progress of work during construction
- To reduce wear and tear of communication route
- To provide safety of the moving vehicle

Classification of Drainage System

Drainage system is classified as :

1. Drainage system provided at the time of construction or temporary drainage system.
2. Drainage system provided in complete tunnel or permanent drainage system

(1) Temporary Drainage System : This is provided to remove groundwater from the tunnel at the time of construction. in this system water is removed either by

(a) open- ditch drainage system or

(b) pumping system

   (a) Open- Ditch Drainage System : In this system, water is collected and removed in open ditches, laid with proper slopes at some distance away from the place of work. This is suitable for impermeable soil and rock bases.

   (b) Pumping System : In this system sumps are constructed at regular intervals. Water is collected in the sumps and is pumped out.

(2) Temporary Drainage System : Permanent drainage system is provided in one of the following methods.

   (a) by providing a central drain

   (b) by providing side drains

   (c) by providing corrugated iron shed and side drains

(a) By Providing a Central Drain

A central drain is provided between two railway tracks or under pavement. It should have enough capacity to handle the expected water in the tunnel. Is should be provided with facilities for inspection and clearing. Inspection manholes are also provided at 30 m to 50 m interval.

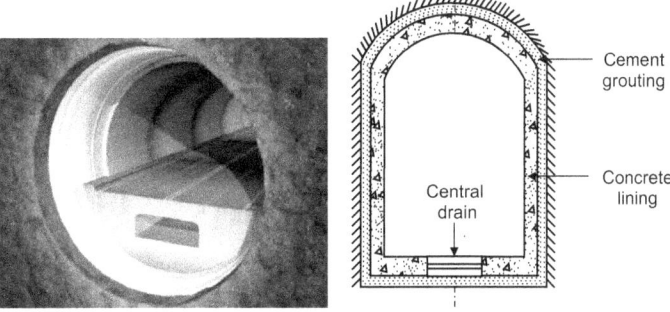

Fig. 18.20 : Central drain system

(b) By Providing a Side Drain

This system is suitable in single lane road or railway tunnel and where the quantity of water to be drained is small. In this system drains are provided in either side of the track or road

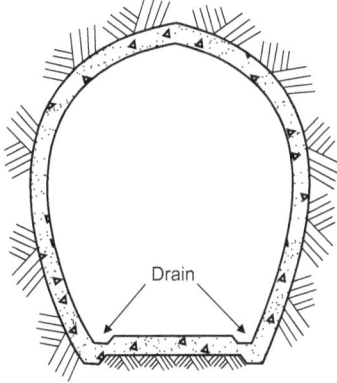 

Fig. 18.21 : By providing a side drain

(c) By Providing Corrugated Iron Shed and Side Drain

This is provided in tunnels in which water leaks from the roof and side wall of tunnels. By providing corrugated iron shed. Shaped to the contour of the roof, water is prevented from dropping on the ck. the corrugated shed guides the water to the side drains and is drained out.

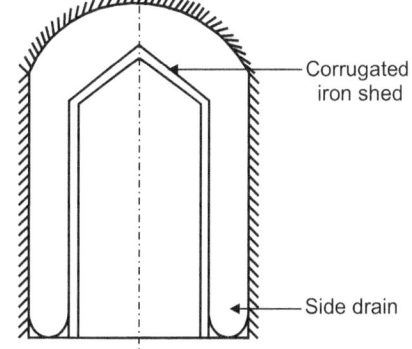

Fig. 18.22 : Corrugated iron shed and side drain

18.9 DUST CONTROL

Lot of dust is produced during drilling, blasting and mucking operations. If silica is present in the rock encountered, there is possibility of workers inhaling silica, leading to its entry into lungs, piercing lungs/leading to disease called silicosis.

Following corrective methods are adopted :

- Sprinking of water over excavated muck, so that while mucking dust is not produced.
- Providing continuous supply of water while drilling. This water not only cools drilling bit, but provides lubrication and eliminates production of dust.
- Providing hood around drill steel at rock face, which is connected to suction hose. This method is used in dry drilling i.e. only pneumatic air is used for drilling.
- Asking workers to use respirators, which filter air, allowing only air to inhale and removing dust.

18.10 SAFETY IN TUNNEL

Tunneling work is widely carried out in the country in the construction of railway, road and hydel projects. The work involved is of a specialized and hazardous nature. Cramped working space in the heading, wet and slippery flooring, artificial lighting - all too often inadequate, difficult ventilation, obnoxious gases, unseen weaknesses in the rock, handling of explosives, leading and hauling muck, etc, might contribute to accidents. In order to avoid hazards, it is necessary to lay down the safety precautions for the use of machinery, electrical installations and labour in tunnels, during the construction period, and arrange for their compliance. Safety Code for Tunneling Work- **IS : 4756 – 1978** code has, therefore, been formulate & to lay down the safety rules for tunneling in rocks and soft strata and underground excavations in rocks.

Safety Precautions in Tunneling

Construction Engineering and safety go hand in hand. Underground construction is inherently a dangerous undertaking. Work goes on in a noisy environment, in close quarters often with moving heavy machinery. Careful attention must be paid to the layout of the worksites; workers must be protected at all times. The overriding philosophy must be that, "everyone goes home safely at the end of their shift".

Every step of the operation should be planned with safety in mind. The normal surface safety concerns are also appropriate for underground construction. Workers must be safeguarded from falling off of the work platforms used in the mining process. Workers must be protected from being struck by the moving equipment used throughout the mining process. Workers most be protected from being electrocuted. However there are also many additional hazards that workers must be protected from and guarded against

- Educate the workers to obey safety regulations.
- Handle explosive with acre and in accordance to rules and instructions
- Anticipate hazards and take remedial measures.
- Provide competent and safety supervisions.
- Inculcate discipline among workers
- Do not overload machinery or equipment
- Use electrical energy with care
- Permit only the trained workers to handle machinery
- Demand strict obedienance of alarms and sign
- Adopt rational approach in tunneling based upon investigation and experience.

The Tunnel Construction Engineer must also be certain to make sure that the job specifications require strict compliance with all safety measures and regulations local, state and national. The Engineer must stress to the designer and the owner that money spent on worker and job site safety is money well spent since the cost of accidents and replacing structures damaged or destroyed by a fire event is so high.

Safety Equipment in Road Tunnels

- **Tunnel Lighting :** The lighting systems enable the human eye to adapt quickly to the reduced visibility in tunnels. Emergency exists and stations are fitted with continuous lighting.
- **Ventilation Systems :** In the event of a fire the ventilation system extracts smoke from the tunnel. in this case leave as quickly as possible the smoke area.
- Emergency exits are clearly marked by appropriate sign and lights. in the event of a fire, always leave your vehicle immediately and follow emergency lights showing the escape route to emergency or tunnel exists.
- **Traffic Surveillance :** If an emergency call comes from inside the tunnel, the image from the camera in that particular section appears automatically on the monitor in the tunnel operator's control room. Video system automatically checks all tunnel area, including the highest permitted speed and the smallest distance between vehicles.
- **Emergency Lanes and Lay-bye :** are used vehicles in the case of braking down or accident.
- **Emergency Stations :** are located in the tunnel at frequent intervals. they are equipped with : emergency phones connected with tunnel, push-button help and fire annunciator and portable fire extinguishers.

Review Questions

1. Write sequence of operations of tunneling.
2. Define mucking. State methods of mucking.
3. Write short notes on :
   (a) Dust control
   (b) Methods of Ventilation
   (c) Lighting in tunnel
   (d) Tunnel drainage
4. What are the methods of ventilation? Explain.
5. What are the objects of lining in the tunnel? Explain any one method of tunnel lining in detail.
6. Describe the various methods for the effective drainage during and after the construction of the tunnels?
7. Write short notes on the safety measures to be adopted in tunnel construction.
8. Write short notes on the safety measures to be adopted in road tunnel.
9. Enlist various methods of tunneling in hard rock Describe any one in detail.
10. What are the various types of explosives used in the tunneling work?
11. Write short notes on :
    (a) Lighting of tunnels.
    (b) Dust control.

CHAPTER 19
TUNNELING IN SOFT MATERIALS

19.1 INTRODUCTION

While tunneling through soft and hard rock more energy and attention is given on excavation and less on the problem of supporting roof, seepage of water, whereas while tunneling through soft soil, more attention is required to be paid on supporting of roof, preventing ingress of water etc. A number of methods, including conventional method of fore poling, shield tunneling (with or without use of compressed air) to Modern Tunnel Boring Machining (TBM) with Earth Pressure Balance (EPB) arrangement are available. A brief introduction of these methods is given below :

Methods

Following methods of tunneling are accepted while tunneling through soft soil :

(a) Fore poling method.

(b) Shield tunneling in free air.

(c) Shield tunneling using compressed air.

(d) Special shield tunneling methods.

    For large diameter tunnels (Diameter > 3 m)

- Slurry shield tunneling.
- Earth pressure balance shield.
- Slim shields.

(e) No dig/trenchless tunneling/Pipe jacking for tunnels of small diameter (i.e. less than 3m).

Factors Influencing Choice of Method

Various factors which influence choice of methods are :

- Ground conditions.
- Size of tunnel.
- Initial and running cost.
- Rate of advance.
- Factors related to time for procurement of new equipment, installation time, space required.
- Support lining etc.

Table 19.1 gives comparison of various methods of tunneling through soft ground.

Table 19.1 : Comparison of Different Methods of Soft Ground Tunneling

Item		Manual Excavation	Shield- Manual or Backhoe or Boom Excavation	Full Face Machine	Full Face Slurry/ Bentonite Machine
Costs	Initial cost	Low	Medium	High	Very high
	Running cost	High	Medium	Medium	High
Rate of Advance m/100 hr	Favourable ground	30	100	400	75
	Mixed ground	10-15	10-15	–	–
	New equipment delivery time	Available	6-9 months	12 months	12 months
	Installation time	Nil	4 weeks	8-10 weeks	15-20 weeks
Installation	Space required	No restriction	Shaft or chamber 1.2 × tunnel diameter	Shaft or chamber 1.2 × tunnel diameter	Shaft or chamber 1.2 × tunnel diameter
Application		Traditional method for short drives	Mixed ground conditions	Homogeneous ground conditions	Water bearing homogeneous ground
General access for operations and maintenance		Good	Good	Fair	Fair
Tunnel size, m		Any	Any	Fair	Fair
Support/lining type		Insitu, segmental	Segmental	Segmental	Segmental

(**Source :** Tunneling in soft ground ... by D. G. Kadkade, Director, Technical, Industries Ltd., in Civil Engineering and Construction Review, July 1994.)

19.2 Needle Beam Method

When a short length weak strata is encountered, it is difficult to make arrangement for modern equipment to deal such situation and particularly in a short interval of time. In such a case, if the strata is strong enough to stand, without any support for short interval, needle beam method can be used. It consists of transmitting load of roof through jacks resting on needle beam having wider flanges as shown in Fig. 19.1

Needle beam is flitched beam comprising of two channel sections of steel and in between these channels, sufficiently deep and wide wooden beam is provided. The wooden beam is fixed to channel, with suitable nut-bolt arrangement. Sufficiently thick and wide wooden plank is provided at the top and bottom of flitched beam to transmit the load over wider area.

On the top of the beam, hydraulic jacks are provided to take the load of roof.

The work is carried out as follows :

- Small pocket hole/notch is made in the roof to accommodate desired thickness and shape of brick masonry.

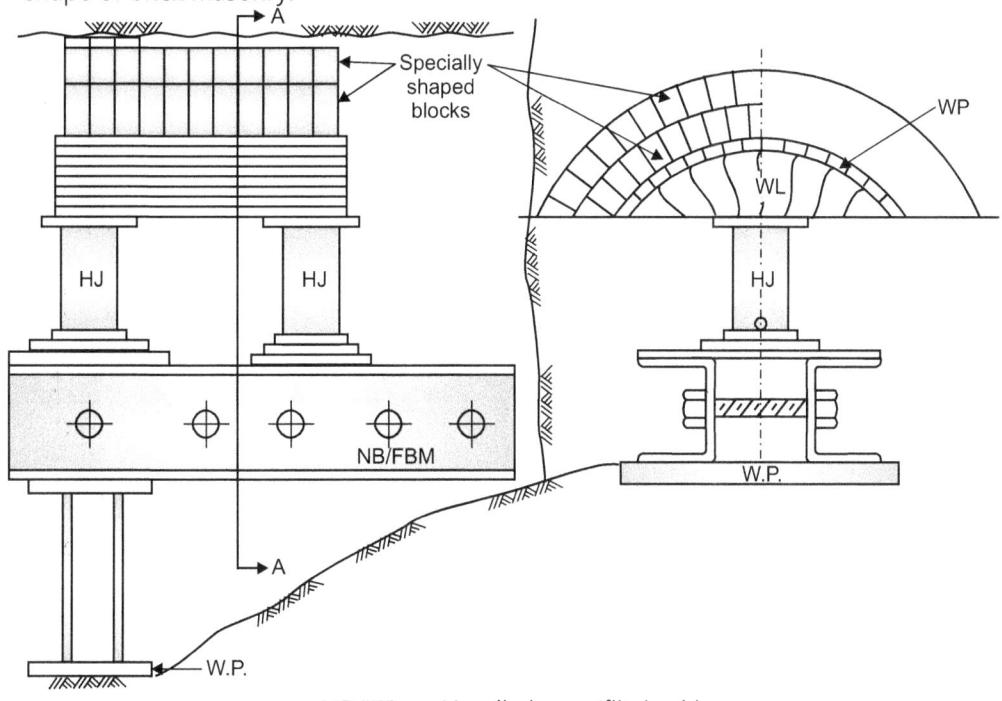

NB/FIB = Needle beam/flitched beam
WP = Wooden plank
HJ = Hydraulic jack
WL = Wooden lagging

Fig. 19.1 : Needle beam method

- Wooden lagging of suitable size and shape is placed below the notch and the lagging is supported by hydraulic jack resting on flitched beam.
- In the excavated notch brick arches out of specially prepared bricks or concrete blocks are provided. The brick arch is supported by wooden lagging, which is self supported by hydraulic jacks resting in flitched beam.
- In the similar fashion, work is extended on either side to cover entire span, carefully giving support to the lining and lagging by hydraulic jacks. Due to arch action, load of roof is transferred on sides, and no tensile stresses are developed.
- Load on hydraulic jack is released gradually and the needle beam together with jacks is pushed forward and work is continued.
- Any uneven settlement in the side wall will lead to heavy stresses and collapse of roof. Precautions are taken to guard this.

This method is relatively slow and labour intensive, hence is suitable for a weak strata of short length only.

Needle beam method, showing method of support to roof by providing arched brick lining.

19.3 NEW AUSTRIAN TUNNELING METHOD (NATM)

At present this method is gaining world-wide recognition. NATM not only takes into account the strength of surrounding ground but also considers support provided by primary support and temporary support.

- It allows flexible tunnel design, which can be readily and continuously updated to suit strata encountered and is therefore suitable for soft ground and hard or medium hard rock as well.
- Strength of rock mass can be mobilized by minimizing rock deformation and preventing of loosening of rock mass.

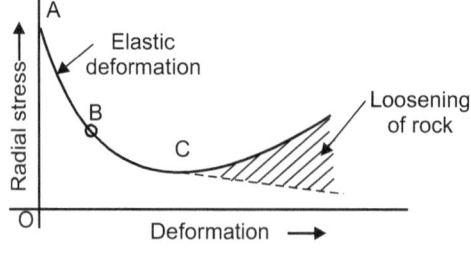

Fig. 19.2

- Installation of instrument in the roof of excavated rock, provides information regarding rock mass deformation. This gives vital information about stability of tunnel and allows optimization of support system.

NATM for Soft Ground Tunneling

As against full face excavation adopted in soft soil using shield driven tunnels, NATM uses face excavation with a stepped face inclined at 60° as shown in Fig. 19.3.

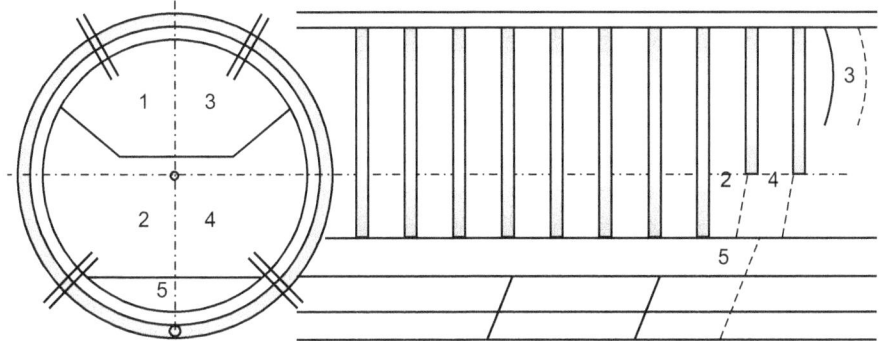

Fig. 19.3 : NATM method

In order to facilitate rapid closing of invert, full face excavation in small advances is permitted. Invert is closed after every alternate advance of crown. Thus, for every 1 m progress in crown portion, invert is closed 4 m behind the crown portion. Depending upon the nature of strata encountered suitable temporary support system and or soil stabilizing measures such as shotcreting, soil reinforcement, grouting, dewatering methods are employed.

Advantages : Use of NATM concept in soft ground tunneling has following advantages :

- It allows use of free excavation area and is therefore cheap.
- Excavated portion of tunnel can be kept effectively dry (even where appreciable water pressure exists), by adopting suitable water proofing membranes.
- Most important, it permits flexibility to suit unforeseen ground conditions.

NATM for Tunneling in Rock

Various measures are taken to control ground deformations, so that resulting ground pressure is not activated.

- **Temporary Support :** Temporary support is provided by use of shotcrete, rock bolting, providing weld mesh and steel ribs.
- **Depth of Round :** It will be noticed that, shorter the depth of round, lesser will be the shortening of horizontal diameter, due to rearrangement of stresses around the face area. This increases stability of tunnel, however it reduces rate of advance of tunnel per round.
- **Pilot Heading :** NATM takes into account the effect of closing of invert. As clarified earlier, in case of soft ground, invert is closed as early as possible to limit ground movement, whereas when hard strata is encountered, invert is closed at a certain distance behind the face. This permits distressing of rock mass.

19.4 TBM

While tunneling through soft soil, many problems like dewatering, collapse of roof, strengthening of roof etc. are required to be tackled. In the early years of 20th century, these were tackled by providing shield tunneling, which consist of forcing sharp edged steel shield in the crown portion, ahead of excavation, and then removing the soil below mechanically or manually. Essentially, Tunnel Boring Machines [TBM] are modern versions of shield tunnel. Initially, TBMs were developed, for tunneling in soft soil, but with the new developments, different types of TBMs are available, so that tunneling can be carried out in various types of soils and rocks. In India recently TBM has been used for tunneling through rock for disposal of sewage, as well as for supply of water.

19.4.1 Types of TBMs

Following types of TBMs are available :
- Unshielded open type.
- Shielded type.
- Double shielded.
- Closed face slurry type.
- Earth pressure balance type.

Tunnels in soft soil are often constructed as bored tunnels, when the use of cut and cover tunnel techniques is not possible or too costly an option. Bored tunnelling techniques cover both tunnels constructed by the use of a Tunnel Boring Machine (TBM) and tunnels constructed by hand tools and machines, using an observational approach with temporary support of the excavation. The latter is often called sprayed concrete lined (SCL) tunnels.

Tunnel Boring Machines

Two typical TBM types are the earth pressure balance (EPB) machine and the slurry machine. During construction, the former is able to counterbalance the ground and water pressures in front of the TBM by the use of one or two screws between the cutterhead and the conveyer belt. The latter uses a technique where bentonite slurry is pumped into the cutterhead and mixed with the excavated material. The mixed slurry is then pumped out of the tunnel where the bentonite and the excavated material are separated again. This system also provides stability in front of the TBM during tunnel construction. During recent years is has become possible to build larger diameter TBM bored tunnels, mainly due to improved technology and the development of larger diameter TBMs. This has opened the market for bored road tunnels significantly, as road tunnels often require a greater cross-section than e.g. rail tunnels, but also bi-directional rail tunnels are now possible to construct. The large diameter tunnels involve large challenges during construction in terms of TBM operation, risk of settlements etc., due to the larger volumes of ground being excavated, but also ring building, with the very large concrete lining segments, is an extra challenge.

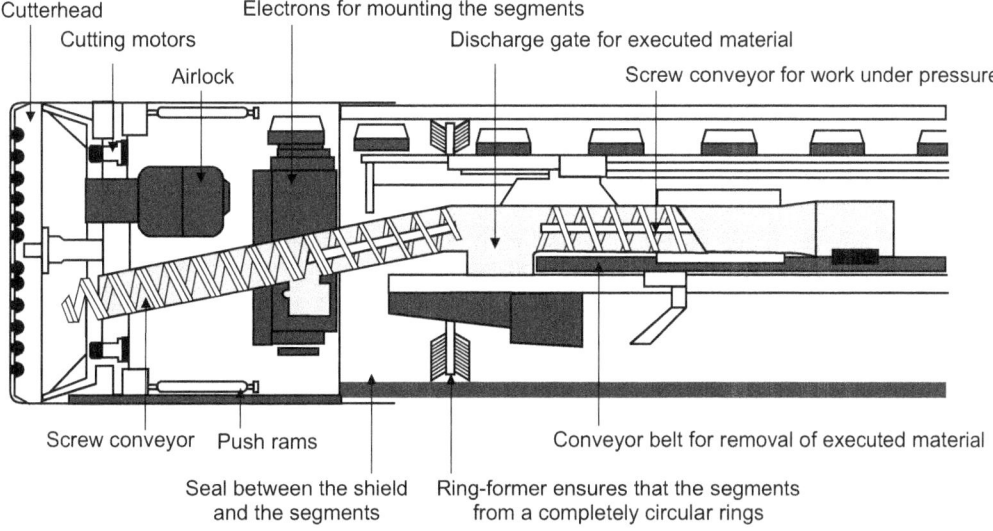

Fig. 19.4

TBM Bored Tunnels
Tunnels constructed by a TBM are typically circular and used in soft ground for long tunnels. TBM tunnels are used both in urban and non-urban areas in soft soil and in a sub-aqueous environment. Compared to SCL tunnel TBM bored tunnels can be constructed in less competent ground and where water pressures are high or impossible to drain. TBM bored tunnels are typically lined with a prefabricated segmental concrete lining.

SCL Bored Tunnels
SCL Bored tunnels are often used for construction of non-circular tunnels or shorter tunnels in relative competent ground conditions, where the ground can be drained during construction. The SCL cross-section can be excavated in sections to suit the actual conditions, and excavations are temporarily lined with a primary lining consisting of shotcrete. The permanent secondary internal lining is built as an in-situ cast concrete lining.

19.4.2 Advantages of TBM
- Very high rates of penetration can be achieved, by selecting appropriate type of equipment.
- Working with TBM is quite safe for people working.
- Use of explosives and consequential dangers thereof can be avoided.
- Does not involve, drilling, blasting, shocks, settlement of buildings in nearby area.
- Excavated surface is of designed diameter and there is no overcutting or under cutting.
- Collapse of roof, and seepage problem can be reduced to great extent.

19.4.3 Disadvantages
- Initial cost of equipment is very high and unless continuity of work is assured, investment is uneconomical.

- The equipment is required to be booked well in advance.
- Replacement of equipment becomes extremely difficult, if incorrect equipment is deployed/or if the strata encountered is unsuitable for the equipment.

19.5 MUCKING

After proper drilling and blasting, excavated/blasted rock is required to be removed and dumped off at suitable place called dumping yard. The process of removing excavated rock and placing in suitable dumpers or wagons is called as mucking.

19.5.1 Methods of Removal of Muck

Methods of removal of muck depend upon
(a) Width and height of tunnel.
(b) Equipment available.

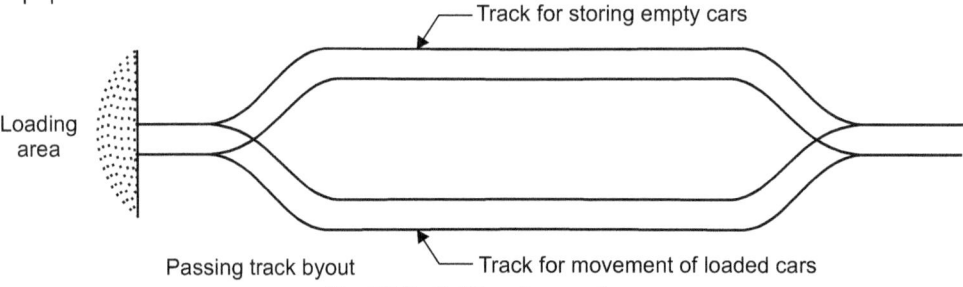

Fig. 19.5 : California crossing

- **California Crossing Method :** When width of tunnel is adequate, two parallel tracks with a California crossing in between as shown in Fig. 19.5 is provided. Empty wagons from one track is allowed to come to near loader, through California crossing. The wagon is then loaded with muck and is allowed to go on another parallel track, in opposite direction outside the tunnel for disposal. This method is not suitable, when width of tunnel is too small to accommodate two tracks.

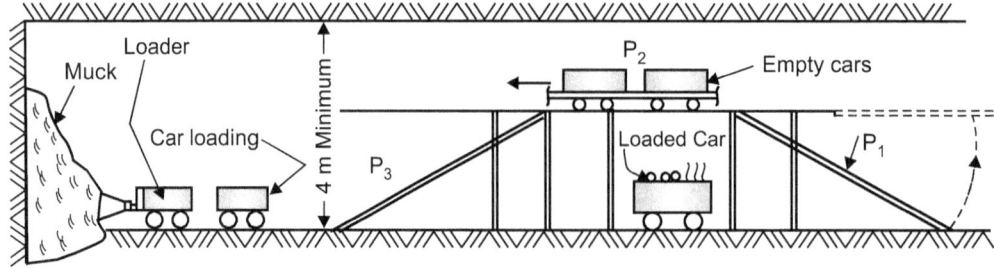

Fig. 19.6

- **Grass Hopper Method :** As shown in Fig. 19.6 empty wagon is stacked on raised platform (2), through inclined platform (1) which can be raised or lowered by mechanical means. The empty wagon, on raised platform (2), is brought down by another inclined platform (3), pushed towards loader, loader fills the empty wagon with muck. The loaded wagon is taken outside, below the raised platform. While the loader fills the wagon, platform (1) is lowered, and empty wagon is stacked on platform (2) and the process continues.

- **Cherry Picker Method :** Instead of providing platform, as in previous method, an arrangement is made to provide a gantry girder, of sufficient height, with an arrangement to hang empty or loaded wagon and move the same horizontally as desired. The process involved is as under :
  - Engine with empty wagons, pushes wagons to the face, where excavated muck is loaded in the last wagon with the help of loader.
  - The engine takes this loaded wagon, just below the gantry girder and this loaded wagon is decoupled and raised with chain and pulley block arrangement and kept hanging.
  - The empty wagons are pushed back in such a way, that if the loaded wagon is lowered, it will be the first wagon behind the engine.
  - The engine is decoupled and taken forward.
  - The fully loaded wagon is lowered and coupled with balanced empty wagon and the engine.
  - The process is repeated, till all the wagons are fully loaded.
  - The engine takes all the wagons together outside to suitable dumping place.
  - The process is repeated.

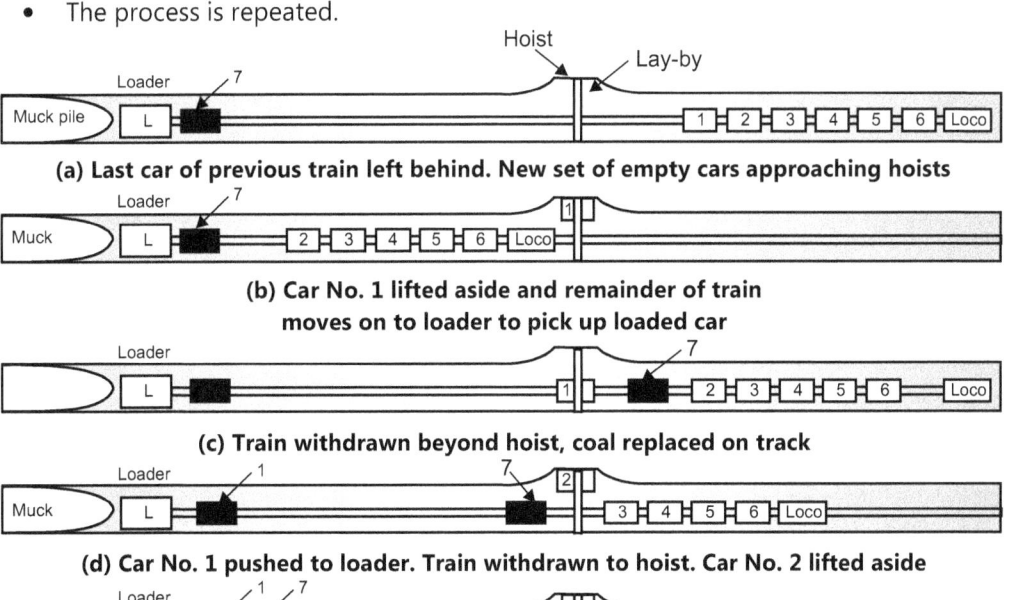

(a) Last car of previous train left behind. New set of empty cars approaching hoists

(b) Car No. 1 lifted aside and remainder of train moves on to loader to pick up loaded car

(c) Train withdrawn beyond hoist, coal replaced on track

(d) Car No. 1 pushed to loader. Train withdrawn to hoist. Car No. 2 lifted aside

(e) Train moved to loader to pull Car No. 1, which is full

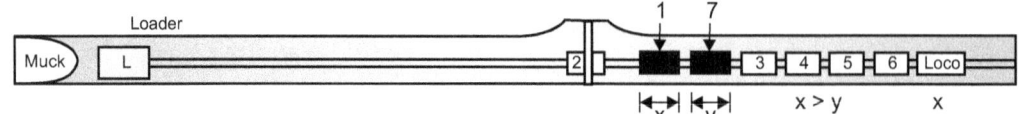

(f) Car No. 1 taken beyond hoist. Car No. 2 replaced on track and ready for pushing to loader. Repeat for all cars

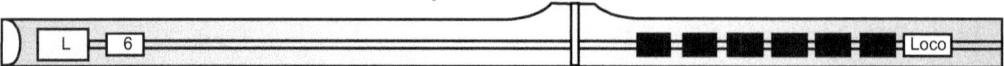

(g) Last empty Car No. 6 left behind, to be pulled etc. in next operation

Fig. 19.7 : Grass Hopper method of mucking

19.5.2 Methods of Mucking based on Equipment Available

- Battery operated or electrically operated mucking system.

Methods explained in (a) above come in this category.

- Use of dumpers : In place of railway track, use of dumpers is made. However, this has two disadvantages :
  - Lot of diesel gas is emitted while plying of dumpers and proper ventilation is required to be arranged.
  - There is lot of wear and tear of tyres plying on rock and suitable protective arrangement has to be made.
  - For turning of trucks through 180°, suitable space/enlargement is required to be made.
- **Use of Conveyor Belts :** Excavated muck is placed over conveyor belt, to carry muck, upto suitable place in tunnel, wherefrom it is hauled to dumping yard. This method is suitable is tunnel of small diameter, full of various types of pipelines etc. However, as tunnel progresses, suitable changes in conveyor belt has to be made

REVIEW QUESTIONS

1. Write factors affecting methods of tunneling.
2. Write short notes on :
   (a) Needle beam method.
   (b) NATM method.
   (c) Shied methods
   (d) California crossing method of mucking
3. Explain TBM method.
4. What are the advantages and disadvantages of TBM method?
5. Describe various methods used for mucking?

www.ingramcontent.com/pod-product-compliance
Lightning Source LLC
Chambersburg PA
CBHW060504300426
44112CB00017B/2540